D0210474

Rome

"All you've got to do is decide to go
and the hardest part is over.

So go!"

TONY WHEELER, COFOUNDER – LONELY PLANET

THIS EDITION WRITTEN AND RESEARCHED BY

Abigail Blasi, Duncan Garwood

Contents

Plan Your Trip — 4

Explore Rome — 46

Understand Rome — 223

Survival Guide — 265

Rome Maps — 297

(left) **Via del Boschetto p154** One of Monti's best shopping streets.

(above) **Basilica di Santa Maria Maggiore p143** Stained-glass window.

(right) **A gelateria store display p33**

Welcome to Rome

A heady mix of haunting sights, awe-inspiring art and vibrant street life, Italy's Eternal City is one of the world's most beautiful capitals.

Historical Legacies

The result of 3000 years of ad hoc urban development, Rome's cityscape is an exhilarating spectacle. Ancient icons recall Rome's time as the fearsome hub of the Roman Empire, the *caput mundi* (capital of the world), while catacombs and clandestine churches hark back to the early days of Christianity. Lording it over the Vatican, St Peter's Basilica is the greatest of the city's basilicas, a masterpiece of Renaissance architecture. Elsewhere, ornate piazzas and elaborate churches add a baroque flourish to the city's streets.

Artistic Riches

Few cities can rival Rome's artistic heritage. Throughout history, the city has starred in the great upheavals of Western art, drawing the top artists of the day and inspiring them to push the boundaries of creative achievement. The result is a city awash with priceless treasures. Ancient statues adorn world-class museums, Byzantine mosaics and Renaissance frescoes dazzle in the city's art-rich churches, baroque facades flank medieval piazzas. Walk around the centre and you'll come across masterpieces by the giants of the artistic pantheon – sculptures by Michelangelo, canvases by Caravaggio, Raphael frescoes and fountains by Bernini.

Living the Lifestyle

A trip to Rome is as much about lapping up the *dolce vita* (sweet life) as gorging on art and culture. It's about relaxing into the city's rhythms and idling around the picturesque streets. Whiling away hours at streetside cafes and people-watching on pretty piazzas are an integral part of the experience. The tempo rises as the heat of the day fades into the evening cool and the fashionably dressed *aperitivo* (aperitif) crowd descends on the city's bars and cafes. Restaurants and trattorias hum with activity and cheerful hordes mill around before heading off to cocktail bars and late-night clubs.

Roman Feasting

Eating out is one of Rome's great pleasures and the combination of romantic al fresco settings and superlative food is a guarantee of good times. For fine dining and five-star wine there are any number of refined restaurants, but for a truly Roman meal search out the city's boisterous pizzerias and convivial trattorias. These are where locals indulge their passion for crispy pizzas, humble but delicious pastas, and cool white wine from the nearby Castelli Romani hills.

Why I Love Rome

By Duncan Garwood, Author

I'm a walker and I love exploring Rome on foot, losing myself in the tangled lanes of the historic centre and neighbourhoods like Trastevere and Monti. I love the aroma of freshly ground coffee that comes out of the cafes and sharing a carafe of local wine over lunch in a trattoria. I enjoy the gruff humour of the locals and the way they have an opinion on everything. I'm also a history buff, and after 15 years in the city, I still get a kick every time I see the Colosseum or spy St Peter's dome looming over the skyline.

For more about our authors, see p328.

Top: Alfresco restaurant tables on a Roman street

Rome's
Top 10

Colosseum (p52)

1 No photograph can prepare you for the thrill of seeing the Colosseum for the first time. For 2000 years this muscular arena has stood as the symbol of Roman power, as the striking embodiment of the terrible awe that Rome once inspired, and it's looking more splendid than ever following a recent restoration. As you climb its steeply stacked stands, try to imagine them full of spectators screaming for blood – a chilling thought.

⊙ *Ancient Rome*

Museo e Galleria Borghese (p183)

2 Everybody's heard of Michelangelo and the Sistine Chapel, but Rome is as much about baroque art as it is the Renaissance, and the Museo e Galleria Borghese is the place to see it. You'll need to book ahead but it's a small price to pay to see Bernini's amazing baroque sculptures, as well as works by Canova, Caravaggio, Raphael and Titian. And afterwards, the surrounding Villa Borghese park is the perfect place to digest what you've just seen.

RIGHT: BERNINI'S *RATTO DI PROSERPINA* (RAPE OF PROSERPINA)

⊙ *Villa Borghese & Northern Rome*

Pantheon (p72)

3 The best preserved of Rome's ancient monuments, the Pantheon is a truly remarkable building. Its huge columned portico and thick-set walls impress, but it's only when you get inside that you get the full measure of the place. It's vast, and you'll feel very small as you look up at the record-breaking dome soaring above your head. Adding to the effect are the shafts of light that stream in through the central oculus (the circular opening at the dome's apex), illuminating the royal tombs set into the circular marble-clad walls.

⊙ *Centro Storico*

Vatican Museums (p126)

4 Rome boasts many artistic highlights, but few are as overpowering as Michelangelo's frescoes in the Sistine Chapel. A kaleidoscopic barrage of colours and images, they come as the grand finale of the Vatican Museums, Rome's largest and most popular art museum. Inside the vast complex, kilometre upon kilometre of corridors are lined with classical sculptures, paintings and tapestries as they lead inexorably towards the Raphael Rooms, a suite of four rooms brilliantly frescoed by Raphael, and, beyond that, the Sistine Chapel. RIGHT: GALLERY OF MAPS

⊙ *Vatican City, Borgo & Prati*

St Peter's Basilica *(p122)*

5 You don't have to be a believer to be bowled over by St Peter's Basilica, Rome's largest and most spectacular church. Everything about the place is astonishing, from the sweeping piazza that announces it to the grandiose facade and unbelievably opulent interior. Topping everything is Michelangelo's extraordinary dome, a mouldbreaking masterpiece of Renaissance architecture and one of Rome's landmark sights. This is a building that was designed to inspire awe, and even in a city of churches like Rome it stands head and shoulders above everything else.

◉ *Vatican City, Borgo & Prati*

Via Appia Antica (p195)

6 The most famous of Rome's ancient roads, and one of the city's most sought-after addresses, the Appian Way is a gorgeous place to be on a clear, sunny morning. Running through lush green fields and littered with piles of greying ruins, it's the very picture of pastoral Italian beauty. But the bucolic scenery belies the road's bloodstained history. It was here that Spartacus and 6000 of his slave army were crucified, and it was here that the early Christians buried their dead in the catacombs.

⦿ *Southern Rome*

Capitoline Museums (p61)

7 In ancient times, the Campidoglio (Capitoline Hill) was home to Rome's two most important temples. Nowadays, the main reason to make the short, steep climb to the top is to admire the views and visit the Capitoline Museums on Piazza del Campidoglio. The world's oldest public museums harbour some fantastic classical statuary, including the celebrated *Lupa Capitolina* (Capitoline Wolf), an icon of early Etruscan art, and some really wonderful paintings. And make sure you bring your camera for the masonry littered around the entrance courtyard. RIGHT: STATUE OF CONSTANTINE

⦿ *Ancient Rome*

An Evening in Trastevere (p163)

8 One of the great joys of Rome is eating and drinking well, especially in summer when it's warm enough to dine al fresco, and the city's animated streets are packed until the early hours. And nowhere is better for a night out than the picture-perfect neighbourhood of Trastevere. Over the river from the historic centre, its medieval lanes, hidden piazzas and pastel-hued *palazzi* (mansions) harbour hundreds of bars, cafes, trattorias and restaurants catering to a nightly crowd of up-for-it Romans and besotted visitors.

✗ *Trastevere & Gianicolo*

Trevi Fountain (p102)

9 A stop at Rome's largest and most famous fountain is a traditional rite of passage for visitors to Rome. Every day crowds gather to toss coins into the fountain's water and ensure that one day they'll return to the Eternal City. The fountain, designed by Nicola Salvi in the 18th century, is a gloriously over-the-top rococo affair depicting wild horses, mythical figures and cascading rock falls. After a lengthy restoration, unveiled in 2015, it's looking particularly splendid, and is most spellbinding when illuminated after night falls.

👁 *Tridente, Trevi & the Quirinale*

Roman Forum & Palatine (p57)

10 To walk through the tumbledown ruins of the Roman Forum is to retrace the footsteps of the great figures of Roman history, such as Julius Caesar and Pompey. However broken the remains, it's a stirring experience to stand at the heart of the Roman Empire. Nearby, the Palatino (Palatine Hill), a green expanse of evocative ruins, is where it all began, where Romulus supposedly killed Remus and founded the city in 753 BC, and where the ancient Roman emperors lived in unimaginable luxury.

👁 *Ancient Rome*

What's New

Street Culture

Forget fine art and five-star dining, street culture is all the rage in Rome right now. Urban art has exploded onto Rome's walls in the past few years, while street food has become the city's latest foodie fad. For a sight of the former, check out the colourful murals on Via del Porto Fluviale (p202) in the trendy Ostiense district; for a taste of the latter hotfoot it to Supplizio (p87)in the historic centre or Pianostrada Laboratorio di Cucina in Trastevere (p165).

Domus Aurea

One of Rome's buried gems, Nero's vast Domus Aurea complex is now re-opening for weekend guided tours. (p144)

Co.So

Join hipsters, mixologists and aficionados at Co.So, one of the city's new breed of cocktail bars in the bohemian Pigneto district. (p151)

Venchi

Rome just got better for chocoholics with the arrival of Venchi. There are two gelaterie, one in the historic centre and one near Piazza di Spagna. (p113)

Enoteca La Torre

After years of success in Viterbo, chef Danilo Ciavattino has transferred his fine-dining restaurant Enoteca La Torre to the romantic riverside environs of Villa Laetitia. (p137)

Casa Fabbrini

With its magazine-worthy interiors and a prime location in Rome's upscale shopping district, B&B Casa Fabbrini is making a mark. (p219)

Cinecittà Film Studios

Tour Rome's legendary Cinecittà Film Studios and see where classics like *Ben Hur*, *Cleopatra* and *La Dolce Vita* were shot. (p204)

Pasticceria De Bellis

Pastry making becomes fine art at Pasticceria De Bellis, a designer pastry shop selling a range of edible mini-masterpieces in the historic centre. (p88)

Temakinho

The vibrant Monti neighbourhood sets the stage for sushi, sake and cocktails at the popular Brazilian-Japanese Temakinho. (p148)

Margutta Glamour Studios

Set up home in one of Rome's most enchanting streets at the artfully decorated Margutta Glamour Studios. (p218)

La Ciambella

A laid-back eatery serving everything from breakfast to pizzas and cocktails, La Ciambella sits over an ancient baths complex near the Pantheon. (p84)

Spot

Refined mid-century furnishings, glassware and objets d'art take centre stage at Spot, a fascinating shop in Monti. (p154)

For more recommendations and reviews, see **lonelyplanet. com/rome**

Need to Know

For more information, see Survival Guide (p265)

Currency
Euro (€)

Language
Italian

Visas
Not required by EU citizens. Not required by nationals of Australia, Canada, New Zealand and the USA for stays of up to 90 days.

Money
ATMs are widespread. Major credit cards are widely accepted but some smaller shops, trattorias, and *pensioni* (small hotels or guesthouses) might not take them.

Mobile Phones
Local SIM cards can be used in European, Australian and unlocked US phones. Other phones must be set to roaming.

Time
Western European Time (GMT/ UTC plus one hour)

Tourist Information
Information points (9.30am to 7pm) around town for maps, brochures and the Roma Pass. Also a telephone line (✆06 06 08) for museum bookings, accommodation and transport help.

Daily Costs
**Budget:
Less than €100**
- ➡ Dorm bed: €15–30
- ➡ Double room in a budget hotel: €50–110
- ➡ Pizza or pasta: €6–12

**Midrange:
€100–250**
- ➡ Double room in a hotel: €110–200
- ➡ Lunch and dinner in local restaurants: €25–50
- ➡ Museum admission: €4–15
- ➡ Roma Pass, a three-day card covering museum entry and public transport: €36

**Top end:
More than €250**
- ➡ Double room in a four- or five-star hotel: €200–450
- ➡ Top restaurant dinner: €50–150
- ➡ Opera ticket: €40–200
- ➡ City-centre taxi ride: €10–15
- ➡ Auditorium concert tickets: €25–90

Advance Planning
Two months before Book high-season accommodation.

Three to four weeks before Book tickets for Domus Aurea (www.coopculture.it). Check for concerts at www.auditorium. com and www.operaroma.it.

One to two weeks before Reserve tables at A-list restaurants. Sort out tickets to the pope's weekly audience at St Peter's. Book ahead for a visit to Palazzo Valentini (www. palazzovalentini.it).

A few days before Book for the Museo e Galleria Borghese (compulsory) and for the Vatican Museums (to avoid queues).

Useful Websites
Lonely Planet (www.lonely-planet.com/rome) Destination lowdown, hotel bookings and traveller forum.

060608 (www.060608.it) Rome's official tourist website.

Coopculture (www.coopculture. it) Information and ticket booking for Rome's monuments.

Vatican Museums (www. vatican.va) Book tickets and avoid the queues.

Auditorium (www.auditorium. com) Check concert listings.

WHEN TO GO

In spring and early autumn there's good weather and many festivals and outdoor events. It's also busy and peak rates apply.

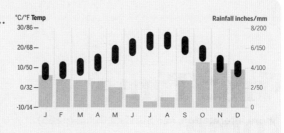

Arriving in Rome

Leonardo da Vinci (Fiumicino) Airport Direct trains to Stazione Termini 6.23am to 11.23pm, €14; slower trains to Trastevere, Ostiense and Tiburtina stations 5.57am to 11.27pm, €8; buses to Stazione Termini 5.35am to midnight, €4 to €9; private transfers from €10.50 per person; taxis €48 (fixed fare to within the Aurelian walls).

Ciampino Airport Buses to Stazione Termini 7.45am to 11.59pm, €4; private transfers from €9.49 per person; taxis €30 (fixed fare to within the Aurelian walls).

Stazione Termini Airport buses and trains, and international trains arrive at Stazione Termini. From here, continue by bus, metro or taxi.

For much more on **arrival** see p266

Getting Around

Rome's public transport includes buses, trams, metro and suburban trains. The main hub is Stazione Termini, the only point at which the two main metro lines cross. The metro is quicker than surface transport but the network is limited and the bus is often better. Children under 10 travel free.

➡ **Metro** The main lines are: A (orange; 5.30am to 9.30pm Thursday to Sunday, replacement bus MA1-MA2 to 11.30pm, to 1.30am Saturday) and B (blue; 5.30am to 11.30pm Monday to Thursday, to 1.30am Friday and Saturday). Line C runs between Monte Compatri and Parco di Centocelle, and is as yet of little use to tourists.

➡ **Buses** Most routes pass through Stazione Termini. Buses run 5.30am to midnight, with limited night services.

For more on **getting around** see p268 ➡

Sleeping

Rome is expensive and busy year-round, so you'll want to book as far ahead as you can to secure the best deal and the place you want.

Accommodation ranges from palatial five-star hotels to hostels, B&Bs, convents, *pensioni*, and a good range of Airbnb options. Hostels are the cheapest, offering dorm beds and private rooms. B&Bs range from simple home-style set-ups to chic boutique outfits with prices to match, while religious institutions provide basic, value-for-money accommodation but may insist on a curfew. Hotels are plentiful and there are many budget, family-run *pensioni* in the Termini area.

Useful Websites

➡ **060608** (www.060608.it) Lists all official accommodation.

➡ **Santa Susanna** (www. santasusanna.org/coming-ToRome/convents.html) Religious accommodation.

➡ **Bed & Breakfast Association of Rome** (www.b-b.rm.it) Search for B&Bs and apartments.

For much more on **sleeping** see p214

ORGANISED TOURS

A tour is a good way of seeing a lot in a short time or investigating a sight in depth. Several outfits run hop-on hop-off bus tours, typically costing about €20 per person. Both the Colosseum and Vatican Museums offer official guided tours, but for a more personalised service you'll be better off with a private guide.

First Time Rome

For more information, see Survival Guide (p265)

Checklist

➡ Check the validity of your passport

➡ Organise travel insurance

➡ Inform your credit/debit card company of your travel plans

➡ Check if you can use your mobile phone

➡ Book for popular sights like the Vatican Museums, Museo e Galleria Borghese and also for A-list restaurants, concerts and accommodation

➡ If coming at Christmas or Easter, check details of religious services at St Peter's Basilica and other big churches

What to Pack

➡ Trainers or comfy walking shoes – you'll walk a lot over cobbled streets

➡ Smart-casual evening clothes – Romans dress up to go out

➡ Sun lotion – it's usually pricier in Italy

➡ Purse with strap – petty theft can be a problem

➡ Water bottle – refill it at Rome's drinking-water fountains

Top Tips For Your Trip

➡ Don't try and cover everything. Focus on a few sights/areas and leave the rest for next time.

➡ Rome's historic centre is made for leisurely strolling, so allow time for mapless wandering. Half the fun of Rome is discovering what's around the corner – and there's always something.

➡ When choosing where to eat, never judge a place by its appearance. Some of the best meals are had in modest-looking trattorias.

➡ When it's very hot – which it is in summer – adjust to the local rhythm: go out in the morning, rest after lunch and head out again late afternoon or early evening.

What to Wear

Appearances matter in Rome. That said, you'll need to dress comfortably because you'll be walking a lot. Suitable clothing for men is generally trousers (pants) and shirts or polo shirts, and for women, skirts, trousers or dresses. Shorts, T-shirts and sandals are fine in summer, but bear in mind that strict dress codes are enforced at St Peter's Basilica and the Vatican Museums. For evening wear, smart casual is the norm. A light sweater or waterproof jacket is useful in spring and autumn.

Be Forewarned

➡ Rome is a safe city but petty theft can be a problem and pickpockets are active in touristy areas and on crowded public transport. Use common sense and watch your valuables.

➡ There aren't any no-go areas, but keep your wits about you around Stazione Termini.

➡ August is Italy's main holiday period. Romans desert the city in droves and many shops and eateries close for a week or two around 15 August. Many museums close on Mondays.

➡ Expect queues at major sights such as the Colosseum, St Peter's Basilica and Vatican Museums. Booking tickets in advance costs extra but saves waiting time.

Money

Bancomat (ATMs) are common, but be aware of transaction fees. If an ATM rejects your card, try another before assuming the problem is with your card. Save money by drinking coffee standing at the bar rather than taking a seat. Also carry a water bottle and fill it at Rome's many fountains (nicknamed '*nasoni*', meaning 'big noses'). Many museums are free on the first Sunday of the month, while the Vatican Museums are free on the last Sunday of the month.

For more information, see p273.

Taxes & Refunds

A 20% value-added tax known as IVA *(Imposta sul Valore Aggiunta)* is included in the price of most goods and services. Tax-free shopping (p275) is available at some shops.

All stays in the city are subject to an accommodation tax – the exact sum depends on the length of your sojourn and type of accommodation.

Tipping

Romans are not big tippers, but the following is a rough guide:

➡ **Taxis** Optional, but most people round up to the nearest euro.

➡ **Restaurants** Service *(servizio)* is generally included; if it's not, a euro or two is fine in pizzerias, 10% in restaurants.

➡ **Bars** Not necessary, although many people leave small change if drinking at the bar.

Language

You can get by with English, but you'll improve your experience no end by mastering a few basic words and expressions. This is particularly true in restaurants where menus don't always have English translations and some places rely on waiters to explain what's on. For more on language, see p278.

① **What's the local speciality?**
Qual'è la specialità di questa regione?
kwa-le la spe-cha-lee-ta dee kwes-ta re-jo-ne

A bit like the rivalry between medieval Italian city-states, these days the country's regions compete in speciality foods and wines.

② **Which combined tickets do you have?**
Quali biglietti cumulativi avete?
kwa-lee bee-lye-tee koo-moo-la-tee-vee a-ve-te

Make the most of your euro by getting combined tickets to various sights; they are available in all major Italian cities.

③ **Where can I buy discount designer items?**
C'è un outlet in zona? che oon owt-let in zo-na

Discount fashion outlets are big business in major cities – get bargain-priced seconds, samples and cast-offs for *la bella figura*.

④ **Let's meet at 6pm for pre-dinner drinks.**
Ci vediamo alle sei per un aperitivo.
chee ve-dya-mo a-le say per oon a-pe-ree-tee-vo

At dusk, watch the main piazza get crowded with people sipping colourful cocktails and snacking the evening away: join your new friends for this authentic Italian ritual!

Etiquette

Despite appearances, Italy is quite a formal society and the niceties of social interaction are observed.

➡ **Greetings** Greet people in bars, shops, trattorias etc with a *buongiorno* (good morning) or *buonasera* (good evening).

➡ **Dress** Cover up to visit churches and go smart when eating out.

➡ **Eating** Eat pasta with a fork; it's OK to eat pizza with your hands.

Roma Pass

These useful passes are available online, from tourist information points or from participating museums.

➡ **Three-day classic pass (€36)** Provides free admission to two museums or sites, unlimited city transport, and discounted entry to other sites, exhibitions and events.

➡ **48-hour pass (€28)** Gives free admission to one museum or site and then as per the classic pass for transport and discounts.

Top Itineraries

Day One

Ancient Rome (p50)

 Start the day at the **Colosseum**, Rome's huge gladiatorial arena – try to get there early to avoid the queues. Then head down to the **Palatino** to poke around crumbling ruins and admire sweeping views. From the Palatino, follow on to the **Roman Forum**, an evocative area of tumbledown temples, sprouting columns and ruined basilicas.

> **Lunch** Sample regional specialities at the Terre e Domus (p67).

Ancient Rome (p50)

After lunch climb the Cordonata to the glorious, harmonious **Piazza del Campidoglio** and the **Capitoline Museums**, where you'll find sensational ancient sculpture and wondrous works by Caravaggio. To clear your head afterwards, pop next door to **Il Vittoriano** and take the lift to the top for Rome's best 360-degree views.

> **Dinner** Dine on quality seafood at Vecchia Roma (p89).

Centro Storico (p70)

Start the evening by exploring the **Jewish Ghetto**, and linger over dinner at **Vecchia Roma**, a classy restaurant on an epically pretty piazza. Next, wander through cobbled streets, past the Pantheon, and over to **Salotto 42** for cocktails with a view onto the worn columns of the Temple of Hadrian.

Day Two

Vatican City, Borgo & Prati (p120)

 On day two, hit the Vatican. First up, grab a *cornetto* (croissant) from **Dolce Maniera**, then plunge into the **Vatican Museums**. Once you've blown your mind on the Sistine Chapel and the other highlights, complete your tour at **St Peter's Basilica**. If you have the energy, climb its Michelangelo-designed dome for fantastic views over the piazza. If the queues are bad, though, or you're suffering art overload, stop first for an early lunch.

> **Lunch** Eat Rome's most perfect pizza at Pizzarium (p138).

Centro Storico (p70)

Dedicate the afternoon to sniffing around the historic centre. Here you'll come across some of Rome's great sights, including the enormous **Piazza Navona** and the incredible **Pantheon**, with its oculus open to the sky. Art lovers can admire paintings by Caravaggio in the **Chiesa di San Luigi dei Francesi** and fashion-conscious shoppers can browse the boutiques on **Via del Governo Vecchio**.

> **Dinner** Enjoy great Roman cooking at Armando al Pantheon (p84).

Centro Storico (p70)

After dinner stop in the centre for a taste of *dolce vita* bar life. Depending on what you're after, you could spend a relaxed evening at chic, laid-back **Etablì** near Piazza Navona, join the student drinkers on lively **Campo de' Fiori**, or chat over coffee at **Caffè Sant'Eustacchio**, which serves some of Rome's (and possibly the world's) best coffee.

NIKADA / GETTY IMAGES ©

St Peter's Square (p134)

Day Three

Villa Borghese & Northern Rome (p181)

 Day three starts with a trip to the **Museo e Galleria Borghese** to marvel at amazing baroque sculpture. Afterwards, walk off what you've just seen in the shady avenues of **Villa Borghese**.

 Lunch Enjoy fresh Roman cooking at antique-packed Casa Conti. (p113)

Tridente, Trevi & the Quirinale (p98)

 In the afternoon investigate the area around **Piazza di Spagna**. Plan your moves while sitting on the **Spanish Steps**, visit the poignant **Keats–Shelley House**, then dive down **Via dei Condotti** to window shop at the flagship designer stores. From Via del Corso, at the bottom, you can make your way up to the **Trevi Fountain**, where tradition dictates you throw in a coin to ensure your return to Rome.

Dinner Go for innovative Glass Hostaria (p168), or traditional Da Olindo (p165).

Trastevere & Gianicolo (p158)

 Over the river, the charmingly photogenic Trastevere neighbourhood bursts with life in the evening as locals and tourists flock to its many eateries and bars. Get into the mood with an aperitif at **Freni e Frizioni**, before eating some Roman soul food at an atmospheric, rough-and-ready trattoria, or enjoying the playful creativity of somewhere more upmarket.

Day Four

Southern Rome (p193)

 On day four it's time to venture out to **Via Appia Antica**. The main attractions here are the catacombs, and it's a wonderfully creepy sensation to duck down into these sinister pitch-black tunnels. Back above ground, you'll find the remains of an ancient racetrack at the nearby **Villa di Massenzio**.

Lunch Eat on the Appia, at Qui Non se More Mai. (p201)

Monti, Esquilino & San Lorenzo (p140)

 Start the afternoon by visiting the **Museo Nazionale Romano: Palazzo Massimo alle Terme**, a superb museum full of classical sculpture and stunning mosaics. Then drop by the monumental **Basilica di Santa Maggiore**, famous for its mosaics, and the **Basilica di San Pietro in Vincoli**, home to Michelangelo's muscular Moses sculpture. Finish up by exploring the pretty lanes of the Monti district.

Dinner Dine at creative Umbrian restaurant L'Asino d'Oro (p148).

Monti, Esquilino & San Lorenzo (p140)

 Either hang out longer in Monti, catching a live gig at **Blackmarket**, or take a trip out to trendy **Pigneto**, where you'll find plenty of bar action, and often live music.

If You Like...

Museums & Galleries

Vatican Museums One of the world's great museums, with a vast collection of classical art culminating in the Sistine Chapel. (p126)

Museo e Galleria Borghese Houses the best baroque sculpture in town and some seriously good Old Masters. (p183)

Museo Nazionale Romano: Palazzo Massimo alle Terme Fabulous Roman frescoes and wall mosaics are the highlight of this overlooked gem. (p142)

Capitoline Museums The world's oldest public museums are a must for anyone interested in ancient sculpture. (p61)

Galleria Doria Pamphilj Hidden behind a grimy exterior, this lavish private gallery is full of major works by big-name Italian artists. (p82)

Galleria Nazionale d'Arte Antica: Palazzo Barberini A sumptuous baroque palace laden with paintings by such giants as Caravaggio, Raphael and Hans Holbein. (p110)

Museo Nazionale Etrusco di Villa Giulia A lovely museum housing a huge collection of Etruscan art and artefacts. (p186)

Roman Relics

Colosseum One of the world's most famous buildings, this breathtaking arena encapsulates all the drama of ancient Rome. (p52)

View of Rome from Gianicolo Hill (p161)

Pantheon With its revolutionary design, this awe-inspiring Roman temple has served as an architectural blueprint for millennia. (p72)

Palatino Ancient emperors languished in luxury on the Palatino, the oldest and most exclusive part of imperial Rome. (p54)

Terme di Caracalla The hulking remains of this vast baths complex hint at the scale that ancient Rome was built to. (p176)

Roman Forum This was ancient Rome's bustling centre full of temples, basilicas, shops and streets. (p57)

Domus Aurea Nero's Golden House lies underground, and a small but astounding section is sometimes open to visitors. (p144)

Via Appia Antica March down Rome's oldest road, built in the 4th century BC, en route to the catacombs. (p195)

Church Art

Sistine Chapel Michelangelo's frescoes are among the world's most famous works of art. (p130)

St Peter's Basilica Marvel at Michelangelo's *Pietà* and many other celebrated masterpieces. (p122)

Chiesa di San Luigi dei Francesi An ornate baroque church boasting a trio of Caravaggio paintings. (p77)

Chiesa di Santa Maria del Popolo Works by Caravaggio, Raphael and Bernini adorn this magnificent Renaissance church. (p101)

Basilica di San Pietro in Vincoli Face up to Michelangelo's muscular *Moses* sculpture. (p144)

Basilica di Santa Maria in Trastevere An ancient basilica celebrated for its golden apse mosaics. (p160)

Going Underground

Basilica di San Clemente Descend into the bowels of this multilayered basilica to discover a pagan temple and 1st-century house. (p174)

Vatican Grottoes Extending beneath St Peter's Basilica, these underground chambers contain the tombs of several popes. (p122)

Catacombs Via Appia Antica is riddled with catacombs where the early Christians buried their dead. (p198)

Terme di Caracalla Explore an ancient temple and the underground tunnels where slaves once fed furnaces at this huge baths complex. (p176)

Palazzo Valentini A multimedia display brings excavated ruins to life beneath the seat of the Province of Rome. (p105)

Case Romane Poke around the houses where Sts John and Paul lived before they were executed. (p175)

Sweeping Views

Il Vittoriano Not recommended for vertigo sufferers, the summit of this marble monolith towers over the rest of Rome. (p66)

For more top Rome spots, see the following:

➡ Eating (p28)

➡ Drinking & Nightlife (p36)

➡ Entertainment (p40)

➡ Shopping (p44)

Gianicolo Rising above Trastevere, the Gianicolo Hill affords sweeping panoramas over Rome's rooftops. (p161)

Orti Farnesiani A viewing terrace in the Palatino's medieval gardens commands grandstand views over the Roman Forum. (p55)

St Peter's Basilica Climb the dome and you're rewarded with huge 360-degree views. (p124)

Street Life

Trastevere Students, tourists, locals, diners, drinkers, junkies and street-hawkers mingle on Trastevere's vivacious streets. (p161)

Spanish Steps Find a space and settle back to watch the ever-changing spectacle on the square below. (p100)

Piazza Navona This beautiful baroque arena provides the stage for a colourful cast of street artists, performers, waiters and tourists. (p74)

Pigneto With its noisy market and vibrant bar scene, this hip district is always lively. (p151)

Campo de' Fiori Market stall holders holler at each other during the day and student drinkers strut their stuff by night. (p78)

Month by Month

January

As New Year celebrations fade, the winter cold digs in. It's a quiet time of year but the sales are a welcome diversion.

🛍 Shopping Sales

Running from early January to mid-February, the winter sales offer savings of between 20% and 50%.

February

Rome's quiet is shattered by high-spirited carnival celebrations, which signal that spring is on the way.

✷ Carnevale Romano

Rome really goes to town for Carnevale, with leaping horse shows on Piazza del Popolo, costumed parades down Via del Corso, street performers on Piazza Navona, and kids in fancy dress.

March

The onset of spring brings blooming flowers, rising temperatures and unpredictable rainfall. Unless Easter falls in late March, the city is fairly subdued and low-season prices still apply.

🏃 Maratona di Roma

Sightseeing becomes sport at Rome's annual marathon (www.maratonadiroma. it). The 42km route starts and finishes near the Colosseum, taking in many of the city's big sights.

April

April is a great month, with lovely, sunny weather, fervent Easter celebrations and festivities. Expect high-season prices.

✷ Easter

In the capital of the Catholic world, Easter is a big deal. On Good Friday the pope leads a candlelit procession around the Colosseum, and there are other smaller parades around the city. At noon on Easter Sunday the Pope blesses the crowds in St Peter's Sq.

✷ Natale di Roma

Rome celebrates its birthday on 21 April with music, historical re-creations and fireworks. Events are staged throughout the city but the focus is Campidoglio and Circo Massimo.

✷ Mostra delle Azalee

From mid-April to early May, the Spanish Steps are decorated with 600 vases of blooming, bright azaleas.

May

May is a busy, high-season month. The weather's perfect and the city is looking gorgeous with blue skies and spring flowers.

☆ Primo Maggio

Thousands of fans troop to Piazza di San Giovanni in Laterano for Rome's free May Day rock concert. It's a mostly Italian affair with big-name local performers, but you might catch the occasional foreign guest star.

June

Summer has arrived and with it hot weather and the Italian school holidays.

✿ Lungo il Tevere

Nightly crowds converge on the river Tiber for this popular summer-long event. Stalls, clubs, bars, restaurants and dance floors line the river bank as Rome's nightlife goes al fresco.

☆ Isola del Cinema

The Isola Tiberina (www. isoladelcinema.com) provides the picturesque backdrop for this open-air film festival, which screens a range of Italian and international films with a focus on independent productions.

☆ Roma Incontro Il Mondo

Villa Ada (www.villaada. org) is transformed into a colourful multi-ethnic village for this popular event. There's a laid-back party vibe and an excellent program of concerts, from Roman rap to jazz and world music.

✿ Festa dei Santi Pietro e Paolo

On 29 June Rome celebrates its two patron saints, Peter and Paul, with a mass at St Peter's Basilica and a street fair on Via Ostiense near the Basilica di San Paolo Fuori-le-Mura.

July

Hot summer temperatures make sightseeing a physical endeavour, but come the cool of evening, the city's streets burst into life as locals come out to enjoy summer festivities.

✿ Festa di Noantri

Trastevere celebrates its roots with a raucous street party in the last two weeks of the month. Centred on Piazza Santa Maria, events kick off with a religious procession and continue with much eating, drinking, dancing and praying.

August

Rome melts in the heat as locals flee the city for summer. Many businesses shut down around 15 August, but hoteliers offer discounts and there are summer events to enjoy.

✿ Festa della Madonna della Neve

On 5 August rose petals are showered on celebrants in the Basilica di Santa Maria Maggiore to commemorate a miraculous 4th-century snowfall.

October

Autumn is a good time to visit – the warm weather is holding, Romaeuropa ensures plenty of cultural action and, with the schools back, there are far fewer tourists around.

☆ Romaeuropa

International performers join emerging stars at Rome's premier dance and drama festival (www. romaeuropa.net). Events, staged from late September through to November, range from avant-garde dance performances to installations, multimedia shows, recitals and readings.

November

Although the wettest month, November compensates with low-season prices, jazz concerts and no queues at the big sights. Autumn is also great for foodies.

☆ Festival Internazionale del Film di Roma

Held at the Auditorium Parco della Musica, Rome's film festival (www.romacinemafest.it) rolls out the red carpet for Hollywood hotshots and bigwigs from Italian cinema.

☆ Festival Internazionale di Musica e Arte Sacra

Over several days in early November, the Vienna Philharmonic Orchestra and other top ensembles perform a series of classical concerts (www.festivalmusicaeartesacra.net) in Rome's four papal basilicas and other churches.

December

The build-up to Christmas feels festive, as the city twinkles in anticipation, decked out in festive lights. Every church has a *presepe* (nativity scene) displayed, from intricate small tableaux to life-size extravaganzas.

✿ Piazza Navona Christmas Fair

Rome's most beautiful baroque square becomes a marketplace as brightly lit market stalls sell everything from nativity scenes to stuffed toys and teeth-cracking *torrone* (nougat).

With Kids

Despite a reputation as a highbrow cultural destination, Rome has a lot to offer kids. Child-specific sights might be thin on the ground, but if you know where to go there's plenty to keep the little ones occupied and parents happy.

PHILIP AND KAREN SMITH / GETTY IMAGES ©

Viewing the Colosseum (p52)

History for Kids

Colosseum
Everyone wants to see the Colosseum (p52) and it doesn't disappoint, especially if accompanied by tales of bloodthirsty gladiators and hungry lions. For maximum effect prep your kids beforehand with a Rome-based film.

Catacombs
Spook your teens with a trip to the catacombs on Via Appia Antica (p195). These pitch-black tunnels, full of tombs and ancient burial chambers, are fascinating, but not suitable for children under about seven.

Palazzo Valentini
Parents and older kids will enjoy the multimedia tour of Roman excavations beneath Palazzo Valentini (p105).

Museums for Kids

Explora
Near Piazza del Popolo, Explora – Museo dei Bambini di Roma (p188) is a hands-on museum for kids under 12, with interactive displays and a free play park.

Museo delle Cere
Go face to face with popes, rock stars, and footy players at Rome's cheesy wax museum, the Museo delle Cere (p108).

Hands-On Activities

Trevi Fountain
Kids love throwing things, so they'll enjoy flinging a coin into the Trevi Fountain (p102). And if they ask, you can tell them that about €3000 is thrown in on an average day.

Bocca della Verità
Put your hand in the Bocca della Verità (Mouth of Truth; p67). Just don't tell a fib, otherwise the mouth will bite off your hand.

Food for Kids

Pizza

Pizza *al taglio* (sliced pizza) is a godsend for parents. It's cheap (about €1 buys two slices of pizza *bianca* – with salt and olive oil), easy to get hold of (there are hundreds of takeaways around town), and works wonders on flagging spirits.

Gelato

Ice cream is another manna from heaven, served in *coppette* (tubs) or *coni* (cones). Child-friendly flavours include *fragola* (strawberry), *cioccolato* (chocolate), and *bacio* (with hazelnuts).

Run in the Park

When the time comes to let the kids off the leash, head to Villa Borghese (p186), the most central of Rome's parks. There's plenty of space to run around in and you can hire family bikes. Other handy parks are Villa Celimontana (p175) and Villa Torlonia (p189).

Animal-Spotting

Animal Sculptures

Set your kids to spot as many animal sculptures as they can. There are hundreds around town, including an elephant (outside the Chiesa di Santa Maria Sopra Minerva), lions (at the foot of the Cordonata staircase up to Piazza del Campidoglio), bees (in Bernini's fountain just off Piazza Barberini), horses, eagles and, of course, Rome's trademark wolf.

Cats

Cats have had the run of Rome's streets for centuries. These days they like to hang out in the ancient temple ruins on the Largo di Torre Argentina (p75).

Zoo

In Villa Borghese, the **Bioparco** (06 360 82 11; www.bioparco.it; Viale del Giardino Zoologico 1; adult/reduced €15/12; 9.30am-6pm summer, to 5pm winter; Bioparco) isn't the best zoo in the world, but after dragging your loved ones to all those churches and museums, it is an option.

A Family Day Out

Ostia Antica

Many of Rome's ancient sites can be boring for children, but Ostia Antica (p206) is different. Here your kids can run along the ancient town's streets, among shops, and all over its impressive amphitheatre.

Tivoli

Kids love exploring the gardens at Villa d'Este (p207) with their water-spouting fountains and grim-faced gargoyles. Nearby, the extensive ruins of Villa Adriana (p207) provide ample opportunity for hide and seek.

Seaside

The nearest beach to Rome is at Ostia Lido, but there are nicer ones at Anzio, Fregene and Santa Marinella.

NEED TO KNOW

Getting Around Cobbled streets make getting around with a pram difficult.

Eating Out In a restaurant ask for a *mezza porzione* (child's portion) and *seggiolone* (highchair).

Supplies Buy baby formula and sterilising solutions at pharmacies. Disposable nappies (diapers; *pannolini*) are available from supermarkets and pharmacies.

Transport Under 10s travel free on all public transport.

Like a Local

Gregarious and convivial, Romans enjoy their city. They love hanging out in its piazzas and speeding around the streets in small cars; they like to dress up and they adore going out. They know theirs is a beautiful city, but they're not jealous and everyone is welcome.

Drink Like a Local

Coffee

Prendere un caffè (having a coffee) is one of the great rituals of Roman life. As a rule, locals will stop at a bar for a coffee in the morning before work, and then again after lunch. To fit in with the crowd, ask for *un caffè* (the term *espresso* is rarely used) and drink standing at the bar. Also, never order a cappuccino after lunch.

For a taste of Rome's finest, head to Caffè Sant'Eustachio (p90) in the historic centre or Sciascia Caffè (p138) in Prati.

Aperitivo

Early evening means *aperitivo* (a drink plus food from a buffet) in many of Rome's fashionable bars. Hotspots include Doppiozeroo (p203) in Ostiense, and Momart (p191), a popular bar off Via Nomentana.

Cool Neighbourhoods

Trastevere

A picturesque district full of bars, cafes and trattorias, Trastevere has long been a foreigners' favourite. But Romans love it too, and amid the tourist bustle, you'll find some characteristic city haunts.

Ostiense

With its disused factories, authentic trattorias and university campus, Ostiense is home to hot clubs and hip bars, as well as several cultural gems.

Pigneto

Pigneto, a former working-class district southeast of Termini, is one of the capital's coolest neighbourhoods, a bar-heavy pocket frequented by bohemians, fun-seekers and trendsetting urbanites.

Testaccio

Down by the Tiber, once-proletarian Testaccio retains a workaday neighbourhood vibe with its daily market, traditional Roman trattorias and popular clubs.

Evening Passeggiata

The *passeggiata* (traditional evening stroll) is a quintessential Roman experience. It's particularly colourful at weekends when families, friends and lovers take to the streets to strut and be seen.

To partake in the spectacle, head to Via del Corso around 6pm. Alternatively, park yourself on the Spanish Steps and watch the theatrics unfold beneath you on Piazza di Spagna (p100).

Football at the Stadio Olimpico

Football is a Roman passion, with support divided between the two local teams: Roma and Lazio. Both play their home games at the Stadio Olimpico (p192), Rome's impressive Olympic stadium. If you go to a game, make sure you get it right – Roma play in red and yellow and their supporters stand in the Curva Sud (South Stand); Lazio play in sky blue and their fans fill the Curva Nord (North Stand).

For Free

Although Rome is an expensive city, you don't have to break the bank to enjoy it. A surprising number of its big sights are free and it costs nothing to stroll the historic streets, piazzas and parks, basking in their extraordinary beauty.

Need to Know

Transport
Holders of the Roma Pass are entitled to free public transport.

Wi-Fi
Free wi-fi is available in many hostels, hotels, bars and cafes.

Tours
To take a free tour check out www.newromefreetour.com.

Free Art

Churches
Feast on fine art in the city's churches. They're all free and many contain priceless treasures by big-name artists such as Michelangelo, Raphael, Bernini and Caravaggio. Major art churches include St Peter's Basilica (p122), the Basilica di San Pietro in Vincoli (p144), Chiesa di San Luigi dei Francesi (p77) and Chiesa di Santa Maria del Popolo (p101).

Vatican Museums
Home to the Sistine Chapel and kilometres of awesome art, the Vatican Museums (p126) are free on the last Sunday of the month.

State Museums
Eight of Rome's municipal museums are free, including the Museo Carlo Bilotti (p186) and the Museo Barracco di Scultura Antica (p79). All state-run museums are *gratis* on the first Sunday of the month.

Free Monuments

Pantheon
A pagan temple turned church, the Pantheon (p72) is a staggering work of architecture with its record-breaking dome and echoing interior.

Trevi Fountain
You don't have to spend a penny to admire the Trevi Fountain (p102), although most people throw a coin in to ensure their return to Rome.

Bocca della Verità
According to legend, if you tell a lie with your hand in the Bocca della Verità (p67) (Mouth of Truth), it'll bite your hand off.

Piazzas & Parks

Piazzas
Hanging out and people-watching on Rome's piazzas is a signature Roman experience. Top spots include Piazza Navona (p74), Campo de' Fiori (p78), Piazza di Spagna (p100) and Piazza del Popolo (p103).

Parks
It doesn't cost a thing to enjoy Rome's parks. The most famous is Villa Borghese (p186), but you'll also find greenery at Villa Torlonia (p189), Villa Celimontana (p175), and on the Gianicolo Hill (p161).

TANIA VOLOBUEVA / GETTY IMAGES ©

Different varieties of pizza in a Rome shop

Eating

This is a city that lives to eat. Food feeds the Roman soul, and a social occasion would be nothing without it. Cooking with local, seasonal ingredients is the norm, as it has been for millennia. Over recent decades the restaurant scene has become increasingly sophisticated, but the city's no-frills, local trattorias still provide some of Rome's most memorable gastronomic experiences.

Roman Cuisine

Like most Italian cuisines, Roman cooking was born of careful use of local ingredients – making use of the cheaper cuts of meat, like *guanciale* (pig's cheek), and greens that could be gathered wild from the fields.

There are a few classic dishes that are served by almost every trattoria and restaurant in Rome. These carb-laden comfort foods are seemingly simple, yet notoriously difficult to prepare well. Iconic Roman dishes include *carbonara* (pasta with lardons, egg and parmesan), *alla gricia* (with pig's cheek and onions), *amatriciana* (invented when an enterprising chef from Amatrice added tomatoes to *alla gricia*) and *cacio e pepe* (with cheese and pepper).

The number of special-occasion, creative restaurants is ever rising in Rome, with a buzz around openings such as Chef Riccardo di Giacinto's All'Oro (p112). Roy Carceres continues to wow at Metamorfosi (p190), and Christina Bowerman, director of Trastevere's Glass Hostaria (p168), is one of the few Italian female chefs to have received a Michelin star. Roman fine-dining restaurants usually embrace the dishes that make up the Roman tradition and have fun with them, adding twists and unexpected flavours and combinations.

Another relatively new concept in Rome is all-day dining, with a few notable all-things-to-all-people restaurants including Baccano (p115), Porto Fluviale (p202) and the multi-storey mall Eataly (p202), which has restaurants to suit every mood, from a hankering for *fritti* (fried food) to fine dining.

Artisanal gelatarie have also refined the city's ice-cream habit, with heavenly ice-cream sellers including Fatamorgana (p111), Dei Gracchi (p111) and Fior di Luna (p165). As all-natural gelatarie revolutionised Rome's sweet tooth, gourmet fast food is an innovation on the savoury side. This is the newest feature of the foodie scene, whereby, as in fine dining, Roman traditions are used as inspiration to produce something that's deliciously surprising, at places such as Supplizio (p87) and Trapizzino (p178). *Pasticcerie* (pastry shops) are also being reinvented as places of chic artistry, with De Bellis (p88) the vanguard of this trend.

Neighbourhood Specialities

Most entrenched in culinary tradition is the Jewish Ghetto area, with its hearty Roman-Jewish cuisine. Deep-frying is a staple of *cucina ebraico-romanesca* (Roman-Jewish cooking), which developed between the 16th and 19th centuries when the Jews were confined to the city's ghetto. To add flavour to their limited ingredients – those spurned by the rich, such as courgette (zucchini) flowers – they began to fry everything from mozzarella to *baccalà* (salted cod). Particularly addictive are the locally grown artichokes, which are flattened out to form a kind of flower shape and then deep-fried and salted.

For the heart (and liver and brains) of the *cucina Romana,* head to Testaccio, a traditional working-class district clustered around the city's former slaughterhouse. In the past, butchers who worked in the city abattoir were often paid in cheap cuts of meat as well as money. The Roman staple *coda alla vaccinara* translates as 'oxtail cooked butcher's style'. This is cooked for hours to create a rich sauce with tender slivers of meat. A famous Roman dish that's not for the faint-hearted is pasta with *pajata,* made with the entrails of young veal calves, considered a delicacy since they contain the mother's congealed milk. If you see the word *coratella* in a dish, it means you'll be eating *lights* (lungs), kidneys and hearts.

NEED TO KNOW

Prices

The following price guide refers to the average cost of a meal that includes *primo* (first course), *secondo* (second course) and *dolce* (dessert), plus a glass of wine. Don't be surprised to see *pane e coperto* (bread and cover charge; €1 to €5 per person) added to your bill.

€	less than €25
€€	€25 to €45
€€€	more than €45

Opening Hours

➡ Most restaurants open noon to 3pm and 7.30pm to 11pm, usually closing one day per week (often Sunday or Monday).

➡ Most eateries close for at least a week in August, but the timing varies from year to year. Some restaurants close for the whole month. It's advisable to ring first in August to check that everyone hasn't gone to the beach.

Etiquette

➡ Dress up when eating out; Italians dress relatively smartly at most meals.

➡ Bite through hanging spaghetti rather than slurping it up.

➡ Pasta is eaten with a fork (not fork and spoon).

➡ It's OK to eat pizza with your hands.

➡ In an Italian home you may *fare la scarpetta* (make a little shoe) with your bread and wipe plates clean of sauces.

➡ If invited to someone's home, traditional gifts are a tray of *dolci* (sweets) from a *pasticceria* (pastry shop), a bottle of wine or flowers.

Tipping

Although service is included, leave a tip: anything from 5% in a pizzeria to 10% in a more upmarket place. At least round up the bill.

Seasonal Calendar

As is the custom all over Italy, Romans eat according to what's in season. Fresh, often sun-ripened ingredients zing with flavour, and the best food is *'zero-kilometri'* – the less distance it has had to travel, the better.

Eating by Neighbourhood

Villa Borghese & Northern Rome
Park cafes and smart,
fashionable restaurants (p190)

Vatican City, Borgo & Prati
Sophisticated restaurants,
delicious takeaways,
heavenly gelaterie (p135)

Tridente, Trevi & the Quirinale
Classy neighbourhood
eateries, great gelaterie
and upmarket cafes (p110)

Centro Storico
Romantic hideaways,
old-school trattorias,
top pizzerias (p83)

Monti, Esquilino & San Lorenzo
Ethnic eats, cool bars,
boho restaurants (p148)

Trastevere & Gianicolo
Touristy but terrific
trattorias, gelaterie, bars
and pizzerias (p163)

Ancient Rome
Hidden gems among
the tourist traps (p67)

San Giovanni & Testaccio
Traditional Roman cuisine,
good cheap eats (p177)

Southern Rome
Trendsetting foodie venues in
ex-industrial Ostiense district (p201)

0   1 km
0   0.5 miles

SPRING

Spring is prime time for lamb, usually roasted with potatoes – *agnello al forno con patate*. Sometimes it's described as *abbacchio* (Roman dialect for lamb) *scottadito* ('hot enough to burn fingers').

March is the best season for *carciofo alla giudia* (Jewish-style artichoke), when the big round artichokes from Cerveteri appear on the table (smaller varieties are from Sardinia), but you can continue eating this delicious dish until June.

May and June are favourable fishing months, good for cuttlefish and octopus, and other seafood.

Grass-green *fave* (broad beans) are eaten after a meal (especially on 1 May), accompanied by some salty *pecorino* cheese.

The lighter green, fluted *zucchine romanesche* (Roman courgette) appear on market stalls, usually with the flowers still attached – these orange petals, deep-fried, are a delectable feature of Roman cooking.

SUMMER

Tonno (tuna) comes fresh from the seas around Sardinia; *linguine ai frutti di mare* and *risotto alla pescatora* are good light summer dishes.

Summertime is *melanzane* (aubergine or eggplant) time: tuck into them grilled as antipasti or fried and layered with rich tomato sauce in *melanzane alla parmagiana*. It's also time for leafy greens, and Rome even has its own lettuce, the sturdy, flavourful *lattuga romana*.

Tomatoes are at their full-bodied finest, and seductive heaps of *pesche* (peaches), *albicocche* (apricots), *fichi* (figs) and *meloni* (melons) dominate market stalls.

AUTUMN

Alla cacciatora (hunter-style) dishes are sourced from Lazio's hills, with meats such as *cinghiale* (boar) and *lepre* (hare).

Fish is also good in autumn; you could try fried

fish from Fiumicino, such as *triglia* (red mullet), or mixed small fish, such as *alici* (anchovies).

Autumn equals mushrooms – the meaty porcini, *galletti* and *ovuli*. Heaping the markets are *broccoletti (also called broccolini)*, a cross between broccoli and asparagus, *uva* (grapes), *pere* (pears) and nuts.

WINTER

Winter is the ideal time to eat cockle-warming dishes with *ceci* (chickpeas) and vegetable-rich minestrone, as well as herb-roasted *porchetta di Ariccia* (pork from Ariccia).

Puntarelle ('little points' – Catalonian chicory), found only in Lazio, is a delicious, faintly bitter winter green.

Markets are piled high with *broccolo Romanesco* (Roman broccoli), *aranci* (oranges) and *mandarini* (mandarins).

In February, look out for *frappé* (strips of fried dough sprinkled with sugar), eaten at carnival time.

When to Eat

For *colazione* (breakfast), most Romans head to a bar for a cappuccino and *cornetto* (croissant).

The main meal of the day is *pranzo* (lunch), eaten at about 1.30pm. Many shops and businesses close for one to three hours every afternoon to accommodate the meal and siesta that follows. On Sundays *pranzo* is particularly important.

Many restaurants offer 'brunch' at weekends, but this isn't the breakfast/lunch combination featuring pancakes and eggs that English and American visitors might expect. Brunch in Rome tends to mean a buffet, available from around noon to 3pm.

Aperitivo is a buffet of snacks to accompany evening drinks, usually from around 6pm till 9pm, and costing around €6 to €10 for a drink and unlimited platefuls.

Cena (dinner), eaten any time from about 8.30pm, is usually simple, although this is changing as fewer people make it home for the big lunchtime feast.

A full Italian meal consists of an antipasto (starter), a *primo piatto* (first course), a *secondo piatto* (second course) with an *insalata* (salad) or *contorno* (vegetable side dish), *dolci* (sweet), fruit, coffee and *digestivo* (liqueur). When eating out, however, you can do as most Romans do, and mix and match: order, say, a *primo* followed by an *insalata* or *contorno*.

THE CULINARY CALENDAR

According to the culinary calendar (initiated by the Catholic Church to vary the nutrition of its flock), fish is eaten on Friday and *baccalà* (salted cod) is often eaten with *ceci* (chickpeas), usually on Wednesday. Thursday is gnocchi (dumplings) day. The traditional, heavy Roman recipe uses semolina flour, but you can also find the typical gnocchi with potatoes. Many traditional Roman restaurants still offer dishes according to this calendar.

Where to Eat

Take your pick according to your mood and your pocket, from the frenetic energy of a Roman pizzeria to the warm familiarity of a local trattoria, run for generations by the same family, or from a bar laden with sumptuous *apertivi* to a restaurant where both presentation and the flavours are a work of art.

ENOTECHE (WINE BARS)

Romans rarely drink without eating, and you can eat well at many *enoteche*, wine bars that usually serve snacks (such as cheeses or cold meats, *bruschette* and *crostini*) and hot dishes. Some, such as Palatium (p114) or Casa Bleve (p87), offer full-scale dining.

TRATTORIA, OSTERIA OR RESTAURANT?

Traditionally, trattorias were family-run places that offered a basic, affordable local menu, while *osterie* usually specialised in one dish and *vino della casa* (house wine). There are still lots of these around. *Ristoranti* offer more choices and smarter service, and are more expensive.

PIZZA

Remarkably, pizza was only introduced to Rome post-WWII, by southern immigrants. It caught on. Every Roman's favourite casual (and cheap) meal is the gloriously simple pizza, with Rome's signature wafer-thin bases, covered in fresh, bubbling toppings, slapped down on tables by waiters on a mission. Pizzerias often only open in the evening, as their wood-fired ovens take a while to get going. Most Romans will precede their pizza with a starter of bruschetta or *fritti* (mixed fried foods, such as zucchini flowers, potato, olives etc) and wash it all down with beer. Some places in Rome serve pizza with a thicker, fluffier base, which is the Neapolitan style.

For a snack on the run, Rome's pizza *al taglio* (by the slice) places are hard to beat, with toppings loaded atop thin, crispy, light-as-air, slow-risen bread that verge on the divine. There's been an increase of more gourmet pizza places in the last decade, with their king being Gabriele Bonci's Pizzarium (p138) close to the Vatican

FAST FOOD

Fast food is a long-standing Roman tradition, with plenty of street-food favourites. A *tavola calda* (hot table) offers cheap, pre-prepared pasta, meat and vegetable dishes, while a *rosticceria* sells mainly cooked meats. Neither is best for a romantic meal, but they're often very tasty.

Another favourite on the run are *arancini*, fried risotto balls that have fillings such as mozzarella and ham. These originate from Sicily, but are much loved in Rome too, where they're known as *supplì*.

Fast food is the latest Roman tradition to be reinvented, with a new-fangled offering of gourmet snacks that riff on family favourites. These days you'll find hip new places serving *supplì* or *fritti* with a twist. And these are no victory of style over substance – the new guard takes their gastronomy just as seriously as the old.

DELIS & MARKETS

Rome's well-stocked delis and fresh-produce markets are a fabulous feature of the city's foodscape. Most neighbourhoods have a few local delis and their own daily food market. The markets operate from around 7am to 1.30pm, Monday to Saturday. There are also some excellent farmers markets, mostly taking place at the weekends. The best of these is the one at Circo Massimo, which takes place on Saturday and Sunday.

Rome's most famous markets include the following:

→ **Campo de' Fiori** (p78) The most picturesque, but also the most expensive. Prices are graded according to the shopper's accent.

→ **Mercato di Circo Massimo** (p69) Rome's best and most popular farmers market is a colourful showcase for seasonal, zero-kilometre produce.

→ **Nuovo Mercato Esquilino** (p155) Cheap and the best place to find exotic herbs and spices.

→ **Piazza dell' Unità** (Map p312) Near the Vatican, perfect for stocking up for a picnic.

→ **Piazza San Cosimato** (Map p316) Trastevere's neighbourhood market is still the business with foodstuffs.

→ **Nuovo Mercato di Testaccio** (p180) A purpose-built site crammed with enticing stalls and local shoppers.

LOCAL RECOMMENDATIONS

Rome resident Elizabeth Minchilli, a prolific food journalist, blogger (www.elizabeth-minchilliinrome.com) and author of *Eating Rome,* shares some top tips.

I always suggest going first to the markets to see what's fresh, because so much has to do with what's seasonal. Besides the regular city markets, there are also weekend farmers markets, including one at Circus Maximus.

You should try *pizza bianca* (white pizza), which is typical Roman street food. There is always a discussion about who has the best. Most people cite the **Forno di Campo de' Fiori** (p88), but I prefer **Roscioli** (p88) for *pizza bianca*. If you want pizza with red sauce, go to **Antico Forno Urbani** (p89). You won't find many foreigners there; it's all Italians. The *pizza rossa* is very thin, covered with just a little bit of tomato sauce, really caramelised and fantastic.

In the last few years Rome has been having this renaissance of pizza makers. The king of pizza is Gabriele Bonci; people come from all over the world to have his pizza, so it's well worth going to **Pizzarium** (p138) if you're near the Vatican.

Another thing to try is ice cream. You'll pass lots of places with huge fluffy mounds: ignore those and try and look for the artisanal gelato makers. Again, seasonal is always good, so you'll get strawberry in the summer, chestnut in the winter. For example, over near Piazza Navona is **Gelateria del Teatro** (p86) and Fatamorgana in **Monti** (p148) and Trastevere. And if you want extra creamy, head to Come il Latte, near Via Flavia.

When it comes to eating out in Rome I love going old school. Sora Margherita is a hole-in-the-wall that not only does artichokes, but has ricotta-topped *cacio e pepe*.

GELATERIE

Eating gelato is as much a part of Roman life as morning coffee – try it and you'll understand why. The city has some of the world's finest ice-cream shops, which use only the finest seasonal ingredients, sourced from the finest locations.

In these artisanal gelaterie you won't find a strawberry flavour in winter, for example, and pistachios are from Bronte, almonds from Avola, and so on. It's all come a long way since Nero snacked on snow mixed with fruit pulp and honey. A rule of thumb is to check the colour of the pistachio flavour: ochre-green equals good, bright-green equals bad.

In the height of summer Romans love to eat *grattachecca* (literally 'scratched ice'), with kiosks selling crushed ice topped with fruit and syrup along the riverside from May to September. It's a great way to cool down.

Most places open from around 8am to 1am, with shorter hours in winter. Prices range from around €2 to €3.50 for a *cona* (cone) or *coppetta* (tub or cup).

Food & Wine Courses

Cookery writer Diane Seed, author of *The Top One Hundred Pasta Sauces*, runs her **Roman Kitchen** (Map p304; ☑06 678 57 59; www.italiangourmet.com; per day €200) several times a year from her kitchen in the Palazzo Doria Pamphilj. There are one-, two- and three-day courses (which include a market visit) costing €200 per day.

In Monti you can take a wine-tasting course or a food tour with Vino Roma (p153), which has a state-of-the-art tasting studio.

FOOD TOURS

Eating Italy Food Tours (www.eating-italyfoodtours.com; €75; ☉daily) is run by American expat Kenny Dunn and offers informative four-hour tours around Testaccio or Trastevere, with the chance to taste 12 delicacies on the way. There's a maximum of 12 people to a tour.

Wine specialists **Vino Roma** (p153) offer bespoke three-hour food tours.

Vegetarians, Vegans & Gluten Free

Panic not, vegetarians; you can eat well in Rome, with the choice of bountiful antipasti, pasta dishes, *insalati, contorni* and pizzas.

Be mindful of hidden ingredients not mentioned on the menu – for example, steer clear of anything that's been stuffed (like courgette flowers, often spiced up with anchovies) or check that it's *senza carne o pesce* (without meat or fish). Note that to many Italians vegetarian means you don't eat red meat.

Vegans are in for a tougher time. Cheese is used universally, so you must specify that you want something *senza formaggio* (without cheese). Also remember that *pasta fresca*, which may also turn up in soups, is made with eggs. The safest bet is to self-cater or try a dedicated vegetarian restaurant, which will always have some vegan options.

Most restaurants offer gluten-free options, as there is a good awareness of celiac disease here. Just say *'Io sono celiaco'* or *'senza glutine'* when you sit down, and usually the waiters will be able to recommend you suitable dishes.

Lonely Planet's Top Choices

Metamorfosi (p190) Michelin-starred, chic yet informal.

Glass Hostaria (p168) Italian cuisine as a creative art in Trastevere.

Casa Coppelle (p84) Creative Italian and French-inspired food in romantic surroundings.

Flavio al Velavevodetto (p178) For the real *cucina romana* (Roman kitchen).

L'Asino d'Oro (p148) Fantastic food, stunning value and Umbrian flavours.

Fatamorgana (p111) Incredible artisanal gelato, in Tridente, Vatican, Monti and Trastevere.

Best Roman

Flavio al Velavevodetto (p178) Classic *cucina romana,* served in huge portions.

Da Felice (p179) In the heartland of Roman cuisine, and sticking to a traditional weekly timetable.

Armando al Pantheon (p84) Family-run trattoria offering hearty Roman cuisine in the shadow of the Pantheon.

Ristorante L'Arcangelo (p137) A creative, contemporary take on Roman dishes.

Best Creative

Metamorfosi (p190) Michelin-starred cuisine by wonder-chef Roy Carceres.

All'Oro (p112) Food as art at chef Riccardo Di Giacinto's glamorous Michelin-starred eatery.

Glass Hostaria (p168) Wonderful, innovative food in a contemporary setting in Trastevere.

Open Colonna (p150) Antonello Colonna's glass-roofed restaurant offers creative takes on Roman classics.

Aroma (p178) Beautiful setting, and chef Giuseppe Di Iorio bedazzles with forward-thinking Mediterranean cuisine.

Renato e Luisa (p88) Always-packed trattoria that takes classic Roman cooking and mixes it up.

Best Pizzerias

Pizzeria Da Remo (p178) Spartan but stunning, the frenetic Roman pizzeria experience in Testaccio.

Pizza Ostiense (p202) New on the scene, but offering classic Roman neighborhood pizza.

Panattoni (p163) Streetside tables and fabulous pizza keep hauling in the hoards to 'l'obitorio' (the morgue).

Pizzeria Ivo (p165) Always busy, fiercely traditional, loud-and-gruff Trastevere pizzeria.

Best by Budget

€

Supplizio (p87) Gourmet fried-rice balls surfing the fast-food trend.

Alfredo e Ada (p86) Much-loved, no-frills, family-run trattoria.

Pizzarium (p138) Top-of-the-range *pizza al taglio*.

€€

L'Asino d'Oro (p148) Umbrian creative cuisine at reasonable prices (especially lunch).

Casa Conti (p113) Wonderful lunchtime restaurant-museum, with traditional local dishes amid picturesque antiques.

Casa Coppelle (p84) Good-value French-Italian cuisine with lashings of romance.

€€€

Metamorfosi (p190) Roy Caceres' stupendously good Michelin-starred cooking.

All'Oro (p112) Michelin-starred cuisine combining innovation and tradition under chef Riccardo Di Giacinto.

Enoteca La Torre (p137) Michelin-starred glamour in the Fendi sisters' Villa Laetitia.

Ristorante L'Arcangelo (p137) Fabulous creative restaurant proffering Roman food with a twist.

Glass Hostaria (p168) Wonderful creative restaurant in Trastevere.

Best Regional

Enoteca Regionale Palatium (p114) Wine-bar showcasing the best of Lazio food and drink.

Colline Emiliane (p115) Fantastic roasted meats and hearty pastas from Emilia-Romagna.

Trattoria Monti (p150) Top-notch traditional cooking from the Marches, including heavenly fried things.

Terre e Domus (p67) All ingredients are sourced from the surrounding Lazio region.

Best See & Be Seen

Dal Bolognese (p112) Moneyed, moghuls and models mingle just off Piazza del Popolo.

Settembrini (p137) Beloved of media lovelies, with the RAI (national media company) headquarters nearby.

Ristorante L'Arcangelo (p137) Politicians and celebrities hobnob over creative dishes.

Il Sorpasso (p136) Vintage-cool bar-restaurant.

Temakhino (p148) Of-the-moment Brazilian-sushi hybrid in Monti, mixing up powerful caipirinhas.

Best Pastry Shops

I Dolci di Nonna Vincenza (p88) Heavenly Sicilian pastries.

Pasticceria De Bellis (p88) Work-of-art cakes, pastries and *dolci* at this chic pasticceria.

Andreotti (p202) Poem-worthy treats from buttery *crostate* (tarts) to the piles of golden *sfogliatelle romane* (ricotta-filled pastries).

Innocenti (p163) Classic old-school Trastevere bakery, with piled-high biscuits such as *brutti ma buoni* (ugly but good).

Best Pizza by the Slice

Pizzarium (p138) Pizza slices created by the master, Gabriele Bonci.

Forno Roscioli (p88) Thin and crispy, this is some of the best *pizza rossa* in Rome, if not the world.

Forno di Campo de' Fiori (p88) Food-of-the-gods *pizza rossa* (with tomato and oregano) and *bianca* (with olive oil and rosemary).

Antico Forno Urbani (p89) A kosher bakery in the Ghetto with incredible *pizza bianca*.

Best Settings

Aroma (p178) The Michelin-starred rooftop restaurant of the Palazzo Manfredi hotel has 'marry-me' views over the Colosseum.

La Veranda (p135) A location in Paolo Sorrentino's the Great Beauty; dine beneath 15th-century Pinturicchio frescoes.

Open Colonna (p150) Restaurant on a mezzanine under a soaring glass ceiling in the Palazzo degli Esposizioni.

Casa Bleve (p87) Gracious colonnaded wine bar with a stained-glass ceiling.

Il Palazzetto (p114) A sunny terrace that overlooks the Spanish Steps.

Ristorante Roof Garden Circus (p67) Rooftop of the Forty Seven hotel with glorious views matched by the food.

Best Places to Eat With Locals

Pizzeria Da Remo (p178) The full neighbourhood Roman pizza experience, with lightning-fast waiters serving paper-thin pizzas.

Da Felice (p179) Traditional local cooking in Testaccio, the heartland of Roman cuisine.

Antico Forno Urbani (p89) Queue up with the locals for *pizza al taglio* in the Ghetto.

Pizza Ostiense (p202) Fabulous thin-crust pizza in Rome's ex-industrial, hip neighbourhood of Ostiense.

Best Gelatarie

Fatamorgana (p111) Rome's finest artisanal flavours, now in multiple central locations.

Gelateria del Teatro (p86) Around 40 choices of delicious ice cream, all made on site.

Il Caruso (p115) A small but perfect selection of creamy flavours.

Gelarmony (p136) A Sicilian gelataria with many great tastes, including typically Sicilian pistachio or cassata.

Dei Gracchi (p111) A taste of heaven in several locations across Rome.

Fior di Luna (p165) Great artisanal ice cream in Trastevere.

Best Fast Food

Trapizzino (p178) Home of the *trapizzino*, a cone of doughy bread with fillers like *polpette al sugo* (meatballs in tomato sauce).

Supplizio (p87) Gourmet versions of Rome's favourite fried risotto ball snacks, *supplì*.

Ciuri Ciuri (p148) Sicilian pastry and top savoury snack stop with delicious *arancini* (the Sicilian version of *supplì*).

Dall'Antò (p149) Antonio cooks up intensely good pancakes from ingredients such as chestnut flour, using ancient regional recipes.

Pianostrada Laboratorio di Cucina (p165) All-female-run bakery and casual cafe using superlative ingredients for gourmet sandwiches and snacks.

Best Food Shops

Eataly (p202) Mall-sized, state-of-the-art food emporium, with produce from all over Italy, and multiple restaurants.

Salumeria Roscioli (p89) The rich scents of fine Italian produce, cured meats and cheeses intermingle in this superlative deli.

Volpetti (p180) This super-stocked deli is a treasure trove of gourmet delicacies and helpful staff.

Castroni (p139) An Aladdin's cave of gourmet delicacies.

Cafes line Piazza della Rotonda, outside the Pantheon (p72)

Drinking & Nightlife

Often the best way to enjoy nightlife in Rome is to wander from restaurant to bar, getting happily lost down picturesque cobbled streets. There's simply no city with better backdrops for a drink: you can savour a Campari overlooking the Roman Forum or sample some artisanal beer while watching the light bounce off baroque fountains.

Rome After Dark

Night-owl Romans tend to eat late, then drink at bars before heading off to a club at around 1am. Like most cities, Rome is a collection of districts, each with its own character, which is often completely different after dark. The *centro storico* and Trastevere pull in a mix of locals and tourists as night falls. Ostiense and Testaccio are the grittier clubbing districts, with clusters of clubs in a couple of locations – Testaccio has a parade of crowd-pleasing clubs running over the hill of Monte Testaccio. There are also subtle political divisions. San Lorenzo and Pigneto, to the south of Rome, are popular with a left-leaning, alternative crowd, while areas to the north (such as Ponte Milvio and Parioli) attract a more right-wing, bourgeois milieu.

The *bella figura* (loosely translated as 'looking good') is important. The majority of locals spend evenings checking each other out, partaking in gelato, and not drinking too much. However, this is changing and certain areas – those popular with a younger crowd – can get rowdy with drunk teens and tourists (for example, Campo de' Fiori and parts of Trastevere).

Enoteche (Wine Bars)

The *enoteca* was where the old boys from the neighbourhood used to drink rough local wine poured straight from the barrel. Times have changed: nowadays they tend to be sophisticated but still atmospheric places, offering Italian and international vintages, delicious cheeses and cold cuts.

Bars & Pubs

Bars range from regular Italian cafe-bars that have seemingly remained the same for centuries, to chic, carefully styled places made for esoteric cocktails – such as Co.So (p151) and Salotto 42 (p92) – and laid-back, perennially popular haunts – such as Freni e Frizioni (p169) – that have a longevity rarely seen in other cities. Pubs are also popular, with several long-running Irish-style pubs such as Finnegans (p153) and Druid's Den (p153) filled with chattering Romans, and more pub-like bars opening on the back of the artisanal beer trend.

Nightclubs

Rome has a range of nightclubs, mostly in Ostiense and Testaccio, with music policies ranging from lounge and jazz to dancehall and hip-hop. Clubs tend to get busy after midnight, or even after 2am. Often admission is free, but drinks are expensive. Cocktails can cost from €10 to €20, but you can drink much more cheaply in the studenty clubs of San Lorenzo, Pigneto and the *centri sociali* (social centres).

Centri Sociali

Rome's flip side is a surprising alternative underbelly, centred on left-wing *centri sociali*: grungy, squatter arts centres that host live music and contemporary arts events. They offer Rome's most unusual, cheap and alternative nightlife options. These include Brancaleone (p191) and Esc Atelier (p153).

Rome in Summer (& Winter)

From around mid-June to mid-September, many nightclubs and live-music venues close, some moving to EUR or the beaches at Fregene or Ostia. The area around the Isola Tiberina throngs with life nightly during the Lungo er Tevere...Roma, a summer festival that sprouts bars, stalls and an open-air cinema along the riverbank.

Be aware that in winter, bars often close earlier in the evening, particularly in areas where the norm is to drink outside.

NEED TO KNOW

Opening Hours

➠ Most cafes: 7.30am to 8pm

➠ Traditional bars: 7.30am to 1am or 2am

➠ Most bars, pubs and *enoteche* (wine bars): lunchtime or 6pm to 2am

➠ Nightclubs: 10pm to 4am

Dress Codes

Romans tend to dress up to go out, and most people will be looking pretty sharp in the smarter clubs and bars in the Centro Storico and Testaccio. However, over in Pigneto and San Lorenzo or at the *centri sociali* (social centres), the style is much more alternative.

Online Resources

➠ **Roma 2 Night** (http://2night.it)

➠ **Zero** (http://roma.zero.eu)

PLAN YOUR TRIP DRINKING & NIGHTLIFE

Gay & Lesbian Rome

There is only a smattering of dedicated gay and lesbian clubs and bars in Rome, though many nightclubs host regular gay and lesbian nights. For local information, pick up a copy of the monthly magazine *AUT*, published by Circolo Mario Mieli (www.mariomieli.org). There's also info at AZ Gay (www.azgay.it). Lesbians can find out more about the local scene at Coordinamento Lesbiche Italiano (www.clrbp.it).

Most gay venues (bars, clubs and saunas) require you to have an Arcigay (p273) membership card. These cost €15/8 per year/three months and are available from any venue that requires one.

Lazio Wines

Lazio wines may not be household names yet, but it's well worth trying some local wines while you're here. Although whites dominate Lazio's production – 95% of the region's Denominazione di Origine Controllata (DOC; the second of Italy's four quality classifications) wines are white – there are a few notable reds as well. Palatium (p114) and Terre e Domus (p67) are the best places for sampling Lazio wines.

WHITES

Most of the house white in Rome will be from the Castelli Romani area to the southeast of Rome, centred on Frascati and Marino. New production techniques have led to a lighter, drier wine that is beginning to be taken seriously. Frascati Superiore is now an excellent tipple, Castel de Paolis' Vigna Adriana wins plaudits, while the emphatically named Est! Est!! Est!!!, produced by the renowned wine house Falesco, based in Montefiascone on the volcanic banks of Lago Bolsena, is increasingly drinkable.

REDS

Falesco also produces the excellent Montiano, blended from Merlot grapes. Colacicchi's Torre Ercolana from Anagni is another opulent red that blends local Cesanese di Affile with cabernet sauvignon and merlot. Velvety, complex and fruity, this is a world-class wine.

Craft Beer

In recent years beer drinking has really taken off in Italy, and especially in Rome, with specialised bars and restaurants offering microbrewed beers. Local favourites include Birradamare in Fiumicino, Porto Fluviale in Ostiense, and Birra Del Borgo in Rieti (on the border between Lazio and Abruzzo), which opened local beer haunts Bir & Fud (p168) and Open Baladin (p91). Local beers reflect the seasonality that's so important in Rome – for example, look for winter beers made from chestnuts.

Other important stops on the artisanal beer trail are Porto Fluviale (p203), Ma Che Siete Venuti a Fà (p168) and Birra Piu (p151).

Cocktails & Digestives

Cocktail bars are the current buzz in Rome, some featuring special local creations such as the Carbonara sour at Co.So (p151), featuring vodka infused with pork fat in a homage to the classic Roman pasta sauce. Popular aperitifs are based on bitter alcoholic liqueurs, such Campari Soda or Aperol spritz, which mixes Aperol with prosecco. Crodino is a herbal, medicinal-tasting non-alcoholic aperitif. Italians love to finish off a meal with a digestif. The best of these aren't shop bought, so if it's 'fatta in casa' (made at home), give it a try.

SOCIAL NETWORKING

Friends in Rome (www.friendsinrome.com) is a social organisation that organises regular social events and offers a chance to mingle with an international crowd – a mix of expats, locals and out-of-towners – and find out about the local social scene.

Coffee

For an espresso (a shot of strong black coffee), ask for *un caffè;* if you want it with a drop of hot/cold milk, order *un caffè macchiato* ('stained' coffee) *caldo/freddo*. Long black coffee (as in a watered-down version) is known as *caffè lungo* (an espresso with more water) or *caffè all'american* (a filter coffee). If you fancy a coffee but one more shot will catapult you through the ceiling, you can drink *orzo*, made from roasted barley but served like coffee.

Then, of course, there's the cappuccino (coffee with frothy milk, served warm rather than hot). If you want it without froth, ask for a *cappuccino senza schiuma;* if you want it hot, ask for it *ben caldo*. Italians drink cappuccino only during the morning and never after meals.

In summer, *cappuccino freddo* (iced coffee with milk, usually already sugared), *caffè freddo* (iced espresso) and *granita di caffè* (frozen coffee, usually with cream) top the charts.

A *caffè latte* is a milkier version of the cappuccino with less froth; a *latte macchiato* is even milkier (warmed milk 'stained' with a spot of coffee). A *caffè corretto* is an espresso 'corrected' with a dash of grappa or something similar.

There are two ways to drink coffee in a Roman bar-cafe: either standing at the bar, in which case you pay first at the till and then, with your receipt, order at the counter; or you can sit down at a table and enjoy waiter service. In the latter case you'll pay up to double what you'd pay at the bar.

Drinking & Nightlife by Neighbourhood

➡ **Centro Storico** Bars and a few clubs, a mix of touristy and sophisticated. (p90)

➡ **Trastevere** Everyone's favourite place for a *passeggiata* (evening stroll), with plenty of bars and cafes. (p168)

➡ **Testaccio** With a cluster of mainstream clubs, this nightlife strip offers poptastic choice. (p179)

➡ **Ostiense** Home to Rome's cooler nightclubs, housed in ex-industrial venues. (p203)

➡ **San Lorenzo** Favoured by students, with a concentration of bars and alternative clubs. (p153)

➡ **Pigneto** Bohemian ex-working-class district lined with bars and restaurants. (p151)

Lonely Planet's Top Choices

Ai Tre Scalini (p152) Buzzing *enoteca* that feels as convivial as a pub.

Ma Che Siete Venuti a Fà (p168) Tiny pub that's the heart of Rome's artisanal beer explosion.

Co.So (p151) A real buzz in this Pigneto hotspot, serving up out-there cocktails on bubble-wrap coasters.

Sciascia Caffè (p138) Classy joint serving the *caffè eccellente*, a velvety smooth espresso in a chocolate-lined cup.

Barnum Cafe (p91) Cool vintage armchairs to sink into by day and cocktails by night.

Best Cafes

La Casa del Caffè Tazza d'Oro (p90) With lovely burnished 1940s fittings, great coffee and, in summer, *granita*.

Chiostro del Bramante Caffè (p87) It's hard to beat a Bramante-designed cloister as a setting.

Sciascia Caffè (p138) Delicious coffee in an elegant interior.

Barnum Cafe (p91) Laid-back coffee drinking in comfortable armchairs.

Best for a Lazy Drink

Ombre Rosse (p169) Lovely, relaxed Trastevere bar, with outside seating.

Stravinskij Bar (p116) Hotel de Russie's elegant bar, with its courtyard garden backed by Borghese gardens.

Fandango Incontro (p92) Arty bar owned by cinema company housed in an 18th-century palazzo.

Yeah! Pigneto (www.yeah-pigneto.com; Via Giovanni de Agostini 41; ⏰8pm-2am) Boho bar with plenty of places to sit, with DJs and regular live gigs.

Best Enoteche

Il Tiaso (p151) With a hip, living-room vibe, plentiful wines, and live music.

Fafiuché (p152) A charming warm-orange space with wine and artisanal beers.

La Barrique (p152) Inviting Monti address, with great wines and accompanying meals.

Il Goccetto (p91) An old-school *vino e olio* (wine and oil) shop makes for a great neighbourhood wine bar.

Best Aperitivo

La Meschita (p169) Delicious nibbles in this tiny *enoteca* adjoining La Ferrara restaurant.

Doppiozeroo (p203) Popular Ostiense address with impressive buffet choice.

Momart (p191) Students and local professionals love its expansive array of pizza and other snacks.

Freni e Frizioni (p169) Perenially cool bar with lavish nightly buffet of snacks.

Best for Beer

Ma Che Siete Venuti a Fà' (p168) Pint-sized bar crammed with real-ale choices.

Open Baladin (p91) More than 40 beers on tap and up to 100 bottled brews.

No.Au (p91) 'Know how' offers an impressive list of artisanal craft brews.

Birra Piu (p151) Pigneto hub, with a great range of craft beers.

Best See & Be Seen

Etablì (p91) Chic bar near Campo de'Fiori, filled with vintage French furniture and laid-back cool.

Salotto 42 (p92) A sitting-room-style bar, offering cocktails facing the ancient Roman Stock Exchange.

Co.So (p151) Opened by the Hotel de Russie's former mixologist, this is Pigneto's hippest haunt.

Rec 23 (p179) With NY style and locally inspired cocktails, this is the place to be seen in Testaccio.

Best Alternative

Lanificio 159 (p191) Cool underground venue hosts live gigs and club nights.

Big Bang (p179) Reggae, dancehall, dub and techno in a graffitti-sprayed former slaughterhouse.

Big Star (p169) Backstreet Trastevere bar, with regular DJs and a laid-back crowd.

Best Gay

Coming Out (p272) A friendly, gay bar near the Colosseum, open all day, with gigs, drag shows and karaoke later on.

L'Alibi (p180) Kitsch shows and house, techno and dance pumping up a mixed gay and straight crowd.

My Bar (p272) A mixed crowd by day, and gayer by night, in the shadow of the Colosseum.

Rome's opera house, the Teatro dell'Opera di Roma (p153)

AFP / STRINGER / GETTY IMAGES ©

 # Entertainment

Watching the world go by in Rome is often entertainment enough, but don't overlook the local arts and sports scene. As well as gigs and concerts in every genre, there are fantastic arts festivals, especially in summer, performances with Roman ruins as a backdrop, and football games that split the city asunder.

Music

Rome's abundance of beautiful settings makes it a superb place to catch a concert. Many international stars play at the Auditorium Parco della Musica (p191), a state-of-the-art, Renzo Piano–designed complex that combines architectural innovation with perfect acoustics. However, there are often creative uses of other spaces. In recent years there have been major gigs on the ancient racetrack Circo Massimo (p64), and Coldplay have even played on the Imperial Rome set in Cinecittà studios (p204).

CLASSICAL

Music in Rome is not just about the Auditorium. There are concerts by the Accademia Filarmonica Romana at Teatro Olimpico (p191); the Auditorium Conciliazione (p138), Rome's premier classical music venue before the newer Auditorium was opened, is still a force to be reckoned with; and the Istituzione Universitaria dei Concerti (p154), holds concerts in the Aula Magna of La Sapienza University.

Free classical concerts are often held in many of Rome's churches, especially at Easter and around Christmas and New Year;

look out for information at Rome's tourist kiosks. The Basilica di San Paolo Fuori le Mura (p200) hosts an important choral mass on 25 January and the hymn 'Te Deum' is sung at the Chiesa del Gesù (p81) on 31 December.

OPERA & DANCE

Rome's opera house, the Teatro dell'Opera di Roma (p153), is a magnificent, grandiose venue, lined in gilt and red, but productions can be a bit hit and miss. It's also home to Rome's official Corps de Ballet and has a ballet season running in tandem with its opera performances. Both ballet and opera move outdoors for the summer season at the ancient Roman Terme di Caracalla, which is an even more spectacular setting.

You can also see opera in various other outdoor locations; check listings or at the tourist information kiosks for details.

Rome's Auditorium hosts classical and contemporary dance performances, as well as the Equilibrio Festival della Nuova Danza in February. The Auditorium Conciliazione is another good place to catch contemporary dance companies. Invito alla Danza is a contemporary dance festival in July that encompasses tango, jazz dance, contemporary and more.

JAZZ, ROCK & POP

Besides the Auditorium Parco della Musica, large concerts also take place at Rome's sports stadiums, including Stadio Olimpico (p192) and the racetrack on the Appia Nuova, the Ippodromo La Capannelle.

The *centri sociali,* alternative arts centres set up in venues around Rome, are also good places to catch a gig, especially Brancaleone (p191) in northern Rome, with music policies encompassing hip-hop, electro, dubstep, reggae and dancehall.

Cinema Under the Stars

There are various atmospheric outdoor summer film festivals; check current listings. The following take place annually.

Isola del Cinema (www.isoladelcinema.com) Independent films in the romantic setting of the Isola Tiberina in July and August. This runs in conjunction with the riverside Lungo il Tevere festival.

Notti di Cinema a Piazza Vittorio (www.agisanec.lazio.it; tickets €7) Italian and international releases at two open-air screens in Piazza Vittorio Emanuele II from June to September.

NEED TO KNOW

Internet Resources
➡ **Comune di Roma** (www.060608.it)
➡ **In Rome Now** (www.inromenow.com)
➡ **Roma Musica** (www.romamusica.it)
➡ **Tutto Teatro** (www.tuttoteatro.com)

Tickets

Tickets for concerts, live music and theatrical performances are widely available across the city. Prices range enormously depending on the venue and artist. Hotels can often reserve tickets for guests, or you can contact the venue or organisation directly – check listings publications for booking details. Otherwise you can try the following:
➡ **Hellò Ticket** (www.helloticket.it)
➡ **Orbis** (06 4827915)

PLAN YOUR TRIP ENTERTAINMENT

Theatre

Rome has a thriving local theatre scene, with both traditional theatres and smaller experimental venues. Performances are usually in Italian.

Particularly wonderful are the summer festivals that make use of Rome's archaeological scenery. Performances take place in settings such as Villa Adriana in Tivoli, Ostia Antica's Roman theatre and the Teatro di Marcello. In summer the **Miracle Players** (06 7039 3427; www.miracleplayers.org) perform classic English drama or historical comedy in English next to the Roman Forum and other open-air locations. Performances are usually free.

Spectator Sports

FOOTBALL

In Rome you're either for AS Roma (*giallorossi* – yellow and reds) or Lazio (*biancazzuri* – white and blues), with both teams playing in Serie A (Italy's premier league). A new Roma stadium is currently being built at Tor di Valle, due to be completed in time for the 2017–18 season. Unfortunately, both sets of supporters have a controversial minority who have been known to cause trouble at matches.

From September to May there's a game at home for Roma or Lazio almost every weekend and a trip to Rome's football stadium, the Stadio Olimpico (p192), is an

AS ROMA VS LAZIO

The Rome derby is one of the football season's highest-profile games. The rivalry between Roma and Lazio is fierce and little love is lost between the fans. If you go to the Stadio Olimpico, make sure you get it right – Roma fans (in deep red with a natty gold trim) flock to the Curva Sud (southern stand), while Lazio supporters (in light blue) stand in the Curva Nord (northern stand). If you want to sit on the fence, head to the Tribuna Tevere or Tribuna Monte Mario. For more details on the clubs, check out www.asroma.it and www.sslazio.it (both in Italian).

unforgettable experience. Note that ticket purchase regulations are far stricter than they used to be. Tickets have to bear the holder's name and passport or ID number, and you must present a photo ID at the turnstiles when entering the stadium. Two tickets are permitted per purchase for Serie A, Coppa Italia and UEFA Champions League games. Tickets cost from around €16 to €250. You can buy them from www.ticketone.it, www.listicket.it, from ticket agencies or at one of the A S Roma or Lazio stores around the city. To get to the stadium, take metro line A to Ottaviano–San Pietro and then bus 32.

BASKETBALL

Basketball is a popular spectator sport in Rome, though it inspires nothing like the fervour of football. Rome's team, **Virtus Roma** (www.virtusroma.it), plays throughout the winter months at the **Palalottomatica** (☑06 540901; www.palalottomatica.it/en/; Viale dell' Umanesimo; ⓜEUR Palasport) in EUR.

RUGBY UNION

Italy's rugby team, the Azzurri (Blues), entered the Six Nations tournament in 2000, and has been the competition underdog ever since. However, it has scored some big wins in recent years, with shock wins over France in 2011 and 2013; in 2015 it beat Scotland (but lost all other games).

The team usually plays home international games at Rome's **Stadio Flaminio** (☑06 3685 7309; www.federugby.it; Viale Maresciallo Pilsudski), but as works continue on the stadium, games are being staged at the Stadio Olimpico (p192).

TENNIS

Italy's premier tennis tournament, the Italian International Tennis Championships, is one of the most important events on the European tennis circuit. Every May the world's top players meet on the clay courts at the monumental, Fascist-era **Foro Italico** (☑800 622662; www.foroitalicoticketing.it; Viale del Foro Italico). Tickets can usually be bought at the Foro Italico each day of the tournament, except for the final days, which are sold out weeks in advance.

EQUESTRIAN EVENTS

Rome's top equestrian event is the annual **Piazza di Siena** (www.piazzadisiena.org), an international showjumping competition held in May and gorgeously set in Villa Borghese.

Entertainment by Neighbourhood

➡ **Centro Storico** Great for concerts in churches or theatre (usually in Italian). (p92)

➡ **Trastevere & Gianicolo** A few blues and jazz live-music venues. (p169)

➡ **Monti, Esquilino & San Lorenzo** Several intimate live-music venues. (p153)

➡ **Villa Borghese & Northern Rome** Home to the great Auditorium Parco della Musica, as well as Rome's major sporting venues. (p191)

➡ **San Giovanni & Testaccio** Regular live gigs in the district's clubs. (p180)

Lonely Planet's Top Choices

Auditorium Parco della Musica (p191) An incredible venue hosting an eclectic, must-see program of music, art and more.

Opera di Roma at Terme di Caracalla (p176) Opera and ballet performed with the amazing backdrop of the ruined Roman Baths of Caracalla.

Roma Incontra il Mondo (p188) Cool World music festival in the parklands of Villa Ada.

Blackmarket (p154) Intimate Monti bar with a regular calendar of live acoustic acts.

Best Classical Venues

Auditorium Parco della Musica (p191) Great acoustics, top international classical musicians and multiple concert halls.

Teatro dell'Opera di Roma (p153) Great, red-velvet and gilt interior for Rome's opera and dance companies.

Terme di Caracalla (p176) Wonderful outdoor setting for Rome's opera and ballet companies.

Auditorium Conciliazione (p138) Classical and contemporary concerts, cabarets, dance spectacles, theatre productions, film screenings and exhibitions in a large venue.

Teatro Olimpico (p191) Home to the Accademia Filarmonica Romana.

Best for Live Gigs

Blackmarket (p154) Bar filled with vintage sofas and armchairs, great for eclectic, mainly acoustic live music.

Big Bang (p179) The former slaughterhouse hosts Bababoomtime, Rome's Friday night reggae party.

Locanda Atlantide (p153) Studenty dive in an ex-warehouse basement, with a broad music policy from punk to folk-prog.

Lanificio 159 (p191) Ex-wool factory hosting underground live gigs alongside club nights.

Best for Jazz

Alexanderplatz (p138) Rome's foremost jazz club, with a mix of international and local musicians.

Charity Café (p154) Spindly tables and chairs, in an intimate space, hosting regular live gigs.

Big Mama (p169) An atmospheric Trastevere venue for jazz, blues, funk, soul and R&B.

Gregory's (p117) Popular with local musicians, a smooth venue close to the Spanish Steps.

Fonclea (p138) Pub venue regularly hosting live jazz, moving riverside in the summer.

Best Theatres

Ostia Antica (p206) Wonderful summer theatre in the ancient amphitheatre built by Agrippa.

Teatro Argentina (p92) The main home of the Teatro di Roma, with a wide-ranging program.

Silvano Toti Globe Theatre (p192) Open-air Elizabethan theatre, like London's Globe, but with better weather (plays in Italian).

Teatro India (p204) The alternative home of the Teatro di Roma.

Best Festivals

Roma Incontra il Mondo (p188) Glorious World music acts play close to the lake in Villa Ada.

Lungo il Tevere (p23) Open-air cinema and stalls line the Tiver riverbank and Tiberina island.

Romaeuropa (p23) Autumn celebration of theatre, opera and dance.

Festa di Noantri (p23) Trastevere's raucous street party in July.

Carnevale Romano (p22) Processions, costumes, parties and confetti – a blow-out before Lent, celebrating the end of winter.

Best Sporting Venues

Foro Italico (p188) Magnificent Fascist-era sports complex.

Stadio Olimpico (p192) Rome's 70,000-seat football stadium, part of the fascist-era Foro Italico.

Piazza di Siena (p186) Lovely racecourse in the heart of the Villa Borghese park.

Palalottomatica (p203) Circular stadium near to EUR in Southern Rome.

Shopping

Rome's shops, studios and boutiques make retail therapy diverting enough to distract you from the cityscape. Wander the backstreets and you'll find yourself glancing into dusty workshops of framers, basketweavers and furniture restorers. Narrow lanes are dotted with jewel-like boutiques, and department stores have an old-school glamour. It's not that there are no chain stores in Rome, but the city is still dominated by individual shops.

High Fashion

Big-name designer boutiques gleam in the grid of streets between Piazza di Spagna and Via del Corso. The great Italian and international names are represented here, as well as many lesser-known designers, selling clothes, shoes, accessories and dreams. The immaculately clad high-fashion spine is Via dei Condotti, but there's also lots of high fashion in Via Borgognona, Via Frattina, Via della Vite and Via del Babuino.

Downsizing a euro or two, Via Nazionale, Via del Corso, Via dei Giubbonari and Via Cola di Rienzo are good for midrange clothing stores, with some enticing small boutiques set amid the chains.

ONE-OFF BOUTIQUES & VINTAGE

Best for cutting-edge designer boutiques and vintage clothes is bohemian Via del Governo Vecchio, running from a small square just off Piazza Navona towards the river. Other places for one-off boutiques are Via del Pellegrino and around Campo de' Fiori. Via del Boschetto, Via Urbana and Via dei Serpenti in the Monti area feature unique clothing boutiques, including a couple where you can get your clothes adjusted to fit, as well as jewellery makers. Monti's also a centre for vintage clothes shops, as well as a weekend vintage market, Mercato Monti Urban Market. (p154)

Antiques

For antiques, Via dei Coronari, Via Margutta, Via Giulia and Via dei Banchi Vecchi are the best places – quality is high, as are the prices.

Artisans

Rome's shopping scene has a surprising number of artists and artisans who create their goods on the spot in hidden workshops. There are several places in Tridente where you can get a bag, wallet or belt made to your specifications; in other shops you can commission lamps or embroidery.

Foodstuffs

Rome is deli heaven, of course. Also well worth a visit are Rome's many wonderful food markets – there's usually one in every district – where you can buy cheese, salami and other delicious stuff; note there are now various farmers' markets as well, including at Circo Massimo at weekends.

Shopping by Neighbourhood

➡ **Centro Storico** Boutiques, one-off designers, antiques, vintage and jewellery, as well as some swoon-worthy delicatessens.

➡ **Tridente, Trevi & the Quirinale** From high-fashion designer stores around Via Condotti to affordable chains on busy Via del Corso.

➡ **Monti, Esquilino & San Lorenzo** Independent fashion, homewares and vintage boutiques.

➡ **Trastevere & Gianicolo** Gifts and one-off shops in one of Rome's prettiest neighbourhoods.

➡ **San Giovanni & Testaccio** Browse a colourful food market and glorious delis.

➡ **Southern Rome** Home of mall-like food emporium Eataly.

Lonely Planet's Top Choices

Confetteria Moriondo & Gariglio (p95) A magical chocolate shop.

Vertecchi Art (p118) Art emporium with beautiful paper and notebooks.

Bottega di Marmoraro (p117) Have the motto of your choice carved into a marble slab at this delightful shop.

Pelletteria Nives (p117) Leather artisans make bags, wallets and more to your specifications.

Foodstuffs

Volpetti (p180) Bulging with delicious delicacies, and notably helpful staff.

Eataly (p202) Mall-scale food shop, filled with products from all over Italy, as well as books, cooking utensils and more.

Salumeria Roscioli (p88) The name is a byword for foodie excellence, with mouth-watering Italian and foreign delicacies.

Pio La Torre (p95) Unpretentious, and every cent you spend helps in the fight against the mafia.

Bookshops

Feltrinelli International (p155) An excellent range of the latest releases in English, Spanish, French, German and Portuguese.

Almost Corner Bookshop (p170) A crammed haven full of rip-roaring reads.

Open Door Bookshop (p170) Many happy moments browsing secondhand books in English, Italian, French and Spanish.

Libreria l'Argonauta (p192) Travel bookshop great for sparking dreams of your next trip.

Artisanal

Bottega di Marmoraro (p117) Commission a marble inscription to remind you of Rome.

Le Artigiane (p92) Maintaining Italy's artisanal traditions with a collection of handmade clothes, costume jewellery, ceramics, design objects and lamps.

Officina della Carta (p170) Beautiful hand-decorated notebooks, paper and cards.

Pelletteria Nives (p117) Have a bespoke leather bag made to your own specifications.

Clothing

Luna & L'Altra (p93) Fashion-heaven, with clothes by Comme des Garçons, Issey Miyake, and Yohji Yamamoto.

Tina Sondergaard (p154) Have a retro-inspired dress adjusted to fit perfectly at this Monti boutique.

daDADA 52 (p94) Cocktail dresses and summer frocks to make you stand out from the crowd (in a good way).

Homewares

Spot (p154) A careful selection of beautiful mid-century furnishings.

Mercato Monti Urban Market (p154) Vintage homeware finds cram this weekend market.

Gifts

Vertecchi Art (p118) Classy stationers, selling different hues of paper, notebooks and gifts appropriate to the season.

Arion Esposizioni (p155) Art, architecture and children's books, plus design-conscious presents.

NEED TO KNOW

Opening Hours

➡ Most city-centre shops: 9am to 7.30pm (or 10am to 8pm) Monday to Saturday; some close Monday morning.

➡ Smaller shops: 9am to 1pm and 3.30pm to 7.30pm (or 4pm to 8pm) Monday to Saturday.

Sales

Winter sales run from early January to mid-February, and summer sales from July to early September.

Taxes & Refunds

Non-EU residents who spend over €175 at shops with a 'Tax Free for Tourists' sticker (www.tax-refund.it) are entitled to a tax refund. Complete a form and get it stamped by customs as you leave Italy.

Fabriano (p117) Leather-bound diaries, funky notebooks and products embossed with street maps of Rome, plus beautifully made key rings and more.

AS Roma Store (p95) Trastevere treasure trove perfume store, with hundreds of choices from niche labels.

Shoes

Borini (p94) An unfussy shop filled to the brim with the latest women's footwear fashions.

Danielle (p117) A fast-changing collection of whatever is in for female feet right now, in a rainbow palette of colours, at affordable prices.

Barrilà Boutique (p117) Hundreds of different women's styles, so a good chance of finding the perfect shoe.

Explore Rome

ROME'S TOP SIGHTS

Neighbourhoods
at a Glance

❶ Ancient Rome p50

In a city of extraordinary beauty, Rome's ancient heart stands out. It's here that you'll find the great icons of Rome's past: the Colosseum, the Palatino, the forums, and Campidoglio (Capitoline Hill). Busy with tourists by day, it's quiet at night with few after-hours attractions.

❷ Centro Storico p70

Ideal for unhurried exploration, the historic centre is the Rome many come to find – a tangled chaos of medieval lanes, animated piazzas, Renaissance *palazzi,* cafes, restaurants and stylish bars. The Pantheon and Piazza Navona are the star turns, but you'll also find a host of monuments, museums and art-laden churches.

❸ Tridente, Trevi & the Quirinale p98

Counting the Trevi Fountain and Spanish Steps among its headline sights, this part of Rome is glamorous, debonair and touristy. The streets around Piazza di Spagna ooze money with their designer boutiques, fashionable bars and swish hotels, while the Trevi Fountain area swarms with overpriced eateries and tacky shops. Lording over it all, the presidential Palazzo del Quirinale exudes sober authority.

❹ Vatican City, Borgo & Prati p120

Over the river from the historic centre, the Vatican is home to two of Rome's top attractions – St Peter's Basilica and the Vatican Museums (where you'll find the Sistine Chapel) – as well as batteries of overpriced restaurants and souvenir shops. Nearby, the upscale Prati district offers excellent accommodation, eating and shopping.

❺ Monti, Esquilino & San Lorenzo p140

Centred on transport hub Stazione Termini, this is a large and cosmopolitan area. Hidden behind its busy roads you'll find some amazing churches, one of Rome's best museums (Palazzo Massimo alle Terme), and any number of cool bars and restaurants, mostly in the the Monti, San Lorenzo and Pigneto districts.

❻ Trastevere & Gianicolo p158

With its picture-perfect lanes, colourful *palazzi* and boho vibe, ever-trendy Trastevere is one of Rome's most vibrant neighbourhoods. Attractive by day, it heaves after dark as crowds swarm to its many restaurants, cafes, bars and pizzerias. Rising behind it, the Gianicolo Hill offers a breath of fresh air and superb views.

❼ San Giovanni & Testaccio p171

This sweeping, multifaceted area has something for everyone: medieval churches and monumental basilicas (Basilica di San Giovanni in Laterano above all), towering ruins (Terme di Caracalla), and tranquil parkland (Villa Celimontana). By the river, Testaccio is an earthy, workaday district known for its nose-to-tail Roman cuisine, traditional trattorias and thumping nightlife.

❽ Villa Borghese & Northern Rome p181

This moneyed area encompasses Rome's most famous park (Villa Borghese) and its most expensive residential district (Parioli). Concert-goers head to the Auditorium Parco della Musica, while art-lovers can choose between contemporary installations at MAXXI or baroque treasures at the Museo e Galleria Borghese.

❾ Southern Rome p193

Boasting a wealth of diversions, from ancient roads to futuristic ministries and cutting-edge clubs, this huge area extends to Rome's southern limits. Interest centres on Via Appia Antica, home of the catacombs; post-industrial Ostiense, full of street art, clubs and popular eateries; and EUR, a modernistic suburb in the extreme south of the city.

Ancient Rome

COLOSSEUM | PALATINO | THE FORUMS | CAMPIDOGLIO | PIAZZA VENEZIA | FORUM BOARIUM

Neighbourhood Top Five

1 Getting your first glimpse of the **Colosseum** (p52). Rome's iconic amphitheatre is both an architectural masterpiece and a stark, spine-tingling reminder of the brutality of ancient times.

2 Roaming the haunting ruins of the **Palatino** (p106), ancient Rome's birthplace and most exclusive neighbourhood.

3 Coming face to face with centuries of awe-inspiring art at the historic **Capitoline Museums** (p61).

4 Exploring the basilicas, temples and triumphal arches of the **Roman Forum** (p57).

5 Surveying the city spread out beneath you from atop **Il Vittoriano** (p66).

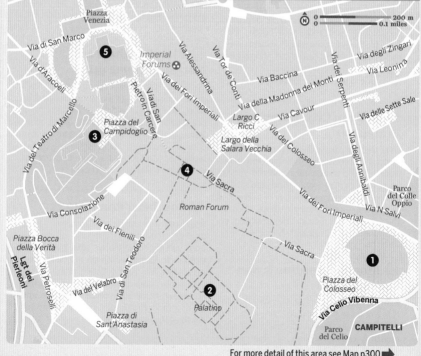

For more detail of this area see Map p300 ➡

Explore: Ancient Rome

Located to the south of the city centre, this area contains the great ruins of the ancient city, all within walking distance of each other. They start to get crowded mid-morning and throng with tourists until mid- to late afternoon, although in peak season they can be busy all day. Apart from the big sights, which you can comfortably cover in a couple of days, there's little in the way of nightlife or after-hours action.

The area has two focal points: the Colosseum to the southeast, and the Campidoglio (Capitoline Hill) to the northwest. In between lie the forums: the Roman Forum to the left of Via dei Fori Imperiali as you walk up from the Colosseum, the Imperial Forums to the right. Rising above the Roman Forum is the Palatino, and behind that the grassy expanse of the Circo Massimo. To the northwest of the Circo, you'll find the Bocca della Verità and a couple of early Roman temples in an area that used to be ancient Rome's cattle market (Forum Boarium).

To explore ancient Rome, the obvious starting point is the Colosseum, which is easily accessible by metro. From there you could go directly up to the Roman Forum, but if you go first to the Palatino (your Colosseum ticket covers the Palatino and Roman Forum), you'll get some wonderful views over the forums. From the Palatino enter the Forum and work your way up to Piazza del Campidoglio and the Capitoline Museums. Nearby, the mammoth white Vittoriano is hard to miss.

Local Life

➜**Exhibitions** While tourists climb all over Il Vittoriano, locals head inside to catch an exhibition at the Complesso del Vittoriano (p66).

➜**Celebrations** Join Romans to celebrate the city's birthday, the Natale di Roma, on 21 April. Events and historical re-enactments are held in and around Rome's ancient sights.

➜**Via Crucis** Crowds gather at the Colosseum (p52) every Good Friday to witness the pope lead the traditional Via Crucis procession.

➜**Jogging** Don your trainers and run with the Romans on the Circo Massimo (p64), a popular jogging venue.

Getting There & Away

➜**Bus** Many buses stop in or near Piazza Venezia, including numbers 40, 64, 87, 170, 492, 916 and H.

➜**Metro** Metro line B has stops at the Colosseum (Colosseo) and Circo Massimo. At Termini follow signs for Line B direzione Laurentina.

Lonely Planet's Top Tip

The big sights in this part of Rome are among the city's most visited. To avoid the worst of the crowds try to visit early morning or in the late afternoon, when it's cooler and the light is much better for taking photos.

Bring bottled water and snacks with you as the bars and snack trucks around the main monuments are a real rip-off.

Best Places to Eat

➜ Terre e Domus (p67)
➜ San Teo (p67)
➜ Ristorante Roof Garden Circus (p67)

For reviews, see p67.➡

Best Places to Drink

➜ 0,75 (p69)
➜ Caffè Capitolino (p69)
➜ Cavour 313 (p69)

For reviews, see p69.➡

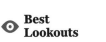

Best Lookouts

➜ Il Vittoriano (p66)
➜ Orti Farnesiani, Palatino (p106)
➜ Tabularium, Capitoline Museums (p61)
➜ Mercati di Traiano Museo dei Fori Imperiali (p65)

For reviews, see p64.➡

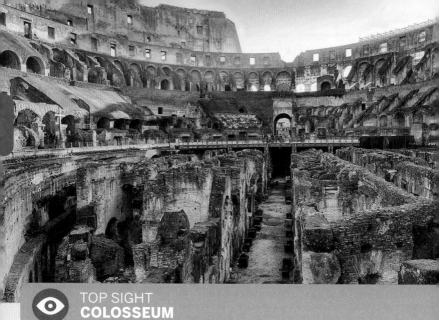

TOP SIGHT
COLOSSEUM

A monument to raw, merciless power, the Colosseum is the most thrilling of Rome's ancient sights. It was here that gladiators met in mortal combat and condemned prisoners fought off wild beasts in front of baying, bloodthirsty crowds. Two thousand years on and it's Italy's top tourist attraction, drawing more than five million visitors a year.

Built by Vespasian (r AD 69–79) in the grounds of Nero's vast Domus Aurea complex, it was inaugurated in AD 80, eight years after it had been commissioned. To mark the occasion, Vespasian's son and successor Titus (r AD 79–81) staged games that lasted 100 days and nights, during which 5000 animals were slaughtered. Trajan (r AD 98–117) later topped this, holding a marathon 117-day killing spree involving 9000 gladiators and 10,000 animals.

The 50,000-seat arena was originally known as the Flavian Amphitheatre, and although it was Rome's most fearsome arena it wasn't the biggest – the Circo Massimo could hold up to 250,000 people. The name Colosseum, when introduced in medieval times, was not a reference to its size but to the *Colosso di Nerone,* a giant statue of Nero that stood nearby.

With the fall of the Roman Empire in the 5th century, the Colosseum was abandoned and gradually became overgrown. In the Middle Ages it served as a fortress for two of the city's warrior families, the Frangipani and the Annibaldi. Later, during the Renaissance and baroque periods it was plundered of its precious travertine, and marble stripped from it was used to make huge palaces such as Palazzo Venezia, Palazzo Barberini and Palazzo Cancelleria.

More recently, pollution and vibrations caused by traffic and the metro have taken their toll. It is currently undergoing a €25-million clean-up, the first in its 2000-year history, and

DON'T MISS...

➡ The stands
➡ The arena
➡ The hypogeum

PRACTICALITIES

➡ Colosseo
➡ Map p300
➡ ☎06 3996 7700
➡ www.coopculture.it
➡ Piazza del Colosseo
➡ adult/reduced incl Roman Forum & Palatino €12/7.50
➡ ⏰8.30am-1hr before sunset
➡ Ⓜ Colosseo

until restoration is finished – at the time of research, this was scheduled for March 2016 – you might find parts of the outer walls covered in scaffolding.

Exterior

The outer walls have three levels of arches, framed by Ionic, Doric and Corinthian columns. These were originally covered in travertine, and marble statues filled the niches on the 2nd and 3rd storeys. The upper level, punctuated with windows and slender Corinthian pilasters, had supports for 240 masts that held up a huge canvas awning over the arena, shielding the spectators from sun and rain. The 80 entrance arches, known as *vomitoria,* allowed the spectators to enter and be seated in a matter of minutes.

Arena

The arena originally had a wooden floor covered in sand to prevent the combatants from slipping and to soak up the blood. It could also be flooded for mock sea battles. Trapdoors led down to the hypogeum, a subterranean complex of corridors, cages and lifts beneath the arena floor.

Stands

The *cavea*, for spectator seating, was divided into three tiers: magistrates and senior officials sat in the lowest tier, wealthy citizens in the middle and the plebs in the highest tier. Women (except for vestal virgins) were relegated to the cheapest sections at the top. And as in modern stadiums, tickets were numbered and spectators were assigned a precise seat in a specific sector – in 2015, restorers uncovered traces of red numerals on the arches, indicating how the sectors were numbered.

The podium, a broad terrace in front of the seats, was reserved for the emperor, senators and VIPs.

Hypogeum

The hypogeum served as the stadium's backstage area. It was here that stage sets were prepared and performers, both human and animal, would gather before showtime.

'Gladiators entered the hypogeum through an underground corridor which led directly in from the nearby Ludus Magnus (gladiator school),' explains the Colosseum's Technical Director, Barbara Nazzaro. 'In side corridors, which stand over a natural spring, boats were kept. When they wanted these boats up in the arena they would let the spring water in and flood the tunnels. Later these passages were used for winch mechanisms, all of which were controlled by a single pulley system. There were about 80 lifts going up to the arena as well as cages where wild animals were kept.'

Games staged at the Colosseum usually involved gladiators fighting wild animals or each other. But contrary to Hollywood folklore, bouts rarely ended in death as the games' sponsor was required to pay compensation to a gladiator's owner if the gladiator died in action.

RICHARD I'ANSON / GETTY IMAGES ©

TOP SIGHT
PALATINO

Rising above the Roman Forum, the Palatino (Palatine Hill) is an atmospheric area of towering pine trees, majestic ruins and memorable views. According to legend, this is where Romulus and Remus were saved by a wolf and where Romulus founded Rome in 753 BC. Archaeological evidence can't prove the myth, but it has dated human habitation here to the 8th century BC.

As the most central of Rome's seven hills, and because it was close to the Roman Forum, the Palatino was ancient Rome's most exclusive neighbourhood. The emperor Augustus lived here all his life and successive emperors built increasingly opulent palaces. But after Rome's fall, it fell into disrepair and in the Middle Ages churches and castles were built over the ruins. Later, wealthy Renaissance families established gardens on the hill.

Most of the Palatino as it appears today is covered by the ruins of the emperor Domitian's vast complex, which served as the main imperial palace for 300 years. Divided into the *Domus Flavia* (imperial palace), *Domus Augustana* (the emperor's private quarters) and a *stadio* (stadium), it was built in the 1st century AD.

DON'T MISS...

➡ Stadio
➡ Domus Augustana
➡ Orti Farnesiani

PRACTICALITIES

➡ Map p300
➡ ☎06 3996 7700
➡ www.coopculture.it
➡ Via di San Gregorio 30 & Via Sacra
➡ adult/reduced incl Colosseum & Roman Forum €12/7.50
➡ ☉8.30am-1hr before sunset
➡ ⓂColosseo

Stadio

On entering the Palatino from Via di San Gregorio, head uphill until you come to the first recognisable construction, the **stadio**. This sunken area, which was part of the main imperial palace, was used by the emperor for private games. To the southeast of the stadium are the remains of a complex built by Septimius Severus, comprising baths (**Terme di Settimio Severo**) and a palace (**Domus Severiana**) where, if they're open, you can visit the **Arcate Severiane** (Severian Arches; ☉Tue & Fri), a series of arches built to facilitate further development.

Domus Augustana & Domus Flavia

Next to the *stadio* are the ruins of the **Domus Augustana** (Emperor's Residence300), the emperor's private quarters in the imperial palace. Over two levels, rooms lead off a *peristilio* (porticoed court-yard) on each floor. You can't get to the lower level, but from above you can see the basin of a fountain and beyond it rooms that were originally paved with coloured marble.

Over on the other side of the Museo Palatino is the **Domus Flavia**, the public part of the palace. The Domus was centred on a grand columned peristyle – the grassy area with the base of an octagonal foun-tain – off which the main halls led. To the north was the emperor's throne room *(aula regia)*; to the west, a basilica (used by the emperor to meet his advisers); and to the south, a large banqueting hall, the *triclinium*.

Museo Palatino

The **Museo Palatino** houses a small collection of finds from the Palatino. The downstairs section illustrates the history of the hill from its origins to the Republican age, while upstairs you'll find arte-facts from the Imperial age, including a beautiful 1st-century bronze, the *Erma di Canefora*.

Casa di Livia & Casa di Augusto

Among the best-preserved buildings on the Palatino is the **Casa di Livia** (incl Casa di Augusto €4; ⊗guided tour 1pm daily, bookings essential), northwest of the Domus Flavia. Home to Augustus' wife Livia, it was built around an atrium leading onto what were once fres-coed reception rooms. Nearby, the **Casa di Augusto** (incl Casa di Livia €4; ⊗guided tour 1pm daily, bookings essential), Augustus' separate residence, contains superb frescoes in vivid reds, yellows and blues.

Criptoportico

Reached from near the Orti Farnesiani, the **criptoportico** is a 128m tunnel where Caligula is said to have been murdered, and which Nero used to connect his Domus Aurea with the Palatino. Lit by a series of windows, it is now used for temporary exhibitions.

Orti Farnesiani

Covering the Domus Tiberiana (Tiberius' palace) in the northwest corner of the Palatino, the **Orti Farnesiani** is one of Europe's earliest botanical gardens. Named after Cardinal Alessandro Farnese, who had it laid out in the mid-16th century, it com-mands breathtaking views over the Roman Forum.

ROMULUS & REMUS

The Palatino is closely associated with the legend of Romulus and Remus. Rome's mythical founders were supposedly brought up here by a shepherd, Faustulus, after a wolf had saved them from death. From near the Casa di Augusto you can look down into the 8th-century-BC **Capanne Romulee** (Romulean Huts), where the twins sup-posedly lived with their adopted father. In 2007 the discovery of a mosaic-covered cave 15m beneath the Domus Augustana reignited interest in the legend. According to some scholars, this was the *Lupercale,* the cave believed by ancient Romans to be where Romulus and Remus were suckled by a wolf.

The best spot for a picnic is the Vigna Barberini (Barberini Vineyard), near the Orti Farnesiani. A grassy area with several benches, it's signposted off the path to the Roman Forum.

PALATINO (PALATINE HILL)

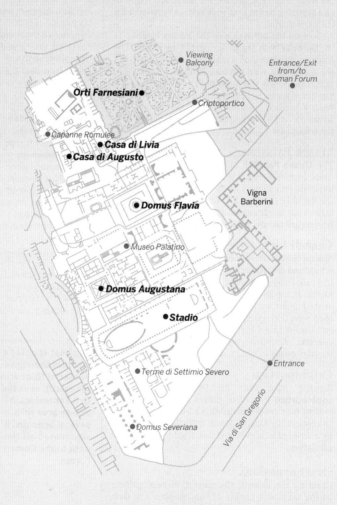

Viewing Balcony

Entrance/Exit from/to Roman Forum

Orti Farnesiani

Criptoportico

Capanne Romulee

Casa di Livia

Casa di Augusto

Domus Flavia

Vigna Barberini

Museo Palatino

Domus Augustana

Stadio

Terme di Settimio Severo

Entrance

Via di San Gregorio

Domus Severiana

S. BORISOV / GETTY IMAGES ©

TOP SIGHT
ROMAN FORUM

The Roman Forum (Foro Romano) was ancient Rome's centrepiece, a grandiose district of temples, basilicas and vibrant public spaces. Nowadays, it's a collection of impressive, if badly labelled, ruins that can leave you drained and confused. But if you can get your imagination going, there's something wonderfully compelling about walking in the footsteps of Julius Caesar and other legendary figures of Roman history.

Originally an Etruscan burial ground, the Forum was first developed in the 7th century BC, growing over time to become the social, political and commercial hub of the Roman Empire. In the Middle Ages it was reduced to pasture land and extensively plundered for its marble. The area was systematically excavated in the 18th and 19th centuries and work continues to this day.

Via Sacra Towards Campidoglio

Entering the Forum from Largo della Salara Vecchia – you can also enter from the Palatino or via an entrance near the Arco di Tito – you'll see the **Tempio di Antonino e Faustina** ahead to your left. Erected in AD 141, this was later transformed into a church, the **Chiesa di San Lorenzo in Miranda**. To your right, the 179 BC **Basilica Fulvia Aemilia** was a 100m-long public hall with a two-storey porticoed facade.

At the end of the path, you'll come to **Via Sacra**, the Forum's main thoroughfare, and the **Tempio di Giulio Cesare** (Tempio del Divo Giulio). Built by Augustus in 29 BC, this marks the spot where Julius Caesar was cremated. Heading right up Via Sacra brings you to the **Curia**, the original seat of the Roman Senate. This barn-like construction was

DON'T MISS...

➡ Curia
➡ Arco di Settimio Severo
➡ Tempio di Saturno
➡ Casa delle Vestali
➡ Basilica di Massenzio
➡ Arco di Tito

PRACTICALITIES

➡ Map p300
➡ ☎06 3996 7700
➡ www.coopculture.it
➡ Largo della Salara Vecchia & Via Sacra
➡ adult/reduced incl Colosseum & Palatino €12/7.50
➡ ⏱8.30am-1hr before sunset
➡ 🚇Via dei Fori Imperiali

Roman Forum

In ancient times, a forum was a market place, civic centre and religious complex all rolled into one, and the greatest of all was the Roman Forum (Foro Romano). Situated between the Palatino (Palatine Hill), ancient Rome's most exclusive neighbourhood, and the Campidoglio (Capitoline Hill), it was the city's busy, bustling centre. On any given day it teemed with activity. Senators debated affairs of state in the **Curia ❶**, shoppers thronged the squares and traffic-free streets, crowds gathered under the **Colonna di Foca ❷** to listen to politicians holding forth from the **Rostrum ❷**. Elsewhere, lawyers worked the courts in basilicas including the **Basilica di Massenzio ❸**, while the Vestal Virgins quietly went about their business in the **Casa delle Vestali ❹**.

Special occasions were also celebrated in the Forum: religious holidays were marked with ceremonies at temples such as **Tempio di Saturno ❺** and **Tempio di Castore e Polluce ❻**, and military victories were honoured with dramatic processions up Via Sacra and the building of monumental arches like **Arco di Settimio Severo ❼** and **Arco di Tito ❽**.

The ruins you see today are impressive but they can be confusing without a clear picture of what the Forum once looked like. This spread shows the Forum in its heyday, complete with temples, civic buildings and towering monuments to heroes of the Roman Empire.

TOP TIPS

» Get grandstand views of the Forum from the Palatino and Campidoglio.

» Visit first thing in the morning or late afternoon; crowds are worst between 11am and 2pm.

» In summer it gets hot in the Forum and there's little shade, so take a hat and plenty of water.

Colonna di Foca & Rostrum
The free-standing, 13.5m-high Column of Phocus is the Forum's youngest monument, dating to AD 608. Behind it, the Rostrum provided a suitably grandiose platform for pontificating public speakers.

Campidoglio (Capitoline Hill)

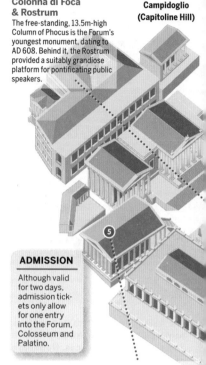

ADMISSION
Although valid for two days, admission tickets only allow for one entry into the Forum, Colosseum and Palatino.

Tempio di Saturno
Ancient Rome's Fort Knox, the Temple of Saturn was the city treasury. In Caesar's day it housed 13 tonnes of gold, 114 tonnes of silver and 30 million sestertii worth

JONATHAN SMITH/GETTY IMAGES ©

LONELY PLANET/GETTY IMAGES ©

Tempio di Castore e Polluce
Only three columns of the Temple of Castor and Pollux remain. The temple was dedicated to the Heavenly Twins after they supposedly led the Romans to victory over the Latin League in 496 BC.

Arco di Settimio Severo

One of the Forum's signature monuments, this imposing triumphal arch commemorates the military victories of Septimius Severus. Relief panels depict his campaigns against the Parthians.

Curia

This big barn-like building was the official seat of the Roman Senate. Most of what you see is a reconstruction, but the interior marble floor dates to the 3rd-century reign of Diocletian.

Basilica di Massenzio

Marvel at the scale of this vast 4th-century basilica. In its original form the central hall was divided into enormous naves; now only part of the northern nave survives.

JULIUS CAESAR

Julius Caesar was cremated on the site where the Tempio di Giulio Cesare now stands.

Via Sacra

Tempio di Giulio Cesare

Casa delle Vestali

White statues line the grassy atrium of what was once the luxurious 50-room home of the Vestal Virgins. The virgins played an important role in Roman religion, serving the goddess Vesta.

Arco di Tito

Said to be the inspiration for the Arc de Triomphe in Paris, the well-preserved Arch of Titus was built by the emperor Domitian to honour his elder brother Titus.

THE VESTAL VIRGINS

Despite privilege and public acclaim, life as a Vestal Virgin was no bed of roses. Every year, six physically perfect patrician girls aged between six and 10 were chosen by lottery to serve Vesta, goddess of hearth and household. Once selected, they faced a 30-year period of chaste servitude at the Tempio di Vesta. During this time their main duty was to ensure that the temple's sacred fire never went out. If it did, the priestess responsible would be flogged. The well-being of the state was thought to depend on the cult of Vesta and on the vestals' chastity, so if a priestess were to lose her virginity, she risked being buried alive as the offending man was flogged to death.

If you're caught short, there are toilets by the Chiesa di Santa Maria Antiqua.

rebuilt on various occasions and what you see today is a 1937 reconstruction of how it looked in the reign of Diocletian (r 284–305).

In front of the Curia, and hidden by scaffolding, is the **Lapis Niger**, a large piece of black marble that's said to cover the tomb of Romulus.

At the end of Via Sacra, the 23m-high **Arco di Settimio Severo** (Arch of Septimius Severus300) is dedicated to the eponymous emperor and his sons, Caracalla and Geta. Close by are the remains of the **Rostrum**, an elaborate podium where Shakespeare had Mark Antony make his famous 'Friends, Romans, countrymen...' speech. Facing this, the **Colonna di Foca** (Column of Phocus) rises above what was once the Forum's main square, **Piazza del Foro**.

The eight granite columns that rise behind the Colonna are all that survive of the **Tempio di Saturno** (Temple of Saturn300), an important temple that doubled as the state treasury. Behind it are (from north to south): the ruins of the **Tempio della Concordia** (Temple of Concord), the **Tempio di Vespasiano** (Temple of Vespasian and Titus) and the **Portico degli Dei Consenti**.

Tempio di Castore e Polluce & Casa delle Vestali

From the path that runs parallel to Via Sacra, you'll pass the stubby ruins of the **Basilica Giulia**, which was begun by Caesar and finished by Augustus. At the end of the basilica, three columns remain from the 5th-century BC **Tempio di Castore e Polluce** (Temple of Castor and Pollux). Nearby, the 6th-century **Chiesa di Santa Maria Antiqua** is the oldest Christian church in the Forum.

Back towards Via Sacra is the **Casa delle Vestali** (House of the Vestal Virgins; currently off-limits), home of the virgins who tended the flame in the adjoining **Tempio di Vesta**.

Via Sacra Towards the Colosseum

Heading up Via Sacra past the **Tempio di Romolo** (Temple of Romulus), you'll come to the **Basilica di Massenzio** (Basilica di Costantino300), the largest building on the forum. Started by Maxentius and finished by Constantine in 315 – it's also known as the Basilica di Costantino – it originally measured approximately 100m by 65m. It's currently out of bounds due to construction work on a new metro line.

Beyond the basilica, the **Arco di Tito** (Arch of Titus300) was built in AD 81 to celebrate Vespasian and Titus' victories against rebels in Jerusalem.

 TOP SIGHT
CAPITOLINE MUSEUMS

The world's oldest public museums, the Capitoline Museums (Musei Capitolini) occupy two stately *palazzi* on Piazza del Campidoglio. Their origins date to 1471, when Pope Sixtus IV donated a number of bronze statues to the city, forming the nucleus of what is now one of Italy's finest collections of classical art. The focus is very much on ancient sculpture but there's also a formidable picture gallery with works by many big-name Italian and Dutch artists.

The museums' entrance is in **Palazzo dei Conservatori**, where you'll find the original core of the sculptural collection on the 1st floor, and the Pinacoteca (picture gallery) on the 2nd storey.

Palazzo dei Conservatori – 1st Floor

Before you head up to start on the sculpture collection proper, take a moment to admire the marble body parts littered around the ground-floor **courtyard**. The mammoth head, hand, and feet all belonged to a 12m-high statue of Constantine that once stood in the Basilica di Massenzio in the Roman Forum.

Of the permanent sculpture collection on the 1st floor, the Etruscan *Lupa Capitolina* (Capitoline Wolf) is the most famous piece. Standing in the **Sala della Lupa**, this 5th-century-BC bronze wolf stands over her suckling wards, Romulus and Remus, who were added to the composition in 1471.

Other crowd-pleasers include the *Spinario,* a delicate 1st-century-BC bronze of a boy removing a thorn from his foot in the **Sala dei Trionfi**, and Gian Lorenzo Bernini's *Medusa* bust in the **Sala delle Oche**.

DON'T MISS...

→ Lupa Capitolina
→ Spinario
→ *La Buona Ventura*
→ Galata Morente
→ Venere Capitolina

PRACTICALITIES

→ Map p300
→ ☑06 06 08
→ www.museicapitolini.org
→ Piazza del Campidoglio 1
→ adult/reduced €11.50/9.50
→ ⊘9.30am-7.30pm, last admission 6.30pm
→ 🚌Piazza Venezia

TREATY OF ROME

With frescoes depicting episodes from ancient Roman history and two papal statues – one of Urban VIII by Bernini and one of Innocent X by Algardi – the **Sala degli Orazi e Curiazi** provided the grand setting for one of modern Europe's key events. On 25 March 1957 the leaders of Italy, France, West Germany, Belgium, Holland and Luxembourg gathered here to sign the Treaty of Rome and establish the European Economic Community, the precursor of the European Union. The hall has a long history of hosting politicians. In the 15th century it was used for the public hearings of the Council of Conservatori (elected magistrates), after whom the *palazzo* is named.

The Caffè Capitolino (p69), the museums' terrace cafe, is on the 2nd floor of Palazzo dei Conservatori. Serving coffee, snacks and fine views, it's an excellent spot for a sightseeing timeout.

Dominating the modern wing known as the **Esedra di Marco Aurelio** is an imposing bronze **equestrian statue** of the emperor Marcus Aurelius – the original of the copy that stands in the piazza outside. Here you can also see the foundations of the Temple of Jupiter, one of the ancient city's most important temples that once dominated the Capitoline Hill.

Palazzo dei Conservatori – 2nd Floor

The 2nd floor is given over to the **Pinacoteca**, the museum's picture gallery. Dating to 1749, the gallery's collection is arranged chronologically with works from the Middle Ages through to the 18th century.

Each room harbours masterpieces, but two stand out: the **Sala Pietro da Cortona**, which features Pietro da Cortona's famous depiction of the *Ratto delle sabine* (Rape of the Sabine Women; 1630), and the **Sala di Santa Petronilla**, named after Guercino's huge canvas *Seppellimento di Santa Petronilla* (The Burial of St Petronilla; 1621–23). This airy hall boasts a number of important canvases, including two by Caravaggio: *La Buona Ventura* (The Fortune Teller; 1595), which shows a gypsy pretending to read a young man's hand while stealing his ring, and *San Giovanni Battista* (John the Baptist; 1602), a sensual and unusual depiction of the New Testament saint.

Tabularium

A tunnel links Palazzo dei Conservatori to Palazzo Nuovo on the other side of the square via the **Tabularium**, ancient Rome's central archive, beneath **Palazzo Senatorio**. The tunnel is lined with panels and inscriptions from ancient tombs, but more inspiring are the views over the Roman Forum from the brick-lined Tabularium.

Palazzo Nuovo

Palazzo Nuovo is crammed to its elegant 17th-century rafters with classical Roman sculpture, including some unforgettable show-stoppers.

From the lobby, where the curly-bearded **Mars** stares ferociously at everyone who passes by, stairs lead up to the main galleries. The first hall you come to is the **Sala del Gladiatore**, home to one of the museum's greatest works – the *Galata Morente* (Dying Gaul). A Roman copy of a 3rd-century-BC Greek original, this sublime sculpture movingly captures the quiet, resigned anguish of a dying Gaul warrior.

Next door, the **Sala del Fauno** takes its name from the red marble statue of a faun.

Another superb piece is the sensual yet demure portrayal of *Venere Capitolina* (Capitoline Venus) in the **Gabinetto della Venere**, off the main corridor, and also worth a look are the busts of philosophers, poets and orators in the **Sala dei Filosofi**.

CAPITOLINE MUSEUMS

GROUND FLOOR

Palazzo Nuovo

Mars

Piazza del Campidoglio

Palazzo Senatorio

Main Entrance

Courtyard

Head of Constantine

stairs

Palazzo dei Conservatori

FIRST FLOOR

Palazzo Nuovo

Gabinetto della Venere

stairs

Sala del Gladiatore

Venere Capitolina

Salone

Fauno

Galata Morente

Sala dei Filosofi

Sala del Fauno

Palazzo dei Conservatori

Sala dei Trionfi

Spinario

Sala degli Orazi e Curiazi

Sala della Lupa

Lupa Capitolina

Medusa

Sala delle Oche

Esedra di Marco Aurelio

Equestrian Statue of Marcus Aurelius

Foundations of Temple of Jupiter

SECOND FLOOR
Palazzo dei Conservatori

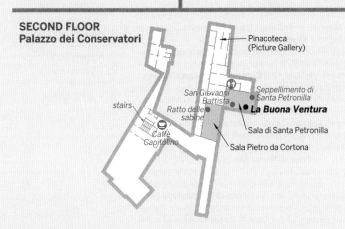

Pinacoteca (Picture Gallery)

San Giovanni Battista

Seppellimento di Santa Petronilla

stairs

Ratto delle sabine

La Buona Ventura

Caffè Capitolino

Sala di Santa Petronilla

Sala Pietro da Cortona

SIGHTS

◉ Colosseum & Palatino

COLOSSEUM RUIN
See p52.

PALATINO ARCHAEOLOGICAL SITE
See p54.

ARCO DI COSTANTINO MONUMENT
Map p300 (Ⓜ Colosseo) On the western side of the Colosseum, this monumental triple arch was built in AD 315 to celebrate the emperor Constantine's victory over his rival Maxentius at the Battle of the Milvian Bridge (AD 312). Rising to a height of 25m, it's the largest of Rome's surviving triumphal arches.

CIRCO MASSIMO HISTORIC SITE
Map p300 (Circus Maximus; Via del Circo Massimo; Ⓜ Circo Massimo) Now little more than a huge basin of dusty grass, the Circo Massimo was ancient Rome's largest chariot racetrack, a 250,000-seater capable of holding up to a quarter of the city's entire population. The 600m track circled a wooden dividing island with ornate lap indicators and Egyptian obelisks.

Chariot races were held here as far back as the 4th century BC, but it wasn't until Trajan rebuilt it after the AD 64 fire that it reached its maximum grandeur.

Restoration work, which is ongoing at the southern end, has unearthed evidence of the taverns and shops that used to flank the track.

◉ The Forums & Around

ROMAN FORUM ARCHAEOLOGICAL SITE
See p57.

**BASILICA DI SS COSMA
E DAMIANO** BASILICA
Map p300 (Via dei Fori Imperiali 1; presepio donation €1; ⊙9am-1pm & 3-7pm, presepio 10am-1pm & 3-6pm Fri-Sun Sep-Jul; 🚌Via dei Fori Imperiali) Backing onto the Roman Forum, this 6th-century basilica incorporates parts of the **Foro di Vespasiano** and **Tempio di Romolo**, visible at the end of the nave. The real reason to visit, though, is to admire the church's vibrant 6th-century apse mosaics, depicting Peter and Paul presenting saints

---

◉ TOP SIGHT
IMPERIAL FORUMS

The sprawl of ruins over the road from the Roman Forum are known collectively as the Imperial Forums (Fori Imperiali). Constructed between 42 BC and AD 112, they were mostly buried in 1933 when Mussolini built Via dei Fori Imperiali through the area. Excavations have since unearthed much of them, but visits are limited to the **Mercati di Traiano** (Trajan's Markets), accessible through the **Museo dei Fori Imperiali**.

Little recognisable remains of the **Foro di Traiano** (Trajan's Forum300), except for some pillars from the **Basilica Ulpia** and the **Colonna di Traiano** (Trajan's Column), whose minutely detailed reliefs depict Trajan's military victories over the Dacians (from modern-day Romania). To the southeast, three columns rise from the **Foro di Augusto** (Augustus' Forum300). The 30m-high wall behind the forum was built to protect it from the fires that frequently swept down from the nearby Suburra slums. The **Foro di Nerva** (Nerva's Forum300) is now largely buried, although part of a temple to Minerva still stands. Originally, it would have connected the Foro di Augusto to the 1st-century **Foro di Vespasiano** (Vespasian's Forum). Over the road, three columns are the most visible remains of the **Foro di Cesare** (Caesar's Forum).

DON'T MISS...

➡ Mercati di Traiano
➡ Colonna di Traiano
➡ Basilica Ulpia

PRACTICALITIES

➡ Map p300
➡ Via dei Fori Imperiali
➡ 🚌Via dei Fori Imperiali

Cosma, Damiano, Theodorus and Pope Felix IV to Christ.

Also worth a look is the 18th-century Neapolitan **presepio** (nativity scene) in a room off the 17th-century cloister.

MERCATI DI TRAIANO MUSEO DEI FORI IMPERIALI MUSEUM

Map p300 (⌖06 06 08; www.mercatiditraiano.it; Via IV Novembre 94; adult/reduced €11.50/9.50; ⊙9.30am-7.30pm, last admission 6.30pm; ☐Via IV Novembre) This striking museum brings to life the **Mercati di Traiano**, emperor Trajan's great 2nd-century market complex, while also providing a fascinating introduction to the **Imperial Forums** with multimedia displays, explanatory panels and a smattering of archaeological artefacts.

Sculptures, friezes and the occasional bust are set out in rooms opening onto what was once the market's Great Hall. But more than the exhibits, the real highlight here is the chance to explore the echoing ruins of the vast complex. The three-storey hemicycle that housed the markets is in remarkably good shape and it doesn't take a huge leap of the imagination to picture it full of traders selling everything from oil and vegetables to flowers, silks and spices.

Rising above the markets is the **Torre delle Milizie** (Militia Tower300), a 13th-century red-brick tower.

CARCERE MAMERTINO HISTORIC SITE

Map p300 (Mamertine Prison; ⌖06 69 89 61; Clivo Argentario 1; admission €3, with tour €5; ⊙9.30am-7pm summer, to 5pm winter; ☐Via dei Fori Imperiali) At the foot of the Campidoglio, the Mamertine Prison was ancient Rome's maximum-security jail. St Peter did time here and while imprisoned supposedly created a miraculous stream of water to baptise his jailers. On the bare stone walls you can just make out early Christian frescoes depicting Jesus and Sts Peter and Paul.

If you just want to nip in and have a look, get the €3 ticket, otherwise guided multimedia tours take about half an hour.

○ Campidoglio

Rising above the Roman Forum, the Campidoglio (Capitoline Hill) was one of the seven hills on which Rome was founded. At its summit were Rome's two most important temples: one dedicated to Jupiter Capitolinus (a descendant of Jupiter, the Roman equivalent of Zeus) and one to the goddess Juno Moneta (which housed Rome's mint). These days, the hill wields political clout as the home of Rome's municipal government.

CAPITOLINE MUSEUMS MUSEUM

See p61.

PIAZZA DEL CAMPIDOGLIO PIAZZA

Map p300 (☐Piazza Venezia) This hilltop piazza, designed by Michelangelo in 1538, is one of Rome's most beautiful squares. You can reach it from the Roman Forum, but the most dramatic approach is via the graceful **Cordonata** (Map p300) staircase up from Piazza d'Ara Coeli.

ⓘ NAVIGATING THE ANCIENT SITES

As fascinating as Rome's ancient ruins are, they are not well labelled and it can be hard to know where to go and what to look at.

Entrances

The Roman Forum and Palatino effectively form a single unified site. They're covered by the same ticket (along with the Colosseum) and once you've entered the site, you can walk freely between the two areas. There are three entrances:

➜ Via di San Gregorio 30 for the Palatino

➜ Largo della Salara Vecchia for the Roman Forum

➜ Via Sacra for both – go left for the Palatino or straight ahead for the Forum.

Specialist Guides

Electa publishes a number of specialist guidebooks to Rome's archaeological sites, including the *Colosseum* (€5); the *Foro, Palatine and Colosseum* (€10); the *Archaeological Guide to Rome* (€12.90); *The Appian Way* (€8); and *The Baths of Caracalla* (€8). All are available at the Colosseum and Roman Forum bookshops.

ⓘ POSING CENTURIONS

Outside the Colosseum, Roman Forum and Vittoriano, you might find yourself been hailed by costumed centurions offering to pose for a photo with you. They're not doing this for love and will expect payment. There's no set rate but €5 is more than enough – and that's €5 in total, not per person.

The piazza is flanked by **Palazzo Nuovo** and **Palazzo dei Conservatori**, together home to the Capitoline Museums, and **Palazzo Senatorio**, seat of Rome city council. In the centre is a copy of an **equestrian statue** of Marcus Aurelius. The original, which dates to the 2nd century AD, is in the Capitoline Museums.

CHIESA DI SANTA MARIA IN ARACOELI   CHURCH

Map p300 (Piazza Santa Maria in Aracoeli; ⊘9am-6.30pm summer, to 5.30pm winter; 🚇Piazza Venezia) Atop the steep 14th-century Aracoeli staircase, this 6th-century Romanesque church marks the highest point of the Campidoglio. Its rich interior boasts several treasures including a wooden gilt ceiling, an impressive Cosmatesque floor and a series of 15th-century Pinturicchio frescoes illustrating the life of St Bernadine of Siena. Its main claim to fame, though, is a wooden baby Jesus that's thought to have healing powers.

In fact, the Jesus doll is a copy. The original, which was supposedly made of wood from the garden of Gethsemane, was pinched in 1994 and has never been recovered.

The church sits on the site of the Roman temple to Juno Moneta and has long had an association with the nativity. According to legend, it was here that the Tiburtine Sybil told Augustus of the coming birth of Christ.

◉ Piazza Venezia

IL VITTORIANO   MONUMENT

Map p300 (Piazza Venezia; ⊘9.30am-5.30pm summer, to 4.30pm winter; 🚇Piazza Venezia) **FREE** Love it or loathe it, as most locals do, you can't ignore Il Vittoriano (aka the Altare della Patria; Altar of the Fatherland), the massive mountain of white marble that towers over Piazza Venezia. Begun in 1885

to honour Italy's first king, Victor Emmanuel II, it incorporates the **Museo Centrale del Risorgimento** (Map p300; www.risorgimento.it; Il Vittoriano , Piazza Venezia; adult/reduced €5/2.50; ⊘9.30am-6.30pm, closed 1st Mon of month; 🚇Piazza Venezia), a small museum documenting Italian unification, and the **Tomb of the Unknown Soldier**.

For Rome's best 360-degree views, take the **Roma dal Cielo** (Map p300; Piazza Venezia; adult/reduced €7/3.50; ⊘9.30am-6.30pm Mon-Thu, to 7.30pm Fri-Sun; 🚇Piazza Venezia) lift to the top.

Housed in the monument's eastern wing is the **Complesso del Vittoriano** (Map p300; ☑06 678 06 64; Via di San Pietro in Carcere; 🚇Via dei Fori Imperiali), a gallery space that regularly hosts major art exhibitions.

ROMAN INSULA   RUIN

Map p300 (Piazza Santa Maria in Aracoeli; 🚇Piazza Venezia) At the bottom of the Campidoglio, next to the Aracoeli staircase, you can see the ruins of a Roman apartment block *(insula)*. Only the upper storeys are visible – the unexcavated ground-floor shops are well below road level – but they provide a fascinating, if fleeting, glimpse into the cramped, squalid conditions that many ancients lived in.

PALAZZO VENEZIA   PALACE

Map p300 (Piazza Venezia; 🚇Piazza Venezia) Built between 1455 and 1464, this was the first of Rome's great Renaissance palaces. For centuries it served as the embassy of the Venetian Republic, but it's most readily associated with Mussolini, who installed his office here in 1929, and famously made speeches from the balcony. Nowadays, it's home to the tranquil **Museo Nazionale del Palazzo Venezia** (Map p300; ☑06 678 01 31; http://museopalazzovenezia.beniculturali.it; Via del Plebiscito 118; adult/reduced €5/2.50; ⊘8.30am-7.30pm Tue-Sun; 🚇Piazza Venezia) and its eclectic collection of Byzantine and early Renaissance paintings, furniture, ceramics, bronze figures, weaponry and armour.

BASILICA DI SAN MARCO   BASILICA

Map p300 (Piazza di San Marco 48; ⊘9am-12.30pm & 4-6pm Tue-Sat, 10am-1pm & 4-8pm Sun; 🚇Piazza Venezia) The early-4th-century Basilica di San Marco stands over the house where St Mark the Evangelist is said to have stayed while in Rome. Its main attraction is the golden 9th-century apse mosaic showing Christ flanked by several saints and Pope Gregory IV.

☉ Forum Boarium & Around

BOCCA DELLA VERITÀ   MONUMENT
Map p300 (Mouth of Truth; Piazza Bocca della Verità 18; admission by donation €0.50; ☺9.30am-5.50pm summer, to 4.50pm winter; 🚇Piazza Bocca della Verità) A bearded face carved into a giant marble disc, the *Bocca della Verità* is one of Rome's most popular curiosities. Legend has it that if you put your hand in the mouth and tell a lie, the Bocca will slam shut and bite your hand off.

The mouth, which was originally part of a fountain, or possibly an ancient manhole cover, now lives in the portico of the **Chiesa di Santa Maria in Cosmedin**, a handsome medieval church.

Originally built in the 8th century, the church was given a major revamp in the 12th century, when the seven-storey bell tower and portico were added and an inlaid Cosmati floor was laid.

FORUM BOARIUM   HISTORIC SITE
Map p300 (Piazza Bocca della Verità; 🚇Piazza Bocca della Verità) Car-choked Piazza Bocca della Verità stands on what was once ancient Rome's cattle market, the Forum Boarium. Opposite the Chiesa di Santa Maria in Cosmedin are two tiny 2nd-century BC temples: the circular **Tempio di Ercole Vincitore** (Map p300; 🕾06 3996 7700; www.coopculture.it; Piazza Bocca della Verità; guided tour €5.50, booking necessary; ☺1st & 3rd Sun of month; 🚇Piazza Bocca della Verità), the oldest marble temple in Rome, and the **Tempio di Portunus** (Map p300; 🕾06 3996 7700; www.coopculture.it; Piazza Bocca della Verità; guided tour €5.50, booking necessary; ☺1st & 3rd Sun of month; 🚇Piazza Bocca della Verità), dedicated to Portunus, god of rivers and ports. Both temples are visitable by guided tour.

Just off the piazza, the 4th-century **Arco di Giano** (Arch of Janus; Map p300; 🚇Piazza Bocca della Verità) is a four-fronted Roman arch where cattle traders used to shelter from the sun and rain. Beyond it is the **Chiesa di San Giorgio in Velabro** (Map p300; Via del Velabro 19; ☺9am-7pm; 🚇Piazza Bocca della Verità), a medieval church whose original 7th-century portico was destroyed by a Mafia bomb attack in 1993.

UNDERGROUND ARTS CENTRE

The sheer depth of Rome's archaeological legacy came to light in 2012, when archaeologists unearthed a 900-seat *athenaeum* (arts centre) 5m below Piazza Venezia. Dating to the 2nd-century reign of Hadrian, the **Auditoria di Adriano** consists of three 13m-high arched halls where spectators would have relaxed on terraced marble seating to be entertained by poets and philosophers.

The discovery came during tunnelling work on a new metro line, illustrating the difficulties that engineers face as they inch through the city's treasure-laden undersoil. The complex is off-limits to visitors.

 EATING

SAN TEO   CAFE, PASTRIES €
Map p300 (Via di San Teodoro 88; snacks & pastries €1-3.50; ☺7am-8pm; 🚇Via dei Cerchi) With *dolci* (sweets) laid out like jewels and an array of artfully crafted tarts and pastries, this *pasticceria*-cum-cafe puts on a great display. Leave the crowds at the Bocca della Verità and sneak off to indulge your sweet tooth with macarons, marrons glacés and creamy *cannoli*. Savoury snacks are also available.

TERRE E DOMUS   LAZIO CUISINE €€
Map p300 (🕾06 6994 0273; Via Foro Traiano 82-4; meals €30; ☺7.30am-12.30am Mon-Sat; 🚇Via dei Fori Imperiali) This modern white-and-glass restaurant is the best option in the touristy Forum area. Overlooking the Colonna di Traiano, it serves a menu of traditional staples, all made with ingredients sourced from the surrounding Lazio region, and a thoughtful selection of regional wines. Lunchtime can be busy but it quietens down in the evening.

RISTORANTE ROOF GARDEN CIRCUS   RISTORANTE €€€
Map p300 (🕾06 678 78 16; www.fortyseven-hotel.com; Hotel Forty Seven, Via Petroselli 47; meals €50; ☺12.30-3pm & 7.30-11.30pm; 🚇Via Petroselli) The rooftop of the Forty Seven hotel sets the romantic stage for chef Vito Grippa's menu of classic Roman dishes and contemporary Italian cuisine. With the Aventino hill rising in the background, you

68

ANCIENT ROME

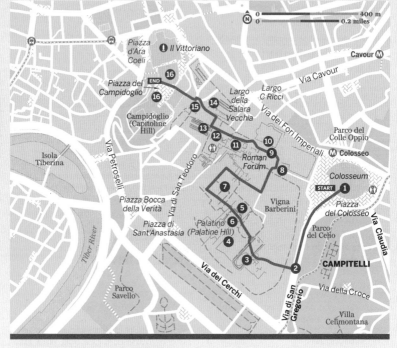

Neighbourhood Walk
Explore the Ruins

START COLOSSEUM
END CAPITOLINE MUSEUMS
LENGTH 1.5KM; FOUR HOURS

Start at the **1 Colosseum** (p52), the great gladiatorial arena that more than any other monument encapsulates the drama of the ancient city. From there, follow Via di San Gregorio down to the **2 Palatino** (p106), 1st-century Rome's most sought-after neighbourhood where the emperor lived alongside the cream of imperial society. The ruins here are confusing, but their scale gives some sense of the luxury in which the ancient VIPs liked to live.

Beyond the **3 stadio** (p54), you can still make out parts of the **4 Domus Augustana** (p55), the emperor's private palace quarters, and the **5 Domus Flavia** (p55), where he would hold official audiences. Take time to pop into the **6 Museo Palatino** (p55), before heading up to the **7 Orti Farnesiani** (p55). These gardens weren't part of the ancient city, but give

good views over the Roman Forum. Next, stroll down to the Forum, entering near the **8 Arco di Tito**, one of the site's great triumphal arches. Beyond this, pick up **9 Via Sacra**, the Forum's main drag. Follow this down, passing the hulking **10 Basilica di Massenzio** (p60), and after a few hundred metres you'll come to the **11 Casa delle Vestali**, where the legendary Vestal Virgins lived tending to their duties and guarding their virtue. Beyond the three columns of the **12 Tempio di Castore e Polluce**, you'll see a flattened area littered with column bases and brick stumps. This is the **13 Basilica Giulia** (p60), where lawyers and magistrates worked in the crowded law courts. Meanwhile, senators debated matters of state in the **14 Curia** (p57), over on the other side of the Forum. From near the Curia, exit the Forum past the **15 Arco di Settimio Severo** (p60) and climb Campidoglio (Capitoline Hill) to the **16 Capitoline Museums** (p61), whose collection of classical art includes some of the city's finest ancient sculpture.

can tuck into stalwarts such as spaghetti *ajo e ojio* (with garlic and olive oil) or push the boat out and opt for something richer like roast guinea fowl with black truffles.

 DRINKING & NIGHTLIFE

0,75 BAR

Map p300 (www.075roma.com; Via dei Cerchi 65; ☻11am-2am; 🛜; 🚇Via dei Cerchi) This welcoming bar on the Circo Massimo is good for a lingering drink, an *aperitivo* (6.30pm onwards) or a light meal (mains €6 to €13.50, salads €5.50 to €7.50). It's a friendly place with a laid-back vibe, an attractive exposed-brick look and cool tunes.

CAFFÈ CAPITOLINO CAFE

Map p300 (Piazzale Caffarelli 4; ☻9am-7.30pm Tue-Sun; 🚇Piazza Venezia) The Capitoline Museums' charming terrace cafe is a good place to relax over a drink or light snack (*panini,* salads and pizza) and enjoy wonderful views across the city's rooftops. Although part of the museum complex, you don't need a ticket to come here as it's accessible via an independent entrance on Piazzale Caffarelli.

CAVOUR 313 WINE BAR

Map p300 (📞06 678 54 96; www.cavour313. it; Via Cavour 313; ☻12.30-2.45pm & 7.30pm-12.30am, closed Sun summer; Ⓜ Cavour) Close to the Forum, wood-panelled Cavour 313 attracts everyone from tourists to actors and politicians. It serves a daily food menu and a selection of salads, cold cuts and cheeses

PICNIC PROVISIONS

Trawling through Ancient Rome's extensive ruins can be hungry work. But rather than stopping off for an overpriced bite in a touristy restaurant, search out **Alimentari Pannella Carmela** (Map p300; Via dei Fienili 61; panini €2-3.50; ☻8.30am-2.30pm Mon-Sat & 5-8pm Mon-Fri; 🚇Via Petroselli) for a fresh, cheap *panino*. A small, workaday food store concealed behind a curtain of creeping ivy, it's a lunchtime favourite supplying many local workers with pizza slices, takeaway salads and hearty ham-and-cheese sandwiches.

(€8 to €12), but the headline act is the wine. And with more than 1200 labels to choose from you're sure to find something to tickle your palate.

SHOPPING

MERCATO DI CIRCO MASSIMO FOOD & DRINK

Map p300 (www.mercatocircomassimo.it; Via di San Teodoro 74; ☻9am-6pm Sat, to 4pm Sun, closed Sun Jul & all Aug; 🚇Via dei Cerchi) Rome's best and most popular farmers market is a colourful showcase for seasonal, zero-kilometre produce. As well as fresh fruit and veg, you can stock up on *pecorino Romano* cheese, milky mozzarella (known locally as *fior di latte*), olive oils, preserves, and *casareccio* bread from the nearby town of Genzano.

Centro Storico

PANTHEON | PIAZZA NAVONA | CAMPO DE' FIORI | JEWISH GHETTO | ISOLA TIBERINA | PIAZZA COLONNA

Neighbourhood Top Five

1 Stepping into the **Pantheon** (p72) and feeling the same sense of awe that the ancients must have felt 2000 years ago. The sight of the dome soaring up above you is a genuinely jaw-dropping spectacle.

2 Exploring **Piazza Navona** (p74) and the warren of medieval lanes that surrounds it.

3 Browsing the fabulous art collection at the **Palazzo e Galleria Doria Pamphilj** (p82).

4 Viewing three Caravaggio masterpieces at the **Chiesa di San Luigi dei Francesi** (p77).

5 Escaping the crowds in the shadowy back streets of the **Jewish Ghetto** (p80).

For more detail of this area see Map p304 and p306 ➡

Explore: Centro Storico

Rome's *centro storico* (historic centre) is made for leisurely strolling and although you could spend weeks exploring its every corner, you can cover most of the main sights in two or three days. Many people enter the area by bus, getting off at Largo di Torre Argentina, from where it's a short walk up to the Pantheon and beyond that to Rome's political nerve-centre Piazza Colonna. Nearby, on Via del Corso, the Palazzo e Galleria Doria Pamphilj houses one of the capital's finest private art collections. Art is thick on the ground in these parts and many of the centre's piazzas and churches harbour extraordinary works by big-name Renaissance and baroque artists. To the west of the Pantheon, the narrow lanes around Piazza Navona, itself one of Rome's great must-see sights, are a magnet for tourists and hip Romans with their bohemian boutiques, cool bars and popular pizzerias.

Over on the other side of Corso Vittorio Emanuele II, the main thoroughfare through the area, all roads lead to Campo de' Fiori, home to a colourful daily market and hectic late-night drinking scene. From 'il Campo' you can shop your way down to the medieval Jewish Ghetto, a wonderfully atmospheric pocket of romantic corners, hidden piazzas and authentic eateries.

Local Life

➡ **Backstreet eating** The restaurants on Piazza Navona and Piazza Rotonda attract a touristy crowd, while Campo de' Fiori (p78) pulls in boozing students. Locals head to places in the quieter backstreets.

➡ **Shopping** Browse retro fashions and indie styles on Via del Governo Vecchio (p76); Via dei Giubbonari is good for frocks and heels.

➡ **Aperitif** Fashion-conscious Romans love to socialise over an evening *aperitivo* in the bars around Piazza Navona (p74).

Getting There & Away

➡ **Bus** The best way to access the *centro storico*. A whole fleet serves the area from Termini, including bus 40 and 64, which both stop at Largo di Torre Argentina and continue down Corso Vittorio Emanuele II. From Via del Tritone near Barberini metro station, bus 492 runs to Corso del Rinascimento for Piazza Navona.

➡ **Metro** There are no metro stations in the neighbourhood but it's within walking distance of Barberini, Spagna and Flaminio stations, all on line A.

➡ **Tram** Catch tram 8 from Piazza Venezia to Trastevere by way of Via Arenula.

Lonely Planet's Top Tip

The *centro storico* is an expensive part of town but there are ways of making your money go further. You can see masterpieces by the likes of Michelangelo, Raphael, Caravaggio and Bernini for nothing by visiting the area's churches, which are all free to enter. Fuel your wanderings with coffee, sliced pizza and ice cream, and fill up with water from the drinking fountains known as *nasoni* (big noses) dotted around the streets.

✗ Best Places to Eat

➡ Casa Coppelle (p84)
➡ La Ciambella (p84)
➡ Supplizio (p88)
➡ Forno Roscioli (p88)
➡ Armando al Pantheon (p84)

For reviews, see p83.➡

☐ Best Places to Drink

➡ Caffè Sant'Eustachio (p90)
➡ Barnum Cafe (p91)
➡ Open Baladin (p91)
➡ Il Goccetto (p91)

For reviews, see p90.➡

◉ Best Art Churches

➡ Chiesa di San Luigi dei Francesi (p77)
➡ Chiesa del Gesù (p81)
➡ Chiesa di Sant'Ignazio di Loyola (p83)
➡ Basilica di Santa Maria Sopra Minerva (p75)

For reviews, see p75.➡

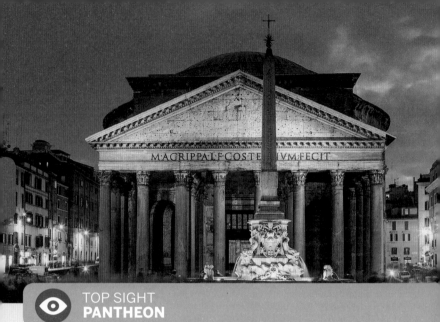

TOP SIGHT
PANTHEON

A striking 2000-year-old temple, now a church, the Pantheon is Rome's best-preserved ancient monument and one of the most influential buildings in the Western world. Its greying, pockmarked exterior might look its age, but inside it's a different story, and it's a unique and exhilarating experience to pass through its vast bronze doors and gaze up at the largest unreinforced concrete dome ever built.

DON'T MISS...

➡ The entrance doors
➡ The dome
➡ Raphael's tomb

PRACTICALITIES

➡ Map p304
➡ Piazza della Rotonda
➡ ⊘8.30am-7.30pm Mon-Sat, 9am-6pm Sun
➡ 🚇Largo di Torre Argentina

History

In its current form the Pantheon dates to around AD 125. The original temple, built by Marcus Agrippa in 27 BC, burnt down in AD 80, and although it was rebuilt by Domitian, it was struck by lightning and destroyed for a second time in AD 110. The emperor Hadrian had it reconstructed between AD 118 and 125, and it's this version that you see today.

Hadrian's temple was dedicated to the classical gods – hence the name Pantheon, a derivation of the Greek words *pan* (all) and *theos* (god) – but in 608 it was consecrated as a Christian church after the Byzantine emperor Phocus donated it to Pope Boniface IV. It was dedicated to the Virgin Mary and all the martyrs and took on the name by which it is still officially known, the Basilica di Santa Maria ad Martyres.

Thanks to this consecration, it was spared the worst of the medieval plundering that reduced many of Rome's ancient buildings to near dereliction. But it didn't escape entirely unscathed – its gilded-bronze roof tiles were removed and, in the 17th century, Pope Urban VIII had the portico's bronze ceiling melted down to make 80 canons for Castel Sant'Angelo and to provide Bernini with bronze for the baldachino at St Peter's Basilica.

During the Renaissance, the building was much admired – Brunelleschi used it as inspiration for his cupola in Florence, and Michelangelo studied it before designing the dome at St Peter's Basilica – and it became an important burial chamber. Today, you'll find the tomb of the artist Raphael here alongside those of kings Vittorio Emanuele II and Umberto I.

Exterior

Originally, the Pantheon was on a raised podium, its entrance facing onto a rectangular porticoed piazza. Nowadays, the dark-grey pitted exterior faces onto busy, cafe-lined Piazza della Rotonda. And while its facade is somewhat the worse for wear, it's still an imposing sight. The monumental entrance **portico** consists of 16 Corinthian columns, each 13m high and each made of Egyptian granite, supporting a triangular **pediment**. Behind the columns, two 20-tonne bronze doors – 16th-century restorations of the original portal – give onto the central rotunda.

Little remains of the ancient decor, although rivets and holes in the brickwork indicate where marble-veneer panels were once placed.

Interior

Although impressive from outside, it's only when you get inside that you can really appreciate the Pantheon's full size. With light streaming in through the **oculus** (the 8.7m-diameter hole in the centre of the dome), the cylindrical marble-clad interior seems vast, an effect that was deliberately designed to cut worshippers down to size in the face of the gods.

Opposite the entrance is the church's main **altar**, over which hangs a 7th-century icon of the *Madonna col Bambino* (Madonna and Child). To the left (as you look in from the entrance) is the tomb of Raphael, marked by Lorenzetto's 1520 sculpture of the *Madonna del Sasso* (Madonna of the Rock). Neighbouring it are the tombs of King Umberto I and Margherita of Savoy. Over on the opposite side of the rotunda is the tomb of King Vittorio Emanuele II.

The Dome

The Pantheon's dome, considered the Romans' most important architectural achievement, was the largest dome in the world until Brunelleschi beat it with his Florentine cupola. Its harmonious appearance is due to a precisely calibrated symmetry – its diameter is exactly equal to the building's interior height of 43.3m. At its centre, the oculus, which symbolically connected the temple with the gods, plays a vital structural role by absorbing and redistributing the dome's huge tensile forces.

Radiating out from the oculus are five rows of 28 coffers (indented panels). These were originally ornamented but more importantly served to reduce the cupola's immense weight.

THE INSCRIPTION

For centuries the Latin inscription over the entrance led historians to believe that the current temple was Marcus Agrippa's original. Certainly, the wording would suggest this, reading: 'M.AGRIPPA.L.F.COS. TERTIUM.FECIT' or 'Marcus Agrippa, son of Lucius, consul for the third time, built this'. However, excavations in the 19th-century revealed traces of an earlier temple and scholars realised that Hadrian had simply placed Agrippa's original inscription over his new temple.

According to the attendants who work at the Pantheon, the question tourists most often ask is: what happens when it rains? The answer is that water gets in through the oculus and drains away through 22 almost-invisible holes in the sloping marble floor.

MASS

The Pantheon is still a working church and mass is celebrated at 5pm on Saturday and 10.30am on Sunday.

TOP SIGHT
PIAZZA NAVONA

With its ornate fountains, exuberant baroque *palazzi* and pavement cafes, Piazza Navona is central Rome's elegant showcase square. Long a hub of local life, it hosted Rome's main market for close on 300 years, and today attracts a colourful daily circus of street performers, hawkers, artists, tourists, fortune-tellers and pigeons.

Stadio di Domiziano

Like many of the city's landmarks, the piazza sits over an ancient monument, in this case the 1st-century-AD **Stadio di Domiziano** (Domitian's Stadium; ☑06 4568 6100; www. stadiodomiziano.com; Via di Tor Sanguigna 3; adult/reduced €8/6; ☺10am-7pm Sun-Fri, to 8pm Sat; ☐Corso del Rinascimento). This 30,000-seat stadium, whose subterranean remains can be accessed from Via di Tor Sanguigna, used to host athletic meets – hence, the name Navona, a corruption of the Greek word *agon,* meaning public games. Inevitably, though, it fell into disrepair and it wasn't until the 15th century that the crumbling arena was paved over and Rome's central market was transferred here from the Campidoglio.

Fountains

The piazza's grand centrepiece is Gian Lorenzo Bernini's **Fontana dei Quattro Fiumi** (Fountain of the Four Rivers). Completed in 1651, this showy fountain features four muscular personifications of the rivers Nile, Ganges, Danube and Plate, representing the four continents of the then-known world. Legend has it that the Nile figure is shielding his eyes from the nearby Chiesa di Sant'Agnese in Agone designed by Bernini's hated rival, Francesco Borromini. In truth, it simply indicated that the source of the Nile was unknown at the time the fountain was created. Towering over the sculpted rock base is a tapering Egyptian obelisk.

The **Fontana del Moro** at the southern end of the square was designed by Giacomo della Porta in 1576. Bernini added the Moor in the mid-17th century, but the surrounding Tritons are 19th-century copies.

At the northern end of the piazza, the 19th-century **Fontana del Nettuno** depicts Neptune fighting with a sea monster, surrounded by sea nymphs.

Chiesa di Sant'Agnese in Agone

With its theatrical facade and rich, domed interior, the **Chiesa di Sant'Agnese in Agone** (www.santagneseinagone.org; Piazza Navona; concerts €13; ☺9.30am-12.30pm & 3.30-7pm Mon-Sat, 10am-1pm & 4-8pm Sun; ☐Corso del Rinascimento) is typical of Francesco Borromini's baroque style. The church, which hosts an annual season of chamber-music concerts, is said to stand on the spot where the martyr Agnes performed a miracle before being killed. According to legend, she was stripped naked by her executioners but miraculously grew her hair to cover her body and preserve her modesty.

Palazzo Pamphilj

The largest building on the square, this elegant baroque **palazzo** (Piazza Navona; ☐Corso del Rinascimento) was built between 1644 and 1650 by Borromini and Girolamo Rainaldi to celebrate Giovanni Battista Pamphilj's election as Pope Innocent X. Inside there are some impressive frescoes by Pietro da Cortona, but the building, which has been the Brazilian Embassy since 1920, is off-limits to the public.

DON'T MISS...

➡ Fontana dei Quattro Fiumi

➡ Chiesa di Sant'Agnese in Agone

➡ Palazzo Pamphilj

PRACTICALITIES

➡ Map p304

➡ ☐Corso del Rinascimento

⊙ SIGHTS

Bound by the River Tiber and Via del Corso, the *centro storico* is made for aimless wandering. Even without trying you'll come across some of Rome's great sights: the Pantheon, Piazza Navona and Campo de' Fiori, as well as a host of monuments, museums and churches. To the south, the Jewish Ghetto has been home to Rome's Jewish community since the 2nd century BC.

⊙ Pantheon & Around

PANTHEON   CHURCH
See p72.

ELEFANTINO   MONUMENT
Map p304 (Piazza della Minerva; 🚇Largo di Torre Argentina) Just south of the Pantheon, the Elefantino is a curious and much-loved statue of a puzzled-looking elephant carrying a 6th-century-BC Egyptian obelisk. Completed in 1667 in honour of Pope Alexander VII, the elephant, symbolising strength and wisdom, was sculpted by Ercole Ferrata to a design by Bernini. The obelisk was taken from the nearby Basilica di Santa Maria Sopra Minerva.

BASILICA DI SANTA MARIA
SOPRA MINERVA   BASILICA
Map p304 (www.santamariasopraminerva.it; Piazza della Minerva 42; ⏱6.45am-7pm Mon-Fri, 6.45am-12.30pm & 3.30-7pm Sat, 8am-12.30pm & 3.30-7pm Sun; 🚇Largo di Torre Argentina) Built on the site of three pagan temples, including one to the goddess Minerva, the Dominican Basilica di Santa Maria Sopra Minerva is Rome's only Gothic church. However, little remains of the original 13th-century structure and these days the main drawcard is a minor Michelangelo sculpture and the colourful, art-rich interior.

Inside, to the right of the altar in the **Cappella Carafa** (also called the Cappella della Annunciazione), you'll find two superb 15th-century frescoes by Filippino Lippi and the majestic tomb of Pope Paul IV.

Left of the high altar is one of Michelangelo's lesser-known sculptures, *Cristo Risorto* (Christ Bearing the Cross; 1520), depicting Jesus carrying a cross while wearing some jarring bronze drapery. This wasn't part of the original composition and was added after the Council of Trent to preserve Christ's modesty.

An altarpiece of the *Madonna and Child* in the second chapel in the northern transept is attributed to Fra Angelico, the Dominican friar and painter, who is also buried in the church.

The body of St Catherine of Siena, minus her head (which is in Siena), lies under the high altar, and the tombs of two Medici popes, Leo X and Clement VII, are in the apse.

LARGO DI TORRE ARGENTINA   SQUARE
Map p304 (🚇Largo di Torre Argentina) A busy transport hub, the Largo di Torre Argentina is set around the sunken **Area Sacra** (Map p304; Largo di Torre Argentina; 🚇Largo di Torre Argentina) and the remains of four Republican-era temples, all built between the 2nd and 4th centuries BC. These ruins, which are among the oldest in the city, are out of bounds to humans but home to a thriving population of around 250 stray cats and a volunteer-run **cat sanctuary** (Map p304; www.romancats.com; ⏱noon-6pm daily).

On the piazza's western flank, Teatro Argentina, Rome's premier theatre, stands near the spot where Julius Caesar was assassinated in 44 BC.

MUSEO NAZIONALE ROMANO:
CRYPTA BALBI   MUSEUM
Map p304 (📞06 3996 7700; www.coopculture.it; Via delle Botteghe Oscure 31; adult/reduced €7/3.50; ⏱9am-7.45pm Tue-Sun; 🚇Via delle Botteghe Oscure) The least known of the Museo Nazionale Romano's four museums, the Crypta Balbi sits over the ruins of several medieval buildings, themselves set atop the Teatro di Balbo (13 BC). Archaeological finds illustrate the urban development of the surrounding area, while the museum's underground excavations, visitable by guided tour, provide an interesting insight into Rome's multilayered past.

⊙ Piazza Navona & Around

PIAZZA NAVONA   PIAZZA
See p74.

VIA DEI CORONARI   AREA
Map p304 (🚇Corso del Rinascimento) Famous for its antique shops, this elegant Renaissance street is a lovely place for a stroll. It

follows the course of the ancient Roman road that connected Piazza Colonna with the Tiber, but owes its name to the medieval *coronari* (rosary-bead sellers) who used to hang out here, hawking their wares to pilgrims as they passed en route to St Peter's Basilica.

CHIESA DI SANTA MARIA DELLA PACE & CHIOSTRO DEL BRAMANTE
CHURCH, GALLERY

Map p304 (www.chiostrodelbramante.it; Via Arco della Pace 5; exhibitions adult/reduced €13/11; ⊙church 9am-11.50pm Mon, Wed & Sat, cloister 10am-8pm; ⬛Corso del Rinascimento) Tucked away in the backstreets behind Piazza Navona, this small church boasts a columned semicircular facade by Pietro da Cortona and a celebrated Raphael fresco, *Sibille* (Sibyls; c 1515). Next door, the **Chiostro del Bramante** (Bramante Cloister) is a masterpiece of High Renaissance architectural styling that is now used to stage art exhibitions and cultural events.

The cloister, which you can visit freely by popping up to the 1st-floor cafe, was originally part of the same monastery complex as the adjoining church. Its sober, geometric lines and perfectly proportioned spaces provide a marked counterpoint to the church's undulating facade, beautifully encapsulating the Renaissance aesthetic that Bramante did so much to promote.

PASQUINO
STATUE

Map p304 (Piazza Pasquino; ⬛Corso Vittorio Emanuele II) This unassuming sculpture is Rome's most famous 'talking statue'. During the 16th century, when there were no safe outlets for dissent, a Vatican tailor named Pasquino began sticking notes to the statue with satirical verses lampooning the church and aristocracy. Soon others joined in and, as the trend spread, talking statues popped up all over town.

Until recently, Romans were still writing messages, known as *pasquinade,* and sticking them to the statue. However, the sculpture is now off-limits and disgruntled Romans have to make do with more contemporary social media.

VIA DEL GOVERNO VECCHIO
AREA

Map p304 (⬛Corso Vittorio Emanuele II) Striking off west from Piazza Pasquino, Via del Governo Vecchio is an atmospheric cobblestoned street full of fashion boutiques, popular eateries and vintage clothes shops. The

road, once part of the papal processional route between the Basilica di San Giovanni in Laterano and St Peter's, acquired its name (Old Government St) in 1755 when the pontifical government relocated from Palazzo Nardini at No 39 to Palazzo Madama.

The Renaissance architect Bramante is thought to have lived at No 123.

CHIESA NUOVA
CHURCH

Map p304 (Piazza della Chiesa Nuova; ⊙7.30am-noon & 4.30-7.15pm Mon-Sat, 8am-1pm & 4.30-7.15pm Sun; ⬛Corso Vittorio Emanuele II) Not exactly *nuova* (new) as the name would suggest, this imposing landmark church, also known as the Chiesa di Santa Maria in Vallicella, boasts a distinguished 17th-century facade and a rich baroque interior. Of particular note are the superb ceiling frescoes by Pietro da Cortona and several paintings by Peter Paul Rubens.

Built in 1575 as part of a complex to house Filippo Neri's Oratorian order, it was originally a large plain church in accordance with Neri's wishes. But when Neri died in 1595 the artists moved in – Rubens painted over the high altar, and Pietro da Cortona decorated the dome, tribune and nave. Neri was canonised in 1622 and is buried in a chapel to the left of the apse.

Next to the church is Borromini's **Oratorio dei Filippini**, and behind it the **Torre dell'Orologio** (Map p304; Piazza dell'Orologio; ⬛Corso Vittorio Emanuele II), a clock tower built to decorate the adjacent convent.

MUSEO DI ROMA
MUSEUM

Map p304 (✆06 06 08; www.museodiroma.it; Piazza di San Pantaleo 10 & Piazza Navona 2; adult/reduced €9.50/7.50; ⊙10am-7pm Tue-Sun; ⬛Corso Vittorio Emanuele II) The baroque Palazzo Braschi houses the Museo di Roma's eclectic collection of paintings, photographs, etchings, clothes and furniture, charting the history of Rome from the Middle Ages to the early 20th century. But as striking as the collection is, the 17th-century *palazzo* itself, with its courtyard, monumental baroque staircase, and frescoed halls is worth a visit.

Among the paintings, look out for Raphael's 1511 portrait of Cardinal Alessandro Farnese, the future Pope Paul III.

Note that ticket prices increase (usually to €11/9) when there's a temporary exhibition on.

CHIESA DI SANT'IVO
ALLA SAPIENZA   CHURCH

Map p304 (Corso del Rinascimento 40; ☻9am-12.30pm Sun; ☐Corso del Rinascimento) Hidden in the porticoed courtyard of **Palazzo della Sapienza**, this tiny church is a masterpiece of baroque architecture. Built by Francesco Borromini between 1642 and 1660, and based on an incredibly complex geometric plan, it combines alternating convex and concave walls with a circular interior topped by a twisted spire.

Palazzo della Sapienza, seat of Rome's university until 1935 and now home to the Italian state archive, is often used to stage temporary exhibitions.

PALAZZO MADAMA   HISTORIC BUILDING

Map p304 (☑06 6706 2177; www.senato.it; Piazza Madama 11; ☻guided tours 10am-6pm 1st Sat of month Jul-Sep; ☐Corso del Rinascimento) **FREE** Seat of the Italian Senate since 1871, the regal Palazzo Madama was originally the 16th-century residence of Giovanni de' Medici, the future Pope Leo X. It was enlarged in the 17th century and later provided office space for several pontifical departments.

The name 'Madama' is a reference to Margaret of Parma, the illegitimate daughter of the Holy Roman Emperor Charles V, who lived here from 1559 to 1567.

CHIESA DI SANT'AGOSTINO   CHURCH

Map p304 (Piazza di Sant'Agostino 80; ☻7.45am-noon & 4-7.30pm; ☐Corso del Rinascimento) The plain white facade of this early Renaissance church, built in the 15th century and renovated in the late 1700s, gives no indication of the impressive art inside. The most famous work is Caravaggio's *Madonna dei Pellegrini* (Madonna of the Pilgrims) but you'll also find a fresco by Raphael and a much-venerated sculpture by Jacopo Sansovino.

The *Madonna del Parto* (Madonna of Childbirth), Sansovino's 1521 statue of the Virgin Mary with baby Jesus, is a favourite with expectant mums who traditionally pray to it for a safe pregnancy. The Madonna also stars in Caravaggio's *Madonna dei Pellegrini*, which caused uproar when it was unveiled in 1604 due to its depiction of Mary's two devoted pilgrims as filthy, badly dressed beggars.

Painting almost a century before, Raphael provoked no such scandal with his fresco of Isaiah, visible on the third pillar on the left side of the nave.

CENTRO STORICO SIGHTS

TOP SIGHT
CHIESA DI SAN LUIGI DEI FRANCESI

Church to Rome's French community since 1589, this opulent baroque *chiesa* is home to a celebrated trio of Caravaggio paintings: the *Vocazione di San Matteo* (Calling of St Matthew), the *Martirio di San Matteo* (Martyrdom of St Matthew) and *San Matteo e l'angelo* (St Matthew and the Angel), known collectively as the St Matthew cycle.

Hanging in the Cappella Contarelli to the left of the main altar, these three canvases are among the earliest of Caravaggio's religious works, painted between 1599 and 1602. But they are inescapably his, featuring a down-to-earth realism and a stunning use of *chiaroscuro* (the bold contrast of light and dark). Caravaggio's refusal to adhere to the artistic conventions of the day and glorify his religious subjects often landed him in hot water and his first version of *San Matteo e l'angelo*, which depicted St Matthew as a bald, bare-legged peasant, was originally rejected by his outraged patron, Cardinal Matteo Contarelli.

Before you leave the church, take a moment to enjoy Domenichino's faded 17th-century frescoes of St Cecilia in the second chapel on the right. St Cecilia is also depicted in the altarpiece by Guido Reni, a copy of a work by Raphael.

DON'T MISS...

➡ *Vocazione di San Matteo*

➡ *Martirio di San Matteo*

➡ *San Matteo e l'angelo*

➡ Domenichino's St Cecilia frescoes

PRACTICALITIES

➡ Map p304

➡ Piazza di San Luigi dei Francesi 5

➡ ☻10am-12.30pm & 3-7pm, closed Thu afternoon

➡ ☐Corso del Rinascimento

◉ Campo De' Fiori & Around

CAMPO DE' FIORI   PIAZZA

Map p304 (◨Corso Vittorio Emanuele II) Noisy, colourful 'Il Campo' is a major focus of Roman life: by day it hosts one of Rome's best-known markets, while at night it morphs into a raucous open-air pub. For centuries the square was the site of public executions, and it was here that the philosopher Giordano Bruno was burned at the stake for heresy in 1600. The spot is marked by a sinister statue of the hooded monk, created by Ettore Ferrari and unveiled in 1889.

The piazza's poetic name (Field of Flowers) explains what stood here before the square was laid out in the mid-15th century.

PALAZZO FARNESE   HISTORIC BUILDING

Map p304 (www.inventerrome.com; Piazza Farnese; admission €5; ⊙guided tours 3pm, 4pm & 5pm Mon, Wed & Fri; ◨Corso Vittorio Emanuele II) Home of the French Embassy, this formidable Renaissance *palazzo,* one of Rome's finest, was started in 1514 by Antonio da Sangallo the Younger, continued by Michel-

angelo and finished by Giacomo della Porta. Inside, it boasts a series of frescoes by Annibale Carracci that are said by some to rival Michelangelo's in the Sistine Chapel. The highlight, painted between 1597 and 1608, is the monumental ceiling fresco *Amori degli Dei* (The Loves of the Gods) in the recently restored Galleria dei Carracci.

Visits to the palazzo are by 45-minute guided tour only, for which you'll need to book at least a week in advance – see the website for details. Photo ID is required for entry and children under 10 are not admitted.

The twin fountains in the square outside are enormous granite baths taken from the Terme di Caracalla.

PALAZZO SPADA   HISTORIC BUILDING

Map p304 (☑06 683 24 09; http://galleriaspada. beniculturali.it; Piazza Capo di Ferro 13; adult/reduced €5/2.50; ⊙8.30am-7.30pm Wed-Mon; ◨Corso Vittorio Emanuele II) With its stuccoed ornamental facade and handsome courtyard, this grand *palazzo* is a fine example of 16th-century Mannerist architecture. Upstairs, a small gallery houses the Spada family art collection with works by Andrea

◉ TOP SIGHT **MUSEO NAZIONALE ROMANO: PALAZZO ALTEMPS**

Just north of Piazza Navona, Palazzo Altemps is a beautiful late-15th-century *palazzo,* housing the best of the Museo Nazionale Romano's formidable collection of classical sculpture. Many pieces come from the celebrated Ludovisi collection, amassed by Cardinal Ludovico Ludovisi in the 17th century.

Prize exhibits include the beautiful 5th-century-BC *Trono Ludovisi* (Ludovisi Throne), a carved marble block whose central relief shows a naked Venus (Aphrodite) being modestly plucked from the sea. In the neighbouring room, the *Ares Ludovisi,* a 2nd-century-BC representation of a young, clean-shaven Mars, owes its right foot to a Gian Lorenzo Bernini restoration in 1622.

Another affecting work is the sculptural group *Galata Suicida* (Gaul's Suicide), a melodramatic depiction of a Gaul knifing himself to death over a dead woman.

The building's baroque frescoes provide an exquisite decorative backdrop. The walls of the **Sala delle Prospettive Dipinte** are decorated with landscapes and hunting scenes viewed through trompe l'oeil windows. These frescoes were painted for Cardinal Altemps, the rich nephew of Pope Pius IV (r 1560–65) who bought the *palazzo* in the late 16th century.

DON'T MISS...

➔ *Trono Ludovisi*
➔ *Ares Ludovisi*
➔ *Galata Suicida*
➔ Sala delle Prospettive Dipinte

PRACTICALITIES

➔ Map p304
➔ ☑06 3996 7700
➔ www.coopculture.it
➔ Piazza Sant'Apollinare 44
➔ adult/reduced €7/3.50
➔ ⊙9am-7.45pm Tue-Sun
➔ ◨Corso del Rinascimento

del Sarto, Guido Reni, Guercino and Titian, while downstairs Francesco Borromini's famous optical illusion, aka the *Prospettiva* (Perspective), continues to confound visitors.

What appears to be a 25m-long corridor lined with columns leading to a hedge and life-sized statue is, in fact, only 10m long. The sculpture, which was a later addition, is actually hip-height and the columns diminish in size not because of distance but because they actually get shorter. And look closer at that perfect-looking hedge – Borromini didn't trust the gardeners to clip a real hedge precisely enough so he made one of stone.

VIA GIULIA   AREA
Map p304 (🚇Via Giulia) Designed by Bramante in 1508 as part of a big urban development program ordered by Pope Julius II, Via Giulia is one of Rome's most charming roads lined with colourful Renaissance *palazzi* and potted orange trees.

At its southern end, the **Fontana del Mascherone** depicts a gormless 17th-century hippy seemingly surprised by water spewing from his mouth. Just beyond it, and spanning the road, is the **Arco Farnese**, an overhead arch designed by Michelangelo as part of an unfinished project to connect Palazzo Farnese with Villa Farnesina on the opposite side of the Tiber.

Continuing north, on the left, in Via di Sant'Eligio, is the lovely Raphael-designed **Chiesa di Sant'Eligio degli Orefici** (🕿06 686 82 60; ⊙by prior reservation only 9am-1pm Mon-Fri).

MUSEO CRIMINOLOGICO   MUSEUM
Map p304 (🕿06 6889 9442; www.museocriminologico.it; Via del Gonfalone 29; admission €2; ⊙9am-1pm Tue-Sat plus 2.30-6.30pm Tue & Thu; 🚇Via Giulia) Check out Rome's dark side at this macabre museum of crime. Housed in a 19th-century prison, its gruesome collection includes torture devices, murder weapons, fake Picassos, and the red cloak of Massimo Titta, the Papal State's official executioner who carried out 516 executions between 1796 and 1865.

CHIESA DI SAN GIOVANNI BATTISTA DEI FIORENTINI   CHURCH
Map p304 (Piazza dell'Oro 2; ⊙7.30am-noon & 5-7pm; 🚇Ponte Vittorio Emanuele II) The last resting place of Francesco Borromini and Carlo Maderno, this graceful 16th-century church was commissioned by Pope Leo X

ARCO DEGLI ACETARI

For one of Rome's most picture-perfect scenes, head to Via del Pellegrino 19, just off Campo de' Fiori. Here you'll come across a dark archway called the **Arco degli Acetari** (Vinegar-Makers' Arch; Map p304; Via del Pellegrino 19; 🚇Corso Vittorio Emanuele II). This in itself isn't especially memorable, but if you duck under it you'll emerge onto a tiny medieval square enclosed by rusty orange houses and full of colourful cascading plants. Cats and bicycles litter the cobbles, while overhead washing hangs off pretty flower-lined balconies.

as a showcase for Florentine artistic talent. Jacopo Sansovino won a competition for its design, which was then executed by Antonio Sangallo the Younger and Giacomo della Porta. Carlo Maderno completed the elongated cupola in 1614, while the travertine facade was added by Alessandro Galilei in the mid-18th century.

PALAZZO DELLA CANCELLERIA   PALACE
Map p304 (Piazza della Cancelleria; exhibition adult/reduced €9/7; ⊙exhibition 9.30am-7.30pm; 🚇Corso Vittorio Emanuele II) As impressive an example of Renaissance architecture as you'll find in Rome, this huge *palazzo* was built for Cardinal Raffaele Riario between 1483 and 1513. It was later acquired by the Vatican and became the seat of the Papal Chancellory. It is still Vatican property and nowadays houses the Tribunal of the Roman Rota, the Holy See's highest ecclesiastical court.

Until April 2016, the *palazzo* is hosting an exhibition dedicated to machines designed by Leonardo da Vinci. But if that doesn't appeal, it's worth nipping through to the courtyard to take a peek at Bramante's glorious double loggia.

Incorporated into the *palazzo*, the 4th-century Basilica di San Lorenzo in Damaso is one of Rome's oldest churches.

MUSEO BARRACCO DI SCULTURA ANTICA   MUSEUM
Map p304 (www.museobarracco.it; Corso Vittorio Emanuele II 166; ⊙10am-4pm Tue-Sun winter, 1-7pm Tue-Sun summer; 🚇Corso Vittorio Emanuele II) **FREE** This charming museum

boasts a fascinating collection of early Mediterranean sculpture. You'll find Greek, Etruscan, Roman, Assyrian, Cypriot and Egyptian works, all donated to the state by Baron Giovanni Barracco in 1902.

The *palazzo* housing the museum, known as the Piccolo Farnesina, was built for a French clergyman, Thomas Le Roy, in 1523.

CHIESA DI SANT'ANDREA DELLA VALLE
CHURCH

Map p304 (Piazza Vidoni 6; ⊘7.30am-noon & 4.30-7.30pm Mon-Sat, 7.30am-12.45pm & 4.30-7.45pm Sun; 🚇Corso Vittorio Emanuele II) A must for opera fans, this towering 17th-century church is where Giacomo Puccini set the first act of *Tosca*. Its most obvious feature is Carlo Maderno's soaring dome, the highest in Rome after St Peter's, but its cavernous baroque interior reveals a wonderful series of frescoes by Matteo Preti and Domenichino, and, in the dome, Lanfranco's heady depiction of the *Gloria del Paradiso* (Glory of Paradise; 1625-28).

Competition between the artists working on the church was fierce and rumour has it that Domenichino once took a saw to Lanfranco's scaffolding, almost killing him in the process.

⊙ Jewish Ghetto

Centred on lively Via Portico d'Ottavia, the Jewish Ghetto is an atmospheric area studded with artisans' studios, vintage clothes shops, kosher bakeries and popular trattorias.

Rome's Jewish community harks back to the 2nd century BC, making it one of the oldest in Europe. At one point there were as many as 13 synagogues in the city, but Titus's defeat of Jewish rebels in Jerusalem in AD 70 changed the status of Rome's Jews from citizens to slaves. Confinement in the Ghetto was first enforced in 1555 when Pope Paul IV ushered in a period of official intolerance that lasted, on and off, until the 20th century.

For local news and tourist information, pop into the **Jewish Info Point** (Map p306; ✆06 9838 1030; www.jewishcommunityofrome. com; Via Santa Maria del Pianto 1; ⊘8.30am-6.30pm Mon-Thu, 8.30am-2pm Fri, 1hr after end of Shabat-11pm Sat, 11am-6pm Sun; 🚇Via Arenula) on the main strip.

MUSEO EBRAICO DI ROMA
SYNAGOGUE, MUSEUM

Map p306 (Jewish Museum of Rome; ✆06 6840 0661; www.museoebraico.roma.it; Via Catalana; adult/reduced €11/8; ⊘10am-6.15pm Sun-Thu, 9am-3.15pm Fri summer, 10am-4.15pm Sun-Thu, 9am-1.15pm Fri winter; 🚇Lungotevere de' Cenci) The historical, cultural and artistic heritage of Rome's Jewish community is chronicled in this small but engrossing museum. Housed in the city's early-20th-century synagogue, Europe's second largest, it displays parchments, precious fabrics, marble carvings, and a collection of 17th-and 18th-century silverware. Documents and photos attest to life in the Ghetto and the hardships suffered by the city's Jewry during WWII.

PALAZZO CENCI
PALACE

Map p306 (Vicolo dei Cenci; ⊘closed to the public; 🚇Via Arenula) A real-life house of horrors, Palazzo Cenci was the scene of one of the 16th century's most infamous crimes, the murder of Francesco Cenci by his long-suffering daughter Beatrice and wife Lucrezia.

Shelley based his tragedy *The Cenci* on the family, and a famous portrait of Beatrice, by Guido Reni, hangs in the Galleria Nazionale d'Arte Antica: Palazzo Barberini (p110). It shows a sweet-faced young girl with soft eyes and fair hair.

FONTANA DELLE TARTARUGHE
FOUNTAIN

Map p306 (Piazza Mattei; 🚇Via Arenula) This playful, much-loved fountain features four boys gently hoisting tortoises up into a bowl of water. Created by Giacomo della Porta and Taddeo Landini in the late 16th century, it's the subject of a popular local legend, according to which it was created in a single night.

The story goes that the Duke of Mattei had it built to save his engagement and prove to his prospective father-in-law that despite gambling his fortune away he was still a good catch. And amazingly, it worked. The father was impressed and allowed Mattei to marry his daughter.

In reality, the fountain was no overnight sensation and took three years to craft (1581-1584). The tortoises, after whom it's named, were added by Bernini during a restoration in 1658.

TOP SIGHT
CHIESA DEL GESÙ

An imposing example of Counter-Reformation architecture, this landmark *chiesa* is Rome's most important Jesuit church. Consecrated in 1584, it's fronted by a harmonious and much-copied facade by Giacomo della Porta. But rather than the masonry, the star turn here is the lavish marble-clad interior. Of the art on display, the most astounding work is the *Trionfo del Nome di Gesù* (Triumph of the Name of Jesus; 1679), the swirling ceiling fresco by Giovanni Battista Gaulli. The artist, better known as Il Baciccia, also created much of the stucco decoration and the cupola frescoes.

In the northern transept, the **Cappella di Sant'Ignazio** houses the tomb of Ignatius Loyola, the Spanish soldier who founded the Jesuits in 1540. Designed by baroque maestro Andrea Pozzo, the altar-tomb is an opulent marble-and-bronze affair with lapis lazuli–encrusted columns, and, on top, a lapis lazuli globe representing the Trinity. On either side are sculptures whose titles neatly encapsulate the Jesuit ethos: to the left, *Fede che vince l'Idolatria* (Faith Defeats Idolatry); to the right, *Religione che flagella l'Eresia* (Religion Lashing Heresy).

The Spanish saint lived in the church from 1544 until his death in 1556.

DON'T MISS...

➡ The *Trionfo del Nome di Gesù* fresco
➡ Cappella di Sant'Ignazio

PRACTICALITIES

➡ Map p304
➡ www.chiesadel-gesu.org
➡ Piazza del Gesù
➡ ⊘7am-12.30pm & 4-7.45pm, St Ignatius rooms 4-6pm Mon-Sat, 10am-noon Sun
➡ 🚇Largo di Torre Argentina

AREA ARCHEOLOGICA DEL TEATRO DI MARCELLO E DEL PORTICO D'OTTAVIA
ARCHAEOLOGICAL SITE

Map p306 (entrances Via del Teatro di Marcello 44 & Via Portico d'Ottavia 29; ⊘9am-7pm summer, 9am-6pm winter; 🚇Via del Teatro di Marcello) **FREE** To the east of the Jewish Ghetto, the **Teatro di Marcello** (Theatre of Marcellus; Map p306; Via del Teatro di Marcello) is the star turn of this dusty archaeological area. This 20,000-seat mini-Colosseum was planned by Julius Caesar and completed in 11 BC by Augustus, who named it after a favourite nephew, Marcellus. In the 16th century, a *palazzo,* which now contains several exclusive apartments, was built on top of the original structure.

Beyond the theatre, the **Portico d'Ottavia**, currently covered in scaffolding, is the oldest *quadriporto* (four-sided porch) in Rome. The dilapidated columns and fragmented pediment once formed part of a vast rectangular portico that was supported by 300 columns and measured 132m by 119m. Erected by a builder called Octavius in 146 BC, it was rebuilt in 23 BC by Augustus, who kept the name in honour of his sister Octavia. From the Middle Ages

until the late 19th century, the portico housed Rome's fish market.

CHIESA DI SAN NICOLA IN CARCERE
CHURCH

Map p306 (☑347 3811874; www.sotterraneidi-roma.it; Via del Teatro di Marcello 46; excavations €3; ⊘10am-7pm, excavations 10am-6pm Mon-Fri, to 5pm Sat & Sun; 🚇Via del Teatro di Marcello) This innocuous-looking 11th-century church harbours some fascinating Roman excavations. Beneath the main church you can poke around the claustrophobic foundations of three Republic-era temples and the remnants of an Etruscan vegetable market. Marble columns from the temples were incorporated into the church's structure and are still visible today.

Visits, led by experts from the Sotterranei di Roma association, are by guided tour only.

◉ Isola Tiberina

One of the world's smallest inhabited islands, the boat-shaped Isola Tiberina (Tiber Island) has been associated with healing since the 3rd century BC, when the Romans

TOP SIGHT
GALLERIA DORIA PAMPHILJ

Hidden behind the grimy exterior of Palazzo Doria Pamphilj, this wonderful gallery boasts one of Rome's richest private art collections, with works by Raphael, Tintoretto, Brueghel, Titian, Caravaggio, Bernini and Velázquez.

Palazzo Doria Pamphilj dates to the mid-15th century, but its current look was largely the work of the current owners, the Doria Pamphilj family, who acquired it in the 18th century. The Pamphilj's golden age, during which the family collection was started, came during the papacy of one of their own, Innocent X (r 1644–55).

The opulent picture galleries, decorated with frescoed ceilings and gilded mirrors, are hung with floor-to-ceiling paintings. Masterpieces abound, but look out for Titian's *Salomè con la testa del Battista* (Salome with the Head of John the Baptist) and two early Caravaggios: *Riposo durante la fuga in Egitto* (Rest During the Flight into Egypt) and *Maddalene Penitente* (Penitent Magdalen). The undisputed star, though, is Velázquez' portrait of an implacable Pope Innocent X, who grumbled that the depiction was 'too real'. For a comparison, check out Gian Lorenzo Bernini's sculptural interpretation of the same subject.

The free audioguide, narrated by Jonathan Pamphilj, brings the place alive with anecdotes and information.

DON'T MISS...

➜ *Salomè con la testa del Battista*

➜ *Riposo durante la fuga in Egitto*

➜ *Ritratto di papa Innocenzo X*

PRACTICALITIES

➜ Map p304

➜ ☑06 679 73 23

➜ www.dopart.it

➜ Via del Corso 305

➜ adult/reduced €11/7.50

➜ ☺9am-7pm, last admission 6pm

➜ 🚇Via del Corso

---

built a temple to the god of medicine Asclepius (aka Aesculapius) here. And still today people come to the Isola to be cured, though they now head to the island's long-standing hospital, the Ospedale Fatebenefratelli.

The island is connected to the mainland by two bridges: the 62 BC **Ponte Fabricio**, Rome's oldest standing bridge, which links with the Jewish Ghetto, and **Ponte Cestio**, which runs over to Trastevere.

Visible to the south are the remains of the **Ponte Rotto** (Broken Bridge), ancient Rome's first stone bridge, which was all but swept away in a 1598 flood.

CHIESA DI SAN BARTOLOMEO   CHURCH

Map p306 (Piazza di San Bartolomeo all'Isola 22; ☺9.30am-1.30pm & 3.30-5.30pm Mon-Sat, 9.30am-1pm Sun; 🚇Lungotevere dei Pierleoni) Built on the ruins of the Roman temple to Aesculapius, the Graeco-Roman god of medicine, the island's 10th-century church is an interesting hybrid of architectural styles: the facade is baroque, as is the richly frescoed ceiling; the bell tower is 12th-century Romanesque, and the 28 columns that divide the interior date to ancient times.

Inside, a marble wellhead is thought to stand over the spring that provided the temple's healing waters.

◉ Piazza Colonna & Around

PIAZZA COLONNA   PIAZZA

Map p304 (🚇Via del Corso) Together with the adjacent Piazza di Montecitorio, this stylish piazza is Rome's political nerve centre. On its northern flank, the 16th-century **Palazzo Chigi** (Map p304; www.governo.it; Piazza Colonna 370; ☺guided visits 9am-1pm Sat Oct-May, bookings required) FREE has been the official residence of Italy's prime minister since 1961. In the centre, the 30m-high **Colonna di Marco Aurelio** (Map p304) was completed in AD 193 to honour Marcus Aurelius' military victories.

The column's vivid reliefs depict scenes from battles against the Germanic tribes (169–173) and the Sarmatians (174–176). In 1589 Marcus was replaced on the top of the column with a bronze statue of St Paul.

PALAZZO DI MONTECITORIO
HISTORIC BUILDING

Map p304 (☏800 012955; www.camera.it; Piazza di Montecitorio; ⊙guided visits noon-2.30pm 1st Sun of month; 🚇Via del Corso) FREE Home to Italy's Chamber of Deputies, this baroque *palazzo* was built by Bernini in 1653, expanded by Carlo Fontana in the late 17th century, and given an art-nouveau facelift in 1918. Visits take in the mansion's lavish reception rooms and the main chamber where the 630 deputies debate beneath a beautiful Liberty-style skyline.

The **obelisk** (Map p304; Piazza di Montecitorio; 🚇Via del Corso) outside was brought from Heliopolis in Egypt by Augustus to celebrate victory over Cleopatra and Mark Antony in 30 BC.

PIAZZA DI PIETRA
PIAZZA

Map p304 (🚇Via del Corso) This charming piazza, surrounded by popular bars and cafes, is overlooked by 11 huge Corinthian columns, all that's left of the 2nd-century **Tempio di Adriano** (Map p304; Piazza di Pietra; 🚇Via del Corso). The temple formerly housed Rome's stock exchange and is now used to host conferences and business events.

CHIESA DI SANT'IGNAZIO DI LOYOLA
CHURCH

Map p304 (Piazza di Sant'Ignazio; ⊙7.30am-7pm Mon-Sat, 9am-7pm Sun; 🚇Via del Corso) Flanking a delightful rococo piazza, this important Jesuit church boasts a Carlo Maderno facade and two celebrated trompe l'oeil frescoes by Andrea Pozzo (1642–1709). One cleverly depicts a fake dome, while the other, on the nave ceiling, shows St Ignatius Loyola being welcomed into paradise by Christ and the Madonna.

For the best views of this dizzying work, stand on the small yellow spot on the nave floor and look up. The ceiling, which is, in fact, flat, appears to curve. But walk a little further into the church and you'll see the carefully created perspective stops working and the deception becomes clear.

The church, which was built by the Jesuit architect Orazio Grassi in 1626, flanks **Piazza di Sant'Ignazio**, an exquisite square laid out in 1727 to resemble a stage set. Note the exits into 'the wings' at the northern end and how the undulating surfaces create the illusion of a larger space.

ROME'S FAVOURITE FOOT

It doesn't appear on any tourist brochures, but the **Piè di Marmo** (Map p304; Via di Santo Stefano del Cacco; 🚇Via del Corso) is one of the Romans' favourite monuments. The giant marble foot started life attached to statue in a 1st-century temple dedicated to the Egyptian gods Isis and Serapis. Some 1600 years later it cropped up on the street that now bears its name, Via del Piè di Marmo. It was moved to its current position in 1878.

CHIESA DI SAN LORENZO IN LUCINA
CHURCH

Map p304 (Piazza San Lorenzo in Lucina 16; ⊙8am-8pm; 🚇Via del Corso) Little remains of the 5th-century church that was originally built here atop a well sacred to Juno. But that shouldn't detract from what is a very pretty church, complete with Romanesque bell tower and a 12th-century columned portico.

Inside, the otherwise standard baroque decor is elevated by Guido Reni's *Crocifisso* (Crucifixion) above the main altar, and a fine bust by Bernini in the Cappella dell'Annunziata. The French painter Nicholas Poussin, who died in 1655, is buried in the church.

✗ EATING

Around Piazza Navona, Campo de' Fiori and the Pantheon you'll find all manner of eateries, including some of the capital's best restaurants (both contemporary and traditional), alongside hundreds of overpriced tourist traps. The atmospheric Ghetto is famous for its Roman-Jewish cuisine.

✗ Pantheon & Around

VENCHI
GELATERIA $

Map p304 (Via degli Orfani 87; gelato from €2.50; ⊙10.30am-10pm Sun-Thu, to 11pm Fri & Sat; 🚇Via del Corso) Forget fancy flavours and gelato experiments, Venchi is all about the unadulterated enjoyment of chocolate. The wall shelves and counter displays feature myriad beautifully packaged delicacies, from pralines to chilli chocolate bars, as well as an assortment of decadent choc-based ice creams.

VICE
GELATERIA **$**

Map p304 (www.viceitalia.it; Corso Vittorio Emanuele II 96; gelato from €2.50; ⊙11am-1am; 🚇Largo di Torre Argentina) Conveniently situated near Largo di Torre Argentina, this contemporary gelateria has a range of classic flavours such as *nocciola* (hazelnut)*, limone* (lemon) and tiramisu, as well as more creative choices like cheesecake and blueberry crumble.

FIOCCO DI NEVE
GELATERIA, CAFE **$**

Map p304 (Via del Pantheon 51; gelato €2.20-4; ⊙10.30am-9pm winter, to 1am summer; 🚇Largo di Torre Argentina) Cheerful, loud staff, locals at the bar, ice cream in natural colours – this pocket-size place has all the hallmarks of a choice Roman gelateria. The fruit flavours are especially good, as is the house speciality, *affogato di zabaglione al caffè*, a coffee with a dollop of zabaglione ice cream plopped in.

ENOTECA CORSI
OSTERIA **$**

Map p304 (☑06 679 08 21; www.enotecacorsi. com; Via del Gesù 87; meals €25; ⊙noon-3.30pm Mon-Sat plus 7.30-10.30pm Thu & Fri; 🚇Largo di Torre Argentina) Join the lunchtime crowds at family-run Corsi, a genuine old-style osteria. The look is no-frills – paper table-cloths, fading framed prints and wine bottles – and the atmosphere one of controlled mayhem. The menu offers no surprises, just filling, homey fare like pasta with potatoes, sausages, and roast chicken.

CIAO CHECCA
FAST FOOD **$**

Map p304 (www.ciaochecca.com; Piazza di Firenze 25-26; meals €10-15; ⊙10.30am-10.30pm; 🚇Corso del Rinascimento) 🍢 When you want a plate of pasta or a quick salad without all the hassle of a restaurant meal, this up-scale fast-food joint is the answer. Expect crowds and recyclable cartons of seasonally inspired dishes ranging from bean soup to ravioli and sweet Sicilian desserts.

ZAZÀ
PIZZA **$**

Map p304 (☑0668801357; Piazza Sant'Eustachio 49; pizza slice around €3; ⊙9am-11pm Mon-Sat, to noon Sun; 🚇Corso del Rinascimento) Handily sandwiched between Piazza Navona and the Pantheon, this bright and breezy take-away dishes up surprisingly good slices of

low-cal pizza, made with carefully sourced organic ingredients. Order to go or grab an outside table and watch the world pass by as you munch.

★CASA COPPELLE
RISTORANTE **$$**

Map p304 (☑06 6889 1707; www.casacoppelle. it; Piazza delle Coppelle 49; meals €35-40; ⊙12-3.30pm & 6.30-11.30pm; 🚇Corso del Rinascimento) Exposed brick walls, flowers and subdued lighting set the stage for creative Italian- and French-inspired food at this intimate, romantic restaurant. There's a full range of starters and pastas, but the real tour de force are the deliciously tender steaks and rich meat dishes. Service is attentive and the setting, on a small piazza near the Pantheon, memorable. Book ahead.

★LA CIAMBELLA
ITALIAN **$$**

Map p304 (www.laciambellaroma.com; Via dell'Arco della Ciambella 20; fixed-price lunch menus €10-25, meals €30; ⊙7.30am-midnight; 🚇Largo di Torre Argentina) From breakfast pastries and lunchtime pastas to afternoon tea, Neapolitan pizzas and aperitif cock-tails, this all-day eatery is a top find. Central but as yet undiscovered by the tourist hordes, it's a spacious, light-filled spot set over the ruins of the Terme di Agrippa, visible through transparent floor panels. The mostly traditional food is spot on, and the atmosphere laid back and friendly.

ARMANDO AL PANTHEON
TRATTORIA **$$**

Map p304 (☑06 6880 3034; www.armandoal-pantheon.it; Salita dei Crescenzi 31; meals €40; ⊙12.30-3pm & 7-11pm Mon-Fri, 12.30-3pm Sat; 🚇Largo di Torre Argentina) An institution in these parts, Armando al Pantheon is a rare find – a genuine family-run trattoria in the touristy Pantheon area. It's been on the go for more than 50 years and has served its fair share of celebs, but it hasn't let fame go to its head and it remains one of the best bets for earthy Roman cuisine. Reservations essential.

OSTERIA DEL SOSTEGNO
TRATTORIA **$$**

Map p304 (☑06 679 38 42; www.ilsostegno.it; Via delle Colonnelle 5; meals €40; ⊙12.30-3pm & 7.30-11.30pm Tue-Sun; 🚇Largo di Torre Argentina) Follow the green neon arrow to the end of a narrow alley and you'll find this well-kept secret. It's an intimate place, a favourite of journalists and politicians who sneak off here to dine on old-school staples such

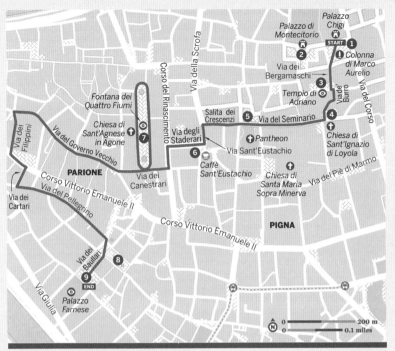

Neighbourhood Walk
Centro Storico Piazzas

START PIAZZA COLONNA
END PIAZZA FARNESE
LENGTH 1.5KM; 3½ HOURS

Start in ❶ **Piazza Colonna** (p82), an elegant square dominated by the 30m-high Colonna di Marco Aurelio and flanked by Palazzo Chigi, the official residence of the Italian prime minister. Next door, facing onto ❷ **Piazza di Montecitorio**, is the impressive seat of Italy's Chamber of Deputies, Palazzo di Montecitorio. From Piazza Colonna follow Via dei Bergamaschi down to ❸ **Piazza di Pietra** (p83), a refined rectangular space overlooked by the 2nd-century Tempio di Adriano. Continue past the columns down Via de' Burro to ❹ **Piazza di Sant'Ignazio**, a small piazza whose resident church boasts some trompe l'oeil frescoes. From here, it's a short walk along Via del Seminario to ❺ **Piazza della Rotonda**, where the Pantheon needs no introduction.

Leaving the Pantheon, head up Salita dei Crescenzi and go left along Via Sant'-Eustachio to ❻ **Piazza Sant'Eustachio**.

On this small, workaday square, the busy Caffè Sant'Eustachio is reckoned by many to serve the best coffee in town. Suitably recharged, follow Via degli Staderari to Corso del Rinascimento, drop a quick left followed by a short right and you'll find yourself emerging onto Rome's showpiece square, ❼ **Piazza Navona** (p74). Here, among the street artists, tourists and pigeons, you can compare the two giants of Roman baroque – Gian Lorenzo Bernini, creator of the Fontana dei Quattro Fiumi, and Francesco Borromini, author of the Chiesa di Sant'Agnese in Agone.

Exit the piazza and follow Via del Governo Vecchio, an atmospheric street lined with fashion boutiques and buzzing eateries. At the end, turn left down Via dei Filippini to Corso Vittorio Emanuele II. Cross over and follow Via dei Cartari down to Via del Pellegrino. Follow on to the noisy market square, ❽ **Campo de' Fiori** (p78), and beyond that, the more sober ❾ **Piazza Farnese** overshadowed by the Renaissance Palazzo Farnese.

as spaghetti carbonara and *saltimbocca* (sliced veal cooked with wine, ham and sage).

LA ROSETTA
SEAFOOD $$$

Map p304 (☑06 686 10 02; www.larosetta.com; Via della Rosetta 8; lunch menu €65, meals €90-120; ◐12.15-2.45pm & 7-10.45pm, closed 3 weeks in Aug; ⬚Corso del Rinascimento) Food fads might come and go but La Rosetta remains what it has long been, one of Rome's top fish restaurants. Hidden down a side street near the Pantheon, it offers classic seafood dishes and a choice of raw delicacies alongside more elaborate modern creations. Bookings essential.

GREEN T
CHINESE $$$

Map p304 (☑06 679 86 28; www.green-tea. it; Via del Piè di Marmo 28; lunch menus €9.50-17.50, meals €50; ◐noon-3pm & 6.30-11.30pm Mon-Sat; ⬚Via del Corso) Flying the flag for quality Chinese food, this five-room feng shui–designed restaurant is one of a kind: a tearoom and boutique serving soups, spicy Sechuan dishes, dim sum and a selection of fine teas. Save money at lunch by opting for one of the daily fixed-price menus.

✖ Piazza Navona & Around

ALFREDO E ADA
TRATTORIA $

Map p304 (☑06 687 88 42; Via dei Banchi Nuovi 14; meals €25; ◐noon-3pm & 7-10pm Tue-Sat; ⬚Corso Vittorio Emanuele II) For an authentic trattoria meal, search out this much-loved local eatery. It's distinctly no-frills with spindly, marble-topped tables and homey clutter, but there's a warm, friendly atmosphere and the traditional Roman food is filling and flavoursome.

BAGUETTERIA DEL FICO
SANDWICHES $

Map p304 (Via della Fossa 12; panini €5-7; ◐11am-2am; ⬚Corso del Risorgimento) A designer baguette bar ideal for a midday bite or late snack. Choose your bread, then select from the rich array of fillers – cured meats, cheeses, marinated vegetables, salads, homemade sauces. For liquid sustenance, there's a choice of bottled craft beers.

GELATERIA DEL TEATRO
GELATERIA $

Map p304 (Via dei Coronari 65; gelato from €2.50; ◐11.30am-midnight; ⬚Corso del Rinascimento) All the ice cream served at this excellent gelateria is prepared on site – look through the window and you'll see how. There are about 40 flavours to choose from, all made from thoughtfully sourced ingredients, including some excellent fruit combos and spicy chocolate.

DA TONINO
TRATTORIA $

Map p304 (Via del Governo Vecchio 18; meals €20-25; ◐noon-3.30pm & 7-11pm Mon-Sat; ⬚Corso Vittorio Emanuele II) A historic presence on Via del Governo Vecchio, Tonino's might be defiantly low-key with its simple wooden tables and yellowing pictures, but it's almost always packed with locals and visitors. Don't expect silver service, or even a menu, just straight-up Roman staples and honest local wine. No credit cards.

PIZZERIA LA MONTECARLO
PIZZA $

Map p304 (☑06 686 18 77; www.lamontecarlo.it; Vicolo Savelli 13; pizzas €5.50-9; ◐11am-11.45pm Tue-Sun; ⬚Corso Vittorio Emanuele II) This historic pizzeria is hugely popular, drawing a mixed crowd of sightseers, locals and even the occasional city celeb. Not the place for a lingering dinner, it can get frantic as the nimble waiters skip around the packed tables dishing out fried starters and crisp, wood-charred pizzas.

LO ZOZZONE
SANDWICHES $

Map p304 (☑06 6880 8575; Via del Teatro Pace 32; panini €6-8; ◐10am-9pm Mon-Fri, to 10.30pm Sat; ⬚Corso del Rinascimento) With a few inside tables and a mile-long menu of *panini,* the affectionately named 'dirty one' is a reliable choice for a quick fill-up. Sandwiches are made with pizza *bianca* (pizza without tomato) and fillings of cured meats, cheeses and vegetables.

CUL DE SAC
WINE BAR, TRATTORIA $$

Map p304 (☑06 6880 1094; www.enotecaculdesacroma.it; Piazza Pasquino 73; meals €30; ◐noon-12.30am; ⬚Corso Vittorio Emanuele II) A perennially popular wine bar just off Piazza Navona, with an always-busy terrace and narrow, bottle-lined interior. Choose your tipple first – the encyclopaedic wine list boasts about 1500 labels – and then pick what to go with it from the ample menu of no-nonsense Roman staples, Gallic-inspired cold cuts, pâtés, and cheeses. Book ahead for the evening.

LA CAMPANA
RISTORANTE **$$**

Map p304 (☑06 687 52 73; www.ristorantelacampana.com; Vicolo della Campana 18; meals €35-40; ☺12.30-3pm & 7.30-11pm Tue-Sun; ☖Via di Monte Brianzo) Caravaggio, Goethe and Federico Fellini are among the luminaries who have dined at what is said to be Rome's oldest trattoria, dating back to around 1518. Nowadays, locals crowd its soberly attired dining rooms to dine on fresh fish and traditional Roman cuisine in a cheerful, pleasantly relaxed atmosphere. Bookings recommended.

DA FRANCESCO
TRATTORIA, PIZZA **$$**

Map p304 (☑06 686 40 09; www.dafrancesco.it; Piazza del Fico 29; pizzas €7-14, meals €35; ☺noon-3.30pm & 7pm-12.30am; ☖Corso Vittorio Emanuele II) Dining at this quintessential Roman pizzeria-cum-trattoria is all about the buzzing atmosphere and cheerful, noisy vibe. With a small interior and tables spilling out onto the pretty piazza outside, it serves Roman-style thin-crust pizzas and a full menu of daily pastas and expertly chargrilled meats. Get here before 8pm or expect to wait.

LILLI
TRATTORIA **$$**

Map p304 (☑06 686 19 16; www.trattorialilli.it; Via di Tor di Nona 23; meals €25-30; ☺12.30-3pm & 7.30-11pm, closed Sun dinner & Mon; ☖Lungotevere Tor di Nona) Few tourists make it to this long-standing neighbourhood trattoria on a cobbled cul-de-sac five minutes' walk from Piazza Navona. But local diners pile in to enjoy its genuine *casareccia* (homestyle) cooking. Bookings recommended.

BAR DEL FICO
ITALIAN **$$**

Map p304 (☑06 6889 1373; Via della Pace 34-35; meals €20-30; ☺8am-2am; ☖Corso Vittorio Emanuele II) Named after the fig tree that shades the chess-playing old boys outside, this fashionable bar-restaurant is good from breakfast through to dinner. The low-key boho decor – rough wooden floors, tin tables and chipped walls – makes for a laid-back ambience for lunchtime pastas and grilled meat dinners. Its Sunday brunch (12.30 to 3pm) is a popular appointment.

LA FOCACCIA
PIZZA, TRATTORIA **$$**

Map p304 (☑06 6880 3312; Via della Pace 11; pizzas €7-9, meals €30-35; ☺11pm-12.30am; ☖Corso del Rinascimento) Hotfoot it to one of the few outside tables at this unsigned pizzeria near the Chiostro del Bramante, or

CHIOSTRO DEL BRAMANTE CAFFÈ

Many of Rome's galleries and museums have in-house cafes but few are as beautifully located as the **Chiostro del Bramante Caffè** (Map p304; www.chiostrodelbramante.it; Via Arco della Pace 5; meals €15-20; ☺10am-8pm Mon-Fri, to 9pm Sat & Sun; ☖Corso del Rinascimento) on the 1st floor of Bramante's elegant Renaissance cloister. With outdoor tables overlooking the central courtyard and an all-day menu, it's a great spot for a break.

settle for a place in the surprisingly large interior. Kick off with a *supplì* (fried rice croquette) or antipasto of fried zucchini before launching into the main event, Neapolitan-style wood-fired pizza.

CASA BLEVE
RISTORANTE, WINE BAR **$$$**

Map p304 (☑06 686 59 70; www.casableve.it; Via del Teatro Valle 48-49; meals €50-65; ☺12.30-3pm & 7.30-10.30pm Mon-Sat; ☖Largo di Torre Argentina) Ideal for a special-occasion dinner, this palatial restaurant–wine bar dazzles with its column-lined dining hall and stained-glass roof. Its wine list, one of the best in town, accompanies a small but considered menu of hard-to-find cheeses, cold cuts, seasonal pastas and refined main courses.

✗ Campo De' Fiori & Around

★ SUPPLIZIO
FAST FOOD **$**

Map p304 (Via dei Banchi Vecchi 143; supplì €3-5; ☺noon-4pm Mon-Sat plus 5.30-10pm Mon-Thu, to 11pm Fri & Sat; ☖Corso Vittorio Emanuele II) Rome's favourite snack, the *supplì* (a fried croquette filled with rice, tomato sauce and mozzarella), gets a gourmet makeover at this elegant new street-food joint. Sit back on the vintage leather sofa and dig into the classic article or throw the boat out and try something different, maybe a mildly spicy fish *suppli* stuffed with anchovies, tuna, parsley, and just a hint of orange.

I DOLCI DI NONNA VINCENZA
PASTICCERIA, CAFE $

Map p304 (www.dolcinonnavincenza.it; Via Arco del Monte 98a; pastries from €2.50; ⊗8am-9pm Sun-Thu, to midnight Fri & Sat; 🚇Via Arenula) Bringing the flavours of Sicily to Rome, this pastry shop is hard to resist. Browse the traditional cakes and tempting *dolci* in the old wooden dressers, before adjourning to the adjacent bar to tear into the heavenly selection of creamy, flaky, puffy pastries.

PASTICCERIA DE BELLIS
PASTICCERIA $

Map p304 (Piazza del Paradiso 56-57; pastries €4; ⊗9am-8pm Tue-Sun; 🚇Corso Vittorio Emanuele II) The beautiful cakes, pastries and *dolci* at this chic pasticceria are miniature works of art. Curated in every detail, they look superb and taste magnificent. You'll find traditional offerings alongside unique creations such as the Assoluta, a decadent concoction combining several chocolate mousses.

FORNO ROSCIOLI
PIZZA, BAKERY $

Map p304 (Via dei Chiavari 34; pizza slices from €2, snacks from €1.50; ⊗7am-7.30pm Mon-Sat; 🚇Via Arenula) This is one of Rome's top bakeries, much loved by lunching locals who crowd here for luscious sliced pizza, prize pastries and hunger-sating *supplì*. There's also a counter serving hot pastas and vegetable side dishes.

FORNO DI CAMPO DE' FIORI
PIZZA, BAKERY $

Map p304 (Campo de' Fiori 22; pizza slices about €3; ⊗7.30am-2.30pm & 4.45-8pm Mon-Sat; 🚇Corso Vittorio Emanuele II) This buzzing bakery on Campo de' Fiori does a roaring trade in *panini* and delicious fresh-from-the-oven *pizza al taglio* (by the slice). Aficionados swear by the *pizza bianca* ('white' pizza with olive oil, rosemary and salt), but the *panini* and *pizza rossa* ('red' pizza, with olive oil, tomato and oregano) taste plenty good, too.

DAR FILETTARO A SANTA BARBARA
FISH & CHIPS $

Map p304 (Largo dei Librari 88; meals €15-20; ⊗5.30-10.45pm Mon-Sat; 🚇Via Arenula) On a tiny, scooter-strewn piazza, this spartan eatery is a classic Roman *friggitoria* (shop selling fried food). The house speciality is battered *baccalà* (cod), but you can also try crisply fried zucchini and anchovies with butter.

RENATO E LUISA
TRATTORIA $$

Map p304 (☎06 686 96 60; www.renatoeluisa.it; Via dei Barbieri 25; meals €45; ⊗8pm-midnight Tue-Sun; 🚇Largo di Torre Argentina) Highly rated locally, this small backstreet trattoria is always packed. Chef Renato takes a creative approach to classic Roman cooking, resulting in dishes that are modern and seasonal yet undeniably local, such as his signature *cacio e pepe e fiori di zucca* (pasta with pecorino cheese, black pepper and courgette flowers). Bookings recommended.

DITIRAMBO
ITALIAN $$

Map p304 (☎06 687 16 26; www.ristoranteditirambo.it; Piazza della Cancelleria 72; meals €40; ⊗1-3pm & 7.20-10.30pm, closed Mon lunch; 🚇Corso Vittorio Emanuele II) Since opening in 1996, Ditirambo has won an army of fans with its informal trattoria vibe and seasonal, organic cuisine. Dishes cover many bases, ranging from old-school favourites to thoughtful vegetarian offerings and more exotic fare such as pasta with Sicilian prawns, basil and lime. Book ahead.

GRAPPOLO D'ORO
ITALIAN $$

Map p304 (☎06 689 70 80; www.hosteriagrappolodoro.it; Piazza della Cancelleria 80; tasting menu €28, meals €35-40; ⊗12.45-3pm & 7-11.30pm, closed Wed lunch; 🚇Corso Vittorio Emanuele II) This informal eatery stands out among the many lacklustre options around Campo de' Fiori. The emphasis is on traditional Roman cuisine, albeit with the occasional twist, so look out for artichoke starters, pastas littered with pecorino, pancetta and black pepper, and mains of no-nonsense braised and grilled meats.

SERGIO ALLE GROTTE
TRATTORIA $$

Map p304 (☎06 686 42 93; Vicolo delle Grotte 27; meals €30-35; ⊗12.30-3.30pm & 6.30-11pm Mon-Sat; 🚇Via Arenula) This is a textbook Roman trattoria: chequered tablecloths, dodgy wall murals, battle-hardened waiters delivering steaming bowls of hearty, down-to-earth pasta followed by steaks grilled over hot coals.

SALUMERIA ROSCIOLI
ITALIAN $$$

Map p306 (☎06 687 52 87; Via dei Giubbonari 21; meals €55; ⊗12.30-4pm & 7pm-midnight Mon-Sat; 🚇Via Arenula) The name Roscioli has long been a byword for foodie excellence, and this luxurious deli-restaurant is the place to experience it. Under a coffered ceiling, you'll find a display of mouth-watering

Italian and foreign delicacies, while behind, in the small restaurant, diners sit down to sophisticated Italian food and some truly outstanding wines.

✖ Jewish Ghetto

ANTICO FORNO URBANI PIZZA, BAKERY **$**

Map p306 (Piazza Costaguti 31; pizza slices from €1.50; ☉7.40am-2.30pm & 5-8.45pm Mon-Fri, 9am-1.30pm Sat & Sun; ☐Via Arenula) A popular kosher bakery, this Ghetto institution makes some of the best pizza *bianca* in town, as well as freshly baked bread, biscuits and focaccias. It gets very busy but once you catch a whiff of the yeasty odours wafting off the counter, there's nothing for it but to grab a ticket and wait your turn.

BOCCIONE BAKERY **$**

Map p306 (☎06 687 86 37; Via del Portico d'Ottavia 1; ☉8am-7.30pm Sun-Thu, 8am-3.30pm Fri; ☐Via Arenula) This tiny, unsigned shop is the Ghetto's most famous bakery, where locals come to buy their special-occasion *dolci* (cakes and pastries). The burnished cakes, served by authentically grumpy ladies, are bursting with fruit, sultanas, and ricotta.

ALBERTO PICA GELATERIA, CAFE **$**

Map p306 (Via della Seggiola 12; gelato €2-3; ☉8.30am-2am; ☐Via Arenula) Recent years have seen an explosion of modern, gourmet gelaterie in Rome, but some of the old places survive. Places like this faded, old-fashioned milk bar, famous for its classic ice creams and rice gelato, which has the flavour and texture of frozen rice pudding.

BEPPE E I SUOI FORMAGGI DELI **$$**

Map p306 (☎06 6819 2210; www.beppeeisuoiformaggi.it; Via Santa Maria del Pianto 9-11; meals €30; ☉9-11am, 11.30am-3.30pm & 7.30-10.30pm Mon-Sat; ☐Via Arenula) It's all in the name – Beppe and his cheeses. This small restaurant, attached to a well-stocked deli selling *formaggi* of all shapes and smells, is a mecca for aficionados, serving cheese throughout the day. Breakfast on ricotta, lunch on robiola, end the day with a dinner of warmed camembert.

PIPERNO RISTORANTE **$$$**

Map p306 (☎06 6880 6629; www.ristorante-piperno.it; Via Monte de' Cenci 9; meals €50-55; ☉12.45-2.20pm & 7.45-10.20pm, closed Mon & Sun dinner; ☐Via Arenula) This historic Ghetto

restaurant, complete with its smart old-school look, is a top spot for traditional Jewish-Roman cooking. Signature dishes include wonderful deep-fried *filetti di baccalà* (cod fillets) and *animelle di agnello con carciofi* (lamb sweetbreads with artichokes). To finish off, try the *tortino al cioccolato* (chocolate cake). Booking recommended.

VECCHIA ROMA RISTORANTE **$$$**

Map p306 (☎06 686 46 04; www.ristorante-vecchiaroma.com; Piazza Campitelli 18; meals €55; ☉12.30-3pm & 8-11pm Thu-Tue; ☐Via del Teatro di Marcello) This old-fashioned restaurant is a picture of formal elegance with its chandeliers, white-jacketed waiters, and candle-lit terrace overlooking a picture-book piazza. But it's not all show and the food is excellent, with some wonderful seafood *antipasti* and top-drawer pastas.

✖ Isola Tiberina

SORA LELLA RISTORANTE **$$$**

Map p306 (☎06 686 16 01; www.soralella.com; Via Ponte Quattro Capi 16; tasting menus €45-58, meals €50; ☉12.30-3pm & 7.30-11pm Wed-Tue; ☐Lungotevere dei Cenci) This long-standing family-run restaurant enjoys a memorable setting in a tower on the Tiber's tiny island. Named after a much-loved Roman actress (the owner's mum), it serves a classic Roman menu spiced up with some wonderful fish dishes. There are also homemade desserts and several tasting menus, including, on Thursdays, one for vegetarians.

✖ Piazza Colonna & Around

GIOLITTI GELATERIA **$**

Map p304 (☎06 699 12 43; www.giolitti.it; Via degli Uffici del Vicario 40; gelato €2.50-4.50; ☉7am-1am; ☐Via del Corso) Rome's most celebrated gelateria started as a dairy in 1900 and still keeps the hoards happy with succulent sorbets and creamy combinations. Gregory Peck and Audrey Hepburn swung by in *Roman Holiday* and, more recently, Barack Obama's daughters stopped off while pops was working at a G8 event. Try the marron glacé, a favourite of Pope John Paul II.

DAL CAVALIER GINO TRATTORIA **$$**

Map p304 (☎06 687 34 34; Vicolo Rosini 4; meals €35; ☉1-3.45pm & 8-11pm Mon-Sat; ☐Via

CENTRO STORICO DRINKING & NIGHTLIFE

KOSHER ROME

If you want to eat kosher in Rome head to Via del Portico d'Ottavia, the main strip through the Jewish Ghetto. Lined with trattorias and restaurants specialising in Roman-Jewish cuisine, it's a lively hang-out, especially on hot summer nights when diners crowd the many sidewalk tables. For a taste of typical Ghetto cooking, try **Nonna Betta** (Map p306; ☑06 6880 6263; www.nonnabetta.it; Via del Portico d'Ottavia 16; meals €30-35; ☺noon-4pm & 6-11pm, closed Fri dinner & Sat lunch; ☐Via Arenula), a small tunnel of a trattoria serving traditional kosher food and local staples such as *carciofi alla guidia* (crisp fried artichokes). Further down the road, the unmarked **Cremeria Romana** (Map p306; Via del Portico d'Ottavia 1b; gelato €2-5; ☺8am-11pm Sun-Thu, to 4pm Fri, 6pm-midnight Sat; ☐Via Arenula) at No 1b has a small selection of tasty kosher gelati.

del Corso) Close to parliament, Gino's is a hidden backstreet trattoria perennially packed with journalists and conspiring politicians. Join the right honourables for well-executed staples such as *tonnarelli cacio e pepe* (pasta with pecorino cheese and black pepper) and *pollo con peperoni* (chicken with pepper), all served under hanging garlic and gaudily painted murals.

OSTERIA
DELL'INGEGNO   ITALIAN $$
Map p304 (☑06 678 06 62; www.osteria-ingegno.it; Piazza di Pietra 45; meals €40; ☺noon-midnight; ☐Via del Corso) A boho-chic restaurant–wine bar with a colourful art-filled interior and a prime location on a charming central piazza. The menu hits all the right notes with a selection of seasonal pastas, creative mains, salads, and homemade desserts, while the 300-strong wine list boasts some interesting Italian labels. *Aperitivo* is served daily from 5pm to 8pm.

MATRICIANELLA   TRATTORIA $$
Map p304 (☑06 683 21 00; www.matricianella. it; Via del Leone 2/4; meals €40; ☺12.30-3pm & 7.30-11pm Mon-Sat; ☐Via del Corso) With its gingham tablecloths, chintzy murals and fading prints, Matricianella is an archetypal trattoria, much loved for its traditional Roman cuisine. Its loyal clientele go crazy for evergreen crowd-pleasers like battered vegetables, artichoke *alla giudia* (fried, Jewish style), and *saltimbocca* (veal cutlet with ham and sage). Booking is essential.

DRINKING & NIGHTLIFE

Nightlife in the *centro storico* clusters on two main areas: the lanes around Piazza Navona, with a number of elegant bars catering to the hip beautiful people; and the rowdier area around Campo de' Fiori, where the crowd is younger and the drinking is heavier. This is where people congregate after football games and foreign students head out on the booze. The *centro storico* also harbours many great cafes.

Pantheon & Around

CAFFÈ SANT'EUSTACHIO   CAFE
Map p304 (www.santeustachioilcaffe.it; Piazza Sant'Eustachio 82; ☺8.30am-1am Sun-Thu, to 1.30am Fri, to 2am Sat; ☐Corso del Rinascimento) This small, unassuming cafe, generally three deep at the bar, is reckoned by many to serve the best coffee in town. Created by beating the first drops of espresso and several teaspoons of sugar into a frothy paste, then adding the rest of the coffee, it's superbly smooth and guaranteed to put some zing into your sightseeing.

LA CASA DEL CAFFÈ TAZZA D'ORO   CAFE
Map p304 (www.tazzadorocoffeeshop.com; Via degli Orfani 84-86; ☺7am-8pm Mon-Sat, 10.30am-7.30pm Sun; ☐Via del Corso) A busy, stand-up cafe with burnished 1940s fittings, this is one of Rome's best coffee houses. Its espresso hits the mark nicely and there's a range of delicious coffee concoctions, including a cooling *granita di caffè*, a crushed-ice coffee drink served with whipped cream.

There's also a small shop and, outside, a coffee *bancomat* for those out-of-hours caffeine emergencies.

Piazza Navona & Around

ETABLÌ
BAR, RISTORANTE

Map p304 (☎06 9761 6694; www.etabli.it; Vicolo delle Vacche 9a; ⊙11am-2am, closed Mon in winter, Sun in summer; ☎; ☒Corso del Rinascimento) Housed in a lofty 16th-century *palazzo*, Etablì is a rustic-chic lounge-bar-restaurant where you can drop by for a morning coffee, have a light lunch or chat over an *aperitivo*. It's laid-back and good-looking, with original French-inspired country decor – think leather armchairs, rough wooden tables, and a crackling fireplace. It also serves weekend brunch, full restaurant dinners (€45), and the occasional jam session.

CIRCUS
BAR

Map p304 (www.circusroma.it; Via della Vetrina 15; ⊙10.30am-2am; ☎; ☒Corso del Rinascimento) A great little bar, tucked around the corner from Piazza Navona. It's a relaxed place popular with out-of-town students who come here to catch up on the news – wi-fi is free and there are international newspapers to read – and hang out over a drink. The atmosphere hots up in the evening when cocktails and shots take over from tea and cappuccino.

NO.AU
BAR

Map p304 (Piazza Montevecchio 16; ⊙6pm-1am Tue-Thu, noon-1am Fri-Sun; ☒Corso del Rinascimento) Opening onto a charming *centro storico* piazza, No.Au – pronounced Know How – is a cool bistrot-bar set-up. Like many fashionable bars, it's big on beer and offers a knowledgeable list of artisanal craft brews, as well as local wines and a small but select food menu.

L'EMPORIO ALLA PACE
CAFE

Map p304 (Via della Pace 28; ⊙6am-2am; ☎; ☒Corso del Rinaascimento) Students sitting solo with a book, gossiping friends, tourists, priests, Romans. This bookshop-cafe caters to a mixed crowd throughout the day, serving cappuccino and cornettos in the morning, *panini* and pastas at lunch, cocktails and midnight beers in the evening.

CAFFÈ DELLA PACE
CAFE

Map p304 (www.caffedellapace.it; Via della Pace 5; ⊙9am-3am Tue-Sun, 4pm-3am Mon; ☒Corso del Rinascimento) For years, this landmark art-nouveau cafe – all stylishly dressed drinkers, polished wood and cascading ivy – was the picture of *dolce vita* poise. In recent times, the cafe has faced a fight for survival against plans to turn it into a five-star hotel, with the public getting behind petitions to save it.

Campo de' Fiori & Around

★BARNUM CAFE
CAFE

Map p304 (www.barnumcafe.com; Via del Pellegrino 87; ⊙9am-10pm Mon, 8.30am-2am Tue-Sat; ☎; ☒Corso Vittorio Emanuele II) A relaxed, friendly spot to check your email over a freshly squeezed orange juice or spend a pleasant hour reading a newspaper on one of the tatty old armchairs in the white bare-brick interior. Come evenings and the scene is cocktails, smooth tunes and coolly dressed-down locals.

OPEN BALADIN
BAR

Map p306 (www.openbaladinroma.it; Via degli Specchi 6; ⊙noon-2am; ☎; ☒Via Arenula) A hip, shabby-chic lounge bar near Campo de' Fiori, Open Baladin is a leading light in Rome's craft-beer scene, with more than 40 beers on tap and up to 100 bottled brews, many from Italian artisanal microbreweries. There's also a decent food menu – *panini*, gourmet burgers and daily specials.

IL GOCCETTO
WINE BAR

Map p304 (Via dei Banchi Vecchi 14; ⊙11.30am-2pm Tue & Sat, 6.30pm-midnight Mon-Sat, closed Aug; ☒Corso Vittorio Emanuele II) This old-school *vino e olio* (wine and oil) shop has everything you could want in a neighbourhood wine bar – a colourful cast of regulars, a cosy, bottle-lined interior, a selection of cheeses and cold cuts, and a serious, 800-strong wine list.

JERRY THOMAS PROJECT
COCKTAIL BAR

Map p304 (☎06 9684 5937; www.thejerrythomasproject.it; Vicolo Cellini 30; ⊙10pm-4am; ☒Corso Vittorio Emanuele II) A self-styled speakeasy with a 1920s look and a password to get in – check the website and call to book – this hidden bar is setting the standards for the cocktail trend currently sweeping Rome. Its hipster mixologists know their stuff and the retro decor lends the place a real Prohibition-era feel.

L'ANGOLO DIVINO
WINE BAR

Map p304 (www.angolodivino.it; Via dei Balestrari 12; ⏲10.30am-3pm Tue-Sat, 5pm-1.30am daily; 🚇Corso Vittorio Emanuele II) A hop and a skip from Campo de' Fiori, this is a warm, woody wine bar. It's an oasis of genteel calm, with a carefully selected wine list and a small daily menu of hot and cold dishes.

Piazza Colonna & Around

SALOTTO 42
BAR

Map p304 (www.salotto42.it; Piazza di Pietra 42; ⏲10.30am-2am Tue-Sun; 🚇Via del Corso) On a picturesque piazza, facing the columns of the Temple of Hadrian, this is a glamorous lounge bar, complete with subdued lighting, vintage 1950s armchairs, Murano lamps and a collection of heavyweight design books. Come for the daily lunch buffet or to hang out with the 'see and be-seen' crowd over an evening cocktail.

FANDANGO INCONTRO
BAR

Map p304 (Via dei Prefetti 22; ⏲10am-9pm Tue-Sun; 🚇Via del Corso) A cultural space run by an Italian film producer and publisher, Fandango Incontro occupies the ground floor of an imposing 18th-century *palazzo*. It's often used to stage events, and its bookshop bar is the ideal spot to sift through comics and discuss art-house cinema over a light lunch or evening aperitif.

GRAN CAFFÈ LA CAFFETTIERA
CAFE

Map p304 (Piazza di Pietra 65; ⏲7am-10pm Mon-Sat, from 9am Sun; 🚇Via del Corso) This stately art-deco cafe with tables on graceful Piazza di Pietra is well-known for its coffee and Neapolitan cakes. For a real taste of Naples go for a *sfogliatella*, a flaky pastry shell stuffed with ricotta and shards of candied fruit.

CIAMPINI
CAFE

Map p304 (Piazza di San Lorenzo in Lucina 29; ⏲7.30am-8.30pm Mon-Sat, to midnight summer; 🚇Via del Corso) Join the neighbourhood's well-heeld locals for an al fresco cappuccino or tip-top gelato at this elegant old cafe on graceful, traffic-free Piazza di San Lorenzo in Lucina. There's also a full food menu of pizzas, pastas, salads and sandwiches.

★ ENTERTAINMENT

TEATRO ARGENTINA
THEATRE

Map p304 (✆06 684 00 03 11; www.teatrodiroma.net; Largo di Torre Argentina 52; tickets €16-29; 🚇Largo di Torre Argentina) Founded in 1732, Rome's top theatre is one of the two official homes of the Teatro di Roma – the other is the Teatro India in the southern suburbs. Rossini's *Barber of Seville* premiered here in 1816 and it today stages a program of drama (mostly in Italian), high-profile dance performances, and classical-music concerts.

TEATRO DELL'OROLOGIO
THEATRE

Map p304 (✆06 687 55 50; www.teatroorologio.com; Via dei Filippini 17a; 🚇Corso Vittorio Emanuele II) A well-known experimental theatre, the three-stage Orologio offers a varied program of contemporary and classic works, including occasional performances in English.

🛍 SHOPPING

🛍 Pantheon & Around

LE ARTIGIANE
CLOTHING, HANDICRAFTS

Map p304 (www.leartigiane.it; Via di Torre Argentina 72; ⏲10am-7.30pm; 🚇Largo di Torre Argentina) A space for local artisans to showcase their wares, this eclectic shop is the result of an ongoing project to sustain and promote Italy's artisanal traditions. It's a browser's dream with an eclectic range of handmade clothes, costume jewellery, ceramics, design objects and lamps.

STILO FETTI
ACCESSORIES

Map p304 (www.stilofetti.it; Via degli Orfani 82; ⏲9am-1pm Tue-Sat, 3.30-7.30pm Mon-Sat; 🚇Via del Corso) Technology might have largely wiped out fountain pens but this old-fashioned family-run shop, on the go since 1893, has a wonderful selection. All styles are covered and you'll find many top brands, from Faber-Castell to Mont Blanc and Montegrappa, the luxury Italian pen-maker favoured by royalty and world leaders.

ALBERTA GLOVES
ACCESSORIES

Map p304 (Corso Vittorio Emanuele II 18; ⏲10am-6.30pm; 🚇Largo di Torre Argentina) From elbow-length silk gloves to tan-coloured driving mitts, this tiny family-run shop sells a wide range of handmade gloves for every conceivable occasion. Scarves and woolly hats too.

🔒 Piazza Navona & Around

SBU
FASHION

Map p304 (www.sbu.it; Via di San Pantaleo 68-69; ⊙10am-7.30pm Mon-Sat; 🚇Corso Vittorio Emanuele II) The flagship store of hip fashion label SBU, aka Strategic Business Unit, occupies a 19th-century workshop near Piazza Navona, complete with cast-iron columns and wooden racks. Pride of place goes to the jeans, superbly cut from top-end Japanese denim, but you can also pick up shirts, jackets, hats, sweaters and T-shirts.

TEMPI MODERNI
JEWELLERY, CLOTHING

Map p304 (Via del Governo Vecchio 108; ⊙9am-1.30pm & 3-7.30pm Mon-Sat; 🚇Corso Vittorio Emanuele II) Klimt prints sit side by side with pop-art paintings and cartoon ties at this kooky curiosity shop on Via del Governo Vecchio. It's packed with vintage costume jewellery, Bakelite pieces from the '20s and '30s, art-nouveau and art-deco trinkets, 19th-century resin brooches and pieces by couturiers such as Chanel, Dior and Balenciaga.

OFFICINA PROFUMO FARMACEUTICA DI SANTA MARIA NOVELLA
BEAUTY

Map p304 (www.smnovella.it; Corso del Rinascimento 47; ⊙10am-7.30pm Mon-Sat; 🚇Corso del Rinascimento) This, the Roman branch of one of Italy's oldest pharmacies, stocks natural perfumes and cosmetics as well as herbal infusions, teas and pot pourri, all shelved in wooden, glass-fronted cabinets under a Murano chandelier. The original pharmacy was founded in Florence in 1612 by the Dominican monks of Santa Maria Novella, and many of its cosmetics are based on 17th-century herbal recipes.

NARDECCHIA
ARTS

Map p304 (Piazza Navona 25; ⊙10am-1pm Tue-Sat, 4.30-7.30pm Mon-Sat; 🚇Corso del Rinascimento) Famed for its antique prints, this historic Piazza Navona shop sells everything from 18th-century etchings by Giovanni Battista Piranesi to more affordable 19th-century panoramas. Bank on at least €150 for a small framed print.

LUNA & L'ALTRA
FASHION

Map p304 (Piazza Pasquino 76; ⊙10am-2pm Tue-Sat, 3.30-7.30pm Mon-Sat; 🚇Corso Vittorio Emanuele II) An address for fashionistas with their fingers on the pulse, this is one of a number of independent boutiques on and around Via del Governo Vecchio. In its austere, gallery-like interior, clothes by Comme des Garçons, Issey Miyake, Yohji Yamamoto and others are exhibited in reverential style.

ALDO FEFÈ
HANDICRAFTS

Map p304 (Via della Stelletta 20b; ⊙8am-7.30pm Mon-Sat; 🚇Corso del Rinascimento) This authentic artisanal workshop produces beautifully hand-painted paper as well as leather-bound notebooks (€32), picture frames and photo albums (from €15). You can also buy Florentine wrapping paper and calligraphic pens.

ZOUZOU
FASHION

Map p304 (www.zouzou.it; Vicolo della Cancelleria 9a; ⊙11am-7.30pm Tue-Sat, 2-7.30pm Mon; 🚇Corso Vittorio Emanuele II) Spice up your Roman romance at this upmarket erotic boutique just off Via del Governo Vecchio. Set up as a Victorian boudoir with crimson walls and corseted mannequins, it sells a range of luxury lingerie, toiletries and toys, all, of course, in the best possible taste.

VESTITI USATI CINZIA
VINTAGE

Map p304 (Via del Governo Vecchio 45; ⊙10am-8pm Mon-Sat, 2-8pm Sun; 🚇Corso Vittorio Emanuele II) Owned by a former costume designer, this is an Aladdin's cave of vintage clothes. Its narrow interior is piled high with jackets (in leather, denim, corduroy and linen), stagy cocktail dresses, screen-printed T-shirts, retro skirts, suede coats, designer sunglasses and colourful bags.

OMERO E CECILIA
VINTAGE

Map p304 (www.omerocecilia.com; Via del Governo Vecchio 110; ⊙10am-8pm Mon-Sat, 2-8pm Sun; 🚇Corso Vittorio Emanuele II) This wonderful tunnel of a place is browsing heaven, stashed full of second-hand leather bags, '70s velvet coats, tweed jackets, '60s Italian dresses, old Burberry trench coats, Church shoes and much more besides.

AI MONASTERI
BEAUTY

Map p304 (www.aimonasteri.it; Corso del Rinascimento 72; ⊙10.30-7.30pm, closed Thu afternoon & Sun; 🚇Corso del Rinascimento) With balms for the body and food for the soul, this monastic apothecary stocks a range of herbal essences, lotions and cosmetics, all made by monks from across Italy, as well as wines, liqueurs and biscuits. There are even elixirs promising love, happiness, and eternal youth.

CASALI ARTS

Map p304 (Via dei Coronari 115; ☺10am-1pm Mon-Sat plus 3.30-7.30pm Sat; ▣Corso del Rinascimento) On lovely Via dei Coronari, Casali deals in original and reproduction etchings and old prints, many delicately hand-coloured. The shop is small but the choice is not, ranging from 16th-century botanical manuscripts to postcard prints of Rome.

LE TELE DI CARLOTTA HANDICRAFTS

Map p304 (Via dei Coronari 228; ☺10.30am-1pm & 3.30-7pm Mon-Fri; ▣Corso del Rinascimento) Search out this tiny sewing box of a shop for hand-embroidered napkins, cushion covers, bags and antique jewellery. If you're stopping long enough in Rome, you can have pieces embroidered to your specifications.

AL SOGNO TOYS

Map p304 (www.alsogno.com; Piazza Navona 53; ☺10am-8pm; ▣Corso del Rinascimento) The extravagant window displays at this landmark toy shop are almost as flamboyant as the sculptural gymnastics on display on Piazza Navona's fountains. Inside, the store is a wonderland of puppets, trolls, fairies, fake Roman weapons, dolls and stuffed animals. The don't-touch atmosphere is best suited to well-behaved little darlings.

⛪ Campo De' Fiori & Around

★IBIZ – ARTIGIANATO
IN CUOIO ACCESSORIES

Map p304 (Via dei Chiavari 39; ☺9.30am-7.30pm Mon-Sat; ▣Corso Vittorio Emanuele II) In their diminutive workshop, Elisa Nepi and her father craft exquisite, well-priced leather goods in simple but classy designs and myriad colours. You can pick up a belt for about €35, while for a bag you should bank on at least €110.

★RACHELE CHILDREN

Map p304 (www.racheleartchildrenswear.it; Vicolo del Bollo 6; ☺10.30am-2pm & 3.30-7.30pm Tue-Sat; ▣Corso Vittorio Emanuele II) Mums looking to update their kids' (under 12s)

wardrobe would do well to look up Rachele in her delightful shop just off Via del Pellegrino. With everything from hats and mitts to romper suits and jackets, all brightly coloured and all handmade, this sort of shop is a dying breed. Most items are around the €40 to €50 mark.

ARSENALE FASHION

Map p304 (www.patriziapieroni.it; Via del Pellegrino 172; ☺10am-7.30pm Tue-Sat, 3.30-7.30pm Mon; ▣Corso Vittorio Emanuele II) Arsenale, the atelier of Roman designer Patrizia Pieroni, is a watchword for original, high-end women's fashion. The virgin white interior creates a clean, contemporary showcase for beautifully cut clothes.

I COLORI DI DENTRO ARTS

Map p304 (www.mgluffarelli.com; Via dei Banchi Vecchi 29; ☺11am-7pm Mon-Sat; ▣Corso Vittorio Emanuele II) Take home some Mediterranean sunshine. Artist Maria Grazia Luffarelli's paintings are a riotous celebration of Italian colours, with sunny yellow landscapes, blooming flowers, Roman cityscapes and comfortable-looking cats. You can buy original watercolours or prints, as well as postcards, T-shirts, notebooks and calendars.

DADADA 52 FASHION

Map p304 (www.dadada.eu; Via dei Giubbonari 52; ☺noon-8pm Mon, 11am-2pm & 3-8pm Tue-Sat, 11.30am-7.30pm Sun; ▣Via Arenula) Girls with an eye for what works should make a beeline for this small boutique. Here you'll find a selection of eye-catching cocktail dresses that can be dressed up or down, print summer frocks, eclectic coats and colourful hats. There's a second **branch** (Map p308; ☏06 6813 9162; Ⓜ Flaminio or Spagna) at Via del Corso 500.

MONDELLO OTTICA FASHION

Map p304 (www.mondelloottica.it; Via del Pellegrino 98; ☺10am-1.30pm & 4-7.30pm Tue-Sat; ▣Corso Vittorio Emanuele II) Eyewear becomes art at this modish optician's on Via del Pellegrino. Known for its avant-garde window displays, often styled by contemporary artists, Mondello Ottica sells frames by leading designers such as Berlin label Kuboraum and Belgian brand Theo. Prescription glasses can be ready the same day.

BORINI SHOES

Map p306 (Via dei Pettinari 86-87; ☺9am-1pm Tue-Sat, 3.30-7.30pm Mon-Sat; ▣Via Arenula) Don't be fooled by the discount, workaday look – those in the know head to this seemingly down-at-heel shop for the latest footwear fashions. Women's styles are displayed in the functional glass cabinets, alongside a small selection of men's leather shoes.

LOCO   SHOES

Map p304 (Via dei Baullari 22; ☺10.30am-7.30pm Tue-Sat, 3.30-7.30pm Mon; 🚇Corso Vittorio Emanuele II) Sneaker fetishists should hotfoot it to Loco for the very latest in big-statement trainers. It's a small shop, but full of attitude, with a jazzy collection of original sneakers (for boys and girls), boots and pumps by international and Italian designers. It also sells bags and costume jewellery.

🏠 Piazza Colonna & Around

★CONFETTERIA MORIONDO & GARIGLIO   FOOD

Map p304 (Via del Piè di Marmo 21-22; ☺9am-7.30pm Mon-Sat; 🚇Via del Corso) Roman poet Trilussa was so smitten with this historic chocolate shop – established by the Torinese confectioners to the royal house of Savoy – that he dedicated several sonnets to it. And we agree, it's a gem. Many of the bonbons and handmade chocolates laid out in ceremonial splendour in the glass cabinets are still prepared according to original 19th-century recipes.

MATERIE   JEWELLERY

Map p304 (www.materieshop.com; Via del Gesù 73; ☺10.30-7.30pm Mon-Sat; 🚇Via del Corso) A showcase for unique handmade jewellery crafted from materials as diverse as silver, perspex, metal, plastic and stone. Each year owner Viviana Violo travels the world on the lookout for new designs to take back and sell in this, her tranquil, central shop. She also stocks a small selection of bags, scarves and other accessories.

TARTARUGHE   FASHION

Map p304 (www.letartarughe.eu; Via del Piè di Marmo 17; ☺10am-7.30pm Tue-Sat, noon-7.30pm Mon; 🚇Via del Corso) Fashionable, versatile and elegant, Susanna Liso's seasonal designs adorn this relaxed, white-walled boutique. Her clothes, which include understated woollen coats, strikingly cut jackets,

LOCAL KNOWLEDGE

HELP FIGHT THE MAFIA

To look at it there's nothing special about **Bottega Pio La Torre** (Map p304; www.liberaterra.it; Via dei Prefetti 23; ☺10.30am-7.30pm Tue-Sat, 10.30am-2.30pm Sun, 3.30-7.30pm Mon; 🚇Via del Corso), a small, unpretentious food store near Piazza del Parlamento. But shop here and you're making a small but concrete contribution to the fight against the mafia. All the gastro goodies on sale, including organic olive oils, pastas, flours, honeys and wine, have been produced on land confiscated from organised crime outfits in Calabria and Sicily.

sweaters, and trousers, provide a vibrant modern update on classic styles. You'll also find a fine line in novel accessories.

BARTOLUCCI   TOYS

Map p304 (www.bartolucci.com; Via dei Pastini 98; ☺10am-10pm; 🚇Via del Corso) It's difficult to resist going into this magical toy shop where everything is carved out of wood. It's guarded by a cycling Pinocchio and a full-sized motorbike, and within are all manner of ticking clocks, rocking horses, planes and more Pinocchios than you'll have ever seen in your life.

A S ROMA STORE   SPORTS

Map p304 (Piazza Colonna 360; ☺10am-7.30pm Mon-Sat, 10.30am-7pm Sun; 🚇Via del Corso) An official club store of A S Roma, one of Rome's two top-flight football teams. There's an extensive array of Roma-branded kit, including replica shirts, caps, T-shirts, scarves, hoodies, keyrings and a whole lot more. You can also buy match tickets here.

DE SANCTIS   CERAMICS

Map p304 (www.desanctis1890.com; Piazza di Pietra 24; ☺10am-1.30pm & 3-7.30pm Mon-Sat, closed Tue morning; 🚇Via del Corso) De Sanctis – in business since 1890 – is full of impressive Sicilian and Tuscan ceramics, with sunbursts of colour decorating crockery, kitchenware and objets d'art. If your purchases are too heavy to carry, it ships worldwide.

Showtime on Rome's Piazzas

From the baroque splendour of Piazza Navona to the clamour of Campo de' Fiori and the majesty of St Peter's Square, Rome's showcase piazzas encapsulate much of the city's beauty, history and drama.

Piazza Navona

In the heart of the historic centre, Piazza Navona (p74) is the picture-perfect Roman square. Graceful baroque *palazzi* (mansions), flamboyant fountains, packed pavement cafes and costumed street artists set the scene for the daily invasion of camera-toting tourists.

St Peter's Square

The awe-inspiring approach to St Peter's Basilica, this monumental piazza (p134) is a masterpiece of 17th-century urban design. The work of Bernini, it's centred on a towering Egyptian obelisk and flanked by two grasping colonnaded arms.

1. Fontana del Nettuno, Piazza Navona (p74) 2. Diners on Campo de' Fiori (p78) 3. St Peter's Square (p134)

Piazza del Popolo

Neoclassical Piazza del Popolo (p103) is a vast, sweeping spectacle. In centuries past, executions were held here; nowadays crowds gather for political rallies, outdoor concerts or just to hang out.

Piazza del Campidoglio

The centrepiece of the Campidoglio (Capitoline Hill), this Michelangelo-designed piazza (p65) is thought by many to be the city's most beautiful. Surrounded on three sides by *palazzi*, it's home to the Capitoline Museums.

Campo de' Fiori

Home to one of Rome's historic markets and a boozy bar scene, Campo de' Fiori (p78) buzzes with activity day and night.

Piazza di Spagna

In Rome's swank shopping district, Piazza di Spagna (p100) has long attracted footsore foreigners who come to sit on the Spanish Steps and watch the world go by.

Tridente, Trevi & the Quirinale

PIAZZA DEL POPOLO | VIA DEL CORSO | PIAZZA DI SPAGNA | TREVI FOUNTAIN |
THE QUIRINALE | PIAZZA BARBERINI | VIA VENETO

Neighbourhood Top Five

1 People-watching, photo-snapping and day-dreaming on the **Spanish Steps** (p100), with a view down the glittering backbone of the Tridente district, designer-clad Via dei Condotti.

2 Gazing at the Caravaggio masterpieces in the artistic treasure trove **Chiesa di Santa Maria del Popolo** (p101).

3 Taking a tour of the **Villa Medici** (p106), with its formal gardens and astounding Rome views, and stopping off in its cafe afterwards.

4 Revelling in the architectural treasures, glut of masterpieces, and breathtaking Cortona ceiling of **Palazzo Barberini** (p110).

5 Visiting the poignant **Keats–Shelley House** (p104), where the young Keats breathed his last in (then) humble rooms overlooking the Spanish Steps.

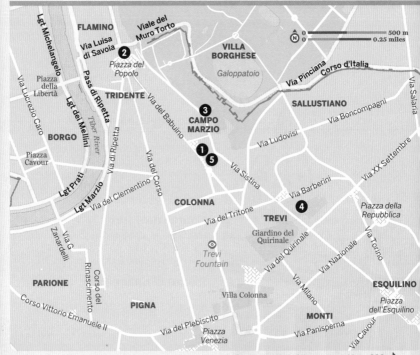

For more detail of this area see Map p308 ➡

Explore: Tridente, Trevi & the Quirinale

Tridente is Rome's most glamorous district, full of designer boutiques, fashionable bars and swish hotels. However, it's not just about shopping, dining and drinking. The area also contains the splendid vast neoclassical showpiece, Piazza del Popolo; the wonderfully frivolous Spanish Steps; the grandiose Villa Medici; the Museo dell'Ara Pacis, a controversial modern museum designed by US architect Richard Meier; artists' street Via Margutta, and several masterpiece-packed churches. To see all the sights here, factoring in some window shopping, would take around half a day to a day, and it's all easily walkable – a short walk from the *centro storico* or Piazza Venezia – and easily accessible from the Spagna and Flaminio metro stations.

Alongside Tridente, the Roman hill of Quirinale is home to the extraordinary Trevi Fountain and the imposing presidential Palazzo del Quirinale, as well as important churches by the twin masters of Roman baroque, Gian Lorenzo Bernini and Francesco Borromini. Other artistic hotspots in the area include the lavish Galleria Colonna and the Galleria Nazionale d'Arte Antica: Palazzo Barberini, a fabulous gallery containing works by a who's who of Renaissance and baroque artists – to see all this at leisure you'll need several days. The Trevi and Quirinale's principal gateway is the Barberini metro stop. Busy during the day, both Tridente and the Quirinale are sleepy after dark.

Local Life

➡ **Ambling** Imagine yourself as part of *Roman Holiday* along the laid-back, cobbled and ivy-draped Via Margutta, and enjoy the upscale neighbourhood feel of this distinctive district.

➡ **Shopping** Commission yourself a handmade bag or a marble motto from one of the area's artisanal shops.

➡ **Coffee** Do as the locals do and grab a caffeine hit, propping up the bar at one of the district's iconic cafes, such as Rosati (p116) or Caffè Greco (p116).

Getting There & Away

➡ **Metro** The Trevi and Quirinale areas are closest to Barberini metro stop, while Spagna and Flaminio stations are perfectly placed for Tridente. All three stops are on line A.

➡ **Bus** Numerous buses run down to Piazza Barberini or along Via Veneto, and many stop at the southern end of Via del Corso and on Via del Tritone, ideal for a foray into Tridente.

Lonely Planet's Top Tip

Local churches are usually locked up for two to three hours over lunch, so if you want to visit the interiors, time your visit for the morning or late afternoon.

 Best Places to Eat

➡ Enoteca Regionale Palatium (p114)

➡ Imàgo (p114)

➡ Fatamorgana (p111)

➡ Colline Emiliane (p115)

➡ Babette (p112)

For reviews, see p110.➡

 Best Places to Drink

➡ Stravinskij Bar – Hotel de Russie (p116)

➡ Il Palazzetto (p114)

➡ Buccone (p111)

For reviews, see p116.➡

◉ **Best Churches**

➡ Chiesa di Santa Maria del Popolo (p101)

➡ Chiesa di Sant'Andrea al Quirinale (p107)

➡ Chiesa di San Carlo alle Quattro Fontane (p107)

➡ Chiesa di Santa Maria della Vittoria (p106)

For reviews, see p103.➡

TRIDENTE, TREVI & THE QUIRINALE

PIAZZA DI SPAGNA & THE SPANISH STEPS

The Spanish Steps and Tridente have been a magnet for foreigners since the 1800s. Charles Dickens wrote, 'these steps are the great place of resort for the artists' "models"... The first time I went up there, I could not conceive why the faces seemed familiar to me... I soon found that we had made acquaintance...on the walls of various Exhibition Galleries.'

The Piazza di Spagna was named after the Spanish Embassy to the Holy See, although the staircase, designed by the Italian Francesco de Sanctis and built in 1725 with a legacy from the French, leads to the French Chiesa della Trinità dei Monti. In the late 1700s the area was much loved by English visitors on the Grand Tour and was known to locals as *er ghetto de l'inglesi* (the English ghetto). Keats lived for a short time in some rooms overlooking the Spanish Steps, and died here of tuberculosis at the age of 25. His landlady's apartment is now a museum devoted to the Romantics, especially Keats.

At the foot of the steps, the fountain of a sinking boat, the Barcaccia (1627), is believed to be by Pietro Bernini, father of the more famous Gian Lorenzo. It's fed from the ancient Roman Acqua Vergine aqueduct, as are the fountains in Piazza del Popolo and the Trevi Fountain. Here there's not much pressure, so it's sunken as a clever piece of engineering. Bees and suns decorate the structure, symbols of the commissioning Barberini family. It was damaged in 2015 by Dutch football fans, and the Dutch subsequently offered to repair the damage. Opposite, Via dei Condotti is Rome's most exclusive shopping street, glittering with big-name designers such as Gucci, Bulgari and Prada.

To the southeast of the piazza, adjacent Piazza Mignanelli is dominated by the Colonna dell'Immacolata, built in 1857 to celebrate Pope Pius IX's declaration of the Immaculate Conception.

DON'T MISS...

➡ The view from the top of the Spanish Steps

➡ Barcaccia

PRACTICALITIES

➡ Map p308

➡ Ⓜ Spagna

TOP SIGHT
CHIESA DI SANTA MARIA DEL POPOLO

This is one of Rome's earliest and richest Renaissance churches, parts of which were designed by Bramante and Bernini. The lavish chapels, decorated by Caravaggio, Bernini, Raphael, Pinturicchio and others, were commissioned by local noble families.

DON'T MISS...

➡ Caravaggio's paintings, Cerasi Chapel

➡ Bernini's work in the Raphael-designed Chigi Chapel

➡ Pinturicchio's frescoes

PRACTICALITIES

➡ Map p308

➡ Piazza del Popolo

➡ ⏱7am-noon & 4-7pm Mon-Sat, 7.30am-1.30pm & 4.30-7.30pm Sun

➡ Ⓜ Flaminio

The Church

The first chapel was built here in 1099, over the tombs of the Domiti family, to exorcise the ghost of Nero, who was secretly buried on this spot and whose malicious spirit was thought to haunt the area. There were subsequent overhauls, but the church's most important makeover came when Bramante renovated the presbytery and choir in the early 16th century and Pinturicchio added a series of frescoes. Also in the Bramante-designed apse are Rome's first stained-glass windows, crafted by Frenchman Guillaume de Marcillat in the early 16th century. The altar houses the 13th-century painting *Madonna del Popolo*. Its most famous works, by Caravaggio, were added in 1601, and Bernini further reworked the church in the 17th century.

Chigi Chapel

Raphael designed the Cappella Chigi, dedicated to his patron, the enormously wealthy banker Agostino Chigi, but never lived to see it completed. Bernini finished the job for him more than 100 years later, contributing statues of Daniel and Habakkuk to the altarpiece, which was built by Sebastiano del Piombo. Only the floor mosaics were retained from Raphael's original design, including that of a kneeling skeleton, placed there to remind the living of the inevitable.

Cerasi Chapel

The church's dazzling highlight is the Cappella Cerasi with its two facing works by Caravaggio: the *Conversion of Saul* and the *Crucifixion of St Peter,* dramatically spotlit via the artist's use of light and shade. The former is the second version, as the first was rejected by the patron. The latter is frighteningly realistic: the artist has used perspective to emphasise the weight of the cross and St Peter's facial expression as he is upturned is heart-rendingly human. The central altarpiece painting is the *Assumption,* by Annibale Carracci.

Della Rovere Chapel

The frescoes in the lunettes, depicting the stories of St Jerome (to whom the chapel is dedicated), and the Nativity with St Jerome above the altar in this chapel were painted by Pinturicchio in the 15th century, and glow with jewel-bright colours.

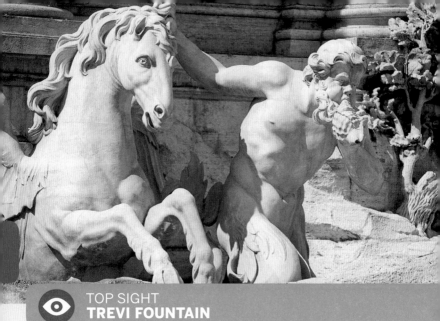

TREVI FOUNTAIN

Fontana di Trevi is a baroque extravaganza, a foaming masterpiece that almost fills an entire piazza. This is where Anita Ekberg cavorted in an iconic black ballgown – apparently wearing waders underneath – in Fellini's *La Dolce Vita* (1960).

The flamboyant baroque ensemble was designed by Nicola Salvi in 1732 and depicts Neptune's chariot being led by Tritons with seahorses – one wild, one docile – representing the moods of the sea. The water still comes from the Aqua Virgo, an underground aqueduct that is over 2000 years old, built by General Agrippa under Augustus and which brings water from the Salone springs around 19km away. The name Trevi refers to the *tre vie* (three roads) that converge at the fountain.

To the eastern side of the fountain is a large round stone urn. The story goes that Salvi, during the construction of the fountain, was harassed by a barber, who had his shop to the east of the fountain and who was critical of the work in progress. Thus the sculptor added this urn in order to block this irritating critic.

The famous tradition (since the film *Three Coins in the Fountain*) is to toss a coin into the fountain, thus ensuring your return to Rome. Around €3000 is thrown into the Trevi on an average day. This money is collected daily and goes to the Catholic charity Caritas, with its yield increasing significantly since the crackdown on criminal elements extracting the money for themselves.

A Fendi-funded €2.18m restoration of the fountain was scheduled for completion in late 2015, and the fountain is thus looking its gleaming best.

DON'T MISS...

➡ The contrasting seahorses, or moods of the sea.

➡ Throwing a coin or three into the fountain.

PRACTICALITIES

➡ Fontana di Trevi

➡ Map p308

➡ Piazza di Trevi

➡ Ⓜ Barberini

SIGHTS

The Piazza del Popolo, the Spanish Steps, the Trevi Fountain, Rome's most fashionable district, Palazzo Barberini and a sprinkling of Caravaggios... and it's all a hop and a skip from Villa Borghese when you're in need of a breather. This area is one of Rome's richest, in terms of cuisine, art and culture (as well as hard cash), and offers an embarrassment of treasures for the visitor.

◉ Piazza del Popolo & Around

CHIESA DI SANTA MARIA DEL POPOLO CHURCH
See p101.

PINCIO HILL GARDENS GARDENS
Map p308 (⊛Flaminio) Overlooking Piazza del Popolo, the 19th-century Pincio Hill is named after the Pinci family, who owned this part of Rome in the 4th century. It's quite a climb up from the piazza, but at the top you're rewarded with lovely views over to St Peter's and the Gianicolo Hill. Alter-

natively, you can approach from the top of the Spanish Steps. From the gardens you can strike out to explore Villa Borghese, the Villa dei Medici, or the Chiesa della Trinità dei Monti at the top of the Spanish Steps.

◉ West of Via Del Corso

MUSEO DELL'ARA PACIS MUSEUM
Map p308 (⊠06 06 08; http://en.arapacis.it; Lungotevere in Auga; adult/reduced €10.50/8.50, audioguide €4; ⊛9am-7pm, last admission 6pm; ⊛Flaminio) The first modern construction in Rome's historic centre since WWII, Richard Meier's controversial and widely detested glass-and-marble pavilion houses the *Ara Pacis Augustae* (Altar of Peace), Augustus' great monument to peace. One of the most important works of ancient Roman sculpture, the vast marble altar – measuring 11.6m by 10.6m by 3.6m – was completed in 13 BC.

The altar was originally positioned near Piazza San Lorenzo in Lucina, slightly to the southeast of its current site. The location was calculated so that on Augustus' birthday the shadow of a huge sundial on Campus Martius would fall directly on it. Over the centuries the altar fell victim to

TRIDENTE, TREVI & THE QUIRINALE SIGHTS

◉ TOP SIGHT
PIAZZA DEL POPOLO

For centuries the site of public executions (the last was in 1826), this public space was once much less grand than today, with a public fountain, horse trough and washing cistern. It was laid out in 1538 to provide a more grandiose entrance to what was then Rome's main northern gateway. Via Flaminia connected the city with the north from here. The piazza has been remodelled several times since, most significantly by Giuseppe Valadier in 1823, who created the gaping ellipse we see today.

In the centre, the 36m-high **obelisk** was brought by Augustus from Heliopolis, in ancient Egypt, and originally stood in Circo Massimo. To the east is the viewpoint of the **Pincio Hill Gardens**. This is not one of Rome's original seven hills, as it lay outside the original city boundary; it was included within the city from the 3rd century.

At the piazza's southern end are Carlo Rainaldi's 17th-century baroque churches, **Chiesa di Santa Maria dei Miracoli** and **Chiesa di Santa Maria in Montesanto**, while on the northern flank is the **Porta del Popolo**, created by Bernini to celebrate Queen Christina of Sweden's defection to Catholicism and arrival in Rome. Its welcoming inscription reads 'FELICI FAUSTOQUE INGRESSUI MDCLV' (For a Happy and Propitious Entrance 1655).

DON'T MISS
➡ The obelisk
➡ The view from the Pincio Hill Gardens

PRACTICALITIES
➡ Map p308
➡ ⊛Flaminio

TOP SIGHT
GALLERIA COLONNA

The only part of Palazzo Colonna open to the public, this dazzlingly opulent gallery houses the Colonna family's small but stunning private art collection. The polished yellow columns represent the 'Colonna' (which also means column) of the family name.

The purpose-built gallery (constructed by Antonio del Grande from 1654 to 1665) has six rooms crowned by fantastical ceiling frescoes, all dedicated to Marcantonio Colonna, the family's greatest ancestor, who defeated the Turks at the naval Battle of Lepanto in 1571. Works by Giovanni Coli and Filippo Gherardi in the Great Hall, Sebastiano Ricci in the Landscapes Room and Giuseppe Bartolomeo Chiari in the Throne Room all commemorate his efforts. Note also the cannonball lodged in the gallery's marble stairs, a vivid reminder of the 1849 siege of Rome.

The art on display features a fine array of 16th- to 18th-century paintings, the highlight of which is Annibale Carracci's vivid *Mangiafagioli* (The Beaneater). A wing opened more recently to the public includes the sumptuous Chapel Hall and the rich 17th-century Artemisia tapestries collection. From May to October a terrace cafe is open.

DON'T MISS...

➡ Fantastic ceiling frescoes

➡ Annibale Carracci's *Mangiafagioli*

PRACTICALITIES

➡ Map p308

➡ ☎06 678 43 50

➡ www.galleriacolonna.it

➡ Via della Pilotta 17

➡ adult/reduced €12/10

➡ ⊙9am-1.15pm Sat, closed Aug

➡ ▣Via IV Novembre

Rome's avid art collectors, and panels ended up in the Medici collection (see the garlanded reliefs embedded in the walls of the Villa Medici), the Vatican and the Louvre. However, in 1936 Mussolini unearthed the remaining parts and decided to reassemble them in the present location.

Of the reliefs, the most important depicts Augustus at the head of a procession, followed by priests, the general Marcus Agrippa and the entire imperial family.

MAUSOLEO DI AUGUSTO   MONUMENT

Map p308 (Piazza Augo Imperatore; ▣Piazza Augusto Imperatore) This mausoleum was built in 28 BC and is the last resting place of Augustus, who was buried here in AD 14, and his favourite nephew and heir Marcellus. Mussolini had it restored in 1936 with an eye to being buried here himself.

Once one of Ancient Rome's most imposing monuments, it's now an unkempt mound of earth, smelly and surrounded by unsightly fences. Work is allegedly ongoing, but there hasn't been much discernible development at the site.

◉ Piazza di Spagna & Around

PIAZZA DI SPAGNA & THE SPANISH STEPS   PIAZZA

See p100.

KEATS–SHELLEY HOUSE   MUSEUM

Map p308 (☎06 678 42 35; www.keats-shelleyhouse.org; Piazza di Spagna 26; adult/reduced €5/4, ticket gives discount for Casa di Goethe; ⊙10am-1pm & 2-6pm Mon-Fri, 11am-2pm & 3-6pm Sat; Ⓜ Spagna) The Keats–Shelley House is where Romantic poet John Keats died of tuberculosis at the age of 25, in February 1821. A year later, fellow poet Percy Bysshe Shelley drowned off the coast of Tuscany. The small apartment evokes the impoverished lives of the poets, and is now a small museum crammed with memorabilia, from faded letters to death masks.

Keats had come to Rome in 1820, on an obviously unsuccessful trip to try to improve his health in the Italian climate.

THE ARTISTS' STREET

Via Margutta has long been associated with art and artists, and today it is still lined with antique shops and art galleries.

'The street's reputation goes back to the 16th century, when it was declared a tax-free zone for artists,' explains Valentina Moncada, owner of the eponymous **gallery** (Map p308; Via Margutta 54; ⊗by appointment only). 'If you were an artist and a resident, you paid no taxes, so artists came from all over Europe. Also there was Villa Medici nearby and all the winners of the Prix de Rome (a prestigious French art scholarship) would often come down here.'

By the late 1800s, the studio that Valentina's family had established in the mid-19th century had grown into a popular meeting point for visiting artists, writers and musicians. 'A string of important musicians visited, including all the Italian opera greats – Puccini, Verdi, Mascagni – as well as the composers Wagner, Liszt and Debussy. The Italian futurists also held their first meetings here and in 1917 Picasso worked here; he met his wife, Olga, in the courtyard of number 54.'

Of the street's more recent residents, the most famous is film director Federico Fellini, who lived at No 110 with his wife Giulietta Masina until his death in 1993.

VIA DEI CONDOTTI   AREA

Map p308 (MSpagna) High-rolling shoppers and window-dreamers take note, this is Rome's smartest shopping strip. At the eastern end, near Piazza di Spagna, Caffè Greco (p116) was a favourite meeting point of 18th- and 19th-century writers. Other top shopping streets in the area include Via Frattina, Via della Croce, Via delle Carrozze and Via del Babuino.

GALLERIA D'ARTE MODERNA   GALLERY

Map p308 (✆06 06 08; www.galleriaartemodernaroma.it; Via F Crispi 24; adult/reduced €7.50/6.50; ⊗10am-6pm Tue-Sun; MBarberini) Housed in an 18th-century Carmelite convent, this interesting collection of art and sculpture from the 20th century includes works by de Chirico and Giorgio Morandi.

Views of Rome, painted by Francesco Trombadori and Riccardo Francalancia in the 1950s, make Villa Borghese and the Colosseum resemble outposts of EUR (the Mussolini-built neoclassical suburb).

CHIESA DELLA TRINITÀ
DEI MONTI   CHURCH

Map p308 (Piazza Trinità dei Monti; ⊗6.30am-8pm Tue-Sun; MSpagna) Looming over the Spanish Steps, this landmark church was commissioned by King Louis XII of France and consecrated in 1585. Apart from the great views from outside, it has some wonderful frescoes by Daniele da Volterra. His *Deposizione* (Deposition), in the second chapel on the left, is regarded as a masterpiece of mannerist painting.

If you don't fancy climbing the steep steps, there's a lift up from Spagna metro station.

MUSEO MISSIONARIO
DI PROPAGANDA FIDE   MUSEUM

Map p308 (✆06 6988 0266; Via di Propaganda 1; admission €8; ⊗2.30-6pm Mon, Wed & Fri; MSpagna) Rome's 'propogation of the faith' museum is housed in a 17th-century baroque masterpiece designed by Gian Lorenzo Bernini and Francesco Borromini, and is an opportunity to peer into Bernini's wooden, Hogwartsesque library, with its ceiling carved with Barberini bees, and Borromini's Chapel of the Magi, where the Wise Men's Epiphany acts an allegory for converts to Christianity.

This little-visited museum houses items brought back from overseas missions, with the eclectic collection including paintings of Japanese life in the 1930s and a Canova portrait of Ezzelino Romano. It was closed for renovation at the time of research, but should have reopened by now.

PALAZZO VALENTINI   ARCHAEOLOGICAL SITE

Map p308 (✆06 3 28 10; www.palazzovalentini. it; Via IV Novembre 119/A; adult/reduced €12/8, advance booking fee €1.50; ⊗9.30am-6.30pm Wed-Mon; MSpagna) Underneath a grand mansion that's been the seat of the Province of Rome since 1873 lie the archaeological remains of several lavish ancient Roman houses; the excavated fragments have been turned into a fascinating multimedia 'experience'. Tours are every 30 minutes, but

ROME'S VERSAILLES

If Napoleon had had his way, the Palazzo del Quirinale would have been Rome's Versailles. Journalist and author Corrado Augias explains:

'Napoleon actually chose Rome as his second capital after Paris. He wanted Versailles at Paris and the Palazzo del Quirinale – incidentally, Rome's greatest and most beautiful palace – in Rome. He set artists and architects to prepare it for him and sent down furniture from Paris. In the end he never came and when he was defeated in 1815 the popes took the *palazzo* back for themselves.'

alternate between Italian, English and French. Book ahead online or by phone, especially during holiday periods.

The visit takes you on a virtual tour of the dwellings, complete with sound effects, vividly projected frescoes and glimpses of ancient life as it might have been lived in the area around the buildings. It's genuinely thrilling and great for older kids.

CASA DI GOETHE
MUSEUM

Map p308 (✆06 3265 0412; www.casadigoethe.it; Via del Corso 18; adult/reduced €5/3; ⊙10am-6pm Tue-Sun; Ⓜ Flaminio) A gathering place for German intellectuals, the Via del Corso apartment where Johann Wolfgang von Goethe enjoyed a happy Italian sojourn (despite complaining of the noisy neighbours) from 1786 to 1788 is now a lovingly maintained small museum. Exhibits include fascinating Piranesi engravings of 18th-century Rome, as well as Goethe's sketches and letters, plus some lovely sketches of him by his friend Tischbein. With advance permission, ardent fans can use the library full of first editions.

★VILLA MEDICI
PALACE

Map p308 (✆06 6 76 11; www.villamedici.it; Viale Trinità dei Monti 1; gardens adult/reduced €12/6; ⊙tours in Italian, French & English Tue-Sun; cafe 11am-6pm Tue-Sun; Ⓜ Spagna) This sumptuous Renaissance palace was built for Cardinal Ricci da Montepulciano in 1540, but Ferdinando dei Medici bought it in 1576. It remained in Medici hands until 1801, when Napoleon acquired it for the French Academy. Take a tour to see the

wonderful landscaped **gardens**, cardinal's painted apartments, and incredible views over Rome. Note the pieces of ancient Roman sculpture from the Ara Pacis embedded in the villa's walls.

The villa's most famous resident was Galileo, who was imprisoned here between 1630 and 1633 during his trial for heresy – though Keith Richards and Anita Pallenberg stayed here in the 1960s. There are up to 19 resident French-speaking artists and musicians, with exhibitions and performances at the end of February and June. There's a lovely, high-ceilinged cafe that sells reasonably priced panini and light lunches (€3 to €12), plus *prosecco* (sparkling wine; €4). You can also stay at the villa, for a price; see the website.

◎ Trevi Fountain to the Quirinale

TREVI FOUNTAIN
FOUNTAIN

See p102.

PALAZZO DEL QUIRINALE
PALACE

See p107.

PIAZZA DEL QUIRINALE
PIAZZA

Map p308 (Ⓜ Barberini) A wonderful spot to enjoy a glowing Roman sunset, this piazza marks the summit of the Quirinale hill. The central **obelisk** was moved here from the Mausoleo di Augusto in 1786 and is flanked by 5.5m statues of **Castor** and **Pollux** reining in a couple of rearing horses.

If you're in the neighbourhood on a Sunday, you can catch the weekly changing of the guard (6pm in summer, 4pm the rest of the year).

★CHIESA DI SANTA MARIA DELLA VITTORIA
CHURCH

(Via XX Settembre 17; ⊙8.30am-noon & 3.30-6pm; Ⓜ Repubblica) This modest church is an unlikely setting for an extraordinary work of art – Bernini's extravagant and sexually charged *Santa Teresa trafitta dall'amore di Dio* (Ecstasy of St Teresa). This daring sculpture depicts Teresa, engulfed in the folds of a flowing cloak, floating in ecstasy on a cloud while a teasing angel pierces her repeatedly with a golden arrow.

Watching the whole scene from two side balconies are a number of figures, including Cardinal Federico Cornaro, for whom the chapel was built. It's a stunning work, bathed in soft natural light filtering through a concealed window. Go in the afternoon for the best effect.

CHIESA DI SANT'ANDREA AL QUIRINALE
CHURCH

Map p308 (Via del Quirinale 29; ⊗8.30am-noon & 2.30-6pm winter, 9am-noon & 3-6pm summer; ⊙Via Nazionale) It's said that in his old age Bernini liked to come and enjoy the peace of this late-17th-century church, regarded by many as one of his greatest. Faced with severe space limitations, he managed to produce a sense of grandeur by designing an elliptical floor plan with a series of chapels opening onto the central area.

The opulent interior, decorated with polychrome marble, stucco and gilding, was a favourite of Pope Alexander VII, who used it while in residence at the Palazzo del Quirinale.

CHIESA DI SAN CARLO ALLE QUATTRO FONTANE
CHURCH

Map p308 (Via del Quirinale 23; ⊗10am-1pm & 3-6pm Mon-Fri, 10am-1pm Sat, noon-1pm Sun; ⊙Via Nazionale) This tiny church is a masterpiece of Roman baroque. It was Borromini's first church, and the play of convex and concave surfaces and the dome illuminated by hidden windows cleverly transform the small space into a place of light and beauty.

The church, completed in 1641, stands at the intersection known as the **Quattro Fontane**, after the late-16th-century fountains on its four corners, representing Fidelity, Strength and the rivers Arno and Tiber. A clean-up job was completed in 2015, and they look better than they have for years – just watch out for traffic as you admire them.

Borromini intended to be buried within the church, but its monks would not permit this because of his suicide.

BASILICA DEI SANTI APOSTOLI
CHURCH

Map p308 (Piazza dei Santissimi Apostoli; ⊗7am-noon & 4-7pm; ⊙Via IV Novembre) This much-altered 6th-century church is dedicated to the apostles James and Philip, whose relics are in the crypt. Its most obvious attraction is the portico with its Renaissance arches and the two-tier facade topped by 13 towering figures. Inside, the flashy baroque interior was completed in 1714 by Carlo and Francesco Fontana. Highlights include the ceiling frescoes by Baciccia and Antonio Canova's grandiose tomb of Pope Clement XIV.

TOP SIGHT
PALAZZO DEL QUIRINALE

Overlooking the high-up Piazza del Quirinale is the imposing presidential palace, formerly the papal summer residence. You can visit by booking at least five days ahead; the shorter tour visits the sumptuous reception rooms, while the longer tour includes the interiors as well as the gardens and the carriages.

The immense Palazzo del Quirinale served as the papal summer residence for almost three centuries, until the keys were begrudgingly handed over to Italy's new king in 1870. Since 1948 it has been home of the Presidente della Repubblica, Italy's head of state.

Pope Gregory XIII (r 1572–85) originally chose the site and over the next 150 years the top architects of the day worked on it, including Bernini, Domenico Fontana and Carlo Maderno.

On the other side of the piazza, the palace's former stables, the **Scuderie Papali al Quirinale** (☑06 3996 7500; www.scuderiequirinale.it; Via XXIV Maggio 16; tickets around €12), is now a magnificent space that hosts art exhibitions; recent shows have included Matisse and Frida Kahlo.

DON'T MISS...

➡ Sunday concerts held in the chapel designed by Carlo Maderno

➡ Splendid exhibitions in the former stables

PRACTICALITIES

➡ Map p308

➡ ☑06 4 69 91

➡ www.quirinale.it

➡ Piazza del Quirinale

➡ admission €10, 30 min tour €1.50, 2½hr tour €10

➡ ⊗9.30am-4pm Tue, Wed & Fri-Sun, closed Aug

➡ Ⓜ Barberini

MIRACULOUS MADONNAS

Overlooking Vicolo delle Bollette, a tiny lane near the Trevi Fountain, there's a small, simple painting of the Virgin Mary. This is the *Madonna della Pietà*, one of the most famous of Rome's *madonnelle* (small madonnas). There are estimated to be around 730 of these roadside madonnas in Rome's historic centre, most placed on street corners or outside historic *palazzi*. Many were added in the 16th and 17th centuries, but their origins date to pagan times when votive wall shrines were set up at street corners to honour the Lares, household spirits believed to protect passers-by. When Christianity emerged in the 4th century AD, these shrines were simply rededicated to the religion's new icons. Their presence was also intended to deter devout Catholics from committing street crime.

The subject of much popular devotion, they are shrouded in myth. The most famous legend dates to 1796 when news of a French invasion is said to have caused 36 *madonnelle*, including the *Madonna della Pietà*, to move their eyes and some even to cry. A papal commission set up to investigate subsequently declared 26 madonnas to be officially miraculous.

As well as food for the soul, the madonnas also provided a valuable public service. Until street lamps were introduced in the 19th century, the candles and lamps that lit up the images were the city's only source of street lighting.

Surrounding the basilica are two imposing baroque palazzi: at the end of the square, **Palazzo Balestra**, which was given to James Stuart, the Old Pretender, in 1719 by Pope Clement XI, and opposite, **Palazzo Odelscalchi**, with its impressive Bernini facade.

CITTÀ DELL'ACQUA ARCHAEOLOGICAL SITE

Map p308 (www.archeodomani.com; Vicolo del Puttarello 25; adult/reduced €3/1; ⊘11am-5.30pm Wed-Fri, 11am-7pm Sat & Sun; Ⓜ Barberini) The little-known excavations of Vicus Caprarius (the name of the ancient street) include a Roman house and a Hadrian-era cistern that connected with the Aqua Virgo cistern. Eight metres deep, they lie just a few paces from the eternal hubbub of the Trevi Fountain – the spring waters that once fed these waterworks now gush forth from the fountain.

This is a chance to appreciate the many layers that lie beneath present-day Rome; mosaics and decorations discovered during the excavations are displayed in a small museum.

MUSEO DELLE CERE MUSEUM

Map p308 (☑06 679 64 82; www.museodellecereroma.com; Piazza dei Santissimi Apostoli 67; adult/reduced €9/7; ⊘9am-9pm; ☐Via IV Novembre) Rome's waxwork museum is said to have the world's third-largest collection, which comprises more than 250 figures, ranging from Barack Obama to Snow White, plus plentiful other popes, poets,

politicians, musicians and murderers. You can also visit the laboratory where the waxworks are created.

◉ Piazza Barberini & Via Veneto

GALLERIA NAZIONALE D'ARTE ANTICA: PALAZZO BARBERINI GALLERY

See p110.

PIAZZA BARBERINI PIAZZA

Map p308 (Ⓜ Barberini) More a traffic thoroughfare than a place to linger, this noisy square is named after the Barberini family, one of Rome's great dynastic clans. In the centre, the Bernini-designed **Fontana del Tritone** (Fountain of the Triton308) depicts the sea-god Triton blowing a stream of water from a conch while seated in a large scallop shell supported by four dolphins. Bernini also crafted the **Fontana delle Api** (Fountain of the Bees308) in the northeastern corner, again for the Barberini family, whose crest featured three bees in flight.

CONVENTO DEI CAPPUCCINI MUSEUM

Map p308 (☑06 487 11 85; Via Vittorio Veneto 27; adult/reduced €8/6, audioguide €4; ⊘9am-7pm; Ⓜ Barberini) This church and convent complex has turned its extraordinary Capuchin cemetery into cash by adding a flashy museum and bumping up the entrance fee. However, it's still worth visiting what is possibly Rome's strangest sight: crypt

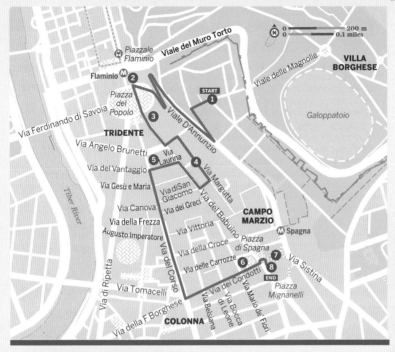

🏃 Neighbourhood Walk
Literary Footsteps

START PINCIO HILL GARDENS
END KEATS–SHELLEY HOUSE
LENGTH 1KM; TWO HOURS

This walk explores the literary haunts, both real and fictional, which speckle the Tridente district.

Begin your walk in ❶**Pincio Hill Gardens** (p103), where Henry James' Daisy Miller walked with Frederick Winterborne. Then make your way downhill to Piazza del Popolo, and visit the church of ❷**Santa Maria del Popolo** (p101). Dan Brown's Angels and Demons made use of this remarkable church in its convoluted plot.

From here it's merely a few steps to ❸**Hotel de Russie** (p219), favoured by the artistic avant-garde in the early 20th century. Jean Cocteau stayed here with Picasso, and wrote a letter home in which he described plucking oranges from outside his window.

Running parallel to Via del Babuino is ❹**Via Margutta** (p105). Famous for its artistic and cinematic connections, this picturesque cobbled street was where Truman Capote wrote his short story Lola about a raven who lived with him at his apartment. Fellini, Picasso, Stravinsky, and Puccini all lived here at some point, and Gregory Peck's character in Roman Holiday had his apartment here (exteriors were shot at No 51).

Next make your way to Via del Corso, to see the ❺**Casa di Goethe** (p106) where Goethe had a whale of a time from 1786 to 1788. Head down Via del Corso then turn left up into Via dei Condotti, where William Thackeray stayed in 1854, stopping at ❻**Caffè Greco** (p116), a former haunt of Casanova, Goethe, Keats, Byron and Shelley. Leaving here, you're almost at the ❼**Spanish Steps** (p100), which Dickens described in his Pictures from Italy. Byron stayed on Piazza di Spagna, at No 25, in 1817. Just south of the steps is the apartments where Keats died of TB, aged just 25. The ❽**Keats–Shelley House** (p104) is now a small museum devoted to the romantic poets.

TOP SIGHT GALLERIA NAZIONALE D'ARTE ANTICA: PALAZZO BARBERINI

The sumptuous Palazzo Barberini is an architectural feast before you even consider the National Art Collection that it houses. This huge baroque palace was commissioned by Urban VIII to celebrate the Barberini family's rise to papal power. Many high-profile architects worked on it, including rivals Bernini and Borromini; the former contributed a large squared staircase, the latter a helicoidal one.

Amid the masterpieces, don't miss Pietro da Cortona's ceiling frescoes in the 1st-floor salon, *Il Trionfo della Divina Provvidenza* (Triumph of Divine Providence; 1632–39). Other must-sees include Hans Holbein's famous portrait of a pugnacious Henry VIII (c 1540), Filippo Lippi's luminous *Annunciazione e due devoti* (Annunciation with two Kneeling Donors) and Raphael's *La Fornarina* (The Baker's Girl). Works by Caravaggio include *San Francesco d'Assisi in meditazione* (St Francis in Meditation), *Narciso* (Narcissus; 1571–1610) and the mesmerisingly horrific *Giuditta e Oloferne* (Judith Beheading Holophernes; c 1597–1600).

DON'T MISS...

➡ Pietro da Cortona's painted ceiling
➡ Raphael's *La Fornarina*
➡ Works by Caravaggio

PRACTICALITIES

➡ Map p308
➡ ☏06 3 28 10
➡ www.galleriabarberini.benicultural.it
➡ Via delle Quattro Fontane 13
➡ adult/reduced €7/3.50, incl Palazzo Corsini
➡ ◷8.30am-7pm Tue-Sun

chapels where everything from the picture frames to the light fittings is made of human bones. The multimedia museum tells the story of the Capuchin order of monks, including a work attributed to Caravaggio: *St Francis in Meditation*.

Between 1528 and 1870 the resident Capuchin monks used the bones of 4000 of their departed brothers to create this mesmerising, macabre memento mori (reminder of death). There's an arch crafted from hundreds of skulls, vertebrae used as fleurs-de-lis and light fixtures made of femurs. Happy holidays!

VIA VITTORIO VENETO   AREA

Map p308 (ⓂBarberini) Curving up from Piazza Barberini to Villa Borghese, Via Vittorio Veneto is the spiritual home of *la dolce vita* – the Rome of the swinging '50s and '60s that was epitomised in Fellini's eponymous film. However, the atmosphere of Fellini's Rome has long gone and the street today, while still a gracious sweep, has the feel of a tourist trap.

Luxury hotels occupy many of the towering streetside *palazzi*, and waistcoated waiters stand on the tree-lined pavement, tempting passers-by into their overpriced restaurants. The huge building on the right as you walk up is the US embassy.

GAGOSIAN GALLERY   GALLERY

Map p308 (☏06 420 86 498; www.gagosian.com; Via Francesco Crispi 16; ◷10.30am-7pm Tue-Sat; ⓂBarberini) **FREE** Since it opened in 2007, the Rome branch of Larry Gagosian's contemporary art empire has hosted the big names of modern art: Cy Twombly, Damien Hirst and Lawrence Weiner, to name a few. The gallery is housed in an artfully converted 1920s bank, and was designed by Roman architect Firouz Galdo and Englishman Caruso St John.

Always worth a look, exhibitions are housed in a dramatic, airy 750 sq m, and the building is fronted by a theatrical neoclassical colonnaded facade.

✖ EATING

Rome's designer shopping district may be fashionista heaven, but it retains a neighbourhood feel, albeit a particularly wealthy one. Lots of classy eateries are sandwiched between the boutiques.

In the Quirinale and Trevi Fountain area, take care selecting where to eat, as there are a lot of unexciting just-for-tourists restaurants. But gems still sparkle among the stones, with some notable restaurants around the presidential palace and parliament – Italian politicians are a discerning bunch when it comes to dining out.

✗ Piazza del Popolo & Around

FATAMORGANA
GELATERIA €

Map p308 (Via Laurina 10; ☺noon-11pm; MFlaminio) The wonderful all-natural Fatamorgana, purveyors of arguably Rome's best artisanal ice cream, now has this handy central branch. Innovative and classic tastes of heaven abound, including flavours such as pear and caramel, all made from the finest seasonal ingredients.

DEI GRACCHI
GELATERIA €

Map p308 (Via di Ripetta 261; ice cream from €2; ☺11.30am-10pm, to midnight Jun-Sep; MFlaminio) A new outpost of the venerable Gelataria dei Gracchi, close to the Vatican, this serves up superb ice cream made from the best ingredients, with an excellent array of classic flavours. It's handily located just off Piazza del Popolo, so you can take your pick and then wander around the square as you revel in your excellent selection.

BUCCONE
RISTORANTE, WINE BAR €

Map p308 (☑06 361 21 54; Via di Ripetta 19; meals €20; ☺12.30-2.30pm & 7.30-10.30pm Mon-Sat; MFlaminio) Step in under the faded gilt-and-mirrored sign and you'll feel as though you've gone back in time. Once a coach house, then a tavern, this building became Buccone in the 1960s, furnished with 19th-century antiques and lined with around a thousand Italian wines. It serves simple food such as mixed plates of cured meat and cheese, but on Saturday offers a proper hot *cena* (dinner).

PIZZA RÉ
PIZZA €

Map p308 (☑06 321 14 68; Via di Ripetta 14; pizzas €7-10; ☺noon-midnight; MFlaminio) Part of a chain, but a good one, this popular pizzeria offers Neapolitan-style pizzas, with thick doughy bases and diverse toppings. The salads are fresh and the antipasti is great – try the fried things or the *mozzarella fresca di bufala e prosciutto San Daniele*

(buffalo mozzarella with San Daniele dry-cured ham). It's a good choice for families.

AL GRAN SASSO
TRATTORIA €€

Map p308 (☑06 321 48 83; www.algransasso.com; Via di Ripetta 32; meals €35; ☺12.30-2.30pm & 7.30-11.30pm Sun-Fri; MFlaminio) A top lunchtime spot, this is a classic, dyed-in-the-wool trattoria specialising in old-school country cooking. It's a relaxed place with a welcoming vibe, garish murals on the walls (strangely often a good sign) and tasty, value-for-money food. The fried dishes are excellent, or try one of the daily specials, chalked up on the board outside.

IL MARGUTTA RISTORARTE
VEGETARIAN €€

Map p308 (☑06 678 60 33; www.ilmargutta.it; Via Margutta 118; meals €40; ☺12.30-3pm & 7-11.30pm; ☑; MSpagna, Flaminio) Vegetarian restaurants in Rome are rarer than parking spaces, and this airy art gallery-restaurant is an unusually chic way to eat your greens. Dishes are excellent and most produce is organic, with offerings such as artichoke hearts with potato cubes and smoked provolone cheese. Best value is the weekday (€15 to €18) and weekend (€25) buffet brunch. There's a vegan menu and live music weekends.

DA PIETRO
OSTERIA €€

Map p308 (☑06 320 88 16; http://hostariadapietro.com; Via Gesù e Maria 18; meals around €45;

ROME'S OPTICAL ILLUSIONS

Aptly for such a theatrical city, Rome contains some magical visual tricks. Overlooking Piazza del Popolo, there are the seemingly twin churches: constructed to look identical while occupying different-sized sites. Then there's Borromini's perspective-defying corridor at **Palazzo Spada** (p78), Andrea Pozzo's amazing trompe l'oeil at the **Chiesa di Sant'Ignazio di Loyola** (p83) and the secret keyhole view from **Priorato dei Cavalieri di Malta** (p176). Strangest of all is the view of St Peter's Dome from **Via Piccolomini** near **Villa Doria Pamphilj** (p162). Here the dome looms, filling the space at the end of the road, framed by trees. But the really curious thing is that as you move towards the cupola it seems to get smaller rather than larger as the view widens.

🕒lunch & dinner Mon-Sat, closed Aug; Ⓜ Spagna) This is an appealing small Roman osteria, occupying several narrow rooms, with patterned tiled floors, arched exposed-stone ceilings, and cheery red tablecloths. Expect robust local cuisine, with dishes such as *saltimbocca alla romana* (veal with prosciutto and sage) or *melanzane alla parmigiana* (layered aubergine with tomato and ham). Pietro's father runs the long-standing Tullio restaurant close to Barberini.

ALL'ORO
ITALIAN €€€

Map p308 (Via del Vantaggio 14; Tasting menu €98, meals €90; Ⓜ Flaminio) A Michelin-starred fine-dining restaurant, All'Oro established itself under chef Riccardo Di Giacinto in the upmarket suburb of Parioli. It's now transferred to the contemporary art-styled First Luxury Art Hotel, with white surroundings and sophisticated dishes such as ravioli filled with mascarpone, duck ragout and red wine reduction, and roasted suckling pig with potatoes and black truffle sauce.

BABETTE
ITALIAN €€€

Map p308 (📞 06 321 15 59; Via Margutta 1; meals €45-55; 🕒 1-3pm Tue-Sun, 7-10.45pm daily, closed Jan & Aug; ✏; Ⓜ Spagna, Flaminio) Babette is run by two sisters who used to produce a fashion magazine, which accounts for its effortlessly chic interior of exposed brick walls and vintage painted signs. You're in for a feast too, as the cooking is delicious, with a sophisticated, creative French twist (think *tortiglioni* with courgette and pistachio pesto). The *torta Babette* is the food of the gods, a light-as-air lemon cheesecake.

The weekend lunch buffet (adult/child €28/18) is a good deal, including water, bread, dessert and coffee.

DAL BOLOGNESE
TRADITIONAL ITALIAN €€€

Map p308 (📞 06 361 14 26; Piazza del Popolo 1; meals €90; 🕒 Tue-Sun, closed Aug; Ⓜ Flaminio) The moneyed and models mingle at this historically chic restaurant. Dine inside, surrounded by wood panelling and exotic flowers, or outside, people-watching with

BERNINI VS BORROMINI

Born within a year of each other, the two giants of Roman baroque hated each other with a vengeance. Gian Lorenzo Bernini (1598–1680), suave, self-confident and politically adept, was the polar opposite of his great rival Francesco Borromini (1599–1677), a solitary and peculiar man who often argued with clients. Borromini's passion for architecture was a matter of life and death: once he caught a man disfiguring some pieces of stone while he was working on rebuilding San Giovanni in Laterano and had him beaten so fiercely that he later died of his injuries (Borromini received a Papal pardon).

Their paths first crossed at St Peter's Basilica. Borromini, who had been working as an assistant to Carlo Maderno, a distant relative and the basilica's lead architect, was furious when Bernini was appointed to take over the project on Maderno's death. Nevertheless, he stayed on as Bernini's chief assistant and actually contributed to the design of the baldachin – a work for which Bernini took full public credit. To make matters worse, Bernini was later appointed chief architect on Palazzo Barberini, again in the wake of Maderno, and again to Borromini's disgust.

Over the course of the next 45 years, the two geniuses competed for commissions and public acclaim. Bernini flourished under the Barberini pope Urban VIII (r 1623–44) and Borromini under his Pamphilj successor Innocent X (r 1644–1655), but all the while their loathing simmered. Borromini accused Bernini of profiting from his (Borromini's) talents, while Bernini claimed that Borromini 'had been sent to destroy architecture'. Certainly, both had very different views on architecture: for Bernini it was all about portraying an experience to elicit an emotional response, while Borromini favoured a more geometrical approach, manipulating classical forms to create dynamic, vibrant spaces.

In their lifetimes, Bernini had the better of the rivalry. His genius was rarely questioned and when he died he was widely regarded as one of Europe's greatest artists. Borromini, in contrast, struggled to win popular and critical support and after a life of depression committed suicide in 1677. Because of the way he died, he couldn't even be buried in the church he'd chosen for himself, San Carlo alle Quattro Fontane.

views over Piazza del Popolo. As the name suggests, Emilia-Romagna dishes are the name of the game; everything is good, but try the tortellini in soup, tagliatelle with ragú, or the damn fine fillet steak.

EDY
TRATTORIA €€€

Map p308 (✆06 3600 1738; Vicolo del Babuino 4; meals €60; ⊙noon-3pm & 6.30-11pm Mon-Sat; Ⓜ Spagna) This classy neighbourhood restaurant's high-ceilinged, intimate interior is peppered with paintings. Despite the tourist-central location, it caters to mainly Italian clientele; the food, such as *linguine al broccoletti,* is delicious. In nice weather there are a few tables outside on the cobbled street.

✗ Piazza di Spagna & Around

PASTIFICIO
FAST FOOD €

Map p308 (Via della Croce 8; pasta, wine & water €4; ⊙lunch 1-3pm Mon-Sat; Ⓜ Spagna) A great find in this pricey 'hood. Pasticcio is a pasta shop that serves up two choices of pasta at lunch time. It's fast food, Italian style – freshly cooked (if you time it right) pasta, with wine and water included. It's no leisurely lunch: there's not much room, so you'll have to nab a chair while you can and eat quickly. This is better than taking away, however; if you do that, you'll miss out on your drink and your pasta will get cold.

GINA
CAFE €

Map p308 (✆06 678 02 51; Via San Sebastianello 7a; snacks €8-16; ⊙11am-8pm; Ⓜ Spagna) Around the corner from the Spanish Steps, this is an ideal place to drop once you've shopped. Comfy white seats are strewn with powder-blue cushions, and it gets packed by a Prada-clad crowd, gossiping and flirting over sophisticated salads and perfect *panini.* You can also order a €40/60 regular/deluxe picnic-for-two to take up to Villa Borghese.

POMPI
DESSERTS €

Map p308 (Via della Croce 82; tiramisu €4; ⊙10.30am-9.30pm; Ⓜ Spagna) Rome's most famous vendor of tiramisu (which literally means 'pick me up') sells takeaway cartons of the deliciously yolky yet light-as-air dessert. As well as classic, it comes in pistachio and strawberry flavours.

You can eat it on the spot or buy frozen portions that will keep for a few hours until you're ready to tuck into it at home. It also sells ice cream.

VENCHI
GELATERIA €

Map p308 (Via della Croce 25; gelato from €2.50; Ⓜ Spagna) Choco-specialists Venchi operate this handily located, usually mobbed gelataria, with a wide range of flavours; when plumping for fruity or creamy, bear in mind they're specialists in all things chocolate.

CASA CONTI
ITALIAN €€

Map p308 (✆06 6920 0735; Via della Croce; meals €40; ⊙1-3pm Mon-Sat; Ⓜ Spagna) This unique place has double-height ceilings and original tiled floors, and is filled with fascinating antiques. With few tables, it's a great hideaway for a simple Roman lunch with a dish of the day such as fettucine, and a wide choice of wines. Delicious desserts may include *cannoli* (custard-filled pastries), *crostate* (jam tarts), tiramisu or chocolate tart.

ANTICA ENOTECA
WINE BAR €€

Map p308 (✆06 679 08 96; Via della Croce 76b; meals €35; ⊙noon-midnight; Ⓜ Spagna) Near the Spanish Steps, locals and tourists alike prop up the 19th-century wooden bar, or sit at outside tables or in the tastefully distressed interior, sampling wines by the glass, snacking on antipasti and ordering well-priced soul food such as soups, pasta, polenta and pizza.

FIASCHETTERIA BELTRAMME
TRATTORIA €€

Map p308 (Via della Croce 39; meals €40; Ⓜ Spagna) With a tiny dark interior whose walls are covered in paintings and sketches right up to the high ceilings, Fiaschetteria (meaning 'wine-sellers') is a discreet, intimate, stuck-in-time place with a short menu and no telephone. Clientele is a mix of tourists and fashionistas with appetites digging into traditional Roman dishes (*pasta e ceci* and so on).

OTELLO ALLA CONCORDIA
TRATTORIA €€

Map p308 (✆06 679 11 78; Via della Croce 81; meals €35; ⊙12.30-3pm & 7.30-11pm Mon-Sat; Ⓜ Spagna) A perennial favourite with both tourists and locals, Otello is a haven near the Spanish Steps. Outside seating is in the vine-covered courtyard of an 18th-century *palazzo* and inside is inviting, with walls hung with pictures.

★ENOTECA REGIONALE
PALATIUM RISTORANTE, BAR €€€

Map p308 (☑06 692 02 132; Via Frattina 94; meals €55; ☺11am-11pm Mon-Sat, closed Aug; ⓜVia del Corso) A rich showcase of regional bounty, run by the Lazio Regional Food Authority, this sleek wine bar serves excellent local specialities, such as *porchetta* (pork roasted with herbs) or *gnocchi alla Romana con crema da zucca* (potato dumplings Roman-style with cream of pumpkin), as well as an impressive array of Lazio wines (try lesser-known drops such as Aleatico). *Aperitivo* is a good bet too. There's also a tantalising array of artisanal cheese and delicious salami and cold cuts.

IMÀGO ITALIAN €€€

Map p308 (☑06 6993 4726; www.imagorestaurant.com; Piazza della Trinità dei Monti 6; veg menus €120, tasting menus €130-140; ☺7-10.30pm; ⓜSpagna) Even in a city of great views, the panoramas from the Hassler Hotel's Michelin-starred romantic rooftop restaurant are special (request the corner table), extending over a sea of roofs to the great dome of St Peter's Basilica. Complementing the views are the bold, mod-Italian creations of culinary whizz, chef Francesco Apreda. Book ahead.

IL PALAZZETTO ITALIAN €€€

Map p308 (☑06 6993 41000; Via del Bottino 8; meals €45; ☺noon-8.30pm Tue-Sun; ⓜSpagna) This sun-trap terrace, ideal for snacks and cocktails, is hidden at the top of the Spanish Steps. It's perfect for a glass of *prosecco* (sparkling wine) and a salad or pasta dish on a sunny day overlooking the comings and goings on the steps. It also does a special margherita pizza plus house wine for €18.

NINO TUSCAN €€€

Map p308 (☑06 679 56 76; Via Borgognona 11; meals €80; ☺12.30-3pm & 7.30-11pm Mon-Sat; ⓜSpagna) With a look of wrought-iron chandeliers, polished dark wood and white tablecloths that has worked since it opened in 1934, Nino is enduringly popular with the rich and famous. Waiters can be brusque if you're not on the A-list, but the food is good hearty fare, including memorable steaks and Tuscan bean soup.

GINGER BRASSERIE €€€

Map p308 (☑06 9603 6390; www.ginger.roma.it; Via Borgognona 43; meals €50; ☺10am-11.30pm; ⓜSpagna) ✐ *Perfecto* for the ladies-who-lunch crowd, this chic, buzzy, white-tiled, high-ceilinged place proffers all-day dining, with a focus on organic dishes including unusual ingredients such as quinoa. There are salads, pricey gourmet sandwiches, pasta dishes, smoothies and shakes.

OSTERIA MARGUTTA TRATTORIA €€€

Map p308 (☑06 323 10 25; www.osteriamargutta.it; Via Margutta 82; meals €60; ☺12.30-3pm & 7.30-11pm Tue-Sun; ⓜSpagna) Theatrical Osteria Margutta is colourful inside and out: inside combines blue glass, rich reds and fringed lampshades, while outside it's flowers and ivy (snap up a terrace table in summer). Plaques on the chairs testify to the famous thespian bums they have supported. The menu combines classic and regional dishes; desserts are homemade, and there's a top wine list.

✗ Trevi Fountain to the Quirinale

DA MICHELE PIZZA €

Map p308 (☑349 2525347; Via dell'Umiltà 31; pizza slices from €3; ☺8am-6pm Mon-Fri, to 10pm summer; ⓜVia del Corso) A handy address in Spagna district: buy your fresh, light and crispy *pizza al taglio* (by the slice), and you'll have a delicious fast lunch. It's all kosher, so meat and cheese is not mixed.

ALICE PIZZA PIZZA €

Map p308 (www.alicepizza.it; Via di San Basilio 56; pizza slices from €3.50; ☺8.30am-4pm Mon-Sat; ⓜBarberini) This hole-in-the-wall *pizza al taglio* place is busy with local workers, tempted in by an enticing range of toppings that proffer something outside the norm, with combinations that might include Emmental and courgette, or aubergine with chilli. There are a couple of seats inside, but they'll only serve as a brief perch.

ANTICO FORNO FAST FOOD €

Map p308 (☑06 679 28 66; Via delle Muratte 8; panini & pizza €3.50; ☺7am-10pm; ⓜVia del Tritone) A mini-supermarket opposite the Trevi Fountain, this busy place has a well-stocked deli where you can choose a filling for your freshly baked *panino* or *pizza bianca,* plus an impressive selection of focaccia and crispy, delicious *pizza al taglio* from the bakery counter at the back. It also sells cold drinks and beers to complete your picnic.

BACCANO
BRASSERIE €€

Map p308 (www.baccanoroma.com; Via delle Muratte 23; meals €45; ⊙8.30am-2am; ⊡Via del Corso) Offering all-day dining in elegant, laid-back surroundings (it's nailed the Balthazar look: polished wood, potted palms, high ceilings, cosy booths). However, if you're in the mood for dinner, burgers, club sandwiches, cocktails, *aperitivi*…you name it, they've got it covered.

IL CHIANTI
TUSCAN €€

Map p308 (⊠06 678 75 50; Via del Lavatore 81-82; meals €45, pizza €8-12; ⊙12.30-3.30pm & 7-11.30pm; ⊡Via del Tritone) This pretty ivy-clad wine bar is bottle-lined and wood-beamed inside, with watch-the-world-go-by streetside seating, backed by a picturesque cascade of ivy, in summer. Cuisine is Tuscan, so the beef is particularly good, but it also serves up imaginative salads and pizza.

NANÀ VINI E CUCINA
TRATTORIA €€

Map p308 (⊠06 6919 0750; Via della Panetteria 37; meals €45; ⊙12.30-3pm & 7-11pm Tue-Sun; ⊡Via del Tritone) An appealing and simple trattoria, specialising in Neapolitan flavours. Eat in the high-ceilinged interior, under huge brass pipes, overlooking the open kitchen, or outside on the *piazzetta*. Try *la carne tenera scaloppine Nanà*, cooked simply in white wine, and other southern dishes.

LE TAMERICI
SEAFOOD €€€

Map p308 (⊠06 6920 0700; Vicolo Scavolino 79; meals €80; ⊙7.30-11pm Mon-Sat, closed Aug; ⊡Via del Tritone) Tucked-away Le Tamerici is a cream-hued, elegant escape from the Trevi Fountain hubbub outside. It impresses with its wine list and range of *digestivi*, as well as with its classy food, including light-as-air homemade pasta. The two intimate rooms with bleached-wood beamed ceilings are a suitably discreet place to settle for an epicurean lunch.

✖ Piazza Barberini & Via Veneto

IL CARUSO
GELATERIA €

(Via Collina 15; ⊙noon-9pm; ⊠Repubblica) Spot Il Caruso by the gelato-licking hordes outside. This artisanal gelateria only does a few strictly seasonal flavours, but they're created to perfection. Try the incredibly creamy pistachio. It also offers two types of *panna:* the usual whipped cream or the verging-on-sublime *zabaglione* (egg and marsala custard) combined with whipped cream.

FORNO CERULLI
PIZZA €

Map p308 (Via di San Nicola da Tolentino 53; pizza from €3; ⊙8am-4pm Mon-Fri; ⊠Barberini) This hidden-away *pizza al taglio* place is much beloved by local office workers and the kind of place you'd blink and miss if you weren't in the know, despite its recent refit. There's now a spacious area inside where you can sit at barstools and eat your slices of delicious, freshly made pizza or foccacia. Eat in or take out.

SAN CRISPINO
GELATERIA €

Map p308 (⊠06 679 39 24; Via della Panetteria 42; tubs from €2.70; ⊙11am-12.30am Sun-Thu, to 1.30am Fri & Sat; ⊠Barberini) This is the original place for gourmet gelato, though it has far more rivals in the capital these days. San Crispino, near the Trevi Fountain, serves strictly natural, seasonal flavours. Quality is high, but helpings are on the small side. No cones, as that'd detract from the taste.

★COLLINE EMILIANE
ITALIAN €€

Map p308 (⊠06 481 75 38; Via degli Avignonesi 22; meals €50; ⊙12.45-2.45pm Tue-Sun & 7.30-10.45pm Tue-Sat, closed Aug; ⊠Barberini) This welcoming, tucked-away restaurant just off Piazza Barberini flies the flag for Emilia-Romagna, the well-fed Italian province that has blessed the world with Parmesan, balsamic vinegar, bolognese sauce and Parma ham. This is a consistently excellent place to eat; there are delicious meats, homemade pasta and rich *ragù*. Try to save room for dessert too.

AL MORO
ITALIAN €€€

Map p308 (⊠06 678 34 96; Vicolo delle Bollette 13; meals €55; ⊙1-3.30pm & 8-11.30pm Mon-Sat; ⊡Via del Corso) This one-time Fellini haunt feels like a step back in time with its picture-gallery dining rooms, Liberty wall lamps, cantankerous buttoned-up waiters and old-money regulars. Join faux royals for soothing classics like *cicoria al brodo* (chicory in broth) or melt-in-your-mouth veal liver with crusty sage and butter.

🍷⚓ DRINKING & NIGHTLIFE

📍 Piazza del Popolo & Around

LA SCENA
BAR

Map p308 (Via della Penna 22; ⊙7am-1am; MFlaminio) Part of the art-deco Hotel Locarno, this bar has a faded Agatha Christie–era feel, and a greenery-shaded outdoor terrace bedecked in wrought-iron furniture. Cocktails cost €13 to €15, or you can partake of afternoon tea from 3pm to 6pm and *aperitivo* from 7pm to 10pm.

STRAVINSKIJ BAR – HOTEL DE RUSSIE
BAR

Map p308 (☑06 328 88 70; Via del Babuino 9; ⊙9am-1am; MFlaminio) Can't afford to stay at the celeb-magnet Hotel de Russie? Then splash out on a drink at its swish bar. There are sofas inside, but best is a drink in the sunny courtyard, with sunshaded tables overlooked by terraced gardens. Impossibly romantic in the best *dolce vita* style, it's perfect for a cocktail (from €20) or beer (€13) and some posh snacks.

ROSATI
CAFE

Map p308 (☑06 322 58 59; Piazza del Popolo 5; ⊙7.30am-11.30pm; MFlaminio) Rosati, overlooking the vast disc of Piazza del Popolo, was once the hang-out of the left-wing chattering classes. Authors Italo Calvino and Alberto Moravia used to drink here while their right-wing counterparts went to the **Canova** (Map p308; ☑06 361 22 31; Piazza del Popolo 16; ⊙8am-midnight; MFlaminio) across the square. Today tourists are the main clientele, and the views are as good as ever.

As usual, drinking standing up at the bar will get you a reasonably priced coffee, while you'll pay a premium for a seat.

📍 Piazza di Spagna & Around

CANOVA TADOLINI
CAFE

Map p308 (☑06 3211 0702; Via del Babuino 150a/b; ⊙9am-10.30pm Mon-Sat; MSpagna) In 1818 sculptor Canova signed a contract for this studio that agreed it would be forever preserved for sculpture. The place is still stuffed with statues and it's a unique experience to sit among the great maquettes and sup an upmarket tea or knock back some wine and snacks.

CAFFÈ GRECO
CAFE

Map p308 (☑06 679 17 00; Via dei Condotti 86; ⊙9am-9pm; MSpagna) Caffè Greco opened in 1760 and is still working the look: penguin waiters, red flock and age-spotted gilt mirrors. Casanova, Goethe, Wagner, Keats, Byron, Shelley and Baudelaire were all once regulars. Now there are fewer artists and lovers and more shoppers and tourists. Prices reflect this, unless you do as the locals do and have a drink at the bar (*caffè* bar/seated €1.50/6).

CIAMPINI 2
CAFE

Map p308 (☑06 678 56 78; Viale Trinità dei Monti; ⊙8am-9pm May-Oct; MSpagna) Hidden away a short walk from the top of the Spanish Steps towards the Pincio Hill Gardens, this graceful cafe-restaurant has a garden-party vibe, with green wooden latticework surrounding the white-clothed tables. There are lovely views over the backstreets behind Spagna, and the gelato is renowned (particularly the chocolate truffle).

📍 Piazza Barberini & Via Veneto

MICCA CLUB
CLUB

Map p308 (☑393 3236244; www.miccaclub.com; Via degli Avignonesi; MBarberini) No longer in its brick-arched cellar in Southern Rome, but now close to Piazza Barberini, Micca Club now has a less arresting interior but still retains its vintage, quirky vibe. This is Rome's burlesque club, where you can sip cocktails while watching shimmying acts upping the kitsch factor. Reserving a table by phone is advised.

MOMA
CAFE

Map p308 (☑06 4201 1798; Via di San Basilio; ⊙8am-midnight Mon-Sat, closed Aug; MBarberini) *Molto* trendy, this cafe-restaurant is a find. It's sleekly sexy and popular with workers from nearby offices. There's a small stand-up cafe downstairs, with a nice little deck outside where you can linger longer over coffee and delicious *dolcetti*. Upstairs is a recommended *cucina creativa* (creative cuisine) restaurant (meals €70).

⭐ ENTERTAINMENT

GREGORY'S
LIVE MUSIC

Map p308 (☑06 679 63 86; www.gregorysjazz.com; Via Gregoriana 54d; ☺7pm-2am Tue-Sun Sep-Jun; ⓂBarberini, Spagna) If Gregory's were a tone of voice, it'd be husky: unwind in the downstairs bar, then unwind some more on squashy sofas upstairs to some slinky live jazz and swing, with quality local performers, who also like to hang out here.

TEATRO QUIRINO
THEATRE

Map p308 (☑06 679 45 85; www.teatroquirino.it; Via delle Vergini 7; 🚇Via del Tritone) Within splashing distance of the Trevi Fountain, this grand 19th-century theatre produces the odd new work and a stream of well-known classics – expect to see works (in Italian) by Arthur Miller, Tennessee Williams, Shakespeare, Seneca and Luigi Pirandello.

TEATRO SISTINA
THEATRE

Map p308 (☑06 420 07 11; www.ilsistina.com; Via Sistina 129; ⓂBarberini) Big-budget theatre spectaculars, musicals, concerts and comic star turns are the staples of the Sistina's ever-conservative, ever-popular repertoire.

🔒 SHOPPING

🛍 Piazza del Popolo & Around

BOTTEGA DI MARMORARO
ARTS

Map p308 (Via Margutta 53b; ☺8am-7.30pm Mon-Sat; ⓂFlaminio) A particularly charismatic hole-in-the-wall shop lined with marble carvings, where you can get marble tablets engraved with any inscription you like (€15). Peer inside at lunchtime and you might see the cheerfully quizzical *marmoraro*, Enrico Fiorentini, cooking pasta for his lunch next to the open log fire.

DANIELLE
SHOES

Map p308 (☑06 679 24 67; Via Frattina 85a; ☺10.30am-7.30pm; ⓂSpagna) If you're female and in need of an Italian shoe fix, this is an essential stop on your itinerary. It sells both classic and fashionable styles – foxy heels, boots and ballet pumps – at extremely reasonable prices. Shoes are soft leather and come in myriad colours.

SPAS

The glamorous and gorgeous day spa **Hotel de Russie Wellness Zone** (Map p308; ☑06 3288 8820; www.hotelderussie.it; Via del Babuino 9; ☺6.30am-10pm; ⓂFlaminio) is in one of Rome's best hotels, and allows entrance to the gym and steam room. Treatments are also available, including shiatsu and deep-tissue massage; a 50-minute massage costs around €95. Another soothing retreat is **Kami Spa** (Map p308; ☑06 4201 0039; www.kamispa.com; Via Degli Avignonesi 11-12; massage €120-160; ⓂBarberini), close to Piazza Barberini, which has treatment rooms and a pool.

PELLETTERIA NIVES
ACCESSORIES

Map p308 (☑333 3370831; Via delle Carrozze 16; ☺9am-1pm & 4-8pm Mon-Sat; ⓂSpagna) Take the rickety lift to this workshop, choose from the softest leathers, and you will shortly be the proud owner of a handmade, designer-style bag, wallet, belt or briefcase – take a design with you. Bags cost €200 to €350 and take around a week to make.

FABRIANO
ARTS, CRAFTS

Map p308 (☑06 3260 0361; www.fabrianoboutique.com; Via del Babuino 173; ☺10am-8pm; ⓂFlaminio, Spagna) Fabriano makes stationery sexy, with deeply desirable leather-bound diaries, funky notebooks and products embossed with street maps of Rome. It's perfect for picking up a gift, with other items including beautifully made leather key rings (€10) and quirky paper jewellery by local designers.

BARRILÀ BOUTIQUE
SHOES

Map p308 (Via del Babuino 34; ☺10am-8pm; ⓂFlaminio, Spagna) For classic, handmade Italian women's shoes that won't crack the credit card, head to Barrilà. This boutique stocks myriad styles in soft leather. From the window they all look a bit traditional, but you're bound to find something you'll like in the jam-packed interior.

DISCOUNT DELL'ALTA MODA
CLOTHING

Map p308 (☑06 361 37 96; Via Gesù e Maria 14; ☺10.30am-1.30pm & 2.30-7.30pm Tue-Sat, 3.30-7.30pm Mon; ⓂFlaminio, Spagna) Discount dell'Alta Moda sells big names, such as Dolce & Gabbana and Gucci, at knock-down prices (around 50% off). It's worth a rummage.

🏛 West of Via Del Corso

MERCATO DELLE STAMPE
MARKET

Map p308 (Largo della Fontanella di Borghese; ⊘7am-1pm Mon-Sat; 🚇Piazza Augusto Imperatore) The Mercato delle Stampe (Print Market) is well worth a look if you're a fan of vintage books and old prints. Squirrel through the permanent stalls and among the tired posters and dusty back editions, and you might turn up some interesting music scores, architectural engravings or chromolithographs of Rome.

L'OLFATTORIO
BEAUTY

Map p308 (🖉06 361 23 25; Via di Ripetta 34; ⊘10.30am-7.30pm Mon-Sat, 11am-7pm Sun; 🚇Flaminio) This is like an *enoteca* (wine bar), but with perfume instead of drinks: scents are concocted by names such as Artisan Parfumeur, Diptyque, Les Parfums de Rosine and Coudray. The assistants will guide you through different combinations of scents to work out your ideal fragrance. Exclusive perfumes are available to buy. Smellings are free but you should book ahead.

IL MARE
BOOKS

Map p308 (🖉06 361 20 91; Via Del Vantaggio 19; 🚇Flaminio) Ahoy there. Specialising in everything *mare* (sea) related, this friendly bookshop has maritime books in Italian, English and French, nautical charts, binoculars, pirate flags, model yachts, posters and Lonely Planet guidebooks.

TOD'S
SHOES

Map p308 (🖉06 6821 0066; Via della Fontanella di Borghese 56; 🚇Via del Corso) Tod's trademark is its rubber-studded loafers (the idea was to reduce those pesky driving scuffs), perfect weekend footwear for kicking back at your country estate.

🏛 Piazza di Spagna & Around

VERTECCHI ART
ARTS

Map p308 (Via della Croce 70; ⊘3.30-7.30pm Mon, 10am-7.30pm Tue-Sat; 🚇Spagna) Ideal for last-minute gift buying, this large paperware and art shop has beautiful printed paper, cards and envelopes that will inspire you to bring back the art of letter writing, plus an amazing choice of notebooks, art stuff and trinkets.

LUCIA ODESCALCHI
JEWELLERY

Map p308 (🖉06 6992 5506; Palazzo Odescalchi, Piazza dei Santissimi Apostoli 81; ⊘9.30am-2pm Mon-Fri; 🚇Spagna) If you're looking for a unique piece of statement jewellery that will make an outfit, this is the place to head to. Housed in the evocative archives of the family *palazzo*, the avant-garde pieces often have an almost medieval beauty, and run from incredible polished steel and chain mail to pieces created out of pearls and fossils. Beautiful. Prices start at around €140.

C.U.C.I.N.A.
HOMEWARES

Map p308 (🖉06 679 12 75; Via Mario de' Fiori 65; ⊘3.30-7.30pm Mon, 10am-7.30pm Tue-Fri, 10.30am-7.30pm Sat; 🚇Spagna) If you need a foodie gadget, C.U.C.I.N.A. is the place. Make your own *cucina* (kitchen) look the part with the designerware from this famous shop, with myriad devices you'll decide you simply must have, from jelly moulds to garlic presses.

FURLA
ACCESSORIES

Map p308 (🖉06 6920 0363; Piazza di Spagna 22; ⊘10am-8pm Mon-Sat, 10.30am-8pm Sun; 🚇Spagna) Simple, good-quality bags in soft leather and a brilliant array of colours is why the handbagging hordes keep flocking to Furla, where all sorts of accessories, from sunglasses to shoes, are made. There are many other branches dotted across Rome.

SERMONETA
ACCESSORIES

Map p308 (🖉06 679 19 60; www.sermonetagloves. com; Piazza di Spagna 61; ⊘9.30am-8pm Mon-Sat, 10am-7pm Sun; 🚇Spagna) Buying leather gloves in Rome is a rite of passage for some, and its most famous glove-seller is the place to do it. Choose from a kaleidoscopic range of quality leather and suede gloves lined with silk and cashmere. An expert assistant will size up your hand in a glance. Just don't expect them to crack a smile.

ANGLO-AMERICAN BOOKSHOP
BOOKS

Map p308 (🖉06 679 52 22; Via della Vite 102; ⊘10.30am-7.30pm Tue-Sat, 3.30-7.30pm Mon; 🚇Spagna) Particularly good for university reference books, the Anglo-American is well stocked and well known. It has an excellent range of literature, travel guides, children's books and maps, and if it hasn't got the book you want, they'll order it.

FENDI CLOTHING

Map p308 (⏶06 69 66 61; Largo Goldoni 420; ⏲10am-7.30pm Mon-Sat, 11am-2pm & 3-7pm Sun; ⓂSpagna) A temple to subtly bling-ing accessories, this multistorey art-deco building is the Fendi mothership: this is the global headquarters, as the brand was born in Rome. Fendi is particularly famous for its products made of leather and (more controversially) fur.

FOCACCI FOOD

Map p308 (⏶06 679 12 28; Via della Croce 43; ⏲8am-8pm; ⓂSpagna) One of several smash-ing delis along this pretty street, this is the place to buy cheese, cold cuts, smoked fish, caviar, pasta, olive oil and wine.

FRATELLI FABBI FOOD

Map p308 (⏶06 679 06 12; Via della Croce 27; ⏲8am-7.30pm Mon-Sat; ⓂSpagna) A small but flavour-packed delicatessen, this is a good place to pick up all sorts of Italian delica-cies – fine cured meats, buffalo mozzarella from Campania, *parmigiano reggiano,* olive oil, *porchetta* from Ariccia – as well as Iranian caviar.

BULGARI JEWELLERY

Map p308 (⏶06 679 38 76; Via dei Condotti 10; ⏲10am-5pm Tue-Sat, 11am-7pm Sun & Mon; ⓂSpagna) If you have to ask the price, you can't afford it. Sumptuous window displays mean you can admire the world's finest jew-ellery without spending a *centesimo.*

FAUSTO SANTINI SHOES

Map p308 (⏶06 678 41 14; Via Frattina 120; ⏲11am-7.30pm Mon, 10am-7.30pm Tue-Sat, 11am-2pm & 3-7pm Sun; ⓂSpagna) Rome's best-known shoe designer, Fausto Santini is famous for his beguilingly simple, archi-tectural shoe designs, with beautiful boots and shoes made from butter-soft leather. Colours are beautiful, the quality impecca-ble. Seek out the end-of-line discount shop (p155) if this looks out of your price range.

⌂ Trevi Fountain to the Quirinale

LIBRERIA GIUNTI AL PUNTO BOOKS

Map p308 (⏶06 699 41 045; www.giuntial-punto.it; Piazza dei Santissimi Apostoli 59-65; ⏲9.30am-7.30pm Mon-Sat; ⛁Piazza Venezia) The 'Straight to the Point' children's book-shop is an ideal place to distract your kids. Large, colourful and well stocked, it has thousands of titles in Italian and a selec-tion of books in French, Spanish, German and English, as well as a good range of toys, from Play Doh to puzzles.

LA RINASCENTE DEPARTMENT STORE

Map p308 (⏶06 679 76 91; Galleria Alberto Sordi, Piazza Colonna; ⏲10am-9pm; ⛁Via del Corso) La Rinascente is a stately, upmarket department store, with a particularly buzz-ing cosmetics department, all amid art-nouveau interiors.

GALLERIA ALBERTO SORDI SHOPPING CENTRE

Map p308 (Piazza Colonna; ⏲10am-10pm; ⛁Via del Corso) This elegant stained-glass arcade appeared in Alberto Sordi's 1973 classic, *Polvere di Stelle,* and has since been re-named for Rome's favourite actor, who died in 2003. It's a serene place to browse stores such as Zara and Feltrinelli, and there's an airy cafe ideal for a quick coffee break.

⌂ Piazza Barberini & Via Veneto

UNDERGROUND MARKET

Map p308 (⏶06 3600 5345; Via Francesco Crispi 96, Ludovisi underground car park; ⏲3-8pm Sat & 10.30am-7.30pm Sun, 2nd weekend of the month Sep-Jun; ⓂBarberini) Monthly market held underground in a car park near Villa Borghese. There are more than 150 stalls selling everything from antiques and col-lectables to clothes and toys.

TRIDENTE, TREVI & THE QUIRINALE SHOPPING

Vatican City, Borgo & Prati

VATICAN CITY | BORGO | PRATI | AURELIO

Neighbourhood Top Five

1 Gazing heavenwards at Michelangelo's masterpieces in the **Sistine Chapel** (p108) – on the ceiling, his cinematic Old Testament frescoes; on the western wall, his terrifying vision of the *Last Judgment*.

2 Being blown away by the super-sized opulence of **St Peter's Basilica** (p122).

3 Trying to line up the columns on **St Peter's Square** (p134) – it is possible.

4 Revelling in the wonderful rooftop views from **Castel Sant'Angelo** (p134).

5 Marvelling at the vibrant colours of the fabulously frescoed **Stanze di Raffaello** (p108).

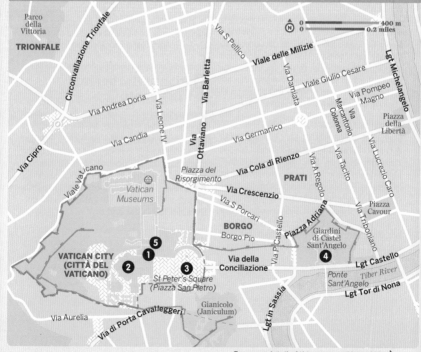

For more detail of this area see Map p312 ➡

Explore: Vatican City, Borgo & Prati

The Vatican, the world's smallest sovereign state (a mere 0.44 sq km), sits atop the low-lying Vatican hill a few hundred metres west of the Tiber. Centred on the domed bulk of St Peter's Basilica, it boasts some of Italy's most revered artworks, many of which are housed in the vast Vatican Museums.

You'll need at least a morning to do justice to the Vatican Museums. The highlight is the Michelangelo-decorated Sistine Chapel, but there's enough art on display to keep you busy for years. If you're with a tour guide, or if you can sneakily join onto a group, you can pass directly from the Sistine Chapel through to St Peter's Basilica; otherwise you'll have to walk around and approach from St Peter's Sq, itself one of the Vatican's most dramatic sights. Once finished in the basilica, you'll be ready for a break. There are few good eating options in the Vatican itself, but the nearby Prati district is full of excellent trattorias, takeaways and restaurants.

Between the Vatican and the river lies the medieval district of the Borgo – before Mussolini bulldozed Via dei Conciliazione through the area, all the streets around St Peter's were like this. The big sight here is Castel Sant'Angelo, the large, drum-shaped castle overlooking the river.

The Vatican, Borgo and Prati districts are all easy to reach by public transport.

Local Life

→**Fast Food** Rather than having a full-length midday meal, local office workers tend to grab a snack from the many excellent takeaways in Prati. Join them and lunch on *pizza al taglio* (pizza by the slice), *arancine* (deep-fried rice balls stuffed with cheese and vegetables) and gelato.

→**Shopping** Spearing off Piazza del Risorgimento, Via Cola di Rienzo is a popular shopping strip lined with department stores and midrange clothes shops.

→**Catch a Gig** Join the locals for sweet melodies at Alexanderplatz (p138), Rome's oldest and most famous jazz joint. Another top venue is the basement pub Fonclea (p138).

Getting There & Away

→**Bus** From Termini, bus 40 is the quickest one to the Vatican – it'll drop you off near Castel Sant'Angelo. You can also take bus 64, which runs a similar route but stops more often. Bus 492 runs from Stazione Tiburtina to Piazza del Risorgimento and Cipro metro station, passing through Piazza Barberini and the *centro storico*.

→**Metro** Take metro line A to Ottaviano–San Pietro. From the station, signs direct you to St Peter's.

Lonely Planet's Top Tip

Be wary of the touts around Ottaviano metro station selling queue-jumping tours of the Vatican Museums. These guys are on commission to round up clients and the tours they offer might well cost more than those sold on the museums' official website.

Note that if you want to attend Easter or Christmas mass at St Peter's you'll have to book (free) tickets through the **Prefettura della Casa Pontificia** (www.vatican.va/various/prefettura/index_en.html).

Best Places to Eat

→ Pizzarium (p138)

→ Romeo (p136)

→ Velavevodetto Ai Quiriti (p136)

→ Enoteca La Torre (p137)

For reviews, see p135.➡

Best Places to Drink

→ Sciascia Caffè (p138)

→ Makasar (p138)

→ Art Studio Café (p138)

→ Passaguai (p138)

For reviews, see p138.➡

Best Overground & Underground

→ Dome of St Peter's Basilica (p122)

→ Terrace of Castel Sant'Angelo (p134)

→ Tomb of St Peter (p125)

→ Vatican Grottoes (p125)

For reviews, see p134.➡

VATICAN CITY, BORGO & PRATI

◉ TOP SIGHT
ST PETER'S BASILICA

In a city of outstanding churches, none can hold a candle to St Peter's, Italy's largest, richest and most spectacular basilica. A monument to centuries of artistic genius, it contains some spectacular works of art, including three of Italy's most celebrated masterpieces: Michelangelo's *Pietà*, his breathtaking dome, and Bernini's *baldachin* (canopy) over the papal altar.

Note that the basilica gets very busy so expect queues most days. Also, strict dress codes are enforced: no shorts, mini-skirts or bare shoulders.

History

The original St Peter's, which lies beneath the current basilica, was commissioned by the emperor Constantine and built around 349 on the site where St Peter is said to have been buried between AD 64 and 67. But like many medieval churches, it eventually fell into disrepair and it wasn't until the mid-15th century that efforts were made to restore it, first by Pope Nicholas V and then, rather more successfully, by Julius II.

In 1506 construction began on Bramante's design for a new basilica based on a Greek-cross plan, with four equal arms and a huge central dome. But on Bramante's death in 1514, building ground to a halt as architects, including Raphael and Antonio da Sangallo, tried to modify his original plans. Little progress was made and it wasn't until Michelangelo took over in 1547 at the age of 72 that the situation changed. Michelangelo simplified Bramante's plans and drew up designs for what was to become his greatest architectural achievement: the dome. He never lived to see it built, though, and it was left to Giacomo della Porta and Domenico Fontana to finish it in 1590.

DON'T MISS...

➡ *Pietà*
➡ Statue of St Peter
➡ The dome
➡ The baldachin
➡ *Cattedra di San Pietro*

PRACTICALITIES

➡ Basilica di San Pietro
➡ Map p312
➡ www.vatican.va
➡ St Peter's Sq
➡ ⊙7am-7pm summer, to 6.30pm winter
➡ Ⓜ Ottaviano-San Pietro

With the dome in place, Carlo Maderno inherited the project in 1605. He designed the monumental facade and lengthened the nave towards the piazza.

The basilica was finally consecrated in 1626.

Facade

Built between 1608 and 1612, Maderno's immense facade is 48m high and 118.6m wide. Eight 27m-high columns support the upper attic on which 13 statues stand representing Christ the Redeemer, St John the Baptist and the 11 apostles. The central balcony, the **Loggia della Benedizione**, is where the pope stands to deliver his *Urbi et Orbi* blessing at Christmas and Easter.

Behind the columns in the grand atrium, the **Porta Santa** (Holy Door) is opened only in Jubilee Years.

Interior – Right Nave

At the beginning of the right aisle is Michelangelo's hauntingly beautiful **Pietà**. Sculpted when the artist was 25 (in 1499), it's the only work he ever signed – his signature is etched into the sash across the Madonna's breast.

Nearby, a **red floor disk** marks the spot where Charlemagne and later Holy Roman emperors were crowned by the pope.

On a pillar just beyond the *Pietà*, Carlo Fontana's gilt and bronze **monument to Queen Christina of Sweden** commemorates the far-from-holy Swedish monarch who converted to Catholicism in 1655.

Moving on, you'll come to the **Cappella di San Sebastiano**, home of Pope John Paul II's tomb, and the **Cappella del Santissimo Sacramento**, a sumptuously decorated baroque chapel with works by Borromini, Bernini and Pietro da Cortona.

Beyond the chapel, the grandiose **monument to Gregory XIII** sits near the roped-off **Cappella Gregoriana**, a chapel built by Gregory XIII from designs by Michelangelo.

Much of the right transept is closed off, but you can still make out the **monument to Clement XIII**, one of Canova's most famous works.

Interior – Central Nave

Dominating the centre of the basilica is Bernini's 29m-high **baldachin**. Supported by four spiral columns and made with bronze taken from the Pantheon, it stands over the **papal altar**, also known as the Altar of the Confession. In front, Carlo Maderno's **Confessione** stands on the site where St Peter was originally buried.

Above the baldachin, Michelangelo's **dome** soars to a height of 119m. Based on Brunelleschi's cupola

CHRISTINA, QUEEN OF SWEDEN

Famously portrayed by Greta Garbo in the 1933 film *Queen Christina*, the Swedish monarch is one of only three women buried in St Peter's Basilica – the other two are Queen Charlotte of Cyprus, a minor 15th-century royal, and Agnesina Colonna, a 16th-century Italian aristocrat. Christina earned her place by abdicating the Swedish throne and converting to Catholicism in 1655. As Europe's most high-profile convert, she became a Vatican darling and spent much of her later life in Rome, where she enjoyed fame as a brilliant patron of the arts. Her active private life was the subject of much salacious gossip, and rumours abounded of affairs with courtiers and acquaintances of both sexes.

Free English-language tours of the basilica are run from the Centro Servizi Pellegrini e Turisti at 9am every Tuesday and Thursday. In certain periods, volunteers from the Pontifical North American College also lead tours. The timetable for these varies, but they typically start at 2.15pm Monday through Friday.

in Florence, it's supported by four massive stone **piers** named after the saints whose statues adorn the Bernini-designed niches. These saints are all associated with the basilica's four major relics: the lance **St Longinus** used to pierce Christ's side; the cloth with which **St Veronica** wiped Jesus' face; a fragment of the Cross collected by **St Helena**; and the head of **St Andrew**.

At the base of the **Pier of St Longinus** is Arnolfo di Cambio's much-loved 13th-century bronze **statue of St Peter**, whose right foot has been worn down by centuries of caresses.

Dominating the tribune behind the altar is Bernini's extraordinary **Cattedra di San Pietro**. A vast gilded bronze throne held aloft by four 5m-high saints, it's centred on a wooden seat that was once thought to have been St Peter's but in fact dates to the 9th century. Above, light shines through a yellow window framed by a gilded mass of golden angels and adorned with a dove to represent the Holy Spirit.

To the right of the throne, Bernini's **monument to Urban VIII** depicts the pope flanked by the figures of Charity and Justice.

Interior – Left Nave

In the roped-off left transept, the **Cappella della Madonna della Colonna** takes its name from the Madonna that stares out from Giacomo della Porta's marble altar. To its right, above the **tomb of St Leo the Great**, is a fine relief by Alessandro Algardi. Under the next arch is Bernini's last work in the basilica, the **monument to Alexander VII**.

Halfway down the left aisle, the **Cappella Clementina** is named after Clement VIII, who had Giacomo della Porta decorate it for the Jubilee of 1600. Beneath the altar is the **tomb of St Gregory the Great** and, to the left, a **monument to Pope Pius VII** by Thorvaldsen.

The next arch shelters Alessandro Algardi's 16th-century **monument to Leo XI**. Beyond it, the richly decorated **Cappella del Coro** was created by Giovanni Battista Ricci to designs by Giacomo della Porta. The **monument to Innocent VIII** by Antonio Pollaiuolo in the next aisle arch is a re-creation of a monument from the old basilica.

Continuing on, the **Cappella della Presentazione** contains two of St Peter's most modern works: a black relief **monument to John XXIII**, by Emilio Greco, and a **monument to Benedict XV**, by Pietro Canonica.

Under the next arch are the so-called **Stuart monuments**. On the right is the monument to Clementina Sobieska, wife of James Stuart, by Filippo Barigioni, and on the left is Canova's vaguely erotic monument to the last three members of the Stuart clan, the pretenders to the English throne who died in exile in Rome.

Dome

From the entrance of the **dome** (with/without lift €7/5; ☉8am-5.45pm summer, to 4.45pm winter; ⓜOttaviano-San Pietro) on the right of the basilica's main portico, you can walk the 551 steps to the top or take a small lift halfway and then follow on foot for the last 320 steps. Either way, it's a long, steep climb. But make it to the top, and you're rewarded with stunning views from a perch 120m above St Peter's Square.

Museo Storico Artistico

Accessed from the left nave, the **Museo Storico Artistico** (Tesoro; adult/reduced €7/5; ☉9am-6.15pm summer, to 5.15pm winter; ⓜOttaviano-San Pietro) sparkles with sacred relics. Highlights include a tabernacle by Donatello; the Colonna Santa, a 4th-century Byzantine column from the earlier church; and the 6th-century Crux Vaticana (Vatican Cross), a jewel-encrusted crucifix presented by the emperor Justinian II to the original basilica.

Inside the dome of St Peter's Basilica

Vatican Grottoes

Extending beneath the basilica, the **Vatican Grottoes** (⊙9am-6pm summer, to 5pm winter) **FREE** contain the tombs and sarcophagi of numerous popes, as well as several columns from the original 4th-century basilica. The entrance is in the Pier of St Andrew.

Tomb of St Peter

Excavations beneath the basilica have uncovered part of the original church and what archaeologists believe is the **Tomb of St Peter** (☑06 6988 5318; admission €13, over 15yr only). In 1942 the bones of an elderly, strongly built man were found in a box hidden behind a wall covered by pilgrims' graffiti. And while the Vatican has never definitively claimed that the bones belong to St Peter, in 1968 Pope Paul VI said that they had been identified in a way that the Vatican considered to be 'convincing'.

The excavations can only be visited by guided tour. To book a spot, email the Ufficio Scavi (scavi@fsp.va) as early as possible.

FACE IN THE BALDACHIN

The frieze on Bernini's baldachin contains a hidden narrative that begins at the pillar to the left (looking with your back to the entrance). As you walk clockwise around the baldachin, note the woman's face carved into the frieze of each pillar. On the first three pillars her face seems to express the increasing agony of childbirth; on the last one, it's replaced by that of a smiling baby. The woman was a niece of Pope Urban VIII and gave birth as Bernini worked on the baldachin.

Contrary to popular opinion, St Peter's Basilica is not the world's largest church – the Basilica of Our Lady of Peace in Yamoussoukro on the Ivory Coast is bigger. Bronze floor plates in the central aisle indicate the respective sizes of the 14 next-largest churches.

VATICAN CITY, BORGO & PRATI ST PETER'S BASILICA

ROGER DE LA HARPE / GETTY IMAGES ©

Visiting the Vatican Museums (Musei Vaticani) is a thrilling and unforgettable experience. With some 7km of exhibitions and more masterpieces than many small countries, this vast museum complex contains one of the world's greatest art collections. Highlights include a spectacular collection of classical statuary, a suite of rooms painted by Raphael, and the Michelangelo-decorated Sistine Chapel.

Founded by Pope Julius II in the early 16th century, the museums are housed in the lavishly decorated halls and galleries of the Palazzo Apostolico Vaticano. This immense 5.5-hectare building consists of two palaces – the Vatican palace (nearer to St Peter's) and the Belvedere Palace – joined by two long galleries. On the inside are three court-yards: the Cortile della Pigna, the Cortile della Biblioteca and, to the south, the Cortile del Belvedere. You'll never cover it all in one day, so it pays to be selective.

Pinacoteca

Often overlooked by visitors, the papal picture gallery displays paintings dating from the 11th to 19th centuries, with works by Giotto, Fra Angelico, Filippo Lippi, Perugino, Titian, Guido Reni, Guercino, Pietro da Cortona, Caravaggio and Leonardo da Vinci.

Look out for a trio of paintings by Raphael in Room VIII – the *Madonna di Foligno* (Madonna of Folignano), the *Incoronazione della Vergine* (Crowning of the Virgin), and *La Trasfigurazione* (Transfiguration), which was completed by his students after his death in 1520. Other highlights include Filippo Lippi's *L'Incoronazione della Vergine con Angeli, Santo e donatore* (Coronation of the Virgin with Angels, Saints, and donors), Leonardo da

DON'T MISS...

➡ Sistine Chapel
➡ *Stanze di Raffaello*
➡ Apollo Belvedere & Laocoön, Museo Pio-Clementino
➡ *La Trasfigurazione*, Pinacoteca

PRACTICALITIES

➡ Map p312
➡ ☏06 6988 4676
➡ http://mv.vatican.va
➡ Viale Vaticano
➡ adult/reduced €16/8, last Sun of month free
➡ ⊙9am-4pm Mon-Sat, 9am-12.30pm last Sun of month
➡ Ⓜ Ottaviano-San Pietro

Vinci's haunting and unfinished *San Gerolamo* (St Jerome), and Caravaggio's *Deposizione* (Deposition from the Cross).

Museo Chiaramonti

This museum is effectively the long corridor that runs down the lower east side of the Belvedere Palace. Its walls are lined with thousands of statues and busts representing everything from immortal gods to playful cherubs and ugly Roman patricians. Near the end of the hall, off to the right, is the **Braccio Nuovo** (New Wing; currently closed for restoration), which contains a famous statue of the Nile as a reclining god covered by 16 babies.

Museo Pio-Clementino

This stunning museum contains some of the Vatican's finest classical statuary, including the peerless *Apollo Belvedere* and the 1st-century BC *Laocoön*, both in the **Cortile Ottagono** (Octagonal Courtyard). Before you go into the courtyard, take a moment to admire the 1st-century *Apoxyomenos,* one of the earliest known sculptures to depict a figure with a raised arm.

To the left as you enter the courtyard, the *Apollo Belvedere* is a 2nd-century Rome copy of a 4th-century-BC Greek bronze. A beautifully proportioned representation of the sun god Apollo, it's considered one of the great masterpieces of classical sculpture. Nearby, the *Laocoön* shows a Trojan priest and his sons in mortal struggle with two sea serpents.

Back inside, the **Sala degli Animali** is filled with a selection of sculpted creatures and some magnificent 4th-century mosaics. Continuing on, you come to the **Sala delle Muse** (Room of the Muses), centred on the *Torso Belvedere,* another must-see. A fragment of a muscular 1st-century BC Greek sculpture, this was found in Campo de' Fiori and used by Michelangelo as a model for his *ignudi* (male nudes) in the Sistine Chapel. It's undergoing restoration.

The next room, the **Sala Rotonda** (Round Room), contains a number of colossal statues, including a gilded-bronze *Ercole* (Hercules) and an exquisite floor mosaic. The enormous basin in the centre of the room was found at Nero's Domus Aurea and is made out of a single piece of red porphyry stone.

Museo Gregoriano Egizio

Founded by Pope Gregory XVI in 1839, the Egyptian museum displays pieces taken from Egypt in ancient Roman times. The collection is small, but there are fascinating exhibits including the *Trono di Rameses II* (part of a statue of the seated king), vividly painted sarcophagi from about 1000 BC, and a couple of macabre mummies.

JUMP THE QUEUE

Avoiding the queues is largely a matter of luck, but there are some things you can do to reduce waiting time. Book tickets online (http://biglietteriamusei.vatican.va/musei/tickets/do; €4 booking fee). On payment, you'll receive email confirmation, which you should print and present, along with valid ID, at the museum entrance. Alternatively, book a tour with a reputable guide. Time your visit: Tuesdays and Thursdays are quietest; Wednesday mornings are good as everyone is at the pope's weekly audience; afternoon is better than the morning; avoid Mondays when many other museums are shut.

On the whole, exhibits are not well labelled, so consider hiring an audioguide (€7) or buying the excellent *Guide to the Vatican Museums and City* (€14). The museums are well equipped for visitors with disabilities, and wheelchairs are available free of charge from the Special Permits desk in the entrance hall. They can also be reserved by emailing accoglienza.musei@scv.va. Strollers can be taken into the museums.

Museo Gregoriano Etrusco

At the top of the Simonetti staircase, this fascinating museum contains artefacts unearthed in the Etruscan tombs of northern Lazio, as well as a superb collection of vases and Roman antiquities. Of particular interest is the *Marte di Todi* (Mars of Todi), a black bronze of a warrior dating to the late 5th century BC.

Galleria dei Candelabri & Galleria degli Arazzi

Originally an open loggia, the **Galleria dei Candelabri** is packed with classical sculpture and several elegantly carved candelabras that give the gallery its name. The corridor continues through to the **Galleria degli Arazzi** (Tapestry Gallery) and its huge hanging tapestries. The best, on the left, were woven in Brussels in the 16th century.

Galleria delle Carte Geografiche & Sala Sobieski

One of the unsung heroes of the Vatican Museums, the 120m-long Map Gallery is hung with 40 huge topographical maps. These were created between 1580 and 1583 for Pope Gregory XIII based on drafts by Ignazio Danti, one of the leading cartographers of his day. Beyond the gallery, the **Sala Sobieski** is named after an enormous 19th-century painting depicting the victory of the Polish King John III Sobieski over the Turks in 1683.

continued on p130

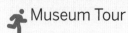

Museum Tour

Vatican Museums

LENGTH THREE HOURS

Pass through the entrance complex and head up the modern spiral ramp to the ❶**Cortile delle Corazze**, the start point for all routes through the museums. Take a moment to nip out to the terrace for views over St Peter's dome and the Vatican Gardens. Re-enter and follow through to the ❷**Cortile della Pigna**, named after the huge Augustan-era bronze pine cone in the monumental niche. Cross the courtyard and enter the long corridor that is the ❸**Museo Chiaramonti**. Don't stop here, but continue left, up the stairs, to the Museo Pio-Clementino for the Vatican's finest classical statuary. Follow the flow of people through to the ❹**Cortile Ottagono** (Octagonal Courtyard), where you'll find the mythical masterpieces, the *Laocoön* and *Apollo Belvedere*. Continue through a series of rooms – the ❺**Sala degli Animali** (Animal Room), the ❻**Sala delle Muse** (Room

of the Muses), home of the famous *Torso Belvedere*, and the ❼**Sala Rotonda** (Round Room), centred on a vast red basin. From the neighbouring ❽**Sala Croce Greca** (Greek Cross Room), the Simonetti staircase leads up to the ❾**Galleria dei Candelabri** (Gallery of the Candelabra), the first of three galleries along a lengthy corridor. It gets crowded up here as you're funnelled through the ❿**Galleria degli Arazzi** (Tapestry Gallery) and onto the ⓫**Galleria delle Carte Geografiche** (Map Gallery), a 120m long hall hung with huge topographical maps. At the end of the corridor, carry on through the ⓬**Sala Sobieski** to the ⓭**Sala di Costantino**, the first of the four Stanze di Raffaello (Raphael Rooms) – the others are the ⓮**Stanza d'Eliodoro**, the ⓯**Stanza della Segnatura**, featuring Raphael's superlative *La Scuola di Atene*, and the ⓰**Stanza dell'Incendio di Borgo**. Anywhere else these magnificent frescoed chambers would be the star attraction, but here they serve as the warm-up for the grand finale, the Sistine Chapel.

VATICAN MUSEUMS

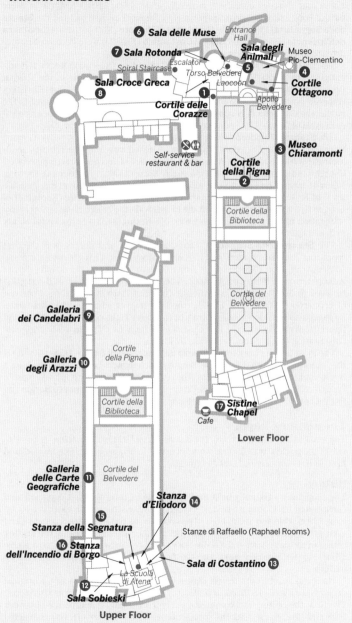

6 *Sala delle Muse*

7 *Sala Rotonda*

Entrance Hall

Sala degli Animali **5**

Museo Pio-Clementino

Spiral Staircase *Escalator*

Torso Belvedere

Sala Croce Greca **8**

Laocoön

Cortile Ottagono **4**

1

Cortile delle Corazze

Apollo Belvedere

3 **Museo Chiaramonti**

✗ ♿

Self-service restaurant & bar

Cortile della Pigna

2

Cortile della Biblioteca

Cortile del Belvedere

Galleria dei Candelabri **9**

Cortile della Pigna

Galleria degli Arazzi **10**

Cortile della Biblioteca

Sistine Chapel **17**

Cafe

Lower Floor

Galleria delle Carte Geografiche **11**

Cortile del Belvedere

Stanza d'Eliodoro **14**

15

Stanze di Raffaello (Raphael Rooms)

Stanza della Segnatura

16 **Stanza dell'Incendio di Borgo**

Sala di Costantino **13**

La Scuola di Atene

12

Sala Sobieski

Upper Floor

Stanze di Raffaello

These four frescoed chambers, currently undergoing partial restoration, were part of Pope Julius II's private apartments. Raphael himself painted the **Stanza della Segnatura** (1508–11) and the **Stanza d'Eliodoro** (1512–14), while the **Stanza dell'Incendio** (1514–17) and **Sala di Costantino** (1517–24) were decorated by students following his designs.

The first room you come to, the **Sala di Costantino** (Reception Room) is dominated by the *Battaglia di Costantino contro Maxentius* (Battle of the Milvian Bridge), a huge fresco showing the victory of Constantine, Rome's first Christian emperor, over his rival Maxentius. Leading off the *sala,* but usually closed to the public, the **Cappella di Niccolo V**, Pope Nicholas V's private chapel, boasts a superb cycle of frescoes by Fra Angelico.

The **Stanza d'Eliodoro**, which was used for private audiences, takes its name from the *Cacciata d'Eliodoro* (Expulsion of Heliodorus from the Temple), an allegorical work referring to Pope Julius II's policy of forcing foreign powers off Church lands. To its right is the *Messa di Bolsena* (Mass of Bolsena), showing Julius II paying homage to the relic of a 13th-century miracle at the lakeside town of Bolsena. Next is the *Incontro di Leone Magno con Attila* (Encounter of Leo the Great with Attila), and, on the fourth wall, the *Liberazione di San Pietro* (Liberation of St Peter), a brilliant work illustrating Raphael's masterful ability to depict light.

The **Stanza della Segnatura**, Pope Julius' study and library, was the first room that Raphael painted, and it's here that you'll find his great masterpiece, *La Scuola di Atene* (The School of Athens), featuring philosophers and scholars gathered around Plato and Aristotle. The seated figure in front of the steps is believed to be Michelangelo, while the figure of Plato is said to be a portrait of Leonardo da Vinci, and Euclide (the bald man bending over) is Bramante. Raphael also included a self-portrait in the lower right corner (he's the second figure from the right in the black hat). Opposite is *La Disputa del Sacramento* (Disputation on the Sacrament), also by Raphael.

The most famous work in the **Stanza dell'Incendio di Borgo** (Dining Room) is the *Incendio di Borgo* (Fire in the Borgo), which depicts Leo IV extinguishing a fire by making the sign of the cross. The ceiling was painted by Raphael's master, Perugino. From the Raphael Rooms, stairs lead to the **Appartamento Borgia** and the Vatican's collection of modern religious art.

The Sistine Chapel

The jewel in the Vatican crown, the Sistine Chapel (*Cappella Sistina)* is home to two of the world's most famous works of art – Michelangelo's ceiling frescoes and his *Giudizio Universale* (Last Judgment).

History

The chapel was originally built for Pope Sixtus IV, after whom it is named, and consecrated on 15 August 1483. It's a big, barnlike structure, measuring 40.2m long, 13.4m wide and 20.7m high – the same size as the Temple of Solomon – and even pre-Michelangelo it would have been impressive. Frescoes by the leading artists of the day adorned the walls, the vaulted ceiling was coloured to resemble a blue sky with golden stars, and the floor had an inlaid polychrome marble pattern.

However, apart from the wall frescoes and floor, little remains of the original decor, which was sacrificed to make way for Michelangelo's two masterpieces. The first, the ceiling, was commissioned by Pope Julius II and painted between 1508 and 1512; the second, the spectacular *Giudizio Universale*, was completed almost 30 years later in 1541.

Both were controversial works influenced by the political ambitions of the popes who commissioned them. The ceiling came as part of Julius II's drive to transform Rome into the Church's showcase capital, while Pope Paul III intended the *Giudizio Universale* to serve as a warning to Catholics to toe the line during the Reformation, which was then sweeping through Europe.

Restoration

In recent years debate has centred on the chapel's multimillion-dollar restoration, which finished in 1999 after nearly 20 years. In removing almost 450 years' worth of dust and candle soot, restorers finally revealed the frescoes in their original technicolour glory. But some critics claimed that they also removed a layer of varnish that Michelangelo had added to darken them and enhance their shadows. Whatever the truth, the Sistine Chapel remains a truly spectacular sight.

The Ceiling & the Ignudi

The Sistine Chapel provided the greatest challenge of Michelangelo's career, and painting the 800-sq-metre vaulted ceiling at a height of more than 20m pushed him to the limits of his genius.

When Pope Julius II first approached him – some say on the advice of his chief architect, Bramante, who was keen for Michelangelo to fail – he was reluctant to accept. He regarded himself as a sculptor and had had virtually no experience painting frescoes. However, Julius was determined and in 1508 he persuaded Michelangelo to accept the commission for a fee of 3000 ducats (more or less €1.5 to €2 million in today's money).

Originally, Pope Julius wanted Michelangelo to paint the twelve apostles and a series of decorative architectural elements. But the artist rejected this and came up with a much more complex design to cover the entire ceiling based on stories from the book of Genesis. And it's this that you see today.

The focus of the ceiling frescoes are the nine central panels, but set around them are 20 athletic male nudes, known as *ignudi*. These muscle-bound models caused a scandal when they were first revealed and today art historians are still divided over their meaning – some claim they are angels, others say that they represent Michelangelo's neo-Platonic vision of ideal man.

Wall Frescoes

If you can tear your eyes away from the Michelangelos, the Sistine Chapel also boasts some superb wall frescoes. These formed part of the original chapel decoration and were painted between 1481 and 1482

CONCLAVE

The Sistine Chapel plays an important religious function as the place where the conclave meets to elect a new pope. Dating to 1274, give or take a few modifications, the rules of the voting procedure are explicit: between 15 and 20 days after the death of a pope, the entire College of Cardinals (comprising all cardinals under the age of 80) is locked in the chapel to elect a new pontiff. Four secret ballots are held every day until a two-thirds majority has been secured. News of the election is communicated by emitting white smoke through a specially erected chimney.

The heat and humidity caused by the chapels' six million annual visitors pose a constant threat to the frescoes, and the Vatican Museums' director has hinted at the possibility of having to limit the number of daily visitors to 20,000.

NIGHT OPENINGS

From mid-April to October, the Museums open late (7pm to 11pm) every Friday evening. Online booking is necessary for these night visits.

SISTINE CHAPEL CEILING

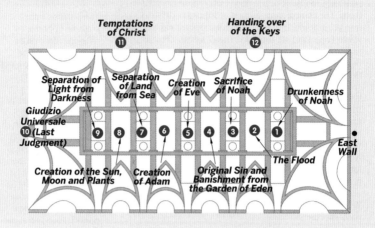

Temptations of Christ 11

Handing over of the Keys 12

Separation of Light from Darkness

Separation of Land from Sea

Creation of Eve

Sacrifice of Noah

Drunkenness of Noah

Giudizio Universale 10 **(Last Judgment)**

9 8 7 6 5 4 3 2 1

East Wall

Creation of the Sun, Moon and Plants

Creation of Adam

Original Sin and Banishment from the Garden of Eden

The Flood

VATICAN CITY, BORGO & PRATI VATICAN MUSEUMS

🏃 Museum Tour

Sistine Chapel

LENGTH 30 MINUTES

On entering the chapel head over to the main entrance in the far (east) wall for the best views of the ceiling.

Michelangelo's ceiling design – which took him four years to complete – covers the entire 800-sq-m surface. With painted architectural features and a colourful cast of biblical figures, it centres on nine central panels depicting the Creation, Adam and Eve, the Fall, and the plight of Noah.

As you look up from the east wall, the first panel is the ❶ **Drunkenness of Noah**, followed by ❷ **The Flood**, and the ❸ **Sacrifice of Noah**. Next, ❹ **Original Sin and Banishment from the Garden of Eden** famously depicts Adam and Eve being sent packing after accepting the forbidden fruit from Satan, represented by a snake with the body of a woman coiled around a tree. The ❺ **Creation of Eve** is then followed by the ❻ **Creation of**

Adam. This, one of the most famous images in Western art, shows a bearded God pointing his finger at Adam, thus bringing him to life. Completing the sequence are the ❼ **Separation of Land from Sea**, the ❽ **Creation of the Sun, Moon and Plants** and the ❾ **Separation of Light from Darkness**, featuring a fearsome God reaching out to touch the sun.

Straight ahead of you on the west wall is Michelangelo's mesmeric ❿ **Giudizio Universale** (Last Judgment), showing Christ (in the centre near the top) passing sentence over the souls of the dead as they are torn from their graves to face him. The saved get to stay up in heaven (in the upper right), the damned are sent down to face the demons in hell (in the bottom right).

The chapel's side walls also feature stunning Renaissance frescoes, representing the lives of Moses (to your left) and Christ (to the right). Look out for Botticelli's ⓫ **Temptations of Christ** and Perugino's ⓬ **Handing over of the Keys**.

by a team of Renaissance artists, including Botticelli, Ghirlandaio, Pinturicchio, Perugino and Luca Signorelli. They represent events in the lives of Moses (to the left, looking at the *Giudizio Universale*) and Christ (to the right).

Giudizio Universale (Last Judgment)

Michelangelo's second stint in the Sistine Chapel, from 1535 to 1541, resulted in the *Giudizio Universale* (Last Judgment), his highly charged depiction of Christ's second coming on the 200-sq-metre western wall.

The project, which was commissioned by Pope Clement VII and encouraged by his successor Paul III, was controversial from the start. Critics were outraged when Michelangelo destroyed two Perugino frescoes when preparing the wall – it had to be replastered so that it tilted inwards to protect it from dust – and when it was unveiled in 1541, its dramatic, swirling mass of 391 predominantly naked bodies provoked outrage. So fierce were feelings that the Church's top brass, meeting at the 1564 Council of Trent, ordered the nudity to be covered up. The task fell to Daniele da Volterra, one of Michelangelo's students, who added fig leaves and loincloths to 41 nudes, earning himself the nickname *il braghettone* (the breeches maker).

For his part Michelangelo rejected the criticism. He even got his own back on one of his loudest critics, Biagio de Cesena, the papal master of ceremonies, by depicting him as Minos, judge of the underworld, with donkey ears and a snake wrapped around him.

Another famous figure is St Bartholomew, just beneath Christ, holding his own flayed skin. The face in the skin is said to be a self-portrait of Michelangelo, its anguished look reflecting the artist's tormented faith.

HEAVENLY BLUE

One of the striking features of the *Giudizio Universale* is the amount of ultramarine blue in the painting – in contrast with the ceiling frescoes, which don't have any. In the 16th century, blue paint was made from the hugely expensive stone lapis lazuli, and artists were reluctant to use it unless someone else was paying. In the case of the *Giudizio Universale*, the pope picked up the tab for all of Michelangelo's materials; on the ceiling, however, the artist had to cover his own expenses and so used less costly colours.

It's often said that Michelangelo worked alone. He didn't. Throughout the job, he employed a steady stream of assistants to help with the plasterwork (producing frescoes involves painting directly onto wet plaster).

MYTHS DEBUNKED

A popular myth is that Michelangelo painted lying down, as portrayed by Charlton Heston in the film *The Agony and the Ecstasy*. In fact, Michelangelo designed a curved scaffolding system that allowed him to work standing up, albeit in an awkward, leaning-back position.

◉ SIGHTS

Boasting priceless treasures at every turn, the Vatican is home to some of Rome's most popular sights. The Vatican Museums and St Peter's Basilica are the star attractions, but Castel Sant'Angelo, one of the city's most recognisable landmarks, is also well worth a visit.

◉ Vatican City

ST PETER'S BASILICA   BASILICA
See p122.

VATICAN MUSEUMS   MUSEUM
See p126.

ST PETER'S SQUARE   PIAZZA
Map p312 (Piazza San Pietro; MOttaviano-San Pietro) Overlooked by St Peter's Basilica, the Vatican's central square was laid out between 1656 and 1667 to a design by Gian Lorenzo Bernini. Seen from above, it resembles a giant keyhole with two semi-circular colonnades, each consisting of four rows of Doric columns, encircling a giant ellipse that straightens out to funnel believers into the basilica. The effect was deliberate – Bernini described the colonnades as representing 'the motherly arms of the church'.

SEPARATE ENTRANCES

It's a common misunderstanding, but many people think that St Peter's Basilica, the Vatican Museums and the Sistine Chapel share a single entrance. They don't. The entrance to St Peter's Basilica is on St Peter's Sq, while the entrance to the Vatican Museums is on Viale Vaticano – follow the Vatican walls westwards from Piazza del Risorgimento. The Sistine Chapel is in the Vatican Museums and can only be accessed through the museums.

You can, if you're sly, pass from the Sistine Chapel through to St Peter's Basilica, athough officially this short cut is reserved for guided groups. You cannot, however, go from St Peter's to the Sistine Chapel.

The scale of the piazza is dazzling: at its largest it measures 340m by 240m. There are 284 columns and, atop the colonnades, 140 saints. The 25m **obelisk** in the centre was brought to Rome by Caligula from Heliopolis in Egypt and later used by Nero as a turning post for the chariot races in his circus.

Leading off the piazza, the monumental approach road, **Via della Conciliazione**, was commissioned by Mussolini and built between 1936 and 1950.

VATICAN GARDENS   GARDENS
Map p312 (http://biglietteriamusei.vatican.va/musei/tickets/do; adult/reduced incl Vatican Museums €32/24; ⊗by reservation only; MOttaviano-San Pietro) Up to half the Vatican is covered by the perfectly manicured Vatican Gardens, which contain fortifications, grottoes, monuments and fountains. Visits are by two-hour guided tour only, for which you'll need to book at least a week in advance. Note that after the tour you're free to visit the Vatican Museums on your own.

NECROPOLI VIA TRIUMPHALIS   ARCHAEOLOGICAL SITE
Map p312 (http://biglietteriamusei.vatican.va/musei/tickets/do; adult/reduced incl Vatican Museums €26/20, incl Vatican Museums & Gardens €37/29; ⊗by reservation only; MOttaviano-San Pietro) Not to be confused with the Tomb of St Peter, this ancient Roman cemetery extends beneath the Vatican hill. Guided tours, which must be pre-booked, follow modern walkways through the ongoing excavations, taking in tombs and burial chambers unearthed during construction of an underground car park.

◉ Borgo

CASTEL SANT'ANGELO   MUSEUM, CASTLE
Map p312 (☑06 681 91 11; http://castelsantangelo.beniculturali.it; Lungotevere Castello 50; adult/reduced €7/3.50; ⊗9am-7.30pm Tue-Sun; ☐Piazza Pia) With its chunky round keep, this castle is an instantly recognisable landmark. Built as a mausoleum for the emperor Hadrian, it was converted into a papal fortress in the 6th century and named after an angelic vision that Pope Gregory the Great had in 590. Nowadays, it houses the **Museo Nazionale di Castel Sant'Angelo** and its eclectic collection of

paintings, sculpture, military memorabilia and medieval firearms.

Many of these weapons were used by soldiers fighting to protect the castle, which, thanks to a secret 13th-century passageway to the Vatican (the *Passetto di Borgo*), provided sanctuary to many popes in times of danger. Most famously, Pope Clemente VI holed up here during the 1527 sack of Rome.

The castle's upper floors are filled with lavishly decorated Renaissance interiors, including the beautifully frescoed **Sala Paolina**. Two storeys up, the **terrace**, immortalised by Puccini in his opera *Tosca,* offers unforgettable views over Rome.

Note that ticket prices may increase during temporary exhibitions.

PONTE SANT'ANGELO BRIDGE

Map p312 (🚇Piazza Pia) The emperor Hadrian built the Ponte Sant'Angelo in 136 to provide an approach to his mausoleum, but it was Bernini who brought it to life, designing the angel sculptures in 1668. The three central arches of the bridge are part of the original structure; the end arches were restored and enlarged in 1892–94 during the construction of the Lungotevere embankments.

✗ EATING

Beware, hungry travellers: there are an unholy number of overpriced tourist-traps around the Vatican and St Peter's. A better bet is nearby Prati, which has lots of excellent eateries catering to the lawyers and media execs who work in the area, many at the headquarters of RAI, the Italian state broadcaster.

✗ Vatican City

OLD BRIDGE GELATERIA €

Map p312 (www.gelateriaoldbridge.com; Viale dei Bastioni di Michelangelo 5; gelato €2-5; ⊙9am-2am Mon-Sat, 2.30pm-2am Sun; 🚇Piazza del Risorgimento, 🚇Piazza del Risorgimento) Ideal for a pre- or post-Vatican pick-me-up, this tiny gelateria has been cheerfully dishing up huge portions of delicious gelato for over 20 years. Alongside all the traditional flavours, there are also yoghurts and refreshing sorbets.

PAPAL AUDIENCES

At 11am on Wednesdays, the pope addresses his flock at the Vatican (in July and August in Castel Gandolfo near Rome). For details of how to apply for free tickets, see the **Vatican website** (www.vatican.va/various/prefettura/index_en.html).

When he's in Rome, the Pope blesses the crowd in St Peter's Sq on Sundays at noon. No tickets are required.

✗ Borgo

LA VERANDA RISTORANTE €€€

Map p312 (📞06 687 29 73; www.laveranda.net; Borgo Santo Spirito 73; meals €60-70, brunch €18-27; ⊙12.30-3pm & 7.30-11pm Tue-Sun; 🚇Piazza Pia) A location in Paolo Sorrentino's Oscar-winning film *The Great Beauty,* this fine-dining restaurant sets a memorable stage for quality Italian cuisine. Inside, you can dine under 15th-century Pinturicchio frescoes, while in the warmer months, you can opt for a shady table in the garden. To enjoy the atmosphere for a snip of the regular price, stop by for Sunday brunch.

✗ Prati

FATAMORGANA GELATERIA €

Map p312 (www.gelateriafatamorgana.it; Via Bettolo 7; gelato from €2; ⊙noon-11pm; 🚇Ottaviano–San Pietro) It's off the beaten track, but this superb gelateria is well worth the walk. As well as all the classic flavours there are some wonderfully original creations, such as a mouth-wateringly good *agrumi* (citrus fruit) and a strange but delicious *basilico, miele e noci* (basil, honey and hazelnuts).

FA-BÌO SANDWICHES €

Map p312 (📞06 6452 5810; www.fa-bio.com; Via Germanico 43; sandwiches €5; ⊙10am-5.30pm Mon-Fri, to 4pm Sat) 🍃 Sandwiches, salads and smoothies are all prepared with speed, skill and fresh organic ingredients at this tiny takeaway. Locals and in-the-know visitors come to grab a quick lunchtime bite, and if you can squeeze in the door you'd do well to follow suit.

MONDO ARANCINA
FAST FOOD €

Map p312 (Via Marcantonio Colonna 38; arancine from €2.50; ☺10am-midnight; MLepanto) All sunny yellow ceramics, cheerful crowds and tantalising snacks, this bustling takeaway brings a little corner of Sicily to Rome. Star of the show are the classic fist-sized *arancine,* deep-fried rice balls stuffed with fillers ranging from classic *ragù* to more exotic fare such as truffle risotto and quail's eggs.

GELARMONY
GELATERIA €

Map p312 (Via Marcantonio Colonna 34; gelato €1.50-3; ☺10am-late; MLepanto) Sweet-tooths are spoiled for choice at this popular Sicilian gelateria. There's an ample selection of gelati, but for a typically Sicilian flavour go for pistachio or *cassata* (sponge cake with cream, marzipan, chocolate and candied fruit).

CACIO E PEPE
TRATTORIA €

Map p312 (☎06 321 72 68; Via Avezzana 11; meals €25; ☺12.30-3pm Mon-Sat, 7.30-11pm Mon-Fri; 🚈Piazza Giuseppe Mazzini) This humble eatery is about as hardcore as it gets with its menu of traditional Roman dishes, spartan interior and no-frills service. If you can find a free seat at one of the pavement tables, keep it simple with the namesake *cacio e pepe* (pasta with pecorino cheese and black peppper).

ROMEO
PIZZA, RISTORANTE €€

Map p312 (☎06 3211 0120; www.romeo.roma. it; Via Silla 26a; pizza slices €2.50, meals €45; ☺9am-midnight; MOttaviano–San Pietro) This chic, contemporary outfit is part bakery, part deli, part takeaway, and part restaurant. For a quick bite, there's delicious sliced pizza or you can have a *panino* made up at the deli counter; for a full restaurant meal, the à la carte menu offers a mix of traditional Italian dishes and forward-looking international creations.

SNACK HEAVEN

There are hundreds of bars, cafes and takeaways in the Prati area, but for a quick, cheap bite nowhere beats **Dolce Maniera** (Map p312; Via Barletta 27; snacks €0.30-1; ☺24hr; MOttaviano–San Pietro), an unmarked basement bakery that serves freshly made *cornetti* (€0.30), as well as slabs of pizza, *panini* and an indulgent array of cakes and biscuits.

VELAVEVODETTO AI QUIRITI
LAZIO CUISINE €€

Map p312 (☎06 3600 0009; www.ristorantevelavevodetto.it; Piazza dei Quiriti 5; meals €35; ☺12.30-2.30pm & 7.30-11.30pm; MLepanto) This welcoming restaurant continues to win diners over with its unpretentious, earthy food and honest prices. The menu reads like a directory of Roman staples, and while it's all pretty good, standout choices include *fettuccine con asparagi, guanciale e pecorino* (pasta ribbons with asparagus, guanciale and pecorino cheese) and *polpette di bollito* (fried meat balls).

IL SORPASSO
ITALIAN €€

Map p312 (www.sorpasso.info; Via Properzio 31-33; meals €20-35; ☺7am-1am Mon-Fri, 9am-1am Sat; 🚈Piazza del Risorgimento) A bar-restaurant hybrid sporting a vintage cool look – vaulted stone ceilings, hanging hams, white bare-brick walls – Il Sorpasso is a hot ticket right now. Open throughout the day, it caters to a fashionable neighbourhood crowd, serving everything from pasta specials to aperitifs, *trapizzini* (pyramids of stuffed pizza), and a full dinner menu.

HOSTARIA DINO E TONY
TRATTORIA €€

Map p312 (☎06 3973 3284; Via Leone IV 60; meals €25-30; ☺12.30-3pm & 7-11pm, closed Sun & Aug; MOttaviano-San Pietro) An authentic old-school trattoria, Dino e Tony offers simple, no-frills Roman cooking. Kick off with the monumental antipasto, a minor meal in its own right, before plunging into the trattoria's signature *rigatoni all'amatriciana* (pasta tubes with bacon-like guanciale, chilli and tomato sauce). No credit cards.

DEL FRATE
RISTORANTE, WINE BAR €€

Map p312 (☎06 323 64 37; www.enotecadelfrate. it; Via degli Scipioni 122; meals €40; ☺noon-3pm & 6pm-11.45 Mon-Sat; MOttaviano–San Pietro) Locals love this upmarket wine bar with its simple wooden tables and high-ceilinged brick-arched rooms. There's a formidable wine and cheese list with everything from Sicilian ricotta to Piedmontese gorgonzola, and a small but refined menu of tartars, salads, fresh pastas and main courses.

DAL TOSCANO
TUSCAN €€

Map p312 (☎06 3972 5717; www.ristorantedaltoscano.it; Via Germanico 58-60; meals €45; ☺12.30-3pm & 8-11.15pm Tue-Sun; MOttaviano-San Pietro) Immerse yourself in the tastes of Tuscany at this old-fashioned *ristorante.*

THE VATICAN: A POTTED HISTORY

Established under the terms of the 1929 Lateran Treaty, the Vatican is the modern vestige of the Papal States, the papal fiefdom that ruled Rome and much of central Italy until Italian unification in 1861. It's an independent nation – the world's smallest – and as such has a head of state (the pope) and government, as well as its own postal service and army – the nattily dressed Swiss Guards.

The Vatican's association with Christianity dates to the 1st century when St Peter was crucified head down in Nero's Circus (roughly where St Peter's Sq now stands). To commemorate this, the emperor Constantine commissioned a basilica to be built on the site where the saint was buried.

For centuries, St Peter's Basilica stood at the centre of a densely populated quarter, but it wasn't until the 12th century that the Palazzo Apostolico Vaticano was built. Like much of the Vatican, this fell into disrepair during the exile of the papacy to Avignon (1305–78) and the Great Schism (the period between 1378 and 1417 when rival popes ruled in Rome and Avignon).

Life returned to the Vatican in the 15th and 16th centuries when a series of ambitious Renaissance popes revamped St Peter's and modernised the Palazzo Apostolico Vaticano. The baroque 17th century saw further transformations, most notably the laying of St Peter's Sq.

Meat is a highlight, with cured hams and salamis served as starters, and grilled steaks providing the mains. But before you embark on the colossal char-grilled *bistecca alla Fiorentina* (Florentine-style steak), try the *ribollito,* a thick Tuscan soup. Reservations advised.

OSTERIA DELL'ANGELO　　TRATTORIA €€

Map p312 (✔06 372 94 70; Via Bettolo 24; fixed-price menu €25-35; ⊘12.30-2.30pm Tue-Fri, 8.30-11pm Mon-Sat; ⓂOttaviano–San Pietro) With rugby paraphernalia on the walls and basic wooden tables, this laid-back neighbourhood trattoria is a popular spot for genuine local cuisine. The fixed-price menu features a mixed antipasti, a robust Roman-style pasta and a choice of hearty mains with a side dish. To finish off, spiced biscuits are served with sweet dessert wine. Reservations recommended.

PIZZERIA AMALFI　　PIZZA €€

Map p312 (✔06 3973 3165; Via dei Gracchi 12; pizzas €6.50-9.50, meals €25-30; ⊘noon-3pm & 7pm-12.30am; ⓂOttaviano–San Pietro) This brassy, brightly coloured pizzeria-cum-restaurant flies the flag for Neapolitan cuisine with its buffalo mozzarella starters, soft, doughy pizzas and calzones. If pizza doesn't appeal, you can choose from a lengthy list of grilled meats, pastas, salads and fish dishes. Note that there's a second branch across the road at Via dei Gracchi 5.

ENOTECA LA TORRE　　RISTORANTE €€€

(✔06 4566 8304; www.enotecalatorreroma. com; Villa Laetitia, Lungotevere delle Armi 22; fixed-price lunch menu €55, meals €110; ⊘12.30-2.30pm Tue-Sat, 7.30-10pm Mon-Sat; ⓡLungotevere delle Armi) The art-nouveau Villa Laetitia provides the romantic setting for this refined Michelin-starred restaurant. A relative newcomer to the capital's fine-dining scene, chef Danilo Ciavattino has quickly established himself with his original culinary style and love of authentic country flavours.

RISTORANTE L'ARCANGELO　　RISTORANTE €€€

Map p312 (✔06 321 09 92; www.larcangelo. com; Via Belli 59-61; lunch/dinner tasting menus €25/55, meals €60; ⊘12.30-2.30pm Mon-Fri, 8-11pm Mon-Sat; ⓡPiazza Cavour) Styled as an informal bistro with wood-panelling, leather banquettes and casual table settings, L'Arcangelo enjoys a stellar local reputation. The highlight for many are the classic Roman staples such as carbonara and *amatriciana,* but there's also a limited selection of more innovative modern dishes. The wine list is a further plus, boasting some interesting Italian labels.

SETTEMBRINI　　RISTORANTE €€€

Map p312 (✔06 323 26 17; www.viasettembrini.it; Via Settembrini 25; menus lunch €28-38, dinner €48-65; ⊘12.30-3pm Mon-Fri, 8-11pm Mon-Sat; ⓡPiazza Giuseppe Mazzini) All labels, suits and media gossip, this fashionable restaurant is part of the ever-growing Settembrini empire. Next door is a stylish all-day cafe, while over the way, Libri & Cucina is a laid-back bookshop eatery, and L'Officina an upscale food store. At the casually chic main restaurant expect contemporary Italian cuisine and quality wine to match.

✖ Aurelio

★ PIZZARIUM
PIZZA €

Map p312 (Via della Meloria 43; pizza slices from €3; ⊙11am-10pm; Ⓜ Cipro–Musei Vaticani) Pizzarium, or 'Bonci pizza rustica #pizzarium', as it has recently re-branded itself, serves some of Rome's best sliced pizza. Scissor-cut squares of meticulously crafted dough are topped with original combinations of seasonal ingredients and served on paper trays for immediate consumption. There's also a daily selection of freshly fried *supplì* (crunchy rice croquettes).

🍷 DRINKING & NIGHTLIFE

The quiet area around the Vatican and Prati harbours a few charming wine bars and cafes.

🍷 Prati

★ SCIASCIA CAFFÈ
CAFE

Map p312 (Via Fabio Massimo 80/A; ⊙7.30am-6.30pm Mon-Sat; Ⓜ Ottaviano–San Pietro) The timeless elegance of this polished cafe is perfectly suited to the exquisite coffee it makes. There are various options but nothing can beat the *caffè eccellente*, a velvety smooth espresso served in a delicate cup that has been lined with melted chocolate. The result is nothing short of magnificent.

MAKASAR
WINE BAR, TEAHOUSE

Map p312 (www.makasar.it; Via Plauto 33; ⊙noon-midnight Tue-Thu, to 2am Fri & Sat, 5.30-11.30pm Sun; 🚇 Piazza del Risorgimento) Recharge your batteries with a quiet drink at this oasis of bookish tranquillity. Pick your tipple from the nine-page tea menu or opt for an Italian wine and sit back in the casually stylish, softly lit interior. For something to eat,

there's a small menu of salads, bruschette, baguettes and healthy hot dishes.

PASSAGUAI
WINE BAR

Map p312 (☎06 8745 1358; www.passaguai.it; Via Leto 1; ⊙10am-2am Mon-Fri, 6pm-2am Sat & Sun; 🛜; 🚇 Piazza del Risorgimento) A cosy basement bar with tables in a vaulted interior and on a quiet sidestreet, Passaguai feels pleasingly off-the-radar. It's a great spot for a beer or glass of wine – there's an excellent choice of both – accompanied by cheese and cold cuts, or even a full meal from the limited menu. Free wi-fi.

ART STUDIO CAFÉ
CAFE

Map p312 (☎06 3260 9104; www.artstudiocafe. it; Via dei Gracchi 187a; ⊙7.30am-9pm Mon-Sat; Ⓜ Lepanto) This artsy, light-filled cafe is a lovely spot for a light lunch, afternoon tea or evening aperitif (€6 to €8 depending on your choice of drink). And for the artist in you, it also offers a series of mosaic and craftwork courses (p139).

☆ ENTERTAINMENT

ALEXANDERPLATZ
JAZZ

Map p312 (☎06 3972 1867; www.alexanderplatz-jazzclub.com; Via Ostia 9; ⊙8.30pm-2am, concerts 9.45pm; Ⓜ Ottaviano-San Pietro) Small, intimate and underground, Rome's most celebrated jazz club draws top Italian and international performers and a respectful cosmopolitan crowd. Book a table for the best stage views or if you want to dine to the tunes. Check the website for upcoming gigs.

FONCLEA
LIVE MUSIC

Map p312 (☎06 689 63 02; www.fonclea.it; Via Crescenzio 82a; ⊙7pm-2am Sep-May; 🚇 Piazza del Risorgimento) Fonclea is a great little pub venue, serving up nightly gigs by bands playing everything from jazz and soul to funk, rock and Latin (concerts start at around 9.30pm). Get in the mood with a drink during happy hour (7pm to 8.30pm daily). From June to August, the pub ups sticks and moves to a site by the Tiber.

AUDITORIUM CONCILIAZIONE
LIVE PERFORMANCE

Map p312 (☎06 3281 0333; www.auditoriumconciliazione.it; Via della Conciliazione 4; 🚇 Piazza Pia) On the main approach road to St Peter's Basilica, this large auditorium plays host to a wide range of events – classical and contemporary concerts, cabarets, dance spectacles, theatre productions, film screenings and exhibitions.

TEATRO GHIONE
THEATRE

Map p312 (☑06 637 22 94; www.teatroghione.it; Via delle Fornaci 37; ☑Via di Porta Cavalleggeri) The Teatro Ghione is a big 500-seat theatre near St Peter's that offers a varied program of classic and modern plays, concerts and musicals.

 # SHOPPING

ENOTECA COSTANTINI
WINE

Map p312 (www.pierocostantini.it; Piazza Cavour 16; ☺9am-1pm Tue-Sat, 4.30-8pm Mon-Sat; ☐Piazza Cavour) If you're after a hard-to-find grappa or something special for your wine collection, this historic *enoteca* is the place to try. Opened in 1972, Piero Costantini's superbly stocked shop is a point of reference for aficionados across town with an 800-sq-m basement cellar and a colossal collection of Italian and world wines and more than 1000 spirits.

ANTICA MANUFATTURA CAPPELLI
ACCESSORIES

Map p312 (☑06 3972 5679; www.antica-cappelleria.it; Via degli Scipioni 46; ☺9am-7pm Mon-Fri; ⓂOttaviano–San Pietro) A throwback to a more elegant age, the atelier-boutique of milliner Patrizia Fabri offers a wide range of beautifully crafted hats. Choose from the off-the-peg line of straw Panamas, vintage cloches, felt berets and tweed deerstalkers, or have one made to measure. Prices range from about €70 to €300 and ordered hats can be delivered within the day.

ARTS & CRAFTS COURSES

If the sight of so much art in the Vatican has inspired you, head to the **Art Studio Café** (p138), a bright cafe that doubles as a mosaic and craft school. There are various courses on offer but if time is tight, the one to go for is a two-hour introduction to mosaic-making (€50 or €35 for children). If you're in town for longer, you could sign up for an eight-lesson course in ceramics (€300) or for six lessons in drawing and painting (€180).

Note that short courses can be arranged in English.

RECHICLE
VINTAGE CLOTHING

Map p312 (Piazza dell'Unità 21; ☺11am-1.30pm Tue-Sat, 2.30-7.30pm Mon-Sat; ☐Via Cola di Rienzo) Search out this discreet boutique behind the covered market on Piazza dell'Unità for secondhand styles and vintage fashions. Designer labels are in evidence among the racks of women's clothes, shoes, bags and accessories displayed alongside the occasional vintage piece.

CASTRONI
FOOD & DRINK

Map p312 (www.castronicoladirienzo.com; Via Cola di Rienzo 196; ☺7.45am-8pm Mon-Sat, 9.30am-8pm Sun; ☐Via Cola di Rienzo) This is a real Aladdin's cave of gourmet treats. Towering, ceiling-high shelves groan under the weight of Italian wines and foodie specialties, classic foreign delicacies, and all manner of sweets and chocolates. Adding to the atmosphere are the coffee odours that waft up from the in-store bar.

Monti, Esquilino & San Lorenzo

MONTI | ESQUILINO | PIAZZA DELLA REPUBBLICA & AROUND | SAN LORENZO & BEYOND | SAN LORENZO

Neighbourhood Top Five

1 Visiting the **Palazzo Massimo alle Terme** (p142), with its incredible frescoes from imperial Rome.

2 Lingering at wine bars and pottering around the bohemian-chic neighbourhood of **Monti** (p145).

3 Hobnobbing with the bohos in Pigneto (p151), the iconic working-class district immortalised by Pasolini.

4 Taking in the splendours of **Basilica di Santa Maria Maggiore** (p143).

5 Exploring the underground wonders of **Domus Aurea** (p144), Nero's great, golden palace that now lies beneath Oppian Hill.

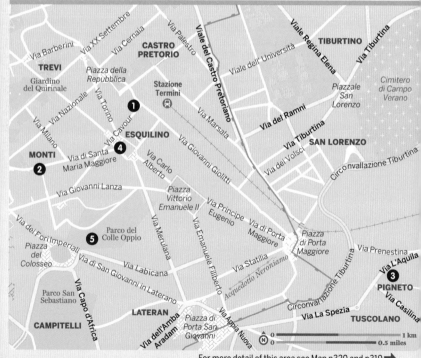

For more detail of this area see Map p320 and p319 ➡

Explore: Monti, Esquilino & San Lorenzo

Esquilino is one of Rome's seven hills, and the area encompasses the sometimes scruffy area around Stazione Termini and Piazza Vittorio Emanuele II. It is also home to some fantastic sights, including some of Rome's finest medieval churches, and the Museo Nazionale Romano: Palazzo Massimo alle Terme, which displays stunning classical art.

Heading downhill, Monti was the ancient city's notorious Suburra slum – a red-light district and the childhood home of Julius Caesar – but is now a charming neighbourhood of inviting eateries, shops and *enoteche* (wine bars) that's ever more popular with tourists and hip locals.

San Lorenzo is a lively student quarter east of Termini, home to the beautiful but little-visited Basilica di San Lorenzo Fuori le Mura. It was the area most damaged by Allied bombing during WWII, which is ironic given the area's vehemently anti-Fascist politics. By day the area feels hungover, a grid of graffitied streets that nonetheless harbour some gemlike boutiques, but after dark it shows its true colours as a student nightlife haunt; it's also home to some excellent restaurants.

A quick tram ride (and on Metro line C when it's finished) southeast, Pigneto also has edge, the Roman equivalent of London's Dalston. Its ever-burgeoning bars and restaurants attract a regular crowd of artists and boho urbanites.

Local Life

➡**Hang-outs** While away an hour or so at Monti's La Bottega del Caffè (p152), watching the world go by.
➡**Shopping** Potter around the vintage and fashion boutiques of Via Serpenti and Via Boschetto in Monti.
➡**Drinking** Have a drink amid artists, bohos, hipsters, and wannabes in buzzing Pigneto.

Getting There & Away

➡**Metro** The Cavour metro stop (line B) is most convenient for Monti, while the Termini (lines A and B), Castro Pretorio (line B) and Vittorio Emanuele (line A) stations are useful for Esquilino. The section of line C that will serve Pigneto won't be completed until 2020.
➡**Bus** Termini is the city's main bus hub, connected to places all over the city. Access Monti from buses stopping on Via Nazionale or Via Cavour. San Lorenzo is served by buses 71 and 492; Pigneto is served by buses 81, 810 and 105, and night bus n12.
➡**Tram** This is an easy way to access San Lorenzo (tram 3) or Pigneto and Centocelle (trams 5, 14 or 19).

Lonely Planet's Top Tip

Don't neglect to visit the oft-overlooked patriarchal **Basilica di San Lorenzo Fuori le Mura** (p147) – it's starkly beautiful.

✕ Best Places to Eat

➡ L'Asino d'Oro (p148)
➡ Trattoria Monti (p150)
➡ Open Colonna (p150)
➡ Panella l'Arte del Pane (p149)

For reviews, see p148.➡

🍷 Best Places to Drink

➡ Ai Tre Scalini (p152)
➡ La Bottega del Caffè (p152)
➡ Il Tiaso (p151)
➡ Co.So (p151)

For reviews, see p152.➡

◉ Best Works of Art

➡ Frescoes at Palazzo Massimo alle Terme (p142)
➡ Michelangelo's colossal Moses (p144)
➡ Fuga's 13th-century facade mosaics (p143)
➡ Richard Meier's modernist Chiesa Dio Padre Misericordioso (p145)

For reviews, see p144.➡

MONTI, ESQUILINO & SAN LORENZO

TOP SIGHT **MUSEO NAZIONALE ROMANO: PALAZZO MASSIMO ALLE TERME**

One of Rome's finest museums, this light-filled treasure trove is packed with spectacular classical art yet remains off the beaten track. It's not to be missed.

We recommend you start your visit on the 2nd floor, so you see its wonders when you're fresh. The sensational frescoes give a more complete picture of the inside of grand ancient Roman villas than you'll see anywhere else in the world. They include scenes from nature, mythology, and domestic and sensual life, using rich, vivid (and expensive) colours.

The showstopper is the decoration covering an entire room from Villa Livia, one of the homes of Augustus' wife Livia Drusilla. The frescoes depict a paradisiacal garden full of a wild tangle of roses, violets, pomegranates, irises and camomile under a deep-blue sky. These decorated a summer triclinium, a large living and dining area built half underground to provide protection from the heat. The lighting mimics the modulation of daylight and highlights the richness of the millennia-old colours.

The ground and 1st floors are devoted to sculpture, examining imperial portraiture as propaganda and including some breathtaking works of art, including the 2nd-century-BC Greek bronzes, the *Boxer* and the *Prince*, a crouching Aphrodite from Villa Adriana, the 2nd-century-BC *Sleeping Hermaphrodite* (pictured above), and the idealised vision of the *Discus Thrower*. Also fascinating are the elaborate bronze fittings that belonged to Caligula's ceremonial ships.

In the basement, the coin collection is far more absorbing than you might expect, tracing the Roman Empire's propaganda offensive via coinage. There's also jewellery dating back several millennia that looks as good as new, and the disturbing remains of a mummified eight-year-old girl, the only known example of mummification dating from the Roman Empire.

DON'T MISS...

➡ The *Boxer*
➡ *Sleeping Hermaphrodite*
➡ Frescoes from Villa Livia

PRACTICALITIES

➡ Map p320
➡ ☎06 3996 7700
➡ www.coopculture.it
➡ Largo di Villa Peretti 1
➡ adult/reduced €7/3.50
➡ ⊙9am-7.45pm Tue-Sun
➡ Ⓜ Termini

TOP SIGHT
BASILICA DI SANTA MARIA MAGGIORE

One of Rome's four patriarchal basilicas, this monumental church stands on the summit of the Esquilino Hill, on the spot where snow is said to have fallen in the summer of AD 358. To commemorate the event, every year on 5 August thousands of white petals are released from the basilica's coffered ceiling.

Outside, the 18.78m-high column came from the basilica of Massenzio in the Roman Forum. The church exterior is decorated by 13th-century mosaics, protected by a baroque porch. The 75m belfry, the highest in Rome, is 14th-century Romanesque.

The great interior retains its 5th-century structure, as well as the original mosaics in the triumphal arch and nave. The central image in the apse, signed by Jacopo Torriti, dates from the 13th century.

Twelfth-century Cosmati paving covers the nave floor. The baldachin over the high altar practically squirms with gilt cherubs; the altar itself is a porphyry sarcophagus, said to contain the relics of St Matthew and other martyrs. Gian Lorenzo Bernini and his father Pietro are buried to the right of the altar, their graves marked by a simple stone embedded in the floor.

Don't miss the upper loggia, the extraordinary creation of Ferdinando Fuga, where you'll get a closer look at the 13th-century mosaics, created by Filippo Rusuti. You'll also see Bernini's baroque helical staircase.

DON'T MISS...

➡ The loggia
➡ Cosmatesque floor
➡ Jacopo Torriti apse mosaics

PRACTICALITIES

➡ Map p320
➡ Piazza Santa Maria Maggiore
➡ basilica/museum/loggia/archaeological site free/€3/5/5
➡ ⊘7am-7pm, museum & loggia 9am-5.30pm
➡ ▣Piazza Santa Maria Maggiore

◉ SIGHTS

◉ Monti

BASILICA DI SAN PIETRO
IN VINCOLI
BASILICA

Map p320 (Piazza di San Pietro in Vincoli 4a; ⏰8am-12.20pm & 3-7pm summer, to 6pm winter; Ⓜ︎Cavour) Pilgrims and art lovers flock to this 5th-century basilica for two reasons: to marvel at Michelangelo's colossal *Moses* (1505) sculpture and to see the chains that supposedly bound St Peter when he was imprisoned in the Carcere Mamertino (near the Roman Forum).

Access to the church is via a flight of steps through a low arch that leads up from Via Cavour.

The church was built specially to house the shackles of St Peter, which had been sent to Constantinople after the saint's death, but were later returned as relics. They arrived in two pieces and legend has it that when they were reunited they miraculously joined together. They are now displayed under the altar.

To the right of the altar, Michelangelo's *Moses* forms the centrepiece of his unfinished tomb for Pope Julius II. The prophet strikes a muscular pose with well-defined biceps, a magnificent waist-length beard and two small horns sticking out of his head. These were inspired by a mistranslation of a biblical passage: where the original said that rays of light issued from Moses' face, the translator wrote 'horns'. Michelangelo was aware of the mistake, but gave Moses horns anyway. Flanking Moses are statues of Leah and Rachel, probably completed by Michelangelo's students.

The tomb, despite its imposing scale, was never finished – Michelangelo originally envisaged 40 statues, but got sidetracked by the Sistine Chapel – and Pope Julius II was buried in St Peter's Basilica.

◉ Esquilino

BASILICA DI SANTA
MARIA MAGGIORE
BASILICA

See p143.

DOMUS AUREA
ARCHAEOLOGICAL SITE

Map p320 (Golden House; ☑06 3996 7700; www.coopculture.it; Viale della Domus Aurea; admisson €10; ⏰guided tours Sat & Sun; Ⓜ︎Colosseo) Nero had his Domus Aurea constructed after the fire of AD 64 (which it's rumoured he had started to clear the area). Named after the gold that lined its facade and interiors, it was a huge complex covering up to a third of the city. The excavated part of the site has been repeatedly closed due to flooding, but opened for weekend guided tours from late 2014; check the website for current opening status.

The palace was full of architectural invention, a more splendid palace than had ever been seen before. However, Nero's successors attempted to raze all trace of his megalomania. Vespasian drained Nero's ornamental lake and, in a symbolic gesture, built the Colosseum in its place. Domitian built a palace on the Palatino, while Trajan sacked and destroyed the 1st floor and then entombed the lower level in earth and used it for the foundations of his public baths complex, which was abandoned by the 6th century. This burial of the palace preserved it; the section that has been excavated lies beneath Oppian Hill. Wear warm clothes when visiting as the palace now lies underground and is damp. Remarkably, the humidity has helped preserve the frescoes in the chambers, though this may only be seen in one small cleaned area – the rest have not been restored. Tours last an hour and 15 minutes and are guided by archaeologists who are extremely knowledgable about the site.

During the Renaissance, artists lowered themselves into the ruins, climbing across the top of Trajan's rubble to study the frescoed grottoes, and Raphael reproduced some of their motifs in his work on the Vatican.

MUSEO NAZIONALE D'ARTE
ORIENTALE
MUSEUM

Map p320 (☑06 4697 4823; www.museorientale.beniculturali.it; Via Merulana 248; adult/reduced €6/3; ⏰9am-2pm Tue, Wed & Fri, 9am-7.30pm Thu, Sat & Sun; Ⓜ︎Vittorio Emanuele) This little-visited but impressive collection is housed in the grandiose 19th-century Palazzo Brancaccio. It includes 5th-century-BC Iranian glassware, items from the ancient settlement of Swat in Pakistan, 12th-century homewares from Afghanistan, engraved ritual vessels from China dating to between 800 BC and 900 BC, and a new Korean gallery with bronzes, seals and contemporary art.

CHIESA DI SANTA CROCE IN
GERUSALEMME
CHURCH

Map p319 (www.santacroceroma.it; Piazza di Santa Croce in Gerusalemme 12; ⏰7am-12.45pm & 3.30-7.30pm; ▣Piazza di Porta Maggiore)

One of Rome's seven pilgrimage churches, the Chiesa di Santa Croce was founded in 320 by St Helena, mother of the emperor Constantine, in the grounds of her palace. It takes its name from the Christian relics here – including a piece of Christ's cross and St Thomas' doubting finger – that St Helena brought to Rome from Jerusalem, housed in a chapel to the left of the altar.

Of particular note are the lovely 15th-century Renaissance apse frescoes representing the legends of Christ's cross.

NATIONAL MUSEUM OF MUSICAL INSTRUMENTS
MUSEUM

Map p319 (✆06 3 28 10; Piazza di Santa Croce in Gerusalemm; adult/reduced €5/2.50; ⊙9am-7pm Tue-Sun; 🚇Piazza di Porta Maggiore) This little-known museum behind the church of Santa Croce stands on the site of the former home of St Helena. It's undeservedly and re-freshingly deserted, with a collection of over 3000 exquisite musical instruments that in-cludes gorgeously painted, handle-operated 18th-century Neapolitan street pianos, and one of the oldest known pianos (1722).

CHIESA DI SANTA PUDENZIANA
CHURCH

Map p320 (www.stpudenziana.org; Via Urbana 160; ⊙9am-noon & 3-6pm; Ⓜ Cavour) The church of Rome's Filipino community contains a spar-kling 4th-century apse mosaic, the oldest of its kind in the city. An enthroned Christ is flanked by two female figures who are crowning St Peter and St Paul; on either side of them are the apostles dressed as Roman senators. Unfortunately, you can only see 10 of the original 12 apostles, as a barbarous 16th-century facelift lopped off two and am-putated the legs of the others.

CHIESA DI SANTA PRASSEDE
CHURCH

Map p320 (Via Santa Prassede 9a; ⊙7.30am-noon & 4-6.30pm; 🚇Piazza Santa Maria Maggiore) Famous for its brilliant mosaics, this 9th-century church is dedicated to St Praxedes, an early Christian heroine who hid Chris-tians fleeing persecution and buried those she couldn't save in a well. The position of the well is now marked by a marble disc on the floor of the nave.

The mosaics, produced by artists who were specially brought in by Pope Paschal I from Byzantium, bear all the hallmarks of their eastern creators, with bold gold back-grounds and a marked Christian symbol-ism. The apse mosaics depict Christ flanked by Sts Peter, Pudentiana and Zeno on the right, and Paul, Praxedes and Pope Paschal

WORTH A DETOUR

CHIESA DIO PADRE MISERICORDIOSO

It's worth making the effort to visit Rome's minimalist church, **Chiesa Dio Padre Misericordioso** (www.diopadre-misericordioso.it/; Via Francesco Tovaglieri 147; ⊙7.30am-12.30pm & 4-7.30pm; 🚇Via Francesco Tovaglieri 147), for a refreshing departure from the excesses of baroque or classicism. This beautiful white Richard Meier creation is pared down, resulting in a remarkable-feeling purity. It's built out of white concrete, stucco, gleaming travertine and 976 sq m of glass, making use of the play of light both inside and out.

on the left. All the figures have golden ha-los except for Paschal, whose head is shad-owed by a blue nimbus to indicate that he was still alive at the time. Further treasures await in the heavily mosaiced **Cappella di San Zenone**, including a piece of the col-umn to which Christ was tied when he was flogged, brought back from Jerusalem – it's in the glass case on the right.

CHIESA DI SAN MARTINO AI MONTI
CHURCH

Map p320 (Viale del Monte Oppio 28; ⊙9 am-noon & 4.30-7pm; Ⓜ Cavour) This was already a place of worship in the 3rd century, when Christians would meet in what was then the home of a Roman named Equitius. In the 4th century, after Christianity was le-galised, a church was constructed, and later rebuilt in the 6th and 9th centuries. It was then completely transformed by Filippo Ga-gliardi in the 1650s.

It's of particular interest for Gagliardi's frescoes showing the Basilica di San Gio-vanni in Laterano before it was rebuilt in the mid-17th century and St Peter's Basilica before it assumed its present 16th-century look. Remnants of the more distant past include the ancient Corinthian columns di-viding the nave and aisles.

CHIESA DI SANTA LUCIA IN SELCI
CHURCH

Map p320 (Via in Selci 82; ⊙8am-noon & 2-6pm; Ⓜ Cavour) The small Chiesa di Santa Lucia in Selci is a convent church devoted to the 4th-century martyr St Lucy. It dates to some time before the 8th century, but was reconstructed by Carlo Maderno in the 16th century, who kept it within the then monastery, hence the lack of a facade. It

ℹ COMBINED TICKET

Note that the ticket (adult/reduced €7/3.50, or €10/6.50 when there's an exhibition) for the Crypta Balbi and Palazzo Altemps (Centro Storico), Palazzo Massimo, Terme di Diocleziano, and Aula Ottagona (Termini) combines admission for all five sites but is only valid for three days, so plan accordingly. Another worthwhile investment could be an Archaeologia Card (€27.50; valid seven days), which covers these sights as well as the Colosseum, Palatino, Terme di Caracalla, Villa dei Quintilli and Cecilia Metella. It's available at any of the sights.

was later restored by Borromini in the 17th century.

PIAZZA VITTORIO EMANUELE II   PIAZZA

Map p320 (Ⓜ️Vittorio Emanuele) Laid out in the late 19th century as the centrepiece of an upmarket residential district, but today with a rundown, seedy feel, Rome's biggest square is a grassy expanse, surrounded by speeding traffic, porticoes and bargain stores. Within the fenced-off central section are the ruins of **Trofei di Mario**, once a fountain at the end of an aqueduct.

In the northern corner, the **Chiesa di Sant'Eusebio** is popular with pet-owners who bring their companions to be blessed on St Anthony's feast day (17 January).

PORTA MAGGIORE   MONUMENT

Map p319 (Piazza di Porta Maggiore; 🚋Porta Maggiore) Porta Maggiore was built by Claudius in AD 52. Then, as now, it was a major road junction under which passed the two main southbound roads, Via Prenestina and Via Labicana (modern-day Via Casilina). The arch supported two aqueducts – the Acqua Claudia and the Acqua Aniene Nuova – and was later incorporated into the Aurelian Wall.

MUSEO STORICO DELLA LIBERAZIONE   MUSEUM

Map p319 (✒️06 700 38 66; www.viatasso.eu; Via Tasso 145; ⊙9.30am-12.30pm Tue-Sun, 3.30-7.30pm Tue, Thu & Fri; Ⓜ️Manzoni) FREE Now a small, chilling museum, Via Tasso 145 was the headquarters of the German SS during the Nazi occupation of Rome (1943–44). Members of the Resistance were interro-

gated, tortured and imprisoned in the cells and you can still see graffiti scrawled on the walls by condemned prisoners.

Exhibits chart the events of the occupation, covering the persecution of the Jews, the underground resistance and the Fosse Ardeatina massacre.

⊙ Piazza della Repubblica & Around

MUSEO NAZIONALE ROMANO: PALAZZO MASSIMO ALLE TERME   MUSEUM

See p142.

MUSEO NAZIONALE ROMANO: TERME DI DIOCLEZIANO   MUSEUM

Map p320 (✒️06 3996 7700; www.coopculture.it; Viale Enrico de Nicola 78; adult/reduced €7/3.50; ⊙9am-7.30pm Tue-Sun; Ⓜ️Termini) The Terme di Diocleziano was ancient Rome's largest bath complex, covering about 13 hectares and with a capacity for 3000 people. Today its ruins constitute part of the impressive Museo Nazionale Romano. This branch of the National Roman Museum supplies a fascinating insight into Roman life through memorial inscriptions and other artefacts. Outside, the vast, elegant cloister was constructed from drawings by Michelangelo.

It's lined with classical sarcophagi, headless statues and huge sculptured animal heads, thought to have come from the Foro di Traiano.

Elsewhere in the museum, look out for exhibits relating to cults and the early development of Christianity and Judaism. There's a particularly interesting section about amulets and spells, which were cast on neighbours and acquaintances to bring them bad luck and worse. Upstairs exhibits tomb objects dating from the 11th to 9th centuries BC, including jewellery and amphora.

As you wander the museum, you'll see glimpses of the original complex, which was completed in the early 4th century as a state-of-the-art combination of baths, libraries, concert halls and gardens – the Aula Ottagona and Basilica di Santa Maria degli Angeli buildings were also once part of this enormous endeavour. It fell into disrepair after the aqueduct that fed the baths was destroyed by invaders in about AD 536.

AULA OTTAGONA   ARCHAEOLOGICAL SITE

Map p320 (Piazza della Repubblica; ⊙varies; Ⓜ️Repubblica) The soaring, atmospheric Octagonal Hall was part of the ancient structure of the Terme di Diocleziano, and today forms a beautiful vaulted space that houses temporary exhibitions, often of sculpture.

BASILICA DI SANTA MARIA
DEGLI ANGELI   BASILICA

Map p320 (www.santamariadegliangeliroma.it; Piazza della Repubblica; Ⓜ Repubblica) This hulking basilica occupies what was once the central hall of Diocletian's baths complex. It was originally designed by Michelangelo, but only the great vaulted ceiling remains from his plans.

CHIESA DI SAN PAOLO
ENTRO LE MURA   CHURCH

Map p320 (www.stpaulsrome.it; cnr Via Nazionale & Via Napoli; ⊗9.30am-4.30pm Mon-Fri; 🚇Via Nazionale) With its stripy neo-Gothic exterior, Rome's American Episcopal church has some unusual 19th-century mosaics, designed by the Birmingham-born artist Edward Burne-Jones.

PALAZZO DELLE
ESPOSIZIONI   CULTURAL CENTRE

Map p320 (☑06 3996 7500; www.palazzoesposizioni.it; Via Nazionale 194; ⊗10am-8pm Tue-Thu & Sun, to 10.30pm Fri & Sat; 🚇Via Nazionale) This huge neoclassical palace was built in 1882 as an exhibition centre, though it has since served as HQ for the Italian Communist Party, a mess hall for Allied servicemen, a polling station and even a public loo. Nowadays it's a splendid cultural hub, with cathedral-scale exhibition spaces hosting blockbuster art exhibitions and sleekly designed art labs, as well as a bookshop and cafe.

The building also hosts everything from multimedia events to concert performances, film screenings and conferences, and has an excellent glass-roofed restaurant that proffers a bargain buffet lunch (€16) Monday to Friday; weekend brunch costs €30.

PIAZZA DELLA REPUBBLICA   PIAZZA

Map p320 (Ⓜ Repubblica) Flanked by grand 19th-century neoclassical colonnades, this landmark piazza was laid out as part of Rome's post-unification makeover. It follows the lines of the semicircular *exedra* (benched portico) of Diocletian's baths complex and was originally known as Piazza Esedra.

First built in 1888 to designs by Alessandro Guerrieri that featured four lions, **Fontana delle Naiadi** aroused puritanical ire when it was unveiled by architect Mario Rutelli in 1901. The nudity of the four naiads (water nymphs) who surround the

central figure of Glaucus wrestling a fish, was considered too provocative – how Italy has changed! Each reclines on a creature symbolising water in a different form: a water snake (rivers), a swan (lakes), a lizard (streams) and a sea-horse (oceans).

⊙ San Lorenzo & Beyond

★BASILICA DI SAN LORENZO
FUORI LE MURA   BASILICA

Map p319 (www.basilicasanlorenzo.it; Piazzale San Lorenzo; ⊗8am-noon & 4-6.30pm; 🚇Piazzale del Verano) This is one of Rome's four patriarchal basilicas and is an atmospheric, tranquil edifice that's starker than many of the city's grand churches, a fact that only adds to its breathtaking beauty. It was the only one of Rome's major churches to have suffered bomb damage in WWII, and although it is a hotchpotch of rebuilds and restorations, it still feels harmonious.

St Lawrence was burned to death in AD 258, and Constantine had the original basilica constructed in the 4th century over his burial place, which was rebuilt 200 years later. Subsequently, a nearby 5th-century church dedicated to the Virgin Mary was incorporated into the building, resulting in the church you see today. The nave, portico and much of the decoration date to the 13th century.

Highlights are the Cosmati floor and the frescoed portico, depicting events from St Lawrence's life. The remains of St Lawrence and St Stephen are in the church crypt beneath the high altar. A pretty barrel-vaulted cloister contains inscriptions and sarcophagi and leads to the Catacombe di Santa Ciriaca, where St Lawrence was initially buried.

CIMITERO DI CAMPO VERANO   CEMETERY

Map p319 (☑06 4923 6349; www.cimiteridiroma.it; Piazzale del Verano; ⊗7.30am-6pm Apr-Sep, to 5pm Oct-Mar; 🚇Piazzale del Verano) The city's largest cemetery dates to the Napoleonic occupation of Rome between 1804 and 1814, when an edict ordered that the city's dead must be buried outside the city walls. Between the 1830s and the 1980s virtually all Catholics who died in Rome (with the exception of popes, cardinals and royalty) were buried here. If you're in the area, it's worth a look for its grand tombs. On 2 November (All Souls' Day), thousands of Romans flock to the cemetery to leave flowers on the tombs of loved ones.

MONTI, ESQUILINO & SAN LORENZO SIGHTS

148

VILLA ALDOBRANDINI

If you're in need of a breather around Via Nazionale or are in search of somewhere for a picnic, then take Via Mazzarino off the main road and walk up the steps, past 2nd-century ruins, where you'll find a graceful, sculpture-dotted garden, with gravelled paths and tranquil lawns, raised approximately 10m above street level.

These are the grounds of **Villa Aldobrandini** (Map p320; ⊙garden dawn-dusk; ⊠Via Nazionale), overlooked by the house built here in the 16th century by Cardinal Pietro Aldobrandini to hold his extensive art collection. Today the villa is closed to the public and houses the headquarters of an international law institute.

PASTIFICIO CERERE
GALLERY

Map p319 (☎06 4542 2960; www.pastificiocerere.com; Via degli Ausoni 7; ⊙3-7pm Mon-Fri, 4-8pm Sat; ⊠Via Tiburtina) An elegant former pasta factory that hung up its spaghetti racks in 1960 after 55 years of business, this is now a hub of Rome's contemporary art scene, with regular shows in the building's gallery and courtyards.

The Pastificio came to prominence in the 1980s as home of the Nuova Scuola Romana (New Roman School), a group of six artists who are still here, alongside a new generation that includes Maurizio Savini, famous for his pink chewing gum sculptures.

 EATING

Monti

CIURI CIURI
PASTRIES €

Map p320 (☎06 4544 4548; Via Leonina 18; snacks around €3; ⊙8.30am-midnight Sun-Thu, to 2am Fri & Sat; ⊠Cavour) Oh yes...what's not to love about a Sicilian ice-cream and pastry shop? Pop by for delectable homemade sweets such as freshly filled *cannoli* (ricotta-filled tubes), *cassata* (sponge with cream, marzipan, chocolate and candied fruit) and *pasticini di mandorla* (almond pastries), all available in bite-sized versions. It's not all sweet: there are also excellent freshly made *arancine* (fried rice balls) and other snacks. Eat in or out.

FATAMORGANA – MONTI
GELATERIA €

Map p320 (Piazza Zingari; gelato from €2.50; ⊙1pm-12.30am; ⊠Cavour) Not only is Fatamorgana one of Rome's finest artisanal gelaterias, offering delicious, gluten-free flavours, but you can sit and eat your choice out on the pretty square. The large photo behind the counter is from the classic film *La Banda degli Onesti* (starring Totò), as the scene was shot on this corner.

GELATARIA DELL'ANGELETTO
GELATERIA

Map p320 (Via dell'Angeletto 15; gelato from €2.50; ⊙noon-midnight; ⊠Cavour) An outpost of gelato-masters Dei Gracchi, who have their original gelateria close to the Vatican, this has many wonderful seasonal flavours, from pear and caramel to apple and cinnamon, and particularly *fantastico* pistachio.

FORNO DA MILVIO
PIZZA €

Map p320 (☎06 4893 0145; Via dei Serpenti 7; pizza slice from €3.50; ⊙6.30am-midnight; ⊠Cavour) A small *pizza al taglio* (by the slice) place that's always busy and serves up a great range of deliciously light and crispy pizza. It's a fast-and-tasty option when you want a cheap lunch in the Colosseum–Monti area. Eat in or takeaway.

★L'ASINO D'ORO
ITALIAN €€

Map p320 (☎06 4891 3832; Via del Boschetto 73; meals €45; ⊙12.30-2.30pm Sat, 7.30-11pm Tue-Sat; ⊠Cavour) This fabulous restaurant was transplanted from Orvieto and its Umbrian origins resonate in Lucio Sforza's delicious, exceptional cooking. It's unfussy yet innovative, with dishes featuring lots of flavourful contrasts, such as lamb meatballs with pear and blue cheese. Save room for the amazing desserts. For such excellent food, this intimate, informal yet classy place is one of Rome's best deals. Hours are changeable so call ahead.

TEMAKINHO
SUSHI €€

Map p320 (www.temakinho.com; Via dei Serpenti 16; meals €40; ⊙12.30-3.30pm & 7pm-midnight; ⊠Cavour) In a city where most food is still resolutely (though deliciously) Italian, this Brazilian-Japanese hybrid serves up sushi and ceviche, and makes for a refreshing, sensational change. As well as delicious, strong *caipirinhas*, which combine Brazilian *cachaça*, sugar, lime and fresh fruit, there are *sakehinhas* made with sake. It's very popular so make sure you book.

DALL'ANTÒ
CREPERIE

Map p320 (☎06 678 07 12; Via della Madonna dei Monti 16; ☺noon-11pm Tue-Sat, noon-3pm Sun; Ⓜ Cavour) In an unusual little labour of love, the owner, Antonio, takes ancient recipes from Tuscany and Liguria, and creates pancakes, which you can watch him creating on the state-of-the-art cooking equipment. Choose from *farinata* (made from chickpea flour), *testarolo* (a wheat pancake with pesto), or *necci* (made from chestnut flour). He's hugely enthusiastic and this is a unique place.

DA VALENTINO
TRATTORIA €€

Map p320 (☎06 488 06 43; Via del Boschetto; meals €25-30; ☺1-2.45pm & 7.30-11.30pm Mon-Sat; Ⓜ Cavour) The vintage 1930s sign outside says 'Birra Peroni', and inside the lovely old-fashioned feel indicates that not much has changed here for years, with black-and-white photographs on the walls, white tablecloths and tiled floors. Come here when you're in the mood for grilled *scamorza* (a type of Italian cheese, similar to mozzarella), as this is the main focus of the menu, with myriad variations: served with tomato and rocket, tomato and gorgonzola, cheese and artichokes, grilled meats, hamburgers and so on.

URBANA 47
ITALIAN €€

Map p320 (☎06 4788 4006; Via Urbana 47; meals €45; Ⓜ Cavour) Opened by the owners of a vintage furniture store, this urbane, informal restaurant is filled with retro furnishings that are all for sale. Chef Alessandro Miotto operates the '0km' rule (as much as possible), meaning that most things you eat here will be sourced from Lazio.

LA CARBONARA
TRATTORIA €€

Map p320 (☎06 482 51 76; Via Panisperna 214; meals €40; ☺Mon-Sat; Ⓜ Cavour) On the go since 1906, this busy restaurant was favoured by the infamous Ragazzi di Panisperna, the group of young physicists whose discoveries led to the construction of the first atomic bomb. The waiters are brusque, it crackles with energy and the interior is covered in graffiti – tradition dictates that diners should leave their mark in a message on the wall.

✖ Esquilino

PANELLA L'ARTE DEL PANE
BAKERY, CAFE €

Map p320 (☎06 487 24 35; Via Merulana 54; snacks about €3.50; ☺8am-11pm Mon-Thu, to

midnight Fri & Sat, 8.30am-4pm Sun; Ⓜ Vittorio Emanuele) With a magnificent array of *pizza al taglio, arancini*, focaccia, fried croquettes and pastries, this smart bakery-cum-cafe is good any time of the day. The outside tables are ideal for a leisurely breakfast or chilled evening drink, or you can perch on a high stool and lunch on something from the sumptuous counter display.

ROSCIOLI
PIZZA, BAKERY €

Map p320 (Via Buonarroti 48; pizza slices €3.50; ☺7am-8pm Mon-Sat; Ⓜ Vittorio Emanuele) Off-the-track branch of this splendid deli-bakery-pizzeria, with delish *pizza al taglio*, pasta dishes and other goodies that make it ideal for a swift lunch or picnic stock-up. It's on a road leading off Piazza Vittorio Emanuele II.

PASTICCERIA REGOLI
BAKERY €

Map p320 (Via dello Statuto 60; ☺6.30am-8.20pm Wed-Sun; Ⓜ Vittorio Emanuele) Buns filled with whipped cream, light-as-air little cream puffs (perfect as a present when you're invited to someone's house for a meal), *crostata* (latticed jam tarts), and excellent ice cream are the name of the game at this much-loved Roman institution, with elegant pale-brick arches, chandeliers, and a cafe next door.

GAINN
KOREAN €

Map p320 (☎06 4436 0160; Via dei Mille 18; meals around €25; ☺lunch & dinner Mon-Sat; Ⓜ Termini) A serene choice close to Rome's main train station, where you'll get a warm, friendly welcome, and dishes come with an array of enticing little salads and pickles, known as kimchi. The diners here are mainly Korean and Chinese, and the good food makes for a refreshing change if you're hankering after something non-Italian.

LA GALLINA BIANCA
PIZZA €

Map p320 (☎06 474 37 77; Via A Rosmini 9; pizzas €7-10; ☺noon-3pm & 6pm-midnight; Ⓜ Termini) The 'White Hen' is a friendly, handy pizzeria amid the minefield of tourist trash around Termini, serving thick-crust Neapolitan pizzas made from slow-risen dough. It's large and airy, decorated in cool pale blue and old wood, with shaded outside seating on a not-too-busy street.

PALAZZO DEL FREDDO DI GIOVANNI FASSI
GELATERIA €

Map p319 (☎06 446 47 40; www.palazzodel-freddo.it; Via Principe Eugenio 65; gelato from

€1.60; ⊙noon-midnight Tue-Sat, 10am-midnight Sun; Ⓜ️Vittorio Emanuele) A great back-in-time barn of a place, sprinkled with vintage gelato-making machinery, Fassi is a classic Rome experience, hugely popular with Korean and Chinese residents and visitors, specialising in flavours such as *riso* (rice), pistachio and *nocciola* (hazelnut). The granita, served with dollops of cream, deserves special mention.

INDIAN FAST FOOD INDIAN €

Map p320 (☎️06 446 07 92; Via Mamiani 11; curries €6-7.50; ⊙11am-10.30pm; Ⓜ️Vittorio Emanuele) Formica tables, Hindi hits, neon lights, chapatti and naan, lip-smacking samosas and bhajis, and a simple selection of main curry dishes: when you're feasting at this authentic joint you can almost imagine yourself in India.

TRATTORIA MONTI RISTORANTE €€

Map p320 (☎️06 446 65 73; Via di San Vito 13a; meals €45; ⊙12.45-2.45pm Tue-Sun, 7.45-11pm Tue-Sat, closed Aug; Ⓜ️Vittorio Emanuele) The Camerucci family runs this elegant brick-arched place, proffering top-notch traditional cooking from the Marches region. There are wonderful *fritti* (fried things), delicate pastas and ingredients such as *pecorino di fossa* (sheep's cheese aged in caves), goose, swordfish and truffles. Try the egg-yolk *tortelli* pasta. Desserts are delectable, including apple pie with *zabaglione*. Word has spread, so book ahead.

TRIMANI RISTORANTE, WINE BAR €€

Map p320 (☎️06 446 96 30; Via Cernaia 37b; meals €45; ⊙11.30am-3pm & 5.30pm-12.30am Mon-Sat; Ⓜ️Termini) Part of the Trimani family's wine empire (their shop just round the corner stocks about 4000 international labels), this is an unpretentious yet highly professional *enoteca*, with knowledgable, multilingual staff. It's Rome's biggest wine bar and has a vast selection of Italian regional wines as well as an ever-changing food menu – tuck into local salami and cheese or fresh oysters.

AGATA E ROMEO ITALIAN €€€

Map p320 (☎️06 446 61 15; Via Carlo Alberto 45; meals €120; ⊙12.30-2.30pm & 7.30-11.30pm Mon-Fri; Ⓜ️Vittorio Emanuele) This elegant, restrained place was one of Rome's gastronomic pioneers and still holds its own as one of the city's most gourmet takes on Roman cuisine. Chef Agata Parisella prepares the menus and runs the kitchen, offering

creative uses of Roman traditions; husband Romeo curates the wine cellar; and daughter Maria Antonietta chooses the cheeses. Bookings essential.

✖ Piazza della Repubblica & Around

DOOZO JAPANESE €€

Map p320 (☎️06 481 56 55; Via Palermo 51; set lunch €16-26, set dinner €15-25; ⊙12.30-3pm & 7.30-11pm Tue-Sat, 7.30-10.30pm Sun; ▣Via Nazionale) Doozo (meaning 'welcome') is a spacious, Zen restaurant-bookshop and gallery that offers tofu, sushi, *soba* (buckwheat noodle) soup and other Japanese delicacies, plus beer and green tea in wonderfully serene surroundings. It's a little oasis, particularly the shady courtyard garden.

★OPEN COLONNA ITALIAN €€€

Map p320 (☎️06 4782 2641; www.antonellocolonna.it; Via Milano 9a; meals €20-80; ⊙12.30-3.30pm Tue-Sun, 8-11.30pm Tue-Sat; ▣; ▣Via Nazionale) Spectacularly set at the back of Palazzo delle Esposizioni, superchef Antonello Colonna's superb restaurant is tucked onto a mezzanine floor under an extraordinary glass roof. The cuisine is new Roman: innovative takes on traditional dishes, cooked with wit and flair. The best thing? There's a more basic but still delectable fixed two-course lunch for €16, and Saturday and Sunday brunch is €30, served in the dramatic, glass-ceilinged hall, with a terrace for sunny days.

✖ San Lorenzo & Beyond

FORMULA UNO PIZZA €

Map p319 (☎️06 445 38 66; Via degli Equi 13; pizzas from €6.50; ⊙7.30pm-1.30am Mon-Sat; ▣Via Tiburtina, ▣Via dei Reti) This basic, historic San Lorenzo pizzeria is as adrenaline-fuelled as its name: waiters zoom around under whirring fans, delivering tomato-loaded bruschetta, fried courgette flowers, *supplì al telefono* and bubbling thin-crust pizza to eternal crowds of feasting students and wallet-savvy locals and tourists.

TRAM TRAM OSTERIA €€

Map p319 (☎️06 49 04 16; www.tramtram.it; Via dei Reti 44; meals around €45; ⊙12.30-3.30pm & 7.30-11.30pm Tue-Sun; ▣Via Tiburtina) This trendy yet old-style lace-curtained trattoria takes its name from the trams that

PIGNETO & CENTOCELLE

If you feel like a night bar-hopping to see where the evening takes you, head to Pigneto. Over the past decade, this working-class quarter has undergone a rapid metamorphosis to arty, hipster nightlife zone. It was previously immortalised by film-maker Pier Paolo Pasolini, who used to hang out at Necci and filmed *Accattone* (1961) here. There's a small-town feel, with low-rise houses and graffiti-covered narrow streets. The action centres on Via del Pigneto, but there are also bars in the surrounding streets. The area also harbours some of Rome's best street art (listed on the street art map available from tourist kiosks). To reach here, take a tram from Termini to Via Prenestina. Nearby Centocelle is becoming a good place to to eat amid in-the-know Roman foodies. It's accessible via Tram 5, the Metro Parco di Centocelle, or buses 14, 105 or 150.

Eating

I Porchettoni (Via del Pigneto; meals around €25; ⊘noon-1am) Lively spot where you can feast on *porchetta* (pork roasted with herbs), mozzarella, earthy cured meats and simple pastas at paper-table-clothed trestle tables.

Osteria Qui se Magna! (☑06 27 48 03; Via del Pigneto 307; meals €25; ⊘Mon-Sat) A small, simple place adorned with gingham paper tablecloths with a couple of outside tables, here you can eat heavenly, hearty, home-cooked food.

Necci (☑06 9760 1552; www.necci1924.com; Via Fanfulla da Lodi 68; dinner around €45, lunch mains around €8; ⊘8am-2am; 🛜) Necci opened as gelataria in 1924 and later became a favourite of Pasolini. Good for a drink or a meal, it serves up sophisticated Italian cooking to an eclectic crowd of all ages, with a lovely, leafy garden terrace.

Primo (☑06 701 38 27;www.primoalpigneto.it; Via del Pigneto 46;meals around €45; ⊘7.30pm-2am Tue-Sat, Sun lunch) Flagship of the Pigneto scene, Primo is still buzzing after several years. Service is slow, though.

Mazzo (☑06 6496 2847; info@thefooders.it; Via delle Rose 54; meals €45; ⊘6pm-midnight Tue-Sun, lunch Sun) Roman cuisine is given a twist here by innovative young chefs, Francesca Barreca and Marco Baccanelli. Sitting times are 8pm and 10pm; book via email.

Drinking

Il Tiaso (Map p319; ☑06 4547 4625; www.iltiaso.com; Via Perugia 20; 🛜; 🚇Circonvallazione Casilina) Think living room with zebra-print chairs, walls of indie art and Lou Reed biographies shelved between wine bottles. Well-priced wine, a chilled vibe, and live music.

Birra Piu (☑06 7061 3106; Via del Pigneto 105; beer €5; ⊘5pm-midnight Mon-Thu, to 2am Fri & Sat, 7pm-midnight Sun; 🚇Circonvallazione Casilina) A small, relaxed bar, with craft beer and a laid-back crowd draped over blonde-wood bar stools and tables.

Co.So (Via Braccio da Montone 80; cocktails €10; ⊘7pm-3am Mon-Sat) This tiny place is buzzing and is hipster to the hilt, with its Carbonara Sour cocktail (with vodka infused with pork fat), bubble-wrap coasters, and popcorn and M&M bar snacks.

Yeah! Pigneto (☑06 6480 1456; www.yeahpigneto.com; Via Giovanni de Agostini 41; small beer €3; aperitivo €7; ⊘8pm-2am) A relaxed boho-feeling bar with DJs playing jazz and the walls covered in collages and classic album covers. Regular live gigs.

rattle past outside. It's a family-run concern whose menu is an unusual mix of Roman and Pugliese (southern Italian) dishes, featuring taste sensations such as *tiella riso*, *patata* and *cozze* (baked rice dish with rice, potatoes and mussels). Book ahead.

POMMIDORO   TRATTORIA €€
Map p319 (☑06 445 26 92; Piazza dei Sanniti 44; meals €35; ⊘12.30-3.30pm & 7-11pm Mon-Sat,

closed Aug; 🚇Via Tiburtina) Throughout San Lorenzo's metamorphosis from down-at-heel working-class district to down-at-heel student enclave, Pommidoro has remained the same. It was a favourite of controversial film director Pasolini and contemporary celebs stop by, but it's an unpretentious place with superb-quality traditional food, specialising in grilled meats.

PASTIFICIO SAN LORENZO — ITALIAN €€€

Map p319 (☑06 9727 3519; Via Tiburtina 135; meals €50; ⊘from 7pm; ▣Via Tiburtina, ▣Via dei Reti) The biggest buzz in San Lorenzo is to be found at this brasserie-style restaurant, housed in a corner of the former pasta factory that is now Rome's contemporary art hub as it's also home to a collective of artists' studios. The place is packed, the vibe is 'this is where it's at', and the food...is fine – nothing to shout about, but perfectly scrumptious old favourites served up in a stylish fashion with equivalent prices.

SAID — ITALIAN €€€

Map p319 (☑06 446 92 04; Via Tiburtina 135; meals €50; ⊘10am-12.30am Mon-Thu, to 1.30am Sat & Sun; ▣Via Tiburtina, ▣Via dei Reti) Said is one of San Lorenzo's chicest haunts, housed in a 1920s chocolate factory. It includes a glorious chocolate shop, selling delights such as Japanese pink-tea pralines, and a stylish restaurant-bar, all cosy urban chic, with battered sofas, industrial antiques and creative cuisine.

🍷 DRINKING & 🍸 NIGHTLIFE

🍷 Monti

⭐AI TRE SCALINI — WINE BAR

Map p320 (Via Panisperna 251; ⊘12.30pm-1am; ⓂCavour) The 'Three Steps' is always packed, with crowds spilling out into the street. Apart from a tasty choice of wines, it sells the damn fine Menabrea beer, brewed in northern Italy. You can also tuck into a heart-warming array of cheeses, salami and dishes such as *polpette al sugo* (meatballs with sauce; €7.50).

FAFIUCHÉ — WINE BAR

Map p320 (☑06 699 09 68; www.fafiuche.it; Via della Madonna dei Monti 28; ⊘5.30pm-1am Mon-Sat; ⓂCavour) Fafiuché means 'light-hearted fun' in the Piedmontese dialect, and this place lives up to its name. The narrow, bottle-lined warm-orange space exudes charm: come here to enjoy wine and artisanal beers, eat delicious dishes originating from Puglia to Piedmont, or buy delectable foodstuffs. *Aperitivo* is from 6.30pm to 9pm.

LA BOTTEGA DEL CAFFÈ — CAFE

Map p320 (Piazza Madonna dei Monti 5; ⊘8am-2am; ⓂCavour) Ideal for frittering away any balmy section of the day, this appealing cafe-bar, named after a comedy by Carlo Goldoni, has greenery-screened tables out on the pretty Piazza Madonna dei Monti. As well as drinks, it serves snacks, from simple pizzas to cheeses and salamis.

LA BARRIQUE — WINE BAR

Map p320 (Via del Boschetto 41b; ⊘12.30-3.30pm & 5.30pm-1am Mon-Sat; ⓂCavour) This appealing *enoteca*, with wooden furniture and whitewashed walls, is a classy yet informal place to hang out and sample excellent French, Italian and German wines; a choice of perfectly cooked, delicious main courses provide a great accompaniment, or you can stick to artisanal cheeses and cold cuts.

AL VINO AL VINO — WINE BAR

Map p320 (Via dei Serpenti 19; ⊘6pm-1am, shop open all day; ⓂCavour) A rustic *enoteca* that's a favourite with the locals, mixing ceramic tabletops and contemporary paintings, this is an attractive spot to linger over a fine collection of wines, particularly *passiti* (sweet wines). The other speciality is *distillati* – grappa, whisky and so on – and there are snacks to help it all go down, including some Sicilian delicacies.

BOHEMIEN — BAR

Map p320 (Via degli Zingari 36; ⊘6pm-2am Wed-Sun; ⓂCavour) 🍷 This little bar lives up to its name; it feels like something you might stumble on in Left Bank Paris. It's small, with mismatched chairs and tables and an eclectic crowd drinking wine by the glass, and tea and coffee.

ICE CLUB — BAR

Map p320 (www.iceclubroma.it; Via della Madonna dei Monti 18; ⊘6pm-2am; ⓂColosseo) Novelty value is what the Ice Club is all about. Pay €15 (you get a free vodka cocktail served in a glass made of ice), put on a thermal cloak and mittens, and enter the bar, in which everything is made of ice (temperature –5°C). Most people won't chill here for long – the record is held by a Russian (four hours).

🍷 Esquilino

BAR ZEST AT THE RADISSON BLU ES — BAR

Map p320 (Via Filippo Turati 171; ⊘9am-1am; ▣Via Cavour) In need of a cocktail in the Termini district? Pop up to the 7th-floor bar at the slinkily designed Radisson Blu Es. Waiters are cute, chairs are by Jasper Morrison, views are through plate-glass and there's a sexy rooftop pool to look at.

CASTRONI
CAFE

Map p320 (Via Nazionale 7; ⊙7.30am-8pm Mon-Sat, 9.30am-8pm Sun; 🚇Via Cavour) This gourmet shop sells foodstuffs from all over the world. Although this branch doesn't have as large a range as that on Via Cola di Rienzo, it still has the fab cafe, which has great coffee, *panini* and other snacks, and you can stand at the bar or sit at a few booth tables.

FIDDLER'S ELBOW
PUB

Map p320 (Via dell'Olmata 43; ⊙5pm-2am; 🚇Via Cavour) Near the Basilica di Santa Maria Maggiore, the granddaddy of Rome's Irish pubs sticks to the formula that has served it so well over the last 25 years or so: Guinness, darts, crisps and big games, attracting a mix of Romans, expats and tourists. There are regular live-music and open-mic nights.

FINNEGANS
PUB

Map p320 (www.finneganpub.com; Via Leonina 66; 🚇Cavour) At first glance this seems like an identikit Irish pub, but look closer and the craic here has Italian twists – the clientele are well-groomed expats and Romans, and you can order Bellinis as well as Guinness. It's Irish-run and shows all the big football and rugby games, and there's occasional live music.

DRUID'S DEN
PUB

Map p320 (www.druidspubrome.com; Via San Martino ai Monti 28; ⊙5pm-2am; 🚇Cavour) When in Rome...do as the Romans do and head to an Irish pub. The Druid's Den attracts a cheerful crowd of young expats and Roman Anglophiles. The atmosphere is convivial, the walls are wood-panelled, Celtic paraphernalia is everywhere, Guinness is on tap and it shows all the big games.

📍 San Lorenzo & Beyond

LOCANDA ATLANTIDE
CLUB, LIVE MUSIC

Map p319 (📞06 4470 4540; www.locandatlantide.it; Via dei Lucani 22b; admission free, shows €3-5; ⊙9pm-2am Oct-Jun; 🚇Via Tiburtina, 🚌Scalo San Lorenzo) Come, tickle Rome's grungy underbelly. Descend through a door in a graffiti-covered wall into this cavernous basement dive, packed to the rafters with studenty, alternative crowds and featuring everything from prog-folk to DJ-spun electro music. It's good to know that punk is not dead.

WINE-TASTING

With beautifully appointed 1000-year-old cellars and a chic tasting studio, **Vino Roma** (Map p320; 📞328 4874497; www.vinoroma.com; Via in Selci 84/G; 2hr tastings per person €50) guides novices and experts in tasting wine, under the knowledgable stewardship of sommelier Hande Leimer and his expert team. Tastings are in English, but German, Japanese, Italian and Turkish sessions are available on special request. It also offers a wine-and-cheese dinner (€60), with snacks, cheeses and cold cuts to accompany the wines, and bespoke three-hour food tours. Book online.

GENTE DI SAN LORENZO
BAR

Map p319 (📞06 445 44 25; Via degli Aurunci 42; ⊙7am-2am; 🚇Via dei Reti) On the corner of San Lorenzo's Piazza dell'Immacolata, which gets thronged with students on balmy nights, this is a relaxed place for a drink and a snack or meal. The interior is airy, with warm wooden floors and brick arches, and there are some outdoor tables as well as regular DJs and occasional live music.

ESC ATELIER
CLUB

Map p319 (www.escatelier.net; Via dei Volsci 159; ⊙varies; 🚇Via Tiburtina, 🚌Via dei Reti) This left-wing alternative arts centre hosts live gigs and club nights: expect electronica DJ sets featuring live sax, discussions, exhibitions, political events and more. Admission and drinks are cheap.

VICIOUS CLUB
CLUB

Map p319 (📞06 7061 4349; www.viciousclub.com; Via Achille Grandi 3a; admission varies; ⊙10pm-4.30am Tue & Thu-Sat, to 4am Sun; 🚇Roma Laziali) Vicious is a gay-friendly club that welcomes all to dance and chatter to a soundtrack of electro, no wave, deep techno, glam indie, and deep house. It's small enough to feel intimate; try Alchemy every Saturday.

⭐ ENTERTAINMENT

TEATRO DELL'OPERA DI ROMA
OPERA

Map p320 (📞06 481 70 03; www.operaroma.it; Piazza Beniamino Gigli; ballet €12-80, opera €17-150; ⊙9am-5pm Tue-Sat, to 1.30pm Sun; 🚇Repubblica) Rome's premier opera house boasts a

SWIMMING AT THE RADISSON BLU ES

This swish, cutting-edge **hotel** (Map p320; ☏06 44 48 41; www.radissonblu.com/eshotel-rome; Via Filippo Turati 171; d €130-250; ❄ @ ☲; Ⓜ Vittorio Emanuele II) close to Termini has a sexy rooftop pool open to nonguests for €45/55 per weekday/weekend, with a 50% discount for children (under three years old free). A cocktail bar and restaurant are located alongside.

plush and gilt interior, a Fascist 1920s exterior and an impressive history: it premiered Puccini's *Tosca*, and Maria Callas once sang here. Opera and ballet performances are staged between September and June.

BLACKMARKET   LIVE MUSIC

Map p320 (www.black-market.it; Via Panisperna 101; ⊙5.30pm-2am; Ⓜ Cavour) A bit outside the main Monti hub, this charming, living-room-style bar filled with eclectic vintage furniture is a small but rambling place, great for sitting back on mismatched armchairs for a leisurely, convivial drink. It hosts regular acoustic indie and folk gigs, which feel a bit like having a band in your living room.

CHARITY CAFÉ   LIVE MUSIC

Map p320 (☏328 8452915; www.charitycafe.it; Via Panisperna 68; ⊙7pm-2am; Ⓜ Cavour) Think narrow space, spindly tables, dim lighting and a laid-back vibe: this is a place to snuggle down and listen to some slinky live jazz. It's civilised, relaxed, untouristy and very Monti. Gigs usually take place from 10pm, with live music and *aperitivo* on Sundays. There's open mic from 7pm on Monday and Tuesday.

ISTITUZIONE UNIVERSITARIA DEI CONCERTI   LIVE MUSIC

Map p319 (IUC; ☏06 361 00 51; www.concertiiuc.it; Piazzale Aldo Moro 5; Ⓜ Castro Pretorio) The IUC organises a season of concerts in the Aula Magna of La Sapienza University, including many visiting international artists and orchestras. Performances cover a wide range of musical genres, including baroque, classical, contemporary and jazz.

TEATRO AMBRA JOVINELLI   THEATRE

Map p319 (☏06 8308 2884; www.ambrajovinelli.org; Via G Pepe 43-47; Ⓜ Vittorio Emanuele) A home from home for many famous Italian comics, the Ambra Jovinelli is a historic venue for alternative comedians and satirists. Between government-bashing, the theatre hosts productions of classics, musicals, opera, new works and the odd concert.

SHOPPING

Monti

MERCATO MONTI URBAN MARKET   MARKET

Map p320 (www.mercatomonti.com; Via Leonina 46; ⊙10am-8pm Sat & Sun; Ⓜ Cavour) Vintage clothes, accessories, one-off pieces by local designers, this market in the hip hood of Monti is well worth a rummage.

TINA SONDERGAARD   CLOTHING

Map p320 (☏334 3850799; Via del Boschetto 1d; ⊙3-7.30pm Mon, 10.30am-7.30pm Tue-Sat, closed Aug; Ⓜ Cavour) Sublimely cut and whimsically retro-esque, these handmade threads are a hit with female fashion cognoscenti, including Italian rock star Carmen Consoli and the city's theatre and TV crowd. You can have adjustments made (included in the price), and dresses cost around €140.

SPOT   HOMEWARES

Map p320 (☏338 9275739; Via del Boschetto; ⊙10.30am-7.30pm Mon-Sat; Ⓜ Cavour) This small shop has an impeccable collection of mid-century furnishings, plus glassware designed by the owners and papier-mâché vases designed by their friends. It's frequented by the likes of Paolo Sorrentino (who directed *La Grande Bellezza*).

LA BOTTEGA DEL CIOCCOLATO   FOOD

Map p320 (☏06 482 14 73; Via Leonina 82; ⊙9.30am-7.30pm Oct-Aug; Ⓜ Cavour) Run by the younger generation of Moriondo & Gariglio, this is a magical world of scarlet walls and old-fashioned glass cabinets set into black wood, with irresistible smells wafting in from the kitchen and rows of lovingly homemade chocolates on display.

FABIO PICCIONI   JEWELLERY

Map p320 (☏06 474 16 97; Via del Boschetto 148; ⊙10.30am-1pm Tue-Sat, 2-8pm Mon-Sat; Ⓜ Cavour) A sparkling Aladdin's cave of decadent, one-of-a-kind costume jewellery; artisan Fabio Piccioni recycles old trinkets to create remarkable art deco–inspired jewellery.

101
CLOTHING

Map p320 (Via Urbana; ◷10am-1.30pm & 2-8pm; Ⓜ️Cavour) The collection at this individual boutique might include gossamer-light jumpers, broad-brimmed hats, chain-mail earrings and silk dresses: it's always worth a look to discover a special something.

PODERE VECCIANO
FOOD

Map p320 (Ⓙ06 4891 3812; Via dei Serpenti 33; ◷10am-8pm; Ⓜ️Cavour) Selling produce from its Tuscan farm, this shop is a great place to pick up presents, such as different varieties of pesto, honey and marmalade, selected wines, olive-oil-based cosmetics and beautiful olive wood chopping boards. There's even an olive tree growing in the middle of the shop.

CREJE
CLOTHING

Map p320 (Ⓙ06 4890 5227; Via del Boschetto 5A; ◷10am-2.30pm & 3-8pm; Ⓜ️Cavour) This eclectic, inexpensive Monti boutique sells a mix of clothing sourced from exotic places, including Indian dresses, plus dramatic silver costume jewellery and soft leather bags.

ABITO
CLOTHING

Map p320 (Ⓙ06 488 10 17; abito61.blogspot.co.uk; Via Panisperna 61; ◷10.30am-8pm Mon-Sat, noon-8pm Sun; Ⓜ️Cavour) Wilma Silvestre designs elegant clothes with a difference. Choose from the draped, chic, laid-back styles on the rack, and you can have one made up just for you in a day or just a few hours – customise the fabric and the colour. There's usually one guest designer's clothes also being sold at the shop.

GIACOMO SANTINI
SHOES

Map p320 (Ⓙ06 488 09 34; Via Cavour 106; ◷3.30-7.30pm Mon, 10am-1pm & 3.30-7.30pm Tue-Sat; Ⓜ️Cavour) This Fausto Santini outlet store sells end-of-line and discounted boots, shoes and bags, and has bargain signature architectural designs in butter-soft leather at a fraction of the retail price. Sizes are limited.

⛪ Esquilino

ARION ESPOSIZIONI
BOOKS

Map p320 (Ⓙ06 4891 3361; Via Milano 15-17; ◷10am-8pm Sun-Thu, to 10.30pm Fri & Sat; ⓆVia Nazionale) In cool, gleaming white rooms designed by Firouz Galdo, Arion Esposizioni – the bookshop attached to Palazzo delle Esposizioni – is just made for browsing. There are books on art, architecture and photog-

raphy, DVDs, CDs, vinyl, children's books and gifts for the design-lover in your life.

MAS
DEPARTMENT STORE

Map p320 (Magazzino allo Statuto; Ⓙ06 446 80 78; Via dello Statuto 11; ◷9am-12.45pm & 3.45-7.45pm; Ⓜ️Vittorio Emanuele) Glorious MAS is a multistorey temple of glorious didn't-know-I-needed-it, cheap-as-chips practical goods: thermal vests, bags, watches, pants and the kitchen sink.

NUOVO MERCATO ESQUILINO
MARKET

Map p319 (Via Lamarmora; ◷5am-3pm Mon-Sat; Ⓜ️Vittorio Emanuele) Cheap, colourful food market, and the best place to find exotic herbs and spices.

⛪ Piazza della Repubblica & Around

FELTRINELLI INTERNATIONAL
BOOKS

Map p320 (Ⓙ06 482 78 78; Via VE Orlando 84; ◷9am-8pm Mon-Sat, 10.30am-1.30pm & 4-8pm Sun; Ⓜ️Repubblica) The international branch of Italy's ubiquitous bookseller has a splendid collection of books in English, Spanish, French, German and Portuguese. You'll find everything from recent bestsellers to dictionaries, travel guides, DVDs and an excellent assortment of maps.

IBS.IT
BOOKS

Map p320 (Via Nazionale 254-255; ◷9am-8pm Mon-Sat, 10am-1.30pm & 4-8pm Sun; ☎; Ⓜ️Repubblica) IBS.it, on three floors, has a good range of Italian literature, reference books and travel guides, as well as CDs, half-priced books (general-fiction paperbacks), a cheery children's section and a few books in English and French.

⛪ San Lorenzo

LA GRANDE OFFICINA
JEWELLERY

Map p319 (Ⓙ06 445 03 48; lagrandeofficinagioielli.blogspot.co.uk; Via dei Sabelli 165B; ◷11am-7.30pm Tue-Fri, 11am-2pm Sat, 1-7.30pm Mon; ⒬Via Tiburtina) Under dusty workshop lamps, husband-and-wife team Giancarlo Genco and Daniela Ronchetti turn everything from old clock parts and Japanese fans into beautiful work-of-art jewellery. Head here for something truly unique.

1. The courtyard garden of Basilica di San Paolo Fuori le Mura (p200) 2. Basilica di Santa Maria in Trastevere (p160) 3. *Ecstasy of St Teresa*, by Gian Lorenzo Bernini, in Chiesa di Santa Maria della Vittoria (p106).

Rome's Churches

Rome is a feast, and whatever your faith, it's impossible not to be awestruck by its riches. Nowhere will you be able to visit such a splendid array and wealth of ecclesiastic architecture, from the stark simplicity of Basilica di Santa Sabina (p176) and the tiny perfection of Bramante's Tempietto (p162) to the awe-inspiring grandeur of St Peter's Basilica (the world's greatest church; p122) and the Sistine Chapel (p130), Rome's other inspirational pilgrimage sites include huge edifices such as the basilicas of San Lorenzo Fuori le Mura (p147), Santa Maria Maggiore (p143), San Giovanni in Laterano (p173) and the Chiesa di Santa Croce in Gerusalemme (p144).

Ancient Architecture

Whether they're baroque, medieval or Renaissance, many churches also feature a form of recycling that's uniquely Roman, integrating leftover architectural elements from imperial Rome. For example, you'll see ancient columns in Santa Maria in Trastevere (p160), and the famous ancient manhole, the Bocca della Verità, in the beautiful medieval Chiesa di Santa Maria in Cosmedin (p67). Taking the idea to the limit, the mesmerising Pantheon (p72) is an entire Roman temple converted into a church.

Divine Art

Rome's churches, which dot almost every street corner, also serve as free art galleries, bedecked in gold, inlay-work, mosaic and carvings. The wealth of the Roman Catholic church has benefited from centuries of virtuoso artists, architects and artisans who descended here to create their finest and most heavenly works in the glorification of God. Without paying a cent, anyone can wander in off the street to see this glut of masterpieces, including works by Michelangelo (in San Pietro in Vincoli, p144, and St Peter's Basilica), Caravaggio (in Santa Maria del Popolo, p101, and San Luigi dei Francesi, p77) and Bernini (in Santa Maria della Vittoria, p106).

Trastevere & Gianicolo

Neighbourhood Top Five

1 Discovering the Piazza di Santa Maria in Trastevere and visiting its beautiful **church** (p160), with its exquisite interior and exterior mosaics.

2 Bar-hopping and people-watching at local haunts such as **Ma Che Siete Venuti a Fà'** (p168).

3 Visiting the nuns' choir of **Basilica di Santa Cecilia in Trastevere** (p164) to see the Cavallini fresco.

4 Feeling as if you're soaring over Rome: the views from **Gianicolo Hill** (p161).

5 Enjoying the breathtakingly beautiful, Renaissance **Villa Farnesina** (p163), with interior decor by Raphael.

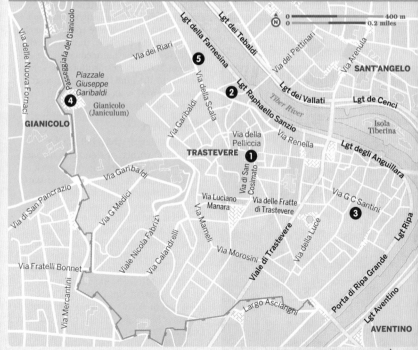

For more detail of this area see Map p316 ➡

Explore: Trastevere & Gianicolo

Trastevere is one of Rome's most vivacious neighbourhoods, an outdoor circus of ochre *palazzi,* ivy-clad facades and photogenic cobblestoned lanes, peopled with a bohemian and eclectic cast of tourists, travellers, students and street hawkers. The bohos and original Romans might be increasingly rubbing shoulders with wealthy expats and American students from the local John Cabot University, as rental prices in this most beguiling district go through the roof, but Trastevere still clings onto its distinct, Roman character. The very name means 'across the Tiber' *(tras tevere),* emphasising the sense of difference.

The area is ideal for aimless, contented wandering, home cooking in local trattorias and an evening drink to watch the world go by: it buzzes after dark, especially on summer evenings. There are also some beautiful sights here: glittering Basilica di Santa Maria is one of Rome's most charming churches, Villa Farnesina is the most breathtaking frescoed mansion you're ever likely to see (home decor by Raphael and others), and exquisitely frescoed Palazzo Corsini is home to a dazzling, almost forgotten-feeling art collection. Close by is its former park, now botanical gardens, and you can hike up Gianicolo (Janiculum Hill) to see Rome laid out before you like a dome-punctuated patchwork. Don't neglect to see Bramante's perfect little Tempietto on your way up. To the east, Basilica di Santa Cecilia is the resting place of Santa Cecilia, patron saint of music, with a wonderful, hidden Cavallini fresco.

Local Life

➡ **Drinking** A coffee or a *sambuca con la mosca* ('with a fly'; sambucca with a coffee bean) at Bar San Calisto (p168).

➡ **Passeggiata** An evening stroll to see and be seen, with a stop for an ice cream.

➡ **Football** Trastevere is a Roma supporters' stronghold: come a big game, the air of excitement is palpable.

Getting There & Away

➡ **Tram** From Largo di Torre Argentina tram 8 runs along the main drag of Viale di Trastevere, ending up at Villa Doria Pamphilj. Tram 3 also stops at the southern end of Viale Trastevere, connecting with Testaccio (Via Marmorata), Colosseo, San Giovanni and Villa Borghese.

➡ **Bus** From Termini, bus H runs to Viale di Trastevere, while the 780 runs from Piazza Venezia. For Gianicolo, if you don't fancy the steep steps from Via G Mameli, take bus 870 from Piazza delle Rovere.

Lonely Planet's Top Tip

Visit Santa Cecilia between 10am and 2.30pm Monday to Saturday, so that you can gain entrance to the hushed convent next door to see the Cavallini fresco.

 ## Best Places to Eat

➡ Glass Hostaria (p168)
➡ La Gensola (p163)
➡ Pianostrada Laboratorio di Cucina (p165)
➡ Fatamorgana (p164)

For reviews, see p163.➡

 ## Best Places to Drink

➡ Ma Che Siete Venuti a Fà (p168)
➡ Ombre Rosse (p169)
➡ Freni e Frizioni (p169)
➡ Bar San Calisto (p168)

For reviews, see p168.➡

Best Works of Art

➡ Basilica di Santa Maria in Trastevere (p160)
➡ Stefano Maderno's sculpture in Santa Cecilia in Trastevere (p164)
➡ Frescoes in Villa Farnesina (p163)
➡ Caravaggios in Galleria Nazionale d'Arte Antica di Palazzo Corsini (p161)

For reviews, see p160.➡

TRASTEVERE & GIANICOLO

TOP SIGHT
BASILICA DI SANTA MARIA IN TRASTEVERE

This glittering church is said to be the oldest church in Rome dedicated to the Virgin Mary. Its facade is decorated with a beautiful medieval mosaic depicting Mary feeding Jesus surrounded by 10 women bearing lamps. Two are veiled and hold extinguished lamps, symbolising widowhood, while the lit lamps of the others represent their virginity.

The church was first constructed in the early 3rd century over the spot where, according to legend, a fountain of oil miraculously sprang from the ground. Its current Romanesque form is the result of a 12th-century revamp. The portico was added by Carlo Fontana in 1702, with its balustrade decorated by four popes.

Inside it's the golden 12th-century mosaics that stand out. In the apse, look out for the dazzling depiction of Christ and his mother flanked by various saints and, on the far left, Pope Innocent II holding a model of the church. Beneath this is a series of six mosaics by Pietro Cavallini (c 1291) illustrating the life of the Virgin.

Note the 21 Roman columns, some plundered from the Terme di Caracalla, the wooden ceiling designed in 1617 by Domenichino and, on the right of the altar, a spiralling Cosmati candlestick, on the exact spot where the oil fountain is said to have sprung. The Cappella Avila is also worth a look for its stunning 17th-century dome. The spiralling Cosmatesque floor was relaid in the 1870s, a re-creation of the 13th-century original.

DON'T MISS...

➡ Facade mosaics
➡ The 13th-century Cavallini mosaics in the apse
➡ Ancient Roman granite columns

PRACTICALITIES

➡ Map p316
➡ Piazza Santa Maria in Trastevere
➡ ⏱7.30am-9pm
➡ 🚌Viale di Trastevere, 🚊Viale di Trastevere

◉ SIGHTS

Trastevere is dotted with exquisite churches and artworks, yet some of its most memorable sights are picturesque glimpses down narrow, ochre-and-orange-shaded lanes. To the north of Trastevere are the slopes of Gianicolo. Today a tranquil and leafy area, it's difficult to imagine that in 1849 this was the scene of fierce and bloody fighting. A makeshift army under Giuseppe Garibaldi defended Rome against French troops sent to restore papal rule.

◉ East of Viale di Trastevere

CHIESA DI SAN FRANCESCO D'ASSISI A RIPA   CHURCH

Map p316 (Piazza di San Francesco d'Assisi 88; ☉7.30am-noon & 2-7.30pm; ☐Viale di Trastevere, ☐Viale di Trastevere) St Francis is said to have stayed here in the 13th century, and you can still see the rock that he used as a pillow and his crucifix in his cell. Rebuilt several times, the church's current incarnation dates from the 1680s. It contains one of Bernini's most daring works, the *Beata Ludovica Albertoni* (Blessed Ludovica Albertoni; 1674), a work of highly charged sexual ambiguity.

It shows Ludovica, a Franciscan nun, in a state of rapture as she reclines, eyes shut, mouth open, one hand touching her breast. The 17th-century church also contains the impressive 18th-century Rospigliosi and Pallavici sculptural monuments.

◉ West of Viale di Trastevere

BASILICA DI SANTA MARIA IN TRASTEVERE   BASILICA

See p160.

GALLERIA NAZIONALE D'ARTE ANTICA DI PALAZZO CORSINI   GALLERY

Map p316 (☏06 6880 2323; www.galleriacorsini. beniculturali.it; Via della Lungara 10; adult/reduced €5/2.50, incl Palazzo Barberini €9/4.50; ☉8.30am-7.30pm Wed-Mon; ☐Lgt della Farnesina, ☐Viale di Trastevere) Once home to Queen Christina of Sweden, whose richly frescoed bedroom witnessed a stready stream of male and female lovers, 16th-century Palazzo Corsini was designed by Ferdinando

Fuga, in grand Versailles style, and houses part of Italy's national art collection. The highlights include Caravaggio's mesmerising *San Giovanni Battista* (St John the Baptist), Guido Reni's unnerving *Salome con la Testa di San Giovanni Battista* (Salome with the Head of John the Baptist), and Fra Angelico's Corsini Triptych, plus works by Rubens, Poussin and Van Dyck.

PIAZZA SANTA MARIA IN TRASTEVERE   PIAZZA

Map p316 (☐Viale di Trastevere, ☐Viale di Trastevere) Trastevere's focal square is a prime people-watching spot. By day it's full of mums with strollers, chatting locals and guidebook-toting tourists; by night it's the domain of foreign students, young Romans and out-of-towners, all out for a good time. The fountain in the centre of the square is of Roman origin and was restored by Carlo Fontana in 1692.

MUSEO DI ROMA IN TRASTEVERE   MUSEUM

Map p316 (☏06 820 59 127; www.museodiromaintrastevere.it; Piazza Sant'Egidio 1b; adult/reduced/child €8.50/7.50/free; ☉10am-8pm Tue-Sun; ☐Viale di Trastevere, ☐Viale di Trastevere) Housed in a 17th-century Carmelite convent, this museum hosts excellent temporary photography exhibitions. Upstairs, the permanent collection contains a selection of 19th-century watercolours depicting Rome, life-size dioramas showing 19th-century Roman life, temporary Rome-related exhibitions, and *Stanza di Trilussa,* an installation relating to the famous Roman poet.

PORTA SETTIMIANA   MONUMENT

Map p316 (☐Lungotevere della Farnesina, Piazza Trilussa) Resembling a crenellated keep, Porta Settimiana marks the start of Via della Lungara, the 16th-century road that connects Trastevere with the Borgo. It was built in 1498 by Pope Alexander VI over a small passageway in the Aurelian Wall and later altered by Pope Pius VI in 1798.

From Porta Settimiana, Via Santa Dorotea leads to Piazza Trilussa, a popular evening hang-out with local youth, and Ponte Sisto, which connects with the *centro storico.*

◉ Gianicolo

GIANICOLO HILL   HILL

Gianicolo (Janiculum) is dotted with monuments to Garibaldi and his army, who fought the French on this spot in 1849. The Italian hero is commemorated with a massive **monument** in Piazzale Giuseppe Garibaldi, while his Brazilian-born wife, Anita, has her own **equestrian monument** about 200m away in Piazzale Anita Garibaldi; she died from malaria shortly after the siege, together with their unborn child.

The Gianicolo is a superb viewpoint, with sweeping panoramas over Rome's rooftops, and has several summer-only bars that are blessed with thrilling views. There are also regular children's puppet shows on the hill, a long-standing tradition.

ORTO BOTANICO   GARDENS

Map p316 (☑06 499 17 107; Largo Cristina di Svezia 24; adult/reduced €8/4; ☺9am-6.30pm Mon-Sat Apr-Oct, to 5.30pm Nov-Mar; ☐Lungotevere della Farnesina, Piazza Trilussa) Formerly the private grounds of Palazzo Corsini, Rome's 12-hectare botanical gardens are a little-known, slightly neglected-feeling gem and a great place to unwind in a tree-shaded expanse covering the steep slopes of the Gianicolo, though the admission charge is unfortunately also a bit steep. Plants have been cultivated here since the 13th century.

However, in their present form, the gardens were established in 1883, when the grounds of Palazzo Corsini were given to the University of Rome. They now contain up to 8000 species, including some of Europe's rarest plants. There are also various architectural delights, including the Scalineta delle Undici Fontane (Staircase of 11 Fountains) designed by Ferdinando Fuga, who was also responsible for the Palazzo Corsini and the loggia at Santa Maria in Maggiore (p143).

GIANICOLO CANNON

If you're meandering through Trastevere, or further afield, and hear a loud crack, panic not, it's just the midday cannon salute from the top of the Gianicolo. In 1847 Pope Pius IX ordered that a cannon fire blank shells at this time daily to set a standard for all the city's bells. Since 1904 it's been shot from the Gianicolo, as it's a little less disturbing from there, but it can still be heard across the city. It wasn't fired during the World Wars, but recommenced in 1959.

TEMPIETTO DI BRAMANTE & CHIESA DI SAN PIETRO IN MONTORIO   CHURCH

Map p316 (www.sanpietroinmontorio.it; Piazza San Pietro in Montorio 2; ☺Chiesa 8.30am-noon & 3-4pm Mon-Fri, Tempietto 9.30am-12.30pm & 2-4.30pm Tue-Fri, 9am-3pm Sat; ☐Via Garibaldi) Considered the first great building of the High Renaissance, Bramante's sublime Tempietto (Little Temple; 1508) is a perfect surprise, squeezed into the courtyard of the Chiesa di San Pietro in Montorio, on the spot where St Peter is said to have been crucified. Small, but perfectly formed, the church has a classically inspired design and ideal proportions that epitomise the Renaissance *zeitgeist*.

It has a circular interior surrounded by 16 columns and topped by a classical frieze, elegant balustrade and dome. More than a century later, in 1628, Bernini added a staircase. Bernini also contributed a chapel to the adjacent church, the last resting place of Beatrice Cenci, an Italian noblewoman who helped murder her abusive father in the 16th century, and subsequently was tried and beheaded on Ponte Sant'Angelo.

It's quite a climb uphill, but you're rewarded by the views. To cheat, take bus 870 from Via Paola just off Corso Vittorio Emanuele II near the Tiber.

FONTANA DELL'ACQUA PAOLA   FOUNTAIN

Map p316 (Via Garibaldi; ☐Via Garibaldi) Just up from the Chiesa di San Pietro in Montorio, this monumental white fountain was built in 1612 to celebrate the restoration of a 2nd-century aqueduct that supplied (and still supplies) water from Lago di Bracciano, 35km to the north of Rome. Four of the fountain's six pink-stone columns came from the facade of the old St Peter's Basilica, while much of the marble was pillaged from the Roman Forum. Originally the fountain had five small basins, but these were replaced by a large granite basin, added by Carlo Fontana, in 1690.

VILLA DORIA PAMPHILJ   PARK

(☺sunrise-sunset; ☐Via di San Pancrazio) Rome's largest park is Rome's favourite place to escape the city noise and bustle. Once a vast private estate, it was laid out around 1650 for Prince Camillo Pamphilj, nephew of Pope Innocent X. It's a huge expanse of rolling parkland, shaded by Rome's distinctive umbrella pines. At its centre is the prince's summer residence, the **Casino del Belrespiro**, and its manicured

TOP SIGHT
VILLA FARNESINA

Serenely and symmetrically proportioned on the outside, this 16th-century villa's interior is fantastically frescoed.

Villa Farnesina was built for Agostino Chigi, the immensely wealthy papal banker. At his banquets he'd encourage his guests to throw their solid gold plates out of the window once they'd finished (servants would stand beneath the windows to catch them in nets). The house was bought by Cardinal Alessando Farnese in 1577.

The architect was Baldassare Peruzzi, formerly Bramante's assistant; he also painted several of the frescoes. On the ground floor is the Loggia of Galatea, attributed to Raphael and depicting a sea nymph, with the vault frescoed by Peruzzi, and mythological scenes by Sebastiani del Piombio. Next door, the Loggia of Cupid and Psyche was also frescoed by Raphael and seethes with naked figures and muscular cupids.

On the 1st floor, Peruzzi's frescoes in the Salone delle Prospettive are a superb illusionary perspective of a panorama of 16th-century Rome, while Chigi's bedchamber is filled with cavorting cherubs, gods and goddesses.

DON'T MISS...

➡ Frescoes by Sebastiano del Piombo

➡ Raphael-attributed loggia decoration

➡ Peruzzi's panoramas in the Salone delle Prospettive

PRACTICALITIES

➡ Map p316

➡ www.villafarnesina.it

➡ Via della Lungara 230

➡ adult/reduced €6/5

➡ ⊗9am-2pm, to 5pm 2nd Sun of month

➡ ⌂Lgt della Farnesina, ⌂Viale di Trastevere

---

gardens and citrus trees. It's now used for official government functions.

EATING

Picturesque Trastevere is packed with restaurants, trattorias, cafes and pizzerias. The better places dot the side streets, and it pays to be selective, as many are bog-standard tourist traps. But there are not just tourists here – Romans like to eat in Trastevere too.

East of Viale di Trastevere

INNOCENTI   BAKERY €
Map p316 (☑06 580 39 26; Via delle Luce 21; ⊗8am-8pm Mon-Sat, 9.30am-2pm Sun; ⌂Viale di Trastevere, ⌂Viale di Trastevere) It's at reassuring spots like this that you can feel that the world never changes, in some corners at least. Here you can buy light-as-air *crostata,* and stock up on biscuits such as *brutti ma buoni* (ugly but good).

DA ENZO   TRATTORIA €
Map p316 (☑06 5812 260; www.daenzoal29.com; Via dei Vascellari 29; meals €25; ⊗Mon-Sat; ⌂Viale di Trastevere, ⌂Viale di Trastevere) This snug dining room serves up seasonally based Roman meals, such as spaghetti with clams and mussels or grilled lamb cutlets. There's a tiny terrace on the quintessential Trastevere cobbled street.

PANATTONI   PIZZA €
Map p316 (☑06 580 09 19; Viale di Trastevere 53; pizzas €6.50-9; ⊗6.30pm-1am Thu-Tue; ⌂Viale di Trastevere, ⌂Viale di Trastevere) Known as 'ai Marmi', Panattoni is also nicknamed *l'obitorio* (the morgue) because of its marble-slab tabletops. Thankfully the similarity stops there. This is one of Trastevere's liveliest pizzerias, with paper-thin pizzas, a clattering buzz, testy waiters, street-side seating and fried starters – specialities are *supplì* (rice balls) and *baccalà* (cod).

★LA GENSOLA   SICILIAN €€
Map p316 (☑06 581 63 12; Piazza della Gensola 15; meals €45; ⊗12.30-3pm & 7.30-11.30pm, closed Sun mid-Jun–mid-Sep; ⌂Viale di Trastevere, ⌂Viale di Trastevere) This tranquil, classy yet

unpretentious trattoria thrills foodies with delicious food that has a Sicilian slant and emphasis on seafood, including an excellent tuna tartare, linguine with fresh anchovies and divine *zuccherini* (tiny fish) with fresh mint.

LE MANI IN PASTA
RISTORANTE **€€**

Map p316 (☑06 581 60 17; Via dei Genovesi 37; meals €35; ⊘12.30-3pm & 7.30-11pm Tue-Sun; 🚇Viale di Trastevere, 🚋Viale di Trastevere) Popular and lively, this rustic, snug place has arched ceilings and an open kitchen that serves up delicious fresh pasta dishes such as *fettucine con ricotta e pancetta*. The grilled meats are great, too.

DA TEO
TRATTORIA **€€**

Map p316 (☑06 581 8385; Piazza dei Ponziani 7; meals around €30; ⊘12.30-3pm & 7.30-11.30pm Mon-Sat; 🚇Viale di Trastevere) Tucked away on the quieter side of Trastevere, Da Teo gets packed out with locals dining on its steaming platefuls of Roman standards, such as *cacio e pepe* (cheese and pepper) or fried lambchops. It's great to eat out on the small piazza when the weather suits. Make sure you book.

✖ West of Viale di Trastevere

★FATAMORGANA – TRASTEVERE
GELATERIA **€**

Map p316 (Via Roma Libera 11, Piazza San Cosimato; cones & tubs from €2; ⊘noon-midnight summer, to 10.30pm winter; 🚇Viale di Trastevere, 🚋Viale di Trastevere) One of several Fatamorgana outlets across Rome, this is one of the finest among the city's gourmet gelatarie. Quality natural ingredients are used to produce creative flavour combos such as pineapple and ginger or pear and gorgonzola. Gluten-free.

DA CORRADO
ROMAN **€**

Map p316 (Via della Pelliccia 39; meals €25; ⊘12.30-2.30pm & 7-11pm Mon-Sat; 🚇Viale di Trastevere, 🚋Viale di Trastevere) Don't expect refined service or a fancy interior. This is a proper old-school Roman trattoria, with no outdoor seating, but an unfussy, rough-and-ready atmosphere. It's packed with locals, feasting on hearty Roman soul food, such as *amatriciana* (pasta with bacon and tomato sauce).

◉ TOP SIGHT **BASILICA DI SANTA CECILIA IN TRASTEVERE**

This church, with its remarkable frescoes by Pietro Cavallini, and ancient Roman excavations, is the last resting place of St Cecilia, the patron saint of music. The centrepiece is Stefano Maderno's delicate sculpture, showing how her miraculously preserved body was apparently found when it was unearthed in the Catacombe di San Callisto in 1599.

This basilica stands on the site of a 5th-century church, itself built over the ancient Roman house where it's believed Cecilia was martyred in AD 230. You can visit the network of excavated houses that lie beneath the church.

In the right-hand nave the Cappella del Caldarium, complete with two works by Guido Reni, marks the spot where the saint was allegedly tortured.

But the Basilica's hidden wonder is Cavallini's spectacular 13th-century fresco, showing a section of his *Last Judgment*, in the nun's choir. Much of this late-medieval masterwork was lost during the 18th-century remodelling of the church, but what remains gives an idea of its splendour.

DON'T MISS...

➡ Cavallini's *Last Judgment* fresco

➡ Maderno's sculpture

➡ Excavated buildings

PRACTICALITIES

➡ Map p316

➡ Piazza di Santa Cecilia

➡ fresco €2.50, crypt €2.50

➡ ⊘basilica & crypt 9.30am-1pm & 4-7.15pm, fresco 10am-2.30pm Mon-Sat

➡ 🚇Viale di Trastevere, 🚋Viale di Trastevere

DA AUGUSTO
TRATTORIA €

Map p316 (☑06 580 37 98; Piazza de' Renzi 15; meals €25; ⊗12.30-3pm & 8-11pm; ☐Viale di Trastevere, ☐Viale di Trastevere) For a Trastevere feast, plonk yourself at one of Augusto's rickety tables, either inside or out on the small piazza, and prepare to enjoy some mamma-style cooking. The gruff waiters dish out hearty platefuls of *rigatoni all'amatriciana* and *stracciatella* (clear broth with egg and Parmesan) among a host of Roman classics. Be prepared to queue. Cash only.

CIURI CIURI
SICILIAN €

Map p316 (☑06 9521 6082; www.ciuri-ciuri. it; Piazza San Cosimato 49b; snacks around €3; ⊗10.30am-midnight; ☐Viale di Trastevere, ☐Viale di Trastevere) A splendid Sicilian cafe selling cakes (the *cannoli* – pastry tubes of ricotta – are filled for you then and there), and creamy artisanal ice cream.

FIOR DI LUNA
GELATERIA €

Map p316 (☑06 6456 1314; Via della Lungaretta 96; gelato from €1.70; ⊗noon-12.30am Tue-Sun; ☐Viale di Trastevere, ☐Viale di Trastevere) This busy little hub serves up handmade gelato and sorbet – it's made in small batches and only uses natural, seasonal ingredients, such as hazelnuts from Tonda and pistachios from Bronte. Cones are not available, as they'd detract from the taste. They make a few flavours from donkeys' milk.

PIZZERIA IVO
PIZZA €

Map p316 (☑06 581 70 82; Via di San Francesco a Ripa 158; pizzas from €7; ⊗7pm-midnight Wed-Mon; ☐Viale di Trastevere, ☐Viale di Trastevere) One of Trastevere's most famous pizzerias, Ivo's has been slinging pizzas for some 40 years, and still the hungry come. With the TV on in the corner and the tables full (a few outside on the cobblestoned street), Ivo is a noisy and vibrant place, and the waiters fit the gruff-and-fast stereotype.

OLD BRIDGE
GELATERIA

Map p316 (Via Della Scala 70; gelato from €2; ⊗noon-2am; ☐Piazza Trilussa) The artisanal gelataria Old Bridge has been keeping punters near the Vatican happy for over 25 years, and have now opened this Trastevere outlet, offering large scoops of creamy gelato.

FORNO LA RENELLA
BAKERY €

Map p316 (☑06 581 72 65; Via del Moro 15-16; pizza slices from €2.50; ⊗7am-2am Tue-Sat, to 10pm

GRATTACHECCA

It's summertime, the living is easy, and Romans like nothing better in the sultry evening heat than to amble down to the river and partake of some *grattachecca* (crushed ice covered in fruit and syrup). It's the ideal way to cool down and there are kiosks along the riverbank satisfying this very Roman need; try **Sora Mirella Caffè** (Map p316; grattachecca €3-6; ⊗11am-3am May-Sep), next to Ponte Cestio.

Sun & Mon; ☐Piazza Trilussa) The wood-fired ovens at this historical Trastevere bakery have been going for decades, producing a delicious daily batch of pizza, bread and biscuits. Piled-high toppings (and fillings) vary seasonally. It's popular with everyone from skinheads with big dogs to elderly ladies with little dogs.

DA OLINDO
TRATTORIA €

Map p316 (☑06 581 88 35; Vicolo della Scala 8; meals €25; ⊗7.30-11pm Mon-Sat; ☐Viale di Trastevere) This is your classic family affair: the menu is short, cuisine robust, portions huge, and the atmosphere lively. Expect *baccalà con patate* (salted cod and potatoes) on Fridays and gnocchi on Thursdays, but other dishes – such as *coniglio all cacciatore* (rabbit, hunter-style) or *polpette al sugo* (meatballs in sauce) – whichever day you like.

PIANOSTRADA LABORATORIO DI CUCINA
ITALIAN €

Map p316 (Vicolo del Cedro; meals €25; ⊗1-4pm & 7.30-11.30pm Tue-Sun; ☐Piazza Trilussa) A diminutive, tucked-away place, this all-female-run foodie stop has been attracting attention with its delicious meals such as parmigiana with aubergine and pumpkin, meatballs, burgers, pasta with swordfish and wild fennel, and gourmet sandwiches. It's all exquisitely made and conceived, so squeeze in along the bar or take one of the tiny tables with barstools.

SISINI
PIZZA €

Map p316 (Via di San Francesco a Ripa 137; pizza & pasta from €3, supplì €1.20; ⊗9am-10.30pm Mon-Sat, closed Aug; ☐Viale di Trastevere, ☐Viale di Trastevere) Locals love this fast-food takeaway joint (the sign outside says 'Supplì'), serving up fresh *pizza al taglio* and

Rome Street Life

As in many sunny countries, much of life in Rome is played out on the street. In the morning, you can watch the city slowly wake up. Shop shutters are cranked open, rubbish collectors do the rounds, restaurants set out their tables: Rome is readying itself for its close-up.

Day to Night

During the next phase, the fruit and veg markets in every *rione* (neighbourhood) will swell with people, with a predominance of matriarchs wielding grocery trolleys and showing a reckless disregard for queuing.

Throughout the day, people come and go on Rome's piazzas and public spaces. In Campo de' Fiori (p90), there's a busy food market during the day, then the character of the piazza changes towards the evening when its bars become busy, taking over corners of the square.

Pedestrianised Via del Pigneto (p171), to Rome's northeast, follows a similar trajectory: market in the morning, bars and cafes creating a party atmosphere in the evening. In the historic centre, locals and tourists gather to rest and people-watch on the Spanish Steps (p113), but these empty as night falls.

Day or evening, the stadium-sized Piazza Navona (p84) ebbs and flows with people-watching entertainment, with hawkers, caricaturists and occasional street performers.

La Passeggiata

In the early evening, the *passeggiata* (an early evening stroll) is an important

1. Dinner in the *centro storico* (p70) **2.** Daily market, Campo de' Fiori (p78) **3.** Portrait artist in Piazza Navona (p74)

part of Roman life, as it is elsewhere in Italy. Locals will usually dress up before heading out. Like many other parts of everyday life, such as coffee-drinking, Italians have elevated a seemingly simple practice into something special.

Romans will usually head to the area that's most convenient for them. Trastevere (p181) tends to be a broader mix of tourists and young people. Villa Borghese (p225) and the Pincio Hill Gardens (p118) attract more families and are more tranquil. Via del Corso is popular among younger window-shoppers, while Rome's smartest shopping strip, Via dei Condotti (p119), attracts a mix of ages. In summer, there's the Lungo il Tevere festival (p26) on Isola Tiberina, and stalls along the riverside create a new area for early evening wanders.

Many people out on the stroll will opt, instead of paying €6 or so to sit and drink at a bar, to stop for a more affordable gelato, which they can eat on their way. In summer, you'll see lots of people enjoying *grattachecca* – flavoured, crushed ice – along the banks of the Tiber.

The *bella figura* ('beautiful figure', better explained as 'keeping up appearances') is important here, and the *passeggiata* is as much about checking everyone else out as it is about enjoying the atmosphere. The *passeggiata* reaches its height in summer, as 5pm or 6pm is when the heat of the day subsides. There's not much else to do, so why not head out into the street?

different pasta and risotto dishes served in plastic boxes. It's also worth sampling the *supplì* (fried rice balls), and roast chicken.

BIR & FUD
PIZZA €

Map p316 (Via Benedetta 23; meals €25; ⊙7.30pm-midnight, to 2am Fri & Sat; ❋; 🚇Piazza Trilussa) This orange-and-terracotta, vaulted, yet contemporary-styled pizzeria wins plaudits for its organic take on pizzas, *crostini* and fried things (potato, pumpkin etc) and has a microbrewery on site, so serves seasonable tipples such as Birrificio Troll Palanfrina (winter only; made from chestnuts).

VALZANI
PASTRIES €

Map p316 (☑06 580 37 92; Via del Moro 37; cakes €3; ⊙10am-8pm Wed-Sun, 3-8pm Mon & Tue, closed Jul & Aug; 🚇Piazza Sonnino, 🚇Piazza Sonnino) The speciality of this glorious, stuck-in-time cake shop, opened in 1925 and not redecorated since, is the legendary *torta sacher*, the favourite cake of Roman film director Nanni Moretti. But there are also chocolate-covered *mostaccioli* (biscuits), Roman *pangiallo* (honey, nuts and dried fruit – typical for Christmas) and Roman *torrone* (nougat).

DAR POETA
PIZZA €

Map p316 (☑06 588 05 16; Vicolo del Bologna 46; meals €25; ⊙noon-midnight; 🚇Piazza Trilussa) Locals and tourists flock to Dar Poeta for filling wood-fired pizzas and a buzzing atmosphere. As well as the usual selection of pizzas, served with crusts that are somewhere between wafer-thin Roman and Neapolitan deep pan, it's also famous for its trademark ricotta and Nutella calzone.

GLASS HOSTARIA
ITALIAN €€€

Map p316 (☑06 5833 5903; Vicolo del Cinque 58; meals €90; ⊙7.30-11.30pm Tue-Sun; 🚇Piazza Trilussa) Trastevere's foremost foodie address, the Glass is a modernist-styled, sophisticated setting decorated in warm wood and contemporary gold, with fabulous cooking to match. Chef Cristina Bowerman creates inventive, delicate dishes that combine with fresh ingredients and traditional elements to delight and surprise the palate. There are tasting menus for €75, €80 and €100.

PARIS
RISTORANTE €€€

Map p316 (☑06 581 53 78; www.ristoranteparis.it; Piazza San Calisto 7a; meals €45-55; ⊙7.30-11pm Mon, 12.30-3pm & 7.30-11pm Tue-Sun; 🚇Viale di Trastevere, 🚇Viale di Trastevere) An old-school restaurant set in a 17th-century building with tables on a small piazza, Paris – named for its founder, not the French capital – is the best place outside the Ghetto to sample Roman-Jewish cuisine. Signature dishes include *gran fritto vegetale con baccalà* (deep-fried vegetables with salt cod) and *carciofi alla giudia* (fried artichoke).

DRINKING & NIGHTLIFE

Trastevere is one of the city's most popular areas to wander, drink and decide what to do afterwards. It's crowded in summer, with stalls, bars spilling into the street and a carnival atmosphere.

West of Viale di Trastevere

MA CHE SIETE VENUTI A FÀ
PUB

Map p316 (www.football-pub.com; Via Benedetta 25; ⊙11am-2am; 🚇Piazza Trilussa) Named after a football chant, which translates politely as 'What did you come here for?', this pint-sized Trastevere pub is a beer-buff's paradise, packing in at least 13 international craft beers on tap and even more by the bottle.

BAR SAN CALISTO
CAFE

Map p316 (☑06 589 56 78; Piazza San Calisto 3-5; ⊙6am-1.45am Mon-Sat; 🚇Viale di Trastevere, 🚇Viale di Trastevere) Those in the know head to the down-at-heel 'Sanca' for its basic, stuck-in-time atmosphere and cheap prices (beer €1.50). It attracts everyone from intellectuals to keeping-it-real Romans, alcoholics and American students. It's famous for its chocolate – hot with cream in winter, ice cream in summer. Try the *sambuca con la mosca* ('with a fly' – a raw coffee bean). Expect occasional late-night jam sessions.

DA BIAGIO
WINE BAR

Map p316 (www.dabiagio.it; Via della Scala 64; ⊙10am-1.30pm & 5pm-midnight; 🚇Piazza Sonnino) With the sign 'Vini & Olio' scrawled above the door, this is a hole-in-the-wall Trastevere institution, lined by bottles of grappa and wine-for-sale, but also offering wine and spirits by the glass, shots and beer on tap. The owner is a funny guy, and has been serving up tipples since 1972. In the evening, drinkers spill out on the cobblestoned Trastevere street.

FRENI E FRIZIONI
BAR

Map p316 (☑06 4549 7499; www.freniefrizioni. com; Via del Politeama 4-6; ☺6.30pm-2am; ☐Piazza Trilussa) This perennially cool Trastevere bar is housed in a former mechanic's workshop – hence its name ('brakes and clutches'). It draws a young *spritz*-loving crowd that swells onto the small piazza outside to sip well-priced cocktails (from €7) and to snack on the daily *aperitivo* (€6 to €10; 7pm to 10pm).

OMBRE ROSSE
BAR

Map p316 (☑06 588 41 55; Piazza Sant'Egidio 12; ☺8am-2am Mon-Sat, 11am-2am Sun; ☐Piazza Trilussa) A seminal Trastevere hang-out; grab a table on the terrace and watch the world go by amid a clientele ranging from elderly Italian wide boys to wide-eyed tourists. Tunes are slinky and there's live music (jazz, blues, world) on Thursday evenings from September to April.

BIG STAR
BAR

Map p316 (Via Goffredo Mameli 25; ☺6pm-2am; ☐Viale de Trastevere, ☐Viale de Trastevere) Off the beaten Trastevere track, this is a cool backstreet bar set away from the main action, with an alternative feel and its drink prices scrawled up on a blackboard. It's a small yet airy interior, where you can drink a wide range of beers and cocktails while listening to the hipster DJs, with a laid-back, appealing vibe.

LA MESCITA
WINE BAR

Map p316 (☑06 5833 3920; Piazza Trilussa 41; ☺5pm-midnight Sun-Thu, to 1am Fri & Sat; ☐Piazza Trilussa) This tiny bar inside the entrance to upmarket restaurant Enoteca Ferrara serves delectable *aperitivo* and has a wide range of wines by the glass, from €7. Fancy an intimate tête-à-tête, with fine wines and yummy snacks? This is your place.

BAR LE CINQUE
BAR

Map p316 (Vicolo del Cinque 5; ☺6.30am-2am Mon-Sat; ☐Piazza Sonnino, ☐Piazza Sonnino) There's no sign outside, and it looks like a rundown ordinary bar, but this is a long-standing Trastevere favourite and it always has a small crowd clustered around outside; they're here for the pivotal location, easygoing vibe and cheap drinks.

🍷 Gianicolo

BAR STUZZICHINI
BAR

Map p316 (Piazzale Giuseppe Garibaldi; ☺7.30am-1am or 2am; ☐Passeggiata del Gianicolo) This little kiosk nestles on the top of Gianicolo, and serves up coffees and drinks, including cocktails. There are a few tables to perch at and the views are unmatchable. On New Year's Eve it opens all night.

IL BARRETTO
BAR

Map p316 (☑06 5836 5422; Via Garibaldi 27; ☺6am-2am Mon-Sat, 5pm-2am Sun; ☐Piazza Sonnino, ☐Piazza Sonnino) Venture a little way up the Gianicolo, up a steep flight of steps from Trastevere. Go on, it's worth it: you'll discover this well-kept-secret cocktail bar. The basslines are meaty, the bar staff hip, and the interior mixes vintage with pop art.

☆ ENTERTAINMENT

BIG MAMA
BLUES

Map p316 (☑06 581 25 51; www.bigmama.it; Vicolo di San Francesco a Ripa 18; ☺9pm-1.30am, shows 10.30pm, closed Jun-Sep; ☐Viale di Trastevere, ☐Viale di Trastevere) Head to this cramped Trastevere basement for a mellow night of Eternal City blues. A long-standing venue, it also stages jazz, funk, soul and R&B, as well as popular Italian cover bands.

LETTERE CAFFÈ GALLERY
LIVE MUSIC

Map p316 (☑06 9727 0991; www.letterecaffe.org; Vicolo di San Francesco a Ripa 100/101; ☺7pm-2am, closed mid-Aug–mid-Sep; ☐Viale di Trastevere, ☐Viale di Trastevere) Like books? Poetry? Blues and jazz? Then you'll love this place – a clutter of barstools and books, where there are regular live gigs, poetry slams, comedy and gay nights, plus DJ sets playing indie and new wave.

TEATRO VASCELLO
THEATRE

Map p316 (☑06 588 10 21; www.teatrovascello.it; Via Giacinto Carini 72, Monteverde; ☐Via Giacinto Carini) Left-field in vibe and location, this independent, fringe theatre stages interesting, cutting-edge new work, including avant-garde dance, multimedia events and works by emerging playwrights.

ALCAZAR CINEMA
CINEMA

Map p316 (☑06 588 00 99; Via Merry del Val 14; ☐Viale di Trastevere, ☐Viale di Trastevere) This old-style cinema with plush red seats occasionally shows films in their original language with Italian subtitles.

NUOVO SACHER
CINEMA

Map p316 (⤢06 581 81 16; www.sacherfilm.eu; Largo Ascianghi 1; ☐Viale di Trastevere, ☐Viale di Trastevere) Owned by cult Roman film director Nanni Moretti, this small cinema with red-velvet seats is the place to catch the latest European art-house offering, with regular screenings of films in their original language.

SHOPPING

PORTA PORTESE MARKET
MARKET

Map p316 (Piazza Porta Portese; ◷6am-2pm Sun; ☐Viale di Trastevere, ☐Viale di Trastevere) To see another side of Rome, head to this mammoth flea market. With thousands of stalls selling everything from rare books and fell-off-a-lorry bikes to Peruvian shawls and MP3 players, it's crazily busy and a lot of fun. Keep your valuables safe and wear your haggling hat.

ROMA-STORE
BEAUTY

Map p316 (⤢06 581 87 89; Via della Lungaretta 63; ◷10am-8pm; ☐Viale di Trastevere, ☐Viale di Trastevere) An enchanting perfume shop crammed full of deliciously enticing bottles of scent, including lots of lesser-known brands that will have perfume-lovers practically fainting with joy.

ANTICA CACIARA TRASTEVERINA
FOOD, WINE

Map p316 (Via San Francesco a Ripa 140; ◷7am-2pm & 4-8pm Mon-Sat; ☐Viale di Trastevere, ☐Viale di Trastevere) The fresh ricotta is a prized possession at this century-old deli, and usually snapped up by lunch. If you're too late, take solace in the famous *pecorino romano* or the *burrata pugliese* (a creamy cheese from the Puglia region), or simply lust after the fragrant hams, bread, Sicilian anchovies and local wines.

OFFICINA DELLA CARTA
GIFTS

Map p316 (⤢06 589 55 57; Via Benedetta 26b; ◷10.30am-7.30pm Mon-Sat; ☐Piazza Trilussa) A perfect present pit-stop, this tiny workshop produces attractive hand-painted paperbound boxes, photo albums, recipe books, notepads, photo frames and diaries.

ALMOST CORNER BOOKSHOP
BOOKS

Map p316 (⤢06 583 69 42; Via del Moro 45; ◷10am-7.30pm Mon-Thu, 10am-8pm Fri & Sat, 11am-8pm Sun; ☐Piazza Trilussa) This is how a bookshop should look: a crammed haven full of rip-roaring reads, with every millimetre of wall space containing English-language fiction and nonfiction (including children's) and travel guides.

OPEN DOOR BOOKSHOP
BOOKS

Map p316 (Via della Lungaretta 23; ◷10am-8pm Mon-Sat; ☐Viale di Trastevere, ☐Viale di Trastevere) This lovely crammed secondhand bookshop is a great place to browse and happen on a classic novel or nonfiction book in English, Italian, French and Spanish.

LA CRAVATTA SU MISURA
ACCESSORIES

Map p316 (⤢06 890 69 41; Via di Santa Cecilia 12; ◷10am-7pm Mon-Sat; ☐Viale di Trastevere, ☐Viale di Trastevere) With ties draped over the wooden furniture, this inviting shop resembles the study of an absent-minded professor. But don't be fooled: these guys know their ties. Only the finest Italian silks and English wools are used in neckwear made to customers' specifications. At a push, a tie can be ready in a few hours.

SCALA QUATTORODICI
CLOTHING
CLOTHING

Map p316 (Villa della Scala 13-14; ◷10am-1.30pm & 4-8pm Tue-Sat, 4-8pm Mon; ☐Piazza Trilussa) Make yourself over à la Audrey Hepburn with these classically tailored clothes in beautiful fabrics – either made-to-measure or off-the-peg. Pricey (a frock will set you back €600 plus) but oh so worth it.

San Giovanni & Testaccio

SAN GIOVANNI | CELIO | AVENTINO | TESTACCIO

Neighbourhood Top Five

❶ Facing up to the monumental splendour of the **Basilica di San Giovanni in Laterano** (p173), and feeling very small as you explore the echoing baroque interior of Rome's oldest Christian basilica.

❷ Being over-awed by the colossal ruins of the **Terme di Caracalla** (p176).

❸ Looking through the keyhole of the **Priorato dei Cavalieri di Malta** (p176).

❹ Going underground through layers of history at the **Basilica di San Clemente** (p174).

❺ Grave-spotting in the **Cimitero Acattolico per gli Stranieri** (p177).

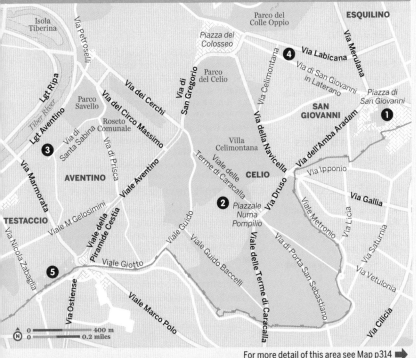

For more detail of this area see Map p314 ➡

Lonely Planet's Top Tip

If you like opera and ballet, check www.operaroma.it for details of summer performances at the Terme di Caracalla. If contemporary art in a gritty urban setting is more your thing, look out for exhibitions and installations at MACRO Testaccio, a gallery space in Rome's former abattoir.

✗ Best Places to Eat

➡ Flavio al Velavevodetto (p178)

➡ Cafè Cafè (p177)

➡ Da Felice (p179)

➡ Pizzeria Da Remo (p178)

➡ Aroma (p178)

For reviews, see p177.➡

🍷 Best Places to Drink

➡ Rec 23 (p179)

➡ Il Pentagrappolo (p179)

➡ Linari (p179)

➡ L'Oasi della Birra (p180)

For reviews, see p179.➡

☉ Best Little-Known Gems

➡ Priorato dei Cavalieri di Malta (p176)

➡ Cimitero Acattolico per gli Stranieri (p177)

➡ Chiesa di Santo Stefano Rotondo (p175)

➡ Basilica di SS Quattro Coronati (p175)

For reviews, see p174.➡

Explore: San Giovanni & Testaccio

Encompassing two of Rome's seven hills, this oft-overlooked part of town offers everything from barnstorming basilicas and medieval churches to ancient ruins, busy markets and hip clubs. The area can easily be divided into two separate patches: San Giovanni and the Celio; and Aventino and Testaccio. A day in each is more than enough to cover the main sights.

Start off at the landmark Basilica di San Giovanni in Laterano, the focal point of the largely residential San Giovanni neighbourhood. It's easily accessible by metro and quite magnificent, both inside and out. Once you've explored the cathedral and surrounding piazza, head down Via di San Giovanni in Laterano towards the Colosseum. Near the bottom, the Basilica di San Clemente is a fascinating church with some thrilling underground ruins. From there, you can walk across to the Celio, the green hill that rises south of the Colosseum. There's not a lot to see, but the graceful Villa Celimontana park is a great place to escape the crowds. Further south, the ruins of the Terme di Caracalla are a thrilling sight.

Further west, on the banks of the Tiber, the once working-class area of Testaccio is a foodie hotspot with a number of excellent trattorias and a popular nightlife district. Rising above it, the Aventino hill boasts a number of serene medieval churches and one of Rome's great curiosities – the famous keyhole view of St Peter's dome.

Local Life

➡ **Romance** Local Lotharios out to impress their loved ones take them to enjoy the sunset views from the Parco Savello (p176) on the Aventino.

➡ **Offal** Testaccio is the spiritual home of 'blood-and-guts' Roman cooking and its popular trattorias and restaurants are the place to try it.

➡ **Parks** You'll often see locals relaxing with a book or going for a leisurely lunchtime stroll in Villa Celimontana (p175).

Getting There & Away

➡ **Bus** Useful bus routes include 85 and 87, both of which stop near the Basilica di San Giovanni in Laterano, and 714, which serves San Giovanni and the Terme di Caracalla.

➡ **Metro** San Giovanni is accessible by metro line A. For Testaccio take line B to Piramide. The Aventino is walkable from Testaccio and Circo Massimo.

➡ **Tram** From San Giovanni tram 3 runs along Viale Aventino to the Piramide area.

TOP SIGHT
BASILICA DI SAN GIOVANNI IN LATERANO

For a thousand years this monumental cathedral was the most important church in Christendom. Dating to the 4th century, it was the first Christian basilica built in the city and, until the late 14th century, it was the pope's main place of worship. It's still Rome's official cathedral and the pope's seat as the bishop of Rome.

The oldest of Rome's four papal basilicas, it was commissioned by the Emperor Constantine and consecrated by Pope Sylvester I in 324. From then until 1309, when the papacy moved to Avignon, it was the principal pontifical church, and the adjacent Palazzo Laterano was the pope's official residence. Both buildings fell into disrepair during the pope's French interlude, and when Pope Gregory XI returned to Rome in 1377 he preferred to decamp to the fortified Vatican.

Over the centuries the basilica has been revamped several times, most notably by Borromini in the 17th century, and by Alessandro Galilei, who added the immense white facade in 1735.

DON'T MISS...

➡ Monument to Pope Sylvester II
➡ The baldachin
➡ The cloister

PRACTICALITIES

➡ Map p314
➡ Piazza di San Giovanni in Laterano 4
➡ basilica/cloister free/€5
➡ ⊙7am-6.30pm, cloister 9am-6pm
➡ Ⓜ San Giovanni

Facade
Surmounted by 15 7m-high statues – Christ with St John the Baptist, John the Evangelist and the 12 Apostles – Galilei's huge facade is an imposing work of late-baroque classicism. Behind the colossal columns there are five sets of doors in the portico. The **central bronze doors** were moved here from the Curia in the Roman Forum, while, on the far right, the **Holy Door** is only opened in Jubilee years.

Interior
The enormous marble-clad interior owes much of its present look to Francesco Borromini, who redecorated it for the 1650 Jubilee. It's a breathtaking sight with a golden **gilt ceiling**, a 15th-century **mosaic floor**, and a wide **central nave** lined with 18th-century sculptures of the apostles, each 4.6m high and set in its own dramatic niche.

At the head of the nave, an elaborate Gothic **baldachin** stands over the papal altar. Dating to the 14th century, this towering ensemble is said to contain the relics of the heads of Sts Peter and Paul. In front, a double staircase leads down to the **confessio** and the Renaissance tomb of Pope Martin V.

Behind the altar, the massive **apse** is decorated with sparkling mosaics. Parts of these date to the 4th century, but most were added in the 1800s.

At the other end of the basilica, on the first pillar in the right-hand nave is an incomplete Giotto fresco. While admiring this, cock your ear towards the next column, where a monument to Pope Sylvester II is said to creak when the death of a pope is imminent.

Cloister
To the left of the altar, the basilica's 13th-century cloister is a lovely, peaceful place with graceful twisted columns set around a central garden. Lining the ambulatories are marble fragments from the original church, including the remains of a 5th-century papal throne and inscriptions of two papal bulls.

SIGHTS

San Giovanni

BASILICA DI SAN GIOVANNI IN LATERANO
BASILICA

See p173.

PALAZZO LATERANO
HISTORIC BUILDING

Map p314 (Piazza di San Giovanni in Laterano; MSan Giovanni) Adjacent to the Basilica di San Giovanni in Laterano, Palazzo Laterano was the official papal residence until the pope moved to the Vatican in 1377. It's still technically Vatican property and today houses offices of the Vicariate of Rome. Much altered over the centuries, it owes its current form to a 16th-century facelift by Domenico Fontana. Overlooking the *palazzo* is Rome's oldest and tallest **obelisk**.

BATTISTERO
CHAPEL

Map p314 (Piazza di San Giovanni in Laterano; ⊘9am-12.30pm & 4-6.30pm; MSan Giovanni) Built by Constantine in the 4th century, this octagonal baptistry served as the prototype for later Christian churches and bell towers. The chief interest, apart from the architecture, is the decorative mosaics, some of which date to the 5th century.

SANTUARIO DELLA SCALA SANTA & SANCTA SANCTORUM
CHAPEL

Map p314 (www.scala-santa.it; Piazza di San Giovanni in Laterano 14; Scala free, Sancta with/without audioguide €5/3.50; ⊘Scala 6am-1pm & 3-7pm summer, to 6.30pm winter, Sancta Sanctorum 9.30am-12.40pm & 3-5.10pm Mon-Sat; MSan Giovanni) The Scala Sancta, said to be the staircase that Jesus walked up in Pontius Pilate's Jerusalem palace, was brought to Rome by St Helena in the 4th century. Pilgrims consider it sacred and climb it on their knees, saying a prayer on each of the 28 steps. At the top, the richly frescoed Sancta Sanctorum (Holy of Holies) was formerly the pope's private chapel.

Behind the sanctuary building you'll see a cut-off cross-section of a building adorned with a showy gold mosaic. This is the **Triclinium Leoninum** (Map p314; MSan Giovanni), an 18th-century reconstruction of a wall from the original Palazzo Laterano.

⊙ TOP SIGHT
BASILICA DI SAN CLEMENTE

This fascinating basilica provides a glimpse into Rome's multilayered past: a 12th-century basilica built atop a 4th-century church, which, in turn, stands over a 2nd-century pagan temple and a 1st-century Roman house. Beneath it all are foundations dating to the Roman Republic.

The ground-floor *basilica superiore* contains some glorious works of medieval art. These include a golden 12th-century apse mosaic, the *Trionfo della Croce* (Triumph of the Cross), showing the Madonna and St John the Baptist standing by a cross on which Christ is represented with 12 white doves (symbolising the apostles). Also impressive are Masolino's 15th-century frescoes in the **Cappella di Santa Caterina**, depicting a crucifixion scene and episodes from the life of St Catherine.

Steps lead down to the 4th-century *basilica inferiore*, mostly destroyed by Norman invaders in 1084, but with some faded 11th-century frescoes illustrating the life of San Clemente. Down another level you'll find yourself walking an ancient lane leading to a 1st-century Roman house and a dark, 2nd-century temple to Mithras, with an altar showing the god slaying a bull. Beneath it all, you can hear the eerie sound of a subterranean river flowing through a Republic-era drain.

DON'T MISS...
→ *Trionfo della Croce*
→ Cappella di Santa Caterina
→ *Basilica inferiore*
→ Temple of Mithras

PRACTICALITIES
→ Map p314
→ www.basilicasan-clemente.com
→ Via di San Giovanni in Laterano
→ excavations adult/reduced €10/5
→ ⊘9am-12.30pm & 3-6pm Mon-Sat, 12.15-6pm Sun
→ ▣Via Labicana

◉ Celio

BASILICA DI SS QUATTRO CORONATI
BASILICA

Map p314 (Via dei Santissimi Quattro Coronati 20; ⊗10-11.45am & 4-5.45pm Mon-Sat, 4-5.45pm Sun; ☐Via di San Giovanni in Laterano) This brooding fortified church harbours some lovely 13th-century frescoes and a delightful hidden cloister. The frescoes, in the **Oratorio di San Silvestro**, depict the story of the Donation of Constantine, a notorious forged document with which the emperor Constantine ceded control of Rome and the Western Roman Empire to the papacy.

To access the Oratorio, ring the bell in the entrance courtyard. You might also have to ring for the cloister, which is situated off the northern aisle.

The basilica, which dates to the 6th century, took on its present form in the 12th-century after the original was destroyed by Normans in 1084. Its name – the Basilica of the Four Crowned Martyrs – is a reference to four Christian sculptors who were supposedly killed by Diocletian for refusing to make a statue of a pagan god.

The basilica's frescoed **Aula Gotica** (Gothic Hall) was recently reopened to occasional guided tours. For details, see www.aulagoticasantiquattrocoronati.it.

CASE ROMANE
CHRISTIAN SITE

Map p314 (☑06 7045 4544; www.caseromane.it; adult/reduced €6/4; ⊗10am-1pm & 3-6pm Thu-Mon; ☐Via Claudia) According to tradition, the apostles John and Paul lived in these subterranean houses beneath the Basilica di SS Giovanni e Paolo before they were beheaded by the emperor Julian. There's actually no direct evidence for this, although research has revealed that the houses were used for Christian worship. There are more than 20 rooms, many of them richly decorated. Entry is to the side of the basilica on the Clivo di Scauro.

CHIESA DI SAN GREGORIO MAGNO
CHURCH

Map p314 (Piazza di San Gregorio 1; ⊗9am-1pm & 3.30-7pm, Cappella di Sant'Andrea 9.30am-12.30pm Tue, Thu, Sat & Sun; Ⓜ Colosseo or Circo Massimo) Ring for admission to this landmark church, which stands on the spot where Pope Gregory supposedly dispatched St Augustine to convert the British. It was originally the pope's family home, but in

THE SUBTERRANEAN CULT OF MITHRAISM

The cult of Mithraism was hugely popular with the ancient Roman military. According to its mythology, Mithras, a young, handsome god, was ordered to slay a wild bull by the Sun. As the bull died, it gave life, its blood causing wheat and other plants to grow.

Mithraic temples, known as Mithraeums, were almost always in underground locations or caves, reflecting the belief that caverns represented the cosmos. In these Mithraeums, devotees underwent complex initiation rites, and ate bread and water as a representation of the body and the blood of the bull. Sound familiar? The early Christians thought so too, and were fervently opposed to the cult.

575 he converted it into a monastery. It was rebuilt in the 17th century and given a baroque makeover a century later.

Inside, look out for the **Cappella Salviati**, a 16th-century chapel by Carlo Maderno, which contains a fresco of a *Madonna with Child*. Outside, the **Cappella di Sant'Andrea** is the most interesting of three small chapels, with frescoes by Domenichino, Guido Reni and Giovanni Lanfranco.

VILLA CELIMONTANA
PARK

Map p314 (⊗7am-sunset; ☐Via della Navicella) With its grassy banks and colourful flower beds, this leafy park is a wonderful place to escape the crowds and enjoy a summer picnic. At its centre is a 16th-century villa housing the Italian Geographical Society.

CHIESA DI SANTO STEFANO ROTONDO
CHURCH

Map p314 (www.santo-stefano-rotondo.it; Via di Santo Stefano Rotondo 7; ⊗10am-1pm & 2-5pm winter, 10am-1pm & 3-6pm summer; ☐Via della Navicella) Set in its own secluded grounds, this haunting church boasts a porticoed facade and a round, columned interior. But what really gets the heart racing is the graphic wall decor – a cycle of 16th-century frescoes depicting the tortures suffered by many early Christian martyrs.

Describing them in 1846, Charles Dickens wrote: 'Such a panorama of horror and butchery no man could imagine in his

TOP SIGHT
TERME DI CARACALLA

The remains of the emperor Caracalla's vast baths complex are among Rome's most awe-inspiring ruins. Inaugurated in 216, the original 10-hectare complex comprised baths, gyms, libraries, shops and gardens. Between 6000 and 8000 people passed through every day, while, underground, hundreds of slaves sweated in 9.5km of tunnels, tending to the intricate plumbing systems.

The baths remained in continuous use until 537, when the invading Visigoths cut off Rome's water supply. Excavations in the 16th and 17th centuries unearthed a number of important sculptures, many of which found their way into the Farnese family's art collection.

Most of the ruins are what's left of the central bath house. This was a huge rectangular edifice bookended by two **palestre** (gyms) and centred on a **frigidarium** (cold room), where bathers would stop after spells in the warmer **tepidarium** and dome-capped **caldaria** (hot room).

As you traverse the ruins towards the *palestra orientale*, look out for a slab of white, pockmarked marble on your right. This is a board from an ancient game called *tropa* (the hole game).

In summer the ruins are used to stage spectacular opera and ballet performances.

DON'T MISS...

➡ The *frigidarium*
➡ The *caldaria*
➡ The *palestre*

PRACTICALITIES

➡ Map p314000
➡ 📞06 3996 7700
➡ www.coopculture.it
➡ Viale delle Terme di Caracalla 52
➡ adult/reduced €6/3
➡ ⏰9am-1hr before sunset Tue-Sun, 9am-2pm Mon
➡ 🚌Viale delle Terme di Caracalla

---

sleep, though he were to eat a whole pig, raw, for supper.'

The church, one of Rome's oldest, dates to the late 5th century, although it was subsequently altered in the 12th and 15th centuries.

⊙ Aventino & Around

BASILICA DI SANTA SABINA
BASILICA

Map p314 (📞06 5 79 41; Piazza Pietro d'Illiria 1; ⏰6.30am-12.45pm & 3-8pm; 🚌Lungotevere Aventino) This solemn basilica, one of Rome's most beautiful medieval churches, was founded by Peter of Illyria in around AD 422. It was enlarged in the 9th century and again in 1216, just before it was given to the newly founded Dominican order – note the tombstone of Muñoz de Zamora, one of the order's founding fathers, in the nave floor. A 20th-century restoration returned it to its original look.

One of the few features to have survived since the 4th century are the basilica's cypress-wood doors. They feature 18 carved panels depicting biblical events, including one of the oldest Crucifixion scenes in existence. It's quite hard to make out in the top

left, but there's a depiction of Jesus and the two thieves, although, strangely, not their crosses.

Inside, 24 custom-made columns support an arcade decorated with a faded red-and-green frieze. Light streams in from high nave windows that were added in the 9th century, along with the carved choir, pulpit and bishop's throne.

Behind the church is a garden and a meditative 13th-century cloister.

PARCO SAVELLO
PARK

Map p314 (Via di Santa Sabina; ⏰7am-6pm Oct-Feb, to 8pm Mar & Sep, to 9pm Apr-Aug; 🚌Lungotevere Aventino) Known to Romans as the *Giardino degli Aranci* (Orange Garden), this pocket-sized park is a romantic haven. Grab a perch at the small panoramic terrace and watch the sun set over the Tiber and St Peter's dome.

PRIORATO DEI CAVALIERI DI MALTA
HISTORIC BUILDING

Map p314 (Piazza dei Cavalieri di Malta; ⏰closed to the public; 🚌Lungotevere Aventino) Fronting an ornate cypress-shaded piazza, the Roman headquarters of the *Cavalieri di Mal-*

ta (Knights of Malta) boast one of Rome's most celebrated views. It's not immediately apparent but look through the keyhole in the Priorato's green door and you'll see the dome of St Peter's Basilica perfectly aligned at the end of a hedge-lined avenue.

⊙ Testaccio

CIMITERO ACATTOLICO
PER GLI STRANIERI   CEMETERY
Map p314 (www.cemeteryrome.it; Via Caio Cestio 5; voluntary donation €3; ⊙9am-5pm Mon-Sat, to 1pm Sun; ⓂPiramide) Despite the roads that surround it, Rome's 'non-Catholic' Cemetery is a verdant oasis of peace. An air of Grand Tour romance hangs over the site where up to 4000 people lie buried, including poets Keats and Shelley, and Italian political thinker Antonio Gramsci.

Among the gravestones and cypress trees, look out for the *Angelo del Dolore* (Angel of Grief), a much-replicated 1894 sculpture that US artist William Wetmore Story created for his wife's grave.

PIRAMIDE DI CAIO CESTIO   LANDMARK
Map p314 (☎06 3996 7700; www.coopculture.it; admission €5.50; ⊙guided tour 11am 2nd & 4th Sat of month; ⓂPiramide) Sticking out like, well, an Egyptian pyramid, this distinctive landmark looms over a busy traffic junction near Piramide metro station. A 36m-high marble-and-brick tomb, it was built for Gaius Cestius, a 1st-century-BC magistrate, and some 200 years later was incorporated into the Aurelian walls near Porta San Paolo. The surrounding area is today known as Piramide.

MONTE TESTACCIO   HISTORIC SITE
Map p314 (☎06 06 08; Via Nicolo Zabaglia 24, cnr Via Galvani; adult/reduced €4/3 plus cost of tour; ⊙group visits only, reservation necessary; ⓆVia Marmorata) In the heart of the eponymous neighbourhood, Monte Testaccio, aka Monte dei Cocci, is an artificial grass-covered hill made of smashed amphorae (*testae* in Latin, hence the area's name, Testaccio).

Between the 2nd century BC and the 3rd century AD, Testaccio was Rome's river port. Supplies of olive oil were transported here in huge terracotta amphorae, which, once emptied, were broken and the fragments stacked in a huge pile near the storehouses. Over time, this pile grew into a substantial 49m-high hill – Monte Testaccio.

MACRO TESTACCIO   GALLERY
Map p314 (☎06 06 08; www.museomacro. org; Piazza Orazio Giustiniani 4; adult/reduced €8.50/7.50; ⊙4-10pm Tue-Sun; ⓆVia Marmorata) Housed in Rome's former slaughterhouse, MACRO Testaccio (the second of MACRO's two exhibition spaces) is part of a cultural complex that also includes Rome's Accademia di Belle Arti and the University of Roma Tre's Architecture Faculty. Contemporary art exhibitions are staged in two cavernous industrial halls. Note that the gallery opens only when there's an exhibition on – check the website for details.

✗ EATING

✗ San Giovanni & Celio

★CAFÈ CAFÈ   BISTRO €
Map p314 (☎06 700 87 43; www.cafecafebistrot. it; Via dei Santissimi Quattro Coronati 44; meals €15-20; ⊙9.30am-11pm; ⓆVia di San Giovanni in Laterano) Cosy, relaxed and welcoming, this cafe-bistro is a far cry from the usual impersonal eateries in the Colosseum area. With its rustic wooden tables, butternut walls and wine bottles, it's a charming spot to recharge your batteries over tea and homemade cake, a light lunch or laid-back dinner. There's also brunch on Sundays.

LI RIONI   PIZZA €
Map p314 (☎06 7045 0605; Via dei Santissimi Quattro Coronati 24; meals €15-20; ⊙ 7pm-midnight Thu-Tue, closed Aug; ⓆVia di San Giovanni in Laterano) Locals swear by Li Rioni, arriving for the second sitting around 9pm after the tourists have left. A classic neighbourhood pizzeria, it buzzes most nights as diners squeeze into the kitschy interior – set up as a Roman street scene – and tuck into wood-fired thin-crust pizzas and crispy fried starters.

IL BOCCONCINO   TRATTORIA €€
Map p314 (☎06 7707 9175; www.ilbocconcino. com; Via Ostilia 23; meals €35; ⊙12.30-3.30pm & 7.30-11.30pm Thu-Tue, closed Aug; ⓆVia Labicana) This laid-back trattoria is one of the better options in the touristy pocket near the Colosseum, standing out for its authentic regional cooking and use of locally sourced seasonal ingredients. Daily specials are chalked up on blackboards; plus there's

---

ⓘ MENU DECODER

The hallmark of an authentic Roman menu is the presence of offal. The Roman love of nose-to-tail eating arose in Testaccio around the city abattoir, and many of the area's trattorias still serve traditional offal-based dishes. So whether you want to avoid them or try them, look out for *pajata* (veal's intestines), *trippa* (tripe), *coda alla vaccinara* (oxtail), *coratella* (heart, lung and liver), *animelle* (sweetbreads), *testarella* (head), *lingua* (tongue) and *zampone* (trotters).

---

a regular menu of classic Roman pastas, meaty mains and imaginative desserts.

TAVERNA DEI QUARANTA   TRATTORIA €€

Map p314 (🗹06 700 05 50; www.tavernadeiquaranta.com; Via Claudia 24; meals €30; ⊙noon-3.30pm & 7.30pm-midnight; 🚇Via Claudia) Tasty traditional food and a prime location – near the Colosseum but just off the beaten track – are the hallmarks of this family-run trattoria. There are no great surprises on the menu, but daily specials add variety and the desserts are homemade – always a good sign.

CAFFÈ PROPAGANDA   BISTRO €€

Map p314 (🗹06 9453 4256; www.caffepropaganda.it; Via Claudia 15; meals €30-40; ⊙12.30pm-2am Tue-Sun; 🚇Via Claudia) This Paris-inspired bistro is a good-looking place with a striking zinc bar, 5m-high ceilings, bric-a-brac on the white-tiled walls, and a menu that covers all the bases, with everything from cocktails and cake to traditional Roman pastas, omelettes, salads and *dolci*.

AROMA   RISTORANTE €€€

Map p314 (🗹06 9761 5109; www.aromarestaurant.it; Via Labicana 125; tasting menus €130; ⊙12.30-3pm & 7.30-11.30pm; 🚇Via Labicana) One for a special-occasion dinner, the rooftop restaurant of the Palazzo Manfredi hotel offers 'marry-me' views of the Colosseum and Michelin-starred food that rises to the occasion. Overseeing the kitchen is chef Giuseppe Di Iorio, whose brand of luxurious, forward-thinking Mediterranean cuisine has won widespread applause from critics and diners alike.

✗ Aventino & Around

IL GELATO   GELATERIA €

Map p314 (Viale Aventino 59; gelato €2-4.50; ⊙10am-midnight summer, 11am-9pm winter; 🚇Viale Aventino) This is the Aventine outpost of the gelato empire built by Rome's ice-cream king, Claudio Torcè. His creamy creations are seasonal and preservative free, ranging from the classic to the decidedly not – anyone for salted peanut or green tea?

✗ Testaccio

TRAPIZZINO   FAST FOOD €

Map p314 (www.trapizzino.it; Via Branca 88; trapizzini from €3.50; ⊙noon-1am Tue-Sun; 🚇Via Marmorata) This pocket-size joint is the birthplace of the *trapizzino*, a kind of hybrid sandwich made by stuffing a small cone of doughy bread with fillers like *polpette al sugo* (meatballs in tomato sauce) or *pollo alla cacc*iatore (stewed chicken). They're messy to eat but quite delicious.

PIZZERIA DA REMO   PIZZA €

Map p314 (🗹06 574 62 70; Piazza Santa Maria Liberatrice 44; pizzas from €5.50; ⊙7pm-1am Mon-Sat; 🚇Via Marmorata) For an authentic Roman experience, join the noisy crowds at one of the city's best-known and most popular pizzerias. It's a spartan-looking place, but the thin-crust Roman pizzas are the business, and there's a cheerful, boisterous vibe. Expect to queue after 8.30pm.

MORDI E VAI   FAST FOOD €

Map p314 (www.mordievai.it; Box 15, Nuovo Mercato Testaccio; panini €3; ⊙6am-3pm Mon-Sat; 🚇Via Galvani) This critically acclaimed market stall – 'Bite and Go' in English – is all about fast food. But fast food Roman style, which means bread rolls filled with *allesso di scottona* (tender slow-cooked beef, the stall's signature dish) or plastic plates of no-nonsense meat-and-veg dishes.

FLAVIO AL VELAVEVODETTO   TRATTORIA €€

Map p314 (🗹06 574 41 94; www.ristorantevelavevodetto.it; Via di Monte Testaccio 97-99; meals €30-35; ⊙12.30-3pm & 7.45-11pm; 🚇Via Galvani) Housed in a rustic Pompeian-red villa, this welcoming eatery specialises in earthy, no-nonsense *cucina romana* (Roman cuisine). Expect *antipasti* of cheeses and cured meats, huge helpings of homemade pastas, and uncomplicated meat dishes.

DA FELICE
LAZIO CUISINE €€

Map p314 (☑06 574 68 00; www.felicetestaccio.
it; Via Mastro Giorgio 29; meals €35-40; ☻12.30-
3pm & 7.30-10.30pm; ☐Via Marmorata) Foodies
swear by this historic stalwart, famous for
its unwavering dedication to local culinary
traditions. In contrast to the light-touch
modern decor, the menu is pure old-school
with a classic weekly timetable: *pasta e fa-
gioli* (pasta and beans) on Tuesdays, *bollito
di manzo* (boiled beef) on Thursdays, seafood on Fridays. Reservations essential.

TRATTORIA DA BUCATINO
TRATTORIA €€

Map p314 (☑06 574 68 86; www.bucatino.com;
Via Luca della Robbia 84; meals €30-35; ☻noon-
3pm & 7-11.55pm Tue-Sun; ☐Via Marmorata)
This genuine neighbourhood trattoria is
hugely popular. It's far from refined with
its dated decor and brusque service, but
the typical Roman food is excellent – try its
trademark *bucatini all'amatriciana* – and
helpings are generous.

CHECCHINO DAL 1887
LAZIO CUISINE €€€

Map p314 (☑06 574 63 18; www.checchino-
dal-1887.com; Via di Monte Testaccio 30; tasting
menus €40-65; ☻12.30-3pm & 8pm-midnight
Tue-Sat; ☐Via Galvani) A pig's whisker from
the city's former slaughterhouse, Checchino
is one of the grander restaurants specialising in the *quinto quarto* ('fifth quarter' –
the insides of the animal). Signature dishes
include *coda all vaccinara* (oxtail stew)
and *rigatoni alla pajata* (pasta tubes with
a sauce of tomato and veal intestines).

🍷 DRINKING & NIGHTLIFE

🍷 San Giovanni & Celio

IL PENTAGRAPPOLO
WINE BAR

Map p314 (Via Celimontana 21b; ☻noon-3pm &
6pm-1am Tue-Fri, 6pm-1am Sat & Sun; Ⓜ Colosseo) This vaulted, softly lit bar is the perfect antidote to sightseeing overload. Join
the mellow crowd for an evening of wine
and jazz courtesy of the frequent live gigs.
There's also lunch and a daily aperitif.

COMING OUT
BAR

Map p314 (www.comingout.it; Via di San Giovanni
in Laterano 8; ☻7am-2am; ☐Via Labicana) On
warm evenings, with lively crowds on the

GAY STREET

The bottom end of Via di San Giovanni
di Laterano, the sloping street that
runs from the Basilica di San Giovanni
in Laterano to near the Colosseum, is a
favourite haunt of Rome's gay community. Not so much during the day, but
in the evening, bars like **Coming Out**
(p179) and **My Bar** (Map p314; Via di
San Giovanni in Laterano 12; ☻9am-2am;
☐Via Labicana) burst into life, attracting large crowds of mainly gay men.

street and the Colosseum as a backdrop,
there are few finer places to sip at than this
friendly, gay bar. It's open all day but is at
its best in the evening when the the atmosphere hots up and the gigs, drag shows and
karaoke nights get under way.

🍷 Testaccio

REC 23
BAR

Map p314 (☑06 8746 2147; www.rec23.com; Piazza dell'Emporio 2; ☻6.30pm-2am daily & 12.30-
3.30pm Sat & Sun; ☐Via Marmorata) All plate
glass and exposed brick, this popular, New
York–inspired venue caters to all moods,
serving aperitifs, restaurant meals, and
a weekend brunch. Arrive thirsty to take
on the Testaccio Mule, one of a long list of
cocktails, or get to grips with the selection
of Scottish whiskies and Latin American
rums. It also hosts regular live gigs.

LINARI
CAFE

Map p314 (Via Nicola Zabaglia 9; ☻7am-11pm
Wed-Mon; ☐Via Marmorata) An authentic local hang-out, Linari has the busy clatter of
a good bar, with excellent pastries, splendid
coffee and plenty of bar-side banter. There
are a few outside tables, ideal for a cheap
lunch, but you'll have to outfox the neighbourhood ladies to get one.

BIG BANG
CLUB

Map p314 (www.bigbangroma.org; Via di Monte
Testaccio 22; ☻10pm-4.30am Fri & Sat; ☐Via
Galvani) For one of the capital's best reggae
parties, head to the Bababoomtime Friday-
night session at Big Bang. The club, housed
in Rome's graffiti-splayed former slaughterhouse, draws a casual, music-loving
crowd who know their reggae, dancehall,
dub and techno.

L'OASI DELLA BIRRA   BAR

Map p314 (☎06 574 61 22; Piazza Testaccio 41; ☺4.30pm-2am; ◧Via Marmorata) In a local bottle shop, this cramped cellar bar is exactly what it says it is – an Oasis of Beer. With up to 500 labels, from Teutonic heavyweights to boutique brews, as well as wines, cheeses, cold cuts and the like, it's ideally set up for elbow-to-elbow quaffing.

L'ALIBI   CLUB

Map p314 (Via di Monte Testaccio 44; ☺11.30pm-5am Thu-Sun; ◧Via Galvani) A historic gay club, L'Alibi does high-camp with style, putting on kitsch shows and playing house, techno and dance to a mixed gay and straight crowd. It's spread over three floors, and if the sweaty atmosphere on the dance floors gets too much, head up to the spacious summer terrace. Saturday's Tommy Night is the hot date right now.

 ENTERTAINMENT

CONTESTACCIO   LIVE MUSIC

Map p314 (www.contestaccio.com; Via di Monte Testaccio 65b; ☺7pm-4am Tue-Sun; ◧Via Galvani) With an under-the-stars terrace and cool, arched interior, ConteStaccio is one of the top venues on the Testaccio clubbing strip. It's something of a multipurpose outfit with a cocktail bar, a pizzeria and a restaurant but is best known for its daily concerts. Gigs by emerging groups set the tone, spanning indie, rock, acoustic, funk and electronic.

 SHOPPING

VOLPETTI   FOOD & DRINK

Map p314 (www.volpetti.com; Via Marmorata 47; ☺8am-2pm & 5-8.15pm Mon-Sat; ◧Via Marmorata) This superstocked deli, considered by many the best in town, is a treasure trove of gourmet delicacies. Helpful staff will guide you through the extensive selection of smelly cheeses, homemade pastas, olive oils, vinegars, cured meats, veggie pies, wines and grappas. It also serves excellent sliced pizza.

NUOVO MERCATO DI TESTACCIO   MARKET

Map p314 (entrances Via Galvani, Via Beniamino Franklin; ☺6am-3pm Mon-Sat; ◧Via Marmorata) Even if you don't need to buy anything, a trip to Testaccio's daily food market is fun. Occupying a modern, purpose-built site, it hums with activity as locals go about their daily shopping, picking, prodding and sniffing the brightly coloured produce and cheerfully shouting at all and sundry.

CALZATURE BOCCANERA   SHOES

Map p314 (Via Luca della Robbia 36; ☺9.30am-1.30pm Tue-Sat & 3.30-7.30pm Mon-Sat,; ◧Via Marmorata) From just-off-the-runway heels to classic driving shoes, high-end trainers and timeless lace-ups, this historic shoe shop stocks a wide range of footwear by top international brands, as well as bags, belts and leather accessories.

SOUL FOOD   MUSIC

Map p314 (www.haterecords.com; Via di San Giovanni in Laterano 192; ☺10.30am-1.30pm & 3.30-8pm Tue-Sat; ◧Via di San Giovanni in Laterano) Run by Hate Records, Soul Food is a laid-back record store with an eclectic collection of vinyl that runs the musical gamut, from '60s garage and rockabilly to punk, indie, new wave, folk, funk and soul. You'll also find retro-design T-shirts, fanzines and other groupie clobber.

VIA SANNIO   MARKET

Map p314 (☺9am-1.30pm Mon-Sat; ⓂSan Giovanni) This clothes market in the shadow of the Aurelian Walls is awash with wardrobe staples. It has a good assortment of new and vintage clothes, bargain-price shoes, jeans and leather jackets.

Villa Borghese & Northern Rome

VILLA BORGHESE | FLAMINIO | SALARIO | NOMENTANO | PARIOLI

Neighbourhood Top Five

1 Getting to grips with artistic genius at the lavish **Museo e Galleria Borghese** (p183), where Bernini's sculptures steal the show, but you'll also find masterpieces by Canova, Caravaggio, Titian and Raphael.

2 Strolling the leafy lanes of Rome's most famous park, **Villa Borghese** (p186).

3 Applauding the sophistication of Etruscan art at the **Museo Nazionale Etrusco di Villa Giulia** (p186).

4 Going face to face with the greats of modern art at the **Galleria Nazionale d'Arte Moderna e Contemporanea** (p187).

5 Catching a world-class concert at the **Auditorium Parco della Musica** (p191).

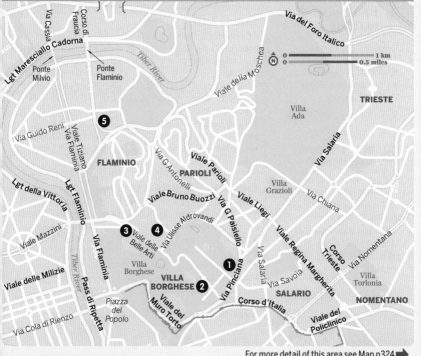

For more detail of this area see Map p324

Lonely Planet's Top Tip

Be sure to book your visit to the Museo e Galleria Borghese. It only takes a quick phone call and you won't get in without a reservation.

On football and rugby match days – usually a Saturday or Sunday – the routes into the Stadio Olimpico get very busy, so watch out around Piazza Mancini and in the river area near the stadium.

 Best Places to Eat

➡ Metamorfosi (p191)

➡ Neve di Latte (p190)

➡ Molto (p191)

➡ Bar Pompi (p190)

For reviews, see p190.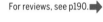

Best Places to Drink

➡ Momart (p191)

➡ Brancaleone (p191)

➡ Lanificio 159 (p191)

➡ Chioschetto di Ponte Milvio (p191)

For reviews, see p191.

Best Museums & Galleries

➡ Museo e Galleria Borghese (p183)

➡ Museo Nazionale Etrusco di Villa Giulia (p186)

➡ Galleria Nazionale d'Arte Moderna e Contemporanea (p187)

➡ MAXXI (p187)

➡ MACRO (p188)

For reviews, see p186.

Explore Villa Borghese & Northern Rome

Although less packed with traditional sights than elsewhere, this large swathe of northern Rome is rich in interest. The obvious starting point is Villa Borghese, an attractive park counting the city's zoo, its largest modern art gallery, and a stunning Etruscan museum among its myriad attractions. But its great scene-stealing highlight is the Museo e Galleria Borghese, one of Rome's top art museums.

From Piazzale Flaminio, a tram heads up Via Flaminia to two of Rome's most important modern buildings: Renzo Piano's arts centre, the Auditorium Parco della Musica, and Zaha Hadid's contemporary art gallery, MAXXI. Continue up the road and you come to Ponte Milvio, a handsome footbridge and scene of an ancient Roman battle. Over the river and to the west, the Stadio Olimpico is Rome's impressive football stadium.

To the east of Villa Borghese, Via Salaria, the old Roman *sale* (salt) road, runs through a smart residential and business district. To the north, Villa Ada expands northwards while, to the south, Via Nomentana traverses acres of housing as it heads out of town. On Via Nomentana, Villa Torlonia is a captivating park, and the Basilica di Sant'Agnese fuori le Mura claims Rome's oldest Christian mosaic.

Local Life

➡**Concerts & Events** Romans are avid supporters of concerts at the Auditorium Parco della Musica (p191). Also check for events at the MAXXI and MACRO art galleries.

➡**Parks** Tourists tend to stop at Villa Borghese (p186), but locals often head to Villa Torlonia (p189) and Villa Ada (p188).

➡**Hang-outs** Piazzale Ponte Milvio is a favourite lunchtime haunt and an evening meeting point for young locals.

Getting There & Away

➡**Bus** Buses 116 and 53 head up to Villa Borghese from Via Vittorio Veneto near Barberini metro station. There are regular buses along Via Nomentana and Via Salaria.

➡**Metro** Villa Borghese is accessible from Flaminio and Spagna stations (both line A).

➡**Tram** Tram 2 trundles up Via Flaminia from Piazzale Flaminio; tram 3 connects Villa Borghese with San Lorenzo, San Giovanni and Testaccio; tram 19 runs from Piazza del Risorgimento (near the Vatican) to Villa Borghese and Viale Regina Margherita.

TOP SIGHT
MUSEO E GALLERIA BORGHESE

If you have time, or inclination, for only one art gallery in Rome, make it this one. Housing what's often referred to as the 'queen of all private art collections', it boasts some of the city's finest art treasures, including a series of sensational sculptures by Gian Lorenzo Bernini and important paintings by the likes of Caravaggio, Titian, Raphael and Rubens.

To limit crowds, visitors are admitted at two-hourly intervals, so you'll need to book your ticket and get an entry time.

The Villa

The museum's collection was formed by Cardinal Scipione Borghese (1579–1633), the most knowledgable and ruthless art collector of his day. It was originally housed in the cardinal's residence near St Peter's but in the 1620s he had it transferred to his new villa just outside Porta Pinciana. And it's here, in the villa's central building, the Casino Borghese, that you'll see it today.

Over the centuries the villa has undergone several overhauls, most notably in the late 1700s when Prince Marcantonio Borghese added much of the lavish neoclassical decor (including the Mariano Rossi fresco pictured above). But while the villa remained intact, the collection did not. Much of the antique statuary was carted off to the Louvre in the early 19th century, and other pieces were gradually sold off. In 1902 the Italian State bought the Casino, but it wasn't until 1997 that the collection was finally put on public display.

The villa is divided into two parts: the ground-floor museum, with its superb sculptures, intricate Roman floor mosaics and hypnotic trompe l'oeil frescoes; and the upstairs picture gallery.

DON'T MISS

➡ Ratto di Proserpina
➡ Venere Vincitrice
➡ Ragazzo col Canestro di Frutta
➡ La Deposizione di Cristo
➡ Amor Sacro e Amor Profano

PRACTICALITIES

➡ Map p324, F6
➡ 06 3 28 10
➡ www.galleria-borghese.it
➡ Piazzale del Museo Borghese 5
➡ adult/reduced €11/6.50
➡ 9am-7pm Tue-Sun
➡ Via Pinciana

CARDINAL SCIPIONE BORGHESE

Cardinal Scipione Caffarelli Borghese (1576–1633) was one of the most influential figures in Rome's baroque art world. Blessed with wealth, power and position – his uncle Pope Paul V made him a cardinal when he was just 26 – he sponsored the greatest artists of the day, including Caravaggio, Bernini, Domenichino, Guido Reni and Peter Paul Rubens. Yet while he promoted the artists he didn't always see eye to eye with them and he was quite prepared to play dirty to get his hands on their works: he had the fashionable painter Cavaliere d'Arpino flung into jail in order to confiscate his canvases and had Domenichino arrested to force him to surrender *La Caccia di Diana* (The Hunt of Diana).

For a restorative coffee, there's a cafe next to the bookshop in the basement reception hall.

Ground Floor

The **entrance hall** features 4th-century floor mosaics of fighting gladiators and a 2nd-century *Satiro Combattente* (Fighting Satyr). High on the wall is a gravity-defying bas-relief of a horse and rider falling into the void by Pietro Bernini (Gian Lorenzo's father).

Sala I is centred on Antonio Canova's daring depiction of Napoleon's sister, Paolina Bonaparte Borghese, reclining topless as *Venere Vincitrice* (Venus Victrix; 1805–08). Its suggestive pose and technical virtuosity is typical of Canova's elegant, mildly erotic neoclassical style.

But it's Gian Lorenzo Bernini's sculptures – flamboyant depictions of pagan myths – that really steal the show. Just look at Daphne's hands morphing into leaves in the swirling *Apollo e Dafne* (1622–25) in **Sala III**, or Pluto's hand pressing into the seemingly soft flesh of Persephone's thigh in the *Ratto di Proserpina* (Rape of Proserpina; 1621–22) in **Sala IV**.

Caravaggio, one of Cardinal Scipione's favourite artists, dominates **Sala VIII**. You'll see a dissipated *Bacchino malato* (Young Sick Bacchus; 1593–94), the strangely beautiful *La Madonna dei Palafrenieri* (Madonna of the Palafrenieri; 1605–06), and *San Giovanni Battista* (St John the Baptist; 1609–10), probably his last work. There's also the much-loved *Ragazzo col Canestro di Frutta* (Boy with a Basket of Fruit; 1593–95) and dramatic *Davide con la Testa di Golia* (David with the Head of Goliath; 1609–10) – Goliath's head is said to be a self-portrait.

Picture Gallery

With works representing the best of the Tuscan, Venetian, Umbrian and northern European schools, the upstairs picture gallery offers a wonderful snapshot of Renaissance art.

In **Sala IX** don't miss Raphael's extraordinary *La Deposizione di Cristo* (The Deposition; 1507) and his charming *Dama con Liocorno* (Lady with a Unicorn; 1506). In the same room you'll find Fra Bartolomeo's superb *Adorazione del Bambino* (Adoration of the Christ Child; 1499) and Perugino's *Madonna col Bambino* (Madonna and Child; early 16th century).

Next door, Correggio's *Danäe* (1530–31) shares wall space with a willowy Venus, as portrayed by Cranach in his *Venere e Amore che Reca Il Favo do Miele* (Venus and Cupid with Honeycomb; 1531).

Moving on, **Sala XIV** boasts two self-portraits by Bernini, and **Sala XVIII** contains two significant works by Rubens: *Compianto su Cristo morto* (The Deposition; 1603) and *Susanna e I Vecchioni* (Susanna and the Elders; 1605–07).

To finish, Titian's early masterpiece *Amor Sacro e Amor Profano* (Sacred and Profane Love; 1514) in **Sala XX** is one of the collection's most prized works.

MUSEO E GALLERIA BORGHESE

Services and Amenities Level (Basement)

First Floor

Ground Floor

◉ SIGHTS

◉ Villa Borghese & Around

MUSEO E GALLERIA BORGHESE   MUSEUM
See p183.

VILLA BORGHESE   PARK
Map p324 (entrances at Piazzale San Paolo del Brasile, Piazzale Flaminio, Via Pinciana, Via Raimondo, Largo Pablo Picasso; ⊘dawn-dusk; ◻Porta Pinciana) Locals, lovers, tourists, joggers – no one can resist the lure of Rome's most celebrated park. Originally the 17th-century estate of Cardinal Scipione Borghese, it covers about 80 hectares of wooded glades, gardens and grassy banks. Among its attractions are several excellent museums, the landscaped **Giardino del Lago** (boat hire per person €3 for 20 minutes; ⊘7am-9pm), and **Piazza di Siena** (◻Porta Pinciana), a dusty arena used for Rome's top equestrian event in May.

Film buffs should head to the area around the Piazzale San Paolo del Brasile entrance, where the Casa del Cinema (p192) hosts regular film-related events, and the **Cinema dei Piccoli** (☑06 855 34 85; www. cinemadeipiccoli.it; Viale delle Pineta 15; tickets Mon-Fri €5, Sat & Sun €6; ◻Porta Pinciana) is the world's smallest cinema.

Bike hire is available at various points, including Largo Pablo Picasso, for €5/15 per hour/day. Note that Monday is not a good day to explore Villa Borghese, as all the museums and galleries are shut – they open Tuesday through Sunday.

MUSEO CARLO BILOTTI   GALLERY
Map p324 (☑06 06 08; www.museocarlobilotti. it; Viale Fiorello La Guardia; ⊘10am-4pm Tue-Fri winter, 1-7pm Tue-Fri summer, 10am-7pm Sat & Sun year-round; ◻Porta Pinciana) **FREE** The Orangery of Villa Borghese provides the handsome setting for the art collection of billionaire cosmetics magnate Carlo Bilotti. The main focus are 18 works by Giorgio de Chirico (1888–1978), one of Italy's foremost modern artists, but also of note is a Warhol portrait of Bilotti's wife and daughter.

GALLERIA NAZIONALE D'ARTE MODERNA E CONTEMPORANEA   GALLERY
Map p324 (☑06 3229 8221; www.gnam.beniculturali.it; Viale delle Belle Arti 131, disabled entrance

---

◉ TOP SIGHT **MUSEO NAZIONALE ETRUSCO DI VILLA GIULIA**

Pope Julius III's 16th-century villa provides the charming setting for Italy's finest collection of Etruscan and pre-Roman treasures. Exhibits, many of which came from tombs in the surrounding Lazio region, range from bronze figurines and black *bucchero* tableware to temple decorations, terracotta vases and dazzling jewellery.

Must-sees include a polychrome terracotta statue of Apollo, from the Etruscan town of Veio, just north of Rome, and the *Euphronios Krater*, a celebrated Greek vase that was returned to Italy in 2008 after a 30-year tug of war between the Italian government and New York's Metropolitan Museum of Art. But perhaps the museum's most famous piece is the 6th-century BC *Sarcofago degli Sposi* (Sarcophagus of the Betrothed). This astonishing work, originally unearthed in a tomb in Cerveteri, depicts a husband and wife reclining on a stone banqueting couch. And although called a sarcophagus, it was actually designed as an elaborate urn for the couple's ashes.

Further finds relating to the pre-Roman Umbri and Latin peoples are on show in the nearby **Villa Poniatowski** (☑06 321 96 98, Sunday tours ☑06 4423 9949; www. villagiulia.beniculturali.it; ⊘9am-1.30pm Tue-Sat, booking necessary).

DON'T MISS
➡ *Sarcofago degli Sposi*
➡ *Apollo di Veio*
➡ *Euphronios Krater*

PRACTICALITIES
➡ Map p324
➡ www.villagiulia. beniculturali.it
➡ Piazzale di Villa Giulia
➡ adult/reduced €8/4
➡ ⊘8.30am-7.30pm Tue-Sun
➡ ◻Via delle Belle Arti

Via Gramsci 73; adult/reduced €8/4; ⊙8.30am-7.30pm Tue-Sun; 🚇Piazza Thorvaldsen) Housed in a vast belle époque palace, this oft-overlooked gallery is an unsung gem. Its superlative collection runs the gamut from neoclassical sculpture to abstract expressionism with works by many of the most important exponents of 19th- and 20th-century art.

There are canvases by the *macchiaioli* (Italian Impressionists) and futurists Boccioni and Balla, as well as sculptures by Canova and major works by Modigliani, De Chirico and Guttuso. International artists represented include Van Gogh, Cézanne, Monet, Klimt, and Alberto Giacometti, whose trademark stick-figures share a room with a Jackson Pollock canvas, a curvaceous Henry Moore sculpture, and a hanging mobile by Alexander Calder.

⊙ Flaminio

AUDITORIUM PARCO
DELLA MUSICA   CULTURAL CENTRE
Map p324 (☑06 8024 1281; www.auditorium. com; Viale Pietro de Coubertin 10; guided tours adult/reduced €9/7; ⊙11am-8pm Mon-Sat, 10am-6pm Sun; 🚇Viale Tiziano) Designed by archistar Renzo Piano and inaugurated in 2002, Rome's flagship cultural centre is an audacious work of architecture consisting of three grey pod-like concert halls set round a 3000-seat amphitheatre.

Excavations during its construction revealed remains of an ancient Roman villa, which are now on show in the Auditorium's small **Museo Archeologico** (www.auditorium.com; Auditorium Parco della Musica, Viale Pietro de Coubertin; ⊙10am-8pm Mon-Sat summer, 11am-6pm Mon-Sat winter, 10am-6pm Sun year-round; 🚇Viale Tiziano) **FREE**.

Guided tours (for a minimum of 10 people) depart hourly between 11.30am and 4.30pm Saturday and Sunday, and by arrangement from Monday to Friday.

MUSEO NAZIONALE DELLE ARTI
DEL XXI SECOLO (MAXXI)   GALLERY
Map p324 (☑06 320 19 54; www.fondazionemaxxi.it; Via Guido Reni 4a; adult/reduced €11/8; ⊙11am-7pm Tue-Sun, to 10pm Sat; 🚇Viale Tiziano) As much as the exhibitions, the highlight of Rome's leading contemporary art gallery is the Zaha Hadid–designed building it occupies. Formerly a barracks, the curved concrete structure is striking inside and out with a multilayered geometric facade and a cavernous light-filled interior full of snaking walkways and suspended staircases.

The gallery has a small permanent collection, but more interesting are the temporary exhibitions. In recent times these have included installations by avant-garde Chinese sculptor Hang Yong Ping and an exhibition of contemporary Iranian art.

PONTE MILVIO   BRIDGE
Map p324 (🚇Ponte Milvio) A cobblestoned footbridge, Ponte Milvio is best known as the site of the ancient Battle of the Milvian Bridge. The bridge was first built in 109 BC to carry Via Flaminia over the Tiber and survived intact until 1849, when

---

THE BATTLE OF THE MILVIAN BRIDGE
....

Constantine's defeat of Maxentius at the Battle of the Milvian Bridge on 28 October 312 is one of the most celebrated victories in Roman history.

The battle came as the culmination of a complex seven-year power struggle for control of the Western Roman Empire. Constantine and his vastly outnumbered army approached Rome from the north along Via Flaminia, meeting Maxentius' forces on the northern bank of the Tiber. Fighting was short and bloody, leaving Maxentius dead, his army in tatters, and the path to Rome unopposed.

But while this is historically significant, the real reason for the battle's mythical status is the Christian legend that surrounds it. According to the Roman historian Lactantius, Constantine dreamt a message telling him to paint a Christian symbol on his troops' shields. A second historian, Eusebius, provides a more dramatic account, recounting how on the eve of the battle Constantine saw a cross in the sky, accompanied by the words, 'In this sign, conquer.' Whatever the case, the reality is that Constantine won a resounding victory and in so doing set the seeds for the spread of Christianity in the Roman world.

GOING UNDERGROUND IN VILLA TORLONIA

Beneath the greenery of Villa Torlonia lie reminders of a dark chapter in Rome's history. Between 1940 and 1943, Mussolini had two air-raid shelters and an underground **bunker** (Map p324; ☑347 3811874; www.sotterraneidiroma.it; guided tour €7, reservations obligatory; ☒Via Nomentana) built beneath what was, at the time, his family estate. Guided tours take you down into these bare underground chambers, complete with anti-gas doors and air filtration systems. The bunker, whose 4m-thick walls lie 6m below the **Casino Nobile**, was still being worked on when the Duce was arrested on 25 July 1943.

Garibaldi's troops blew it up to stop advancing French soldiers. Pope Pius IX had it rebuilt a year later. On the northern end, the **Torretta Valadier** was formerly used to stage art exhibitions.

FORO ITALICO   ARCHITECTURE
Map p324 (Viale del Foro Italico; ☒Piazzale della Farnesina) At the foot of the heavily wooded **Monte Mario**, the Foro Italico is a grandiose Fascist-era sports complex, centred on the Stadio Olimpico (p192), Rome's 70,000-seat football stadium. Most people pass through en route to a football or rugby match, but if you're interested in Fascist architecture, it's worth a look.

Designed by the architect Enrico Del Debbio, it remains much as it was originally conceived. A 17m-high marble **obelisk** stands at the beginning of a broad avenue leading down to the **Stadio dei Marmi**, a running track surrounded by 60 marble nudes, and the Stadio Olimpico.

EXPLORA – MUSEO DEI BAMBINI DI ROMA   MUSEUM
Map p324 (☑06 361 37 76; www.mdbr.it; Via Flaminia 82; adult/reduced €8/5; ☺enter at 10am, noon, 3pm & 5pm Tue-Sun; Ⓜ Flaminio) Rome's only dedicated kids' museum, Explora is aimed at the under-12s. It's divided into thematic sections and has everything from a supermarket to a play pool and fire engine, it's a hands-on, feet-on, full-on experience that your nippers will love. Out-

side there's also a free play park open to all. Booking is recommended.

◉ Salario

MUSEO D'ARTE CONTEMPORANEA DI ROMA (MACRO)   ART GALLERY
Map p324 (☑06 06 08; www.museomacro.org; Via Nizza 138, cnr Via Cagliari; adult/reduced €9.50/7.50; ☺10.30am-7.30pm Tue-Sun; ☒Via Nizza) Along with MAXXI, this is Rome's most important contemporary art gallery. Occupying a converted Peroni brewery, it hosts temporary exhibitions and displays works from its permanent collection of post-1960s Italian art.

Vying with the exhibits for your attention is the museum's sleek black-and-red interior. The work of French architect Odile Decq, this retains much of the building's original structure while also incorporating a sophisticated steel-and-glass finish.

CATACOMBE DI PRISCILLA   CHRISTIAN SITE
Map p324 (☑06 8620 6272; www.catacombepriscilla.com; Via Salaria 430; guided visit adult/reduced €8/5; ☺8.30am-noon & 2.30-5pm Tue-Sun; ☒Via Salaria) Dug between the 2nd and 5th centuries, this network of creepy tunnels was known as the Queen of Catacombs. It was an important early Christian burial site and numerous martyrs and popes were buried in the tombs and chambers that line the 13km of tunnels.

Visits take in a decorated Greek chapel and a scratchy fresco of the Virgin Mary. Dating to around 230 AD, this is thought to be the oldest ever image of the Madonna.

VILLA ADA   PARK
Map p324 (entrances at Via Salaria, Via Ponte Salario, Via di Monte Antenne, Via Panama; ☺7am-sunset; ☒Via Salaria) Once the private property of King Vittorio Emanuele III, Villa Ada is a big rambling park with shady paths, lakes, lawns and woods. It's popular with locals and explodes into life in summer when outdoor concerts are staged during the Roma Incontro il Mondo festival.

◉ Nomentano

PORTA PIA   GATE
Map p324 (Piazzale Porta Pia; ☒Via XX Settembre) Michelangelo's last architectural work, this crenellated structure was commis-

sioned by Pope Pius IV to replace Porta Nomentana, one of the original gates in the Aurelian walls.

Bitter street fighting took place here in 1870 as Italian troops breached the adjacent walls to wrest the city from the pope and claim it for the nascent kingdom of Italy.

VILLA TORLONIA   PARK

Map p324 (Via Nomentana 70; ⊙7am-7.30pm winter, to 8.30pm summer; ⌂Via Nomentana) Full of towering pine trees, atmospheric palms and scattered villas, this splendid 19th-century park once belonged to Prince Giovanni Torlonia (1756–1829), a powerful banker and landowner. His large neoclassical villa, **Casino Nobile**, later became the Mussolini family home (1925–43) and, in the latter part of WWII, Allied headquarters (1944–47). These days it houses an art museum.

MUSEI DI VILLA TORLONIA   MUSEUM

Map p324 (⌨06 06 08; www.museivillatorlonia.it; Via Nomentana 70; Casino Nobile adult/reduced €7.50/6.50, Casina delle Civitte adult/reduced €6/5, combined adult/reduced €9.50/7.50; ⊙9am-7pm Tue-Sun; ⌂Via Nomentana) Housed in three villas – Casino Nobile, Casina delle Civette and Casino dei Principi – this museum boasts an eclectic collection of sculpture, paintings, furnishings, and decorative stained glass. The main ticket office is just inside the Via Nomentana entrance to Villa Torlonia.

With its oversized neoclassical facade, designed by Giuseppe Valadier, **Casino Nobile** (www.museivillatorlonia.it; Villa Torlonia, Via Nomentana 70; adult/reduced €7.50/6.50; ⊙9am-7pm Tue-Sun; ⌂Via Nomentana) makes quite an impression. In the lavishly decorated interior you can admire the Torlonia family's fine collection of classically inspired sculpture and early-20th-century paintings from the Scuola Romana (Roman School of Art).

To the northeast, the much smaller **Casina delle Civette** (www.museivillatorlonia. it; Villa Torlonia, Via Nomentana 70; ⊙9am-7pm Tue-Sun; ⌂Via Nomentana) is a bizarre mix of Swiss cottage, Gothic castle and twee farmhouse decorated in art-nouveau style. Built between 1840 and 1930, it's now a museum dedicated to stained glass.

Casino dei Principi (Villa Torlonia, Via Nomentana 70; adult/reduced incl Casino Nobile €7.50/6.50; ⊙9am-7pm Tue-Sun; ⌂Via Nomentana), which houses the archive of the Scuola Romana, stages temporary exhibitions.

BASILICA DI SANT'AGNESE FUORI LE MURA & MAUSOLEO DI SANTA COSTANZA   BASILICA, CATACOMBS

(www.santagnese.com; entrances at Via Nomentana 349 & Via di Sant Agnese 3; basilica & mausoleo free, catacombs guided visit adult/reduced €8/5; ⊙basilica 7.30am-noon & 4-7.30pm, mausoleo 9am-noon & 4-6pm, catacombs 9-11.30am Mon-Sat & 3-4.30pm daily; ⌂Via Nomentana) Although a bit of a hike, it's well worth searching out this intriguing medieval church complex, comprising the Basilica di Sant'Agnese Fuori le Mura and the 4th-century Mausoleo di Santa Costanza, home to some of Christendom's earliest mosaics.

The current basilica, whose origins date to the 7th century BC, was built over the **catacombs** where St Agnes was buried. It has been much modified over the centuries but its golden **apse mosaic**, one of the best examples of Byzantine art in Rome, has survived intact. It shows St Agnes, flanked by popes Honorius and Symmachus, standing over the signs of her martyrhood – a sword and a flame. According to tradition, the 13-year-old Agnes was sentenced to be burnt at the stake, but when the flames failed to kill her she was beheaded on Piazza Navona and buried beneath this church.

Up from the main basilica is the Mausoleo di Santa Costanza. This squat circular building has a dome supported by 12 pairs of granite columns and a vaulted ambulatory decorated with beautiful 4th-century mosaics.

QUARTIERE COPPEDÈ

Best entered from the corner of Via Tagliamento and Via Dora, the compact **Quartiere Coppedè** (Map p324; ⌂Viale Regina Margherita) is a fairy-tale neighbourhood of Tuscan turrets, Liberty sculptures, Moorish arches, Gothic gargoyles, frescoed facades and palm-fringed gardens. The mind behind the madness belonged to the little-known Florentine architect, Gino Coppedè, who designed and built the quarter between 1913 and 1926.

At the heart of the district is the whimsical **Fontana delle Rane** (Fountain of the Frogs; Map p324; Piazza Mincio; ⌂Viale Regina Margherita), a modern take on the better known Fontana delle Tartarughe in the Jewish Ghetto.

VILLA BORGHESE & NORTHERN ROME SIGHTS

LOCAL KNOWLEDGE

HIDDEN GELATO GEMS

This neck of Rome harbours some outstanding gelaterie. They're not the easiest to find, though, and unless you know where to look you're unlikely to stumble on them. A typical case in point is **Neve di Latte** (Map p324; Via Poletti 6; gelato €2.50-5; ☺noon-10pm Sun-Thu, to 11pm Fri & Sat), an innocuous looking place near MAXXI that serves some of the best classical ice creams in town. Over the river, **Al Settimo Gelo** (Map p324; www.alsettimogelo. it; Via Vodice 21a; gelato €2-5; ☺10-8pm Mon-Sat winter, to 11pm summer, 11.30am-2pm & 3.30-8pm Sun; ☐Piazza Giuseppe Mazzini) is another much-lauded gelateria, known for its creative flavours and use of natural ingredients.

EATING

Villa Borghese & Around

SERENELLA
PIZZA €

Map p324 (Via Salaria 70; pizza slices from €1.50; ☺8am-10pm; ☐Via Salaria) It's a bit out of the way, but this humble pizza takeaway makes for a top pit-stop. It uses natural yeast in its pizza bases, which come with a selection of imaginative toppings. For a cheap, easy-to-eat snack, the *pizza bianca* (with salt and olive oil) is excellent.

CINECAFFÈ
CAFE €

Map p324 (www.cinecaffe.it; Casina delle Rose, Largo Marcello Mastroianni 1; meals €15-25; ☺8.30am-8.30pm; ☐Porta Pinciana) Part of the Casa del Cinema (p192) complex, this modern cafe is one of the few places to get a decent bite in Villa Borghese. Stop by for a morning coffee or claim a table on the sunny deck and tuck into an ample lunch buffet (€15 for one plate, €25 for no-limits access).

CAFFÈ DELLE ARTI
CAFE, RISTORANTE €€

Map p324 (☎06 3265 1236; www.caffedellearti-roma.com; Via Gramsci 73; meals €45; ☺12.30-3.30pm daily & 7.30-11pm Tue-Sun; ☐Piazza Thorvaldsen) The cafe-restaurant of the Galleria Nazionale d'Arte Moderna (p187) sits in neoclassical splendour in a tranquil corner of Villa Borghese. An elegant venue, it's at its best on sultry summer evenings when you can sit on the terrace and revel in the romantic atmosphere over coffee, cocktails or an al fresco dinner of classic Italian cuisine.

Flaminio

BAR POMPI
PASTRIES €

Map p324 (Via Cassia 8; tiramisu €3.50; ☺7am-midnight Wed-Mon, 4pm-midnight Tue; ☐Ponte Milvio) This renowned pasticceria serves Rome's most celebrated tiramisu. Alongside the classic coffee, liqueur and cocoa combination, there are several other versions, including strawberry, pistachio, and banana and chocolate.

IL GIANFORNAIO
BAKERY €

Map p324 (Largo Maresciallo Diaz 16; pizza slices €3.50; ☺7.30am-9pm Mon-Sat, 9am-3pm Sun; ☐Ponte Milvio) This popular lunch spot is something of a Jack of all trades, serving a range of sweet and savoury snacks – think *cornettos* (croissants), home-baked biscuits and excellent pizza slices – as well as daily pasta and meat dishes.

PALLOTTA
TRATTORIA, PIZZA €€

Map p324 (☎06 333 42 45; www.ristorantepallotta. it; Piazzale Ponte Milvio 23; meals €30, pizzas from €7; ☺noon-3pm & 7-11.30pm; ☐Ponte Milvio) An unpretentious spot with a shady garden, this landmark trattoria is good for traditional Roman pastas, uncomplicated grilled meats and crispy pizzas. It's well known locally and can get busy, so it's best to book.

Salario

PASTICCERIA GRUÈ
PASTRIES €

Map p324 (Viale Regina Margherita 95; pastries from €2; ☺7am-9pm; ☐Viale Regina Margherita) One of many eateries on Viale Regina Margherita, this sleek pasticceria-cafe is a local hotspot – suits and sharply dressed office workers lunch here and evening sees the local aperitif crowd move in. But its real calling cards are the exquisitely designed pastries and chocolates that stare out from beneath the counter.

Parioli

METAMORFOSI
RISTORANTE €€€

Map p324 (☎06 807 68 39; www.metamorfosiro-ma.it; Via Giovanni Antonelli 30-32; tasting menus

€80-110, lunch menus €45; ◷12.30-2.30pm & 8-10.30pm, closed Sat lunch & Sun; 🖵Via Giovanni Antonelli) Since opening in 2011, chef Roy Carceres' Michelin-starred restaurant has established itself as one of Rome's top dining tickets, offering innovative, contemporary cuisine, impeccable service, and a chic but informal setting. Various tasting menus are available, including a three-course lunch option.

MOLTO RISTORANTE €€€
Map p324 (☎06 808 29 00; www.moltoitaliano. it; Viale Parioli 122; meals €45-50; ◷1-3pm & 8-11pm; 🖵Viale Parioli) Fashionable and quietly glamorous, Molto is a Parioli favourite. The discreet entrance gives onto an elegant, modern interior and open-air terrace, while the menu offers everything from simple, homemade pastas to more decadent truffle-flavoured dishes and succulent roast meats.

DRINKING & NIGHTLIFE

MOMART BAR
(www.momartcafe.it; Viale XXI Aprile 19; ◷noon-2am Mon-Fri, 6pm-2am Sat & Sun; 🖵Via XXI Aprile) A spacious modern bar in the university district near Via Nomentana, Momart serves one of Rome's most popular aperitifs. A mixed crowd of students and local professionals flocks here to fill up on the pizza-led buffet and kick back over cocktails on the pavement terrace.

BRANCALEONE CLUB
(www.brancaleone.eu; Via Levanna 11; ◷hours vary, typically 10.30pm-late; 🖵Via Nomentana) From its anti-establishment roots as a *centro sociale* (social centre), Brancaleone has grown to become one of Rome's top clubs, drawing blockbuster DJs and a young clubbing crowd. Rap, hip-hop, drum'n'bass, and electronica feature heavily, and there's a regular calendar of events and one-off evenings. The club is in the outlying Montesacro district.

LANIFICIO 159 CLUB
(www.lanificio159.com; Via Pietralata 159a; ◷hours vary, typically 11pm-4am; 🖵Via Val Brembana) Occupying an ex-wool factory in Rome's northeastern suburbs, this cool underground venue hosts live gigs and hot clubbing action, led by top Roman crews and international DJs. The club is part of a larger complex that stages more reserved events such as Sunday markets, exhibitions and aperitifs.

CHIOSCHETTO DI PONTE MILVIO BAR
Map p324 (Ponte Milvio 44; ◷6pm-2am summer only; 🖵Ponte Milvio) A local landmark, this green kiosk next to the Ponte Milvio bridge is perennially popular with the young crowd from Rome's wealthy northern suburbs. It might look like a shack – it is a shack – but the mojitos are the business and it does an excellent thirst-quenching *grattachecca* (shaved ice flavoured with fruit syrup).

PIPER CLUB CLUB
Map p324 (www.piperclub.it; Via Tagliamento 9; ◷11pm-5am Fri & Sat; 🖵Viale Regina Margherita) To Rome what Studio 54 was to New York, Piper has been a nightlife fixture for 50 years, and it just keeps on going. Fridays it hosts themed parties, everything from Latin nights to '90s house celebrations, while on Saturdays resident DJs drive the rhythms.

☆ ENTERTAINMENT

AUDITORIUM PARCO DELLA MUSICA CONCERT VENUE
Map p324 (☎06 8024 1281; www.auditorium.com; Viale Pietro de Coubertin 30; 🖵Viale Tiziano) The hub of Rome's thriving cultural scene, the Auditorium is the capital's premier concert venue and one of Europe's most popular arts centres. Its three concert halls offer superb acoustics, and, together with a 3000-seat open-air arena, stage everything from classical-music concerts to jazz gigs, public lectures, and film screenings.

The Auditorium is also home to Rome's world-class **Orchestra dell' Accademia Nazionale di Santa Cecilia** (www.santa-cecilia.it).

TEATRO OLIMPICO THEATRE
Map p324 (☎06 326 59 91; www.teatroolimpico. it; Piazza Gentile da Fabriano 17; 🖵Piazza Mancini, 🖵Piazza Mancini) The Teatro Olimpico is home to the **Accademia Filarmonica Romana** (www.filarmonicaromana.org), a classical-music organisation whose past members have included Rossini, Donizetti and Verdi. The theatre offers a varied program of classical and chamber music, opera, ballet, one-man shows and comedies.

VILLA BORGHESE & NORTHERN ROME SHOPPING

SPORT AT THE OLIMPICO

Watching a game of football (or rugby) at Rome's **Stadio Olimpico** (Map p324; ✆06 3685 7520; Viale dei Gladiatori 2, Foro Italico) is an unforgettable experience, although you'll have to keep your wits about you as crowd trouble is not unheard of.

Throughout the football season (September to May) there's a game most Sundays involving one of the city's two teams: **A S Roma** (www.asroma.it), known as the *giallorossi* (yellow and reds), or **Lazio** (www.sslazio.it), the *biancazzuri* (white and blues). Tickets cost from about €16 depending on the match and can be bought at Lottomatica outlets, at the stadium, at ticket agencies, online (www.listicket.it) or at one of the several Roma or Lazio stores around town. The stadium also hosts Italy's 6 Nations rugby matches between February and March.

CASA DEL CINEMA
CINEMA

Map p324 (✆06 06 08; www.casadelcinema.it; Largo Marcello Mastroianni 1, Villa Borghese; ⊠Porta Pinciana) In Villa Borghese, the Casa del Cinema comprises three projection halls, an exhibition space, and an outdoor theatre. It screens everything from documentaries to shorts, indie flicks and arthouse classics (sometimes in their original language), and hosts a regular program of retrospectives and film-related events.

SILVANO TOTI GLOBE THEATRE
THEATRE

Map p324 (✆06 06 08; www.globetheatreroma.com; Largo Aqua Felix, Villa Borghese; tickets €10-23; ⊠Piazzale Brasile) Like London's Globe Theatre but with better weather, Villa Borghese's open-air Elizabethan theatre serves up Shakespeare (performances mostly in Italian) from July through to September.

 SHOPPING

LIBRERIA L'ARGONAUTA
BOOKS

Map p324 (www.librerialargonauta.com; Via Reggio Emilia 89; ⊙10am-8pm Mon-Fri, 10am-1pm & 4-8pm Sat; ⊠Via Nizza) Near the MACRO museum, this travel bookshop is a lovely place to browse. With its serene atmosphere and shelves of travel literature, guides, maps and photo tomes, it can easily spark daydreams of far-off places.

BULZONI
WINE

Map p324 (www.enotecabulzoni.it; Viale Parioli 36; ⊙8.30am-2pm, 4.30-8.30pm; ⊠Viale Parioli) This historic wine shop has been supplying Parioli with wine since 1929. It has a formidable collection of Italian regional wines, as well as European and New World labels, and a carefully curated selection of champagnes, liqueurs, olive oils and gourmet delicacies.

BAGHEERA
FASHION

Map p324 (www.bagheeraboutique.com; Piazza Euclide 30; ⊙9.30am-1pm Tue-Sat, 3.30-7.30pm Mon-Sat; ⊠Piazza Euclide) This modish boutique has long been a local go-to for the latest fashions. Alongside sandals and vampish high heels you'll find dresses by Dries Van Noten and a selection of bags and accessories by big-name international designers.

ANTICAGLIE A PONTE MILVIO
MARKET

Map p324 (Via Capoprati; ⊙9am-8pm 1st & 2nd Sun of month, closed Aug; ⊠Ponte Milvio) The 2nd-century-BC Ponte Milvio forms the backdrop to this monthly antique market. On the first and second Sunday of every month up to 200 stalls spring up on the riverbank laden with antiques, objets d'art, vintage clothes, period furniture and all manner of collectable clobber.

Southern Rome

VIA APPIA ANTICA | OSTIENSE | SAN PAOLO | GARBATELLA

Neighbourhood Top Five

1 Walking or cycling along the **Via Appia Antica** (p103), tracing the route of a thousand ancient Roman footsteps.

2 Exploring Rome's Christian burial catacombs, such as the **Catacombe di San Sebastiano** (p196).

3 Checking out the colourful, edgy street art in **Ostiense** (p202).

4 Wandering around the ingenious location for the overflow from the Capitoline Museums: **Centrale Montemartini** (p201).

5 Feeling dwarfed by the majesty of **Basilica de San Paolo Fuori Le Mura** (p200).

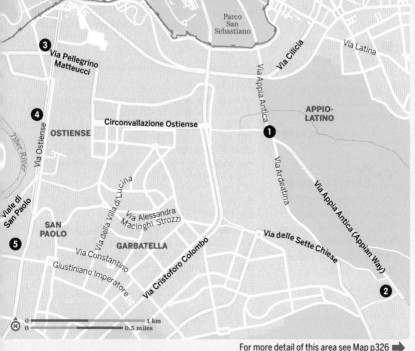

For more detail of this area see Map p326 ➡

Lonely Planet's Top Tip

On Sunday, the first section of Appia Antica is supposedly traffic free, but in recent years this has not been enforced. The first section, stretching 1km from Porta San Sebastiano, is not at all pleasant to walk along, even on supposedly 'traffic free' days. It's best to take bus 118 to the Basilica of San Sebastiano, close to the genuinely traffic-free section.

SOUTHERN ROME

✖ Best Places to Eat

➡ Trattoria Priscilla (p201)
➡ Qui Non se More Mai (p201)
➡ Il Giardino di Giulia e Fratelli (p201)
➡ Andreotti (p202)
➡ Pizza Ostiense (p202)

For reviews, see p201.➡

🍷 Best Places to Drink

➡ Porto Fluviale (p203)
➡ Doppiozeroo (p203)
➡ Neo Club (p203)
➡ Goa (p203)

For reviews, see p203.➡

◉ Best Entertainment

➡ La Casa del Jazz (p204)
➡ Caffè Letterario (p204)
➡ Goa (p203)
➡ Piscina delle Rose (p203)

For reviews, see p204.➡

Explore Southern Rome

Southern Rome is a sprawling neighbourhood that comprises four distinct areas of interest to tourists: Via Appia Antica, famous for its catacombs; hip, post-industrial, street-art-covered Via Ostiense; picturesque Garbatella; and EUR, Mussolini's futuristic building development. It's all quite spread out, but public transport connections are good.

Heading southeast from Porta San Sebastiano, Via Appia Antica (the Appian Way) is one of the world's oldest roads and a much-prized Roman address. It's a beautiful part of town, with crumbling ruins set amid pea-green fields and towering umbrella pines.

To the west, Via Ostiense presents a very different picture. Desolate-looking disused factories and warehouses surprisingly harbour restaurants, pubs, clubs and bars, and the huge Eataly, a restaurant and Italian foodstuffs complex. Planned redevelopments for the ex-Mercati Generali as a 'City of Youth' – comprising leisure, cultural and office space and designed by Rem Koolhaas – have started but stalled.

Ostiense also harbours a couple of gemlike sights: Centrale Montemartini, a disused power plant housing superb classical statuary, and Basilica di San Paolo fuori le Mura, the world's third-largest church. The area also has some of Rome's best street art, with entire buildings covered in rainbows of colour. Nearby, the character-filled Garbatella district merits exploration for its original architecture, while further south, EUR was built by Mussolini as a showcase for his Fascist regime, a fascinating, Orwellian quarter of wide boulevards and linear buildings.

Local Life

➡**Eating** Pick up some delicious pastries at Andreotti (p202) or sampling the virtuoso pizza at Pizza Ostiense (p202).

➡**Clubbing** Some of Rome's coolest clubs are clustered around Via Ostiense.

➡**Cycling** Escape from the frenetic city centre along the beautiful Appian Way (p103).

Getting There & Away

➡**Metro** Metro line B runs to Piramide, Garbatella, Basilica San Paolo, EUR Palasport and EUR Fermi.

➡**Bus** There are bus connections to Porta San Sebastiano (118, 218 and 714), Via Ostiense (23 and 716) and Via Appia Antica (118).

TOP SIGHT
VIA APPIA ANTICA

Heading southeast from Porta San Sebastiano, the Appian Way (Appian Way) was known to the Romans as the *regina viarum* (queen of roads). Named after Appius Claudius Caecus, who laid the first 90km section in 312 BC, it was extended in 190 BC to reach Brindisi, some 540km away on the southern Adriatic coast.

Via Appia Antica has long been one of Rome's most exclusive addresses, a beautiful cobblestoned thoroughfare flanked by grassy fields, Roman structures and towering pine trees. Most splendid of the ancient houses was **Villa dei Quintilli** – so desirable that emperor Commodus murdered its owners and took it for himself.

The Appia Antica, peaceful today, resounds with history: it's where Spartacus and 6000 of his slave rebels were crucified in 71 BC, and around it lie 300km of underground tunnels that were carved out of soft tufa rock, and used as burial chambers by the early Christians. Corpses were wrapped in simple white sheets and usually placed in rectangular niches carved into the walls, which were then closed with marble or terracotta slabs. You can't visit all 300km, but three major catacombs (San Callisto, San Sebastiano and Santa Domitilla) are open for guided exploration.

If you're planning on really doing the sights, think about buying the Appia Antica Card. Near the start of the road, the Appia Antica Regional Park Information Point is very informative. You can buy a map of the park here and hire bikes. To be sure of a bike, arrive early, as they run out quickly. Child-sized bikes aren't available, but child seats (up to 20kg) are; book these in advance as there are not many available. The park runs tours on foot/by bike (€8/12) in English, Spanish and German, which have to be booked by email in advance.

DON'T MISS...

➜ The catacombs
➜ Cycling along the Appia
➜ Villa dei Quintilli

PRACTICALITIES

➜ Map p326
➜ ☎06 513 53 16
➜ www.parcoappia-antica.it
➜ bike hire hr/day €3/15
➜ ⊘Information Point 9.30am-1pm & 2-5.30pm Mon-Fri, 9.30am-6.30pm Sat & Sun, to 5pm winter
➜ ▣Via Appia Antica

TOP SIGHT
BASILICA & CATACOMBE DI SAN SEBASTIANO

The most famous of the catacombs, these contain frescoes, stucco work, epigraphs and several immaculately preserved mausoleums. The catacombs extend for more than 12km and are divided into three levels: 3m, 9m and 12m deep. They once harboured more than 65,000 tombs.

Basilica

The 4th-century **basilica** (Via Appia Antica 136; ⊘8am-1pm & 2-5.30pm; ☐Via Appia Antica) that was built here by Emperor Constantine was mostly destroyed by Saracen raids in the 9th century, and the church you see today mainly dates from the reconstruction initiated by Cardinal Borghese in the 17th century. It is dedicated to St Sebastian, who was martyred and buried here in the late 3rd century. In 826 his body was transferred to St Peter's for safekeeping, but he was re-interred here in the 12th century. In the Capella delle Reliquie you'll find one of the arrows used to kill him and the column to which he was tied. On the other side of the church is a marble slab with Jesus' footprints.

DON'T MISS...

➤ Graffiti to St Peter and St Paul
➤ Mausoleums
➤ Basilica di San Sebastiano

PRACTICALITIES

➤ Map p326, G5
➤ ☏06 785 03 50
➤ www.catacombe.org
➤ Via Appia Antica 136
➤ adult/reduced €8/5
➤ ⊘10am-5pm Mon-Sat, closed Dec
➤ ☐Via Appia Antica

Catacombs

A warren of tunnels that lie beneath the church and beyond, the Catacombe di San Sebastiano were the first catacombs to be so called, the name deriving from the Greek *kata* (near) and *kymbas* (cavity), because they were located near a cave. During the persecution of Christians by the emperor Vespasian from AD 258, it's believed that the catacombs were used as a safe haven for the remains of St Peter and St Paul and became a popular pilgrimage site. A plastered wall is covered with hundreds of invocations, engraved by worshippers in the 3rd and 4th centuries, featuring personalised entreaties such as 'Peter and Paul, pray for Victor'. However, it may be the case that the remains were never kept here, and the catacombs simply served as a focus for worship during those difficult times.

Mausoleums

Within the catacombs there are three beautifully preserved, decorated mausoleums. Each of the monumental facades feature a door, above which are inscribed symbols and the names of the owners. The first mausoleum belonged to Marcus Clodius Ermete, while the second one is named 'of the innocentiores', which is thought to have been the name of an association. During the 3rd century the area was filled in to build a place of pilgrimage where visitors could come to honour St Peter and St Paul, which is why the delicate stucco has remained so immaculately well-preserved.

◉ SIGHTS

The awe-inspiring Appian Way stretches south of Rome, dotted by Roman ruins above and riddled with catacombs below.

◉ Via Appia Antica

CATACOMBE DI
SAN SEBASTIANO CATACOMB
See p196.

VILLA DI MASSENZIO RUINS
Map p326 (⏁06 780 13 24; www.villadimassenzio.it; Via Appia Antica 153; ⏱9am-1pm Tue-Sat; 🚇Via Appia Antica) The outstanding feature of Maxentius' enormous 4th-century palace complex is the **Circo di Massenzio** (Map p326; Via Appia Antica 153; 🚇Via Appia Antica), Rome's best-preserved ancient racetrack – you can still make out the starting stalls used for chariot races. The 10,000-seat arena was built by Maxentius around 309, but he died before ever seeing a race here.

Above the arena are the ruins of Maxentius' imperial residence. Near the racetrack, the **Mausoleo di Romolo** (Tombo di Romolo; Map p326; Via Appia Antica 153; 🚇Via Appia Antica) was built by Maxentius for his 17-year-old son Romulus. The huge mausoleum was originally crowned with a large dome and surrounded by an imposing colonnade, in part still visible. The Torlonia family extended the tomb, turning it into a country house.

MAUSOLEO DI CECILIA METELLA RUIN
Map p326 (⏁06 3996 7700; www.coopculture.it; Via Appia Antica 161; adult/reduced incl Terme di Caracalla & Villa dei Quintili €7/4; ⏱9am-1hr before sunset Tue-Sun; 🚇Via Appia Antica) Dating to the 1st century BC, this great drum of a mausoleum encloses a burial chamber, now roofless. In the 14th century it was converted into a fort by the Caetani family, who were related to Pope Boniface VIII, and used to frighten passing traffic into paying a toll.

The tomb was built for the daughter of the consul Quintus Metellus Creticus. Cecilia Metella was of particular significance as she joined two important families by marriage – she was also daughter-in-law of Crassus, Julius Caesar's banker. The walls are made of travertine and the interior is decorated with a sculpted frieze featuring Gaelic shields, ox skulls and festoons.

CAPO DI BOVE ARCHAEOLOGICAL SITE
(⏁06 7839 2729; Via Appia Antica 222; ⏱9am-1.30pm & 2.30-5pm Mon-Sat) Discovered when excavating the grounds of a private villa to build a swimming pool, the remains of this Roman villa give a sense of how a gracious ancient Roman life was lived, with mosaics and the remains of its private bath house, set amid the countryside of the Appia Antica Regional Park.

VILLA DEI QUINTILI RUIN
(⏁06 3996 7700; www.coopculture.it; Via Appia Nuova 1092; adult/reduced incl Terme di Caracalla & Mausoleo di Cecilia Metella €7/4; ⏱9am-1hr before sunset Tue-Sun; 🚇Via Appia Antica) Towering over green fields, this 2nd-century villa is one of Rome's unsung splendours. It was the luxurious abode of two consuls, the Quintili brothers, but its splendour was their downfall. The emperor Commodus had them both killed, taking over the villa for himself. You may now enter the complex from the Via Appia entrance (previously its only entrance was from Via Appia Nuova), making it much more accessible.

The emperor added to the complex, and the ruins are fabulously impressive. The highlight is the well-preserved baths complex with a pool, *caldarium* (hot room) and *frigidarium* (cold room). There's an interesting small museum.

CATACOMBE DI SAN CALLISTO CATACOMB
Map p326 (⏁06 513 01 51; www.catacombe.roma.it; Via Appia Antica 110 & 126; adult/reduced €8/5; ⏱9am-noon & 2-5pm, closed Wed & Feb; 🚇Via Appia Antica) These are the largest and busiest of Rome's catacombs. Founded at the end of the 2nd century and named after Pope Calixtus I, they became the official cemetery of the newly established Roman Church. In the 20km of tunnels explored to date, archaeologists have found the tombs of 500,000 people and seven popes who were martyred in the 3rd century.

The patron saint of music, St Cecilia, was also buried here, though her body was later removed to the Basilica di Santa Cecilia in Trastevere. When her body was exhumed in 1599, more than a thousand years after her death, it was apparently perfectly preserved, as depicted in Stefano Maderno's softly contoured sculpture, a replica of which is here.

SOUTHERN ROME SIGHTS

Roman Catacombs

Ancient Roman law forbade burying the dead within the city walls, for reasons of hygiene. Rome's persecuted Christian community didn't have their own cemeteries, so in the 2nd century AD they began to build an extensive network of subterranean burial grounds outside the city.

The tombs were dug by specialised gravediggers, who tunnelled out the galleries. Bodies were wrapped in simple shrouds and then either placed individually in carved-out niches, called *loculi*, or in larger family tombs. Many tombs were marked with elaborate decorations, from frescoes to stucco work, which remain remarkably well preserved. A great many tombs discovered here bear touching inscriptions, such as the following: 'Apuleia Crysopolis, who lived for 7 years, 2 months; (her) parents made (this) for their dearest daughter'.

Symbolism

An almost secretive language of symbols had evolved to represent elements of the Christian faith. Since many early Christians could not read and write, these symbols served as both a secret code and a means to communicate among the illiterate. The most common of the symbols include the fish, the Greek word for which is *ichthys*, standing for Iesous Christos Theou Yios Soter (Jesus Christ, son of God, Saviour). The anchor, which also appears regularly, symbolises the belief in Christ as a safe haven, a comforting thought in times of persecution. It's thought, too, that this was again an example of Greek wordplay: *ankura* resembling *en kuriol*, which means 'in the Lord'. A dove with an olive

1. Crypt of the Popes, Catacombe di San Callisto (p197) **2.** Catacombe di Priscilla (p188) **3.** Wall fresco in Catacombe di San Callisto (p197)

branch in the beak is a reference to the biblical dove, meaning salvation.

Abandonment

The catacombs began to be abandoned as early as 313, when Constantine issued the Milan decree of religious tolerance and Christians were thus able to bury their dead in churchyards.

In about 800, after frequent incursions by invaders, the bodies of the martyrs and first popes were transferred to the basilicas inside the city walls for safe keeping. The catacombs were abandoned and by the Middle Ages many had been forgotten.

Since the 19th century, more than 30 catacombs have been uncovered in the area. The warren of tunnels are fascinating to explore, and sections of three sets of catacombs are accessible via guided tour.

Unless you're passionate about catacombs, visiting one set will be sufficient.

TOP 5 CATACOMB READS

➡ *The Roman Catacombs,* by James Spencer Northcote (1859)

➡ *Tombs and Catacombs of the Appian Way: History of Cremation,* by Olinto L Spadoni (1892)

➡ *Valeria, the Martyr of the Catacombs,* by WH Withrow (1892)

➡ *Christian Rome: Past and Present: Early Christian Rome Catacombs and Basilicas,* by Philippe Pergola (2002)

➡ *The Churches and Catacombs of Early Christian Rome: A Comprehensive Guide* by Matilda Webb (2001)

TOP SIGHT
BASILICA DI SAN PAOLO FUORI LE MURA

The world's third-largest church and the biggest in Rome after St Peter's, this magnificent basilica stands on the site where St Paul was buried after being decapitated in AD 67. Built by Constantine in the 4th century, it was largely destroyed by fire in 1823 .

Much of what you see today is a 19th-century reconstruction, which remained as faithful as possible to the original building. However, not everything was decimated in the fire; many treasures survived, including the 5th-century **triumphal arch**, with its heavily restored mosaics, and the Gothic marble tabernacle over the high altar. Arnolfo di Cambio designed this around 1285, together with another artist, possibly Pietro Cavallini.

Doom-mongers should check out the papal portraits beneath the nave windows. Every pope since St Peter is represented and legend has it that when there is no room for the next portrait, the world will fall.

The stunning 13th-century Cosmati mosaic work in the **cloisters** of the adjacent Benedictine abbey also survived the 1823 fire, and is well worth a visit. Here, unusually, the mosaic work decorated the spiralled, twisted and straight columns.

DON'T MISS...

➡ 5th-century triumphal arch and mosaics
➡ Papal portraits
➡ Cloister

PRACTICALITIES

➡ Map p326
➡ www.abbaziasan-paolo.net
➡ Via Ostiense 190
➡ cloisters €4, archaeological walk €4, audioguide €5
➡ ⊙7am-6.30pm
➡ Ⓜ San Paolo

MAUSOLEO DELLE FOSSE ARDEATINE
MONUMENT

Map p326 (✆06 513 67 42; Via Ardeatina 174; ⊙8.15am-3.30pm Mon-Fri, to 4.30pm Sat & Sun; 🚌Via Appia Antica) FREE This moving mausoleum is dedicated to the victims of Rome's worst WWII atrocity. Buried here, outside the Ardeatine Caves, are 335 Italians shot by the Nazis on 24 March 1944. Following the massacre, ordered in reprisal for a partisan attack, the Germans used mines to explode sections of the caves and bury the bodies. After the war, the bodies were exhumed, identified and reburied in a mass grave, now marked by a huge concrete slab and sculptures.

The site also has a tiny museum dedicated to the Italian Resistance (doors close 15 minutes before the rest of the site).

CATACOMBE DI SANTA DOMITILLA
CATACOMB

Map p326 (✆06 511 03 42; www.domitilla.info; Via delle Sette Chiese 283; adult/reduced €8/5; ⊙9am-noon & 2-5pm Wed-Mon, closed Jan; 🚌Via Appia Antica) Among Rome's largest and oldest, these wonderful catacombs stretch for about 18km. They were established on the private burial ground of Flavia Domitilla, niece of the emperor Domitian and a member of the wealthy Flavian family. They contain Christian wall paintings and the haunting underground **Chiesa di SS Nereus e Achilleus**, a 4th-century church dedicated to two Roman soldiers martyred by Diocletian.

CHIESA DEL DOMINE QUO VADIS?
CHURCH

Map p326 (Via Appia Antica 51; ⊙8am-6.30pm Mon-Fri, 8.15am-6.45pm Sat & Sun winter, to 7.30pm summer; 🚌Via Appia Antica) This pint-sized church marks the spot where St Peter, fleeing Rome, met a vision of Jesus going the other way. When Peter asked: 'Domine, quo vadis?' (Lord, where are you going?), Jesus replied, 'Venio Roman iterum crucifigi' (I am coming to Rome to be crucified again). Reluctantly deciding to join him, Peter tramped back into town where he was arrested and executed.

In the aisle are copies of Christ's footprints; the originals are in the Basilica di San Sebastiano.

MUSEO DELLE MURA
MUSEUM

Map p326 (☑06 7047 5284; www.museodel-lemuraroma.it; Via di Porta San Sebastiano 18; ⊗9am-2pm Tue-Sun; ◻Porta San Sebastiano) Marking the start of Via Appia Antica, the 5th-century Porta San Sebastiano is the largest of the gates in the Aurelian Wall. During WWII the Fascist Party secretary Ettore Muti lived here; today it houses the modest Museo delle Mure, which offers the chance to walk along the top of the walls for around 50m as well as displaying the history of the city's fortifications.

The gate was originally known as Porta Appia but took on its current name in honour of the thousands of pilgrims who passed under it on their way to the Catacombe di San Sebastiano.

⊙ Ostiense, San Paolo & Garbatella

Heading south from Stazione Roma-Ostia, the gritty Via Ostiense encompasses clubs in converted warehouses and a couple of notable sights. Street-art fans are in for a treat, particularly on Via del Porto Fluviale.

CAPITOLINE MUSEUMS AT CENTRALE MONTEMARTINI
MUSEUM

Map p326 (☑06 06 08; www.centralemonte-martini.org; Via Ostiense 106; adult/reduced €7.50/6.50, incl Capitoline Museums €16/14, valid 7 days; ⊗9am-7pm Tue-Sun; ◻Via Ostiense) Housed in a former power station, this fabulous outpost of the Capitoline Museums (Musei Capitolini) boldly juxtaposes classical sculpture against diesel engines and giant furnaces. The collection's highlights are in the **Sala Caldaia**, where ancient statuary strike poses around the giant furnace. Beautiful pieces include *Fanciulla Seduta* (Seated Girl) and *Musa Polimnia* (Muse Polyhymnia), and there are also some exquisite Roman mosaics, depicting favourite subjects such as hunting scenes and foodstuffs.

QUARTIERE GARBATELLA
AREA

Map p326 (Ⓜ Garbatella) A favourite location for TV and film-makers, Quartiere Garbatella was originally conceived as a workers' residential quarter, but in the 1920s the Fascists hijacked the project and used the area to house people who'd been displaced by construction work in the city. Many people were moved into *alberghi suburbani* (suburban hotels), big housing blocks designed by

Innocenzo Sabbatini, the leading light of the 'Roman School' of architecture. The most famous, **Albergo Rosso** (Map p326; Piazza Michele da Carbonara), is typical of the style. Other trademark buildings are the **Scuola Cesare Battisti** (Map p326; Piazza Damiano Sauli) on Piazza Damiano Sauli and **Teatro Palladium** on Piazza Bartolomeo Romano.

 EATING

The increasingly fashionable southern neighbourhoods of Ostiense and Garbatella feature some excellent restaurants, including those in Ostiense's Eataly complex. You can also eat well in a rural setting close to Via Appia Antica.

✗ Via Appia Antica

TRATTORIA PRISCILLA
TRATTORIA €€

Map p326 (☑06 513 63 79; Via Appia Antica 68; meals €30; ⊗1-3pm daily, 8-11pm Mon-Sat; ◻Via Appia Antica) Set in a 16th-century former stable, this intimate family-run trattoria has been feeding hungry travellers along the Appian Way for more than a hundred years, serving up traditional *cucina Romana,* so think *carbonara, amatriciana* (bacon and tomato sauce) and *cacio e pepe* (cheese and pepper). The tiramisu wins plaudits.

QUI NON SE MORE MAI
ITALIAN €€

Map p326 (☑06 780 3922; Via Appia Antica 198; meals around €40; ⊗12.30-3pm & 6.30-11.30pm Tue-Sat; ◻Via Appia Antica) This small, charismatically rustic restaurant has an open fire for grilling, plus a small terrace for when the weather's good. The menu offers Roman classics such as pasta *amatriciana, carbonara, alla gricia* (with pig's cheek), *cacio e pepe,* and so on. Just the thing to set you up for the road ahead.

IL GIARDINO DI GIULIA E FRATELLI
ITALIAN €€

Map p326 (☑347 5092772; Via Appia Antica 176; meals €25-30; ⊗noon-3pm & 7-11.30pm Tue-Sat; ◻Via Appia Antica) Almost opposite the tomb of Cecilia Metella, this is lovely, especially when the weather is good, as there's seating out in the garden, as well as inside with greenery-filled views. It's ideal for lunch or *aperitivo*, and a particularly good family choice. There's a simple menu of mains such as lasagne or meatballs.

✗ Ostiense, San Paolo & Garbatella

PIZZA OSTIENSE
PIZZA €

Map p326 (Via Ostiense 56; ☺6.30pm-1am; MPyramide) Run by folk formerly of the much-lauded classic Roman pizzeria Remo, in Testaccio, Pizza Ostiense offers similarly paper-thin, crispy bases and delicious fresh toppings and scrumptious *fritti* (fried things) in unfussy surroundings, with a friendly vibe.

ANDREOTTI
PASTRIES €

Map p326 (☑06 575 07 73; Via Ostiense 54; ☺7.30am-9.30pm; ⊋Via Ostiense) Film director and Ostiense local Ferzan Ozpetek is such a fan of the pastries here he's been known to cast them in his films. They're all stars, from the buttery *crostate* (tarts) to the piles of golden *sfogliatelle romane* (ricotta-filled pastries). You can also eat a cheap lunch or dinner here from the tasty *tavola calda* (hot table), with pasta dishes ringing in at €5.

EATALY
ITALIAN €

Map p326 (☑06 9027 9201; www.eataly.net/it_en; Air Terminal Ostiense, Piazzale XII Ottobre 1492; ☺shop 10am-midnight, restaurants noon-11.30pm; MPyramide) Eataly is an enormous, mall-like complex, a glittering, gleaming, somewhat confusing department store, entirely devoted to Italian food. As well as foodstuffs from all over the country, books, and cookery implements, the store is also home to 19 cafes and restaurants, including excellent pizzas, pasta dishes, ice cream and more.

PORTO FLUVIALE
TRATTORIA, PIZZA €€

Map p326 (☑06 574 31 99; www.portofluviale.com; Via del Porto Fluviale 22; meals €35; ☺10.30am-2am; MPyramide) A hip, buzzing restaurant in the industrial-chic vein, Porto Fluviale is a great space and a good place to go with families: it's lively, spacious and good value, offering pasta, pizza and *cicchetti* (tapas-style appetisers, such as artichoke and ham bruschetta) that are served until late.

OSTIENSE STREET ART

Rome's street-art scene has exploded in recent years, with many of Rome's less picturesque suburbs given a burst of colour via some astounding, mammoth murals. Rome's tourist kiosks are even offering a free street-art map to help you explore, and different street-art itineraries for various areas are available online at www.turismo-roma.it.

The ex-industrial units and alternative culture of Ostiense have created an ideal marriage between edgy street artists and grey wallspace in need of some colour. With over 30 works, this area is one of the best parts of Rome to wander and enjoy the outdoor gallery.

Rome's annual Outdoor Festival was the source of many works, while others were supported by the gallery **999 Contemporary** (www.999gallery.com), which has a detailed map of works in Ostiense online at www.ostiensedistrict.it.

Highlights include the murals on a **former military warehouse** (Map p326; Via del Porto Fluviale), where the entire building is covered in a rainbow of sinister faces, incorporating the building's 48 arched windows as eyes. These apparently represent the evils of homelessness, on a building that has been a long-term squat. A fantastical mural on the side of the building shows a boat topped by cranes and robots. These are all the work of Italian artist **Blu** (www.blublu.org), from Bologna, who completed the works in 2014.

Another place to look out for (but mind the traffic as you explore) is the underpass on Via delle Conce, with works by artists Lucamaleonte and Gaucholadri, among others. Further up Via Ostiense, near Centrale Montmartini, is another work by Blu depicting interlocking yellow cars that covers the entire facade of the social centre, **Alexis** (Map p326; Via Ostiense 122). The centre is named for Alexis Grigoropoulos, the 15-year-old student who was killed, allegedly by a police bullet, during demonstrations in Greece in 2008 – the mural incorporates his portrait and the date of his death

Other areas to look out for some great street art include Pigneto, San Basilio, San Lorenzo and Testaccio.

🍷 DRINKING & NIGHTLIFE

The ex-industrial area of Ostiense is fertile clubbing land, with its many warehouses, workshops and factories given a new lease of life as pockets of nightlife nirvana. This is where Rome's serious clubbers lose countless hours worshipping at the shrines of electro, nu-house, nu-funk and all sorts of other eclectica.

DOPPIOZEROO   BAR

Map p326 (☑06 5730 1961; www.doppiozeroo. com; Via Ostiense 68; ☺7am-2am Mon-Sat; ⓂPiramide) This easygoing bar was once a bakery, hence the name ('double zero' is a type of flour). But today the sleek, modern interior attracts hungry, trendy Romans like bees to honey, especially for the cheap lunches (*primo/secondo* €4.50/6.50) and famously lavish, dinnertastic *aperitivo* between 6pm and 9pm.

PORTO FLUVIALE   BAR

Map p326 (☑06 574 31 99; www.portofluviale. com; Via del Porto Fluviale 22; ☺10.30am-2am; ⓂPiramide) A large bar in a converted factory, this has an ex-industrial look – dark-green walls and a brickwork floor – and is a relaxing, appealing place for morning coffee, *aperitivo* or an evening drink to a soundtrack of plinky jazz. In line with Rome's current love of artisanal brews, it serves its own Porto Fluviale craft beer (medium €5.50).

GOA   CLUB

Map p326 (☑06 574 82 77; www.goaclub.com; Via Libetta 13; ☺11.30pm-4.30am Thu-Sat; ⓂGarbatella) Goa is Rome's serious super-club, with international names, ethnic-styling, a fashion-forward crowd, podium dancers and heavies on the door.

NEO CLUB   CLUB

Map p326 (Via degli Argonauti 18; ☺11pm-4am Fri & Sat; ⓂGarbatella) This small, dark two-level club has an underground feel and is one of the funkiest choices in the zone, featuring

---

WORTH A DETOUR

ROMAN UNIVERSAL EXHIBITION (EUR)

One of the few planned developments in Rome's history, EUR was built for an international exhibition in 1942. Although war intervened and the exhibition never took place, the name stuck – Esposizione Universale di Roma (Roman Universal Exhibition) or EUR. There are a few museums but the area's interest lies in its spectacular rationalist architecture. It's unique, if not on a particularly human scale, and the style is beautifully expressed in a number of distinctive *palazzi*, including the iconic **Palazzo della Civiltà del Lavoro** (Palace of the Workers; Quadrato della Concordia; ⓂEUR Magliana), dubbed the Square Colosseum. The Palace of the Workers is EUR's architectural icon, a rationalist masterpiece clad in gleaming white travertine. Designed by Giovanni Guerrini, Ernesto Bruno La Padula and Mario Romano, and built between 1938 and 1943, it consists of six rows of nine arches, rising to a height of 50m. It's recently become Fendi's headquarters.

Elsewhere, other monumentalist architecture includes the **Chiesa Santi Pietro e Paolo** (Piazzale Santi Pietro e Paolo), the **Palazzetto dello Sport (Palalottomatica)** (Piazzale dello Sport) and the wonderful **Palazzo dei Congressi** (Piazza JF Kennedy). Massimiliano Fuksas' cutting-edge Nuvola ('cloud') congress centre is the most recent dramatic architectural addition to the area, but work has stalled, due to lack of funding.

The **Museo della Civiltà Romana** (☑06 06 08; Piazza G Agnelli 10; ☺closed for renovations; ⓂEUR Fermi) covers Roman history, and was founded by Mussolini in 1937 to glorify imperial Rome. Children will enjoy the models and weapons. It adjoins the **Museo Astronomico & Planetario** (☑06 06 08; www.planetarioroma.it; ☺closed for renovation), show in Italian. Both were being renovated at the time of research, but were expected to reopen in 2016.

Also in EUR is Rome's largest public swimming pool, **Piscina delle Rose** (☑06 5422 0333; www.piscinadellerose.it; Viale America 20; before/after 1pm €16/14, 3hr Mon-Fri €10, under 10yr free; ☺10am-10pm Mon-Fri, 9am-7pm Sat & Sun mid-May–Sep; ⓂEUR Palasport). It gets crowded, so arrive early to grab a deck chair.

WORTH A DETOUR

CINECITTÀ, CINEMA CITY

Cinecittà (☑ 06 88816182; cinecittastudios.it; Via Tuscolana 1055; adult/child €20/10 set tours (Italian/English) & exhibitions; ⏲ 9.30am-7pm Wed-Mon; Ⓜ Cinecittà), Italy's foremost film studio, was founded in 1937 by Mussolini, and used for many iconic Italian and international films. It's now possible to take a tour of the studios, where you get to visit several impressive sets, including 1500s Florence and ancient Rome, and there are interesting exhibitions, one dedicated to the work of Fellini, and another exploring the history of the studios, with some hands-on exhibits, and, most excitingly, an American submarine set.

Originally intended by Mussolini to turn out propaganda pictures, the studios were used during WWII variously as a refugee camp and hospital, but postwar they went from strength to strength. In the 1950s many major Hollywood films were made here, including Cleopatra, and Rome became nicknamed Hollywood on the Tiber. This was also to become Fellini's stomping ground – he even had a bedroom here – and *La Dolce Vita* was filmed in Theatre 5, within which the director re-created Via Veneto. Later, spaghetti westerns dominated the schedule, as directors such as Sergio Leone directed films such as *A Fistful of Dollars* and *The Good, the Bad & the Ugly*. Recent blockbusters to have been made here include *Ben Hur* and *Zoolander 2*.

a dancetastic mish-mash of breakbeat, techno and old-skool house.

LA SAPONERIA   CLUB
Map p326 (☑ 06 574 69 99; Via degli Argonauti 20; ⏲ 11pm-4.30am Tue-Sun Oct-May; Ⓜ Garbatella) Formerly a soap factory, nowadays La Saponeria is a cool space that's all exposed brick and white walls and brain-twisting light shows. It lathers up the punters with guest DJs spinning everything from nu-house to nu-funk, minimal techno, dance, hip-hop and 1950s retro.

RASHOMON   CLUB
Map p326 (www.rashomonclub.com; Via degli Argonauti 16; ⏲ 11pm-4am Fri & Sat Oct-May; Ⓜ Garbatella) Rashomon is sweaty, not posey, and where to head when you want to dance your ass off. Shake it to a music-lovers' feast of the sound of the underground, especially house, techno and electronica.

⭐ ENTERTAINMENT

LA CASA DEL JAZZ   JAZZ
Map p326 (☑ 06 70 47 31; www.casajazz.it; Viale di Porta Ardeatina 55; admission varies; ⏲ gigs around 8-9pm; Ⓜ Piramide) In the middle of a 2500-sq-m park in the southern suburbs, the Casa del Jazz is housed in a three-storey 1920s villa that once belonged to a Mafia boss. When he was caught, the Comune di Roma (Rome Council) converted it into a jazz-fuelled complex, with a 150-seat auditorium, rehearsal rooms, a cafe and a restaurant. Some events are free.

CAFFÈ LETTERARIO   LIVE MUSIC
Map p326 (☑ 06 5730 2842, 340 3067460; www.caffeletterarioroma.it; Via Ostiense 83, 95; ⏲ 10am-2am Tue-Fri, 4pm-2am Sat & Sun; 🚇 Via Ostiense) Caffè Letterario is an intellectual hang-out housed in the converted, post-industrial space of a former garage. It combines designer looks, a bookshop, a gallery, performance space and a lounge bar. There are regular gigs from 10pm to midnight, ranging from soul and jazz to Indian dance.

XS LIVE   LIVE MUSIC
Map p326 (☑ 06 5730 5102; www.xsliveroma.com; Via Libetta 13; ⏲ 11.30pm-4am Thu-Sun Sep-May; Ⓜ Garbatella) A rocking live music and club venue, hosting regular gigs. Big names playing here in recent times range from Peter Doherty to Jefferson Starship, and club nights range from Cool Britannia–themed trips to '80s odysseys.

TEATRO INDIA   THEATRE
Map p326 (☑ 06 8400 0311; www.teatrodiroma.net; Lungotevere dei Papareschi; tickets €10-30; 🚇 Via Enrico Fermi) Inaugurated in 1999 in the post-industrial landscape of Rome's southern suburbs, the India is the younger sister of Teatro Argentina. It's a stark modern space in a converted industrial building, a fitting setting for its cutting-edge program, with a calendar of international and Italian works.

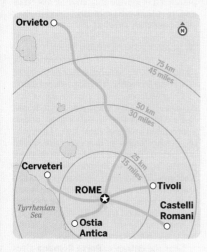

Day Trips from Rome

Ostia Antica p206
Wander through complete streets, gape at ancient toilets and clamber over an amphitheatre at the ancient port of Ostia Antica, Rome's very own Pompeii.

Tivoli p207
A hilltop town home to two Unesco World Heritage sites: Villa Adriana, the emperor Hadrian's colossal country estate, and Villa d'Este, famous for its landscaped gardens and lavish fountains.

Castelli Romani p208
Located south of Rome, the pretty Colli Albani (Alban Hills) and their 13 towns have long provided a green escape for overheated Romans.

Cerveteri p210
The evocative tombs and archaeological treasures of this once important Etruscan city provide a window into a mysterious ancient world.

Orvieto p211
Home to one of Italy's most awe-inspiring Gothic cathedrals, this hilltop Umbrian town makes for a rewarding day trip.

Ostia Antica

Explore

Half a day or more would be ideal to explore the impressive remains of Ostia Antica. This ancient Roman city was a busy working port, and its extensive ruins are substantial and well preserved. Most of the headline sights are situated on or near the main drag, the Decumanus Maximus, which runs for more than a kilometre from the main entrance (Porta Romana) to Porta Marina, the city gate that originally led to the sea. The site gets busy at weekends.

The Best...

➡**Sight** Terme di Nettuno
➡**Place to Eat** Ristorante Monumento

Top Tip

Bring a picnic or time your visit so that you can eat at a restaurant as the on-site canteen gets extremely busy.

Getting There & Away

➡**Car** Take Via del Mare and follow signs for the *scavi* (ruins).

➡**Train** Take the Ostia Lido train from Stazione Porta San Paolo (next to Piramide metro station) and get off at Ostia Antica. Trains leave every 15 minutes or so and the trip, which is covered by a standard Rome public-transport ticket, takes 25 minutes. On arrival, walk over the pedestrian bridge and continue until you see the castle to your right and the ruins straight ahead.

Need to Know

➡**Location** 25km southwest of Rome

◉ SIGHTS

First settled in the 4th century BC, Ostia (the name means the mouth or *ostium* of the Tiber) grew to become a great port and an important commercial centre with a population of around 50,000.

Decline set in after the fall of the Roman Empire, and by the 9th century the city had largely been abandoned, its citizens driven off by barbarian raids and outbreaks of malaria. Over subsequent centuries, it was plundered of marble and building materials and its ruins were gradually buried in river silt, hence their survival.

★**SCAVI ARCHEOLOGICI DI OSTIA ANTICA** ARCHAEOLOGICAL SITE

(☑06 5635 0215; www.ostiaantica.beniculturali. it; Viale dei Romagnoli 717; adult/reduced €10/6; ◷8.30am-6.15pm Tue-Sun summer, earlier closing winter) An easy train ride from Rome, Ostia Antica is one of Italy's most under-appreciated archaeological sites. The ruins of ancient Rome's main seaport are spread out and you'll need a few hours to do them justice. Highlights include the **Terme di Nettuno** (Baths of Neptune), a steeply stacked amphitheatre, and an ancient cafe, complete with bar and traces of the original menu frescoed on the wall.

Note that the site gets busy at weekends, but is much quieter on weekdays.

Near the entrance, **Porta Romana** gives onto the **Decumanus Maximus**, the site's central strip, which runs over 1km to **Porta Marina**, the city's original sea-facing gate.

On the Decumanus, the Terme di Nettuno is a must-see. This baths complex, one of 20 that originally stood in town, dates to the 2nd century and boasts some superb mosaics, including one of Neptune driving his sea-horse chariot. In the centre of the complex are the remains of an arcaded **Palestra** (gym).

Next to the Terme is the **Teatro**, an amphitheatre built by Agrippa and later enlarged to hold 4000 people.

The grassy area behind the amphitheatre is the **Piazzale delle Corporazioni** (Forum of the Corporations), home to the offices of Ostia's merchant guilds. The mosaics that line the perimeter are thought to represent the businesses housed on the square: ships and dolphins indicated shipping agencies, while the elephant probably referred to a business involved in the ivory trade.

The **Forum**, Ostia's main square, is overlooked by what remains of the **Capitolium**, a temple built by Hadrian and dedicated to Jupiter, Juno and Minerva.

Nearby is another highlight: the **Thermopolium**, an ancient cafe. Check out the bar, the frescoed menu, the kitchen and the small courtyard where customers would have relaxed next to a fountain.

Across the road are the remains of the 2nd-century **Terme del Foro**, originally the city's largest baths complex. Here, in the *forica* (public toilet), you can see 20 well-preserved latrines set sociably in a long stone bench.

For more modern facilities, there's a cafeteria-bar complex with toilets and a gift shop to the north of the Decumanus (head up Via dei Mulini).

EATING

RISTORANTE MONUMENTO RISTORANTE €€
(☎06 565 00 21; www.ristorantemonumento.it; Piazza Umberto I 8; fixed-price lunch menu €14, meals €30; ☺12.30-3.30pm & 8-11pm) This historic restaurant started life in the 19th century, catering to the men working on reclaiming the local marshlands. Nowadays, it feeds sightseers fresh out of the nearby ruins, serving homemade pastas and excellent seafood. A fixed-price lunch menu is available Monday through Friday.

Tivoli

Explore

Throughout its history, Tivoli has provided a summer haven for rich Romans. Testifying to this are its two historic playgrounds, both Unesco World Heritage Sites: Villa Adriana, the emperor Hadrian's sprawling country estate just outside town; and the 16th-century Villa d'Este, an aristocratic Renaissance retreat up in the hilltop centre.

You can visit both in a day, though you'll have to start early. The best way is to visit Villa d'Este first, then have lunch in the centre before heading down to Villa Adriana.

The Best...

→**Sight** The *canopo* at Villa Adriana
→**Place to Eat** Sibilla (p208)

Top Tip

Villa Adriana is at its best when the spring flowers are out, but if you suffer hay fever, make sure you take antihistamines.

Getting There & Away

→**Bus** Tivoli is accessible by Cotral bus (€2.20, 50 minutes, every 15 to 20 minutes) from Ponte Mammolo metro station. To get to Villa Adriana from Tivoli's historic centre, take local CAT bus 4 or 4X (€1, 10 minutes, half-hourly) from Largo Garibaldi.

→**Car** Take either Via Tiburtina (SS5) or the faster Rome–L'Aquila autostrada (A24).
→**Train** From Stazione Tiburtina (€2.60, one hour, at least hourly).

Need to Know
→**Location** 30km east of Rome
→**Tourist Information Point** (☎0774 31 35 36; Piazzale delle Nazione Unite; ☺9.30am-5.30pm Tue-Sun) In the hilltop centre near where the bus arrives.

SIGHTS

VILLA ADRIANA ARCHAEOLOGICAL SITE
(☎0774 38 27 33; www.villaadriana.beniculturali.it; adult/reduced €8/4; ☺9am-1hr before sunset) The ruins of Hadrian's vast country villa, 5km outside Tivoli proper, are quite magnificent, easily on a par with anything you'll see in Rome. Built between AD 118 and 138, the villa was one of the largest in the ancient world, encompassing more than 120 hectares, of which about 40 are now open to the public. You'll need several hours to explore.

Must-sees include the **canopo**, a landscaped canal overlooked by a *nymphaeum* (shrine to the water nymph), and the **Teatro Marittimo**, Hadrian's personal refuge.

Hadrian, a great traveller and enthusiastic architect, designed much of the villa himself, basing his ideas on buildings he'd seen around the world. The **pecile**, the large pool area near the walls, is a reproduction of a building in Athens. Similarly, the *canopo* is a copy of a sanctuary in the Egyptian town of Canopus, with a narrow 120m-long pool flanked by sculptural figures. At its head, the **Serapaeum** is a semicircular *nymphaeum* that was used to host summer banquets. Flanking the water, the **antiquarium** is used to stage temporary exhibitions (note that when these are on, admission to the Villa costs slightly more than usual).

Parking (€3) is available at the site.

VILLA D'ESTE HISTORIC BUILDING
(☎0774 31 20 70; www.villadestetivoli.info; Piazza Trento; adult/reduced €8/4; ☺8.30am-1hr before sunset Tue-Sun) In Tivoli's hilltop centre, the steeply terraced grounds of Villa d'Este are a superlative example of a Renaissance garden, complete with monumental fountains, elegant tree-lined avenues and landscaped grottoes. The villa, originally a Benedictine convent, was converted into a luxury retreat

by Lucrezia Borgia's son, Cardinal Ippolito d'Este, in the late 16th century. It later provided inspiration for composer Franz Liszt, who stayed here between 1865 and 1886 and immortalised it in his 1877 piano composition *The Fountains of the Villa d'Este*.

Outside, the manicured gardens feature water-spouting gargoyles and shady lanes flanked by cypresses and fountains. Look out for the Bernini-designed **Fountain of the Organ**, which uses water pressure to play music through a concealed organ, and the 130m-long **Avenue of the Hundred Fountains**.

 EATING

TRATTORIA DEL FALCONE   TRATTORIA €€

(☑0774 31 23 58; Via del Trevio 34; meals €30; ☉noon-4pm & 6.30-11pm) Near Villa d'Este, this cheerful, family-run trattoria has been serving pizzas, classic pastas, meat and seafood since 1918. Boasting exposed stone decor and a small internal courtyard, it's popular with both tourists and locals.

SIBILLA   RISTORANTE €€€

(☑0774 33 52 81; Via della Sibilla 50; meals €50; ☉12.30-3pm & 7.30-10.30pm) With tables set out by two ancient Roman temples and water cascading down the green river gorge below, the Sibilla's outdoor terrace sets a romantic stage for seasonally driven menus and superlative wine.

Castelli Romani

Explore

A pretty pocket of verdant hills and volcanic lakes 20km south of Rome, the Colli Albani (Alban Hills) and their 13 towns are collectively known as the Castelli Romani. Since early Roman days they've provided a green refuge from the city, and still today Romans flock to the area on summer weekends. The easiest towns to get to are Frascati, renowned for its white wine, and Castel Gandolfo, a handsome hilltop centre. Also of interest is Grottaferrata, which has a fine medieval abbey, and Lago Albano, a scenic volcanic lake.

The Best...
→**Sight** Lago Albano
→**Place to Eat** Cacciani (p210)
→**Place to Drink** Frascati (p210)

Top Tip

In Frascati, search out a *cantina* (cellar-cum-trattoria) and settle down for a simple feast of *porchetta* (herb-roasted pork) and fresh local wine.

Getting There & Away

→**Car** For Frascati and Grottaferrata take Via Tuscolana (SS215); for Castel Gandolfo and Lago Albano take Via Appia Nuova (SS7), following signs for Ciampino Airport.

→**Train** There are buses to Frascati, but the best way to reach it is by train from Stazione Termini (€2.10, 30 minutes, hourly Monday to Saturday, every two hours Sunday). There are also regular trains to Castel Gandolfo from Termini (€2.10, 45 minutes). There are no trains between Frascati and Castel Gandolfo.

Getting Around

→**Bus** From Frascati's Piazza Marconi Cotral buses connect with Grottaferrata (€1.10, 10 minutes, twice hourly) and Castel Gandolfo (€1.10, 30 minutes).

Need to Know

→**Location** 20km southeast of Rome
→**Frascati Point Tourist Office** (☑06 9401 5378; Piazza Marconi 5; ☉8am-8pm Mon-Fri, 10am-8pm Sat & Sun)

◉ SIGHTS

◉ Frascati

SCUDERIE ALDOBRANDINI   MUSEUM

(☑06 941 71 95; Piazza Marconi 6; adult/reduced €5.50/3; ☉10am-6pm Tue-Fri, 10am-7pm Sat & Sun) The former stables of Villa Aldobrandini, restored by architect Massimiliano Fuksas, house Frascati's single museum of note, the **Museo Tuscolano**. Dedicated to local history, its collection includes ancient

ESCAPE TO THE BEACH

When you start wilting in Rome's heat, it's time to hit the beach. The nearest is at Ostia Lido, but there are better options further afield:

Fregene A popular resort backed by a tall pine forest. Good for nightlife and beach posing. Regular Cotral buses (€2.20, 50 minutes) run here from Cornelia metro station.

Lago di Bracciano A beautiful volcanic lake with a popular beach at Anguillara Sabazia. Half-hourly trains serve Anguillare from Termini (€2.60, 55 minutes).

Santa Severa Has a lovely strip of sand overlooked by a brooding castle. Nearby **Santa Marinella** is another good option. Hourly trains runs to Santa Severa from Termini (€4, one hour).

Anzio South of Rome, Anzio boasts sandy beaches and some excellent seafood restaurants. Trains run from Termini (€3.60, 70 minutes) every hour (two hourly on Sundays).

Sabaudia Harder to get to, but you're rewarded with clean waters and a fabulous stretch of dune-backed sand. Hourly Cotral buses head here from Laurentina metro station (€5, two hours).

Sperlonga A fashionable spot with a crescent of white sand and a steeply stacked medieval town. From Termini take the train to Fondi (€6.90, 1¼ hours, hourly), then a bus.

Roman artefacts and several interesting models of local villas.

VILLA ALDOBRANDINI GARDENS   GARDENS
(Via Cardinal Massai 18; ⊘9am-5.30pm Mon-Fri) **FREE** Looming over Frascati's main square, Villa Aldobrandini is a haughty 16th-century villa designed by Giacomo della Porta and built by Carlo Maderno. It's closed to the public, but you can visit its impressive baroque gardens during the week.

◉ Grottaferrata

MONASTERO ESARCHICO DI SANTA MARIA DI GROTTAFERRATA   CHURCH
(www.abbaziagreca.it; Viale San Nilo; ⊘9am-noon & 4-7pm Mon-Sat) Better known as the Abbazia Greca di San Nilo, this fortified monastery was founded in 1004. The walls and battlements were added some 400 years later to provide a protective perimeter to the Chiesa di Santa Maria di Grottaferrata. This bejewelled, icon-laden church features a series of 17th-century frescoes by Domenichino and a revered Byzantine image of Santa Maria.

◉ Castel Gandolfo

One of the Castelli's prettiest towns, Castel Gandolfo is a refined hilltop *borgo* (medieval town). There are no must-see sights, but **Piazza della Libertà** is a lovely spot for an ice cream, and the views over Lago Alba-

no are gorgeous. Facing onto the piazza is the pope's 17th-century summer residence, the **Palazzo Pontificio** (closed to the public), where he holds his regular weekly audiences in July and August.

BARBERINI GARDENS   GARDENS
(http://biglietteriamusei.vatican.va/musei/tickets/do; guided tours €26; ⊘by reservation Mon-Sat) Castel Gandolfo's Palazzo Pontificio might be off-limits, but you can explore its gardens on a guided visit. The 90-minute tours, which must be booked online, take in Roman ruins and sweeping views as they navigate the garden's immaculately manicured lanes.

◉ Lago Albano

The largest and most developed of the Castelli's two volcanic lakes – the other is Lago di Nemi – Lago Albano is set in a steeply banked, wooded crater. It's a popular hangout, particularly in spring and summer, when Romans flock here to top up their tans and eat in the many lakeside eateries.

✗ EATING & DRINKING

✗ Frascati

The Frascati area is famous for its white wine. Frascati itself is dotted with *cantine,* down-to-earth eateries where you can try the local *porchetta* and jugs of fresh young wine. Alternatively, you can pick up a *panino con porchetta* (pork roll) from one of the stands on and around around Piazza del Mercato.

CANTINA SIMONETTI OSTERIA €

(www.cantinasimonetti.com; Piazza San Rocco 4; meals €20; ⊙7.45-midnight Wed-Sun & 1-4pm Sat & Sun, longer hours summer) For an authentic dining experience, search out this traditional *cantina* and sit down to a casual meal of *porchetta*, cold cuts and cheese, accompanied by local white wine. In keeping with the food, the decor is rough-and-ready rustic with plain wooden tables and paper tablecloths.

CACCIANI RISTORANTE €€€

(☑06 942 03 78; www.cacciani.it; Via Armando Diaz 13; fixed-price lunch menu €25, meals from €45; ⊙12.15-3pm & 7-11pm Tue-Sat, 12.15-3pm Sun) Frascati's most renowned restaurant offers fine food and twinkling terrace views over Rome. The menu lists modern creative dishes, but it's the classics like *cannelloni con ragù* (cannelloni with meat sauce) that really stand out. There's also a weighty wine list and a couple of fixed-price menus, including a €25 weekday lunch option.

✗ Castel Gandolfo

ANTICO RISTORANTE
PAGNANELLI RISTORANTE €€€

(☑06 936 00 04; www.pagnanelli.it; Via Antonio Gramsci 4, Castel Gandolfo; meals €60-70; ⊙noon-3.30pm & 6.30-11.45pm) Housed in a wisteria-clad villa, this celebrated restaurant is a great place for a romantic meal. It's no casual trattoria, erring on the formal and touristy side, but the seasonally driven menu is excellent, there's a colossal wine list and the views over Lago Albano are unforgettable.

Cerveteri

Explore

The quiet provincial town of Cerveteri is home to one of Italy's greatest Etruscan treasures – the weird and magnificent Necropoli di Banditaccia. Situated in the verdant countryside just outside the modern town, this Unesco-listed burial complex is the only surviving trace of the once-powerful Etruscan city that stood here from the 9th century BC.

Spend the morning wandering around the necropolis, a veritable city of the dead where you half expect to see hobbits popping out of the grassy mounds, then lunch in the medieval town centre, before completing your day with a visit to the fascinating archaeological museum.

The Best...

➡**Sight** Necropoli di Banditaccia
➡**Place to Eat** Antica Locanda le Ginestre

Top Tip

Don't miss Cerveteri's Etruscan museum, which provides context for the tombs and brings the ancient era to life.

Getting There & Away

➡**Bus** Take the Cotral bus (€2.80, 55 minutes, half-hourly) from outside Cornelia metro station. To get to the necropolis from the town centre, bus G runs approximately hourly from the main square (€1.10, five minutes).
➡**Car** Take either Via Aurelia (SS1) or the Civitavecchia autostrada (A12) and exit at Cerveteri–Ladispoli.

Need to Know

➡**Location** 35km northwest of Rome
➡**Tourist Information Point** (☑06 9955 2637; Piazza Aldo Moro; ⊙9.30am-12.30pm winter, 9.30am-12.30pm & 4-6pm spring, 9.30am-12.30pm & 5.30-7.30pm summer)

◉ SIGHTS

Cerveteri (Kysry to the Etruscans and Caere to Latin speakers) was one of the most important commercial centres in the Mediterranean from the 7th to the 5th centuries BC. But the city was largely built of wood and as such very little has survived. Only the necropolis, carved underground, remains to hint at the splendours of the Etruscan city.

Cerveteri's fortunes faded as Roman power grew, and in 358 BC the city was annexed by Rome. After the fall of the Roman Empire, the spread of malaria and repeated Saracen invasions caused further decline. In the 13th century there was a mass exodus from the city to the nearby town of Ceri, and

WORTH A DETOUR

TARQUINIA

For a full immersion in Etruscan culture, push on to Tarquinia, about 50km north of Cerveteri. This, the second of Lazio's great Etruscan towns, is famous for its extraordinary frescoed tombs. The **Museo Archeologico Nazionale Tarquiniese** (0766 85 00 80; www.tarquinia-cerveteri.it; Via Cavour 1; adult/reduced €6/3, incl necropoli €8/4; ⊙8.30am-7.30pm Tue-Sun) displays innumerable treasures, notably a terracotta frieze of winged horses (the *Cavalli Alati*), and several painted tombs. To see Etruscan tombs in situ, head to the Unesco-listed **Necropoli di Monterozzi** (⊘0766 84 00 00; www.tarquinia-cerveteri.it; Via Ripagretta; adult/reduced €6/3, incl museum €8/4; ⊙8.30am-7.30pm Tue-Sun summer, to 1hr before sunset winter), 1.5km outside the centre.

To reach Tarquinia from Cerveteri, take a Cotral bus to Ladispoli station and then a train to Tarquinia (€3.60, 35 minutes, hourly). Returning to Rome, there are direct trains to Termini (€6.90, 1 hour 20 minutes, hourly).

Caere became Caere Vetus (Old Caere), from which its current name derives. The early 19th century saw the first tentative archaeological explorations in the area, and in 1911 systematic excavations began in earnest.

★NECROPOLI DI
BANDITACCIA   ARCHAEOLOGICAL SITE

(⊘06 994 06 51; www.tarquinia-cerveteri.it; Via della Necropoli 43/45; adult/reduced €8/5, incl museum €10/6; ⊙8.30am-1hr before sunset) This haunting 12-hectare necropolis is a veritable city of the dead, with streets, squares and terraces of *tumuli* (circular tombs cut into the earth and capped by turf). Some tombs, including the 6th-century-BC **Tomba dei Rilievi**, retain traces of painted reliefs, many of which illustrate endearingly domestic household items, as well as figures from the underworld.

Another interesting tomb is the 7th-century BC **Tumulo Mengarelli**, whose plain interior shows how the tombs were originally structured.

To bone up on the site's history, you can watch short films in the **Sala Mengarelli** every half past the hour. You can also take a tour that features 3D installations reconstructing the tombs' frescoes and funerary items.

MUSEO NAZIONALE CERITE   MUSEUM

(⊘06 994 13 54; www.tarquinia-cerveteri.it; Piazza Santa Maria 4; adult/reduced €8/5, incl necropolis €10/6; ⊙8.30am-7.30pm Tue-Sun) Housed in a medieval fortress on what was once ancient Caere's acropolis, this splendid museum charts the history of the Etruscan city, housing archaeological treasures unearthed at the necropolis. On the ground floor, a multimedia display illustrates the stories behind some of the collection's prize exhibits.

 EATING

ANTICA LOCANDA
LE GINESTRE   REGIONAL ITALIAN €€

(⊘06 994 33 65; www.anticalocandaleginestre.com; Piazza Santa Maria 5; fixed-price menus €20-30, meals €40-45; ⊙12.30-2.30pm & 7.30-10.30pm Tue-Sun) On a delightful *centro storico* piazza, this family-run restaurant is a top choice for quality regional food. Dishes such as risotto with asparagus tips and saffron are prepared with seasonal local produce and served in an elegant dining room and flower-filled courtyard. Book ahead.

Orvieto

Explore

Strategically located on the main train line between Rome and Florence, the spectacularly sited hilltop town of Orvieto is home to one of Italy's most awe-inspiring cathedrals. The humbug-striped Gothic Duomo is a truly breathtaking site as it towers over the town's medieval centre. Unsurprisingly, it's a tourist honeypot, attracting hordes of visitors, particularly in summer. But don't let that deter you. It's well worth the effort and the surrounding streets are a wonderful place to stroll and enjoy a leisurely lunch.

The Best...

➜**Sight** Duomo di Orvieto (p213)

➜**Place to Eat** Trattoria del Moro Aronne (p213)

➜**Place to Drink** Vinosus (p213)

POMPEII & NAPLES IN A DAY

Just over an hour's fast train ride south of Rome, Naples is one of Italy's most exhilarating cities, a combustible mix of bombastic streetlife, world-class museums and a Unesco-listed historic centre. Further around the bay, Pompeii is an unforgettable sight, an ancient Roman city preserved almost in its entirety. A port and thriving commercial centre, the city was buried by volcanic debris when Vesuvius erupted in AD 79 and its ruins today provide a unique model of a working Roman town. You can cover both on a day trip from Rome, but you'll need to be fired up and full of energy.

To get to Pompeii by mid-morning, take the 7.35am (or 8.45am) Frecciarossa train from Termini to Napoli Centrale (around €40 one way). On arrival, follow signs for the Circumvesuviana (beneath the main station) and catch the earliest available train to Pompei-Scavi-Villa dei Misteri (€3.20). **Pompeii** (☑081 857 53 47; www.pompeiisites.org; entrances at Porta Marina, Piazza Esedra & Piazza Anfiteatro; adult/reduced €11/5.50, incl Herculaneum €20/10; ⊗8.30am-7.30pm summer, to 5pm winter) is huge and you'll need three hours to cover its greatest hits, which include the Forum, Lupanare (an ancient brothel), amphitheatre, and Villa dei Misteri. Pick up a free site map when you buy your ticket.

For lunch, grab a panino from the on-site cafeteria or push onto Pompeii town for a more refined meal at **President** (☑081 850 72 45; www.ristorantepresident.it; Piazza Schettini 12; meals €35; ⊗noon-4pm & 7pm-midnight, closed Mon Oct-Apr; ⓡFS to Pompei, ⓡCircumvesuviana to Pompei Scavi-Villa dei Misteri).

Back in Naples, spend the afternoon exploring the *centro storico*. If you can handle more ancient treasures, head to the **Museo Archeologico Nazionale** (☑081 442 21 49; http://cir.campania.beniculturali.it/museoarcheologiconazionale; Piazza Museo Nazionale 19; adult/reduced €8/4; ⊗9am-7.30pm Wed-Mon; ⓜMuseo, Piazza Cavour), whose stunning collection of classical art includes many prize finds from Pompeii. Also worth a look is the **Cappella Sansevero** (☑081 551 84 70; www.museosansevero.it; Via Francesco de Sanctis 19; adult/reduced €7/5; ⊗9.30am-6.30pm Mon & Wed-Sat, to 2pm Sun; ⓜDante).

You'll need to dine early to make your evening train, so head to **Pizzeria Gino Sorbillo** (☑081 44 66 43; www.accademiadellapizza.it; Via dei Tribunali 32; pizzas from €3.30; ⊗noon-3.30pm & 7pm-1am Mon-Sat; ⓜDante) for a taste of authentic Neapolitan pizza.

The last fast train back to Rome leaves at 7.30pm, but there's a slower Intercity at 8.31pm or a snail-paced *regionale* at 8.48pm.

Top Tip

Stay overnight to experience the medieval atmosphere of the town once all the day trippers have ebbed away.

Getting There & Away

➡**Car** The city is on the A1 north–south autostrada. There's metered parking on Piazza Cahen and in designated areas outside the city walls, including Campo della Fiera.

➡**Train** Trains run to Orvieto from Stazione Termini (€7.50 to €17, 1¼ hours, hourly).

Getting Around

➡**Funicular** From the train station take the funicular (€1.30) up to Piazza Cahen in the historic centre. The fare includes a bus ride from Piazza Cahen up to Piazza Duomo.

➡**Bus** Bus 1 runs to the old town from the train station (€1.30), and bus A connects Piazza Cahen with Piazza Duomo.

Need to Know

➡**Location** 120km northwest of Rome
➡**Tourist Office** (☑0763 34 17 72; www.orvieto.regioneumbria.eu; Piazza Duomo 24; ⊗8.15am-1.50pm & 4-7pm Mon-Fri, 10am-1pm & 3-6pm Sat & Sun)

◉ SIGHTS

Sitting astride a volcanic plug of rock above fields streaked with vines, olive and cypress trees, Orvieto's *centro storico* harbours Etruscan antiquities and underground caves besides its magnificent cathedral.

DUOMO DI ORVIETO — CATHEDRAL

(☎0763 34 24 77; www.opsm.it; Piazza Duomo 26; admission €3; ⊙9.30am-6pm Mon-Sat, 1-5.30pm Sun, shorter hours winter) Nothing can prepare you for the visual feast that is Orvieto's soul-stirring Gothic cathedral. Dating to 1290, it sports a black-and-white banded exterior fronted by what is perhaps the most astonishing facade to grace any Italian church: a mesmerising display of rainbow frescoes, jewel-like mosaics, bas-reliefs and delicate braids of flowers and vines.

The building took 30 years to plan and three centuries to complete. It was started by Fra Bevignate and later additions were made by Sienese master Lorenzo Maitani, Andrea Pisano (of Florence Cathedral fame) and his son Nino Pisano, Andrea Orcagna and Michele Sanicheli.

Of the art on show inside, it's Luca Signorelli's magnificent *Giudizio Universale* that draws the crowds. The artist began work on the vast fresco in 1499 and over the course of the next four years covered every inch of the **Cappella di San Brizio** with a swirling and, at times, grotesque depiction of the Last Judgment. Michelangelo is said to have taken inspiration from the work. Indeed, to some, Michelangelo's masterpiece runs a close second to Signorelli's creation.

On the other side of the transept, the **Cappella del Corporale** houses a 13th-century altar cloth stained with blood that miraculously poured from the communion bread of a priest who doubted the transubstantiation.

MUSEO DELL'OPERA DEL DUOMO DI ORVIETO — MUSEUM

(☎0763 34 24 77; www.museomodo.it; Piazza Duomo 26; admission €5; ⊙9.30am-7pm) Housed in the former papal palace, this museum contains a fine collection of religious relics from the cathedral, as well as Etruscan antiquities and paintings by artists such as Arnolfo di Cambio and the three Pisanos (Andrea, Nino and Giovanni).

TORRE DEL MORO — HISTORIC BUILDING

(Moor's Tower; Corso Cavour 87; adult/reduced €2.80/2; ⊙10am-8pm) From the Piazza Duomo, head northwest along Via del Duomo to Corso Cavour and the 13th-century Torre del Moro. Climb all 250 steps for sweeping views of the city.

ORVIETO UNDERGROUND — HISTORIC SITE

(www.orvietounderground.it; Piazza Duomo 24; adult/reduced €6/5; ⊙tours 11am, 12.15pm, 4pm & 5.15pm daily) The coolest place in Orvieto (literally), this series of 440 caves has been used for millennia by locals for various purposes, including as WWII bomb shelters, refrigerators, wells and, during many a pesky Roman or barbarian siege, as dovecotes to trap the usual one-course dinner: pigeon (still seen on local restaurant menus as *palombo*).

EATING & DRINKING

TRATTORIA DEL MORO ARONNE — TRATTORIA €€

(☎0763 34 27 63; www.trattoriadelmoro.info; Via San Leonardo 7; meals €25-30; ⊙noon-2.30pm & 7.30-9.30pm Wed-Mon) This welcoming trattoria has a convivial feel, authentic food and honest prices. The focus is on traditional cooking and strong regional flavours. Warm up with a goat cheese and fig marmalade starter before hitting your stride with a healthy cut of grilled beef.

LE GROTTE DEL FUNARO — UMBRIAN €€

(☎0763 34 32 76; www.grottedelfunaro.it; Via Ripa Serancia 41; pizza €4-8.50, meals €25-35; ⊙noon-3pm & 7pm-midnight) What could be more romantic – well, at least in a fairytale kind of way – than dining in a proper underground grotto? But this restaurant has more going for it than the novelty factor. Alfredo and Sandra make a cracking kitchen duo, preparing wood-fire-oven pizzas alongside Umbrian dishes like truffle-ricotta-filled ravioli and braised Chianina beef.

VINOSUS — WINE BAR

(Piazza Duomo 15; ⊙11am-4pm & 7pm-midnight Tue-Sun) In photo-op range of the cathedral's northwest wall is this wine bar and eatery. Try the cheese platter with local honey and pears for an elegant addition to wine.

🛏 SLEEPING

⭐ B&B LA MAGNOLIA — B&B €

(☎0763 34 28 08, 349 4620733; www.bblamagnolia.it; Via del Duomo 29; d €60-90; ❄) Tucked down a side street north of the Duomo (the sign is easily missed), this light-filled Renaissance residence has delightful rooms and apartments, an English-speaking owner, a large shared kitchen and a balcony overlooking the rooftops. The owner, Serena, can tell you all about Orvieto – whatever you want to know, just ask.

Sleeping

From opulent five-star palaces to chic boutique hotels, family-run pensions, B&Bs, hostels and convents, Rome has accommodation to please everyone. But while there's plenty of choice, rates are universally high and you'll need to book early to get the best deal.

Pensions & Hotels

The bulk of Rome's accommodation consists of *pensioni* (pensions) and *alberghi* (hotels).

A *pensione* is a small, family-run hotel, often in a converted apartment. Rooms are usually fairly simple, though most come with a private bathroom.

Hotels are rated from one to five stars. Most hotels in Rome's historic centre tend to be three-star and up. As a rule, a three-star room will come with a hairdryer, a minibar (or fridge), a safe, air-con and wi-fi. Some may also have satellite TV. Note that Roman hotel rooms tend to be small, especially in the *centro storico* and Trastevere, where hotels are often housed in centuries-old *palazzi*.

B&Bs & Guesthouses

Alongside traditional B&Bs, Rome has many boutique-style guesthouses offering chic accommodation at midrange to top-end prices.

Breakfast in a Roman B&B usually consists of bread rolls, croissants, yoghurt, ham and cheese.

Hostels

Rome's hostels cater to everyone from backpackers to budget-minded families. Many offer hotel-style rooms alongside traditional dorms.

Some hostels don't accept reservations for dorm beds, so it's first come, first served.

Religious Institutions

Many of Rome's religious institutions offer cheap(ish) rooms. These often impose strict curfews and are fairly short on frills. Book well ahead.

Rental Accommodation

For longer stays, renting an apartment will generally work out cheaper than an extended hotel sojourn. Bank on about €900 per month for a studio apartment or one-bedroom flat. For longer stays, you'll probably have to pay bills plus a building maintenance charge.

Seasons & Rates

Rome doesn't have a low season as such but rates are at their lowest from November to March (excluding Christmas and New Year) and from mid-July through August. Expect to pay top whack in spring (April to June) and autumn (September and October) and over the main holiday periods (Christmas, New Year and Easter). Most midrange and top-end hotels accept credit cards. It's always best to check in advance.

Accommodation Websites

➡ **Lonely Planet** (www.lonelyplanet.com/italy/rome/hotels) Consult a list of author-reviewed accommodation options and book online.

➡ **060608** (www.060608.it/en/accoglienza/dormire) Official Comune di Roma site with accommodation lists. Details are not always up to date.

➡ **Bed & Breakfast Association of Rome** (www.b-b.rm.it) Lists B&Bs and short-term apartment rentals.

➡ **Bed & Breakfast Italia** (www.bbitalia.it) Rome's longest-established B&B network.

➡ **Rome As You Feel** (www.romeasyoufeel.com) Apartment rentals, from cheap studio flats to luxury apartments.

Lonely Planet's Top Choices

Palm Gallery Hotel (p222)
Arty retreat in elegant surroundings.

Babuino 181 (p219) Chic luxury on top shopping street.

Arco del Lauro (p221) Minimalist comfort in Trastevere B&B.

Villa Spalletti Trivelli (p221) Stately style in a city-centre mansion.

Best by Budget

€

Arco del Lauro (p221) A cool bolthole in happening Trastevere.

Althea Inn (p222) Designer comfort at budget prices.

Beehive (p220) Classy hostel near Termini.

€€

Palm Gallery Hotel (p222) A delightful villa hotel.

Residenza Maritti (p216) Welcoming hideaway near the forums.

Daphne Inn (p218) Boutique hotel with superlative service.

€€€

Babuino 181 (p219) Bask in understated luxury

Villa Spalletti Trivelli (p221) Live like country-house nobility

Best for Location

Albergo Abruzzi (p217)
Wake up to the Pantheon.

Casa di Santa Brigida (p217) A convent overlooking Piazza Farnese.

Best for Romance

Hotel Sant'Anselmo (p222) Escape to this beautiful Liberty-style villa.

Hotel Locarno (p219) Star in your own romance at this art-deco gem.

Best B&Bs

Maria-Rosa Guesthouse (p221) Your Trastevere home from home.

La Piccola Maison (p218) Quiet comfort near Piazza Barberini.

Best Value for Money

Althea Inn (p222) A hidden gem near Testaccio.

Le Stanze di Orazio (p219) Get your money's worth at this Vatican B&B.

La Controra (p218) Quality hostel in upscale area.

SLEEPING

NEED TO KNOW

Price Ranges
These price ranges are for a high-season double room with private bathroom:

€	under €110
€€	€110 to €200
€€€	over €200

Breakfast is included unless otherwise stated.

Reservations
➡ Always try to book ahead, especially for the major religious festivals.

➡ Ask for a *camera matrimoniale* for a room with a double bed; a *camera doppia* has twin beds.

Checking In & Out
➡ When you check in you'll need to present your passport or ID card.

➡ Checkout is usually between 10am and noon. In hostels it's around 9am.

➡ Some guesthouses and B&Bs require you to arrange a time to check in.

Where to Stay

Neighbourhood	For	Against
Ancient Rome	Close to major sights such as Colosseum, Roman Forum and Capitoline Museums; quiet at night.	Not cheap and has few budget options; restaurants are touristy.
Centro Storico	Atmospheric area with everything on your doorstep – Pantheon, Piazza Navona, restaurants, bars, shops.	Most expensive part of town; few budget options; can be noisy.
Tridente, Trevi & the Quirinale	Good for Spanish Steps, Trevi Fountain and designer shopping; excellent midrange to top-end options; good transport links.	Upmarket area with prices to match; subdued after dark.
Monti, Esquilino & San Lorenzo	Lots of budget accommodation around Stazione Termini; top eating options in Monti and good nightlife in San Lorenzo; good transport links.	Some dodgy streets in Termini area, which is not Rome's most characterful.
San Giovanni & Testaccio	Authentic atmosphere with good eating and drinking options; Aventino, a quiet, romantic area; Testaccio, a top food and nightlife district.	Few options available; not many big sights.
Trastevere & Gianicolo	Gorgeous, atmospheric area; party vibe with hundreds of bars, cafes, and restaurants; some interesting sights.	Very noisy, particularly on summer nights; expensive.
Vatican City, Borgo & Prati	Near St Peter's Basilica and Vatican Museums; decent range of accommodation; some excellent shops and restaurants; on the metro.	Expensive near St Peter's; not much nightlife; sells out quickly for religious holidays.
Villa Borghese & Northern Rome	Largely residential area good for the Auditorium and some top museums; generally quiet after dark.	Out of the centre; few budget choices.

🛏 Ancient Rome

⭐**RESIDENZA MARITTI**   GUESTHOUSE €€
Map p300 (📞06 678 82 33; www.residenzamaritti.com; Via Tor de' Conti 17; s €50-120, d €80-170, tr €100-190; ❄🛜; ⓂCavour) Boasting stunning views over the forums, this gem has rooms spread over several floors. Some are bright and modern, others are more cosy in feel, with antiques and family furniture. There's no breakfast but you can use a fully equipped kitchen.

NERVA BOUTIQUE HOTEL   BOUTIQUE HOTEL €€
Map p300 (📞06 678 18 35; www.hotelnerva.com; Via Tor de' Conti 3; s €70-180, d €90-300; ❄🛜; ⓂCavour) Fresh from a recent makeover, this friendly hotel is tucked away behind the Imperial Forums. Its snug rooms display a contemporary look in shades of cream, grey and black, with padded leather bedsteads, hanging lamps, and the occasional art tome.

FORTY SEVEN   BOUTIQUE HOTEL €€€
Map p300 (📞06 678 78 16; www.fortysevenhotel.com; Via Petroselli 47; r €170-300; ❄🛜; 🚇Via Petroselli) Near the Bocca della Verità, the plain grey facade of this classy four-star gives onto a bright modern interior, full of sunshine and sharply designed guest rooms. There's also a rooftop restaurant and, in the basement, a gym and Turkish bath.

HOTEL FORUM   HISTORIC HOTEL €€€
Map p300 (📞06 679 24 46; www.hotelforum.com; Via Tor de' Conti 25-30; r €180-350; ❄🛜; ⓂCavour) The stately Forum offers formal elegance and inspiring views. From the rooftop restaurant you can survey a sea of ruins, while inside it's all antiques, wood-panelling and dangling chandeliers. Rooms are small and classically attired. Parking is available for €40 per day.

⇌ Centro Storico

HOTEL PENSIONE BARRETT   PENSION €
Map p304 (☑06 686 84 81; www.pensionebar-rett.com; Largo di Torre Argentina 47; s €115, d €125, tr €150; ❋🛜; ⬚Largo di Torre Argentina) This charming pension boasts a convenient central location and an exuberant decor that marries leafy pot plants with statues, busts and vibrant stucco. Rooms are cosy and come with thoughtful extras like foot spas and fully stocked fridges.

ALBERGO DEL SOLE   HOTEL €
Map p304 (☑06 687 94 46; www.solealbiscione.it; Via del Biscione 76; s €70-100, d €100-145, tr €120-180; ❋🛜; ⬚Corso Vittorio Emanuele II) This simple, no-frills place is supposedly the oldest hotel in Rome, dating to 1462. There's nothing special about the functional rooms, but each floor has its own outdoor terrace, and the location near Campo de' Fiori is excellent. No breakfast.

ALBERGO CESÀRI   HISTORIC HOTEL €€
Map p304 (☑06 674 97 01; www.albergocesari.it; Via di Pietra 89/A; s €70-150, d €110-250; ❋🛜; ⬚Via del Corso) This friendly three-star has been welcoming guests since 1787 and both Stendhal and Mazzini are said to have slept here. Modern visitors can expect traditional rooms, a stunning rooftop terrace, and a wonderful central location.

HOTEL DUE TORRI   HOTEL €€
Map p304 (☑06 6880 6956; www.hotelduetorriroma.com; Vicolo del Leonetto 23; s €70-140, d €110-220, tr €140-240; ❋🛜; ⬚Via di Monte Brianzo) If the rooms at this refined hotel could talk, they'd have some stories to tell. The Due Torri might now be a classically attired three-star with period furniture and 26 cosy rooms, but in centuries past it housed a cardinals' residence and a brothel.

ARGENTINA RESIDENZA   BOUTIQUE HOTEL €€
Map p304 (☑06 6819 3267; www.argentinaresidenza.com; Via di Torre Argentina 47; r €120-200; ❋🛜; ⬚Largo di Torre Argentina) Escape the hustle and relax in the comfort of this quiet boutique hotel on Largo di Torre Argentina. Its six decently sized rooms sport a low-key contemporary look with design touches and elegant furnishings.

HOTEL NAVONA   HOTEL €€
Map p304 (☑06 6821 1392; www.hotelnavona.com; Via dei Sediari 8; s €60-170, d €60-260;

❋🛜; ⬚Corso del Rinascimento) This small hotel offers a range of handsome, modern rooms in a 15th-century *palazzo* near Piazza Navona. They come in various shapes and looks, but the most striking feature a showy silver-and-grey design. Breakfast costs €10 extra.

HOTEL TEATRO DI POMPEO   HOTEL €€
Map p304 (☑06 6830 0170; www.hotelteatrodipompeo.it; Largo del Pallaro 8; s €90-165, d €110-220; ❋@🛜; ⬚Corso Vittorio Emanuele II) Tucked away behind Campo de' Fiori, this charming hotel sits atop the 1st-century-BC Theatre of Pompey – the basement breakfast room is actually in the theatre's ruins. Rooms are attractive with classic wooden furniture, terracotta floor tiles and, in some, sloping wood-beamed ceilings.

DIMORA DEGLI DEI   BOUTIQUE HOTEL €€
Map p304 (☑06 6819 3267; www.pantheondimoradeglidei.com; Via del Seminario 87; r €80-200; ❋🛜; ⬚Largo di Torre Argentina) Location and discreet style are the selling points of this elegant bolthole near the Pantheon. On the 1st floor of a centuries-old *palazzo*, it has six high-ceilinged tastefully furnished rooms. Breakfast (€10) is optional.

CASA DI SANTA BRIGIDA   RELIGIOUS ACCOMMODATION €€
Map p304 (☑06 6889 2596; www.brigidine.org; Piazza Farnese 96, entrance Via di Monserrato 54; s/d €120/200; ❋🛜; ⬚Corso Vittorio Emanuele II) Named after the Swedish St Brigid who died here in 1373, this tranquil convent enjoys a superb location overlooking Piazza Farnese. Rooms are simple, clean and decidedly lowtech – entertainment here is limited to a piano in the communal room, a small library and views from the roof terrace.

★**HOTEL CAMPO DE' FIORI**   BOUTIQUE HOTEL €€€
Map p304 (☑06 687 48 86; www.hotelcampodefiori.com; Via del Biscione 6; r €90-400, apt €80-350; ❋@🛜; ⬚Corso Vittorio Emanuele II) This rakish four-star has got the lot – baroque boudoir decor, an enviable location, professional staff and a fabulous panoramic roof terrace. The interior feels delightfully decadent with its boldly coloured walls, low wooden ceilings, gilt mirrors and restored bric-a-brac. Also available are 13 apartments.

ALBERGO ABRUZZI   HOTEL €€€
Map p304 (☑06 679 20 21; www.hotelabruzzi.it; Piazza della Rotonda 69; d €120-340, tr €150-400,

q €180-450; ❄ 🛜; 🚇 Largo di Torre Argentina) As locations go, the Abruzzi's tops the charts, bang opposite the Pantheon. Its recently refurbished rooms sport a smart look with blown-up photos printed on white walls and dark wood flooring. They are small, though, and late-night noise might be a problem.

🛏 Tridente, Trevi & the Quirinale

⭐ LA CONTRORA HOSTEL €

(📞 06 9893 7366; Via Umbria 7; dm €20-40, d €80-110; ❄ @ 🛜; Ⓜ Barberini, Ⓜ Repubblica) Quality budget accommodation is thin on the ground in the upmarket area north of Piazza Repubblica, but this great little hostel is a top choice. It has a friendly laid-back vibe, cool staff, double rooms and bright, airy mixed dorms (for three and four people), with parquet floors, air-con and private bathrooms.

HOTEL PANDA PENSION €

Map p308 (📞 06 678 01 79; www.hotelpanda.it; Via della Croce 35; s €65-90, d €85-130, tr €120-150, q €160-190; ❄ 🛜; Ⓜ Spagna) Near the Spanish Steps, in an area where a bargain is a Bulgari watch bought at the sales, the Panda flies the flag for budget accommodation. It's a friendly place with high-ceilinged rooms and simple, tasteful decor. Air-con is free in summer, but €6 in other periods.

LA PICCOLA MAISON B&B €€

Map p308 (📞 06 4201 6331; www.lapiccolamaison. com; Via dei Cappuccini 30; s €50-180, d €70-270; ❄ 🛜; Ⓜ Barberini) The excellent Piccola Maison is housed in a 19th-century building in a great location close to Piazza Barberini, and has pleasingly plain, neutrally decorated rooms and thoughtful staff. It's a great deal.

HOTEL TAX

Everyone overnighting in Rome has to pay a room-occupancy tax on top of their regular bill.

➡ €3 per person per night in one- and two-star hotels

➡ €3.50 in B&Bs and room rentals

➡ €4/6/7 in three-/four-/five-star hotels.

The tax is applicable for a maximum of 10 consecutive nights. Prices in reviews do not include the tax.

DAPHNE INN BOUTIQUE HOTEL €€

Map p308 (📞 06 8745 0086; www.daphne-rome. com; Via di San Basilio 55; s €115-180, d €130-240, ste €190-290, without bathroom s €70-130, d €90-160; ❄ 🛜; Ⓜ Barberini) Run by an American-Italian couple, the Daphne has helpful English-speaking staff and chic, comfortable rooms. They come in various shapes and sizes, but the overall look is smart contemporary. There's a second branch, Daphne Trevi, at Via degli Avignonesi 20.

HOTEL SUISSE PENSION €€

Map p308 (📞 06 678 36 49; www.hotelsuisse-rome.com; Via Gregoriana 54; s €80-100, d €135-170, tr €180-200; @ 🛜; Ⓜ Spagna, Ⓜ Barberini) An air of old-school elegance pervades at this delightful family-run pension. Attractive antique furniture and creaking, polished parquet floors set the tone for the 12 tasteful, modestly decorated rooms.

GREGORIANA HOTEL €€

Map p308 (📞 06 679 42 69; www.hotelgregoriana. it; Via Gregoriana 18; s €120-168, d €150-288; ❄; Ⓜ Spagna) This low-key, polished art-deco hotel is fantastically set behind the Spanish Steps. Beds have beautiful, circular maple-wood headboards, snow-white linen and lots of gleaming rosewood. Staff are friendly and unpretentious.

MARGUTTA GLAMOUR STUDIOS APARTMENT €€

Map p308 (📞 333 7982702; www.marguttaglamourstudios.com; Via Margutta 54-55; apt €150-180; Ⓜ Spagna) Four charming apartments on one of Rome's prettiest streets, which has a village feel despite being in the thick of Tridente. All are decorated with flair, and the two larger apartments, in former artists' studios, are spectacular, with double height ceilings; the smaller two are charming, with pretty outlooks.

HOTEL MOZART HOTEL €€

Map p308 (📞 06 3600 1915; www.hotelmozart. com; Via dei Greci 23b; r €140-200; ❄ @ 🛜; Ⓜ Spagna) The Mozart has classic, immaculate rooms, decorated in dove greys, eggshell blues, golden yellows and rosy pinks, with comfortable beds, gleaming linen and polished wooden furniture; deluxe rooms have jacuzzis and small terraces.

It also administers the Vivaldi Luxury Suites and several apartments nearby. Look out for special offers on the website, where rooms can go for as little as €80.

HOTEL BAROCCO
HOTEL €€

Map p308 (📞06 487 20 01; www.hotelbarocco.com; Piazza Barberini 9; d €160-290; ❄ @ 🛜; Ⓜ Barberini) Very central, this well-run, welcoming 41-room hotel overlooking Piazza Barberini (the pricier rooms have views) has a classic feel, with rooms featuring oil paintings, spotless linen, gentle colour schemes and fabric-covered walls. Breakfast is ample and served in a wood-panelled room.

HOTEL LOCARNO
HOTEL €€

Map p308 (📞06 361 08 41; www.hotellocarno.com; Via della Penna 22; s €90-260, d €120-270; ❄ @ 🛜; Ⓜ Flaminio) With its ivy-clad exterior, stained-glass doors and rattling cagelift, the Locarno is an art-deco classic – the kind of place Hercule Poirot might stay if he were in town. Many rooms have silk wallpaper and period furniture, and are occasionally in need of TLC, but full of charm. There's a roof garden, a restaurant and an atmospheric bar.

HOTEL MODIGLIANI
HOTEL €€

Map p308 (📞06 4281 5226; www.hotelmodigliani.com; Via della Purificazione 42; s €100-160, d €100-270; ❄ 🛜; Ⓜ Barberini) Run by an artistic couple, the Modigliani is all about attention to detail and service. The 23 dove-grey rooms are spacious and light, and the best ones have views and balconies, either outside or over the quiet courtyard garden.

★ BABUINO 181
BOUTIQUE HOTEL €€€

Map p308 (📞06 3229 5295; www.romeluxurysuites.com/babuino; Via del Babuino 181; r €240-715; ❄ 🛜; Ⓜ Flaminio) A beautifully renovated old *palazzo*, Babuino offers discreet luxury, with great attention to detail, a sleek roof terrace and modern, chic rooms with touches such as a Nespresso machine and fluffy bathrobes. A new annexe across the street has added more suites and rooms that continue the theme of understated elegance. The same company runs the similarly impressive **Margutta 54** (Map p308; 📞06 322 95 295; www.romeluxurysuites.com/margutta/default-en.html; Via Margutta 54; d from €250; Ⓜ Spagna) and Mario de' Fiori 37.

CASA FABBRINI
B&B €€€

Map p308 (📞06 324 3706; www.casafabbrini.it; Vicolo delle Orsoline 13; r €280; Ⓜ Spagna) A beautifully styled boutique B&B that could have sprung from the pages of *Elle Decoration*, with antique doors as bedheads, coloured-glass lamps and painted furniture.

CROSSING CONDOTTI
GUESTHOUSE €€€

Map p308 (📞06 6992 0633; www.crossingcondotti.com; Via Mario de' Fiori 28; r €240-470; ❄ 🛜; Ⓜ Spagna) This is one of Rome's breed of upmarket guesthouses, where all the fittings, linen and comforts are top of the range, and the pretty, though not large, rooms have lots of character and antique furnishings. There's also a well-stocked kitchen with drinks and a Nespresso machine. The more expensive rooms, recently added, have walk-in showers and a kitchenette, and the top choice has a Turkish bath.

HOTEL DE RUSSIE
HOTEL €€€

Map p308 (📞06 32 88 81; www.hotelderussie.it; Via del Babuino 9; d €550-850; ❄ @; Ⓜ Flaminio) The historic de Russie is almost on Piazza del Popolo, and has exquisite terraced gardens. The decor is softly luxurious in many shades of grey, and the rooms offer state-of-the-art entertainment systems, massive mosaic-tiled bathrooms and all the luxuries. There's a lovely courtyard bar.

🛏 Vatican City, Borgo & Prati

HOTEL SAN PIETRINO
HOTEL €

Map p312 (📞06 370 01 32; www.sanpietrino.it; Via Bettolo 43; s €45-75, d €55-112; ❄ @ 🛜; Ⓜ Ottaviano–San-Pietro) Within easy walking distance of St Peter's, family-run San Pietrino is an excellent budget choice. Its 11 cosy rooms are characterful and prettily decorated with terracotta-tiled floors and the occasional statue. No breakfast.

COLORS HOTEL
HOTEL €

Map p312 (📞06 687 40 30; www.colorshotel.com; Via Boezio 31; s €30-90, d €45-122; ❄ 🛜; 🖵 Via Cola di Rienzo) Popular with young travellers, this welcoming hotel impresses with its fresh, artful design and vibrantly coloured rooms. These come in various shapes and sizes, including some cheaper ones with shared bathrooms and, from June to August, dorms for guests under 38. Breakfast on request costs €6.50.

LE STANZE DI ORAZIO
B&B €€

Map p312 (📞06 3265 2474; www.lestanzediorazio.com; Via Orazio 3; r €85-135; ❄ @ 🛜; Ⓜ Lepanto) This small boutique B&B is excellent value for money. It has five bright, playfully decorated rooms – think shimmering rainbow wallpaper, lilac accents, and designer bathrooms – and a small breakfast area.

FABIO MASSIMO DESIGN HOTEL
BOUTIQUE HOTEL €€

Map p312 (☑06 321 30 44; www.hotelfabiomassimo.com; Viale Giulio Cesare 71; r €89-229; ❄️🛜; ⓂOttaviano-San Pietro) Walkable from Ottaviano metro station, this sleek design hotel is convenient as well as stylish. From the 4th-floor reception and breakfast area, corridors lead off to nine rooms, each furnished in contemporary reds and slate greys, with flower motifs and hanging lamps.

HOTEL BRAMANTE
HISTORIC HOTEL €€

Map p312 (☑06 6880 6426; www.hotelbramante.com; Vicolo delle Palline 24-25; s €100-160, d €140-240, tr €175-260, q €190-300; ❄️🛜; 🚇Borgo Sant'Angelo) Nestled under the Vatican walls, the Bramante exudes country-house charm with its cosy internal courtyard, wood-beamed ceilings and antique furniture. It's housed in the 16th-century building where architect Domenico Fontana once lived.

★VILLA LAETITIA
BOUTIQUE HOTEL €€€

(☑06 322 67 76; www.villalaetitia.com; Lungotevere delle Armi 22; r €200-280, ste €500; ❄️🛜; 🚇Lungotevere delle Armi) Villa Laetitia is a stunning boutique hotel in a riverside art-nouveau villa. Its 20 rooms, each individually designed by Anna Venturini Fendi of the famous fashion house, marry modern design touches with vintage pieces and rare finds, such as an original Picasso in the Garden Room.

🛏 Monti, Esquilino & San Lorenzo

★BEEHIVE
HOSTEL €

Map p320 (☑06 4470 4553; www.the-beehive.com; Via Marghera 8; dm €25-35, s €50-80, d €90-100, without bathroom s €60-70, d €70-80, tr €95-105; ❄️🛜; ⓂTermini) 🌿 More boutique chic than backpacker dive, the Beehive is Rome's best hostel; book well ahead. There's a spotless, eight-person mixed dorm or six private double rooms, some with air-con. Original artworks and funky modular furniture add colour, and there's a cafe. Some off-site rooms, sharing communal bathrooms and kitchen, are another bargain (single €40 to €50, double €60 to €80).

BLUE HOSTEL
HOSTEL €

Map p320 (☑340 925 85 03; www.bluehostel.it; Via Carlo Alberto 13, 3rd fl; d €60-150, apt €100-180; ❄️🛜; ⓂVittorio Emanuele) A hostel in name only, this pearl offers small, hotel-standard rooms, each with its own ensuite bathroom, and decorated in tasteful low-key style – beamed ceilings, wooden floors, French windows, black-and-white framed photos. There's also an apartment, with kitchen, that sleeps up to four. No lift and no breakfast.

WELROME HOTEL
HOTEL €

Map p320 (☑06 4782 4343; www.welrome.it; Via Calatafimi 15-19; d/tr/q €110/148/187; ❄️🛜; ⓂTermini) A small, spotless hotel in a quiet backstreet not far from Termini. Owners Mary and Carlo take great pride in looking after their guests and will enthusiastically advise you on where to eat, what to do and where to avoid. Their seven simply decorated rooms are clean and comfortable. No breakfast but kettles and fridges are provided, and there are plenty of nearby bars for a *cornetto* (croissant) and coffee.

PAPA GERMANO
HOTEL €

Map p320 (☑06 48 69 19; www.hotelpapagermano.it; Via Calatafimi 14a; d €50-110, without bathroom dm €15-35, s €30-65, d €40-85; ❄️@🛜; ⓂTermini) Easygoing and popular, Papa Germano is a budget stalwart. There are various sleeping options, ranging from four-person dorms to private rooms with or without bathrooms. It has a family-run feel, the decor is plain and fairly smart, and all rooms are scrupulously clean.

ALESSANDRO PALACE HOSTEL
HOSTEL €

Map p320 (☑06 446 19 58; www.hostelsalessandro.com; Via Vicenza 42; dm €19-35, d €70-110, tr €85-120; ❄️@🛜; ⓂCastro Pretorio) This well-kept favourite offers spick-and-span, terracotta-floored doubles and triples, as well as dorms sleeping from four to eight, all with cheery bedspreads. Every room has its own bathroom with hairdryer. There's a basement bar, and it runs local tours.

HOTEL ARTORIUS
HOTEL €€

Map p320 (☑06 482 11 96; www.hotelartoriusrome.com; Via del Boschetto 13; d €86-140; ❄️@🛜; ⓂCavour) The art-deco lobby looks promising, and the rest delivers too in this 10-room Monti hotel with a family-run feel. Rooms are simple and plain – not large, but perfectly comfortable – and one (room 109) has a terrace. Book well ahead.

DUCA D'ALBA
HOTEL €€

Map p320 (☑06 48 44 71; www.hotelducadalba.com; Via Leonina 14; r €115-380; ❄️🛜; ⓂCavour)

This appealing four-star hotel in the Monti district has small but charming rooms: most have fabric-covered or handpainted walls, wood-beamed ceilings and big flat-screen TVs.

RESIDENZA CELLINI GUESTHOUSE €€

Map p320 (☑06 4782 5204; www.residenza-cellini.it; Via Modena 5; s €100-135, d €115-150; ❄@❖; MRepubblica) With grown-up furnishings featuring potted palms, polished wood, pale-yellow walls, oil paintings and a hint of chintz, this charming, family-run place on a quiet road parallel to Via Nazionale offers spacious, elegant rooms, all with satellite TV and jacuzzi or hydro-massage shower. There's a sunny flower-surrounded terrace for summer breakfasts.

★VILLA SPALLETTI TRIVELLI HOTEL €€€

Map p320 (☑06 4890 7934; www.villaspalletti.it; Via Piacenza 4; r €450-620; ❄@❖; MSpagna) With 12 rooms in a glorious mansion in central Rome, Villa Spalletti Trivelli was built by Gabriella Rasponi, widow of Italian senator Count Venceslao Spalletti Triveli and the niece of Carolina Bonaparte (Napoleon's sister). It's a soujourn in a stately home: rooms are soberly and elegantly decorated, and the sitting rooms are hung with 16th-century tapestries or lined with antique books. There's a basement spa.

🛏 Trastevere & Gianicolo

MARIA-ROSA GUESTHOUSE B&B €

Map p316 (☑338 7700067; www.maria-rosa.it; Via dei Vascellari 55; s €45-65, d €65-80, tr €80-120; @❖; ⬛Viale di Trastevere, ⬛Viale di Trastevere) This is a delightful B&B on the 3rd floor of a Trastevere townhouse. It's a simple affair with two guestrooms sharing a single bathroom and a small living room, but the homey decor, pot plants and books create a lovely, warm atmosphere. The owner, Sylvie, also has a further three rooms on the floor above at **La Casa di Kaia** (Map p316; ☑338 7700067; www.kaia-trastevere.it; Via dei Vascellari 55; with shared bathroom s €45-55, d €65-75; ❖; ⬛Viale di Trastevere, ⬛Viale di Trastevere). There's no lift.

LA FORESTERIA ORSA MAGGIORE HOSTEL €

Map p316 (☑06 689 37 53; www.casainternazionaledelledonne.org; 2nd fl, Via San Francesco di Sales 1a; dm €26, s/d €75/110, without bathroom €52/72; @❖; ⬛Piazza Trilussa) This lesbian-friendly, women-only guesthouse (boys

aged 12 or younger are welcome) is housed in a lovely 16th-century convent, close to the river. It is run by the Casa Internazionale delle Donne (International Women's House) and offers safe, well-priced accommodation in Trastevere. Reception is open from 7am to 3am. The 13 simple rooms sleep two, four, five or eight, and some have views onto the internal garden. It's wheelchair accessible.

★ARCO DEL LAURO B&B €€

Map p316 (☑346 2443212, 9am-2pm 06 9784 0350; www.arcodellauro.it; Via Arco de' Tolomei 27; s €72-132, d €132-145; ❄❖; ⬛Viale di Trastevere, ⬛Viale di Trastevere) This fab six-room B&B occupies a centuries-old *palazzo* on a narrow cobbled street. Its gleaming white rooms combine rustic charm with a modern look and comfortable beds. The owners are welcoming and always ready to help.

RELAIS LE CLARISSE HOTEL €€

Map p316 (☑06 5833 4437; www.leclarisse.com; Via Cardinale Merry del Val 20; r €80-230; ❄❖; ⬛Viale di Trastevere, ⬛Viale di Trastevere) Set hacienda-style around a pretty internal courtyard with an olive tree and a smattering of cast-iron tables, this is a delightful oasis in Trastevere's bustling core. In contrast to the urban mayhem outside, the hotel is a picture of farmhouse charm with rooms, each named after a plant, decorated in rustic style with wrought-iron bedsteads and wood-beamed ceilings.

RESIDENZA ARCO DE' TOLOMEI HOTEL €€

Map p316 (☑06 5832 0819; www.bbarcodeitolomei.com; Via Arco de' Tolomei 27; d €155-205; ❄❖; ⬛Viale di Trastevere, ⬛Viale di Trastevere) This gorgeous place is decorated with polished antiques and rich contrasting chintzes that make the interiors feel like a country cottage. It's a lovely place to stay, and the owners are friendly and helpful.

BUONANOTTE GARIBALDI GUESTHOUSE €€

Map p316 (☑06 5833 0733; www.buonanottegaribaldi.com; Via Garibaldi 83; r €210-280, closed 7 Jan–7 Mar; ❄@❖; ⬛Piazza Sonnino, ⬛Piazza Sonnino) With only three rooms, this is a haven: an upmarket B&B in a divinely pretty inner-city villa, set around a courtyard. The rooms are beautifully decorated and there are works of art and sculpture all over the place – this is artist Luisa Longo's house. Pick of the rooms is Blue, upstairs, which opens onto a greenery-shaded terrace.

SLEEPING TRASTEVERE & GIANICOLO

HOTEL SANTA MARIA HOTEL €€

Map p316 (⌂06 589 46 26; www.hotelsantamaria. info; Vicolo del Piede 2; s €90-225, d €100-290, tr €130-330; ❄@☎; ⊟Viale di Trastevere, ⊟Viale di Trastevere) Walk along the ivy-lined approach and you'll enter a tranquil haven. Surrounding a spacious modern cloister (a former convent site), shaded by orange trees, rooms are cool and comfortable, decorated in sunny colours, and with terracotta floors. There are some larger family rooms. The staff is professional, and there's access for people with a disability. Nearby **Residenza Santa Maria** (Map p316; ⌂06 5833 5103; www.residenzasantamaria.com; Via dell'Arco di San Calisto 20; s €90-190, d €100-230; @☎) is its smaller sister.

VILLA DELLA FONTE B&B €€

Map p316 (⌂06 580 37 97; www.villafonte.com; Via della Fonte dell'Olio 8; r €80-230; ❄☎; ⊟Viale di Trastevere, ⊟Viale di Trastevere) A terracotta-hued, ivy-shrouded gem, Villa della Fonte is a romantic choice, occupying a 17th-century building in a street off Piazza Santa Maria in Trastevere. It has five rooms, all of which are simply decorated but have pretty outlooks, good bathrooms and comfortable beds. The sunny garden terrace is a plus.

★DONNA CAMILLA SAVELLI HOTEL €€€

Map p316 (⌂06 58 88 61; www.hoteldonnacamillasavelli.com; Via Garibaldi 27; d €165-250; ❄@☎; ⊟Viale di Trastevere, ⊟Viale di Trastevere) It's seldom you have such an exquisite opportunity as to stay in a converted convent designed by Borromini. It's been beautifully updated; muted colours complement the serene concave and convex curves of the architecture, and service is excellent. The pricier of the 78 rooms overlook the cloister garden or have views of Rome, and are decorated with antiques – it's worth forking out that bit extra.

🛏 San Giovanni & Testaccio

★ALTHEA INN B&B €

Map p314 (⌂339 4353717, 06 9893 2666; www. altheainn.com; Via dei Conciatori 9; d €70-125; Ⓜ Piramide) In a workaday apartment block, this friendly B&B offers superb value for money and easy access to Testaccio's bars, clubs and restaurants. Its spacious, light-filled rooms sport a modish look with white walls and tasteful modern furniture. Each also has a small terrace.

HOTEL LANCELOT HOTEL €€

Map p314 (⌂06 7045 0615; www.lancelothotel. com; Via Capo d'Africa 47; s €100-128, d €130-196; ❄☎; ⊟Via di San Giovanni in Laterano) A great location near the Colosseum, striking views, and helpful English-speaking staff – the family-run Lancelot scores across the board. The lobby and communal areas gleam with marble and crystal while the spacious rooms exhibit a more classic style.

HOTEL ROMANCE HOTEL €€

Map p314 (⌂06 8929 5106; www.hotelromance. it; Via Marco Aurelio 37a; s €70-140, d €70-200; ❄☎; ⓂColosseo) A warm welcome awaits at this family-run three-star near the Colosseum. It has quiet, comfy rooms decorated in traditional Roman style and views over a lush garden next door.

★HOTEL SANT'ANSELMO HOTEL €€€

Map p314 (⌂06 57 00 57; www.aventinohotels. com; Piazza Sant'Anselmo 2; s €90-265, d €99-290; ❄☎; ⊟Via Marmorata) A ravishing romantic hideaway in the elegant Aventino district. Its rooms are not the biggest but they are stylish, juxtaposing four-poster beds, Liberty-style furniture and marble bathrooms with modern touches.

🛏 Villa Borghese & Northern Rome

★PALM GALLERY HOTEL HOTEL €€

Map p324 (⌂06 6478 1859; www.palmgalleryhotel.com; Via delle Alpi 15d; s €100-120, d €100-210; ❄☎; ⊟Via Nomentana, ⊟Viale Regina Margherita) Housed in an early-20th-century villa, this gorgeous hotel sports an eclectic look that effortlessly blends African and Middle Eastern art with original art-deco furniture, exposed brickwork and hand-painted tiles. Rooms are individually decorated, with the best offering views over the wisteria and thick greenery in the surrounding streets.

🛏 Southern Rome

HOTEL ABITART HOTEL €€

Map p326 (⌂06 454 31 91; www.abitarthotel. com; Via Matteucci 12; d €130-150; ⓂPiramide, ⊟Ostiense) Located in the gritty, trendy Ostiense area, the Abitart is decorated with a pop-arty feel, and is close to some good restaurants.

Understand Rome

Rome Today

Recent events have left Rome shaken and angry. In late 2014 the city was shocked to the core as details emerged of deep-rooted corruption in city hall and links to organised crime. This, coming after a year of spending cuts and economic uncertainty, was a bitter pill for the city's already weary residents to swallow. On the plus side, restoration work concluded on several high-profile monuments, and Pope Francis continues to win over fans in the Vatican.

Best on Film

La grande bellezza (The Great Beauty; 2013) Paolo Sorrentino's Fellini-esque homage to the Eternal City.

Roma Città Aperta (Rome Open City; 1945) A neo-realist study of desperation in Nazi-occupied Rome.

Dear Diary (1994) Cult director Nanni Moretti scoots around a semideserted Rome.

The Talented Mr Ripley (1999) Murderous intrigue on Piazza di Spagna and in other Italian locations.

Best in Print

The Secrets of Rome: Love & Death in the Eternal City (Corrado Augias; 2007) Journalist Augias muses on little-known historical episodes.

Roman Tales (Alberto Moravia; 1954) Short stories set in Rome's poorest neighbourhoods.

Rome (Robert Hughes; 2012) A personal portrait of the city by the straight-talking Australian art critic.

Michelangelo & the Pope's Ceiling (Ross King; 2003) Fascinating account of the painting of the Sistine Chapel.

Scandal Rocks the City

Rome is no stranger to controversy but even hardened observers were shocked by the Mafia Capitale scandal that rocked the city in late 2014.

The controversy centred on a criminal gang that had infiltrated city hall and was making millions by milking off funds earmarked for immigration centres and camps for the city's Roma population. Thirty-seven people were arrested and up to 100 politicians and public officials, including former mayor Gianni Alemanno, were placed under police investigation. The Romans, not unused to the colourful behaviour of their elected officials, were appalled and a feeling of genuine outrage swept the city.

The man charged with cleaning up the mess – quite literally in some places as the gang had also muscled in on waste disposal contracts – was mayor Ignazio Marino. A former surgeon who likes to cycle around town, Marino has not had an easy ride since taking over from Alemanno in mid-2013. He has had to deal with the city's parlous finances – Rome narrowly avoided bankruptcy in early 2014 – while also managing local exasperation at the state of degradation and neglect in the city.

He has come under enormous pressure to resign but so far he has resisted, and, in a defiant move to promote the city, he recently backed a bid for Rome to host the 2024 Olympics.

Restoration & Urban Art

Rome's recent economic straits have put an enormous strain on the city's capacity to maintain its historical monuments. But walk around town today and you'll see several high-profile monuments gleaming in the wake of recent makeovers.

Despite the very public nature of these restoration projects, most of them were actually financed by private money. In the past few years Rome's cultural administrators have been actively courting private investment to help shore up municipal budgets. And while this has attracted heated debate, it has proved successful: the Colosseum clean-up was sponsored by Tod's, the Fendi fashion house footed the bill for work on the Trevi Fountain, and Bulgari has pledged €1.5 million towards an overhaul of the Spanish Steps.

But away from the spotlight, it's been a very different story. Little private money has been pouring into Rome's suburbs, so the locals have taken it on themselves to brighten things up. Street art has exploded onto the scene in recent times, and giant murals have become a real feature of some of the city's lesser-known neighbourhoods.

The Pope's Charm Offensive

Over on the west bank of the Tiber, the Vatican continues to capture the world's attention.

In April 2014 an estimated 800,000 people flocked to St Peter's to witness the dual canonisation of Popes John Paul II and John XXIII. Overseeing events was Pope Francis, the popular Argentinian pontiff whose papacy has done much to resurrect the Church's image in the wake of Benedict XVI's troubled tenure.

His humble, everyman style has proved a hit, and efforts to put social and environmental issues at the centre of the Church agenda have won him widespread applause.

In a surprise recent move, he generated much excitement, as well as a fair degree of panic, by proclaiming a Jubilee Year to run from December 2015 to November 2016. A Jubilee or Holy Year is one in which the Church offers a plenary indulgence to Catholics who visit one of Rome's patriarchal basilicas and observe certain religious conditions. City officials, while delighted at the prospect of all the money the pilgrims will bring, are understandably daunted at the prospect of having to prepare for such a huge event in such a short time.

Tourism Thrives

As well as wooing Catholics back to the fold, Pope Francis has had a positive effect on tourism, and in 2014 he was credited with inspiring a 28% increase in the number of Argentinian visitors to the city.

Surprisingly, Rome's recent tribulations haven't adversely affected tourism, which continues to go from strength to strength – arrivals in 2014 were up on previous years, confirming the recent upward trend.

But a rise in tourist numbers, while generally a good thing for the city, has proved a mixed blessing for the Sistine Chapel. This, the star attraction of the Vatican Museums, is full to bursting, and in March 2015 the Museums' director announced that he would have to limit daily visits if visitor numbers continued to grow.

if Rome were 100 people

51 would commute by car
28 would use public transport
15 would commute by scooter
6 would commute on foot

nationality
(% of population)

Italian — 88
Others — 12

population per sq km

ROME / ITALY

≈ 200 people

History

Rome's history spans three millennia, from the classical myths of vengeful gods to the follies of Roman emperors, from Renaissance excess to swaggering 20th-century fascism. Emperors, popes and dictators have come and gone, playing out their ambitions and conspiring for their place in history. Everywhere you go in this remarkable city, you're surrounded by the past. Martial ruins, Renaissance *palazzi* and flamboyant baroque basilicas all have tales to tell – of family feuding, historic upheavals, artistic rivalries, intrigues and dark passions.

Ancient Rome, the Myth

Excavations under the Lapis Niger in the Roman Forum have unearthed a wall dating to between the end of the 9th century BC and the early 8th century BC. This would suggest that Rome was founded a century or so before its traditional birth date of 753 BC.

As much a mythical construct as a historical reality, ancient Rome's image has been carefully nurtured throughout history. Intellectuals, artists and architects have sought inspiration from this skilfully constructed legend, while political and religious rulers have invoked it to legitimise their authority and serve their political ends.

Imperial Spin Doctors

Rome's original myth-makers were the first emperors. Eager to reinforce the city's status as *caput mundi* (capital of the world), they turned to writers such as Virgil, Ovid and Livy to create an official Roman history. These authors, while adept at weaving epic narratives, were less interested in the rigours of historical research and frequently presented myth as reality. In the *Aeneid,* Virgil brazenly draws on Greek legends and stories to tell the tale of Aeneas, a Trojan prince who arrives in Italy and establishes Rome's founding dynasty. Similarly, Livy, a writer celebrated for his monumental history of the Roman Republic, makes liberal use of mythology to fill the gaps in his historical narrative.

Ancient Rome's rulers were sophisticated masters of spin, and under their tutelage, art, architecture and elaborate public ceremony were employed to perpetuate the image of Rome as an invincible and divinely sanctioned power. Monuments such as the Ara Pacis, the Colonna di Traiano and the Arco di Costantino celebrated imperial glories, while gladiatorial games highlighted the Romans' physical superiority.

TIMELINE	753 BC	509 BC	146 BC
	According to legend, Romulus kills his twin brother Remus and founds Rome. Archaeological evidence exists of an 8th-century settlement on the Palatino.	On the death of the king Tarquinius Superbus, the Roman Republic is founded, paving the way for Rome's rise to European domination.	Carthage is razed to the ground at the end of the Third Punic War and mainland Greece is conquered by rampant legionaries. Rome becomes undisputed master of the Mediterranean.

ROMULUS & REMUS, ROME'S LEGENDARY TWINS

The most famous of Rome's many legends is the story of Romulus and Remus and the foundation of the city on 21 April 753 BC. According to myth, Romulus and Remus were the children of the vestal virgin Rhea Silva and the god of war, Mars. While still babies they were set adrift on the Tiber to escape a death penalty imposed by their great-uncle Amulius, who at the time was battling with their grandfather Numitor for control of Alba Longa. However, they were discovered near the Palatino by a she-wolf, who suckled them until a shepherd, Faustulus, found and raised them.

Years later the twins decided to found a city on the site where they'd originally been saved. They didn't know where this was, so they consulted the omens. Remus, on the Aventino, saw six vultures; his brother over on the Palatino saw 12. The meaning was clear and Romulus began building, much to the outrage of his brother. The two subsequently argued and Romulus killed Remus.

Romulus continued building and soon had a city. To populate it he created a refuge on the Campidoglio, Aventino, Celio and Quirinale Hills, to which a ragtag population of criminals, ex-slaves and outlaws soon decamped. However, the city still needed women. Romulus therefore invited everyone in the surrounding country to celebrate the Festival of Consus (21 August). As the spectators watched the festival games, Romulus and his men pounced and abducted all the women, an act that was to go down in history as the Rape of the Sabine Women.

The Colosseum, the Roman Forum and the Pantheon were not only sophisticated feats of engineering, they were also impregnable symbols of Rome's eternal might.

The Past as Inspiration

During the Renaissance, a period in which ancient Rome was hailed as the high point of Western civilisation, the city's great monuments inspired a whole generation of artists and architects. Bramante, Michelangelo and Raphael modelled their work on classical precedents as they helped rebuild Rome as the capital of the Catholic Church.

But more than anyone, it was Italy's 20th-century Fascist dictator Benito Mussolini who invoked the glories of ancient Rome. *Il Duce* spared no effort in his attempts to identify his fascist regime with imperial Rome – he made Rome's traditional birthday, 21 April, an official Fascist holiday, he printed stamps with images of ancient Roman emperors, and he commissioned archaeological digs to unearth further proof of Roman might. His idealisation of the Roman Empire underpinned much of his colonialist ideology.

Nowadays, the myth of Rome is used less as a rallying cry and more as an advertising tool – and with some success. However cynical and

Historical Sites

Palatino

Largo di Torre Argentina

Capitoline Hill

Roman Forum

Castel Sant'Angelo

Palazzo Venezia

73–71 BC	49 BC	15 March 44 BC	AD 14
Spartacus leads a slave revolt against dictator Cornelius Sulla. Defeat is inevitable; punishment is brutal. Spartacus and 6000 followers are crucified along Via Appia Antica.	*'Alea iacta est'* ('The die is cast'). Julius Caesar leads his army across the River Rubicon and marches on Rome. In the ensuing civil war, Caesar defeats rival Pompey.	On the Ides of March, soon after Julius Caesar is proclaimed dictator for life, he is stabbed to death in the Teatro di Pompeo (on modern-day Largo di Torre Argentina).	Augustus dies after 41 years as Rome's first emperor. His reign is successful, unlike those of his mad successors, Tiberius and Caligula, who go down in history for their cruelty.

world-weary you are, it's difficult to deny the thrill of seeing the Colosseum for the first time or of visiting the Palatino, the hill where Romulus is said to have founded the city.

Legacy of an Empire

Rising out of the bloodstained remains of the Roman Republic, the Roman Empire was the Western world's first great superpower. At its zenith under the emperor Trajan (r AD 98–117), it extended from Britannia in the north to North Africa in the south, from Hispania (Spain) in the west to Palestina (Palestine) and Syria in the east. Rome itself had more than 1.5 million inhabitants and the city sparkled with the trappings

A WHO'S WHO OF ROMAN EMPERORS

Of the 250 or so emperors of the Roman Empire, only a few were truly heroic. Here we highlight 10 of the best, worst and completely insane.

Augustus (27 BC–AD 14)	Rome's first emperor. Ushers in a period of peace and security; the arts flourish and many monuments are built, including the Ara Pacis and Pantheon.
Caligula (37–41)	Emperor number three after Augustus and Tiberius. Remains popular until illness leads to the depraved behaviour for which he becomes infamous. Is murdered by his bodyguards on the Palatino.
Claudius (41–54)	Expands the Roman Empire and conquers Britain. Is eventually poisoned, probably at the instigation of Agrippina, his wife and Nero's mother.
Nero (54–68)	Initially rules well but later slips into madness – he has his mother murdered, persecutes the Christians, and attempts to turn half the city into a palace, the Domus Aurea. He is eventually forced into suicide.
Vespasian (69–79)	First of the Flavian dynasty, he imposes peace and cleans up the imperial finances. His greatest legacy is the Colosseum.
Trajan (98–117)	Conquers the east and rules over the empire at its zenith. He revamps Rome's city centre, adding a forum, marketplace and column, all of which still stand.
Hadrian (117–38)	Puts an end to imperial expansion and constructs walls to mark the empire's borders. He rebuilds the Pantheon and has one of the ancient world's greatest villas built at Tivoli.
Aurelian (270–75)	Does much to control the rebellion that sweeps the empire at the end of the 3rd century. Starts construction of the city walls that still today bear his name.
Diocletian (284–305)	Splits the empire into eastern and western halves in 285. Launches a savage persecution of the Christians as he struggles to control the empire's eastern reaches.
Constantine I (306–37)	Although based in Byzantium (later renamed Constantinople in his honour), he legalises Christianity and embarks on a church-building spree in Rome.

64	67	80	285
Rome is ravaged by a huge fire that burns for five and a half days. Some blame Nero, although he was in Anzio when the conflagration broke out.	St Peter and St Paul become martyrs as Nero massacres Rome's Christians. The persecution is a thinly disguised ploy to win back popularity after the great fire of 64 AD.	The 50,000-seat Flavian Amphitheatre, better known as the Colosseum, is inaugurated by the emperor Titus. Five thousand animals are slaughtered in the 100-day opening games.	To control anarchy within the Roman Empire, Diocletian splits it into two. The eastern half is later incorporated into the Byzantine Empire; the western half falls to the barbarians.

The Roman Empire

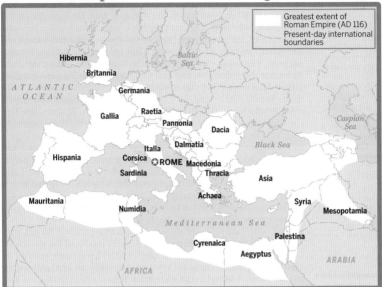

of imperial splendour. Decline eventually set in during the 3rd century, and by the latter half of the 5th century, Rome was in barbarian hands.

Europe Divided

The empire's most immediate legacy was the division of Europe into east and west. In AD 285 the emperor Diocletian, prompted by widespread disquiet across the empire, split the Roman Empire into eastern and western halves – the west centred on Rome, the east on Byzantium (later called Constantinople) – in a move that was to have far-reaching consequences. In the west, the fall of the Western Roman Empire in AD 476 paved the way for the emergence of the Holy Roman Empire and the Papal States, while in the east, Roman (later Byzantine) rule continued until 1453 when the empire was conquered by Ottoman armies.

Democracy & the Rule of Law

In cultural terms, Roman innovations in language, law, government, art, architecture, engineering and public administration remain relevant.

Ancient Rome on Screen

Spartacus (1960; Stanley Kubrick)

Quo Vadis (1951; Mervyn LeRoy)

Gladiator (2000; Ridley Scott)

I, Claudius (1976; BBC)

Rome (2005–07; HBO)

313	476	754	800
A year after his victory at the Battle of Milvian Bridge, the emperor Constantine issues the Edict of Milan, officially establishing religious tolerance and legally ending Christian persecution.	The fall of Romulus Augustulus marks the end of the Western Empire. This has been on the cards for years: in 410 the Goths sack Rome; in 455 the Vandals follow suit.	Pope Stephen II and Pepin, king of the Franks, cut a deal resulting in the creation of the Papal States. The papacy is to rule Rome until Italian unification.	Pope Leo III crowns Pepin's son, Charlemagne, Holy Roman Emperor during Christmas mass at St Peter's Basilica. A red disk in the basilica marks the spot where it happened.

One of the Romans' most striking contributions to modern society was democratic government. Democracy had first appeared in 5th-century-BC Athens, but it was the Romans, with their genius for organisation, who took it to another level. Under the Roman Republic (509–47 BC), the Roman population was divided into two categories: the Senate and the Roman people. Both held clearly defined responsibilities. The people, through three assembly bodies – the Centuriate Assembly, the Tribal Assembly and the Council of the People – voted on all new laws and elected two annual tribunes who had the power of veto in the Senate. The Senate, for its part, elected and advised two annual consuls who acted as political and military leaders. It also controlled the Republic's purse strings and, in times of grave peril, could nominate a dictator for a six-month period.

This system worked pretty well for the duration of the Republic, and remained more or less intact during the empire – at least on paper. In practice, the Senate assumed the assemblies' legislative powers and the emperor claimed power of veto over the Senate, a move that pretty much gave him complete command.

The observance of law was an important element in Roman society. As far back as the 5th century BC, the Republic had a bill of rights, known as the Twelve Tables. This remained the foundation stone of Rome's legal system until the emperor Justinian (r 527–65) produced his mammoth *Corpus Iurus Civilis* (Body of Civil Law) in 529. This not only codified all existing laws, but also included a systematic treatise on legal philosophy. In particular, it introduced a distinction between *ius civilis* (civil law; laws particular to a state), *ius gentium* (law of nations; laws established and shared by states) and *ius naturale* (natural law; laws concerning male-female relationships and matrimony).

Latin

More than the laws themselves, Rome's greatest legacy to the legal profession was the Latin language. Latin was the lingua franca of the Roman Empire and was later adopted by the Catholic Church, a major reason for its survival. It is still one of the Vatican's official languages and until the second Vatican Council (1962–65) it was the only language in which Catholic Mass could be said. As the basis for modern Romance languages such as Italian, French and Spanish, it provides the linguistic roots of many modern words.

Roman Roads

Just as many words lead to Latin, so all roads lead to Rome. The ancient Romans were the master engineers of their day, and their ability to travel quickly was an important factor in their power to rule. The queen

Via Appia Antica is named after Appius Claudius Caecus, the Roman censor who initiated its construction in 312 BC. He also built Rome's first aqueduct, the Aqua Appia, which brought in water from the Sabine Hills.

Virgil (70 BC–19 BC), real name Publius Vergilius Maro, was born near the northern Italian town of Mantua to a wealthy family. He studied in Cremona, Milan, Rome and Naples, before becoming Rome's best-known classical poet. His most famous works are the *Eclogues*, *Georgics* and the *Aeneid*.

1084	1300	1309	1347
Rome is sacked by a Norman army after Pope Gregory VII invites them in to help him against the besieging forces of the Holy Roman Emperor Henry IV.	Pope Boniface VIII proclaims Rome's first ever Jubilee, offering a full pardon to anyone who makes the pilgrimage to the city. Up to 200,000 people are said to have come.	Fighting between French-backed pretenders to the papacy and Roman nobility ends in Pope Clement V transferring to Avignon. Only in 1377 does Pope Gregory XI return to Rome.	Cola di Rienzo, a local notary, declares himself dictator of Rome. Surprisingly, he's welcomed by the people; less surprisingly he's later driven out of town by the hostile aristocracy.

of all ancient roads was Via Appia Antica, which connected Rome with the southern Adriatic port of Brindisi. Via Appia survives to this day, as do many of the other consular roads: Via Aurelia, Via Cassia, Via Flaminia and Via Salaria among them.

Christianity & Papal Power

For much of its history Rome has been ruled by the pope, and still today the Vatican wields immense influence over the city.

The ancient Romans were remarkably tolerant of foreign religions. They themselves worshipped a cosmopolitan pantheon of gods, ranging from household spirits and former emperors to deities appropriated from Greek mythology (Jupiter, Juno, Neptune, Minerva etc). Religious cults were also popular – the Egyptian gods Isis and Serapis enjoyed a mass following, as did Mithras, a heroic saviour-god of vaguely Persian origin, who was worshipped by male-only devotees in underground temples.

Emergence of Christianity

Christianity entered this religious cocktail in the 1st century AD, sweeping in from Judaea, a Roman province in what is now Israel and the West Bank. Its early days were marred by persecution, most notably under Nero (r 54–68), but it slowly caught on, thanks to its popular message of heavenly reward and the evangelising efforts of Sts Peter and Paul. However, it was the conversion of the emperor Constantine (r 306–37) that really set Christianity on the path to European domination. In 313 Constantine issued the Edict of Milan, officially legalising Christianity, and later, in 378, Theodosius (r 379–95) made Christianity Rome's state

The patron saints of Rome, Peter and Paul, were both executed during Nero's persecution of the Christians between 64 and 68. Paul, who as a Roman citizen was entitled to a quick death, was beheaded, while Peter was crucified head down on the Vatican Hill.

HISTORY CHRISTIANITY & PAPAL POWER

DONATION OF CONSTANTINE

The most famous forgery in medieval history, the Donation of Constantine is a document in which the Roman emperor Constantine purportedly grants Pope Sylvester I (r 314–35) and his successors control of Rome and the Western Roman Empire, as well as primacy over the holy sees of Antioch, Alexandria, Constantinople, Jerusalem and all the world's churches.

No one is sure when the document was written but the consensus is that it dates to the mid- or late 8th century. This fits with the widespread theory that the author was a Roman cleric, possibly working with the knowledge of Pope Stephen II (r 752–57).

For centuries the donation was accepted as genuine and used by popes to justify their territorial claims. But in 1440 the Italian philosopher Lorenzo Valla proved that it was a forgery. By analysing the Latin used in the document he was able to show that it was inconsistent with the Latin used in the 4th century.

1378–1417	1506	1508	1527
Squabbling between factions in the Catholic Church leads to the Great Schism. The pope rules in Rome while the alternative anti-pope sits in Avignon.	Pope Julius II employs 150 Swiss mercenaries to protect him. The 100-strong Swiss Guard, all practising Catholics from Switzerland, are still responsible for the pope's personal safety.	Michelangelo starts painting the Sistine Chapel, while down the hall Raphael begins to decorate Pope Julius II's private apartments, better known as the Stanze di Raffaello (Raphael Rooms).	Pope Clement VII takes refuge in Castel Sant'Angelo as Rome is sacked by troops loyal to Charles V, king of Spain and Holy Roman Emperor.

The Roman Inquisition was set up in the 16th century to counter the threat of Protestantism. It was responsible for prosecuting people accused of heresy, blasphemy, immorality and witchcraft, and although it did order executions, it often imposed lighter punishments such as fines and the recital of prayers.

religion. By this time, the Church had developed a sophisticated organisational structure based on five major sees: Rome, Constantinople, Alexandria, Antioch and Jerusalem. At the outset, each bishopric carried equal weight, but in subsequent years Rome emerged as the senior party. The reasons for this were partly political – Rome was the wealthy capital of the Roman Empire – and partly religious – early Christian doctrine held that St Peter, founder of the Roman Church, had been sanctioned by Christ to lead the universal Church.

Papal Control

But while Rome had control of Christianity, the Church had yet to conquer Rome. This it did in the dark days that followed the fall of the Roman Empire. And although no one person can take credit for this, Pope Gregory the Great (r 590–604) did more than most to lay the groundwork. A leader of considerable foresight, he won many friends by supplying free bread to Rome's starving citizens and restoring the city's water supply. He also stood up to the menacing Lombards, who presented a very real threat to the city.

It was this threat that pushed the papacy into an alliance with the Frankish kings, an alliance that resulted in the creation of the two great powers of medieval Europe: the Papal States and the Holy Roman Empire. In Rome, the battle between these two superpowers translated into endless feuding between the city's baronial families and frequent attempts by the French to claim the papacy for their own. This political and military fighting eventually culminated in the papacy transferring to the French city of Avignon between 1309 and 1377, and the Great Schism (1378–1417), a period in which the Catholic world was headed by two popes, one in Rome and one in Avignon.

As both religious and temporal leaders, Rome's popes wielded influence well beyond their military capacity. For much of the medieval period, the Church held a virtual monopoly on Europe's reading material (mostly religious scripts written in Latin) and was the authority on virtually every aspect of human knowledge. All innovations in science, philosophy and literature had to be cleared by the Church's hawkish scholars, who were constantly on the lookout for heresy.

You'll see the letters SPQR everywhere in Rome. They were adopted during the Roman Republic and stand for Senatus Populusque Romanus (the Senate and People of Rome).

Modern Influence

Almost a thousand years on and the Church is still a major influence on modern Italian life. Its rigid stance on social and ethical issues such as abortion, same-sex marriage and euthanasia informs much public debate, often with highly divisive results. A famous example was a right-to-die case in 2008 that saw the Vatican try to block a High Court decision allowing doctors to cease treatment of a long-term coma patient.

1540	1555	1626	1632
Pope Paul III officially recognises the Society of Jesus, aka the Jesuits. The order is founded by Ignatius de Loyola, who spends his last days in the Chiesa del Gesù.	As fear pervades Counter-Reformation Rome, Pope Paul IV confines the city's Jews to the area known as the Jewish Ghetto. Official intolerance continues on and off until the 20th century.	After more than 150 years of construction, St Peter's Basilica is consecrated. The hulking basilica remains the largest church in the world until well into the 20th century.	Galileo Galilei is summoned to appear before the Inquisition. He is forced to renounce his belief that the earth revolves around the sun and is exiled to Florence.

The relationship between the Church and Italy's modern political establishment has been a fact of life since the founding of the Italian Republic in 1946. For much of the First Republic (1946–94), the Vatican was closely associated with the Christian Democrat party (DC, Democrazia Cristiana), Italy's most powerful party and an ardent opponent of communism. At the same time, the Church, keen to weed communism out of the political landscape, played its part by threatening to excommunicate anyone who voted for Italy's Communist Party (PCI, Partito Comunista Italiano).

Today, no one political party has a monopoly on Church favour, and politicians across the spectrum tread warily around Catholic sensibilities. But this reverence isn't limited to the purely political sphere; it also informs much press reporting and even law enforcement. In September 2008 Rome's public prosecutor threatened to prosecute a comedian for comments made against the pope, invoking the 1929 Lateran Treaty under which it is a criminal offence to 'offend the honour' of the pope and Italian president. The charge, which ignited a heated debate on censorship and the right to free speech, was eventually dropped by the Italian justice minister.

Renaissance – a New Beginning

Bridging the gap between the Middle Ages and the modern era, the Renaissance (Rinascimento in Italian) was a far-reaching intellectual, artistic and cultural movement. It emerged in 14th-century Florence but quickly spread to Rome, where it gave rise to one of the greatest makeovers the city had ever seen.

Humanism & Rebuilding

The movement's intellectual cornerstone was humanism, a philosophy that focused on the central role of humanity within the universe, a major break from the medieval world view, which had placed God at the centre of everything. It was not anti-religious, though. Many humanist scholars were priests and most of Rome's great works of Renaissance art were commissioned by the Church. In fact, it was one of the most celebrated humanist scholars of the 15th century, Pope Nicholas V (r 1447–84), who is generally considered the harbinger of the Roman Renaissance.

When Nicholas became pope in 1447, Rome was not in good shape. Centuries of medieval feuding had reduced the city to a semideserted battleground, and its bedraggled population lived in constant fear of plague, famine and flooding (the Tiber regularly broke its banks). In political terms, the papacy was recovering from the trauma of the Great Schism and attempting to face down Muslim encroachment in the east.

Longest-Serving Popes

St Peter
(r 30–67)

Pius XI
(r 1846–78)

John Paul II
(r 1978–2005)

Leo XIII
(r 1878–1903)

Pius Vi
(r 1775–99)

The Borgias, led by family patriarch Rodrigo, aka Pope Alexander VI (r 1492–1503), were one of Renaissance Rome's most notorious families. Machiavelli supposedly modelled *Il Principe* (The Prince) on Rodrigo's son, Cesare, while his daughter, Lucrezia, earned notoriety as a femme fatale with a penchant for poisoning her enemies.

1656–67	1798	1870	1885
Gian Lorenzo Bernini lays out St Peter's Sq for Pope Alexander VII. Bernini, along with his great rival Francesco Borromini, are the leading exponents of Roman baroque.	Napoleon marches into Rome, forcing Pope Pius VI to flee. A republic is announced, but it doesn't last long and in 1801 Pius VI's successor Pius VII returns to Rome.	Nine years after Italian unification, Rome's city walls are breached at Porta Pia and Pope Pius IX is forced to cede the city to Italy. Rome becomes the Italian capital.	To celebrate Italian unification and honour Italy's first king, Vittorio Emanuele II, construction work begins on Il Vittoriano, the mountainous monument dominating Piazza Venezia.

It was against this background that Nicholas decided to rebuild Rome as a showcase for Church power. To finance his plans, he declared 1450 a Jubilee year, a tried and tested way of raising funds by attracting hundreds of thousands of pilgrims to the city (in a Jubilee year, anyone who comes to Rome and confesses receives a full papal pardon).

Over the course of the next 80 years or so, Rome underwent a complete overhaul. Pope Sixtus IV (r 1471–84) had the Sistine Chapel built and, in 1471, gave the people of Rome a selection of bronzes that became the first exhibits of the Capitoline Museums. Julius II (r 1503–13) laid Via del Corso and Via Giulia, and ordered Bramante to rebuild St Peter's Basilica. Michelangelo frescoed the Sistine Chapel and designed the dome of St Peter's, while Raphael inspired a whole generation of painters with his masterful grasp of perspective.

The Sack of Rome & Protestant Protest

But outside Rome an ill wind was blowing. The main source of trouble was the long-standing conflict between the Holy Roman Empire, led by the Spanish Charles V, and the Italian city states. This simmering tension came to a head in 1527 when Rome was invaded by Charles' marauding army and ransacked while Pope Clement VII (r 1523–34) hid in Castel Sant'Angelo. The sack of Rome, regarded by most historians as the nail in the coffin of the Roman Renaissance, was a hugely traumatic event. It left the papacy reeling and gave rise to the view that the Church had been greatly weakened by its own moral shortcomings. That the Church was corrupt was well known, and it was with considerable public support that Martin Luther pinned his 95 Theses to a church door in Wittenberg in 1517, thus sparking the Protestant Reformation.

The Counter-Reformation

The Counter-Reformation, the Catholic response to the Reformation, was marked by a second wave of artistic and architectural activity as the Church once again turned to bricks and mortar to restore its authority. But in contrast to the Renaissance, the Counter-Reformation was also a period of persecution and official intolerance. With the full blessing of Pope Paul III, Ignatius Loyola founded the Jesuits in 1540, and two years later the Holy Office was set up as the Church's final appeals court for trials prosecuted by the Inquisition. In 1559 the Church published the *Index Librorum Prohibitorum* (Index of Prohibited Books) and began to persecute intellectuals and freethinkers. Galileo Galilei (1564–1642) was forced to renounce his assertion of the Copernican astronomical system, which held that the earth moved around the sun. He was summoned by the Inquisition to Rome in 1632 and exiled to Florence for the rest of his life. Giordano Bruno (1548–1600), a free-

Historical Reads

The Pursuit of Italy (David Gilmour)

Rome: The Biography of a City (Christopher Hibbert)

The Families Who Made Rome: A History and a Guide (Anthony Majanlahti)

Absolute Monarchs (John Julius Norwich)

The pope's personal fiefdom, the Papal States were established in the 8th century after the Frankish King Pepin drove the Lombards out of northern Italy and donated large tracts of territory to Pope Stephen II. At the height of their reach, the States encompassed Rome and much of central Italy.

1922	1929	1944	1946
Some 40,000 fascists march on Rome. King Vittorio Emanuele III, worried about the possibility of civil war, invites the 39-year-old Mussolini to form a government.	Keen to appease the Church, Mussolini signs the Lateran Treaty, creating the state of the Vatican City. To celebrate, Via della Conciliazione is bulldozed through the medieval Borgo.	On 24 March, 335 Romans are shot by Nazi troops in an unused quarry on Via Ardeatina. The massacre is a reprisal for a partisan bomb attack in Via Rasella.	The Italian republic is born after a vote to abolish the monarchy. Two years later, on 1 January 1948, the Italian constitution becomes law.

thinking Dominican monk, fared worse. Arrested in Venice in 1592, he was burned at the stake eight years later in Campo de' Fiori. The spot is today marked by a sinister statue.

Despite, or perhaps because of, the Church's policy of zero tolerance, the Counter-Reformation was largely successful in re-establishing papal prestige. And in this sense it can be seen as the natural finale to the Renaissance that Nicholas V had kicked off in 1450. From being a rural backwater with a population of around 20,000 in the mid-15th century, Rome had grown to become one of Europe's great 17th-century cities.

Power & Corruption

The exercise of power has long gone hand in hand with corruption. And no one enjoyed greater power than Rome's ancient emperors and Renaissance popes.

Imperial Follies & Papal Foibles

Of all ancient Rome's cruel and insane leaders, few are as notorious as Caligula. A byword for depravity, he was hailed as a saviour when he inherited the empire from his hated great-uncle Tiberius in AD 37. But this optimism was soon to prove ill-founded, and after a bout of serious illness, Caligula began showing disturbing signs of mental instability. He made his senators worship him and infamously tried to make his horse a senator. By AD 41 everyone had had enough of him, and on 24 January the leader of his own Praetorian Guard stabbed him to death.

Debauchery on such a scale was rare in the Renaissance papacy, but corruption was no stranger to the corridors of ecclesiastical power. It was not uncommon for popes to father illegitimate children and nepotism was rife. The Borgia pope Alexander VI (r 1492–1503) had two illegitimate children with the first of his two high-profile mistresses. The second, Giulia Farnese, was the sister of the cardinal who was later to become Pope Paul III (r 1534–59), himself no stranger to earthly pleasures. When not persecuting heretics during the Counter-Reformation, the Farnese pontiff managed to father four children.

Tangentopoli

Corruption has also featured in modern Italian politics, most famously during the 1990s *Tangentopoli* (Kickback City) scandal. Against a backdrop of steady economic growth, the controversy broke in Milan in 1992 when a routine corruption case – accepting bribes in exchange for contracts – blew up into a nationwide crusade against corruption.

Led by magistrate Antonio di Pietro, the Mani Pulite (Clean Hands) investigations exposed a political and business system riddled with

Political Reads

Good Italy: Bad Italy
(Bill Emmott)

The Dark Heart of Italy
(Tobias Jones)

Modern Italy: A Political History
(Denis Mack Smith)

Gladiatorial combat was part of the public games (*ludi*) that the state put on at the Colosseum. Gladiators were prisoners of war, condemned criminals or volunteers who would fight in bouts of 10 to 15 minutes. Surprisingly, these rarely ended in death.

1957	1960	1968	1978
Leaders of Italy, France, West Germany, Belgium, Holland and Luxembourg meet in the Capitoline Museums to sign the Treaty of Rome and establish the European Economic Community.	Rome stages the Olympic Games while Federico Fellini films *La Dolce Vita* at Cinecittà studios. Three years later Elizabeth Taylor falls for Richard Burton while shooting *Cleopatra* at Cinecittà.	Widespread student unrest results in mass protests across Italy. In Rome, students clash with police at La Sapienza's architecture faculty, an event remembered as the Battle of Valle Giulia.	Former PM Aldo Moro is kidnapped and shot by a cell of the extreme left-wing Brigate Rosse (Red Brigades) during Italy's *anni di piombo* (years of lead).

corruption. Politicians, public officials and business people were investigated and for once no one was spared, not even the powerful Bettino Craxi (prime minister between 1983 and 1989), who rather than face trial fled Rome in 1993. He was subsequently convicted in absentia on corruption charges and died in self-imposed exile in Tunisia.

Contemporary Controversies

Controversy and lurid gossip were a recurring feature of Silvio Berlusconi's three terms as prime minister (1994, 2000–06, and 2008–11). In 2010, one of his right-hand men, Guido Bertolaso, was caught up in a police probe into the allocation of construction contracts for the 2009 G8 conference, while Berlusconi himself faced a series of trials, mostly for business-related tax offences. His prosecutors finally got him in 2012 when he was convicted of tax fraud and sentenced to community service and a two-year ban on holding public office.

More recently, city hall became the focus of a massive corruption investigation in late 2014 as allegations surfaced that members of the city's municipal council had been colluding with criminals to skim the cream off public funds.

> The most salacious scandal of the Berlusconi era was the Rubygate affair. This centred on claims that Berlusconi had paid for sex with an underage dancer called Ruby Rubacuore. After a two-year trial, Berlusconi was found guilty, but in July 2014 his conviction was overturned on appeal.

The First Tourists

Pilgrims have been pouring into Rome for centuries but it was the classically minded travellers of the 18th and 19th centuries who established the city's reputation as a modern holiday hotspot.

Religious Pilgrimages

As seat of the Catholic Church, Rome was already one of the main pilgrim destinations in the Middle Ages, when, in 1300, Pope Boniface VIII proclaimed the first ever Holy Year (Jubilee). Promising full forgiveness for anyone who made the pilgrimage to St Peter's Basilica and the Basilica di San Giovanni in Laterano, his appeal to the faithful proved a resounding success. Hundreds of thousands answered his call and the Church basked in popular glory.

Some 700 years later and the Holy Year tradition is still going strong. Up to 24 million visitors descended on the city for Pope John Paul II's 2000 Jubilee, a feat that the Vatican will be hoping to repeat in the Holy Year that Pope Francis has declared for 2016.

> Romantic poet John Keats lived the last months of his short life in a house by the Spanish Steps. He died in February 1821 and, along with fellow poet Percy Bysshe Shelley, was buried in Rome's Cimitero Acattolico per gli Stranieri.

The Grand Tour

While Rome has a long past as a pilgrimage site, its history as a modern tourist destination can be traced back to the late 1700s and the fashion for the Grand Tour. The 18th-century version of a gap year, the Tour

1992–93	2000	2001	2005
A nationwide anti-corruption crusade, Mani Puliti (Clean Hands), shakes the political and business worlds. High-profile figures are arrested and former PM Bettino Craxi flees the country.	Pilgrims pour into Rome from all over the world to celebrate the Catholic Church's Jubilee year. A highpoint is a mass attended by two million people at Tor Vergata university.	Colourful media tycoon Silvio Berlusconi becomes prime minister for the second time. His first term in 1994 was a short-lived affair; his second lasts the full five-year course.	Pope John Paul II dies after 27 years on the papal throne. He is replaced by his long-standing ally Josef Ratzinger, who takes the name Benedict XVI.

was considered an educational rite of passage for wealthy young men from northern Europe, and Britain in particular. In the 19th century it became fashionable for young ladies to travel, chaperoned by spinster aunts, but in the late 1700s it was largely a male preserve.

The overland journey through France and into Italy followed the medieval pilgrim route, entering Italy via the St Bernard Pass and descending the west coast before cutting in to Florence and then down to Rome. After a sojourn in the capital, tourists would venture down to Naples, where the newly discovered ruins of Pompeii and Herculaneum were causing much excitement, before heading up to Venice.

Rome, enjoying a rare period of peace, was perfectly set up for this English invasion. The city was basking in the aftermath of the 17th-century baroque building boom, and a craze for all things classical was sweeping Europe. Rome's papal authorities were also crying out for money after their excesses had left the city coffers bare, reducing much of the population to abject poverty.

Thousands came, including Goethe, who stopped off to write his travelogue *Italian Journey* (1817), as well as Byron, Shelley and Keats, who all fuelled their romantic sensibilities in the city's vibrant streets. So many English people stayed around Piazza di Spagna that locals christened the area *er ghetto de l'inglesi* (the English ghetto).

Artistically, rococo was the rage of the moment. The Spanish Steps, built between 1723 and 1726, proved a major hit with tourists, as did the exuberant Trevi Fountain.

In his 1818 work *Childe Harold's Pilgrimage*, the English poet Lord Byron quotes the words of the 8th-century monk Bede: 'While stands the Coliseum, Rome shall stand; When falls the Coliseum, Rome shall fall! And when Rome falls – the World.'

HISTORY THE GHOSTS OF FASCISM

The Ghosts of Fascism

Rome's fascist history is a highly charged subject. In recent years historians on both sides of the political spectrum have accused each other of recasting the past to suit their views: left-wing historians have criticised their right-wing counterparts for glossing over the more unpleasant aspects of Mussolini's regime, while right-wingers have attacked their left-wing colleagues for whitewashing the facts to perpetuate an overly simplistic anti-fascist narrative.

Mussolini

Benito Mussolini was born in 1883 in Forlì, a small town in Emilia-Romagna. As a young man he was a member of the Italian Socialist Party, but service in WWI and Italy's subsequent descent into chaos led to a change of heart, and in 1919 he founded the Italian Fascist Party. Calling for rights for war veterans, law and order, and a strong nation, the party won support from disillusioned soldiers, many of whom joined the squads of Blackshirts that Mussolini used to intimidate his political enemies.

2008	2011	2012	2013
Gianni Alemanno, a former member of the neo-fascist party MSI (Movimento Sociale Italiano), sweeps to victory in Rome's mayoral elections. The news makes headlines across the world.	PM Berlusconi resigns as Italy's debt crisis threatens to spiral out of control. He is replaced by economist Mario Monti.	On 31 October the Church's top brass meet in the Sistine Chapel to celebrate the 500th anniversary of Michelangelo's ceiling frescoes.	Pope Benedict XVI becomes the first pope to resign since Gregory XII in 1415. He is replaced by the Argentinian cardinal Jorge Mario Bergoglio who is elected Pope Francis.

Now an established political player, former comedian Beppe Grillo hit the big time when his Five Star Movement took a quarter of the vote in Italy's 2013 election. A charismatic rabble-rouser, Grillo articulated the anger felt by many Italians against the country's pampered political elite.

In 1921 Mussolini was elected to the Chamber of Deputies. His parliamentary support was limited but on 28 October 1922 he marched on Rome with 40,000 black-shirted followers. Fearful of civil war between the fascists and socialists, King Vittorio Emanuele III responded by inviting Mussolini to form a government. His first government was a coalition of fascists, nationalists and liberals, but victory in the 1924 elections left him better placed to consolidate his power, and by the end of 1925 he had seized complete control of Italy. In order to silence the Church he signed the Lateran Treaty in 1929, which made Catholicism the state religion and recognised the sovereignty of the Vatican State.

On the home front, Mussolini embarked on a huge building program: Via dei Fori Imperiali and Via della Conciliazione were laid out; parks were opened on the Oppio Hill and at Villa Celimontana; the Imperial Forums and the temples at Largo di Torre Argentina were excavated; and the monumental Foro Italico sports complex and EUR were built.

Abroad, Mussolini invaded Abyssinia (now Ethiopia) in 1935 and sided with Hitler in 1936. In 1940, standing on the balcony of Palazzo Venezia, he announced Italy's entry into WWII to a vast, cheering crowd. The good humour didn't last, as Rome suffered, first at the hands of its own Fascist regime, then, after Mussolini was ousted in 1943, at the hands of the Nazis. Rome was liberated from German occupation on 4 June 1944.

Post-War Period

Defeat in WWII didn't kill off Italian fascism, and in 1946 hardline Mussolini supporters founded the Movimento Sociale Italiano (MSI; Italian Social Movement). For close on 50 years this overtly fascist party participated in mainstream Italian politics, while on the other side of the spectrum the Partito Comunista Italiano (PCI; Italian Communist Party) grew into Western Europe's largest communist party. The MSI was finally dissolved in 1994, when Gianfranco Fini rebranded it as the post-Fascist Alleanza Nazionale (AN; National Alliance). AN remained an important political player until it was incorporated into Silvio Berlusconi's Popolo della Libertà party in 2009.

Outside the political mainstream, fascism (along with communism) was a driving force of the domestic terrorism that rocked Rome and Italy during the *anni di piombo* (years of lead), between the late 1960s and the early '80s. Terrorist groups emerged on both sides of the ideological spectrum, giving rise to a spate of politically inspired violence. In one of the era's most notorious episodes, the communist Brigate Rosse (Red Brigades) kidnapped and killed former prime minister Aldo Moro in 1978, leaving his bullet-ridden body in the boot of a car on Via Michelangelo Caetani near the Jewish Ghetto.

2013	2014	2014	2015
Work gets underway on a three-year €23 million clean-up of the Colosseum, the first in the arena's 2000-year history.	The former mayor of Florence, 39-year-old Matteo Renzi, ousts PD party colleague Enrico Letta to become Italy's youngest ever prime minister.	Ex-mayor Gianni Alemanno and up to 100 politicians and public officials are placed under police investigation as the so-called Mafia Capitale scandal rocks Rome.	Rome's presidential palace, Palazzo del Quirinale, gets a new resident as Sergio Mattarella replaces 89-year-old Giorgio Napolitano as Italy's Presidente della Repubblica.

The Arts

Rome's turbulent history and magical cityscape have long provided inspiration for painters, sculptors, film-makers, writers and musicians. The great classical works of Roman antiquity fuelled the imagination of Renaissance artists; Counter-Reformation persecution led to baroque art and popular street satire; the trauma of Mussolini and WWII found expression in neo-realist cinema. More recently, the story has been of street art and film-making in the face of austerity and funding cutbacks.

Painting & Sculpture

Home to some of the Western world's most recognisable art, Rome is a visual feast. Its churches alone contain more masterpieces than many small countries, and the city's galleries are laden with works by world famous artists.

Etruscan Groundwork

Laying the groundwork for much later Roman art, the Etruscans placed great importance on their funerary rites and they developed sepulchral decoration into a highly sophisticated art form. Elaborate stone sarcophagi were often embellished with a reclining figure or a couple, typically depicted with a haunting, enigmatic smile. A stunning example is the *Sarcofago degli Sposi* (Sarcophagus of the Betrothed) in the Museo Nazionale Etrusco di Villa Giulia. Underground funerary vaults, such as those unearthed at Tarquinia, were further enlivened with bright, exuberant frescoes. These frequently represented festivals or scenes from everyday life, with stylised figures shown dancing or playing musical instruments, often with little birds or animals in the background.

The Etruscans were also noted for their bronze work and filigree jewellery. Bronze ore was abundant and was used to craft everything from chariots to candelabras, bowls and polished mirrors. One of Rome's most iconic sculptures, the 5th-century-BC *Lupa Capitolina* (Capitoline Wolf), now in the Capitoline Museums, is, in fact, an Etruscan bronze. Etruscan jewellery was unrivalled throughout the Mediterranean and goldsmiths produced elaborate pieces using sophisticated filigree and granulation techniques that were only rediscovered in the 20th century.

For Italy's best collection of Etruscan art, head to the Museo Nazionale Etrusco di Villa Giulia; to see Etruscan treasures in situ head up to Cerveteri and Tarquinia.

Roman Developments

In art, as in architecture, the ancient Romans borrowed heavily from the Etruscans and Greeks. In terms of decorative art, the Roman use of mosaics and wall paintings was derived from Etruscan funerary decoration. By the 1st century BC, floor mosaics were a popular form of home decor. Typical themes included landscapes, still lifes, geometric patterns and depictions of gods. Later, as production and artistic techniques improved, mosaics were displayed on walls and in public buildings. In the Museo Nazionale Romano: Palazzo Massimo alle

---

Top Galleries & Museums

Vatican Museums

Museo e Galleria Borghese

Capitoline Museums

Museo Nazionale Romano: Palazzo Massimo alle Terme

The best-surviving examples of Etruscan frescoes are found in Tarquinia, where up to 6000 tombs have been discovered. Particularly impressive are the illustrations in the Tomba delle Leonesse (Tomb of the Lionesses).

Terme, you'll find some spectacular wall mosaics from Nero's villa in Anzio, as well as a series of superb 1st-century-BC frescoes from Villa Livia, one of the homes of Livia Drusilla, Augustus' wife.

Sculpture

Sculpture was an important element of Roman art, and was largely influenced by Greek styles. In fact, early Roman sculptures were often made by Greek artists or were, at best, copies of imported Greek works. They were largely concerned with the male physique and generally depicted visions of male beauty in mythical settings – the *Apollo Belvedere* and *Laocoön* in the Vatican Museums' Museo Pio-Clementino are classic examples.

However, over time Roman sculpture began to lose its obsession with form and to focus on accurate representation, mainly in the form of sculptural portraits. Browse the collections of the Capitoline Museums or the Museo Nazionale Romano: Palazzo Massimo alle Terme and you'll be struck by how lifelike – and often ugly – so many of the marble faces are.

In terms of function, Roman art was highly propagandistic. From the time of Augustus (r 27 BC–AD 14), art was increasingly used to serve the state, and artists came to be regarded as little more than state functionaries. This new narrative art often took the form of relief decoration illustrating great military victories – the Colonna di Traiano and Ara Pacis are stunning examples of the genre.

One of Rome's great medieval artists was Pietro Cavallini (c 1240–1330). Little is known about this Roman-born painter, but his most famous work is the *Giudizio Universale* (Last Judgment) fresco in the Chiesa di Santa Cecilia in Trastevere.

Early Christian Art

The earliest Christian art in Rome are the traces of biblical frescoes in the Catacombe di Priscilla and the Catacombe di San Sebastiano. These, and other early works, are full of stock images: Lazarus being raised from the dead, Jesus as the good shepherd, the first Christian saints. Symbols also abound: the dove representing peace and happiness, the anchor or trident symbolising the cross, fish in reference to an acrostic from the ancient Greek word for fish (Ichthys), which spells out Jesus Christ, Son of God, Saviour.

Mosaics

With the legalisation of Christianity in the 4th century, these images began to move into the public arena, appearing in mosaics across the city. Mosaic work was the principal artistic endeavour of early Christian Rome and mosaics adorn many of the churches built in this period, including the Chiesa di Santa Pudenziana, the Mausoleo di Santa Costanza, and the Basilica di Santa Maria Maggiore.

TOP ART CHURCHES

St Peter's Basilica	Michelangelo's divine *Pietà* is just one of the many masterpieces on display at the Vatican's showcase basilica.
Basilica di San Pietro in Vincoli	Moses stands as the muscular centrepiece of Michelangelo's unfinished tomb of Pope Julius II.
Chiesa di San Luigi dei Francesi	Frescoes by Domenichino are outshone by three Caravaggio canvases depicting the life and death of St Matthew.
Chiesa di Santa Maria del Popolo	A veritable gallery with frescoes by Pinturicchio, a Raphael-designed chapel, and two paintings by Caravaggio.
Chiesa di Santa Maria della Vittoria	The church's innocuous exterior gives no clues that this is home to Bernini's extraordinary *Santa Teresa traffitta dall'amore di Dio* (Ecstasy of St Teresa).
Chiesa di Santa Prassede	The Cappella di San Zenone features some of Rome's most brilliant Byzantine mosaics.

NEOCLASSICISM

Emerging in the late 18th and early 19th centuries, neoclassicism signalled a departure from the emotional abandon of the baroque and a return to the clean, sober lines of classical art. Its major exponent was the sculptor Antonio Canova (1757–1822), whose study of Paolina Bonaparte Borghese as *Venere Vincitrice* (Venus Victrix) in the Museo e Galleria Borghese is typical of the mildly erotic style for which he became known.

Eastern influences became much more pronounced between the 7th and 9th centuries, when Byzantine styles swept in from the East, leading to a brighter, golden look. The best examples in Rome are in the Basilica di Santa Maria in Trastevere and the 9th-century Chiesa di Santa Prassede.

The Renaissance

Originating in late-14th-century Florence, the Renaissance had already made its mark in Tuscany and Venice before it arrived in Rome in the latter half of the 15th century. But over the next few decades it was to have a profound impact on the city as the top artists of the day were summoned to decorate the many new buildings going up around town.

Michelangelo & the Sistine Chapel

Rome's most celebrated works of Renaissance art are Michelangelo's paintings in the Sistine Chapel – his cinematic ceiling frescoes, painted between 1508 and 1512, and the *Giudizio Universale* (Last Judgment), which he worked on between 1536 and 1541. Regarded as the high point of Western artistic achievement, these two works completely outshine the chapel's wall paintings, themselves masterpieces of 15th-century fresco art by Pietro Vannucci (Perugino; 1446–1523), Sandro Botticelli (1445–1510), Domenico Ghirlandaio (1449–94), Cosimo Rosselli (1439–1507), Luca Signorelli (c 1445–1523) and Bernadino di Betto (Pinturicchio; 1454–1513).

Michelangelo Buanarroti (1475–1564), born near Arezzo in Tuscany, was the embodiment of the Renaissance spirit. A painter, sculptor, architect and occasional poet, he, more than any other artist of the era, left an indelible mark on the Eternal City. The Sistine Chapel, his *Pietà* in St Peter's Basilica, sculptures in the city's churches – his masterpieces are legion and they remain city highlights to this day.

Raphael, Master of Perspective

Renaissance art, inspired by humanism, which held man to be central to the God-created universe and beauty to represent a deep inner virtue, focused heavily on the human form. This, in turn, led artists to develop a far greater appreciation of perspective. Early Renaissance painters made great strides in formulating rules of perspective, but they still struggled to paint harmonious arrangements of figures. And it was this that Raffaello Sanzio (Raphael; 1483–1520) tackled in his great masterpiece *La Scuola di Atene* (The School of Athens; 1510–11) in the Vatican Museums.

Originally from Urbino, Raphael arrived in Rome in 1508 and went on to become the most influential painter of his generation. A paid-up advocate of the Renaissance exaltation of beauty, he painted many versions of the Madonna and Child, all of which epitomise the Western model of 'ideal beauty' that perseveres to this day.

Counter-Reformation & the Baroque

The baroque burst onto Rome's art scene in the early 17th century in a swirl of emotional energy. Combining a dramatic sense of dynamism

---

Key Renaissance Works

Pietà (St Peter's Basilica)

La Scuola di Atene (Vatican Museums)

Deposizione di Cristo (Galleria e Museo Borghese)

Handing over of the Keys (Sistine Chapel)

Michelangelo and Raphael didn't get on. Despite this, Raphael felt compelled to honour his elder after sneaking into the Sistine Chapel to look at Michelangelo's half-finished ceiling frescoes. He was so impressed with what he saw that he painted Michelangelo into his masterpiece *La Scuola di Atene*.

Big-Name
Baroque
Artists

Annibale Carracci
(1560–1609)

Caravaggio
(1573–1610)

Domenichino
(1581–1641)

Pietro da Cortona
(1596–1669)

Gian Lorenzo Bernini
(1598–1680)

with highly charged emotion, it was enthusiastically appropriated by the Catholic Church, which used it as a propaganda tool in its persecution of Counter-Reformation heresy. The powerful popes of the day eagerly championed the likes of Caravaggio, Gian Lorenzo Bernini, Domenichino, Pietro da Cortona and Alessandro Algardi.

Not surprisingly, much baroque art has a religious theme and you'll often find depictions of martyrdoms, ecstasies and miracles.

Caravaggio

One of the key painters of the period was Caravaggio (1573–1610), the Milan-born *enfant terrible* of Rome's art world. A controversial and often violent character, he arrived in Rome around 1590 and immediately set about rewriting the artistic rule books. While his peers and Catholic patrons sought to glorify and overwhelm, he painted subjects as he saw them. He had no time for 'ideal beauty' and caused uproar with his lifelike portrayal of hitherto sacrosanct subjects – his *Madonna dei Pellegrini* (Madonna of the Pilgrims), in the Chiesa di Sant'Agostino, is typical of his audacious approach.

Gian Lorenzo Bernini

While Caravaggio shocked his patrons, Gian Lorenzo Bernini (1598–1680) delighted them with his stunning sculptures. More than anyone else before or since, Bernini was able to capture a moment, freezing emotions and conveying a sense of dramatic action. His depiction of *Santa Teresa traffita dall'amore di Dio* (Ecstasy of St Teresa) in the Chiesa di Santa Maria della Vittoria does just that, blending realism, eroticism and theatrical spirituality in a work that is widely considered one of the greatest of the baroque period. You'll find further evidence of his genius in his mythical sculptures at the Museo e Galleria Borghese.

Frescoes

Fresco painting continued to provide work for artists well into the 17th century. Important exponents include Domenichino (1581–1641), whose decorative works adorn the Chiesa di San Luigi dei Francesi and the Chiesa di Sant'Andrea della Valle; Pietro da Cortona (1596–1669), author of the *Trionfo della Divina Provvidenza* (Triumph of Divine Providence) in Palazzo Barberini; and Annibale Carracci (1560–1609), the genius behind the frescoes in Palazzo Farnese, said by some to equal those of the Sistine Chapel.

20th-Century Futurism

Often associated with fascism, Italian futurism was an ambitious wide-ranging movement, embracing not only the visual arts but also architecture, music, fashion and theatre. The futurists, who first met in 1906 in a studio on Via Margutta, were evangelical advocates of modernism and their works highlighted dynamism, speed, machinery and technology.

Emerging around 1520, mannerism bridged the gap between the Renaissance and baroque era. Signature traits include the use of artificial colours, and figures with elongated limbs posed in florid settings.

One of the movement's founding fathers, Giacomo Balla (1871–1958) encapsulated the futurist ideals in works such as *Espansione dinamica Velocità* (Dynamic Expansion and Speed), one of a series of paintings exploring the dynamic nature of motion, and *Forme Grido Viva l'Italia* (The Shout Viva l'Italia), an abstract work inspired by the futurists' desire for Italy to enter WWI. Both are on show at the Galleria Nazionale d'Arte Moderna.

Contemporary Scene

Rome's contemporary art scene is centred on the capital's two flagship galleries: the Museo Nazionale delle Arti del XXI Secolo, better known as MAXXI, and the Museo d'Arte Contemporanea di Roma, aka MAC-

RO. Both have struggled since opening in 2010 and 2011 respectively, but the 2013 appointment of Chinese art critic and curator Hou Hanru as MAXXI's artistic director has shaken up the scene, and recent exhibitions have provoked considerable interest, both locally and abroad.

Rome also has a burgeoning gallery scene with an increasing number of private galleries across town.

Street art has really taken off in Rome, particularly in the suburbs of Ostiense, Pigneto, San Basilio, San Lorenzo and Testaccio, where giant murals have been painted on housing blocks, abandoned buildings and disused factories. Providing an impetus is the Out Door Festival, an urban art event now in its sixth year.

Literature

A history of authoritarian rule has given rise to a rich literary tradition, encompassing everything from ancient satires to dialect poetry and anti-fascist prose. As a backdrop, Rome has inspired authors as diverse as Goethe and Dan Brown.

Cicero, Virgil et al – the Classics

Famous for his blistering oratory, Marcus Tullius Cicero (106–43 BC) was the Roman Republic's pre-eminent author. A brilliant barrister, he became consul in 63 BC and subsequently published many philosophical works and speeches. Fancying himself as the senior statesman, he took the young Octavian under his wing and attacked Mark Antony in a series of 14 speeches, the *Philippics*. But these proved fatal, for when Octavian changed sides and joined Mark Antony, he demanded, and got, Cicero's head.

> A number of Rome's churches boast impressive ornamental floors with geometrical arrangements of coloured marble. This revolutionary paving style was developed in the 12th and 13th centuries by a group of Roman stoneworking families, collectively known as the Cosmati.

THE ARTS LITERATURE

SAINTS GLOSSARY

As befits the world's Catholic capital, Rome is overrun by saints. Roads are named after them, churches commemorate them and paintings portray them in all their righteous glory. Here we list some of the big-name *santi* (saints) you'll come across in Rome.

Santa Cecilia (2nd century, b Rome)	St Cecilia is the patron of music and musicians. She was buried in the Catacombe di San Callisto and later moved to the Basilica di Santa Cecilia in Trastevere.
San Giovanni (d c 101)	Author of the gospel of St John and the Book of Revelation, St John was a travelling companion of Jesus and friend of St Peter. The Basilica di San Giovanni in Laterano is dedicated to him and St John the Baptist.
San Lorenzo (c 225–258, b Huesca, Spain)	St Lawrence safeguarded the assets of the 3rd-century Roman Church when not helping the sick, poor and crippled. His patronage of chefs and cooks results from his indescribably awful death – he was grilled to death on a griddle iron.
San Marco (1st century AD, b Libya)	St Mark is said to have written the second gospel while in Rome. The Basilica di San Marco stands over the house where he used to stay when in town.
San Paolo (c 3–65, b Turkey)	St Paul was beheaded in Rome during Nero's persecution of the Christians. Along with St Peter, he's the capital's patron saint. Their joint feast day, a holiday in Rome, is 29 June.
San Pietro (d 64, b Galilee)	One of Rome's two patron saints, St Peter is said to have founded the Roman Catholic Church after Jesus gave him the keys to the Kingdom of Heaven. He was crucified head down and buried on the spot where St Peter's Basilica now stands.
San Sebastiano (d c 288, b France)	St Sebastian distinguished himself in Diocletian's imperial army before converting to Christianity. As punishment, Diocletian had him tied to a tree and turned into an archery target. He survived, only to be beaten to death.

Poetry & Satire

A contemporary of Cicero, Catullus (c 84–54 BC) cut a very different figure. A passionate and influential poet, he is best known for his epigrams and erotic verse.

On becoming emperor, Augustus (aka Octavian) encouraged the arts, and Virgil (70–19 BC), Ovid, Horace and Tibullus all enjoyed freedom to write. Of the works produced in this period, it's Virgil's rollicking *Aeneid* that stands out. A glorified mix of legend, history and moral instruction, it tells how Aeneas escapes from Troy and after years of mythical mishaps ends up landing in Italy where his descendants Romulus and Remus eventually found Rome.

Little is known of Decimus Iunius Iuvenalis, better known as Juvenal, but his 16 satires have survived as classics of the genre. Writing in the 1st century AD, he combined an acute mind with a cutting pen, famously scorning the masses as being interested in nothing but 'bread and circuses'.

> Virgil gave us some of our most famous expressions: 'fortune favours the bold', 'love conquers all' and 'time flies'. However, it was Juvenal who issued the classic warning: *'quis custodiet ipsos custodes?'* or 'who guards the guards?'

Ancient Histories

The two major historians of the period were Livy (59 BC–AD 17) and Tacitus (c 56–116). Although both wrote in the early days of empire they displayed very different styles. Livy, whose history of the Roman Republic was probably used as a school textbook, cheerfully mixed myth with fact to produce an entertaining and popular tome. Tacitus, on the other hand, took a decidedly colder approach. His *Annals* and *Histories,* which cover the early years of the Roman Empire, are cutting and often witty, although imbued with an underlying pessimism.

Street Writing & Popular Poetry

Rome's tradition of street writing goes back to the dark days of the 17th-century Counter-Reformation. With the Church systematically suppressing criticism, disgruntled Romans began posting *pasquinades* (anonymous messages; named after the first person who wrote one) on the city's so-called speaking statues. These messages, often archly critical of the authorities, were sensibly posted in the dead of night and then gleefully circulated around town the following day. The most famous speaking statue stands in Piazza Pasquino near Piazza Navona.

Dialect Verse

Poking savage fun at the rich and powerful was one of the favourite themes of Gioacchino Belli (1791–1863), one of a trio of poets who made their names writing poetry in Roman dialect. Born poor, Belli started his career with conventional and undistinguished verse, but found the crude and colourful dialect of the Roman streets better suited to his outspoken attacks on the chattering classes.

Carlo Alberto Salustri (1871–1950), aka Trilussa, is the best known of the trio. He also wrote social and political satire, although not exclusively so, and many of his poems are melancholy reflections on life, love and solitude. One of his most famous works, the anti-fascist poem *All'Ombra* (In the Shadow), is etched onto a plaque in Piazza Trilussa, the Trastevere square named in his honour.

The poems of Cesare Pescarella (1858–1940) present a vivid portrait of turn-of-the-century Rome. Gritty and realistic, they pull no punches in their description of the everyday life of Rome's forgotten poor.

> Rome's most influential contribution to literature was the Vulgate Bible. This dates to the 4th century when Pope Damasus (r 366–384) had his secretary Eusebius Hieronymous, aka St Jerome, translate the bible into accessible Latin. His version is the basis for the bible currently used by the Catholic Church.

Rome as Inspiration

With its magical cityscape and historic atmosphere, Rome has provided inspiration for legions of foreign authors.

PIER PAOLO PASOLINI, MASTER OF CONTROVERSY

....

Poet, novelist and film-maker Pier Paolo Pasolini (1922–75) was one of Italy's most important and controversial 20th-century intellectuals. His works, which are complex, unsentimental and provocative, provide a scathing portrait of Italy's postwar social transformation.

Although he spent much of his adult life in Rome, he had a peripatetic childhood. He was born in Bologna but moved around frequently and rarely spent more than a few years in any one place.

Politically, he was a communist, but he never played a part in Italy's left-wing establishment. In 1949 he was expelled from the *Partito Comunista Italiano* (PCI; Italian Communist Party) after a gay sex scandal and for the rest of his career he remained a sharp critic of the party. His most famous outburst came in the poem *Il PCI ai giovani*, in which he dismisses left-wing students as bourgeois, and sympathises with the police, whom he describes as *figli di poveri* (sons of the poor). In the context of 1968 Italy, a year marked by widespread student agitation, this was a highly incendiary position to take.

Pasolini was no stranger to controversy. His first novel *Ragazzi di Vita* (The Ragazzi), set in the squalor of Rome's forgotten suburbs, earned him success and a court case for obscenity. Similarly, his early films – *Accattone* (1961) and *Mamma Roma* (1962) – provoked righteous outrage with their relentlessly bleak depiction of life in the Roman underbelly.

True to the scandalous nature of his art, Pasolini was murdered in 1975. It was originally thought that his death was linked to events in the gay underworld but, revelations in 2005 hinted that it might, in fact, have been a politically motivated killing.

Romantic Visions

In the 18th century the city was a hotbed of literary activity as historians and Grand Tourists poured in from northern Europe. The German author Johann Wolfgang von Goethe captures the elation of discovering ancient Rome and the colours of the modern city in his celebrated travelogue *Italian Journey* (1817).

Rome was also a magnet for the English Romantic poets. John Keats, Lord Byron, Percy Bysshe Shelley, Mary Shelley and other writers all spent time in the city. Keats came to Rome in 1821 in the hope that it would cure his ill health, but it didn't and he died of tuberculosis in his lodgings at the foot of the Spanish Steps.

Later, in the 19th century, American author Nathaniel Hawthorne took inspiration from a sculpture in the Capitoline Museums to pen his classic *The Marble Faun* (1860).

Rome as Backdrop

In the first decade of the 2000s it became fashionable for novelists to use Rome as a backdrop. Most notably, Dan Brown's thriller *Angels and Demons* (2001) is set in Rome, as is Jeanne Kalogridis sumptuous historical novel *The Borgia Bride* (2006).

Robert Harris's accomplished fictional biographies of Cicero, *Imperium* (2006) and *Lustrum* (*Conspirata* in the US; 2010), are just two of many books set in ancient Rome. Other popular books in the genre include Lindsey Davis' Falco series of ancient murder mysteries.

Literature & Fascism

A controversial figure, Gabriele D'Annunzio (1863–1938) was the most flamboyant Italian writer of the early 20th century. A WWI fighter pilot and ardent nationalist, he was born in Pescara and settled in Rome in 1881. Forever associated with fascism, he wrote prolifically, both poetry and novels.

In 1559 Pope Paul IV published the *Index Librorum Prohibitorum* (Index of Prohibited Books), a list of books forbidden by the Catholic Church. Over the next 400 years it was revised 20 times, the last edition appearing in 1948. It was officially abolished in 1966.

The Anti-Fascists

On the opposite side of the political spectrum, Roman-born Alberto Moravia (1907–90) was banned from writing by Mussolini and, together with his wife, Elsa Morante (1912–85), was forced into hiding for a year. The alienated individual and the emptiness of fascist and bourgeois society are common themes in his writing. In *La Romana* (The Woman of Rome; 1947) he explores the broken dreams of a country girl, Adriana, as she slips into prostitution and theft.

The novels of Elsa Morante are characterised by a subtle psychological appraisal of her characters and can be seen as a personal cry of pity for the sufferings of individuals and society. Her 1974 masterpiece, *La Storia* (History), is a tough tale of a half-Jewish woman's desperate struggle for dignity in the poverty of occupied Rome.

Taking a similarly anti-fascist line, Carlo Emilio Gadda (1893–1973) combines murder and black humour in his classic whodunnit, *Quer Pasticciaccio Brutto de Via Merulana* (That Awful Mess on Via Merulana; 1957). Although the mystery is never solved, the book's a brilliant portrayal of the pomposity and corruption that thrived in Mussolini's Rome.

Roman Reads

Roman Tales (Alberto Moravia)

That Awful Mess on Via Merulana (Carlo Emilio Gadda)

The Secrets of Rome, Love & Death in the Eternal City (Corrado Augias)

Writing Today

Born in Rome in 1966, Niccolò Ammaniti is the best known of the city's crop of contemporary authors. In 2007 he won the Premio Strega, Italy's top literary prize for his novel, *Come Dio comanda* (As God Commands), although he's probably best known for *Io Non Ho Paura* (I'm Not Scared; 2001), a soulful study of a young boy's realisation that his father is involved in a child kidnapping.

Another name to look out for is Andrea Bajani (b 1975), who has already scooped an impressive number of awards in his short writing career. The only one of his books that has so far been translated into English is *Ogni promessa* (Every Promise; 2010), a slow, beautifully written novel exploring themes of relationships, vulnerability, and coming to terms with the past.

Cinema

Rome has a long cinematic tradition, spanning the works of the postwar neo-realists and film-makers as diverse as Federico Fellini, Sergio Leone, and Paolo Sorrentino, the Oscar-winning director of *La grande bellezza* (The Great Beauty).

The Golden Age

Dramatically ensconced in a Richard Meier–designed pavilion, the *Ara Pacis* is a key work of ancient Roman sculpture. The vast marble altar is covered with detailed reliefs, including one showing Augustus with his family.

For the golden age of Roman film-making you have to turn the clocks back to the 1940s, when Roberto Rossellini (1906–77) produced a trio of neo-realist masterpieces. The first and most famous was *Roma Città Aperta* (Rome Open City; 1945), filmed with brutal honesty in the Prenestina district east of the city centre. Vittorio de Sica (1901–74) kept the neo-realist ball rolling in 1948 with *Ladri di Biciclette* (Bicycle Thieves), again filmed in Rome's sprawling suburbs.

Federico Fellini (1920–94) took the creative baton from the neo-realists and carried it into the following decades. His disquieting style demands more of audiences, abandoning realistic shots for pointed images at once laden with humour, pathos and double meaning. Fellini's greatest international hit was *La Dolce Vita* (1960), starring Marcello Mastroianni and Anita Ekberg.

The films of Pier Paolo Pasolini (1922–75) are similarly demanding. A communist Catholic homosexual, he made films such as *Accattone*

(The Scrounger; 1961) that not only reflect his ideological and sexual tendencies but also offer a unique portrayal of Rome's urban wasteland.

Contemporay Directors

Born in Naples but Roman by adoption, Paolo Sorrentino is the hottest property in Italian cinema right now. His 2013 hit *La grande bellezza* (The Great Beauty) won worldwide critical acclaim and a host of major awards, including the Oscar for Best Foreign Language Film. The movie, which focuses on a world-weary habitué of Rome's *dolce vita* society, presents Italy's ancient capital as a complex, suffocating city whose lavish beauty masks a decadent, morally bankrupt heart.

In contrast to Sorrentino, a Neapolitan best known for a film about Rome, Matteo Garrone (b 1968) is a Roman best known for a film about Naples. *Gomorra* (Gomorrah; 2008), a hard-hitting exposé of of the Neapolitan *camorra* (mafia), pulls no punches as it unflinchingly depicts the grim realities of Naples' criminal underbelly.

Other Roman directors to have enjoyed recent critical acclaim include Emanuele Crialese (b 1965), author of *Terraferma,* a thought-provoking study of the effects of immigration on a small Sicilian island, and Saverio Costanzo (b 1975), who hit the bullseye with his 2010 adaptation of Paolo Giordano's bestselling book *La solitudine dei numeri primi* (The Solitude of Prime Numbers). Gabriele Muccino (b 1967), director of the 2001 smash *L'Ultimo Bacio* (The Last Kiss), returned to his earlier success in 2010 with *Baciami ancora* (Kiss Me Again)*,* a sequel to *L'Ulltimo Baccio.*

Before Muccino, Rome was generally represented by Carlo Verdone (b 1950) and Nanni Moretti (b 1953). A comedian in the Roman tradition, Verdone has made a name for himself satirising his fellow citizens in a number of bittersweet comedies, such as the 1995 *Viaggi di Nozze* (Honeymoons).

Moretti, on the other hand, falls into no mainstream tradition. A politically active writer, actor and director, his films are often whimsical and self-indulgent. Arguably his best work, *Caro Diario* (Dear Diary; 1994) earned him the Best Director prize at Cannes in 1994 – an award that he topped in 2001 when he won the Palme d'Or for *La Stanza del Figlio* (The Son's Room).

Since its inception in 2006, the Festa del Cinema di Roma has established itself on the European circuit. But harsh economic realities have seen it scale back its ambitions and it now strives to champion home-grown talent.

THE ARTS CINEMA

SERGIO LEONE, MR SPAGHETTI WESTERN

Best known for virtually single-handedly creating the spaghetti western, Sergio Leone (1929–89) is a hero to many. Astonishingly, though, he only ever directed seven films.

The son of a silent-movie director, Leone cut his teeth as a screenwriter on a series of sword-and-sandal epics, before working as assistant director on *Quo Vadis?* (1951) and *Ben-Hur* (1959). He made his directorial debut three years later on *Il Colosso di Rodi* (The Colossus of Rhodes; 1961).

However, it was with his famous dollar trilogy – *Per un pugno di dollari* (A Fistful of Dollars; 1964), *Per qualche dollari in piu* (For a Few Dollars More; 1965) and *Il buono, il brutto, il cattivo* (The Good, the Bad and the Ugly; 1966) – that he really hit the big time. The first, filmed in Spain and based on the 1961 samurai flick *Yojimbo,* set the style for the genre. No longer were clean-cut, morally upright heroes pitted against cartoon-style villains, but characters were complex, often morally ambiguous and driven by self-interest.

Stylistically, Leone introduced a series of innovations that were later to become trademarks. Chief among these was his use of musical themes to identify his characters. And in this he was brilliantly supported by his old schoolmate, Ennio Morricone. One of Hollywood's most prolific composers, Morricone (b 1928) has worked on more than 500 films, but his masterpiece remains his haunting score for *Il buono, il brutto, il cattivo*.

On Location in Rome

Recently, the big news in cinema circles has been the return of international film-making to Rome. In 2015 Daniel Craig was charging around town in a souped-up Aston Martin for the next James Bond outing, *Spectre,* while Ben Stiller was camping it up for *Zoolander 2,* the follow-up to his 2001 hit fashion comedy. Down in the city's southern reaches, a remake of *Ben-Hur* was filmed at the Cinecittà film studios, the very same place where the original sword-and-sandal epic was shot in 1959.

This renaissance in the city's cinematic fortunes is largely due to a series of tax breaks that Matteo Renzi's government has introduced to lure film-makers back to Rome and tackle the crisis that has been afflicting the city's film industry. For years Rome was a favourite film location, drawing big-name American directors and earning itself the nickname 'Hollywood on the Tiber'. However, competition from cheaper eastern European countries, combined with a fall in domestic production and cuts in government funding, led to a serious decline in fortunes in the late noughties and early part of this decade.

Inaugurated in 1937, Rome's Cinecittà studios are part of cinematic folklore. *Ben-Hur, Cleopatra, La Dolce Vita* and Martin Scorsese's 2002 epic *Gangs of New York* are among the classics that were filmed at the studios' vast 40-hectare site.

Music

Despite years of austerity-led cutbacks, Rome's music scene is bearing up well. International orchestras perform to sell-out audiences, jazz greats jam in steamy clubs and rappers rage in underground venues.

Choral & Sacred Music

In a city of churches, it's little wonder that choral music has deep roots in Rome. In the 16th and 17th centuries, Rome's great Renaissance popes summoned the top musicians of the day to tutor the papal choir. Two of the most famous were Giovanni Pierluigi da Palestrina (c 1525–94), one of Italy's foremost Renaissance composers, and the Naples-born Domenico Scarlatti (1685–1757).

The papal choirs were originally closed to women and the high parts were taken by *castrati,* boys who had been surgically castrated to preserve their high voices. The use of *castrati* lasted until the early 20th century, when in, 1913, Alessandro Moreschi (1858–1922), the last known *castrato,* retired from the Sistine Chapel choir.

ROME IN THE MOVIES

Rome's monuments, piazzas and atmospheric streets provide the backdrop to many classic, and some not so classic, films.

Roma Città Aperta (1945)	Neo-realist masterpiece shot on the streets of Prenestina.
Ladri di Biciclette (1948)	Classic drama that ranges from the city's desolate outskirts to Porta Portese market.
Roman Holiday (1953)	Gregory Peck and Audrey Hepburn scoot around Rome's headline sights.
La Dolce Vita (1960)	The Trevi Fountain stars in Fellini's great Roman masterpiece.
The Talented Mr Ripley (1999)	Rome sets the stage for this chilling psychological thriller.
Pranzo di Ferragosto (Midsummer Lunch; 2008)	A gentle comedy-drama set in a deserted Trastevere.
Il Divo (2008)	Paolo Sorrentino's stylised portrait of controversial politician Giulio Andreotti.
Angels & Demons (2009)	Characters bounce between locations in this glossy Dan Brown adaption.
To Rome with Love (2012)	Rome gets the Woody Allen treatment in this cliche-ridden comedy.
La grande belleza (2013)	Rome's beauty masks cynicism and moral decadence in Sorrentino's Oscar-winner.

To support the pope's musicians, Sixtus V established the Accademia di Santa Cecilia in 1585. Originally it was involved in the publication of sacred music, but it later developed a teaching function, and in 1839 it completely reinvented itself as an academy with wider cultural and academic goals. Today it is a highly respected conservatory with its own world class orchestra and chorus.

Opera

Rome is often snubbed by serious opera buffs who prefer their Puccini in Milan, Venice or Naples. However, performances at the city's main opera house, the Teatro dell'Opera, are passionately followed. The Romans have long been keen opera-goers and in the 19th century a number of important operas were premiered in Rome, including Rossini's *Il Barbiere di Siviglia* (The Barber of Seville; 1816), Verdi's *Il Trovatore* (The Troubadour; 1853) and Giacomo Puccini's *Tosca* (1900).

Tosca not only premiered in Rome but is also set in the city. The first act takes place in the Chiesa di Sant'Andrea della Valle, the second in Palazzo Farnese, and the final act in Castel Sant'Angelo, the castle from which Tosca jumps to her death.

Jazz, Rap & Hip Hop

Jazz has long been a mainstay of Rome's music scene. Introduced by US troops during WWII, it grew in popularity during the postwar period and took off in the 1960s with the opening of the mythical Folkstudio club. Since then, it has gone from strength to strength and the city now boasts some fabulous jazz clubs, including Alexanderplatz, Big Mama, and the Casa del Jazz. Big names to look out for include Enrico Pieranunzi, a Roman-born pianist and composer, and Doctor 3, whose idiosyncratic sound has earned it considerable acclaim.

Rome also has a vibrant rap and hip-hop scene. Hip hop, which arrived in the city in the late 1980s and spread via the *centro sociale* (organised squat) network, was originally highly politicised and many early exponents associated themselves with Rome's alternative left-wing scene. Since then, exposure and ever-increasing commercialisation has diluted, though not entirely extinguished, this political element. Names to look out for include Colle der Formento, Cor Veleno, Jesto, and the ragamuffin outfit Villa Ada Posse.

Theatre & Dance

Surprisingly for a city in which art has always been appreciated, Rome has no great theatrical tradition. That said, theatres such as Teatro Vascello and Teatro India stage wide-ranging programs offering everything from avant-garde dance to cutting-edge street theatre.

Although not strictly speaking a Roman, Dacia Maraini (b 1936) has produced her best work while living in Rome. Considered one of Italy's most important feminist writers, she has more than 30 plays to her name, many of which continue to be translated and performed around the world.

Dance is a major highlight of Rome's big autumn festival, Romaeuropa. But while popular, performances rarely showcase homegrown talent, which remains thin on the ground.

Major ballet performances are staged at the Teatro dell'Opera, home to Rome's principal ballet company, the Balletto del Teatro dell'Opera, led by the Sicilian director, Eleonora Abbagnato.

Throughout the 1960s and '70s Italy was a prolific producer of horror films. Rome's master of terror was, and still is, Dario Argento (b 1940), director of the 1975 cult classic *Profondo Rosso* (Deep Red) and more than 20 other movies.

Niccolò Ammaniti's 2009 *Che la festa cominci* (Let the Games Begin) offers debauchery, laughs, and Satanic sects as it gleefully satires the bizarre excesses of modern society.

Architecture

From ancient ruins and Renaissance basilicas to baroque churches and hulking fascist *palazzi*, Rome's architectural legacy is unparalleled. Michelangelo, Bramante, Borromini and Bernini are among the architects who have stamped their genius on its remarkable cityscape. But it's not all about history. In recent times high-profile building projects have drawn the world's top architects to Rome.

The Ancients

Architecture was central to the success of the ancient Romans. In building their great capital, they were among the first people to use architecture to tackle problems of infrastructure, urban management and communication. For the first time, architects and engineers designed houses, roads, aqueducts and shopping centres alongside temples, tombs and imperial palaces. To do this, the Romans advanced methods devised

Above: Basilica di Santa Maria in Trastevere (p164)

by the Etruscans and Greeks, developing construction techniques and building materials that allowed them to build on a massive and hitherto unseen scale.

Etruscan Roots

By the 7th century BC the Etruscans were the dominant force on the Italian peninsula, with important centres at Tarquinia, Caere (Cerveteri) and Veii (Veio). These city-states were fortified with defensive walls, and although little actually remains – the Etruscans generally built with wood and brick, which don't age well – archaeologists have found evidence of aqueducts, bridges and sewers, as well as sophisticated temples. In Rome, you can still see foundations of an Etruscan temple on the Campidoglio (Capitoline Hill).

Much of what we now know about the Etruscans derives from findings unearthed in their elaborate tombs. Like many ancient peoples, the Etruscans placed great emphasis on their treatment of the dead and they built impressive cemeteries. These were constructed outside the city walls and harboured richly decorated stone vaults covered by mounds of earth. The best examples are to be found in Cerveteri, north of Rome.

Roman Developments

When Rome was founded in 753 BC (or earlier if recent archaeological findings are to be believed), the Etruscans were at the height of their power and Greek colonists were establishing control over southern Italy. In subsequent centuries a three-way battle for domination ensued, with the Romans emerging victorious. Against this background, Roman architects borrowed heavily from Greek and Etruscan traditions.

Ancient Roman architecture was monumental in form and often propagandistic in nature. Huge amphitheatres, aqueducts and temples joined muscular and awe-inspiring basilicas, arches and thermal baths in trumpeting the skill and vision of the city's early rulers and the nameless architects who worked for them.

Temples

Early Republican-era temples were based on Etruscan designs, but over time the Romans turned to the Greeks for their inspiration. But whereas Greek temples had steps and colonnades on all sides, the classic Roman temple had a high podium with steps leading up to a deep porch. Good examples include the Tempio di Portunus near Piazza della Bocca della Verità, and, though they're not so well preserved, the temples in the Area Sacra di Largo di Torre Argentina. These temples also illustrate another important feature of Roman architectural thinking. While Greek temples were designed to stand apart and be viewed from all sides, Roman temples were built into the city's urban fabric, set in busy central locations and positioned to be approached from the front.

The Roman use of columns was also Greek in origin, even if the Romans preferred the more slender Ionic

MAIN ARCHITECTURAL PERIODS

c 8th–3rd centuries BC

The Etruscans in central Italy and the Greeks in their southern Italian colony, Magna Graecia, lay the groundwork for later Roman developments. Particularly influential are Greek temple designs.

c 4th century BC–5th century AD

The ancient Romans make huge advances in engineering techniques, constructing monumental public buildings, bridges, aqueducts, housing blocks and an underground sewerage system.

4th–12th centuries

Church building is the focus of architectural activity in the medieval period as Rome's early Christian leaders seek to stamp their authority on the city.

15th–16th centuries

Based on humanism and a reappraisal of classical precepts, the Renaissance hits an all-time high in the first two decades of the 16th century, a period known as the High Renaissance.

17th century

Developing out of the Counter-Reformation, the baroque flourishes in Rome, fuelled by Church money and the genius of Gian Lorenzo Bernini and Francesco Borromini.

18th century

A short-lived but theatrical style born out of the baroque, the florid rococo gifts Rome some of its most popular sights.

and Corinthian columns to the plain Doric pillars – to see how the columns differ, study the exterior of the Colosseum, which incorporates all three styles.

Aqueducts & Sewers

The Romans used a variety of building materials. Wood and tufa, a soft volcanic rock, were used initially but travertine, a limestone quarried in Tivoli, later took over as the favoured stone. Marble, imported from across the empire, was used mainly as decorative panelling, attached to brick or concrete walls.

One of the Romans' crowning architectural achievements was the development of a water supply infrastructure, based on a network of aqueducts and underground sewers. In the early days, Rome got its water from the Tiber and natural underground springs, but as its population grew so demand outgrew supply. To meet this demand, the Romans constructed a complex system of aqueducts to bring water in from the hills of central Italy and distribute it around town.

The first aqueduct to serve Rome was the 16.5km Aqua Appia, which became fully operational in 312 BC. Over the next 700 years or so, up to 800km of aqueducts were built in the city, a network capable of supplying up to one million cubic metres of water a day.

This was no mean feat for a system that depended entirely on gravity. All aqueducts, whether underground pipes, as most were, or vast overland viaducts, were built at a slight gradient to allow the water to flow. There were no pumps to force the water along so this gradient was key to maintaining a continuous and efficient flow.

At the other end of the water cycle, waste water was drained away via an underground sewerage system known as the Cloaca Maxima (Great Sewer) and emptied downstream into the river Tiber. The Cloaca was commissioned by Rome's seventh and last king, Tarquin the Proud (r 535–509 BC), as part of a project to drain the valley where the Roman Forum now stands. It was originally an open ditch, but from the beginning of the 2nd century BC it was gradually built over.

Residential Housing

Rome's ancient ruins are revealing in many ways, but the one thing they lack is colour. Ancient Rome would have been a vivid, brightly coloured place with buildings clad in coloured marble, gaudily painted temples and multicoloured statues.

While Rome's emperors and aristocrats lived in luxurious palaces on the Palatino (Palatine Hill), the city's poor huddled together in large residential blocks called *insulae*. These were huge, poorly built structures, sometimes up to six or seven storeys high, that accommodated hundreds of people in dark, unhealthy conditions. Little remains of these early *palazzi* but near the foot of the Aracoeli staircase – the steps that lead up to the Chiesa di Santa Maria in Aracoeli – you can see a section of what was once a typical city-centre *insula*.

Concrete & Monumental Architecture

Most of the ruins that litter modern Rome are the remains of the ancient city's big, show-stopping monuments – the Colosseum, the Pantheon, the Terme di Caracalla, the Forums. These grandiose constructions are not only reminders of the sophistication and intimidatory scale of ancient Rome – just as they were originally designed to be – they are also monuments to the vision and bravura of the city's ancient architects.

OBELISKS

More readily associated with ancient Egypt than Rome, obelisks are a distinctive feature of the Roman cityscape. Many were brought over from Egypt after it was conquered by Augustus in 31 AD and used to decorate the *spina* (central spine) of the city's circuses (chariot-racing arenas). Later the Romans began to make their own for their elaborate mausoleums.

The highest, and one of the oldest – it dates to the 15th century BC – towers 32.1m over Piazza San Giovanni in Laterano. The most curious sits atop Bernini's famous Elefantino statue outside the Chiesa di Santa Maria Sopra Minerva.

One of the key breakthroughs the Romans made, and one that allowed them to build on an ever-increasing scale, was the invention of concrete in the 1st century BC. Made by mixing volcanic ash with lime and an aggregate, often tufa rock or brick rubble, concrete was quick to make, easy to use, and cheap. Furthermore, it freed architects from their dependence on skilled masonry labour – up to that point construction techniques required stone blocks to be specially cut to fit into each other. Concrete allowed the Romans to develop vaulted roofing, which they used to span the Pantheon's ceiling and the huge vaults at the Terme di Caracalla.

Concrete wasn't particularly attractive, though, and while it was used for heavy-duty structural work it was usually lined with travertine and coloured marble, imported from Greece and North Africa. Brick was also an important material, used both as a veneer and for construction.

Early Christian

The history of early Christianity is one of persecution and martyrdom. Introduced in the 1st century AD, it was legalised by the emperor Constantine in 313 AD and became Rome's state religion in 378. The most startling reminders of early Christian activity are the catacombs, a series of underground burial grounds built under Rome's ancient roads. Christian belief in the resurrection meant that the Christians could not cremate their dead, as was the custom in Roman times, and with burial forbidden inside the city walls they were forced to go outside the city.

Church Building

The Christians began to abandon the catacombs in the 4th century and increasingly opted to be buried in churches the emperor Constantine was building in the city. Although Constantine was actually based in Byzantium, which he renamed Constantinople in his own honour, he nevertheless financed an ambitious building program in Rome. The most notable of the many churches he commissioned is the Basilica di San Giovanni in Laterano. Built between 315 and 324 and re-worked into its present shape in the 5th century, it was the

late 18th–19th centuries

Piazza del Popolo takes on its current form and Villa Torlonia gets a facelift courtesy of Rome's top neoclassical architect, Giuseppe Valadier.

late 19th century

Rome gets a major post-unification makeover – roads are built, piazzas are laid, and residential quarters spring up to house government bureaucrats.

early 20th century

Muscular and modern, Italian rationalism plays to Mussolini's vision of a fearless, futuristic Rome, a 20th-century *caput mundi* (world capital).

1990s–

Rome provides the historic stage upon which some of the world's top contemporary architects experiment. Criticism and praise are meted out in almost equal measure.

ALL ROADS LEAD TO ROME

The Romans were the great road builders of the ancient world. Approximately 80,000km of surfaced highways spanned the Roman Empire, providing vital military and communication links. Many of Rome's modern roads retain the names of their ancient forebears and follow almost identical routes.

Via Appia	The 'queen of roads' ran down to Brindisi on the southern Adriatic coast.
Via Aurelia	Connected Rome with France by way of Pisa and Genoa.
Via Cassia	Led north to Viterbo, Siena and Tuscany.
Via Flaminia	Traversed the Apennines to Rimini on the east coast.
Via Salaria	The old salt road linked with the Adriatic port of Castrum Truentinum, south of modern-day Ancona.

model on which many subsequent basilicas were based. Other period showstoppers include the Basilica di Santa Maria in Trastevere and the Basilica di Santa Maria Maggiore.

A second wave of church-building hit Rome in the period between the 8th and 12th centuries. As the early papacy battled for survival against the threatening Lombards, its leaders took to construction to leave some sort of historical imprint, resulting in the Basilica di Santa Sabina, the Chiesa di Santa Prassede and the 8th-century Chiesa di Santa Maria in Cosmedin, home of the Bocca della Verità (Mouth of Truth).

The 13th and 14th centuries were dark days for Rome as internecine fighting raged between the city's noble families. While much of northern Europe and even parts of Italy were revelling in Gothic arches and towering vaults, little of lasting value was being built in Rome. The one great exception is the city's only Gothic church, the Chiesa di Santa Maria Sopra Minerva.

Basilica Style

In design terms, these early Christian churches were modelled on, and built over, Rome's great basilicas. In ancient times, a basilica was a large rectangular hall used for public functions, but as Christianity took hold they were increasingly appropriated by the city's church-builders. The main reason for this was that they lent themselves perfectly to the new style of religious ceremonies that the Christians were introducing, rites that required space for worshippers and a central focus for the altar. Rome's pagan temples, in contrast, had been designed as symbolic cult centres and were not set up to house the faithful – in fact, most pagan ceremonies were held outside, in front of the temple, not inside as the Christian services required.

ROME'S SIGNATURE BUILDINGS

Rome's cityscape is a magical mix of ruins, monuments, palaces, piazzas and churches. Here are some of the city's most significant buildings.

Colosseum	Rome's iconic arena bears the hallmarks of ancient Roman architecture: arches, the use of various building materials, unprecedented scale.
Pantheon	The dome, one of the Romans' most important architectural innovations, finds perfect form atop this revolutionary structure.
Basilica di Santa Maria Maggiore	Although much modified over the centuries, this hulking cathedral exemplifies the Christian basilicas being built in the early Middle Ages.
Tempietto di Bramante	A masterpiece of harmonious design, Bramante's 1502 temple beautifully encapsulates High Renaissance ideals.
St Peter's Basilica	Michelangelo's dome and Carlo Maderno's facade are the key architectural features of this, the greatest of Rome's Renaissance churches.
Chiesa del Gesù	One of Rome's finest Counter-Reformation churches with a much-copied facade by Giacomo della Porta and an ornate baroque interior.
Chiesa di San Carlo alle Quattro Fontane	A prized example of baroque architecture, Francesco Borromini's church boasts convex and concave surfaces, hidden windows, and a complex elliptical plan.
Palazzo della Civiltà del Lavoro	Nicknamed the 'Square Colosseum', this EUR landmark is a masterpiece of 1930s Italian rationalism.
Auditorium Parco della Musica	Renzo Piano's audacious arts complex is the most influential contemporary building in Rome.
MAXXI	Zaha Hadid's award-winning 2010 building provides a suitably striking setting for Rome's flagship contemporary arts museum.

BRAMANTE, THE ARCHITECT'S ARCHITECT

One of the most influential architects of his day, Donato Bramante (1444–1514) was the godfather of Renaissance architecture. His peers, Michelangelo, Raphael and Leonardo da Vinci, considered him the only architect of their era equal to the ancients.

Born near Urbino, he originally trained as a painter before taking up architecture in his mid-30s in Milan. However, it was in Rome that he enjoyed his greatest success. Working for Pope Julius II, he developed a monumental style that while classical in origin was pure Renaissance in its expression of harmony and perspective. The most perfect representation of this is his Tempietto, a small but much-copied temple. His original designs for St Peter's Basilica also revealed a classically inspired symmetry with a Pantheon-like dome envisaged atop a Greek-cross structure.

Rich and influential, Bramante was an adept political operator who was not above badmouthing his competitors. It's said, for example, that he talked Pope Julius II into giving Michelangelo the contract for the Sistine Chapel ceiling in the hope that it would prove the undoing of his young Tuscan rival.

Over time, basilica design became increasingly standardised. A principal entrance would open onto an atrium, a courtyard surrounded by colonnaded porticoes, which, in turn, would lead to the porch. The interior would be rectangular and divided by rows of columns into a central nave and smaller, side aisles. At the far end, the main altar and bishop's throne (cathedra) would sit in a semicircular apse. In some churches a transept would bisect the central nave to form a Latin cross.

The Renaissance

Florence, rather than Rome, is generally regarded as Italy's great Renaissance city. But while many of the movement's early architects hailed from Tuscany, the city they turned to for inspiration was Rome. The Eternal City might have been in pretty poor nick in the late 15th century, but as the centre of classical antiquity it was much revered by budding architects and a trip to study the Colosseum and the Pantheon was considered a fundamental part of an architect's training.

One of the key aspects they studied, and which informs much Renaissance architecture, is the concept of harmony. This was achieved through the application of symmetry, order and proportion. To this end many Renaissance buildings incorporated structural features copied from the ancients – columns, pilasters, arches and, most dramatically, domes. The Pantheon's dome, in particular, proved immensely influential, serving as a blueprint for many later works.

Early Years

It's impossible to pinpoint the exact year the Renaissance arrived in Rome, but many claim it was the election of Pope Nicholas V in 1447 that sparked off the artistic and architectural furore that was to sweep through the city in the next century or so. Nicholas believed that as head of the Christian world Rome had a duty to impress, a theory that was eagerly taken up by his successors, and it was at the behest of the great papal dynasties – the Barberini, Farnese and Pamphilj – that the leading artists of the day were summoned to Rome.

The Venetian Pope Paul II (r 1464–71) commissioned many works, including Palazzo Venezia, Rome's first great Renaissance *palazzo*. His successor, Sixtus IV (r 1471–84), had the Sistine Chapel built, and enlarged the Chiesa di Santa Maria del Popolo.

Architecture Reads

Rome (Amanda Claridge)

The Genius in the Design: Bernini, Borromini and the Rivalry that Transformed Rome (Jake Morrissey)

Rome and Environs: An Archaeological Guide (Filippo Coarelli)

Giuseppe Valadier (1762–1839) was the popes' go-to architect in the early 19th century. He is best known for his neoclassical revamp of Piazza del Popolo and the Pincio Hill, but also worked on important restorations of Ponte Milvio and the Arco di Tito.

High Renaissance

It was under Pope Julius II (1503–13) that the Roman Renaissance reached its peak, thanks largely to a classically minded architect from Milan, Donato Bramante (1444–1514).

Considered the high priest of Renaissance architecture, Bramante arrived in Rome in 1499. Here, inspired by the ancient ruins, he developed a refined classical style that was to prove hugely influential. His 1502 Tempietto, for example, perfectly illustrates his innate understanding of proportion. Similarly harmonious is his 1504 cloister at the Chiesa di Santa Maria della Pace near Piazza Navona.

In 1506 Julius commissioned him to start work on the job that would eventually finish him off – the rebuilding of St Peter's Basilica. The fall of Constantinople's Aya Sofya (Church of the Hagia Sofia) to Islam in the mid-14th century had pricked Nicholas V into ordering an earlier revamp, but the work had never been completed and it wasn't until Julius took the bull by the horns that progress was made. However, Bramante died in 1514 and he never got to see how his original Greek-cross design was developed.

St Peter's Basilica occupied most of the other notable architects of the High Renaissance, including Giuliano da Sangallo (1445–1516), Baldassarre Peruzzi (1481–1536) and Antonio da Sangallo the Younger (1484–1546). Michelangelo (1475–1564) eventually took over in 1547, modifying the layout and creating the basilica's crowning dome. Modelled on Brunelleschi's cupola for the Duomo in Florence, this is considered the artist's finest architectural achievement and one of the most important works of the Roman Renaissance.

Mannerism

As Rome's architects strove to build a new Jerusalem, the city's leaders struggled to deal with the political tensions arising outside the city walls. These came to a head in 1527 when the city was invaded and savagely routed by troops of the Holy Roman Emperor, Charles V. This traumatic event forced many of the artists working in Rome to flee the city and ushered in a new style of artistic and architectural expression. Mannerism was a relatively short-lived form but in its emphasis on complexity and decoration, in contrast to the sharp, clean lines of traditional Renaissance styles, it hinted at the more ebullient designs that would arrive with the advent of the 17th-century baroque.

One of mannerism's leading exponents was Baldassarre Peruzzi, whose Palazzo Massimo alle Colonne on Corso Vittorio Emanuele II reveals a number of mannerist elements – a pronounced facade, decorative window mouldings, showy imitation stonework.

The Vittoriano, Rome's largest and hardest to miss monument, was built to honour King Vittorio Emanuele II, united Italy's first king. Completed in 1935 after 50 years' construction, it boasts some impressive statistics, standing 135m wide and rising to a height of 81m.

ROCOCO FRILLS

In the early 18th century, as baroque fashions began to fade and neoclassicism waited to make its 19th-century entrance, the rococo burst into theatrical life. Drawing on the excesses of the baroque, it was a short-lived fad but one that left a memorable mark.

The Spanish Steps, built between 1723 and 1726 by Francesco de Sanctis, provided a focal point for the many Grand Tourists who were busy discovering Rome's classical past. A short walk to the southwest, Piazza Sant'Ignazio was designed by Filippo Raguzzini (1680–1771) to provide a suitably melodramatic setting for the Chiesa di Sant'Ignazio di Loyola, Rome's second most important Jesuit church.

Most spectacular of all, however, was the Trevi Fountain, one of the city's most exuberant and enduringly popular monuments. It was designed in 1732 by Nicola Salvi (1697–1751) and completed three decades later.

/ GETTY IMAGES ©

The Counter-Reformation-style facade of Chiesa del Gesù (p81)

The Baroque

As the principal motor of the Roman Renaissance, the Catholic Church became increasingly powerful in the 16th century. But with power came corruption and calls for reform. These culminated in Martin Luther's *95 Theses* and the far-reaching Protestant Reformation. This hit the Church hard and prompted the Counter-Reformation (1560–1648), a vicious and sustained campaign to get people back into the Catholic fold. In the midst of this great offensive, baroque art and architecture emerged as a highly effective form of propaganda. Stylistically, baroque architecture aims for a dramatic sense of dynamism, an effect that it often achieves by combining spatial complexity with clever lighting and a flamboyant use of decorative painting and sculpture.

One of the first great Counter-Reformation churches was the Jesuit Chiesa del Gesù, designed by the leading architect of the day, Giacomo della Porta (1533–1602). In a move away from the style of earlier Renaissance churches, the facade has pronounced architectural elements that create a contrast between surfaces and a play of light and shade.

The end of the 16th century and the papacy of Sixtus V (1585–90) marked the beginning of major urban-planning schemes. Domenico Fontana (1543–1607) and other architects created a network of major thoroughfares to connect previously disparate parts of the sprawling city and decorative obelisks were erected at vantage points across town. Fontana also designed the main facade of Palazzo del Quirinale, the immense palace that served as the pope's summer residence for almost three centuries. His nephew, Carlo Maderno (1556–1629), also worked on the *palazzo* when not amending Bramante's designs for St Peter's Basilica.

Key Bernini Works

St Peter's Square

Chiesa di Sant'Andrea al Quirinale

Fontana dei Quattro Fiumi

Palazzo di Montecitorio

Bernini vs Borromini

No two people did more to fashion the face of Rome than the two great figures of the Roman baroque – Gian Lorenzo Bernini (1598–1680) and Francesco Borromini (1599–1667). Two starkly different characters –

Key Borromini Works

....

Chiesa di San Carlo alle Quattro Fontane

....

Chiesa di Sant'Agnese in Agone

....

Chiesa di Sant'Ivo alla Sapienza

....

Prospettiva, Palazzo Spada

The term Scuola romana (Roman School) is used to define a group of architects working in the 1920s and '30s, mainly on large-scale housing projects. Their designs sought to ally modern functionalism with a respect for tradition and a utopian vision of urban development.

Naples-born Bernini was suave, self-confident and politically adept; Borromini, from Lombardy, was solitary and peculiar – they led the transition from Counter-Reformation rigour to baroque exuberance.

Bernini is perhaps best known for his work in the Vatican. He designed St Peter's Sq, famously styling the colonnade as 'the motherly arms of the Church', and was chief architect at St Peter's Basilica from 1629. While working on the basilica, he created the baldachin (altar canopy) over the main altar, using bronze stripped from the Pantheon.

Under the patronage of the Barberini pope Urban VIII, Bernini was given free rein to transform the city, and his churches, *palazzi,* piazzas and fountains remain landmarks to this day. However, his fortunes nose-dived when the pope died in 1644. Urban's successor, Innocent X, wanted as little contact as possible with the favourites of his hated predecessor, and instead turned to Borromini, Alessandro Algardi (1595–1654) and Girolamo and Carlo Rainaldi (1570–1655 and 1611–91, respectively). Bernini later came back into favour with his 1651 Fontana dei Quattro Fiumi in the centre of Piazza Navona, opposite Borromini's Chiesa di Sant'Agnese in Agone.

Borromini, the son of an architect and well versed in stonemasonry and construction techniques, created buildings involving complex shapes and exotic geometry. A recurring feature of his designs was the skilful manipulation of light, often obtained by the clever placement of small oval-shaped windows. His most memorable works are the Chiesa di San Carlo alle Quattro Fontane, which has an oval-shaped interior, and the Chiesa di Sant'Ivo alla Sapienza, which combines a complex arrangement of convex and concave surfaces with an innovative spiral tower.

Throughout their careers, the two geniuses were often at each other's throats. Borromini was deeply envious of Bernini's early successes, and Bernini was scathing of Borromini's complex geometrical style.

Fascism, Futurism & the 20th Century

Rome entered the 20th century in good shape. During the last 30 years of the 19th century it had been treated to one of its periodic makeovers – this time after being made capital of the Kingdom of Italy in 1870. Piazzas were built – Piazza Vittorio Emanuele II, at the centre of a new upmarket residential district, and neoclassical Piazza della Repubblica, over Diocletian's bath complex – and roads were laid. Via Nazionale and Via Cavour were constructed to link the city centre with the new railway station, Stazione Termini, and Corso Vittorio Emanuele II was built to connect Piazza Venezia with the Vatican.

FIVE FLAMBOYANT FOUNTAINS

Trevi Fountain	Wild horses rise out of the rocks at this fantastical rococo extravaganza, Rome's largest and most celebrated fountain.
Fontana dei Quattro Fiumi	Topped by a tapering obelisk, Bernini's opulent baroque display highlights on Piazza Navona.
Fontana delle Naiadi	The naked nymphs languishing around Piazza della Repubblica's scene-stealing fountain caused a scandal when revealed in 1901.
Fontana dell'Acqua Paola	Known to Romans as *il fontanone del Gianicolo,* this grandiose baroque fountain sits atop the Gianicolo Hill.
Barcaccia	The Spanish Steps lead down to this sunken-ship fountain, supposedly modelled on a boat dumped on the piazza by a flood in 1598.

Rationalism & Rebuilding

Influenced by the German Bauhaus movement, architectural rationalism was all the rage in 1920s Europe. In its international form it advocated an emphasis on sharply defined linear forms, but in Italy it took on a slightly different look, thanks to the influence of the Gruppo Sette, its main Italian promoters, and Benito Mussolini, Italy's fascist dictator. Basically, the Gruppo Sette acknowledged the debt Italian architecture owed to its classical past and incorporated elements of that tradition into their modernistic designs. Aesthetically and politically, this tied in perfectly with Mussolini's vision of fascism as the modern bearer of ancient Rome's imperialist ambitions.

A shrewd manipulator of imagery, Mussolini embarked on a series of grandiose building projects, including the 1928–31 Foro Italico sports centre, Via dei Foro Imperiali, and the residential quarter of Garbatella. Garbatella, now a colourful neighbourhood in southern Rome, was originally planned as an English-style garden city to house city workers, but in the 1920s the project was hijacked by the fascist regime, which had its own designs. Central to these were innovative housing blocks, known as *alberghi suburbani* (suburban hotels), which were used to accommodate people displaced from the city centre. The most famous of these hotels, the Albergo Rosso, was designed by Innocenzo Sabbatini (1891–1983), the leading light of the Roman School of architecture.

EUR

Mussolini's most famous architectural legacy is the EUR district in the extreme south of the city. Built for the Esposizione Universale di Roma in 1942, this Orwellian quarter of wide boulevards and huge linear buildings owes its look to the vision of the *razionalisti* (rationalists). In practice, though, only one of their number, Adalberto Libera, actually worked on the project, as by this stage most of the Gruppo Sette had fallen out with the ruling Fascist junta. Libera's Palazzo dei Congressi is a masterpiece of rationalist architecture, but EUR's most iconic building is the 'Square Colosseum', the Palazzo della Civiltà del Lavoro, designed by Giovanni Guerrini, Ernesto Bruno La Padula and Mario Romano.

Postwar Developments

For much of the postwar period, architects in Rome were limited to planning cheap housing for the city's ever-growing population. Swathes of hideous apartment blocks were built along the city's main arteries, and grim suburbs sprang up on land claimed from local farmers.

The 1960 Olympics heralded a spate of sporting construction, and both Stadio Flaminio and Stadio Olimpico date to this period. Pier Luigi Nervi, Italy's master of concrete and a hugely influential innovator, added his contribution in the form of the Palazzetto dello Sport.

Modern Rome

The 21st century has witnessed a flurry of architectural activity in Rome. A clutch of 'starchitects' have worked on projects in the city, including Renzo Piano, Italy's foremost architect, renowned American Richard Meier, Anglo-Iraqi Zaha Hadid, and Odile Decq, a major French architect.

Controversy & Acclaim

The foundations of this building boom date to the early 1990s, when the then mayor Francesco Rutelli launched a major clean-up of the historic centre. As part of the process, he commissioned Richard Meier to build

---

ARCHITECTURE MODERN ROME

Designed by Paolo Portoghesi, Rome's postmodernist mosque is one of Europe's largest. Its critically acclaimed design is centred on a beautiful, luminous interior capped by a cupola and 16 surrounding domes.

Via dei Fori Imperiali, the road that divides the Roman Forums from the Imperial Forums, was one of Mussolini's most controversial projects. Inaugurated in 1932, it was conceived to link the Colosseum (ancient power) with Piazza Venezia (fascist power), but in the process tarmacked over much of the ancient forums.

CONTEMPORARY BRIDGES

In recent years, three new bridges have opened in Rome. In 2011 the Ponte della Musica footbridge was inaugurated after three years' construction. Spanning the Tiber between the Flaminio district and the Foro Italico sports complex, it features a steel arch design by English studio Buro Happold and architects Powell-Williams.

A year later, the Cavalcavia Ostiense was inaugurated in the southern Ostiense district. Known locally as the 'Cobra', this road bridge sports a sinuous white steel arch as it runs over the railway line that had long separated Ostiense from nearby Garbatella.

Also in Ostiense, the foot and cycle bridge Ponte della Scienza was opened in May 2014, spanning the Tiber between the Riva Ostiense and Riva Portuense.

Modern Icons

Palazzo della Civiltà del Lavoro

Auditorium Parco della Musica

Museo dell'Ara Pacis

Museo Nazionale delle Arti del XXI Secolo (MAXXI)

a new pavilion for the 1st-century-AD Ara Pacis. Predictably, Meier's glass-and-steel Museo dell'Ara Pacis caused controversy when it was unveiled in 2006. Vittorio Sgarbi, an outspoken art critic and politician, claimed that the American's design was the first step to globalising Rome's unique classical heritage. The Roman public appreciated the idea of modern architecture in the city centre, but few were entirely convinced by Meier's design.

Meier won far more acclaim for a second project, his striking Chiesa Dio Padre Misericordioso in Tor Tre Teste, a dreary suburb east of the city centre. This was one of a number of churches commissioned by the Vicariate of Rome for the 2000 Jubilee. Another, the Chiesa di Santa Maria della Presentazione, designed by the Rome-based Nemesi studio, sparked interest when it was inaugurated in the outlying Quartaccio neighbourhood in 2002.

Other headline buildings from this period include Renzo Piano's Auditorium Parco della Musica (2002), Zaha Hadid's MAXXI (2010) and Odile Decq's 2010 MACRO building.

Fuksas & Future Plans

Born in Rome in 1944, Massimiliano Fuksas is known for his futuristic vision, and while he has no signature building as such, his design for the Centro Congressi Italia, aka the Nuvola, comes as close as any to embodying his style. A rectangular 30m-high glass shell containing a 3500-sq-m steel-and-Teflon cloud supported by steel ribs and suspended over a vast conference hall, its look is fearlessly modern. Yet it's not without its references to the past: in both scale and form it owes its inspiration to the 1930s rationalist architecture that surrounds it in EUR.

Construction started on the Nuvola in 2007 but work has been hampered by spiralling costs and, at the time of research, completion had been re-scheduled for mid-2016.

But while work struggles ahead in EUR, plans are afoot for a number of high-profile development projects elsewhere in the city. These include a new contemporary arts centre to be built by award-winning French architect Jean Nouvelin in the Forum Boarium area, and, to the north, a vast Città della Scienza (City of Science) complex to be housed in an ex-barracks in the Flaminio district. In the city's southern reaches, initial surveying had just started on a site earmarked for a new 52,500-capacity stadium for the Roma football team, the Stadio della Roma.

Rome's Eataly complex is a masterclass in urban regeneration, bringing life back to a derelict train station. Until the complex opened in 2012, the Air Terminal Ostiense, which had originally been designed to serve airport trains arriving for the 1990 football World Cup, had been an abandoned shell.

Architecture Glossary

apse	a semicircular or polygonal recess with a domed roof over a church's altar
baldachino	(baldachin) a stone canopy built over an altar or tomb; often supported by columns and freestanding
baroque	style of European art, architecture and music of the 17th and 18th centuries
basilica	an oblong hall with an apse at the end of the nave; used in ancient Rome for public assemblies and later adopted as a blueprint for medieval churches
cloister	enclosed court attached to a church or monastery; consists of a roofed ambulatory surrounding an open area
colonnade	a row of columns supporting a roof or other structure
crypt	an underground room beneath a church used for services and burials
cupola	a rounded dome forming part of a ceiling or roof
forum	in ancient Rome, a public space used for judicial business and commerce
frieze	a horizontal band, often with painted or sculptural decoration, that sits between the architrave and cornice
futurism	Italian early-20th-century artistic movement that embraced modern technology
loggia	a gallery or room with one side open, often facing a garden
nave	the central aisle in a church, often separated from parallel aisles by pillars
neoclassicism	dominant style of art and architecture in the late 18th and early 19th centuries; a return to ancient Roman styles
portico	a porch with a roof supported by columns
rationalism	international architectural style of the 1920s; its Italian form, often associated with fascism, incorporates linear styles and classical references
Renaissance	European revival of art and architecture based on classical precedents between the 14th and 16th centuries
rococo	ornate 18th-century style of architecture
stucco	wall plaster used for decorative purposes
trompe l'oeil	a visual illusion tricking the viewer into seeing a painted object as a three-dimensional image
transept	in a cross-shaped church, the two parts that bisect the nave at right angles, forming the short arms of the cross

The Roman Way of Life

As a visitor, it's often difficult to see beyond Rome's spectacular veneer to the large, modern city that lies beneath: a living, breathing capital that's home to almost three million people. How do the Romans live in their city? Where do they work? Who do they live with? How do they let their hair down?

A Day in the Life

English journalist John Hooper examines the contradictions and insecurities that lie beneath the smooth veneer of Italian society in his entertaining 2015 book *The Italians*. Like Luigi Barzini's 1964 classic of the same name, it's an entertaining and informative read full of obscure details and quirky facts.

Rome's Mr Average, Signor Rossi, lives with his wife in a small, two-bedroom apartment in the suburbs and works in a government ministry in the city centre. His working day is typical of the many who crowd *i mezzi* (the means, ie public transport) in the morning rush hour.

His morning routine is the same as city dwellers the world over: a quick breakfast – usually nothing more than a sweet, black espresso – followed by a short bus ride to the nearest metro station. On the way he'll stop at an *edicola* (kiosk) to pick up his daily newspaper (*Il Messaggero*) and share a joke with the kiosk owner. A quick scan of the headlines reveals few surprises – Matteo Renzi promoting his latest reforms; the usual political shenanigans in city hall; Roma and Lazio match reports.

Rome's metro is not a particularly pleasant place to be in *l'ora di punta* (the rush hour), especially in summer when it gets unbearably hot, but the regulars are resigned to the discomfort and bear it cheerfully.

His work, like many in the swollen state bureaucracy, is not the most interesting in the world, nor the best paid, but it's secure and with a much sought-after *contratto a tempo indeterminato* (permanent contract) he doesn't have to worry about losing it. In contrast, many of his younger colleagues work in constant fear that their temporary contracts will not be renewed when they expire.

Lunch, which is typically taken around 1.30pm, is usually a snack or *pizza al taglio* (by the slice) from a nearby takeaway. Before heading back to the office for the afternoon session, there's time for a quick coffee in the usual bar.

Clocking off time in most ministries is typically from 5pm onwards and by about 7pm the evening rush hour is in full swing. Once home, our Signor Rossi catches the 8pm TV news before sitting down to a pasta supper at about 8.30pm.

In 2014 the average salary in Rome was €30,279. This compares to Italy's national average of €28,977, €45,170 in Germany, and €36,980 in France.

Work

Employment in the capital is largely based on Italy's bloated state bureaucracy. Every morning armies of suited civil servants pour into town and disappear into vast ministerial buildings to keep the machinery of government ticking over. Other important employers include the tourist sector, finance, media and culture – Italy's state broadcaster RAI is based in Rome, as is much of the country's film industry, and there are hundreds of museums and galleries across town.

RELIGION IN ROMAN LIFE

Rome is a city of churches. From the great headline basilicas in the historic centre to the hundreds of parish churches dotted around the suburbs, the city is packed with places to worship. And with the Vatican in the centre of town, the Church is a constant presence in Roman life.

Yet the role of religion in modern Roman society is an ambiguous one. On the one hand, most people consider themselves Catholic, but on the other, church attendance is in freefall, particularly among the young, and atheism is growing.

But while Romans don't go to church very often, they are, on the whole, a conformist bunch, and for many the Church remains a point of reference. The Church's line on ethical and social issues might not always meet with widespread support, but it's always given an airing in the largely sympathetic national press. Similarly, more than half of people who get married do so in church, and first communions remain an important social occasion entailing gift-giving and lavish receptions.

Catholicism's hold on the Roman psyche is strong, but an increase in the city's immigrant population has led to a noticeable Muslim presence. This has largely been a pain-free process, but friction has flared on occasion and in November 2014 riot police were forced to intervene after crowds attacked a migrant reception centre in the Tor Sapienza suburb in the far east of the city.

But times are hard and it's tough for young people to get a foot on the career ladder – Rome's youth unemployment has risen over the past few years and currently stands at 33.3%. To land it lucky, it helps to know someone. Official figures are hard to come by, but it's a widely held belief that personal or political connections are the best way of landing a job. This system of *raccomandazioni* (recommendations) is widespread and regularly gives rise to scandal. In recent years high-profile controversies have centred on nepotistic appointments at Rome's La Sapienza University, at the city's public transport operator, and, in the most recent case, at Rome's waste disposal company.

Of course, getting a job is one thing, but finding one to suit your qualifications is quite another, and many young Romans are forced to choose between unemployment or taking a job for which they are overqualified.

Like everywhere in Italy, Rome's workplace remains largely a male preserve. Female unemployment remains an urgent issue and Italian women continue to earn less than their male counterparts. That said, recent signs have been positive, at least at the top end of the scale. The number of women serving on company boards has increased since 2011, and women make up almost a third of Matteo Renzi's current government.

In 2014 the average price for a square metre of residential property was around €3500, with rates topping €8000 in the historic centre. In the suburbs, the going rate was between €3000 and €4000 per square metre.

Home Life & the Family

Romans, like most Italians, live in apartments. These are often small – 75 to 100 sq m is typical – and expensive. House prices in central Rome are among the highest in the country and many first-time buyers are forced to move out of town or to distant suburbs outside the GRA *(grande raccordo anulare)*, the busy ring road that marks the city's outer limit.

Almost all apartments are in self-managed *condomini* (blocks of individually owned flats), a fact that gives rise to no end of neighbourly squabbling. Regular *condominio* meetings are often fiery affairs as neighbours argue over everything from communal repairs to noisy dogs and parking spaces.

Rates of home ownership are relatively high in Rome – about 65% – and properties are commonly kept in the family, handed down from generation to generation. People do rent, but the rental market is largely targeted at Rome's huge student population.

FASHION & THE BELLA FIGURA

Making a good impression (*fare la bella figura*) is extremely important to Romans. For a style-conscious hipster that might mean having the latest tattoos, the right-shaped beard, and a state-of-the-art smartphone. For a middle-aged professional it will involve being impeccably groomed and dressed appropriately for every occasion. This slavish adherence to fashion isn't limited to clothes or accessories. It extends to all walks of life and trend-conscious Romans will frequent the same bars and restaurants, drink the same *aperitivi* and hang out on the same piazzas.

Staying at Home

Italy's single most successful institution, and the only one in which the Romans continue to trust, is the family. It's still the rule rather than the exception for young Romans to stay at home until they marry, which they typically do at around 30. Figures report that virtually one in two 25- to 34-year-olds still live at home with at least one parent. To foreign observers this seems strange, but there are mitigating factors: almost half of these stay-at-homes are out of work and property prices are high. There's also the fact that young Romans are generally reluctant to downgrade and move to a cheaper neighbourhood. Seen from another perspective, it might simply mean that Roman families like living together.

But while faith in the family remains, the family is shrinking. Italian women are giving birth later than ever and having fewer children – there were fewer babies born in 2014 than in any year since modern Italy was founded in 1861. Rome's army of *nonni* (grandparents) berate their children for this, as does the Pope, for whom 'the choice to not have children is selfish'. For their part, Italy's politicians worry that such a perilously low birth rate threatens the future tax returns necessary for funding the country's pension payments.

Rome has the worst traffic in Italy and is the third most congested city in Europe, according to a report by traffic navigator company Tom Tom. Topping Europe's traffic blacklist are Warsaw and Marseille.

Play

Despite the ongoing economic gloom, and all the trials and tribulations of living in Rome – dodgy public transport, iffy services and sky-high prices – few Romans would swap their city for anywhere else. They know theirs is one of the world's most beautiful cities and they enjoy it with gusto. You only have to look at the city's pizzerias, trattorias and restaurants to see that eating out is a much-loved local pastime. It's a cliché of Roman life but food really is central to social pleasure.

Drinking, in contrast, is not a traditional Roman activity, at least not in the sense of piling into a pub for pints of beer. Romans have long enjoyed hanging out and looking cool – just look at all those photos of *dolce vita* cafe society – and an evening out in Rome is as much about flirting and looking gorgeous as it is about consuming alcohol.

Clothes shopping is a popular Roman pastime, alongside cinema-going and football. Interest in Rome's two Serie A teams, Roma and Lazio, remains high and a trip to the Stadio Olimpico to watch the Sunday game is still considered an afternoon well-spent. Depending on the result, of course.

Rome is to get its first official red-light district after mayor Ignazio Marino green-lighted proposals in February 2015 for an area of legally tolerated prostitution in the EUR district. Unsurprisingly, the move met with opposition from right-wing councillors and Church representatives.

Romans are inveterate car-lovers and on hot summer weekends they will often drive out to the coast or surrounding countryside. Beach bums make for nearby Ostia or more upmarket Fregene, while those in search of a little greenery head to the Castelli Romani, a pocket of green hills just south of town famous for its Frascati wine and popular *fraschette* eateries.

Survival Guide

Transport

ARRIVING IN ROME

Most people arrive in Rome by plane, landing at one of its two airports: Leonardo da Vinci (better known as Fiumicino) or Ciampino, hub for European low-cost carrier Ryanair. Flights from New York take around nine hours; from London 2¾ hours; from Sydney at least 22 hours.

Domestic flights connect Rome with airports across Italy.

As an alternative to short-haul flights, trains serve Rome's main station, Stazione Termini, from a number of European destinations, including Paris (about 15 hours), as well as cities across Italy.

Long-distance domestic and international buses arrive at the Autostazione Tiburtina.

You can also get to Rome by boat. Ferries serve Civitavecchia, some 80km north of the city, from a number of Mediterranean ports.

Flights, cars and tours may be booked online at lonelyplanet.com/bookings.

Leonardo da Vinci Airport

Rome's main international airport, **Leonardo da Vinci** (Fiumicino; ☑06 6 59 51; www. adr.it/fiumicino), is 30km west of the city. It's divided into four terminals: Terminals 1, 2 and 3 are for domestic and international flights; Terminal 5 is for American and Israeli airlines flying to the US and Israel.

Terminals 1, 2 and 3 are within easy walking distance of each other in the main airport building; Terminal 5 is accessible by shuttle bus from Terminal 3.

The easiest way to get into town is by train, but there are also buses and private shuttle services.

Train

Leonardo Express Train (one way €14) Runs to/from Stazione Termini. Departures from the airport every 30 minutes between 6.23am and 11.23pm; from Termini between 5.35am and 10.35pm. Journey time is 30 minutes.

FL1 Train (one way €8) Connects to Trastevere, Ostiense and Tiburtina stations, but not Termini. Departures from the airport every 15 minutes (half-hourly on Sundays and public holidays) between 5.57am and 10.42pm; from Tiburtina every 15 minutes between 5.46am and 7.31pm, then half-hourly to 10.02pm.

Bus

SIT Bus (☑06 591 68 26; www.sitbusshuttle.it; one way €6) Regular departures from the airport to Stazione Termini (Via Marsala) from 8.30am to 11.50pm; from Termini between 5am and 8.30pm. All buses stop at the Vatican en route. Tickets are available on the bus. Journey time is approximately one hour.

Cotral Bus (www.cotralspa. it; one way €5, if bought on the bus €7) Runs to/from Fiumicino from Stazione Tiburtina via Termini. Eight daily departures including night services from the airport at 1.15am, 2.15am, 3.30am and 5am, and from Tiburtina at 12.30am, 1.15am, 2.30am and 3.45am. Journey time is one hour.

Terravision Bus (www.terravision.eu; one way €6, online €4) Regular services from the airport to Stazione Termini (Via Marsala) between 5.35am and 11pm; from Termini between 4.40am and 9.50pm. Allow about an hour for the journey.

Private Shuttle

Airport Connection Services (☑06 2111 6248; www.airportconnection.it) Transfers to/from the city centre start at €35 per person.

Airport Shuttle (www. airportshuttle.it) Transfers to/from your hotel for €25 for one person, then €5 for each additional passenger up to a maximum of eight.

Taxi

The set fare to/from the city centre is €48, which is valid for up to four passengers

CLIMATE CHANGE & TRAVEL

Every form of transport that relies on carbon-based fuel generates CO_2, the main cause of human-induced climate change. Modern travel is dependent on aeroplanes, which might use less fuel per kilometre per person than most cars but travel much greater distances. The altitude at which aircraft emit gases (including CO_2) and particles also contributes to their climate change impact. Many websites offer 'carbon calculators' that allow people to estimate the carbon emissions generated by their journey and, for those who wish to do so, to offset the impact of the greenhouse gases emitted with contributions to portfolios of climate-friendly initiatives throughout the world. Lonely Planet offsets the carbon footprint of all staff and author travel.

including luggage. Note that taxis registered in Fiumicino charge more, so make sure you catch a Comune di Roma taxi – these are white with a taxi sign on the roof and Roma Capitale written on the door along with the taxi's licence number. Journey time is approximately 45 to 60 minutes depending on traffic.

Car

Follow signs for Roma out of the airport and onto the autostrada. Exit at EUR, following for the *centro*, to link up with Via Cristoforo Colombo, which will take you directly into the centre.

Ciampino Airport

Ciampino (✆06 6 59 51; www.adr.it/ciampino), 15km southeast of the city centre, is used by Ryanair. It's not a big airport but there's a steady flow of traffic and at peak times it can get extremely busy.

To get into town, the best option is to take one of the dedicated bus services. You can also take a bus to Ciampino station and then pick up a train to Termini.

Bus

Terravision Bus (www.terravision.eu; one way €6, online €4) Twice hourly departures to/from Via Marsala outside Stazione Termini. From the airport services are between 8.15am and 12.15am; from Via Marsala

between 4.30am and 9.20pm. Buy tickets at Terracafè in front of the Via Marsala bus stop. Journey time is 40 minutes.

SIT Bus (✆06 591 68 26; www.sitbusshuttle.com; to/from airport €6/4) Regular departures from the airport to Via Marsala outside Stazione Termini between 7.45am and 11.15pm; from Termini between 4.30am and 9.30pm. Get tickets on the bus. Journey time is 45 minutes.

Atral (www.atral-lazio.com) Runs buses to/from Anagnina metro station (€1.20) and Ciampino train station (€1.20), where you can get a train to Termini (€1.30).

Private Shuttle

Airport Shuttle (www.airportshuttle.it)

Taxi

The set rate to or from the airport is €30. Journey time is approximately 30 minutes depending on traffic.

Car

Exit the station and follow Via Appia Nuova into the centre.

Termini Train Station

Almost all trains arrive at and depart from **Stazione Termini** (Piazza dei Cinquecento; ⓂTermini), Rome's main train station and principal transport hub. There are regular connections to other European countries, all major Italian cities, and many smaller towns.

Train information is available from the Customer Service area on the main

BUSES FROM TERMINI

From Piazza dei Cinquecento outside Stazione Termini buses run to all corners of the city.

DESTINATION	BUS
Campo de' Fiori	40/64
Colosseum	75
Pantheon	40/64
Piazza Navona	40/64
Piazza Venezia	40/64
St Peter's Sq	40/64
Terme di Caracalla	714
Trastevere	H
Trevi Fountain	85
Villa Borghese	910

concourse to the left of the ticket desks. Alternatively, check www.trenitalia.com or phone ☑892021.

From Termini, you can connect with the metro or take a bus from Piazza dei Cinquecento out front. Taxis are outside the main entrance/exit.

Tiburtina Bus Station

Long-distance national and international buses use **Autostazione Tiburtina** (Piazzale Tiburtina; ⓂTiburtina).

From the bus station, cross under the overpass for the Tiburtina train station, where you can pick up metro line B and connect with Termini for onward buses, trains and metro line A.

Civitavecchia Port

The nearest port to Rome is at Civitavecchia, about 80km north of town. Ferries sail here from destinations across the Mediterranean, including Sicily and Sardinia. Check www.traghettiweb.it for route details, prices, and to book.

From Civitavecchia there are half-hourly trains to Stazione Termini (€5 to €15, 40 minutes to 1¼ hours). Civitavecchia's station is about 700m from the entrance to the port.

GETTING AROUND ROME

Rome is a sprawling city, but the historic centre is relatively compact and it's possible to explore much of it on foot. The city's public transport system includes buses, trams, a metro, and a suburban train system. Tickets are valid for all forms of transport.

Metro

➡ Rome has two main metro lines, A (orange) and B (blue), which cross at Termini. A branch line, 'B1', serves the northern suburbs, and a line C runs through the southeastern outskirts.

➡ Trains run between 5.30am and 11.30pm (to 1.30am on Fridays and Saturdays).

➡ All stations on line B have wheelchair access except Circo Massimo, Colosseo and Cavour. On line A, Ottaviano–San Pietro and Termini have lifts.

➡ Take line A for the Trevi Fountain (Barberini), Spanish Steps (Spagna) and St Peter's (Ottaviano–San Pietro).

➡ Take line B for the Colosseum (Colosseo).

Bus & Tram

➡ Rome's buses and trams are run by **ATAC** (☑06 5 70 03; www.atac.roma.it).

➡ The main bus station is in front of Stazione Termini on Piazza dei Cinquecento, where there's an **information booth** (⏱7.30am-8pm).

➡ Other important hubs are at Largo di Torre Argentina and Piazza Venezia.

USEFUL BUS & TRAM ROUTES

SERVICE	ROUTE	OPERATING HOURS	FREQUENCY
Bus H	Termini, Via Nazionale, Piazza Venezia, Viale Trastevere	5.30am-midnight	up to 7 per hr
3 Tram	Ostiense, Testaccio, Viale Aventino, Circo Massimo, Colosseo, San Giovanni, Porta Maggiore, San Lorenzo, Villa Borghese	5.30am-10pm	up to 7 per hr
8 Tram	Piazza Venezia, Via Arenula, Trastevere	5.35am-midnight	up to 7 per hr
Bus 23	Piazzale Clodio, Piazza del Risorgimento, Lungotevere, Testaccio, Ostiense, Basilica di San Paolo	5.15am-midnight	up to 6 per hr
Bus 40	Termini, Via Nazionale, Piazza Venezia, Largo di Torre Argentina, Borgo Sant'Angelo	6am-midnight	up to 12 per hr
Bus 64	Similar route to 40 but slower and with more stops	5am-midnight	up to 12 per hr
Bus 170	Termini, Via Nazionale, Piazza Venezia, Via del Teatro Marcello, Piazza Bocca della Verità, Testaccio, EUR	5.30am-midnight	up to 7 per hr
Bus 492	Stazione Tiburtina, San Lorenzo, Termini, Piazza Barberini, Largo di Torre Argentina, Corso del Rinascimento, Piazza del Risorgimento, Cipro–Vatican Museums	5.15am-midnight	up to 6 per hr
Bus 660	Largo Colli Albani to Via Appia Antica	7am-8.45pm	2 per hr
Bus 714	Termini, Piazza Santa Maria Maggiore, Piazza San Giovanni in Laterano, Viale delle Terme di Caracalla, EUR	5.30am-midnight	up to 7 per hr
Bus 910	Termini, Piazza della Repubblica, Villa Borghese, Auditorium Parco della Musica, Piazza Mancini	5.30am-midnight	up to 6 per hr

➡ Buses run from about 5.30am until midnight, with limited services throughout the night.

➡ Rome's night bus service comprises more than 25 lines, many of which pass Termini and/or Piazza Venezia. Buses are marked with an 'n' before the number and bus stops have a blue owl symbol. Departures are usually every 15 to 30 minutes between about 1am and 5am, but can be much slower.

The most useful routes:

n1 Follows metro line A route.

n2 Follows metro line B route.

n7 Piazzale Clodio, Piazza Cavour, Via Zanardelli, Corso del Rinascimento, Corso Vittorio Emanuele II, Largo di Torre Argentina, Piazza Venezia, Via Nazionale and Stazione Termini.

Car & Motorcycle

Driving around Rome is not recommended. Riding a scooter or motorbike is faster and makes parking easier, but Rome is no place for learners, so if you're not experienced, give it a miss. Hiring a car for a day trip out of town is worth considering.

Most of Rome's historic centre is closed to unauthorised traffic from 6.30am to 6pm Monday to Friday, from 2pm to 6pm (10am to 7pm in some places) Saturday, and from 11pm to 3am Friday and Saturday. Evening restrictions also apply in Trastevere, San Lorenzo, Monti, and Testaccio, typically from 9.30pm or 11pm to 3am on Fridays and Saturdays.

All streets accessing the 'Limited Traffic Zone' (ZTL) are monitored by electronic-access detection devices. If you're staying in this zone, contact your hotel. For further information, check www.agenziamobilita.roma.it.

Driving Licence & Road Rules

All EU driving licences are recognised in Italy. Holders of non-EU licences should get an International Driving Permit (IDP) to accompany their national licence. Apply to your national motoring association.

A licence is required to ride a scooter – a car licence will do for bikes up to 125cc; for anything over 125cc you'll need a motorcycle licence.

Other rules:

➡ Drive on the right, overtake on the left.

➡ It's obligatory to wear seat belts, to drive with your headlights on outside built-up areas, and to carry a warning triangle and fluorescent waistcoat in case of breakdown.

➡ Wearing a helmet is compulsory on all two-wheeled vehicles.

➡ The blood alcohol limit is 0.05%; for drivers under 21 and those who have had their licence for less than three years it's zero.

Unless otherwise indicated, speed limits are as follows:

➡ 130km/h on autostradas

➡ 110km/h on all main, non-urban roads

➡ 90km/h on secondary, non-urban roads

➡ 50km/h in built-up areas

A good source of information is the **Automobile Club d'Italia** (ACI; www.aci.it), Italy's national motoring organisation.

Hire

To hire a car you'll require a driving licence (plus IDP if necessary) and credit card. Age restrictions vary but generally you'll need to be 21 or over. Car hire is available at both Rome's airports and Stazione Termini.

Avis (☏199 100 133; www.avisautonoleggio.it)

Europcar (☏199 30 70 30; www.europcar.it)

Hertz (☏02 6943 0019; www.hertz.it)

Maggiore National (☏199 151 120; www.maggiore.it)

Reckon on at least €60 per day for a small car. Note also that most hire cars have manual transmission.

To hire a scooter, prices range from about €30 to €120 depending on the size of the vehicle.

Reliable operators:

Bici & Baci (☏06 482 84 43; www.bicibaci.com; Via del Viminale 5; ⏱8am-7pm)

Eco Move Rent (☏06 4470 4518; www.ecomoverent.com; Via Varese 48-50; ⏱8.30am-7.30pm)

Treno e Scooter (☏06 4890 5823; www.trenoescooter.com; Piazza dei Cinquecento; ⏱9am-2pm & 4-7pm)

On Road (☏06 481 56 69; www.scooterhire.it; Via Cavour 80; ⏱9am-7pm)

Parking

Blue lines denote pay-and-display parking – get tickets from meters (coins only) and *tabacchi*.

Expect to pay €1.20 per hour between 8am and 8pm (11pm in some places). After 8pm (or 11pm) parking is free until 8am the next morning.

Traffic wardens are vigilant and fines are not uncommon. If your car gets towed away, call ☏06 6769 2303.

There's a comprehensive list of car parks on www.060608.it – click on the transport tab and car parks.

Useful car parks:

Piazzale dei Partigiani (per hr €0.77; ⏱7am-11pm)

Stazione Termini (Piazza dei Cinquecento; per hr/day €2.20/18; ⏱6am-1am)

Villa Borghese (Viale del Galoppatoio 33; per hr/day €2.20/18; ⏱24hr)

Bicycle

The centre of Rome doesn't lend itself to cycling: there are steep hills, treacherous cobbled roads and the traffic is terrible. If you want to

TICKETS, PLEASE

Public-transport tickets are valid on all of Rome's bus, tram and metro lines, except for routes to Fiumicino airport. They come in various forms:

➡ **BIT** (*biglietto integrato a tempo;* valid for 100 minutes and one metro ride) €1.50

➡ **Roma 24h** (valid for 24 hours) €7

➡ **Roma 48h** (valid for 48 hours) €12.50

➡ **Roma 72h** (valid for 72 hours) €18

➡ **CIS** (*carta integrata settimanale;* a weekly ticket) €24

➡ **Abbonamento mensile** (a monthly pass) single-user pass €35; pass that can be used by anyone €53

Buy tickets at *tabacchi,* newsstands and from vending machines at main bus stops and metro stations. They must be purchased before you start your journey and validated in the machines on buses, at the entrance gates to the metro, or at train stations. Ticketless riders risk an on-the-spot €50 fine. Children under 10 years travel free.

The Roma Pass (two/three days €28/36) comes with a two-/three-day travel pass valid within the city boundaries.

Travelling Out of Town

For destinations in the surrounding Lazio region, **Cotral** (☑800 174471; www.cotralspa. it) buses depart from numerous points throughout the city. The company is linked with Rome's public transport system, which means that you can buy tickets that cover city buses, trams, metro, and train lines, as well as regional buses and trains.

There are a range of tickets but your best bet is a daily BIRG (*biglietto integrato regionale giornaliero*) ticket, which allows unlimited travel on all city and regional transport. It's priced according to zones; tickets range from €3.30 to €14. Get tickets from *tabacchi* and authorised ATAC sellers.

---

pedal around town, pick up *Andiamo in Bici a Roma* (€7), a useful map that details Rome's main cycle paths.

➡ Bikes can be transported on certain specified bus and tram routes, and on the metro at weekends and on weekdays from 5.30am to 7am, from 10am to noon, and from 8pm until the end of service.

➡ Bikes can be carried on the Lido di Ostia train on Saturday and Sunday and on weekdays from the beginning of service to 10am and from 8pm until the end of service. You have to buy a separate ticket for the bike.

➡ See www.atac.roma.it (Bike Friendly) for more details.

➡ On regional trains marked with a bike icon on the timetable, you can carry a bike if you pay a €3.50 supplement.

Hire

Reckon on €3 to €6 per hour, €11 to €25 per day.

Top Bike Rental & Tours (☑06 488 28 93; www.topbikerental.com; Via Labicana 49; ☺10am-7pm)

Appia Antica Regional Park Information Point (☑06 513 53 16; www.parcoappiaantica. it; Via Appia Antica 58-60; per hr/day €3/15)

Eco Move Rent (☑06 4470 4518; www.ecomoverent.com; Via Varese 48-50; ☺8.30am-7.30pm)

Villa Borghese (Largo Pablo Picasso)

Taxi

➡ Official licensed taxis are white with an ID number and 'Roma Capitale' on the sides.

➡ Always go with the metered fare, never an arranged price (the set fares to and from the airports are exceptions).

➡ In town (within the ring road) flag fall is €3 between 6am

and 10pm on weekdays, €4.50 on Sundays and holidays, and €6.50 between 10pm and 6am. Then it's €1.10 per kilometre. Official rates are posted in taxis and on www.agenziamobilita. roma.it.

➡ You can hail a taxi, but it's often easier to wait at a rank or phone for one. There are taxi ranks at the airports, Stazione Termini, Piazza della Repubblica, Piazza Barberini, Piazza di Spagna, the Pantheon, the Colosseum, Largo di Torre Argentina, Piazza Belli, Piazza Pio XII, and Piazza del Risorgimento.

➡ You can book a taxi by phoning the Comune di Roma's automated taxi line on ☑06 06 09 or calling a taxi company direct.

➡ The website www.060608. it has a list of taxi companies – click on the transport tab, then 'getting around' and 'by taxi'.

➡ Note that when you call for a cab, the meter is switched on straight away and you pay for the cost of the journey from wherever the driver receives the call.

La Capitale (⌂06 49 94)
Pronto Taxi (⌂06 66 45)
Radio 3570 (⌂06 35 70; www.3570.it)
Samarcanda (⌂06 55 51; www.samarcanda.it)
Tevere (⌂06 41 57)

Train

Apart from connections to Fiumicino airport, you'll probably only need the overground rail network if you head out of town.

➡ Train information is available from the Customer Service area on the main concourse. Alternatively, check www.trenitalia.com or phone ⌂89 20 21.

➡ Buy tickets on the main station concourse, from automated ticket machines, or from an authorised travel agency – look for an FS or *biglietti treni* sign in the window.

➡ Rome's second train station is **Stazione Tiburtina**, four stops from Termini on metro line B. Of the capital's eight other train stations, the most important are **Stazione Roma-Ostiense** and **Stazione Trastevere**.

TOURS

Walking

A Friend in Rome (⌂340 501 92 01; www.afriendinrome. it) Silvia Prosperi organises private tailor-made tours (on foot, bike or scooter) to suit your interests. She covers the Vatican, main historic centre and areas outside the capital. Rates are €50 per hour, with a minimum of three hours for most tours. She also arranges kid-friendly tours, cooking classes, vintage car tours and more.

Roman Guy (http://theromanguy.com) A professional set-up that organises a wide range of group and private tours. Packages, led by English-speaking experts, include early-bird visits to the Vatican Museums (US$84), foodie tours of Trastevere and the Jewish Ghetto (US$84), and a bar hop through the historic centre's cocktail bars.

Dark Rome (⌂06 8336 0561; www.darkrome.com) Runs a range of themed tours, costing from €25 to €150, including skip-the-line visits to the Colosseum and Vatican Museums, and semiprivate visits to the Sistine Chapel. Other popular choices include a Crypts and Catacombs tour, which takes in Rome's buried treasures, and a day trip to Pompeii.

Through Eternity Cultural Association (⌂06 700 93 36; www.througheternity.com) A reliable operator offering private and group tours led by English-speaking experts. Popular packages include a twilight tour of Rome's piazzas and fountains (€39, 2½ hours), a skip-the-line visit to the Vatican Museums by day/night (€56/66, 3½ hours), and a foodie tour of Testaccio (€80, four hours).

Roma Cristiana (⌂06 69 89 61; www.operaromanapellegrinaggi.org) Runs tours, including guided visits to the Vatican Museums (adult/reduced €35/25) and two-hour tours of St Peter's Basilica (€14).

Arcult (⌂339 650 31 72; www.arcult.it) Run by architects, Arcult offers excellent customisable group tours focusing on Rome's contemporary architecture. Prices depend on the itinerary.

Bus

Open Bus Cristiana (www.operaromanapellegrinaggi. org; single tours €15, 24/48hr ticket €20/48; ☉9am-6pm)

The Vatican-sponsored Opera Romana Pellegrinaggi runs a hop-on, hop-off bus departing from Via della Conciliazione and Termini. Stops are situated near to main sights including St Peter's Basilica, Piazza Navona, the Trevi Fountain and the Colosseum. Tickets are available on board or at the meeting point just off St Peter's Sq.

Bike & Scooter

Top Bike Rental & Tours (⌂06 488 28 93; www.topbikerental.com; Via Labicana 49; ☉10am-7pm) Offers a series of bike tours throughout the city, including a four-hour 16km exploration of the city centre (€45) and an all-day 30km ride through Via Appia Antica and environs (€79). Out-of-town tours take in Castel Gandolfo, Civita di Bagnoregio and Orvieto.

Bici & Baci (⌂06 482 84 43; www.bicibaci.com; Via del Viminale 5; ☉8am-7pm) Bici & Baci runs daily bike tours of central Rome, taking in the historical centre, Campidoglio and the Colosseum, as well as tours on vintage Vespas and in classic Fiat 500 cars. Reckon on €49 for the bike tour, €145 for the Vespa ride and €290 for the four-hour guided drive.

Boat

Rome Boat Experience (⌂06 8956 7745; www.romeboatexperience.com; adult/reduced €18/12) From April to October runs hop-on, hop-off cruises along the Tiber. From May to October there are also dinner cruises (€62, two hours) every Friday and Saturday, and daily wine-bar cruise (€25, 1½ hours) from Monday to Thursday. Embarkation points are at Molo Sant'Angelo and Isola Tiberina.

Directory A–Z

Customs Regulations

Within the European Union you are entitled to tax-free prices on fragrances, cosmetics and skincare; photographic and electrical goods; fashion and accessories; and gifts, jewellery and souvenirs where they are available and if there are no longer any allowance restrictions on these tax free items.

If you're arriving from a non-EU country you can import, duty free, 200 cigarettes, 1L of spirits (or 2L fortified wine), 4L wine, 60ml perfume, 16L beer, and goods, including electronic devices, up to a value of €300/430 (travelling by land/sea); anything over this value must be declared on arrival and the duty paid.

On leaving the EU, non-EU residents can reclaim value-added tax (VAT) on expensive purchases.

Emergency

Ambulance	✆118
Fire	✆115
Police	✆112, 113

Electricity

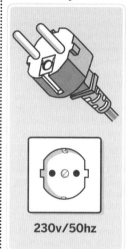

230v/50hz

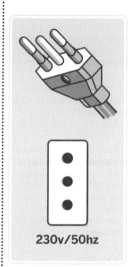

230v/50hz

Gay & Lesbian Travellers

Hardly San Fran on the Med, Rome nevertheless has a thriving, if low-key, gay scene. Close to the Colosseum, San Giovanni in Laterano has several bars dotted along it, including **Coming Out** (Map p314; www.comingout.it; Via di San Giovanni in Laterano 8; ⊗7am-2am; ᄆVia Labicana) and **My Bar** (Map p314; Via di San Giovanni in Laterano 12; ⊗9am-2am; ᄆVia Labicana). There is also a popular gay beach, Settimo Cielo, outside Rome

at Capocotta, accessible via bus 61 from Ostia Lido or bus 70 from EUR.

Homosexuality is legal (over the age of 16) and even widely accepted, but Italy is notably conservative in its attitudes, largely keeping in line with those of the Vatican. However, in 2015, Rome approved the establishment of a civil union register, with the support of Mayor Ignazio Marino; gay marriages conducted abroad may also be transcribed into the register.

The main gay cultural and political organisation is the **Circolo Mario Mieli di Cultura Omosessuale**

(Map p326; 📞800 110611; www.
mariomieli.org; Via Efeso 2a),
which organises debates,
cultural events and social
functions, including Gay
Pride.

The national organisation
for lesbians is the **Coordinamento Lesbiche Italiano**
(Map p316; www.clrbp.it; Via
San Francesco di Sales 1b),
which holds regular conferences and literary evenings.
There is also a women-only
hostel, **La Foresteria Orsa
Maggiore** (p221) located in
Trastevere.

Arcigay Roma (📞06
6450 1102; www.arcigayroma.
it; Via Nicola Zabaglia 14) is the
Roman branch of the na-
tional Arcigay organisation.
Offers counselling, phone
lines and information.

Internet Access

There are plenty of internet cafes to choose from,
particularly clustered around
Termini station. Most hotels
have wi-fi these days, though
with signals of varying
quality. There will usually be
at least one fixed computer
for guest use.

There are lots of wi-fi hotspots, run by **Provincia di
Roma** (www.provincia.roma.it)
and **Roma Wireless** (www.
romawireless.com); to use
these you will need to register online using a credit card
or an Italian mobile number.
Once you've registered,
you'll receive a call to check
the line, and once you've
answered (you don't need to
speak), you'll be able to log
in and use a password.

An easier option is to head
to a cafe or bar offering free
wi-fi. Places offering wi-fi are
indicated by the wi-fi icon
(📶) in this guide.

Legal Matters

The most likely reason for
a brush with the law is to
report a theft. If you do have
something stolen and you
want to claim it on insurance,
you must make a statement
to the police as insurance
companies won't pay up
without official proof of a
crime.

The Italian police is di-
vided into three main bodies:
the *polizia*, who wear navy-
blue jackets; the *carabinieri*,
in a black uniform with a red
stripe; and the grey-clad
guardia di finanza (fiscal
police), responsible for fighting tax evasion and drug
smuggling. If you run into
trouble, you're most likely
to end up dealing with the
polizia or *carabinieri*.

If you're caught with what
the police deem to be a
dealable quantity of hard or
soft drugs, you risk a prison
sentence of between six and
20 years. The offence of
possession for personal use
is punishable by administra-
tive sanctions.

Medical Services

Italy has a public health
system that is legally bound
to provide emergency care
to everyone. EU nationals
are entitled to reduced-cost,
sometimes free, medical
care with a European Health
Insurance Card (EHIC), available from your home health
authority; non-EU citizens
should take out medical
insurance.

For emergency treatment,
you can go to the *pronto
soccorso* (casualty) section
of an *ospedale* (public hospital). For less serious ailments
call the **Guardia Medica**
(📞06 884 01 13; Via Mantova
44; ⏰24hr).

A more convenient
course, if you have insurance
and can afford to pay up
front, would be to call a private doctor for a home visit.
Try the **International Medical Centre** (📞06 488 23 71;
Via Firenze 47; GP call-out &
treatment fee €140, 8pm-9am
& weekends €200; ⏰24hr).

If you need an ambulance,
call 📞118.

Pharmacies

Marked by a green cross,
farmacie (pharmacies) open
from 8.30am to 1pm and
4pm to 7.30pm Monday
to Friday and on Saturday
mornings. Outside these
hours they open on a rota-
tional basis, and all are legally required to post a list of
places open in the vicinity.

If you think you'll need a
prescription while in Rome,
make sure you know the
drug's generic name rather
than the brand name. Regular
medications available over
the counter – such as antihistamines or paracetamol –
tend to be expensive in Italy.

Money

Italy's currency is the
euro. Euro notes come in
denominations of €500,
€200, €100, €50, €20, €10
and €5. Euro coins are in
denominations of €2 and €1,
and 50, 20, 10, five, two and
one cents.

For the latest exchange
rates, check out www.xe.com.

ATMs

ATMs (known in Italy as
bancomat) are widely available in Rome and most will
accept cards tied into the
Visa, MasterCard, Cirrus and
Maestro systems. The daily
limit for cash withdrawal is
€250. Let your bank know
when you are going abroad,
in case they block your
card when payments from
unusual locations appear. If
you are registered for online
banking, you may be able to
do this online.

Remember that every
time you withdraw cash,
your home bank charges you
a foreign exchange fee (usually around 1% to 3%) as well
as a transaction charge of
around 1%. Check with your
bank before you go to find
out their specific charges.

Changing Money

You can change your money
in banks, at post offices or at

a *cambio* (exchange office). There are exchange booths at Stazione Termini and at Fiumicino and Ciampino airports. In the centre, there are numerous bureaux de change, including **American Express** (☑06 6 76 41; Piazza di Spagna 38; ☺9am-5.30pm Mon-Fri, 9am-12.30pm Sat)

Always make sure you have your passport or some form of photo ID when exchanging money.

Credit Cards

Credit cards are widely accepted but it's still a good idea to carry a cash back-up. Virtually all midrange and top-end hotels accept credit cards, as do most restaurants and large shops. You can also use them to obtain cash advances at some banks. Some of the cheaper *pensioni* (guesthouses), trattorias and pizzerias accept nothing but cash.

Major cards such as Visa, MasterCard, Eurocard, Cirrus and Eurocheques are widely accepted. Amex is also recognised, although it's less common than Visa or MasterCard.

Note that using your credit card in ATMs can be costly. On every transaction there's a fee, which can reach US$10 with some credit-card issuers, as well as interest per withdrawal. Check with your issuer before leaving home.

If your card is lost, stolen or swallowed by an ATM, telephone to have an immediate stop put on its use.

The Amex office can issue customers with new cards, usually within 24 hours and sometimes immediately, if they have been lost or stolen.

Opening Hours

Banks 8.30am to 1.30pm and 2.45pm to 4.30pm weekdays

Bars & cafes 7.30am to 8pm, sometimes until 1am or 2am

Shops 9am or 10am to 7.30 or 8pm Monday to Saturday, some 11am to 7pm Sunday; smaller shops closed 1pm-3.30pm

Clubs 10pm to 4am

Restaurants noon to 3pm and 7.30pm to 11pm (later in summer)

Post

Italy's postal system, **Poste Italiane** (☑80 31 60; www. poste.it), is reasonably reliable, though parcels do occasionally go missing.

Stamps *(francobolli)* are available at post offices and authorised tobacconists (look for the official *tabacchi* sign: a big 'T', usually white on black).

Opening hours vary but are typically 8.30am to 6pm Monday to Friday and 8.30am to 1pm on Saturday. All post offices close two hours earlier than normal on the last business day of each month.

Main Post Office (Map p308;☑06 6973 7205; Piazza di San Silvestro 19; ☺8.20am-7.05pm Mon-Fri, 8.20am-12.35pm Sat)

Vatican Post Office (Map p312;☑06 6989 0400; St Peter's Sq; ☺8.30am-6.45pm Mon-Fri, 8.30am-2pm Sat) Letters can be posted in blue Vatican post boxes only if they carry Vatican stamps.

Rates

Letters up to 20g cost €0.95 to Zone 1 (Europe and the Mediterranean Basin), €2.30 to Zone 2 (other countries in Africa, Asia and the Americas) and €3 to Zone 3 (Australia and New Zealand). For

DISCOUNT CARDS

DISCOUNT CARD	PRICE ADULT/ REDUCED	VALIDITY	FEATURES
Archaeologia Card	€25/15	7 days	Entrance to the Colosseum, Palatino, Terme di Caracalla, Museo Nazionale Romano (Palazzo Altemps, Palazzo Massimo alle Terme, Terme di Diocleziano, Crypta Balbi), Mausoleo di Cecilia Metella and Villa dei Quintili.
OMNIA Vatican & Rome	€98/65	3 days	Fast-track entry to the Vatican Museums; St. Peter's Basilica/Vatican Gardens, plus a minibus tour; the Basilica di San Giovanni, Colosseum, Roman Forum and Palatino with audio-guides; and the Mamertine Prison. Free travel on the Roma Cristiana Open Bus; one other site, and reductions for all offered in the Roma Pass; unlimited public transport in Rome.
Roma Pass	€36	3 days	Includes free admission to two museums or sites, plus reduced entry to extra sites, unlimited public transport within Rome, and reduced entry to other exhibitions and events. The 48-hours Roma Pass (€28) is a more limited version.

Note that EU citizens aged between 18 and 25 generally qualify for a discount at most galleries and museums, while those under 18 and over 65 often get in free. In both cases you'll need proof of your age, ideally a passport or ID card.

more important items, use registered mail *(raccomandata)*, which costs €5.30 to Zone 1, €6.20 to Zone 2 and €6.70 to Zone 3.

Public Holidays

Most Romans take their annual holiday in August. This means that many businesses and shops close for at least part of the month, particularly around Ferragosto (Feast of the Assumption) on 15 August.

Public holidays include the following:

Capodanno (New Year's Day) 1 January

Epifania (Epiphany) 6 January

Pasquetta (Easter Monday) March/April

Giorno della Liberazione (Liberation Day) 25 April

Festa del Lavoro (Labour Day) 1 May

Festa della Repubblica (Republic Day) 2 June

Festa dei Santi Pietro e Paolo (Feast of St Peter & St Paul) 29 June

Ferragosto (Feast of the Assumption) 15 August

Festa di Ognisanti (All Saints' Day) 1 November

Festa dell'Immacolata Concezione (Feast of the Immaculate Conception) 8 December

Natale (Christmas Day) 25 December

Festa di Santo Stefano (Boxing Day) 26 December

Safe Travel

Rome is not a dangerous city, but petty crime is a problem. Road safety is also an issue. The highway code is obeyed with discretion, so don't take it for granted that cars and scooters will stop at pedestrian crossings, or even at red lights.

PRACTICALITIES

Media

Vatican Radio (www.radiovaticana.org; 93.3 FM and 105 FM in Rome) In Italian, English and other languages.

RAI-1, RAI-2 and RAI-3 (www.rai.it) National broadcaster, running state TV and radio.

Radio Città Futura (www.radiocittafutura.it) Great for alternative and world music.

Main commercial stations (mostly run by Silvio Berlusconi's Mediaset company) Canale 5 (www.mediaset.it/canale5), Italia 1 (www.mediaset.it/italia1), Rete 4 (www.mediaset.it/rete4) and La 7 (www.la7.it).

Smoking

Smoking is banned in enclosed public spaces, which includes restaurants, bars, shops and public transport. It's also been recently banned in Villa Borghese and all other public parks.

Weights & Measures

Italy uses the metric system.

Taxes & Refunds

A value-added tax of 20%, known as IVA (Imposta di Valore Aggiunto), is slapped on just about everything in Italy. If you are a non-EU resident and you spend more than €175 on a purchase, you can claim a refund when you leave the EU. The refund only applies to purchases from affiliated retail outlets that display a 'Tax Free' sign. When you make your purchase, ask for a tax-refund voucher, to be filled in with the date of your purchase and its value. When you leave the EU, get this voucher stamped at customs and take it to the nearest tax-refund counter where you'll get an immediate refund, either in cash or charged to your credit card.

Telephone
Domestic Calls

Rome's area code is ☎06. Area codes are an integral part of all Italian phone numbers and must be dialled even when calling locally. Mobile-phone numbers are nine or 10 digits long and begin with a three-digit prefix starting with a ☎3. Toll-free numbers are known as *numeri verdi* and usually start with ☎800. Some six-digit national-rate numbers are also in use.

International Calls

To call abroad from Italy, dial ☎00, then the country and area codes, followed by the telephone number.

Try to avoid making international calls from a hotel, as rates are high. It's cheaper to call from a private call centre or from a payphone with an international calling card. These are available at newsstands and tobacconists, and are often good value. Another alternative is to use a direct-dialling service such as AT&T's USA Direct (access number ☎800 172 444) or Telstra's Australia Direct (access number ☎800 172 610), which allows you to make a reverse-charge call at home-country rates. You can also Skype from most internet cafes.

To make a reverse-charge (collect) international call from a public telephone, dial ☎170. All phone operators speak English.

STOP, THIEF!

The greatest risk visitors face in Rome is from pickpockets and thieves. There's no reason for paranoia, but you need to be aware that the problem exists and protect your valuables with this in mind.

Pickpockets go where the tourists go, so watch out around the most touristed and crowded areas, such as the Colosseum, Piazza di Spagna, St Peter's Sq and Stazione Termini. Note that thieves prey on disoriented travellers at the bus stops around Termini, fresh in from airports. Crowded public transport is another hotspot – the 64 Vatican bus is notorious. If travelling on the metro, try to use the end carriages, which are usually less busy.

A money belt with your essentials (passport, cash, credit cards) is a good idea. However, to avoid delving into it in public, carry a wallet with a day's cash. Don't flaunt watches, cameras and other expensive goods. If you're carrying a bag or camera, wear the strap across your body and away from the road – moped thieves can swipe a bag and be gone in seconds. Be careful when you sit down at a streetside table – never drape your bag over an empty chair by the road or put it where you can't see it.

A common method is for one thief to distract you while their assistant makes away with your purse. Beware of gangs of kids or others demanding attention. If you notice that you've been targeted, either take evasive action or shout 'va via!' ('go away!') in a loud, angry voice. Remember also that some of the best pickpockets are well dressed.

In case of theft or loss, always report the incident to the police within 24 hours and ask for a statement.

Mobile Phones

Italian mobile phones operate on the GSM 900/1800 network, which is compatible with the rest of Europe and Australia but not always with the North American GSM or CDMA systems – check with your service provider.

If you have a GSM dual-, tri- or quad-band phone that you can unlock (again, check with your service provider), it can cost as little as €10 to activate a prepaid (*prepagato*) SIM card in Italy. **TIM** (Telecom Italia Mobile; www.tim.it), **Wind** (www.wind.it) and **Vodafone** (www.vodafone.it) all offer SIM cards and have retail outlets across town. Note that by Italian law all SIM cards must be registered, so make sure you have a passport or ID card with you when you buy one.

Public Phones

You can still find public payphones around Rome. Most work and most take telephone cards (*schede telefoniche*), although you'll still find some that accept coins or credit cards. You can buy phonecards (€5, €10 or €20) at post offices, tobacconists and newsstands.

Time

Italy is in a single time zone, one hour ahead of GMT. Daylight-saving time, when clocks move forward one hour, starts on the last Sunday in March. Clocks are put back an hour on the last Sunday in October.

Italy operates on a 24-hour clock, so 6pm is written as 18:00.

Toilets

Public toilets are not widespread and those that do exist are often closed; some make a small charge. The best thing to do is to nip into a cafe or bar, all of which are required by law to have a toilet.

Tourist Information

Phone Resources

Comune Call Centre (06 06 06; 24hr) Very useful for practical questions such as:

Where's the nearest hospital? Where can I park? Staff speak English, Italian and Romanian.

Tourist Information Line (06 06 08; 9am-9pm) A free multilingual tourist line providing info on culture, shows, hotels, transport etc.

Tourist Offices

Centro Servizi Pellegrini e Turisti (Map p312; 06 6988 1662; St Peter's Sq; 8.30am-6pm Mon-Sat) The Vatican's official tourist office.

Rome Tourist Board (APT; 06 06 08; www.turismoroma.it;)

The Comune di Roma runs tourist information points throughout the city, including the following:

Ciampino Airport (International Arrivals, baggage claim area; 9am-6.30pm)

Fiumicino Airport (Terminal 3, International Arrivals; 8am-7.30pm)

Piazza Navona Tourist Information (Map p304; 9.30am-7.15pm) Actually on Piazza delle Cinque Lune.

Stazione Termini Tourist Information (Map p320; ⊙8am-7.45pm) In the hall adjacent to platform 24.

Fori Imperiali Tourist Information (Map p300; Via dei Fori Imperiali; ⊙9.30am-7pm)

Minghetti Tourist Information (Map p308; Via Marco Minghetti; ⊙9.30am-7.15pm) Between Via del Corso and the Trevi fountain.

Via Nazionale Tourist Information (Map p320; Via Nazionale; ⊙9.30am-7.15pm)

Travellers with Disabilities

Rome isn't an easy city for travellers with disabilities. Cobbled streets, blocked pavements and tiny lifts are difficult for wheelchair users, while the relentless traffic can be disorienting for partially sighted travellers or those with hearing difficulties.

Getting around on public transport is difficult. On metro line B all stations have wheelchair access except for Circo Massimo, Colosseo, Cavour and EUR Magliana, while on line A only Cipro–Musei Vaticani and Valle Aurelia have lifts. Bus 590 covers the same route as metro line A and is wheelchair accessible. Newer buses and trams have disabled access; it's indicated on bus stops which routes are wheelchair accessible.

If travelling by train, ring the **national helpline** (☑199 303060) to arrange assistance. At Stazione Termini, the **Sala Blu Assistenza Disabili** (Stazione Termini; ⊙7am-9pm), next to platform 1, can provide information on wheelchair-accessible trains and help with transport in the station. Contact the office 24 hours ahead if you know you're going to need assistance. There

are similar offices at Tiburtina and Ostiense stations.

Airline companies should be able to arrange assistance at airports if you notify them of your needs in advance. Alternatively, contact **ADR Assistance** (www.adr-assistance.it) for assistance at Fiumicino or Ciampino airports.

Some taxis are equipped to carry passengers in wheelchairs; ask for a taxi for a *sedia a rotelle* (wheelchair).

Lonely Planet has the Travel for All community on Google+, which is worth joining for information sharing and making connections.

Sage Traveling (www.sagetraveling.com) is a US-based agency started by wheelchair user John Sage who has visited over 70 countries in Europe; it offers advice and tailor-made tours to assist disabled travellers, specialising in Europe.

Visas

EU citizens do not need a visa to enter Italy. Nationals of some other countries, including Australia, Canada, Israel, Japan, New Zealand, Switzerland and the USA, do not need a visa for stays of up to 90 days.

Italy is one of the 15 signatories of the Schengen Convention, an agreement whereby participating countries abolished customs checks at common borders.

The standard tourist visa for non-European visitors to a Schengen country is valid for 90 days; for more information see www.schengenvisainfo.com/tourist-schengen-visa. You must apply for it in your country of residence and you cannot apply for more than two in any 12-month period. They are not renewable inside Italy.

Permesso di Soggiorno

A *permesso di soggiorno* (permit to stay, also referred to as a residence permit) is required by all non-EU nationals who stay in Italy longer than three months. In theory, you should apply for one within eight days of arriving in Italy. EU citizens do not require a *permesso di soggiorno*, but are required to register with the local registry office (*ufficio anagrafe*) if they stay for more than three months.

To get one, you'll need an application form; a valid passport, containing a stamp with your date of entry into Italy (ask for this, as it's not automatic); a photocopy of your passport with visa, if required; four passport-style photographs; a €16 official stamp; and a contribution of €80 to €200.

Although correct at the time of writing, the documentary requirements change periodically, so always check before you join the inevitable queue. Details are available on www.poliziadistato.it – click on the English tab and then follow the links.

The quickest way to apply is to go with the relevant documents to the **Ufficio Immigrazione** (http://questure.poliziadistato.it; Via Teofilo Patini; ⊙8.30-11.30am Mon-Fri & 3-5pm Tue & Thu) in the city's eastern suburbs.

Women Travellers

Sexual harrassment can be an issue in Rome; if you get groped, a loud '*che schifo!*' (how disgusting!) will draw attention to the incident. Otherwise women should take the usual precautions as they would in any large city, and, as in most places, avoid wandering around alone late at night, especially in the area around Termini.

Language

When in Rome, you'll find that locals appreciate you trying their language, no matter how muddled you may think you sound. Italian is not difficult to pronounce as the sounds used in spoken Italian can all be found in English.

Note that, in our pronunciation guides, ai is pronounced as in 'aisle', ay as in 'say', ow as in 'how', dz as the 'ds' in 'lids', and that r is a strong and rolled sound. Keep in mind too that Italian consonants can have a stronger, emphatic pronunciation – if the consonant is written as a double letter, it should be pronounced a little stronger. This difference in the pronunciation of single and double consonants can mean a difference in meaning, eg *sonno son*·no (sleep) versus *sono so*·no (I am). The Italian ch is is usually pronounced as a hard c, so, for example, 'chiesa' is 'key-esa'.

If you read our coloured pronunciation guides as if they were English, you'll be understood. The stressed syllables are indicated with italics.

BASICS

Italian has two words for 'you' – use the polite form *Lei* lay if you're talking to strangers, officials or people older than you. With people familiar to you or younger than you, you can use the informal form *tu* too.

In Italian, all nouns and adjectives are either masculine or feminine, and so are the articles *il/la* eel/la (the) and *un/una* oon/oo·na (a) that go with the nouns.

In this chapter the polite/informal and masculine/feminine options are included where necessary, separated with a slash and indicated with 'pol/inf' and 'm/f'.

WANT MORE?

For in-depth language information and handy phrases, check out Lonely Planet's *Italian phrasebook*. You'll find it at **shop. lonelyplanet.com**, or you can buy Lonely Planet's iPhone phrasebooks at the Apple App Store.

Hello.	*Buongiorno.*	bwon·*jor*·no
Goodbye.	*Arrivederci.*	a·ree·ve·*der*·chee
Yes.	*Sì.*	see
No.	*No.*	no
Excuse me.	*Mi scusi.* (pol)	mee *skoo*·zee
	Scusami. (inf)	*skoo*·za·mee
Sorry.	*Mi dispiace.*	mee dees·*pya*·che
Please.	*Per favore.*	per fa·*vo*·re
Thank you.	*Grazie.*	*gra*·tsye
You're welcome.	*Prego.*	*pre*·go

How are you?
Come sta/stai? (pol/inf)   *ko*·me sta/stai

Fine. And you?
Bene. E Lei/tu? (pol/inf)   *be*·ne e lay/too

What's your name?
Come si chiama? pol   *ko*·me see *kya*·ma
Come ti chiami? inf   *ko*·me tee *kya*·mee

My name is ...
Mi chiamo ...   mee *kya*·mo ...

Do you speak English?
Parla/Parli   *par*·la/*par*·lee
inglese? (pol/inf)   een·*gle*·ze

I don't understand.
Non capisco.   non ka·*pee*·sko

ACCOMMODATION

Do you have a ... room?	*Avete una camera ...?*	a·*ve*·te oo·na *ka*·me·ra ...
double	*doppia con letto matrimoniale*	*do*·pya kon *le*·to ma·tree·mo·*nya*·le
single	*singola*	*seen*·go·la
How much is it per ...?	*Quanto costa per ...?*	*kwan*·to *kos*·ta per ...
night	*una notte*	oo·na *no*·te
person	*persona*	per·*so*·na

Is breakfast included?
La colazione è la ko·la·*tsyo*·ne e
compresa? kom·*pre*·sa

air-con	*aria*	*a*·rya
	condizionata	kon·dee·tsyo·*na*·ta
bathroom	*bagno*	*ba*·nyo
campsite	*campeggio*	kam·*pe*·jo
guesthouse	*pensione*	pen·*syo*·ne
hotel	*albergo*	al·*ber*·go
youth hostel	*ostello della*	os·*te*·lo de·la
	gioventù	jo·ven·*too*
window	*finestra*	fee·*nes*·tra

DIRECTIONS

Where's ...?
Dov'è ...? do·*ve* ...

What's the address?
Qual'è l'indirizzo? kwa·*le* leen·dee·*ree*·tso

Could you please write it down?
Può scriverlo, pwo *skree*·ver·lo
per favore? per fa·*vo*·re

Can you show me (on the map)?
Può mostrarmi pwo mos·*trar*·mee
(sulla pianta)? (*soo*·la *pyan*·ta)

at the corner	*all'angolo*	a·*lan*·go·lo
at the traffic lights	*al semaforo*	al se·*ma*·fo·ro
behind	*dietro*	*dye*·tro
far	*lontano*	lon·*ta*·no
in front of	*davanti a*	da·*van*·tee a
near	*vicino*	vee·*chee*·no
next to	*accanto a*	a·*kan*·to a
opposite	*di fronte a*	dee *fron*·te a
straight ahead	*sempre*	*sem*·pre
	diritto	dee·*ree*·to
to the left	*a sinistra*	a see·*nee*·stra
to the right	*a destra*	a *de*·stra

EATING & DRINKING

What would you recommend?
Cosa mi consiglia? ko·za mee kon·*see*·lya

What's in that dish?
Quali ingredienti kwa·li een·gre·*dyen*·tee
ci sono in chee *so*·no een
questo piatto? *kwe*·sto *pya*·to

What's the local speciality?
Qual'è la specialità kwa·*le* la spe·cha·*lee*·ta
di questa regione? dee *kwe*·sta re·*jo*·ne

That was delicious!
Era squisito! e·ra skwee·*zee*·to

Cheers!
Salute! sa·*loo*·te

KEY PATTERNS

To get by in Italian, mix and match these simple patterns with words of your choice:

When's (the next flight)?
A che ora è a ke o·ra e
(il prossimo volo)? (eel pro·*see*·mo vo·lo)

Where's (the station)?
Dov'è (la stazione)? do·ve (la sta·*tsyo*·ne)

I'm looking for (a hotel).
Sto cercando sto cher·*kan*·do
(un albergo). (oon al·*ber*·go)

Do you have (a map)?
Ha (una pianta)? a (oo·na *pyan*·ta)

Is there (a toilet)?
C'è (un gabinetto)? che (oon ga·bee·*ne*·to)

I'd like (a coffee).
Vorrei (un caffè). vo·*ray* (oon ka·*fe*)

I'd like to (hire a car).
Vorrei (noleggiare vo·*ray* (no·le·*ja*·re
una macchina). oo·na ma·*kee*·na)

Can I (enter)?
Posso (entrare)? po·so (en·*tra*·re)

Could you please (help me)?
Può (aiutarmi), pwo (a·yoo·*tar*·mee)
per favore? per fa·*vo*·re

Do I have to (book a seat)?
Devo (prenotare *de*·vo (pre·no·*ta*·re
un posto)? oon po·sto)

Please bring the bill.
Mi porta il conto, mee *por*·ta eel *kon*·to
per favore? per fa·*vo*·re

I'd like to reserve a table for ...	*Vorrei prenotare un tavolo per ...*	vo·*ray* pre·no·*ta*·re oon *ta*·vo·lo per ...
(two) people	*(due) persone*	(*doo*·e) per·*so*·ne
(eight) o'clock	*le (otto)*	le (o·to)

I don't eat ...	*Non mangio ...*	non *man*·jo ...
eggs	*uova*	*wo*·va
fish	*pesce*	*pe*·she
nuts	*noci*	*no*·chee
(red) meat	*carne (rossa)*	*kar*·ne (*ro*·sa)

Key Words

bar	*locale*	lo·*ka*·le
bottle	*bottiglia*	bo·*tee*·lya
breakfast	*prima*	*pree*·ma
	colazione	ko·la·*tsyo*·ne

cafe	bar	bar
cold	freddo	fre·do
dinner	cena	che·na
drink list	lista delle bevande	lee·sta de·le be·van·de
fork	forchetta	for·ke·ta
glass	bicchiere	bee·kye·re
grocery store	alimentari	a·lee·men·ta·ree
hot	caldo	kal·do
knife	coltello	kol·te·lo
lunch	pranzo	pran·dzo
market	mercato	mer·ka·to
menu	menù	me·noo
plate	piatto	pya·to
restaurant	ristorante	ree·sto·ran·te
spicy	piccante	pee·kan·te
spoon	cucchiaio	koo·kya·yo
vegetarian (food)	vegetariano	ve·je·ta·rya·no
with	con	kon
without	senza	sen·tsa

Meat & Fish

beef	manzo	man·dzo
chicken	pollo	po·lo
clams	vongole	vong·o·lay
duck	anatra	a·na·tra
fish	pesce	pe·she
herring	aringa	a·reen·ga
lamb	agnello	a·nye·lo
lobster	aragosta	a·ra·gos·ta
meat	carne	kar·ne
mussels	cozze	ko·tse
oysters	ostriche	o·stree·ke
pork	maiale	ma·ya·le
prawn	gambero	gam·be·ro

Signs

Entrata/Ingresso	Entrance
Uscita	Exit
Aperto	Open
Chiuso	Closed
Informazioni	Information
Proibito/Vietato	Prohibited
Gabinetti/Servizi	Toilets
Uomini	Men
Donne	Women

salmon	salmone	sal·mo·ne
scallops	capasante	ka·pa·san·te
seafood	frutti di mare	froo·tee dee ma·re
shrimp	gambero	gam·be·ro
squid	calamari	ka·la·ma·ree
trout	trota	tro·ta
tuna	tonno	to·no
turkey	tacchino	ta·kee·no
veal	vitello	vee·te·lo

Fruit & Vegetables

apple	mela	me·la
beans	fagioli	fa·jo·lee
cabbage	cavolo	ka·vo·lo
capsicum	peperone	pe·pe·ro·ne
carrot	carota	ka·ro·ta
cauliflower	cavolfiore	ka·vol·fyo·re
cucumber	cetriolo	che·tree·o·lo
fruit	frutta	froo·ta
grapes	uva	oo·va
lemon	limone	lee·mo·ne
lentils	lenticchie	len·tee·kye
mushroom	funghi	foon·gee
nuts	noci	no·chee
onions	cipolle	chee·po·le
orange	arancia	a·ran·cha
peach	pesca	pe·ska
peas	piselli	pee·ze·lee
pineapple	ananas	a·na·nas
plum	prugna	proo·nya
potatoes	patate	pa·ta·te
spinach	spinaci	spee·na·chee
tomatoes	pomodori	po·mo·do·ree
vegetables	verdura	ver·doo·ra

Other

bread	pane	pa·ne
butter	burro	boo·ro
cheese	formaggio	for·ma·jo
eggs	uova	wo·va
honey	miele	mye·le
ice	ghiaccio	gya·cho
jam	marmellata	mar·me·la·ta
noodles	pasta	pas·ta
oil	olio	o·lyo
pepper	pepe	pe·pe

rice	riso	ree·zo
salt	sale	sa·le
soup	minestra	mee·nes·tra
soy sauce	salsa di soia	sal·sa dee so·ya
sugar	zucchero	tsoo·ke·ro
vinegar	aceto	a·che·to

Drinks

beer	birra	bee·ra
coffee	caffè	ka·fe
(orange) juice	succo (d'arancia)	soo·ko (da·ran·cha)
milk	latte	la·te
red wine	vino rosso	vee·no ro·so
soft drink	bibita	bee·bee·ta
tea	tè	te
(mineral) water	acqua (minerale)	a·kwa (mee·ne·ra·le)
white wine	vino bianco	vee·no byan·ko

EMERGENCIES

Help!
Aiuto! a·yoo·to

Leave me alone!
Lasciami in pace! la·sha·mee een pa·che

I'm lost.
Mi sono perso/a. (m/f) mee so·no per·so/a

There's been an accident.
C'è stato un incidente. che sta·to oon een·chee·den·te

Call the police!
Chiami la polizia! kya·mee la po·lee·tsee·a

Call a doctor!
Chiami un medico! kya·mee oon me·dee·ko

Where are the toilets?
Dove sono i gabinetti? do·ve so·no ee ga·bee·ne·tee

I'm sick.
Mi sento male. mee sen·to ma·le

It hurts here.
Mi fa male qui. mee fa ma·le kwee

I'm allergic to ...
Sono allergico/a a ... (m/f) so·no a·ler·jee·ko/a a ...

Question Words		
How?	Come?	ko·me
What?	Che cosa?	ke ko·za
When?	Quando?	kwan·do
Where?	Dove?	do·ve
Who?	Chi?	kee
Why?	Perché?	per·ke

SHOPPING & SERVICES

I'd like to buy ...
Vorrei comprare ... vo·ray kom·pra·re ...

I'm just looking.
Sto solo guardando. sto so·lo gwar·dan·do

Can I look at it?
Posso dare un'occhiata? po·so da·re oo·no·kya·ta

How much is this?
Quanto costa questo? kwan·to kos·ta kwe·sto

It's too expensive.
È troppo caro/a. (m/f) e tro·po ka·ro/a

Can you lower the price?
Può farmi lo sconto? pwo far·mee lo skon·to

There's a mistake in the bill.
C'è un errore nel conto. che oo·ne·ro·re nel kon·to

ATM	Bancomat	ban·ko·mat
post office	ufficio postale	oo·fee·cho pos·ta·le
tourist office	ufficio del turismo	oo·fee·cho del too·reez·mo

TIME & DATES

What time is it?	Che ora è?	ke o·ra e
It's one o'clock.	È l'una.	e loo·na
It's (two) o'clock.	Sono le (due).	so·no le (doo·e)
Half past (one).	(L'una) e mezza.	(loo·na) e me·dza

in the morning	di mattina	dee ma·tee·na
in the afternoon	di pomeriggio	dee po·me·ree·jo
in the evening	di sera	dee se·ra

yesterday	ieri	ye·ree
today	oggi	o·jee
tomorrow	domani	do·ma·nee

Monday	lunedì	loo·ne·dee
Tuesday	martedì	mar·te·dee
Wednesday	mercoledì	mer·ko·le·dee
Thursday	giovedì	jo·ve·dee
Friday	venerdì	ve·ner·dee
Saturday	sabato	sa·ba·to
Sunday	domenica	do·me·nee·ka

January	gennaio	je·na·yo
February	febbraio	fe·bra·yo
March	marzo	mar·tso
April	aprile	a·pree·le
May	maggio	ma·jo

June	giugno	joo·nyo
July	luglio	loo·lyo
August	agosto	a·gos·to
September	settembre	se·tem·bre
October	ottobre	o·to·bre
November	novembre	no·vem·bre
December	dicembre	dee·chem·bre

NUMBERS

1	uno	oo·no
2	due	doo·e
3	tre	tre
4	quattro	kwa·tro
5	cinque	cheen·kwe
6	sei	say
7	sette	se·te
8	otto	o·to
9	nove	no·ve
10	dieci	dye·chee
20	venti	ven·tee
30	trenta	tren·ta
40	quaranta	kwa·ran·ta
50	cinquanta	cheen·kwan·ta
60	sessanta	se·san·ta
70	settanta	se·tan·ta
80	ottanta	o·tan·ta
90	novanta	no·van·ta
100	cento	chen·to
1000	mille	mee·lel

TRANSPORT

At what time does the ... leave/arrive?
A che ora | a ke o·ra
parte/arriva ...? | par·te/a·ree·va ...

boat	la nave	la na·ve
bus	l'autobus	low·to·boos
ferry	il traghetto	eel tra·ge·to
metro	la metro·politana	la me·tro·po·lee·ta·na
plane	l'aereo	la·e·re·o
train	il treno	eel tre·no

... ticket	un biglietto ...	oon bee·lye·to
one-way	di sola andata	dee so·la an·da·ta
return	di andata e ritorno	dee an·da·ta e ree·tor·no

bus stop	fermata dell'autobus	fer·ma·ta del ow·to·boos
platform	binario	bee·na·ryo
ticket office	biglietteria	bee·lye·te·ree·a
timetable	orario	o·ra·ryo
train station	stazione ferroviaria	sta·tsyo·ne fe·ro·vyar·ya

Does it stop at ...?
Si ferma a ...? | see fer·ma a ...

Please tell me when we get to ...
Mi dica per favore | mee dee·ka per fa·vo·re
quando arriviamo a ... | kwan·do a·ree·vya·mo a ...

I want to get off here.
Voglio scendere qui. | vo·lyo shen·de·re kwee

I'd like to hire a bicycle.
Vorrei noleggiare | vo·ray no·le·ja·re
una bicicletta. | oo·na bee·chee·kle·ta

I have a flat tyre.
Ho una gomma bucata. | o oo·na go·ma boo·ka·ta

I'd like to have my bicycle repaired.
Vorrei fare riparare la | vo·ray fa·re ree·pa·ra·re la
mia bicicletta. | mee·a bee·chee·kle·ta

GLOSSARY

abbazia – abbey
(pizza) al taglio – (pizza) by the slice
albergo – hotel
alimentari – grocery shop; delicatessen
anfiteatro – amphitheatre
aperitivo – pre-evening meal drink and snack
arco – arch
autostrada – motorway; highway

battistero – baptistry
biblioteca – library
biglietto – ticket
borgo – archaic name for a small town, village or town sector (often dating to Middle Ages)

camera – room
campo – field
cappella – chapel

Cappella Sistina – Sistine Chapel
carabinieri – police with military and civil duties
Carnevale – carnival period between Epiphany and Lent
casa – house
castello – castle
cattedrale – cathedral
catacomba – catacomb
centro sociale –social centre;

often a venue for concerts, club nights, cultural events

centro storico – historic centre

chiesa – church

chiostro – cloister; covered walkway, usually enclosed by columns, around a quadrangle

città – town; city

colonna – column

comune – equivalent to a municipality or county; a town or city council; historically, a self–governing town or city

corso – boulevard

duomo – cathedral

enoteca – wine bar

espresso – short black coffee

EUR (Esposizione Universale di Roma) –outlying district in south Rome known for its rationalist architecture

ferrovia – railway

festa – feast day; holiday

fontana – fountain

foro – forum

fiume – river

gelateria – ice-cream shop

giardino – garden

grattachecca – ice drink flavoured with fruit and syrup

grotta – cave

isola – island

lago – lake

largo – small square

locanda – inn; small hotel

mar, mare – sea

mausoleo – mausoleum; stately and magnificent tomb

mercato – market

museo – museum

necropoli – ancient name for cemetery or burial site

nord – north

osteria – casual tavern or eatery presided over by a host

palazzo – mansion; palace; large building of any type, including an apartment block

palio – contest

Papa – Pope

parco – park

passeggiata – traditional evening stroll

pasticceria – cake/pastry shop

pensione – guesthouse

piazza – square

piazzale – large open square

pietà – literally 'pity' or 'compassion'; sculpture, drawing or painting of the dead Christ supported by the Madonna

pinacoteca – art gallery

PIT (Punto Informativo Turistico) – Tourist Information Point

ponte – bridge

porta – gate; door

porto – port

prenotare – to book or reserve

reale – royal

ristorante – restaurant

rocca – fortress

sala – room; hall

salumeria – delicatessen

santuario – sanctuary; 1. the part of a church above the altar; 2. an especially holy place in a temple (antiquity)

scalinata – staircase

scavi – excavations

spiaggia – beach

stadio – stadium

stazione – station

stazione marittima – ferry terminal

strada – street; road

sud – south

superstrada – expressway; highway with divided lanes

tartufo – truffle

tavola calda – literally 'hot table'; pre-prepared meat, pasta and vegetable selection, often self-service

teatro – theatre

tempietto – small temple

tempio – temple

terme – thermal baths

tesoro – treasury

Tevere – Tiber

torre – tower

trattoria – simple restaurant

Trenitalia – Italian State Railways; also known as Ferrovie dello Stato (FS)

via – street; road

Via Appia Antica – Appian Way

viale – avenue

vico – alley; alleyway

villa – town house; country house; also the park surrounding the house

FOOD GLOSSARY

abbacchio al forno – lamb roasted with rosemary and garlic; usually accompanied by rosemary-roasted potatoes

agnello alla cacciatora – lamb 'hunter-style' with onion and fresh tomatoes

baccalà – salt cod, often served deepfried in the Roman–Jewish tradition

bresaola – wind-dried beef, a feature of Roman-Jewish cuisine; served as a replacement for *prosciutto* (ham)

bruschette – grilled bread rubbed with garlic, splashed with olive oil and sprinkled with salt, most commonly then topped by tomatoes.

bucatini all'amatriciana – thick spaghetti with tomato sauce, onions, pancetta, cheese and chilli; originated in Amatrice, a town east of Rome, as an adaptation of *spaghetti alla gricia*

cacio e pepe – pasta mixed with freshly grated *pecorino romano* (a sharp,salty, sheep's milk cheese), ground black pepper and a dash of olive oil

carciofi alla giudia – deepfried 'Jewish-style' artichokes; the heart is soft and succulent, the leaves taste like delicious crisps

carciofi alla romana – artichokes boiled with oil, garlic and mint

coda alla vaccinara – beef tail stewed with garlic, parsley, onion, carrots, celery and spices; a dish developed when abattoir workers received the cheapest cuts of meat

fiori di zucca – courgette flowers, usually stuffed with mozzarella and anchovies and fried

frutti di mare – seafood; usually served as a sauce with pasta, comprising tomatoes, clams, mussels, and perhaps prawns and calamari

gnocchi alla romana – semolina-based mini-dumplings baked with ragù or tomato sugo; traditionally served on Thursdays

involtini – thin slices of veal or beef,rolled up with sage or sometimes vegetables and mozzarella.

minestra di arzilla con pasta e broccoli – skate soup with pasta and broccoli; Roman-Jewish dish served only at the most traditional restaurants

pasta con lenticchie – popular local dish of pasta with lentils

pasta e ceci – pasta with chickpeas; warms the cockles in winter

pizza bianca – 'white pizza' unique to Rome; a plain pizza brushed with salt, olive oil and often rosemary; can split and fill to make a sandwich

pollo alla romana – chicken cooked in butter, marjoram, garlic, white wine and tomatoes or peppers

polpette al sugo – meatballs with traditional tomato sauce

porchetta – a hog roasted on a spit with herbs and an abundance of finocchio *selvatico* (wild fennel); the best comes from Ariccia, in the hills south of Rome

ragù– classic Italian meat sauce traditionally made by slowly stewing cuts of meat, or mince, in a rich tomato sugo

rigatoni alla pajata – thick ridged pasta tubes with the small intestine of a milk-fed calf or lamb; a Testaccio speciality

saltimbocca alla romana – the deliciously named 'leap in the mouth'; a veal cutlet jazzed up with sparing amounts of prosciutto and sage

spaghetti alla carbonara – sauce of egg, cheese and *guanciale* (cured pig's cheek); the egg is added raw, and stirred into the hot pasta to cook it

spaghetti alla gricia – pasta with pecorino cheese, black pepper and pancetta;

spaghetti con le vongole – spaghetti with clams and a dash of red chilli to pep things up; sometimes served with tomatoes,sometimes without

stracciatella – humble chicken broth given a lift by the addition of Parmesan and whisked egg

sugo – all-purpose tomato sauce served in many dishes; it's traditionally combined with *basilico* (basil)

supplì – rice balls, like large croquettes; if they contain mozzarella, they're called supplì a telefono because when you break one open, the cheese forms a string like a telephone wire between the two halves

trippa alla romana – tripe cooked with potatoes, tomato and mint and sprinkled with pecorino cheese; a typical Saturday-in-Rome dish

Behind the Scenes

SEND US YOUR FEEDBACK

We love to hear from travellers – your comments keep us on our toes and help make our books better. Our well-travelled team reads every word on what you loved or loathed about this book. Although we cannot reply individually to your submissions, we always guarantee that your feedback goes straight to the appropriate authors, in time for the next edition. Each person who sends us information is thanked in the next edition – the most useful submissions are rewarded with a selection of digital PDF chapters.

Visit **lonelyplanet.com/contact** to submit your updates and suggestions or to ask for help. Our award-winning website also features inspirational travel stories, news and discussions.

Note: We may edit, reproduce and incorporate your comments in Lonely Planet products such as guidebooks, websites and digital products, so let us know if you don't want your comments reproduced or your name acknowledged. For a copy of our privacy policy visit lonelyplanet.com/privacy.

OUR READERS

Many thanks to the travellers who used the last edition and wrote to us with helpful hints, useful advice and interesting anecdotes:

Ben Smith, Bettina Pickering, Donna Harshman, Elena Sartore, Fiona Whitfield, Gillian Rooney, John Woodhouse, Josefin Nilsson, Lee Warren, Leo Andrews, Lise Larsen, Marc Bilardie, Mardie Noble, Margaret Chappell, Michelle Slattery, Niko Waesche, Pedro Pacheco, Ricardo Blasco, Rocío Balboa, Viktoria Creteil, Yesika Arranz.

ACKNOWLEDGEMENTS

Illustration pp58–9 by Javier Zarracina

Cover photograph: Street scene in Trastevere district, MATTES Rene/Corbis

AUTHOR THANKS

Abigail Blasi

Molto grazie to Anna Tyler and Duncan Garwood. Thanks to Luca, Anna and Marcello. Gratitude to Barbara Lessona for all her kind assistance, and for their help with research thanks to Marco Messina at the Appia Antica and Paola Zaganelli.

Duncan Garwood

A big thank you to fellow author Abi Blasi for her suggestions and great work, and to Anna Tyler at LP for her unstinting support. For their tips and help with research *grazie* to Silvia Prosperi, Barbara Lessona, Paolo Mazza, and the team at the Roman Guy. As always, a big, heartfelt hug to Lidia and the boys, Ben and Nick.

THIS BOOK

This 9th edition of Lonely Planet's *Rome* guidebook was researched and written by Duncan Garwood and Abigail Blasi, who also wrote the previous edition together. This guidebook was produced by the following:

Destination Editor
Anna Tyler
Product Editors
Briohny Hooper,
Catherine Naghten
Senior Cartographer
Anthony Phelan
Book Designers
Virginia Moreno,
Wibowo Rusli
Assisting Editors
Andrea Dobbin,
Victoria Harrison
Cartographer
Julie Dodkins

Cover Researcher
Naomi Parker
Thanks to Shahara
Ahmed, Imogen Bannister,
Sasha Baskett, Ryan Evans,
Larissa Frost, Andi Jones,
Claire Murphy, Wayne Murphy, Rosie Nicholson, Karyn
Noble, Samantha Russell-
Tulip, Dianne Schallmeiner,
Angela Tinson, Lauren
Wellicome, Tony Wheeler,
Tracy Whitmey

See also separate subindexes for:

✗ **EATING P291**

● **DRINKING & NIGHTLIFE P293**

☆ **ENTERTAINMENT P293**

🔒 **SHOPPING P293**

▭ **SLEEPING P294**

Index

✖ EATING

Rome Maps

Sights
- Beach
- Bird Sanctuary
- Buddhist
- Castle/Palace
- Christian
- Confucian
- Hindu
- Islamic
- Jain
- Jewish
- Monument
- Museum/Gallery/Historic Building
- Ruin
- Shinto
- Sikh
- Taoist
- Winery/Vineyard
- Zoo/Wildlife Sanctuary
- Other Sight

Activities, Courses & Tours
- Bodysurfing
- Diving
- Canoeing/Kayaking
- Course/Tour
- Sento Hot Baths/Onsen
- Skiing
- Snorkelling
- Surfing
- Swimming/Pool
- Walking
- Windsurfing
- Other Activity

Sleeping
- Sleeping
- Camping

Eating
- Eating

Drinking & Nightlife
- Drinking & Nightlife
- Cafe

Entertainment
- Entertainment

Shopping
- Shopping

Information
- Bank
- Embassy/Consulate
- Hospital/Medical
- Internet
- Police
- Post Office
- Telephone
- Toilet
- Tourist Information
- Other Information

Geographic
- Beach
- Gate
- Hut/Shelter
- Lighthouse
- Lookout
- Mountain/Volcano
- Oasis
- Park
- Pass
- Picnic Area
- Waterfall

Population
- Capital (National)
- Capital (State/Province)
- City/Large Town
- Town/Village

Transport
- Airport
- Border crossing
- Bus
- Cable car/Funicular
- Cycling
- Ferry
- Metro station
- Monorail
- Parking
- Petrol station
- S-Bahn/Subway station
- Taxi
- T-bane/Tunnelbana station
- Train station/Railway
- Tram
- Tube station
- U-Bahn/Underground station
- Other Transport

Note: Not all symbols displayed above appear on the maps in this book

Routes
- Tollway
- Freeway
- Primary
- Secondary
- Tertiary
- Lane
- Unsealed road
- Road under construction
- Plaza/Mall
- Steps
- Tunnel
- Pedestrian overpass
- Walking Tour
- Walking Tour detour
- Path/Walking Trail

Boundaries
- International
- State/Province
- Disputed
- Regional/Suburb
- Marine Park
- Cliff
- Wall

Hydrography
- River, Creek
- Intermittent River
- Canal
- Water
- Dry/Salt/Intermittent Lake
- Reef

Areas
- Airport/Runway
- Beach/Desert
- Cemetery (Christian)
- Cemetery (Other)
- Glacier
- Mudflat
- Park/Forest
- Sight (Building)
- Sportsground
- Swamp/Mangrove

TRIESTE

FLAMINIO

PARIOLI

TRIONFALE

VILLA
BORGHESE

4

SALARIO

VATICAN CITY
(CITTÀ DEL
VATICANO)

PRATI

TRIDENTE

SALLUSTIANO

BORGO

CAMPO
MARZIO

2

TREVI

10

TIBURTINO

PONTE

COLONNA

PARIONE

REGOLA

PIGNA

MONTI

SAN LORENZO

3

GIANICOLO

9

ESQUILINO

TRASTEVERE

CAMPITELLI

1

SAN GIOVANNI

8

7

AVENTINO

SAN GIOVANNI

TUSCOLANO

CELIO

11

TESTACCIO

6

MONTEVERDE

GIANCOLENSE

Tiber River

OSTIENSE

APPIO-
LATINO

Marrana della Caffarella

SAN
PAOLO

GARBATELLA

0   2 km
N 0   1 mile

MAP INDEX

ANCIENT ROME Map on p300

ANCIENT ROME

ANCIENT ROME

Key on p299

See map p305

See map p309

See map p321

MONTI

Via Panisperna

Via Cimarra

Via degli Zingari

Piazza Madonna dei Monti

Via Leonina

Via del Boschetto

Via dei Serpenti

Via Baccina

Via di Sant'Agata dei Goti

Via dell'Garotano

Via Mazzarino

Via Baccina

Via della Madonna dei Monti

Largo Magnanapoli

Largo Angelicum

Largo C. Ricci

Via della Salara Vecchia

Via Nazionale

Via IV Novembre

Via Alessandrina

Imperial Forums

Via dei Fori Imperiali

Via di Tulliano

Via di San Pietro in Carcere

Via della Sant'Eufemia

Vicolo di San Bernardo

Via Cesare Battisti

Via dei Fornari

Piazza Venezia

Via del Plebiscito

Piazza di San Marco

Via degli Astalli

Via di San Marco

Piazza d'Ara Coeli

Via San Venazio

Via d'Aracoeli

Tor De' Specchi

Via Margana

Via Tribuna di Tor De' Specchi

Vic. Margana

Via della Villa Caffarelli

Campidoglio (Capitoline Hill)

Via di Monte Tarpeo

Via del Foro Romano

Clivus Capitolinus

Via del Teatro di Marcello

Via d. Villa Caffarelli

Capitoline Museums

Roman Forum Entrance

Largo della Salara Vecchia

Via della Curia

Via Sacra

Fori Imperiali Tourist Information

Via dei Fori Imperiali

Via del Colosseo

Piazza San Francesco di Paola

Via delle Sette sale

Via Eudossiana

Via di San Pietro in Vincoli

Via del Fagutale

Via degli Annibaldi

Via Vittorino da Feltre

Via delle Carine

Via dell'Agnello

Via Frangipane

Via Cavour

Via Monte Oppio

Via della Polveriera

Via Tor de' Conti

3

28

16

39

3

37

29

42

55

45

25

50

53

30

56

49

1

76

51

52

46

12

36

38

40

77

80

81

82

44

70

74

59

67

54

19

9

43

32

66

57

27

60

61

15

14

71

63

65

13

11

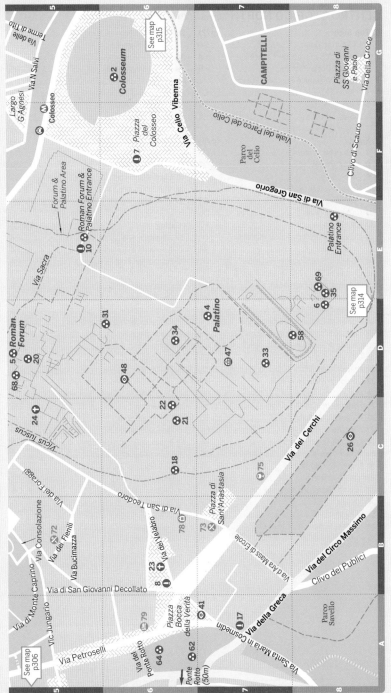

CENTRO STORICO NORTH *Map on p304*

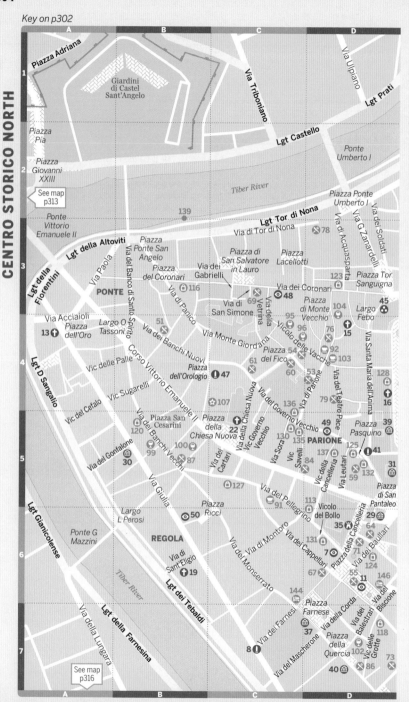

Key on p302

Piazza Adriana

Giardini
di Castel
Sant'Angelo

Via Triboniano

Via Ulpiano

Lgt Prati

Piazza
Pia

Lgt Castello

Ponte
Umberto I

Piazza
Giovanni
XXIII

See map
p313

Tiber River

Piazza Ponte
Umberto I

Via di Tor di Nona

Lgt Tor di Nona

Via G Zanardelli

Via dei Soldati

Ponte
Vittorio
Emanuele II

139

Via di Acquasparta

78

Lgt della Altoviti

Piazza
Ponte San
Angelo

Via di San Salvatore
in Lauro

Piazza di
San Salvatore
in Lauro

Piazza
Lacellotti

123

Piazza Tor
Sanguigna

Lgt della
Fiorentini

Via Paola

Via del Banco di Santo Spirito

Piazza
del Coronari

Via dei
Gabrielli

Via dei Coronari

48

PONTE

116

Via di
San Simone

69

Via della Vetrina

Piazza
di Monte
Vecchio

104

45

Largo
Febo

Via Acciaioli

13

Largo O
Tassoni

51

Via di Panico

95

Vicolo delle Vacche

96

76

15

Via Santa Maria dell'Anima

Piazza
dell'Oro

Corso Vittorio Emanuele II

Via dei Banchi Nuovi

Via Monte Giordana

Piazza
del Fico

54

92

103

Lgt D Sangallo

Vic delle Palle

61

60

53

79

Via di Parione

Via del Teatro Pace

128

16

Vic Sugarelli

Piazza
dell'Orologio

47

107

Via della Chiesa Nuova

136

Via del Governo Vecchio

49

Piazza
Pasquino

39

Vic del Cefalo

Via dei Banchi Vecchi

Piazza San
Cesarini

22

Piazza
della
Chiesa Nuova

Vic Governo
Vecchio

130

135

PARIONE

125

41

120

100

99

87

30

Via del Gonfalone

Via dei
Cartari

Via Sora

Vic
Savelli

137

84

59

132

31

Piazza
di San
Pantaleo

127

91

Via del Pellegrino

113

Vic della
Cancelleria

Via Leutari

Largo
L Perosi

Piazza
Ricci

50

Vicolo
del Bollo

29

35

Ponte G
Mazzini

REGOLA

Via di
Sant'Eligio

19

Via del Monserrato

Via di Montoro

Via dei Cappellari

131

7

67

Via della Cancelleria

Piazza della Cancelleria

71

124

55

11

146

Lgt Gianicolense

Via dei Farnesi

144

8

Lgt dei Tebaldi

Via del Monserrato

Piazza
Farnese

37

Piazza
della
Quercia

40

Via del Mascherone

8

Via della Corda

Via dei
Balestrari

102

Vic delle
Grotte

118

Via del
Biscione

86

73

Tiber River

Via della Lungara

Lgt della Farnesina

See map
p316

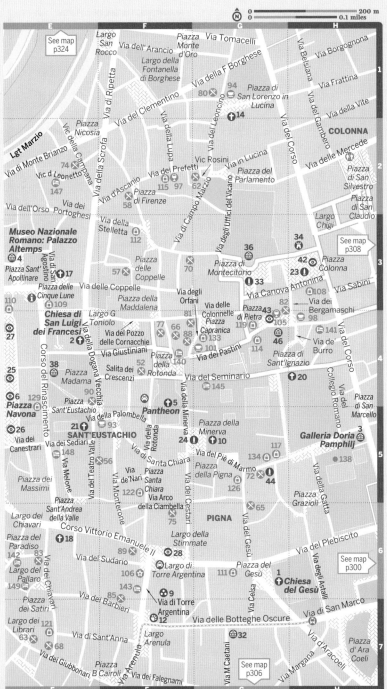

CENTRO STORICO SOUTH

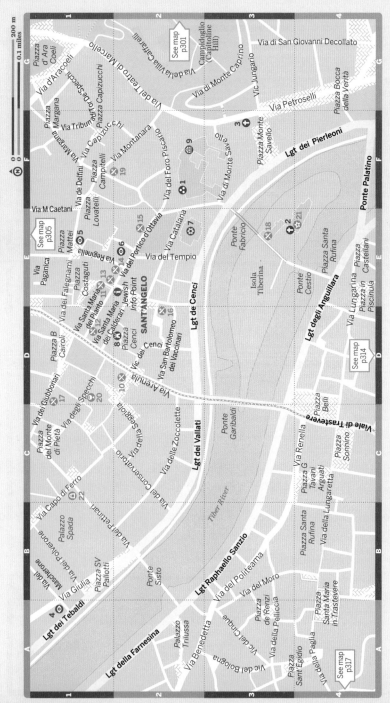

CENTRO STORICO SOUTH

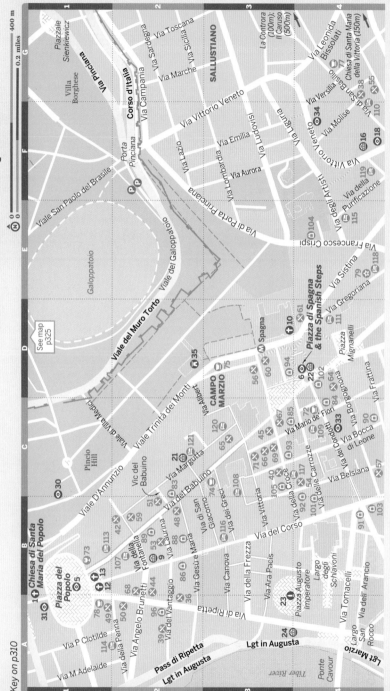

TRIDENTE, TREVI & THE QUIRINALE

See map p325

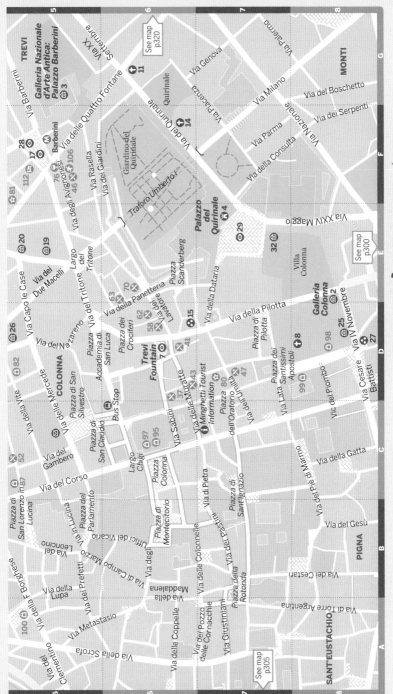

TREVI

Galleria Nazionale
d'Arte Antica:
Palazzo Barberini

Via XX Settembre

See map p320

MONTI

Via Genova

Quirinale

Via del Boschetto

Via dei Serpenti

Via delle Quattro Fontane

Via Barberini

Barberini

Via Piacenza

Via Milano

Via della Consulta

Via Parma

Via Nazionale

Via degli Avignonesi

Via Rasella

Via del Giardini

Giardino del
Quirinale

Via del Quirinale

Traforo Umberto I

Palazzo
del
Quirinale

Via XXIV Maggio

See map p300

Villa
Colonna

Galleria
Colonna

Piazza
Scanderberg

Via della Dataria

Via della Pilotta

Via dei
Due Macelli

Via Capo le Case

Largo
del
Tritone

Via del Tritone

Via della Panetteria

Via delle
Lavatore

Piazza di
San Silvestro

Accademia di
San Luca

Piazza dei
Crociferi

Via della Pilotta

Piazza di
Pilotta

Piazza dei
Santissimi
Apostoli

Via IV Novembre

Via Cesare Battisti

COLONNA

Via del Nazareno

Piazza di
San Claudio

Trevi
Fountain

Via delle Murate

Minghetti Tourist
Information

Piazza
dell'Oratorio

Via dell'Umiltà

Via Lata

Piazza dei
SS. Apostoli

Vic del Piombo

Via della Vite

Via della Mercede

Bus Stop

Via Sabini

Via del
Gambero

Largo
Chigi

Piazza
Colonna

Via di Pietra

Piazza di
Sant'Ignazio

Via del Piè di Marmo

Via della Gatta

PIGNA

Via del Corso

Via del
Parlamento

Piazza di
Montecitorio

Via delle Colonnelle

Via del Gesù

Via del Cestari

Piazza di
San Lorenzo in
Lucina

Via del
Leoncino

Uffici del Vicario

Via in Lucina

Via di Campo Marzio

Via degli

Via della
Maddalena

Via dei Pastini

Piazza della
Rotonda

Via di Torre Argentina

Via della
Lupa

Via della F Borghese

Via dei Prefetti

Via Metastasio

Via della Scrofa

Via delle Coppelle

Via del Pozzo
delle Cornacchie

Via Giustiniani

SANT'EUSTACHIO

Via del
Clementino

See map
p305

TRIDENTE, TREVI & THE QUIRINALE

VATICAN CITY, BORGO & PRATI

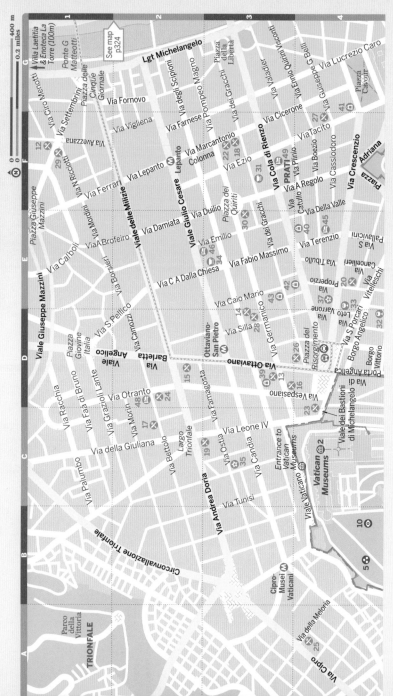

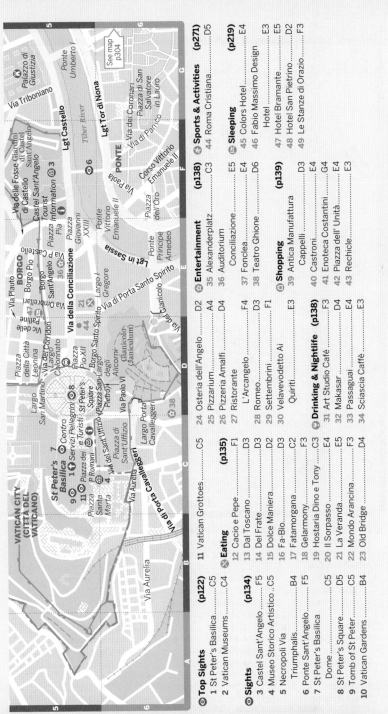

VATICAN CITY, BORGO & PRATI

SAN GIOVANNI & TESTACCIO

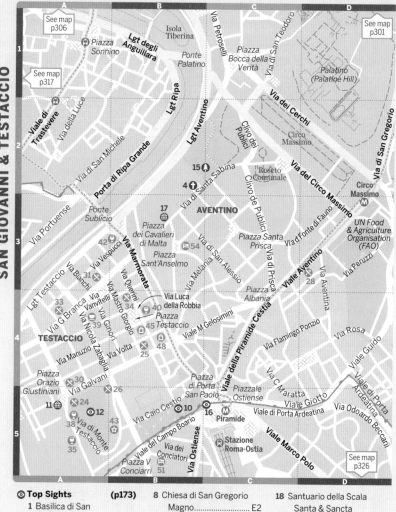

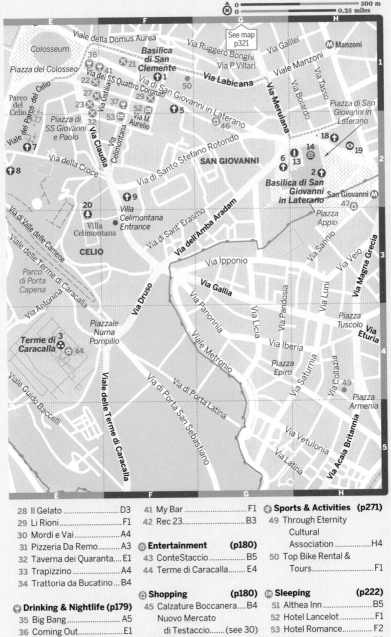

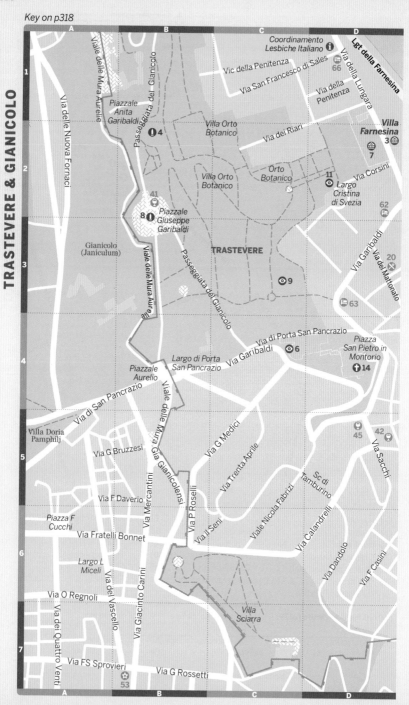

TRASTEVERE & GIANICOLO

Viale delle Mura Aurelie
Via delle Nuova Fornaci
Passeggiata del Gianicolo
Piazzale Anita Garibaldi
4

Coordinamento Lesbiche Italiano
Vic della Penitenza
Via San Francesco di Sales
66
Lgt della Farnesina
Via della Farnesina
Via della Lungara
Via della Penitenza
Villa Orto Botanico
Via dei Riari
Villa Farnesina
3
7

Villa Orto Botanico
Orto Botanico
11
41
8
Piazzale Giuseppe Garibaldi
Via Corsini
Largo Cristina di Svezia
62

Gianicolo (Janiculum)
Viale delle Mura Aurelie
Passeggiata del Gianicolo
TRASTEVERE
9
Via Garibaldi
Via del Mattonato
20
63

Via di Porta San Pancrazio
Via Garibaldi
6
Largo di Porta San Pancrazio
Piazzale Aurelio
Piazza San Pietro in Montorio
14

Villa Doria Pamphilj
Via di San Pancrazio
Viale delle Mura Gia Gianicolensi
Via G Bruzzesi
Via G Medici
Via Trenta Aprile
45
42
Via Sacchi

Via F Daverio
Via Mercantini
Via P Roselli
Via Nicola Fabrizi
Sc di Tamburino
Via Calandrelli

Piazza F Cucchi
Via Fratelli Bonnet
Via il Seni

Largo L Miceli
Via del Vascello
Via Giacinto Carini
Via Dandolo
Via F Casini

Via O Regnoli
Villa Sciarra

Via dei Quattro Venti
Via FS Sprovieri
Via G Rossetti
53

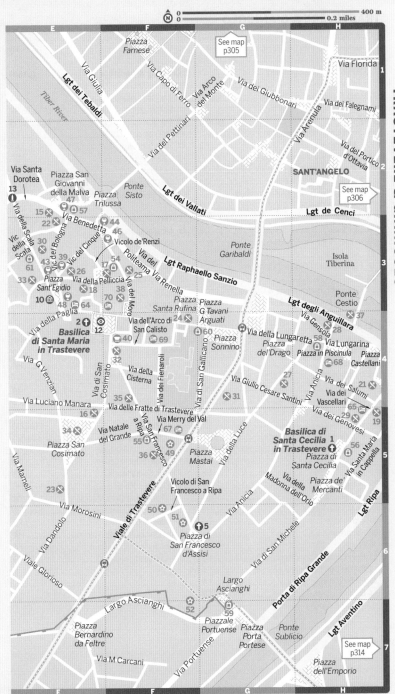

400 m
0.2 miles

E   F   G   H

See map
p305

Via Florida · 1

Via dei Falegnami

Via del Portico
d'Ottavia

SANT'ANGELO · 2

See map
p306

Lgt de Cenci

Piazza Farnese
Via Giulia
Via Capo di Ferro
Via Arco del Monte
Via dei Giubbonari
Via Arenula
Lgt dei Tebaldi
Via dei Pettinari

Via Santa Dorotea · 13

Piazza San Giovanni della Malva · 47

Piazza Trilussa

Ponte Sisto

Lgt dei Vallati

Tiber River

Via della Scala · 15 · 22
Via Benedetta · 44 · 46
Vicolo de'Renzi
Via del Cinque
Vic del Bologna
Vic della Scala
30 · 39 · 43 · 61
26 · 18
33 · Piazza Sant'Egidio · 10 · 48 · 64 · 70
Via della Pelliccia
Via della Paglia
17 · 54
25
Via del Moro

Ponte Garibaldi

Lgt Raphaello Sanzio

Ponte Garibaldi

Isola Tiberina · 3

Ponte Cestio

Lgt degli Anguillara · 37

Basilica di Santa Maria in Trastevere · 2 · 12

Via dell'Arco di San Calisto
Via G Venzian
40
32
Via di San Cosimato
Via della Cisterna
Via delle Fratte di Trastevere
Via dei Fienaroli

Piazza Santa Rufina
Piazza G Tavani Arguati · 24
69 · 60
Piazza Sonnino

Via della Lungaretta · 28 · 58
Via Gensola
Via Lungarina
Piazza in Piscinula · 68
Piazza Castellani · 4

Via Luciano Manara

16
34
Piazza San Cosimato
Via Natale del Grande
55 · 36
Via San Francesco a Ripa
67 · 49
Piazza Mastai
Via della Luce

Piazza del Drago
27
Via Giulio Cesare Santini · 31
Via Anicia
Via dei Salumi · 21 · 65 · 19
Via dei Vascellari
Via dei Genovesi

Basilica di Santa Cecilia in Trastevere · 1 · 56
Piazza di Santa Cecilia
Piazza de' Mercanti
Via Santa Maria in Cappella · 5

Via Mameli
23
Via Morosini
Via Dandolo
Viale di Trastevere
Via della Madonna dell'Orto
Via Anicia
Lgt Ripa

Vicolo di San Francesco a Ripa
50 · 51 · 5
Piazza di San Francesco d'Assisi
Viale Glorioso

Largo Ascianghi
52 · 59
Piazzale Portuense
Piazza Porta Portese
Ponte Sublicio
Porta di Ripa Grande
Lgt Aventino · 7

Piazza Bernardino da Feltre
Via M Carcani
Via Portuense
Via di San Michele
Piazza dell'Emporio

See map
p314

TRASTEVERE & GIANICOLO *Map on p316*

TRASTEVERE & GIANICOLO

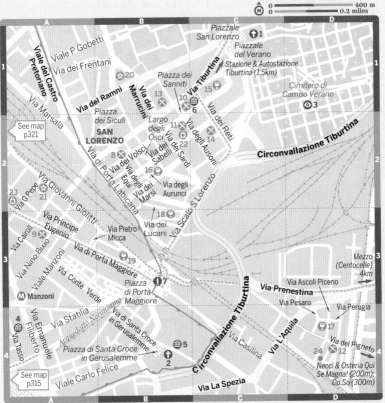

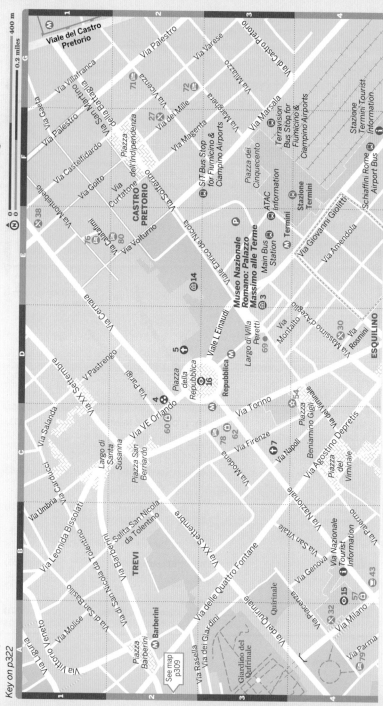

MONTI & ESQUILINO

Key on p322

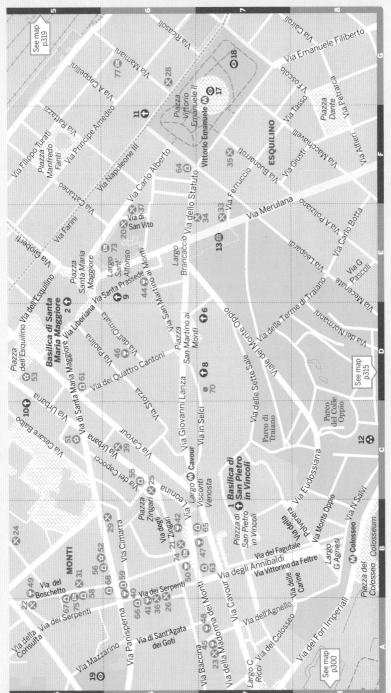

MONTI & ESQUILINO

VILLA BORGHESE & NORTHERN ROME *Map on p324*

VILLA BORGHESE & NORTHERN ROME

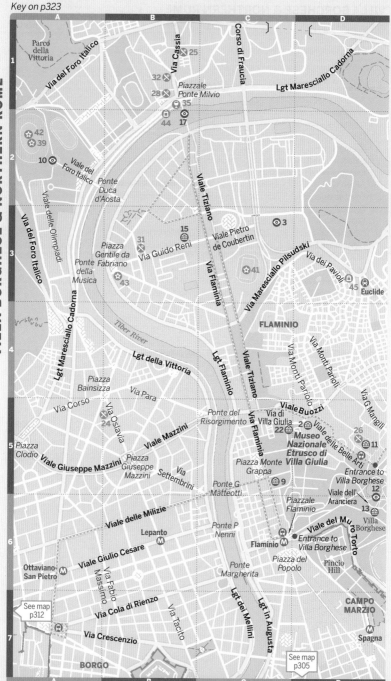

Parco della Vittoria

Via del Foro Italico

Via Cassia 25

32

28

Piazzale Ponte Milvio

35

44 17

Corso di Francia

Lgt Maresciallo Cadorna

42
39

10

Viale del Foro Italico

Ponte Duca d'Aosta

Viale Tiziano

3

Via delle Olimpiadi

Viale del Foro Italico

31

15

Viale Pietro de Coubertin

Piazza Gentile da Fabriano

Via Guido Reni

Via Flaminia

41

Via Maresciallo Piisudski

Via dei Pavioli

45
Euclide

Ponte della Musica

43

Tiber River

FLAMINIO

Lgt Maresciallo Cadorna

Lgt della Vittoria

Lgt Flaminio

Viale Tiziano

Via Monti Parioli

Via Monti Parioli

Via G Mangili

Piazza Bainsizza

Via Para

Via Corso

Via Oslavia

24

Viale Mazzini

Piazza Giuseppe Mazzini

Viale Buozzi

Via di Villa Giulia

22 2

Museo Nazionale Etrusco di Villa Giulia

Viale delle Belle Arti

26

11

Piazza Clodio

Viale Giuseppe Mazzini

Via Settembrini

Ponte del Risorgimento

Via Flaminia

Piazza Monte Grappa

Entrance to Villa Borghese

12

Viale delle Milizie

Lepanto

Ponte P Nenni

Ponte G Matteotti

9

Piazzale Flaminio

Viale dell' Aranciera

13

Villa Borghese

Ottaviano San Pietro

Viale Giulio Cesare

Via Fabio Massimo

Flaminio

Entrance to Villa Borghese

Viale del Muro Torto

Piazza del Popolo

Pincio Hill

CAMPO MARZIO

Ponte Margherita

Via Cola di Rienzo

Via Tacito

See map p312

Via Crescenzio

Lgt dei Mellini

Lgt in Augusta

Spagna

BORGO

See map p305

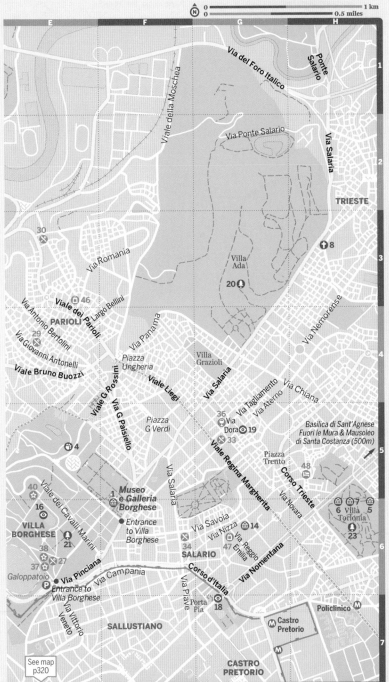

0 _____ 1 km
0 _____ 0.5 miles

SOUTHERN ROME

0 — 1 km
0 — 0.5 miles

See map p314

Via Portuense

1

Ponte Lungo

Via Appia Nuova

Piazza dei Re di Roma

Re di Roma

Via Ivrea

Via Etruria

Via Latina

Via Latina

Via Tabarini

Via Latina

Marrana della Caffarella

Via della Caffarella

2

3

Parco della Caffarella

4

Via Gallia

Piazza Tuscolo

Via Saturnia

Via Acaia

Via Acaia Britannia

Via Cilicia

APPIO-LATINO

Via Appia Antica (Appian Way)

Via Ardeatina

E

Piazza Epiro

Via Vetulonia

Via Latina

Piazza Galeria

Via Appia Antica

Via Appia Antica **3**

10

Viale Metronio

Via di Porta Latina

Via di Porta San Sebastiano

16

25

Circonvallazione Ardeatina

D

Viale delle Terme di Caracalla

Parco San Sebastiano

Viale Guido Baccelli

Viale di Porta Ardeatina

32

Via Odoardo Beccarii

Via Guglielmo Massaia

Via Roberto De Nobili

C

Viale Guido

Via Odoardo Beccarii

Viale Marco Polo

Circonvallazione Ostiense

GARBATELLA

4

Via Rocca da Cesinale

Via Francesco Passino

Via Alessandra Macinghi Strozzi

18

Via Giot

Piazzale dei Partigiani

Stazione Roma-Ostiense

21

Via Ignazio Persico

Via Giovanni Ansaldo

17

Teatro Palladium

Piramide

Stazione Roma-Ostia

Via Giacinto Pullino

B

Viale della Piramide Cestia

Via Pellegrino Matteucci

35

31

OSTIENSE

30 **29**

28

Garbatella

34

Via Giulio Rocco

27

SAN PAOLO

Via Marmorata

TESTACCIO

Piazza V Copelarri

12

20

Via del Porto Fluviale

Via del Commercio

26

6

5

Via Ostiense

Via Libetta

Viale di San Paolo

Lgt di San Paolo

A

Largo GB Marzi

Ponte Testaccio

Via G Branca

Via Nicola Zabaglia

Via B Franklin

Via Pacinotti

33

Tiber River

Lgt dei Papareschi

Via Enrico Fermi

Via Portuense

Lgt Testaccio

Via Calvani

1

2

3

4